THE MARKETER'S

HANDBOOK

THE MARKETER'S
HANDBOOK

Reassessing Marketing Techniques for Modern Business

Laurie Young

A John Wiley & Sons, Ltd., Publication

This edition first published 2011
© 2011 John Wiley & Sons Ltd

Registered office
John Wiley & Sons Ltd, The Atrium, Southern Gate, Chichester, West Sussex, PO19 8SQ, United Kingdom

For details of our global editorial offices, for customer services and for information about how to apply for permission to reuse the copyright material in this book please see our website at www.wiley.com.

Library of Congress Cataloging-in-Publication Data
Young, Laurie, 1955-
    The marketer's handbook : reassessing marketing techniques for modern business / Laurie Young.
        p. cm.
    Includes bibliographical references and index.
    ISBN 978-0-470-74687-5 (hardback)
    1. Marketing. I. Title.
    HF5415.Y7917 2011
    658.8—dc22
                                                                    2011007563

A catalogue record for this book is available from the British Library.

ISBN 978-0-470-74687-5 (hardback) ISBN 978-1-119-97352-2 (ebk)
ISBN 978-1-119-97850-3 (ebk) ISBN 978-1-119-97851-0 (ebk)

Set in 11 on 13 pt Bembo by Toppan Best-set Premedia Limited, Hong Kong
Printed in Great Britain by Antony Rowe Ltd, Chippenham, Wiltshire

For Joyce & Ken, who never had a chance but gave me one.

CONTENTS

PREFACE

Now that I have published several books, I am often asked how long it takes to write one. The normal answer is between eighteen months and three years. This one, though, took thirty-five years.

Its tone was set by an incident which happened when, in my mid twenties, I was asked to be executive assistant to the Deputy Chairman of BT. He (the former Deputy Chair of Barclays Bank) was brought into the company by Prime Minister Margaret Thatcher, to run the privatization. I was his only assistant and was closely involved in the marketing of the float. There followed eighteen months of demanding work with a project that set all kinds of firsts. Afterwards, though, the newly privatized firm had to set up several radically new approaches. One was a mechanism to assess and approve capital projects, a level of spend which dominated the new company because of its extensive backbone network. My boss wanted to set up a "capital appraisal committee" to ensure that more commercially orientated decisions were made at the acquisition and spend of capital investment. He asked me to investigate "discounted cash flow analysis" and "internal rate of return" in order to draft the methods by which this capital spend (which at the time was massive) would be evaluated and approved.

I spent several hours with internal and external accountants, and academics, on this interesting project. At some point it struck me, though, that these concepts (like many management tools) were merely a way to structure the thinking of executives in order to spend shareholder funds to best effect. They looked objective, numerical, and detailed; yet they still called for the judgement of the senior team on where they would allocate scarce resources; they were concepts designed to help reach better decisions. As a result, I went back to source and, with the advice of much more experienced people, set up mechanisms to dramatize the choices, based on the analysis. In other words, we understood the strengths and weaknesses of the tool and adjusted it to suit our circumstances.

Later, I went back into marketing. As I did my postgraduate diploma and MBA I went into concepts like the Boston Box and the Ansoff Matrix in greater depth. I never forgot my former boss's approach, though, and asked myself about both the sources and the use of these concepts to help spend shareholder funds wisely. As my career progressed I used many of them but I have been shocked by some of the things I have found. This book is the result.

Walk into any reputable book shop and you would think that marketing and sales people are really stupid. There are books on the "principles of marketing", "introduction to marketing", "marketing for dummies", "new rules" on various bits of marketing and, most irritating of all, a plethora of opinionated nonsense on the latest whizzo ideas. Admittedly, most marketing people find (as do many others) that, after university, their early jobs contain activities which are nothing at all to do with the concepts they learnt. They might be absorbed in creating email blasts, researching latest fads on the web, preparing PowerPoint presentations for senior people (some of which are never used), or putting out the chairs for events. Some rarely see a marketing plan or a portfolio analysis until they progress in their career.

Yet there comes a time when they might need to express an idea or a new strategy to their boss, their colleagues or, more worryingly, to a customer. It is at this time that many reach for models and concepts taught when they were at college. And then there is a problem. Sometimes business problems are complex and cannot be summarized into a sound bite, one page of A4, or a Twitter comment. Sometimes, "key outcomes" and anodyne bullet points simply will not do. Sometimes, professionals have to be thoughtful, careful, smart, and judicious. It is at those times that the depth, credibility, and effectiveness of marketing concepts come under the microscope. This book is intended to help with those occasions (because not much else does).

Contrary to popular belief, there are thousands upon thousands of people, all over the world, who try to use ideas, tools, and techniques to express the thinking behind marketing initiatives in order to get better decisions for shareholders. Like other professionals, marketing specialists use a range of concepts and models in their work. This book contains descriptions of a number of those that are referred to most commonly (and one or two that I have found useful which are less well known). It does not attempt to be an exhaustive review of all the techniques to which marketers can resort nor does it attempt to provide a detailed description, or critique, of each one. And, it certainly doesn't attempt to make a fortune by joining in on the latest fad or fashion in thinking. Quite the opposite. It tries to understand the historical use of enduring marketing principles and practice. It aims to point to the origin, context, and limitations of some of the better known ideas that are currently used in business.

The book describes each tool or concept and its source. Further reading and quotes are included to help those who want to delve deeper when they actually come to use them. Above all it asks: "How useful and relevant is this concept? Will it improve decision making? Does the damn thing have any credibility and does it work?"

I have to thank a number of people who have read and checked the text; and picked me up on my many errors! In academia: Professor David Carson, University of Ulster, Professor Adrian Payne, University of New South Wales, Professor Silvia Hodges, Fordham Law School, New York, Professor Paul Fifield, University of Southampton, Professor Robert Shaw, Cass Business School Oxford, and Charles Nixon of Cambridge Marketing College. Those working in practical marketing jobs: Tim Westall, founding partner of April Strategy, Simon Phillips, marketing director of Grosvenor Estates, Simon Esenberger and Hamish Pringle, CEO of the Institute of Practitioners in Advertising. Any remaining errors and omissions are mine, but the text is much better for their support.

Thanks also to those who provided case studies, including: Rae Sedel of Russell Reynolds, Tony Rogers of Interoute, David Munn of ITSMA, Mike Aubrey Bugg of Age Concern, Vincent Rousselet and Philip Oliver of Fujitsu, Barbara Jenkins of Microsoft, Ginnie Leatham and Ashley Stockwell of Virgin Media, Julie Meyers, Tom Dolan and Robert Corbishley of Xerox, Kevin Bishop of IBM, Peter Snelling of Michelin, Sir Paul Judge, Diao Yunfeng and Zhung Bin of Haier, Natasha Clay of Diageo, Jonathan Brayne of Allen & Overy, Nichola Murphy and Natasha Jackson of River Publishing. All of these people have been genuinely interested in giving their experience to the marketing community to help improve the profession's understanding.

I should especially like to thank Dawn Southgate at the library of the Chartered Institute of Marketing for her patient support and, as usual, the Wiley team (who I must have driven completely mad by now!). Thanks also to Lucy Sinclair for her help with text preparation.

I cannot thank, but nonetheless owe a debt of gratitude to, the many people over the years who, with a furrowed brow, have puzzled with me over one or other technique en route to a presentation on some matter to our employers. Smart people working for BT, Unisys, Ericsson, PricewaterhouseCoopers, Blakes Marketing, Allen & Overy, and many more have honed our communication of some dusty concept or another. To them all: many thanks. This is, very much, our voice to our profession.

Laurie Young
Winter 2010

THE BLIND MEN AND AN ELEPHANT

by John Godfrey Saxe

It was six men of Indostan
To learning much inclined,
Who went to see the Elephant
(Though all of them were blind),
That each by observation
Might satisfy his mind

The First approached the Elephant,
And happening to fall
Against his broad and sturdy side,
At once began to bawl:
"God bless me! but the Elephant
Is very like a wall!"

The Second, feeling of the tusk,
Cried, "Ho! what have we here
So very round and smooth and sharp?
To me 'tis mighty clear
This wonder of an Elephant
Is very like a spear!"

The Third approached the animal,
And happening to take
The squirming trunk within his hands,
Thus boldly up and spake:
"I see," quoth he, "the Elephant
Is very like a snake!"

The Fourth reached out an eager hand,
And felt about the knee.
"What most this wondrous beast is like
Is mighty plain," quoth he;
"'Tis clear enough the Elephant
Is very like a tree!"

The Fifth, who chanced to touch the ear,
Said: "E'en the blindest man
Can tell what this resembles most;
Deny the fact who can
This marvel of an Elephant
Is very like a fan!"

The Sixth no sooner had begun
About the beast to grope,
Than, seizing on the swinging tail
That fell within his scope,
"I see," quoth he, "the Elephant
Is very like a rope!"

And so these men of Indostan
Disputed loud and long,
Each in his own opinion
Exceeding stiff and strong,
Though each was partly in the right,
And all were in the wrong!

Moral:
So oft in theologic wars,
The disputants, I ween,
Rail on in utter ignorance
Of what each other mean,
And prate about an Elephant

WHAT'S IN AND WHAT'S NOT

WHAT'S IN

Account based marketing: see Account management
AAR model
Account management
Advertising
AIDA
Ansoff and his matrix
Audit (The market audit)

B-to-B: see Business-to-business marketing
Behavioural insights for marketing
Bellwether markets: see Diffusion of innovation
Blueprinting
Boston Matrix
Brands
Business-to-business marketing
Brand valuation: see Brand
Buyer behaviour: see Consumer behaviour or Organizational buying behaviour
Buzz: see Viral marketing

Campaign: see Marketing communication
Category management
Celebrity endorsement
Customer experience management: see Service quality
Channels of distribution
Channel strategy: see Channels of distribution

Closing techniques
Cognitive dissonance: see Behavioural aspects of marketing
Collateral; see Packaging
Co-creation of products and services: see Innovation management
Conjoint research: see Research
Communication: see Marketing communication
Competitive strategy
Concept testing: see Research
Conjoint research: see Research
Consumer behaviour
Contact audit
CRM: see Loyalty
CSR, Corporate social responsibility
Customer experience management: see Service quality
Customer journey: see Blueprinting and Service quality
Customer Value: see Value propositions
Cultural variations

Decision-making unit (DMU)
Differentiation
Diffusion of innovations
Digital marketing
Direct marketing
Directional policy matrix

Entertaining customers: see Hospitality
Event marketing: see Sponsorship
Experience curves: see Boston Matrix

Features analysis
Four Ps: see Marketing mix

Gap Model
GE/McKinsey matrix: see Directional policy matrix
Globalization of markets
Growth/share matrix: see Boston Matrix

Hospitality and customer entertainment

IMC: see Marketing communication
Innovation management
Intangibility: see Services marketing
Integrated marketing communication: see Marketing communication
Internal marketing
International Marketing

Latent markets: see Market maturity
Lifetime value: see Relationship marketing, Loyalty, and Service quality
Loyalty

Market audit: see Audit
Market definition
Market maturity
Market myopia: see Market definition
Market share
Marketing communication
Marketing concept
Marketing management
Marketing measurement
Marketing mix
Marketing plans and planning
Marketing strategy
Mass customization: see Relationship marketing
Mavens: see Diffusion of innovations, Viral marketing.
Maslow's hierarchy of needs: see Behavioural aspects of marketing
Media: see Marketing communication
Micro marketing: see Category management
Molecular modelling

Network marketing: see Relationship marketing, Viral marketing
NPD/NSD (New product design/New service design)

Organizational buying behaviour
Organizational competence in marketing

Packaging
Perceptual maps: see Positioning
PEST: see Market audit
Pestel: see Market audit
Pipeline management
PLC: see Product life cycle
Porter's competitive forces
Portfolio analysis and managment
Positioning
Post purchase distress
Pricing
Prospects: see Pipeline management
Product life cycle (PLC)
Public Relations (PR)

Relationship marketing (RM)
Repositioning

Research

Sales and selling
Scenario planning
Sector marketing
Segmentation
Service quality
Services marketing
Seven Ps: see Marketing mix and Services marketing
Solutions marketing
Sponsorship
STP: see Positioning

Thought leadership

Value propositions
Viral marketing

WHAT'S NOT

Beak even analysis: a financial method of estimating when a business initiative might return more to the company than its costs.

Belbin's team roles: (but see Marketing management). A method of identifying the way individuals behave in teams.

Brand valuation techniques: (but see Brand).

Business process re-engineering: (but see Thought leadership). A rather faddish idea which argued for the re-configuration of opcrational processes.

Business vision: a method of setting the strategic intent of a company.

Core competence: a corporate strategy and operational concept which encourages executives to focus on what their organization excels at.

Corporate strategy: Method of setting direction for the entire firm. Needs to inter-relate with market analysis and marketing strategy.

Customer journey: (but see Service quality). A service quality concept, popular in financial services companies, which focuses attention on customers' experiences.

Critical success factors: (but see Competitive strategy). A method of identifying important competitive issues that executives should focus on.

Discounted cash flow analysis (DCF): an accounting technique to determine payback on an investment and to decide between alternative uses of capital.

Economies of scale (but see Boston Matrix).

Learning curves (but see Boston Matrix).

Mission statement: A method of setting strategic intent of a company.

Myers Briggs: (but see Marketing management). A respected method of identifying personality traits.

Net promoter: (but see loyalty and service quality). A new approach to the measurement of reputation and service quality, relatively unsubstantiated at the time of writing.

O&M: a rather outdated process design approach (but see blueprinting).

Pareto (but see Account management).

Project management: (but see Marketing management) a well developed method of organizing activities in a one-off management task.

Proprietary tools: there are many good methods and techniques which have been developed by agencies and suppliers and are sold to marketers. This book has omitted the more modern of them because it is difficult to assess how far they are generically applicable.

Return on investment: an accounting term used to understand the returns a business might get from an investment, and used very sloppily by marketers to chat about the value of their activities to their boss.

Shareholder value: a slightly faddish concept pushed by some accountants and economists which is supposed to link the managerial levers of a business to the return to investors. Very suspect because there are so many different variables which affect the value of shares.

Six sigma: (but see Service quality) A newish framework for managing improvements in quality.

Strategic business units (SBUs)

SWOT: a generic, well known management concept to summarize competitive issues.

Total Quality Management (TQM): (but see Service quality). A specific approach to quality management. Some marketing specialists tried to ride the publicity wave associated with this by trying to introduce improvements to marketing management under the term "Total Quality Marketing". The latter had some merit but appears a little faddish at the time of writing.

Value-based marketing: a rather dubious attempt to attract the attention of senior executives to marketing by connecting the function with the shareholder value fad; unsubstantiated at the time of writing.

Value chain analysis: (but see Competitive strategy). A corporate strategy technique identifying important and unimportant activities in a firm's processes.

THE RATINGS

As their career progresses, marketing professionals develop their own judgements on the concepts and techniques that they use. Some they dismiss out of hand. Others become familiar, practical approaches.

The ratings in this book are my own, developed over thirty years of use. They are my opinion based on reading into them and discussing them with others. I do not expect anybody to agree with all, or many, of my opinions. I do urge all professionals, though, to develop their own view.

The criteria for my ratings are:

Practical and powerful: the highest compliment I can pay a marketing concept. Not only is it founded on good, analytical, and experiential evidence, but it works well in practice.

Practical: The evidence for these concepts are, in my opinion, primarily experiential, they need more substantiation but that doesn't mean that they are not usable.

Merely conceptual: These are normally theoretical with little evidence of their being useful in practice. Some have been substantiated by good academic rigour and ought to be tried.

Toxic: These, if misunderstood or misapplied, can do real damage to your shareholders' business and your career. That doesn't mean you should not use them, but understand their limitations and their risks.

A

 **AAR MODEL**

Application: business-to-business marketing, planning major account strategy, relationship marketing

The AAR model

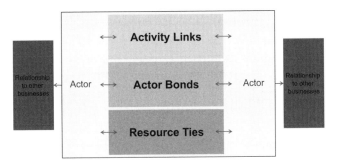

Figure A.1: The actors–activities–resources model
Source: Håkansson and Snehota, 1995

The concept

This little known idea, the "actors-activities-resources" model (see Figure A.1), divides business relationships into three progressive and inter-related layers:

(i) "Activity links" are the work, projects, or other activities, involved in the interaction between two businesses. These vary with the depth of relationship. They range from simple sales and technical projects through to two firms meshing or adapting their systems and business processes to become more efficient. The latter has created sizable business opportunities in areas such as outsourcing over the past few decades.

(ii) "Actor bonds". These occur when two business people interact through a buying or professional advisory process. The academics behind this research suggest that there are three components necessary for them to develop. The first is reciprocity during the process, ensuring that both sides give something to the interaction, even if one is a customer. The second is commitment and the third is trust. All three increase as healthy business relationships develop.

As people interact they form perceptions of each other about: capability, limitations, commitment, and trust. If the relationship develops these perceptions influence the degree and clarity with which the two communicate; and also the degree to which they involve each other in their own professional network. So, for the supplier, the way in which they conduct their work influences the trust their customer develops in them and the degree to which they will be invited further into the organization, and so the possibility of further work.

(iii) "Resource ties" are items used by people during business interactions. They might include: software, intellectual capital, skilled staff, knowledge, experience, and expertise. People who have resources, or control over them, have greater power in professional relationships. This power is the basis of the offer (the customer comes to the supplier because they lack one or more of these resources) but clearly the immediacy or importance of need and the scarcity of resource influences pricing and quality perceptions.

This concept suggests that business becomes more secure and profitable as relationships between organizations deepen through the three levels. So, the thinking behind the model will seem intuitively correct to many people in *business-to-business marketing*. This is its strength, capturing, as it does, the day-to-day experience of many marketers. It allows a firm, when needed, to use a common process and terminology in its approach to customer relationship management. However, it also introduces (perhaps for the first time) a reasonably robust mechanism whereby marketers can analyse and understand in detail what many recognize to be their most important approach to market: relationships with repeat customers.

At its very simplest this model can be used as a basis of discussion with internal colleagues to map the depth of relationships that their company has with its customers. Sales people can be asked to complete formats of their customer relationships using the three levels of the model. Actions arising from discussion of the results (e.g. creating more opportunities for non-task related exchange or making different resources, such as knowledge, available) can be put into account plans.

However, this concept can also be used as the basis of detailed analysis and research. A hypothesis of the professional relationships that exist in a market, and the types of interaction, can be created using the terms of the model. It can then be used as a guide to design a research sample and questionnaire. A two-step, qualitative and quantitative research process based on it is likely to reveal powerful insights into the relationships customers have with the firm and its competitors.

History, context, criticism, and development

This model was developed, during the 1980s and 1990s, by academic researchers interested in both *business-to-business* and *network marketing*. It is relatively unknown and relatively modern. Nonetheless, their work contains detailed and painstaking research together with numerous case studies in, largely, European countries. They also examined international *business-to-business* links; between engineering companies in Australia and their clients in Asia, for example. Yet it appears to be a tool that can also be used for practical purposes within a normal business.

Voices and further reading

- Axelsson, L. and Easton, G., *Industrial Networks: A New View of Reality*. Routledge, 1992.
- Håkansson, H. and Snehota, I., *Developing Relationships in Business Networks*. Routledge, 1995.
- "There is a team effect. Jointly, the two companies can perform activities and utilize resources which none of them could accomplish in isolation. What they can accomplish depends on how the relationship develops. A relationship between two companies does not become automatically a perfect 'team' but the potential is always there. The team effects have to be tried out. They develop as the parties involved experiment with the various connections and learn about their effects. The quality of the relationship is the extent to which this function will be exploited." Håkansson and Snehota, ibid.
- Purchase, S. and Ward, A., "AAR model: cross cultural developments". *International Marketing Review* 20:2, January 2002.
- Ford, D., *The Business Marketing Course*. John Wiley & Sons Ltd, 2002.
- "Resource ties can develop gradually and unconsciously as problems are solved within a relationship. These ties can be substantial and important in old relationships, without the companies being aware of them. In contrast, innovation often occurs when the resources are tied together in new ways between companies and this can lead to the development of offerings with wide application. Both of these issues emphasize the importance for the marketer of auditing each important relationship". Ford, ibid.
- Woodburn, D. and McDonald. M.H.B., *Key Account Management: The Definitive Guide*. John Wiley & Sons Ltd, 2011 (3rd edn).

Things you might like to consider

(i)   This is a relatively unknown theoretical concept which has been tested reasonably rigorously in academic research projects. However, there is not much evidence of it being used extensively in day-to-day sales and marketing within actual businesses. Even though it looks practical it is relatively untested in real businesses.
(ii) It could be the basis of a consistent way of analysing the relationship status of a number of customer accounts. It could also be used as the basis of a research brief.
(iii) It can be the basis of a viral marketing campaign, examining as it does the complex inter-relationships between business people in different groups.
(iv) It could be integrated into a market audit as a means to understand customer behaviour.

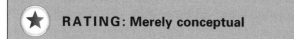

ACCOUNT MANAGEMENT

Application: sales to major customers

Customer organization

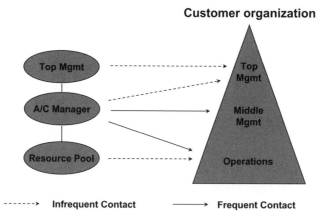

Figure A.2:   The typical approach of major account management

The concept

This concept concentrates specifically on the need to analyse and service important customers. The reality for many firms is that their revenues are dominated by a relatively small number of important, repeat customers. So, for many marketers, their day-to-day job is focused on the needs and opportunities within a small group of significant buyers rather than the mass markets which absorb so much of marketing research and thinking; the so-called Pareto principle. Yet, this perspective is barely covered in marketing courses and tends to be neglected in text books on the generic principles of marketing.

There are several aspects to effective account management:

(i) Prioritizing the customer accounts

Two researchers (Woodburn, D. and McDonald, M.H.B., 2011) found, rather alarmingly, that 85% of Western European companies had no idea whether or not they made or lost money from their major customers. So, marketers have to start by identifying their most important customers. This can be as crude as listing them by volume of business and ranking accordingly. Some focus on their "top 100" (produced in this way) or some version of it. Others have tiered layers of prioritized accounts, each receiving different levels of attention according to the volume of business they generate. Unfortunately, though, these simple approaches won't meet all of the firm's objectives in its market, and it certainly won't reveal that it may only be receiving a small share of these companies' spend in its category. Marketers may, for instance, want to identify customers with the highest potential and penetrate those further. Or they may have more generic strategies, such as wanting to penetrate a sector of the market or to take business from a competitor. Or they may set out to "penetrate" certain types of premium customers in order to be recognized as a high quality supplier. If these "target customers" have low immediate spend, they may be categorized as a "strategic account" and receive the same attention as important customers with a larger immediate business volume. So, effective account selection is critically dependant on the setting of good marketing objectives.

With these different issues to resolve and objectives to achieve, it is sensible to step back, and analyse both the existing major customers and the potential buyers before settling on any strategy or approach toward them. If, for example, customer accounts are mapped in terms of the size of their spend and in terms of the company's share of that spend (as shown in Figure A.3) there will normally be a spread of business. Marketers can use this analysis to determine where best to allocate scarce resources for maximum return. This straightforward analysis suggests four strategies according to where the accounts fall:

- Maintain: the intention here is to hold position with relatively little investment. Some, for example, set up telephone-based account management for those that merit less investment.
- Defend: these accounts are important and effort must be made to both keep the customer excited by the supplier's offer and to keep competition out.

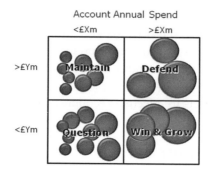

Figure A.3: A representation of prioritized customer accounts

- Question: if there is one weakness that almost all marketers have it's the reluctance to cut out unprofitable or low potential customers. Those in this part of the analysis, though, detract from the resources and attention that should be showered on others. They ought to be culled.
- Win and grow: this group of customers is high potential and effort should be put into penetrating this customer base further. Resources saved from culled accounts and any incremental investment should be put here. It should be the future business.

The size of the circles represents the size of the customers' businesses, so this gives an indication of which accounts are likely to be more lucrative and which to allocate resources to.

The *directional policy matrix (DPM)* can also be used to help prioritize accounts and, at the same time, gain some consensus among the different people involved in account management activities. Involving general managers, account directors, sales, service, and marketing specialists in a project to score and rank accounts brings focus and consistency to account selection. The ability to customize criteria is likely to reveal very powerful insights. A DPM analysis that includes, for instance, the anticipated lifetime value of accounts is likely to make major account selection more relevant and strategically effective.

(ii) Major customer sales strategies

Once the top priority accounts are identified, account managers are assigned to them, taking them beyond the "opportunistic" approach usually adopted by sales teams that focus on new business. Account managers are dedicated to one large customer in order to "develop the account"; in other words: to grow the revenue from it. Their role is to get to know that organization in depth and identify or create opportunities.

Some have, or develop, deep knowledge of the industrial sector in which the customer's business concentrates. This enables them to choose relevant products or services for their customer and even to advise executives within it. They need to be capable of understanding and presenting the whole range of products, skills, and services offered by their firm. At a minimum, excellent communications skills will be needed plus a recognized ability to generate revenue. Successful individuals in this role are also creative, able to spot opportunities and harness their own firm's abilities by forming teams to suggest ideas. They normally deal at middle or senior management level but, on occasion, need to gain access to the heights of their customer's organization (perhaps to discuss strategy) and the very bottom (perhaps to collect data), as shown in Figure A.2. Yet, they must not only be the voice of their employer to the customer, but also the voice of that customer to their own organization.

(iii) Relationship stages

The depth of interaction between an organization and its significant customers goes through several stages. These deepen and become more valuable as the relationship between the two organizations develops. These stages have been identified and categorized by various researchers. The *AAR* model, for instance, identifies three levels of relationship: activity links, actor bonds, and resource ties (see separate entry). The subtlety and depth behind the development of the "actor bonds" level is fascinating and practical. On the other hand, Professor Malcolm McDonald, who established a ten-year research project into major account marketing at Cranfield University, identified five layers to developing relationships: "exploratory", "basic", "cooperative", interdependent", and "integrated" (see Woodburn and McDonald, 2011). They identify the individual needs, the relationship needs, and the benefits at each stage.

These conceptual frameworks can be used to identify the stages in development of the relationship between each account and the supplier. Both generic strategy and practical account plans can be built around them.

(iv) Account plans

The best account management normally involves an "account planning process" of some kind, frequently undertaken on a six-monthly basis, which adds discipline to relationship management. It normally involves an internal meeting of employees who have an interest in the account, led by the account manager. At this meeting, the team discusses a number of issues; including:

- Objectives for the account. These might be financial, relationship building, or strategic;

- Environmental awareness. A review of the customer's market and challenges, used to understand issues and identify potential opportunities;
- Business profile and performance review;
- Creation of potential projects and sales;
- Sales and marketing programmes specifically for that account;
- Proposed annual investment to use within the account.

The team should develop specific sales objectives, such as to win one or more of the opportunities identified. Yet it should also create supporting marketing objectives; such as to reposition the company as a consultancy partner to the account, or to build awareness and preference among important executives for their company. (As important as the objectives themselves is the conversation.) Finally, the account team has to agree how often progress against the objectives will be measured and how it will be reported to senior management.

Sometimes, account leaders will involve members of the customer's organization in planning sessions to add perspective and depth to the debate. This alone tends to engage others with customers and increase the inter-relationships between the two organizations. The output of the planning process, often in the form of an account plan, is shared with relevant people in the firm. The draft plan should be signed off by interested executives including people like an account director, marketing director, service director, and sales director. Once approved, it should form part of the regular account reviews and account governance procedures.

(v) Serious investment in unearthing insight into major accounts

Some marketers have come to the conclusion that, if large business customers are a market in their own right, then analysis should be conducted in a similar way to a full *"market audit"*. For instance, to build an understanding of the account's situation and plans, information can be collected and used in a similar way to which macro-environmental factors are viewed for generic markets; using the "PESTEL" mnemonic, for instance, (see *market audit*) as a structure for this thinking.

Some go one step further and analyse how their customer's market is evolving in much the same way as they analyse their own market. One of the most powerful aspects of his approach is "value chain analysis". The aim of this perspective, used routinely in first rate consultancies, is to focus on what the customer provides for its customers. It examines the contribution of all functions within the organization and what exactly the business does for its buyers. It will enable the account planning team to match its offer to the customer's needs and to be pro-active with proposed projects. In fact, it can unleash powerful, innovative propositions, which revolutionize a customer's business and approaches to its work.

Data is gathered from multiple sources to understand specific customer needs, how products or services can be used to address those needs, and also how best to communicate the value of those offers to the different buyers and influencers in the organization. Publicly available information sources open to the marketer include: the account's website (including investor relations information if it is a public company); press coverage (Google alerts can provide daily media coverage of the account for example); social media (blogs, tweets, and LinkedIn profiles of executives); and conference presentations and articles given or written by its employees. Sources of information available for the marketer to buy include: information aggregators (such as Factiva, One Source, or Boardex), investment analyst reports, industry analyst reports and academic case studies of the organization. External advisors can also contribute. They include: industry analysts, procurement advisors, trade or professional body representatives, journalists or editors, and peers in similar roles in other companies. Many of these can be sought out for opinions on proposals, or as sources of potential suppliers.

A profile is needed of each customer, containing information on its strategy, vision, objectives, its important initiatives, performance and associated issues, organizational structure, culture, and buying priorities. In addition, profiles of the key executives within the business are important. What are their roles, their background, their objectives, and their perceptions of suppliers? Their likely buying behaviours can be understood by creating a history of their previous decisions.

Finally, an overview of the competitive landscape within the account is crucial. How much does it spend on the category and what share do the various suppliers have? What are the perceptions of those suppliers? What is their perception of the quality they receive? How much do they earn from the account and with whom do they have relationships? It is important to understand the competitive personnel and their networks in the account. Every day executives in the customer organization see the supplier's employees and those of competitors. Sometimes they proffer ideas and sales bids on the same issue or needs. What do the executives in the account see and hear? How does it seem to them? What are the strengths and weaknesses of the various sales people offering them advice? A "map" of the important decision makers and influencers is a useful tool. It should reflect their relationships with each other and indicate the strength of influence of each person on the buying decision for a specific category or opportunity, together with their perception of the supplier. Marketing can really add value here, by identifying and profiling executives; and finding ways to open doors for the account team to meet them.

(vi) Creating account specific value propositions

One of the most recent trends in *business-to–business marketing* is the creation of unique and specific *"value propositions"* for individual important customers. Marketers in leading firms set out to specifically create an offer that resonates with and excites their customer. It is a deliberate attempt to move away from vague, meaningless. and commoditized "*solutions*". For each opportunity identified in the account plan, a *value proposition* is created that demonstrates an understanding of the buyers' issues, makes the benefits of the offer clear in their language, highlights how the value of the offer outweighs the price, and reinforces the unique selling points or differentiators of the company. Marketers then try to create a snappy "elevator pitch" for use by the account team when meeting buyers and influencers.

(vii) Designing bespoke *marketing plans* for specific accounts

A large number of business-to-business suppliers are beginning to apply dedicated marketing to important, individual customers and not just generic markets or sectors. This is much more than the usual sales or bid processes dressed up in marketing jargon. It's a tool by which scarce marketing resources are focused on a handful of companies. This approach aims to help companies broaden and strengthen their account relationships, increase awareness and demand for their offer, and ultimately improve their financial results. The approach has been given various titles by the marketers involved (including: client centric, key account, account-based marketing, and one-to-one marketing).

The aim is to create an integrated *sales* and *marketing plan* for one customer, in the same way as is done for a generic market or *segment*. Usually there are two aspects to this: building credibility for the new *value proposition* inside the account; and getting the account team access to the right buyers and influencers for that proposition. Some of the marketing communication tactics include: customized *thought leadership* (on issues uncovered in the account analysis and summarized in the *value proposition*), dedicated portals or extranets, high value *direct marketing*, private seminars and workshops, content-rich *hospitality*, and customized testimonials or case studies. The channels most suitable for the messages and the best sequence of activity should be planned in as much detail as that for a more generic market. It is important to develop an integrated approach that incorporates multiple channels that the buyers and influencers use and trust.

(viii) Establishing a communications infrastructure

As with any marketing programme, success in marketing to specific organizations relies on good marketing management and programme management. This includes: agreeing the timeline for each campaign to each customer, creating a critical path of activities and milestones with each account team, and agreeing the governance process for the overall programme of activities. It is useful, for instance, to agree escalation procedures, as, often, the bespoke *marketing plan* relies on significant time and effort from various members of the account team and company executives, who may all be subject to other priorities and might miss the deadlines set for them.

History, context, criticism, and development

The concept of customer "account management" is based on the fact that certain buyers will give repeat business to a supplier whereas others will not. It developed when product companies found that revenue improved if they took different approaches to existing buyers than those used with "new business prospects". They found that the skills of a sales person focused exclusively on getting new customers were different to those of a "representative" dedicated to managing the orders from existing buyers. The latter is focused on creating longer term relationships and gets involved in many issues other than direct sales (such as complaints, billing, service, or administrative difficulties) which might threaten the business exchanges between the two sides.

Although used in retail, consumer goods, and the car industry, it was when this concept moved into the young computer industry (with its then obsession on its installed base of products) that there was progressive codification of major account management as a discipline. The practices of global market leader IBM, where account managers had been chosen, trained, and fêted for many years, were particularly influential. The concept has since moved into other industries and has been adopted, to a greater or lesser extent, by many different companies.

Even at its best, though, there are limitations to the sales aspects of account management. Much modern practice has been based, for instance, on processes pioneered by IBM in the 1980s. It had client relationship directors and detailed account plans with sophisticated prospecting and sales support. Yet, when (in the early 1990s) the company faced traumas due to dramatic changes in the computer market (like interoperability), it nearly collapsed. This was, in part, due to the fact that its account managers had missed changing customer needs. Similar difficulties occurred at BT. After it was privatized, it invested heavily in account managers but, within five years, its share of its prime market, the city of London, had dropped from 100% to under 20%. Yet, if account management sales theory (which was designed when these markets had semi-monopolistic distortions) was correct, neither should have got into that situation because their account managers would be so close to their customers.

So, account or relationship management as a discipline has its flaws. Account managers might, for instance, hoard information about their customers or miss more general trends because they are so focused on sales deals in one business. In fact, many companies have found that account management needs to be supported by service and marketing strategies to major customers. Leading firms in a range of international industries no longer see this as just a sales strategy or a marketing programme. They are creating products or services, value propositions, marketing strategies and communications programmes for one major customer at a time. This approach seems to have evolved more forcibly in the past decade because company after company has realized that some of their customers have revenues that exceed the GDP of some nation states. Logic suggests that if they were entering a new national market they would resource it with an experienced general manager and a range of operational capabilities. It would be much more than just a sales emphasis and so their most important customers should have more significant resources than just account sales teams. Some companies in business-to-business markets have called this "Account based marketing" (ABM) but it remains to be seen as to whether this becomes a generally recognized term.

Voices and further reading

*   "Client-centric marketing is about managing client perceptions of your services and capabilities . . . to move client perception in a positive direction over the long term. The perception should be able to endure beyond changes in client personnel and changes in the company. Generalist approaches are no longer enough in today's competitive market. No more going to big industry shows and trying to get clients to attend. This time, you customise the show, the round-table and the thought leadership. You still have to do the big shows to create the awareness, but it's no longer the basis of business to business services market-ing – client or account centric marketing will be the model of the future." Dr Charles Doyle, who initiated the original adoption of this technique at Accenture.
*   Cheverton, P., *Key Account Management*. Kogan Page, 1999.
*   Woodburn, D. and McDonald. M.H.B., *Key Account Management: The Definitive Guide*. John Wiley & Sons Ltd, 2011 (3rd edn).
*   "The management of a relationship is not at all like managing a basic or normal selling relationship. Instead of getting on and doing things . . . the key account manager needs to consider how to work through other people in the business, how to coordinate what they do, and how to gain an appropriate level of visibility of activity without drowning in communication and tasks." McDonald, ibid.
*   Bonoma, T.V., "Major sales: who really does the buying?" *Harvard Business Review*. July–August 2006.
*   Shapiro, B. and Posner, R.S., "Making the major sale". *Harvard Business Review*, July–August 2006.
*   ". . . for repetitive major sales the objective should be to develop long-term account relationships, not just sales. The supplier with an established account relationship has a significant competitive advantage. Because risks are high and an intimate buyer/seller relationship builds over time, buyers are hesitant to try new suppliers and tend to remain with established ones . . ." Shapiro and Posner, ibid.

Things you might like to consider

(i)   It is a simple fact that many companies are dominated by relationships with a few repeat customers. It is ridiculous for the marketing function to concentrate on the generic market, the acquisition of new business or generic campaigns if a large percentage of business comes from a few large organizations.

(ii) Just because they are a large customer to your company, it does not mean that you are significant to them. It may be that there is opportunity to penetrate these organizations much further. A marketer dedicated to major accounts should not become immersed in internal perspectives; they need to understand, as objectively as possible, the spend in their category by each of their major customers.

(iii) A surprising number of firms do not know the competitor account managers that deal with their major customers. How can any effective marketing be developed if they are unaware of what others are saying to the customer they value about the same matters they want to communicate?

(iv) Sophisticated marketing communication strategies (such as *network marketing*, *relationship marketing*, and *viral marketing*) should be deployed in marketing to major customers as much as, perhaps more than, to generic markets.

(v) This requires as sophisticated organizational capability as that deployed by leading firms to market to generic mass markets.

Xerox's Evolution of global account management

At the time of writing, Xerox is the world's largest technology and services company that specializes in document management. With sales of $17.6 billion and 57,100 employees in 160 countries, the company helps businesses deploy smart document management strategies and find better ways to work. Global account management is not a recent phenomenon for the firm as it first appointed them in 1988. But with increasing globalization, customer requirements have changed and the need for more strategic account management is even stronger.

Aware of the need to take their global account management to a new level, Xerox recently built a "global accounts community", which concentrates on making it easier for customers to do business with the company on an international basis. It resulted in a 27% revenue growth in two years. Xerox puts this success down to a stronger, more empowered, group of people.

GLOBAL BUSINESS

As with many large corporations, Xerox was international in scope but "not truly global". The company came to realize that although it had, over time, increased its number of global accounts to a hundred, it hadn't allowed for the considerable infrastructure or capabilities it needed to have in place to really support these accounts. It was also apparent that Xerox's approach to national and global accounts was "cookie cutter", with no real customization around the types of different accounts or geographical reach.

To improve its global account marketing, Xerox experimented with a new global programme that had a refined focus on the very top tier global accounts. Twenty-five accounts were selected as being globally strategic to Xerox, and requiring an integrated and coordinated global approach through dedicated client managing directors and virtual teams across the world.

One of the big catalysts that drove Xerox in this direction was its move to being more services focused. When providing services, the supplier no longer talks to just procurement or strategic sourcing, but also to executives running aspects of the business to get realistic input to their work. It's a very different dialogue than the "cost per print" conversation typical in Xerox's market. With the move from a product to a partnership approach, and the capability to offer global services, Xerox has been able to step above a lot of its competition and create a very different offer.

Although integrated into the broader sales structure, this was about strategic account management, not just "sales", and demanded a very different set of skills and capabilities from the account leadership. It was the result of external and internal pressure: to meet both the level of skill required by the customer and Xerox's ambition. Global business was complicated, with a need to ensure good balance between country and global strategies. The elements Xerox attributed their progress to were: leadership, account selection, coverage, infrastructure, and executive support. Removed from geographic boundaries and managed at the global level, the vision and strategy for these accounts was controlled by a much more empowered group of people than under the old regime of managing up through the organization.

LEADERSHIP

Senior leadership became the critical factor for these global accounts, both at general management and account levels. At the outset, Xerox put the top tier of accounts under the Vice President of global account operations, who reported directly to the Chairman and CEO. Later, it moved to the President of Xerox Global Services. The credibility and leverage of someone who sits at the senior table, sharing progress on a consistent basis, was fundamental to success.

At an account level, the client managing directors (CMDs), who owned the global strategy, had to build and maintain trusted relationships across different cultures, geographies, and economies. This demanded a high level of maturity and experience; articulate professionals who knew the industry and how to engage at executive level. The CMD role has proved to be a very different profile than the typical person Xerox would have hired ten years ago to lead accounts; the company had to recruit both internally and externally to find these capabilities.

ACCOUNT SELECTION

Like most companies, Xerox automatically gravitated towards the largest customers. Yet it was important to identify accounts where the relationship was strategically important for both parties. A primary reason to limit the number of global accounts was to maintain clear customer focus. So, Xerox went from a hundred to twenty-five "tier-1 accounts", as it only wanted companies in the programme with a true appetite for global business. Three initial criteria determined whether a company could become a global account:

*   The company had to be truly global, with operations in more than two regions and a substantial part of its business outside its home market;
*   The size of the company, both in existing and potential business;
*   The company needed to be organized in a global way, to have global procurement and willing to collaborate with Xerox in a global manner.

COVERAGE

A clear understanding of the scope of global accounts and determining how to add value delivers considerable return. Xerox had a dedicated person to design global plans for each of the top tier accounts and a clearer strategy for serving the world. It had the ability to take a close look at the client, really study where they are as a business, take advantage of the emerging and growth markets they were pursuing, and set up a coverage scheme that matched the client's needs more effectively than in the past. As a result, Xerox realized much more of its growth from new business in non-domestic areas than before.

INFRASTRUCTURE

Xerox found that delivering the right infrastructure for global operations underpinned performance. This included:

Global bid support – one of the toughest jobs was trying to negotiate pricing from four operating companies and a 160 countries around the world, particularly without a well coordinated pricing or contracting programme. (The importance of a coordinated bid increases considerably when offering services, where you can build a more complex proposition.) In the new programme all four operating companies had bid proposal teams and Xerox was able to pull together a much more effective and professional global account bid response. Whereas previously Xerox tended to bid for everything, it became routine to, first, decide whether to bid at all, through careful qualification criteria. As everybody participated towards a winning bid, Xerox developed the ability to smooth out inconsistencies that occur on the global stage. Certainly, with this programme, Xerox became more creative and differentiated, adding value rather than competing on price.

Global agility – a core capability that needed to be well resourced; global, regional, selective, and responsive. Until recently, only the Xerox global general manager or CMD had the ability to step outside of their country to help pursue a deal. Yet the pursuit teams' cross-border capability was essential to go after these big accounts, particularly with real growth coming from the emerging market regions that don't have the skill-sets required to pursue those opportunities. Xerox became a lot smarter at getting the people and teams who could really own the pursuit of opportunities into a variety of different countries.

Global compensation – Xerox introduced a new compensation plan for the top-tier team to help them drive global revenue. This comprised two key metrics: invoiced revenue and total contract value. Both were multi-year compensation plans to help people think longer term, a fundamental for global accounts. Ultimately, with senior people leading these accounts, a level of P&L responsibility was needed and so they set out to measure bottom line profitability.

As global plans can help to change the company's culture from a more siloed, "local geography" starting point, plans that were 100% country based changed radically to think about global revenues as well. For example, Xerox's Japanese organization had its account reviews at North America headquarters.

Communication this was important for virtual team networks. A good reporting system with alignment throughout the organization assisted a more customer-centric than geographic focus. Xerox's own web-based "DocuShare" has proved a valuable system for internal information sharing, and initiatives such as customized customer portals. From a sales perspective, Salesforce.com has enabled Xerox to manage global accounts more effectively and to provide information back to the countries as and when they needed it.

CORPORATE SPONSORSHIP

This global programme would not have thrived without the full support of senior management. Executive commitment was essential to help meet client expectations and drive the considerable changes needed. But it added most value by its indirect support of the CMDs, which enabled these people to have sufficient power to coordinate activities and influence priorities across traditional geographic and business unit boundaries. Xerox's focused executive programme was revised to ensure that the top ten executives in the organization were aligned to each of these twenty-five top tier accounts.

IN SUMMARY

Xerox built a strong global account community to meet the business needs of its most strategic global clients. It improved global bid success, a higher penetration of its services portfolio, greater levels of customer satisfaction, and many more "C-level" conversations in these priority accounts. It also garnered a "non-domestic" revenue growth of 27%, five times above that achieved in the other global accounts. According to Xerox, becoming a global company "never ends", with the need to constantly evolve as your strategic customers change; "It's a race without a finish".

Source: Based on an SAMA conference presentation by Tom Dolan and agreed for publication.

 RATING: Practical and powerful

 ADVERTISING

Application: communication of propositions, education, preparation for sales

The concept

Advertising is one of those vast subjects that it is very difficult to do justice to in this format. It is one of the best known aspects of marketing and captures the public imagination. People in large companies, in marketing agencies, and in universities dedicate their whole working life to it.

Advertising is, essentially, the practice of buying space in various public media, often called "above the line" (a throwback to the past which it is probably not worth going into) in order to communicate a message to a wide market; and, whatever anyone says, it unquestionably influences buyers (whether businesses or consumers). In fact, it has been behind the success of many of the world's most famous and favourite purchases (like Coca-Cola, Singer, Nike, Apple, Gillette, IBM, and Heinz).

Advertising is attractive because it communicates a message to a large audience very effectively. It is particularly good at communicating messages that require impact, like the launch of a new product or business. It is used extensively by both consumer and business-to-business companies but their commitment to it can be erratic and, as a result, not as effective as it could be. It has been most successful when business leaders have demonstrated a long-term financial commitment to it.

The media used include: broadcast media (television, radio and cinema), print media (newspapers and magazines), online media (websites, online publications, and mobiles), and outdoor media (like posters). Marketers need to plan carefully the use of this method of influencing their intended audience. As a result, advertising campaigns are calculated on the basis of the likelihood of their audience seeing or hearing the message a given number of times over a sustained period.

There are several aspects to good, effective advertising:

(i)   A first rate knowledge of the market and detailed analysis.
(ii) Clear, sometimes unique, insights into the human beings at which it is aimed. (See *behavioural aspects of marketing*).
(iii) A clear communication strategy, often held over many years.
(iv) A distinct, simple message.
(v)   A compelling idea. (This is different from a mere message. It is often the most value that advertising agencies add and there has been debate in the industry about charging for it separately.)
(vi) Organizational capability. (Evidence suggests that companies develop, just as in any other area of business, progressive organizational capability in advertising through, *inter alia,* processes, agency management, and brief clarification. This is at the heart of much success in advertising. There is no doubt that companies are likely to improve advertising effectiveness as they gain experience in more campaigns.)
(vii) Wonderful creative execution. In fact, there is, it seems, a clear link between creative and adverting effectiveness (see Field, P., 2010). This research, commissioned by Thinkbox and the British Institute of Practitioners in Advertising, showed correlation between a campaign's performance across the creative awards recognized by The Gunn Report, and their business performance in the IPA Effectiveness Awards databank (2000–2008). Amongst other findings, the research showed a direct correlation between strong advertising creativity and business success. Creatively-awarded campaigns were, on average, eleven times more efficient. It also revealed that many highly creative campaigns do not have enough media money invested in them. The client misses the opportunity to capitalize on creative excellence and leverage it to gain significant increases in market share.
(viii) Excellent media choice and management. The choice and purchase of media is a highly specialized and precise skill usually the province of dedicated firms (such as, at the time of writing, MediaCom, ZenithOptimedia, Carat, OMD, UM, MEC, PHD, Vizeum, or Mindshare).
(ix) Some form of success, payback or return measure.

Advertising does, however, have a number of drawbacks. Firstly, it can be expensive, requiring large investment to reach audiences through television or radio networks. Yet, the ability to target messages very finely has improved considerably over recent decades as the proliferation of media has occurred and audiences have migrated away from mass media toward the web, DVDs, cable, satellite, and even computer games. This has caused major advertisers to focus their media choices more precisely and has also reduced costs.

This fundamental change in the nature of media has prompted some advertisers to concentrate on prompting customers to access other channels (such as a web page). A business-to-business campaign might, for example, use social networking sites, blogs, radio, business or news-orientated TV channels, and specialist publications (such as in-flight magazines and trade papers). Called "narrow casting", this can sometimes be more effective and less costly than generic broadcast advertising of the past. A buyer listening to a jazz station in the car on the way home or reading a favourite blog online, or viewing a favourite TV channel on a specialized station, may be more influenced by this cheaper media than by a nationwide advert. Now, more than ever, advertising needs to be sophisticated and carefully planned communication run by specialists who manage spend judiciously and target precisely the intended audience. As a result, modern practice tends to emphasize multiple channels, particularly the web, and response management.

Secondly, there is such a deluge of messages aimed at modern buyers that it is hard to make a message stand out. So, advertising campaigns need to be creative and sustained. A well planned and eye-catching campaign running for, say, two years will eventually catch the attention of the intended audience and influence its thinking. The general rule of thumb seems to be that, when a firm's executives become bored or driven to distraction by their own advertising, the market is just beginning to get it.

Finally, the impact of advertising can be hard to measure. It is difficult to understand the return on advertising expenditure, even if it is well remembered or wins industry awards. Firms tend to create their own measures which help them come to a judgment about the return they get for the cost of advertising. One common practice, for instance, is to have one geography reserved as a quiet area, which does not receive the campaign. Differences in the effect on sales can then be estimated. There have been numerous attempts, going back several centuries, to find a universal, "scientific" measure of the financial benefits and economic effect of advertising but, at the time of writing, this is still elusive. Most senior executives in major companies establish some mechanism which indicates return to their own satisfaction.

History, context, criticism, and development

The use of good, effective paid advertising is older than many realize. This is not just an esoteric reference to the odd poster or handbill. Companies have indulged in good, systematic advertising that would be recognized by modern practitioners, for at least 300 years. For example, an advertisement in the British "Mercurius Politicus" of 20 December 1660 was for toothpaste ("Dentifice to scour and cleanse the teeth" see Turner, E.S., 1968). It emphasized the benefits of the product the way advertising would today (". . . making them white as Ivory . . . fastens the teeth, sweetens the breath and preserves the gums . . ."). Business leaders like Josiah Wedgwood (UK 1760s), Henry Heinz (USA 1880s), and Robert Woodruff (Coca-Cola 1920s) used advertising to build lasting brands and companies. One of the first advertising agencies in America, J. Walter Thompson, was created in 1878 and the oldest agency, according to Britain's History of Advertising Trust, was the "Publicke Register for general Commerce", founded in 1611. There were well known advertising consultants in both America (Elmo St Lewis) and the UK (Henry Samson) in the late Victorian period.

There were experienced and insightful advertising campaigns during the eighteenth and nineteenth centuries in at least America and the UK (and probably other developed nations like the Netherlands and Germany). Iconic campaigns have appeared in most cultures and created profit by capturing the imagination and dreams of people. They include: the Guinness animals, Pear's "Bubbles" image, Coke's "the real thing", and Esso's "tiger in your tank". Some (like De Beers' "Diamonds are forever") were long running and some were dramatic one-off's (like Apple's 1984 launch of the Mac at the Super Bowl). The approach has been successful for both consumer and business-to-business suppliers. It has worked for manufacturers, service suppliers, and retailers. It has also been successfully used for political campaigns and public service messages to educate.

Of course, over time, the volume and the methods have changed. At the start of the industrial revolution in the West and during the Edo period in Japan, for instance, handbills, "puffs", and Hikifuda were used. The latter have been described by one source: "as overwhelming as TV today" (Yamaki, T. and Fukatsu, K., 1995). As literacy and media grew, newspaper, radio, and TV advertising expanded, reaching the mass audiences of today.

So, advertising has an unashamedly successful heritage in creating wealth and profits for business leaders. Yet, not only has advertising launched and built brands, it has influenced society, introducing new language, social norms, and concepts. *"Cleanliness is next to godliness"* was, for instance, a 19th century slogan that Pear's soap used to enter the American market (a phrase that some people still think is in Shakespeare or the Bible). Haddon Sundbloom's 1931 adverts fixed Santa Claus, to this day, as a jolly plump man with bushy white beard in, of course, Coca-Cola red (before he had been depicted in various forms, like a tall green elf). The advertising of De Beers, which started in the 1930s, crystallized the habit of diamonds being given as a symbol of a marriage proposal and, in some countries, created the practice. Apart from creating cultural habits, advertising has also launched the careers of many fabulous artists (from William Hogarth, Santō Kyōden, and Toulouse-Lautrec to Salman Rushdie and Alan Parker). Much art in many societies simply would not have existed if advertising had not funded young artists and helped them to succeed.

Voices and further reading

- "Whatever is common is despised. Advertisements are now so numerous that they are very negligently perused, and it is, therefore, necessary to gain attention by magnificence of promises, and by eloquence sometimes sublime and sometimes pathetic. Promise, large promise, is the soul of an advertisement. I remember a wash-ball that had a quality truly wonderful – it gave an exquisite edge to the razor. And there are now to be sold, for ready money only, some duvets for bed-coverings, of down, beyond comparison superior to what is called otter-down, and indeed such, that its many excellencies cannot be here set forth. There are some, however, that know the prejudice of mankind in favour of modest sincerity. The vender of the beautifying fluid sells a lotion that repels pimples, washes away freckles, smoothes the skin, and plumps the flesh; and yet, with a generous abhorrence of ostentation, confesses, that it will not restore the bloom of fifteen to a lady of fifty." Ben Johnson, *The Thunderer* (Newspaper), 1759.

- "…the whole success of this business depends on advertising." King Gillette, 1912 (quoted in Lunn, P., 2010.)
- Ogilvy, D., *Confessions of an Advertising Man*. Southbank Publishing, 2004 (first published 1963).
- "Creating successful advertising is a craft, part inspiration but mostly know-how and hard work . . . its function is not to persuade people to try your product, but to persuade them to use it more often than other brands." Ogilvy, ibid.
- "No one doubts that advertising has done much to raise the standards of physical well-being. It has speeded the introduction of useful inventions to a wide as distinct select circle. It has brought prosperity to communities which did not know how to sell their rotting crops. By widening markets, it has enabled costs of raw materials to be cut, accelerated turnover, lowered selling prices. It has spread seasonal trade and kept people in employment. It has been a guarantee of dependability – for who would buy a nameless motor-car put together in a back-street workshop? The prime objective of the exercise was not, of course, to benefit humanity but to sell more fabrics, more toothpaste, more disinfectant." Turner, E.S., 1968.
- The *Advertising Works* series of books published by WARC annually. (These contain the winning cases from the IPA Effectiveness Awards plus chapters on the key insights from them.)
- Sternthal, B., "Advertising strategy" in Iacobucci, D., *Kellogg on Marketing*. John Wiley & Sons Ltd, 2001.

Things you might like to consider

(i) This method has been selling products and services, and building brands for at least 300 years. The main reason why senior people do not seriously consider using it is that they are inexperienced with it and baulk at the costs; and those that simply reject it need their head examined. Marketers in non-marketing or newer companies have a responsibility to shareholders to make the argument for using this stunningly effective tool.

(ii) To succeed this needs organizational competence and good management by people who know what they are doing. One campaign, however good, does not make the case for embedding this tool as a mechanism of long-term, systematic revenue growth.

(iii) Main media advertising is most effective when combined with other communication methods (like *direct marketing*, *digital marketing*, and *PR*) now described in a concept called "Integrated marketing communication" (see: *marketing communication*).

(iv) To be fair, some business leaders, like the late Anita Roddick (the founder of Body Shop) and Charles Schultz (of Starbucks), have created successful brands whilst being cautious of, or even opposed to, advertising. So, there is an alternative view and alternative choices.

(v) Marketers tend to lazily use the term ROI (return on investment) with regard to debate about the financial benefits of advertising. It is, though, a current account expense, a cost of day-to-day business and not an investment. It is sensible to use judgement about its value to the ongoing operations of the business and practical measures of sales effect. Only where it is directly contributing to the value of an investment might ROI or DCF analysis be appropriate. Modern accountancy tends to view brands, for example, as intangible assets (see *brand*) that can be valued in balance sheets. The investment in advertising to increase the value of these assets has been the subject of ROI and investment analysis in some companies.

(vi) Some argue (Godin, S., 2004) that, with the fundamental changes to TV and mass media, reliance on broadcast advertising should be cast aside. They propose creating word-of-mouth campaigns (see *viral marketing*) for groups of early adopters (see *diffusion of innovations*) to stimulate demand for distinctive new products. They argue that marketers should no longer concentrate messages to large audiences through mass advertising. This, though, seems risky and relies on just one aspect of sophisticated marketing communications (which has, admittedly, been used to grow nascent markets). Marketers, of course, need to be judicious, professional, and cautious in choice of media; but neglecting the full range of marketing communications and over 300 years of successful history seems risky.

Advertising Arthur's Guinness

Guinness is one of the world's most popular and well known drinks. It dates back to the 18th century where it was founded, in Ireland, by Arthur Guinness. The company, which was headquartered in London from 1932 onwards, merged with Grand Metropolitan plc in 1997 and was formed into the multi-national alcohol conglomerate Diageo.

Guinness has a very long history of investment in various aspects of marketing. For instance, its famous and familiar harp logo has been used as its trademark since around 1862. (It is similar to the harp of Brian Boru, a symbol of Ireland since the 16th century. Although the Guinness logo faces right instead of left, and so can be distinguished from the Irish coat of arms.)

Yet the brand's iconic stature is undoubtedly due to a long history of excellent advertising. The most famous and recognizable is probably the campaign run in the 1930s using illustrations of different animals. It was created by an advertising agency called Bensons and drawn by the artist John Gilroy. They used catch phrases such as "Lovely Day for a Guinness", "Guinness Makes You Strong," "My Goodness My Guinness," and most famously, "Guinness is Good For You". The animals included a kangaroo, ostrich, seal, lion, and notably a toucan, which has since became as much a symbol of Guinness as the harp. The novelist Dorothy L. Sayers, a copywriter at Benson at the time, wrote the copy of several of the adverts in question.

Like many successful brands, the commitment to really great, memorable advertising has been continued for decades. In the 1980s, for example, there was a multi-award-winning series of "darkly" humorous adverts, featuring actor Rutger Hauer, with the theme "Pure Genius". Whereas the 1994–1995 "Anticipation campaign" featured actor Joe McKinney dancing to "Guaglione" while his pint settled. It was so popular that it put the song in the charts for several weeks. In 2000, Guinness's 1999 advertisement "Surfer" was named the best television commercial of all time in a UK poll conducted by The Sunday Times and Channel 4.

Their UK commercial "Noitulove", was first broadcast in October 2005 and became the world's most-awarded commercial the following year. In it, three men drink a pint of Guinness, then begin to both walk and evolve backward. Their "reverse evolution" passes through an ancient homo sapiens, a monkey, a flying lemur, a pangolin, an ichthyosaur and a velociraptor until finally settling on a mud skipper drinking dirty water, which then expresses its disgust at the taste of the stuff, followed by the line "Good Things Come To Those Who Wait". The ad was called Noitulove – because it is Evolution backwards.

On 24th September 2009, the company initiated its "To Arthur" campaign which, in tune with modern thinking, went well beyond pure broadcast advertising. The objective of the campaign was to create "a programme of deep and engaging content, rich experiences and events". The aim was to harness 250 years of goodwill; to celebrate and perpetuate the goodness of Guinness. It combined broadcast advertising, modern digital media, event sponsorship, viral marketing and rewards to take advantage of an iconic moment: the 250th anniversary of the brand. The TV advert started with two friends realizing the long history and lifting up their glass saying "to Arthur!". This slowly spread through the bar to the streets outside and then around the world. The advert ended with an invitation to "Join the world-wide celebration".

Known as "Arthur's Day" this was, in fact, a series of events and celebrations taking place around the world to celebrate the life and legacy of Arthur Guinness and the beer which he brought to the world. (It took place for the second time at 17.59pm on 23rd September 2010.) Two versions of the Saatchi & Saatchi global ad featuring a toast to Arthur Guinness ran across the globe.

Apart from attracting the attention of consumers across the world, it was also designed as a way of giving something back to existing drinkers. For instance, Guinness organized a music event on Arthur's Day featuring some of the world's biggest artists (such as The Black Eyed Peas, Mystery Jets, Tom Jones, Johnny Flynn, and The Undertones). The celebrations were held in Dublin and around the world (in cities like New York, Lagos, and Kuala Lumpur). They also planned a series of "Guinness experiences" such as a trip into space on Richard Branson's Virgin Galactic Spaceship and a journey to Guinness' "deep sea bar".

So this highly successful brand has a history of investment in various aspects of marketing, from award-winning television advertisements to experiences, merchandising, and digital marketing. It is now using the full range of marketing communications to engage with modern consumers across the world. When presenting this to the prestigious conference of Britain's Marketing Society, Diageo representative, Natasha Clay, said: "A modern audience wants to be entertained and engaged by long cherished brands. This world-wide integrated campaign used different techniques to do that really effectively. We think we are continuing the tradition of Arthur Guinness in the modern world and the modern way."

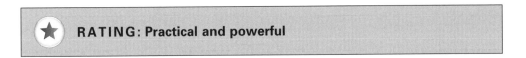

RATING: Practical and powerful

"AIDA"

Use: advertising planning, measurement

Figure A.4:   The AIDA concept

The concept

This little tool (see Figure A.4) is typical of a number of ideas (called "response hierarchy models") intended to be practical mechanisms to design, plan, and measure advertising and to plan sales calls. Although the concepts that they are based on vary, they assume that the buyer "passes through a cognitive, affective and behavioural stage"; to quote Professor Kotler (Kotler, P., 2003). In other words, they assume that buyers move through a number of states of mind in relation to buying any item. AIDA is one of the most widely known and taught. It assumes that people become interested in a product or service after the proposition has first gained their attention. Properly crafted, communication will then cause them to desire it. This, in turn, will prompt them to buy.

Advocates of this approach suggest that this tool can be used to plan the different methods of reaching customers in different states (using, for instance, advertising to gain attention and sales people to stimulate the action of purchase). They argue that this enables marketers to optimize marketing budgets and measure their effect. Suppliers should segment their intended market into groups of buyers who are at different stages in their buying process. Marketers should, first, estimate the total size of the market and the numbers in it. Research can then be used to understand the numbers of people who are in the different states of the model. By multiplying each group by the percentage that the sample is of the total market, the number of buyers in each group can be estimated. If this exercise is repeated after a campaign, the effect of the campaign can be estimated. At the time of writing, some surprisingly large and well known companies have major, worldwide measurement systems built on this concept.

History, context, criticism, and development

This dubious little concept has been very influential in the development of marketing theory. In the 1975, for instance, Professor E. Jerome McCarthy was still using it in the fifth edition of his book (McCarthy, E.J., 1975) as a basis for planning communications to the market. The phrase "integrated marketing communication" (see: *marketing communication*) did not exist then, so he used AIDA to wrap the activities of selling and advertising into one process in order to optimize the use of funds and to maximize effectiveness. As his was the work that codified the simplistic and infamous "*four Ps*", this concept was also built into the mid-century codification of marketing thought. Although logical at the time, it probably shouldn't have been.

It really is obvious that some academics simply do not read the references they quote to support the assertions they make. Several, for instance, quote the source of this idea as an article called "Theories of selling" published by E.K. Strong in 1925. Strong was an academic who specialized in psychology and was at Stanford at the time. In fact, the source is earlier and very different. It appears, for instance, in text books on advertising in the early 1920s (see Tipper et al., 1922). In his article, Strong attributes it to a leading advertising consultant of the late 1800s, E. St Elmo Lewis. Lewis (1872–1948) was nationally recognized in the United Sates as a leading teacher and writer on advertising, co-founding the Association of National Advertisers. He wrote several books and advocated the AIDA approach around 1889. It seems to have caught the imagination of business people as a sales tool, giving a clear framework in America for the very first time. They seem to have been taught to use the idea as a format for controlling the conversation with customers in order to gain a sale.

Ironically, Strong's 1925 article is pointing out that the idea is "dying out to some extent". He refers to developing ideas in "behaviouristic psychology" and combines this with a review of literature of the time to suggest his own structure ("Want, solution, action and satisfaction"). Psychology has, of course, moved on significantly in a hundred years, influencing marketing, selling and, increasingly, economics. The verified, scientific progress in understanding both human behaviour and the physiology of the brain has been applied to marketing problems. Behaviourists would now be much less rigid in suggesting the stages that human beings go through when moving toward buying anything.

Moreover, the concept was first mooted before many marketing media existed, for instance, before the cinema and broadcast radio, let alone television and the internet. The audiences that modern media have to reach are, of course, larger and more sophisticated than they were a hundred years ago. Also, in the years since, thinking around the buying and sales process has changed radically. Neil Rackham's "SPIN selling" (Rackham, N., 1995) has, for example, received wide acclaim. In it he suggests an approach to selling which asks a number of significant questions to get to the heart of a customer's need. As his work is based on analysis of 35,000 sales transactions in different industries, it is reasonably robust. Similarly, recent trends in several industries to "climb the value chain" as a response to harsh buying processes have led to "*solutions selling*" and "*consultative selling*" (see *sales*). Each demands a customized approach and the need to relinquish the sales agenda to the customer. AIDA as a prescribed, controlling sales approach is largely discredited.

Voices and further reading

- "Satisfaction is . . . most important because unless the goods measure up to expectations there will be no repeat orders. When 'want' is emphasized first, 'getting attention and interest' ceases to be a major problem. Whenever one of a prospect's wants is called to his mind, his attention and interest are automatically secured, and are essentially relevant. Consequently, the terms 'attention and interest' can be eliminated from selling and advertising literature." Strong, E., 1925.
- "In practice, few messages take the consumer all the way from awareness through purchase, but the AIDA framework suggests the desirable qualities of any communication." Kotler, P., 2003.

Things you might like to consider

(i) To be fair, despite its age and dubious nature, the thinking behind this idea, and others like it, can still be useful. Reminding marketers involved in communications (particularly advertising agencies) that people need to move progressively towards a purchase can give focus to campaigns.

(ii) This concept is very old and based on a pseudo-scientific, rational view of human behaviour. People are rarely so linear in either their response to communications or their purchase behaviour.

(iii) The tool is sometimes used to set communication objectives. If the marketer knows the attitude of their market, then objectives can be set in the light of that knowledge. If the customers are unaware of an offer, for example, then the very first, simple communication objective is to create awareness.

(iv) It works quite well in indicating the effect of communications on a large market. If, after a campaign, a number of customers indicate that they have been convinced to engage, then it is likely to have had some effect. The precise use of its terms to measure the progressive change in segments of customers is, though, a little risky and misleading.

(v) It is probably wise in a 21st century economy with complex media to be wary of relying too heavily on a 19th century view of human behaviour little developed to cope with even 20th century mass media. Don't you think?

★ **RATING: Toxic**

ANSOFF AND HIS MATRIX

Application: Innovation, acquisition strategy, development of marketing strategy

The Ansoff matrix

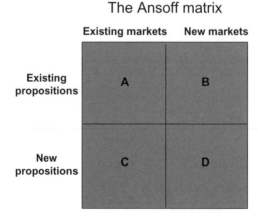

Figure A.5:   The traditional representation of Ansoff's matrix

The concept

Figure A.5 above represents Ansoff's matrix as it is taught in colleges today and as it appears in text books across the world. (It is depressing that many inaccurately quote the source of this diagram as his 1957 *Harvard Business Review* article, where it does not actually appear. That article has the more detailed version below.) As taught, the idea suggests that firms distil their strategic options by focusing their thinking through a review of existing markets, new markets, existing products, and new products. So, even at its simplest, it is a useful mechanism to help leaders reach consensus during strategy debates.

The first step in its use is the analysis of product and market opportunities. This may begin with a simple list of all the existing product/market groups in which the company is established. Then using market reports, research and creative techniques like brainstorming, it is possible to identify other opportunities. Once the analysis is available the options can either be summarized, using judgement, into the simplified version of the tool or crafted into a more thorough analysis by creating a cell for each product/market match (using the original version of Ansoff's work, shown below). The opportunities can either be discussed by the leaders at this stage or prioritized using agreed criteria. Ansoff himself recommended that, due to the risk and cost involved, firms conduct risk analysis of the more likely strategies.

The matrix helps leaders think through four different growth strategies, which require different marketing and communications approaches. They are presented below in what is taught as ascending order of risk:

- "Market penetration" is increasing market share with existing propositions to current markets.
- "Market extension" or market development is targeting existing propositions at new markets.
- "Product development" is developing new propositions for existing markets.
- "Diversification" is growing new businesses with new propositions for new markets.

The matrix helps to clarify leaders' thinking and to illustrate the very different strategic approaches needed for each of the four strategies. Ideally, an operational marketing plan should be created for each strategic option that is finally approved.

History, context, criticism, and development

Professor H. Igor Ansoff (1918–2002) was probably one of the first truly influential corporate strategy professors. In fact, he was nicknamed the "father of strategic management" because, before the publication of his book on corporate strategy, companies had very little guidance on how to plan for the future; most, it seems, simply extrapolated from existing budgets.

A highly accomplished mathematician and engineer, he worked in both academia and industry. Apart from roles at UCLA and what is now the Alliant International University, he was also, for instance, employed by the Rand and Lockheed Aircraft corporations, where he was the corporate planner. He was committed to the view that strategy and plans should not only be clearly and logically linked but should also be based on detailed and thorough data analysis. This combination of the practical and academic made his work appealing to a wide audience. There is some suggestion, for instance, that he coined the phrase "paralysis by analysis".

Ansoff's work was originally presented as corporate strategy, giving direction to the entire business. It is most famous now, though, for his work in what he called the "growth vector"; that is marketing strategy. His concepts are based on such thorough and long-standing analysis that they deserve greater respect and use than the over simplification taught today.

Ansoff's original representation of the concepts he discovered and developed (see Ansoff, H.I., 1957) was more sophisticated than the way it is normally represented in modern publications. It was designed to stimulate wide thinking, innovation, and entrepreneurialism at the top of companies. He was particularly interested in diversification opportunities. His work was based on analysis of M&A activity by American businesses in the first half of the 20th century. He suggested that there were two key bases for diversification, which he made the axes of his diagram. They were:

* "Product lines": referring to both the physical characteristics of the product and its performance characteristics (i.e. services).
* "Markets": He called these "product missions" rather than buyer segments. By this he meant "all the different market alternatives" or the various uses for the product and its potential uses. His reason for defining it in these terms was to make business leaders innovative and open minded about sectors and opportunities.

He proposed his matrix as a way of constructing different "product-market" strategies; those "joint statements of a product line and the corresponding set of missions which the products are designed to fulfil". His original diagram is reproduced below in Figure A.6 (π represents the product line and μ the "missions").

Interestingly, this representation of his work puts much less stress on market penetration than the popularly used version and details the many strategic options that arise from thinking broadly about the fusion of product and market possibilities. In other words, it was designed as an innovation tool.

Teachers who shake their heads alarmingly about the risks of diversification strategies seem to miss the fact that his HBR article was called "strategies *for* diversification". In fact, there is some suggestion that his work, as it became famous, led to some of the hugely successful diversified businesses of the mid century, like Hanson and GE; because it was read and admired by people at the most senior levels of business, who began to accept the idea that top executives should engage in and direct corporate strategy. The introduction to the 1985 reprint of his 1968 book on corporate strategy

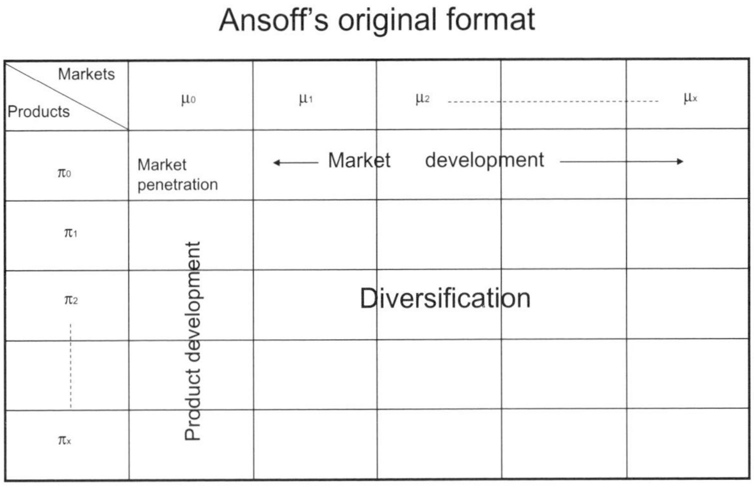

Ansoff's original format

Figure A.6: Ansoff's diagram as it appears in his original 1957 article

(Ansoff, 1985) was, for example, written by Sir John Harvey Jones, the then chairman of ICI, in which he said:

> It is a remarkable tribute to Professor Ansoff's foresight and analytical ability that the book, which was first issued in 1968, continues to sell in such quantity . . . it must rank as one of the most successful business books of all time. . . . planning must be done by the board as a whole . . .

When making the case for diversification, Ansoff pointed out that, without it, companies can fall short of their growth targets (because, for example, of market saturation). He differentiated between horizontal and vertical differentiation; and also argued that it should be based on a "common theme" of the company (an early articulation of what later became known as "the core competence of the corporation").

In fact, the more simplified version of his matrix is just one four by four model that appears in this book. He used it to show that a firm's diversification polices could be based on its "common thread" if they understood the "growth vector of their business". By grounding their innovation and diversification strategy in the heritage of market penetration or product development, risk could be managed.

Voices and further reading

- Ansoff, H. Igor, "Strategies for diversification". *Harvard Business Review*. 35:5, September–October 1957.
- Ansoff, H. Igor, "A model for diversification". *Management Science*, 4:1, July 1958.

- Ansoff, H. Igor, et al., *Twenty Years of Acquisition Behavior in America.* Cassell, 1972. A long term study (1946–65) into the effectiveness of corporate mergers and acquisitions as a means of business growth.
- Ansoff, H, Igor, *Corporate Strategy.* McGraw-Hill, USA, 1965 and Penguin Books, UK, 1985.
- Ansoff, H. Igor, *Business Strategy* (editor and contributor) Penguin Books, 1969.

Things you might like to consider

(i) This is based on personal experience and profound, detailed research over several decades. It is an evidence-based conceptual tool.

(ii) At its simplest, the four box model is a useful summary of strategic choices in growth strategies. It prompts senior people to think through the very different approaches to the four different choices; and is useful, if more precise thinking, consensus, or clarity is what's needed. It is, though, a vast over-simplification which exaggerates market penetration.

(iii) The heart of this tool has been lost. It is, in fact, an innovation stimulation technique. It prompts executives to think of multiple applications for their products and services; and to apply them to different customer opportunities and segments.

(iv) The work was conducted, in America, in the early and mid 20th century with a bias toward the scientific approach and engineering, data-based analysis. It is well received in engineering cultures like technology companies, oil firms, and utilities. It may be less appropriate to service businesses, more intuitively run firms, and some international cultures.

(v) The work was based largely on the experience of manufacturing companies. Many of the modern economies are now dominated by service firms.

(vi) To regard the four strategic choices as an ascending order of risk is naive and superficial. Ansoff argued that each opportunity be considered but sophisticated risk analysis used before decisions are taken. The latter approach is routinely undertaken by people involved in acquisitions. To teach marketing specialists that, for example, diversification should be dismissed as too risky locks them out of potentially highly rewarding growth opportunities.

(vii) This tool is about revenue growth. It makes acquisition as part of growth strategy a routine part of marketers' considerations.

(viii) It is powerful at engaging non-marketing senior executives in the development of growth (i.e. their marketing) strategies.

(ix) Don't you just love Ansoff's description of marketing strategy as the "growth vector of the business"?

 RATING: Practical and powerful

🔍 AUDIT (THE MARKET AUDIT)

Application: market analysis

Overview of a market planning process.

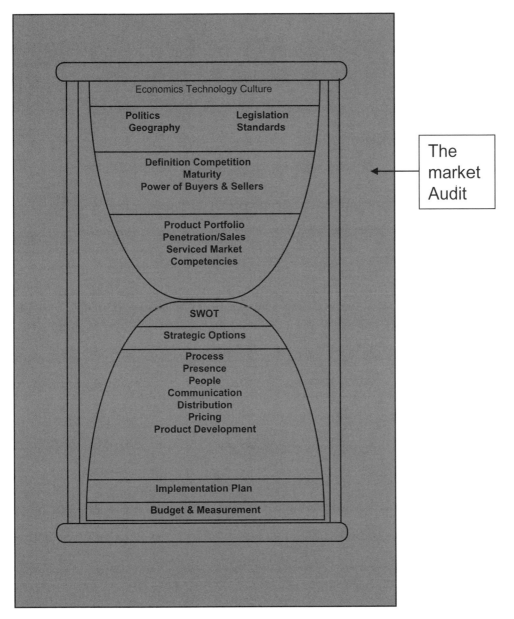

Figure A.7: A representation of a typical linear market planning process, with integral market audit

The concept

The market audit is an attempt to conduct dispassionate, objective, and logical analysis of a market. The aim is to think through a number of aspects of a market as part of a sequential market planning process. As each step is completed, "insights" from that analysis are distilled into a summary of market perspective. These can, in turn, be used as a basis for the development of *marketing strategy* and *marketing plans*.

Figure A.7 attempts to represent this logical, analytical approach to marshalling marketing resources. The top section is the market audit, a sequential set of steps leading to strategic options and detailed planning. Not all need to be started sequentially but each yields insight that supplements others and may cause some to be re-evaluated. Analysis of the macro market and a lack of good data might, for instance, prompt the need for specific, detailed customer or competitor research, unforeseen at the start of the process.

The analysis is conducted in the following steps:

Step 1: Analysis of external forces affecting the market; audit of the marketing environment (sometimes called environmental analysis)

This helps the firm to understand the macro-economic forces shaping markets, creating or destroying opportunities within them. They include:

* The raw forces affecting the market. Changes, for instance, in economics, social demography, and technology affect the prosperity of the market and there is little the firm can do to influence them.
* Human initiatives which moderate the impact of those raw forces on a market such as: politics, law, and industry-specific regulation. Politicians at all levels, for instance, create legal frameworks which affect the efficiency and prosperity of markets. These can be influenced by marketing skills.

By trawling through published data on these issues and drawing them into an integrated perspective, surprisingly powerful insights can be found. They could, for instance, highlight an issue on which firms might need to lobby regulators. In fact, damage can be caused if they are neglected. The elite executive search market, for example, works on the basis that management talent is in demand and needs to be found by specialists. Some cultures, however, regard this as unfair and would prefer all roles to be clearly advertised. This so called "German model" nearly became the standard practice for the European union when it reviewed this market in the late 1990s. The political debate eventually went the other way and a threat to the future profits of the participants in this industry was averted. Interestingly, though, few of them knew it was going on and even fewer set out to influence a debate which could have destroyed their business.

These external forces are often remembered with the mnemonic "PESTEL" (politics, economics, social changes, technology impact, environmental changes, and legislation). Even this limited analysis can yield useable information. If executives in a firm are asked to collect data under each heading and then meet to work through each subject area, profound insights can emerge.

Step 2: Analysis of the market structure

The next significant step in a market audit is to get a perspective on the structure and dynamics of the specific market or markets in which the firm operates.

*   Decide the market's definition. (See *market definition*)
*   Plot the maturity of the market. (See *market maturity*)
*   Determine purchasing power. What is the balance of power between suppliers and buyers?
*   Examine competition. Who are they and what are their strategies? (See *competitive strategy*)
*   Analyse substitutes. Can buyers get the benefits of the offer in any other way?
*   Segment the market. (See *segmentation*)

A powerful method of getting an objective view of these factors in a market is Michael Porter's competitive intensity work (See *Porter's five forces*).

Step 3: Detailed buyer analysis and research

This involves analysis of *research* into the needs and aspirations of existing and intended buyers. It is wise to start by collecting all published research and previously conducted *research* projects in order to identify gaps in knowledge. Marketers may then come to the conclusion that a specific study is needed to fill important gaps in knowledge. If so, this is likely to be the most costly and longest aspect of the market audit. Yet, it can be the most valuable. Marketers should reassess the viability of their *segmentation*, the offer to those segments, *pricing*, and communication approaches in the light of this research.

Step 4: Internal analysis/effectiveness review

This is about understanding the position of the firm within its market by detailed analysis of both its own competencies and the profile of its buyers. It includes: the source of business, revenue and income trends and the potential for growth. This analysis can yield surprising insights. Some firms, for example, believe that their buyers are chief executives, when analysis shows them to be lower level specialists. Others have been surprised to find that larger corporate accounts are less profitable than mid–market, smaller customers. Such insights can yield real benefit for the firm's approach to its market.

Professor Kotler (Kotler, 2003) recommends that the internal analysis covers: "marketing strategy audit" (mission, objectives, and strategy), marketing organization audit (formal structure and functional efficiency), marketing systems audit (CRM, planning, and NPD systems), marketing productivity audit, and the marketing function audit (the four Ps, see *marketing mix*).

The characteristics of the market audit are:

(i)   It should be comprehensive; gaining a perspective on the market and covering all the marketing activities of the business.
(ii) It should be systematic, conducting analysis in a clear, logical order.
(iii) It should be objective and independent. The aim of the approach is to gather knowledge and insight into the market situation in as objective a way as possible.
(iv) It should be undertaken periodically.

The audit starts with a management meeting to agree what data will be collected in what format and by whom. A detailed, timed, and costed programme then needs to be produced.

History, context, criticism, and development

This is quite a recent method, developed (largely) by Professor Malcolm McDonald through his highly successful books on market planning processes. The concept does not seem to appear in marketing texts before the 1970s, for instance. It has been accepted and integrated into the many text books on the "principles" of marketing and is routinely taught as a respected, analytical method. There does not seem to have been rigorous critique of it or diagnosis as to why many companies do not adopt it. It was developed at a time when logical, systematic approaches to strategy and planning were in vogue; and when traditional economic assumptions were commonplace. As promulgated, for instance, it might neglect modern insights into relationship marketing or behavioural economics. Moreover, some strategy specialists are currently saying that the implementation of plans and strategies is never linear. Human dynamics in organizations mean that more fluid perspectives, like complexity theory, are better explanations for what occurs. It is interesting, for instance, that a more flexible technique for capturing market insight, *scenario planning*, has been the preferred method in integrating market analysis into corporate plans; and is moving progressively into marketing functions (see Ringland, G. and Young, L., 2006). The market audit remains, though, as a flexible, logical process to give direction to analysis and to structure thinking. It should be able to assimilate these developing perspectives.

Voices and further reading

- "Study of the market is fully as important as study of the product. Who are the people who form the natural market for the goods you have to sell? Where do they live? How do they live? What are their buying habits? How much can they pay for a product like yours . . . Is the market local, state-wide, national, or international? What about competition? How many competitors have you? What is their relative strength . . . Can the total consumption be increased? Can you get your share increased?" Butler, R.S., 1917.
- "Whereas market analysis should reveal opportunities and identify products and services that might best take advantage of them, the environment should be examined in order to pinpoint any potential obstacles or constraints . . . changes can reveal opportunities as well . . . the environment consist of exogenous variables that exist outside the marketing department and thus beyond its direct control. The six most important are…" (He cites: Competition, the economy, political and legal elements, company objectives and resources, culture, and technology.) Hise, R.T., 1977.
- "A marketing audit is a comprehensive, systematic, independent and periodic examination of a company's or a business unit's marketing environment, objectives, strategies and activities with a view to determining problem areas and opportunities and recommending a plan of action to improve the company's marketing performance." Kotler, 2003.
- "An audit is a systematic, critical and unbiased review and appraisal of the environment and of the company's operations. . . . Often the need for an audit does not manifest itself until things start to go wrong for a company, such as declining sales, falling margins, lost market share, underutilized capacity and so on . . . The audit is a structured approach to the collection and analysis of information and data in the complex business environment and an essential prerequisite to problem-solving." McDonald, M.H.B., 1992.
- McDonald, M.H.B. and Wilson H., *Marketing Plans. How to Prepare Them: How to Use Them*. John Wiley & Sons Ltd, 2011 (7th edn).
- "That's the trouble with the market audit; it's a dispassionate, objective and rational approach to a passionate and emotional environment: a market" Paul Fifield (in correspondence about this book).
- "Relationship marketing adds an extra dimension to marketing planning and the marketing audit. In viewing marketing as part of the interaction and events in a network of relationships, we have to broaden the marketing function beyond marketing and sales departments and company boundaries." Gummerson, E., 2003.

Things you might like to consider

(i)   The market audit is a logical, linear process which suits large organizations with a systematic approach to market planning. It may not be well received in more intuitively run, flexible organizations.

(ii) It is based on a traditional economic view of a market, so there is a danger that behavioural insights will be missed.

(iii) There is some confusion between a market audit (trying to get an objective and detailed view of a market) and a marketing audit (analysis of the marketing capabilities of the firm). It is important to be clear about what is needed and why.

(iv) Although practical and logical, this is still not a widely known or widely taught concept.

(v)   As Professor Alderson said (Alderson, W. 1957) markets develop herd behaviours. Marketers and customers both develop language, concepts, and beliefs which are unique to a market. One of the strengths of the market audit process is its requirement to step back and objectively examine market dynamics. That alone can lead to profound insights that, sometimes, only outsiders and newcomers can see.

 RATING: Practical

BEHAVIOURAL INSIGHTS FOR MARKETING

Application: almost every aspect of marketing but especially segmentation, branding, NPD/NSD, and communication

Maslow's hierarchy of needs

Once a stage has ceased to motivate, the next stage motivates

External events mean that individuals (and organizations) can go down, as well as up

Self Actualization

Esteem

Each stage motivates — until satisfied — then it CEASES to motivate

Belonging & Love

Each stage is a discrete step

Safety

Physiological

Figure B.1: Maslow's hierarchy of needs

The concept

Time and again marketers have succeeded through gaining and exploiting an insight into human beings, their behaviour, and motivations. Whether it is successful branding, clever segmentation, iconic advertising, or stunning product innovation, human insight has been behind many of the successes of marketing. Sometimes this has resulted from the intuition of business leaders, sometimes from the outstanding creativity of a bloody minded or odd individual, sometimes through dogged trial and error and, often, through insights from field *research*. It is without doubt, though, that ever since marketers have sought to study and codify marketing, they have tried to find systematic, credible means to understand human behaviour. This means that they have sought out disciplines in the behavioural sciences like psychology, sociology, anthropology and, more recently, the still controversial behavioural economics. The fundamental view of the people who lead this is, quite sensibly, that marketing is about people, not products. It has led to several sub disciplines in marketing such as *consumer behaviour* and *organizational buying behaviour*.

As a result, marketers in all disciplines borrow concepts from the behavioural sciences in order to try to gain competitive advantage. One of the most commonly known concepts that has been used to understand human motivation is, for example, Maslow's "Hierarchy of needs" (shown in Figure B.1). In his book, (Maslow, A., 1970), Abraham Maslow suggested that human beings have a hierarchy of motives. He argued that, once they have lower needs (like security and hunger) satisfied, they are then motivated to satisfy others which are more esoteric and higher status, like the need for "self actualization" (the desire to make life meaningful). Maslow was not rigid about the layers and acknowledged that people such as artists or priests can be motivated in different ways, neglecting the lower level needs for a greater gain at the higher level.

This model can clearly be related to marketing. The "need to belong" for instance, explains a tendency for people to identify with a brand ("I am a *Vogue* reader"), new social networking sites, and segmentation. Whereas, in the recent recession, the threat to security meant that many consumers would not respond to marketing of higher level products and services even if they had actual cash. This, though, is just one of many useful concepts from the behavioural sciences.

Another famous term used extensively in marketing (often without the first idea what it really means) is "cognitive dissonance"; framed by social scientist Leon Festinger in 1957. He suggested that people hold a number of "cognitions" (types of knowledge) at any one time and that they form irrelevant or dissonant relationships with one another. These might be emotions or values or behaviours. He argued that people avoid information which causes dissonance with what they already know or value. This influences choice of reading or TV viewing. It can be a powerful force affecting the marketing messages that people respond to. It can also be a contributor to *post purchase distress* if customers grow dissatisfied with an important purchase. They will tend to emphasize positives and ignore negatives to reassure themselves that they did the right thing.

In some cases, marketing specialists have cooperated with behavioural disciplines. For example, at Harvard, Gerald Zaltman set up a unit which combined psychologists and marketers. He and Stephen Kosslyn (an expert in cognitive neuroscience) formed their "Mind of the market lab", an interdisciplinary group of scholars who meet to discuss addiction, irrationality, memory, and learning (see Zaltman, G., 2003). It is an unabashed attempt to use developing behavioural and physical science to gain insight for the advantage of marketing.

Behavioural aspects of marketing are, then, the drive to understand human beings and the way they make decisions to buy. A range of concepts from behavioural disciplines have been used to understand: communication, perception, motivation, learning, attitude, personality, and group behaviour (both as part of a family and a work organization). From the very famous (like Freud and Pavlov) to a range of different models or concepts (like transactional analysis, see Harris, T.A., 1973; and even Myers Briggs personality types), different constructs have been used by marketers to understand markets and gain insight into buyer behaviour.

Behavioural economics has a lot to offer in this field. This approach challenges some of the assumptions of traditional economics (for example, that mankind always acts in selfish self-interest operating in free, impersonal markets). It is based on experimentation and observation which should interest any marketer. For example, this branch of economics talks about the "endowment effect", that human beings appear to value something they already own almost twice as much as something they have yet to gain; that something already owned is instinctively valued more highly. Understanding this properly can help loyalty, brand, and marketing communication strategies.

History, context, criticism, and development

Human insight has been at the heart of marketing's contribution to profit for at least 300 years. In 18th century Britain, Josiah Wedgwood raised himself from grinding poverty to millionairedom through understanding that a new "middling class" of people (as he called them), created by the industrial revolution, would spend their new money aping the taste of the wealthy and he tracked changes in fashion as closely as any celebrity designer today. In 19th century America, Henry Heinz not only understood that farmers' wives would value the time saved in their busy lives if there were high quality food preparations but also that the new railways opened up fantastic opportunities in distribution as shop keepers faced an onslaught from fast growing markets. In the depression hit mid 20th century Oppenheimer (and his advertiser JWT) understood that, despite war and pestilence, "diamonds were a girl's best friend" when her potential mate was talking wedding bells. And in the hip, connected, fast moving world on the cusp of the 21st century, Charles Schultz of Starbucks understood that even the independent young needed the sanctuary of that "other place".

Sometimes, these techniques get muddled with existing business lore (as in the case of the *product life cycle* and *the diffusion of innovations*); sometimes they get chosen randomly and out of context; and sometimes (as with Strong's 1925 critique of *AIDA*) they are simply ignored. Other times, profound insight has been criminally neglected. For example, one of the leading marketing academics of the 1950s was Wroe Alderson from Wharton. He published a treatise (Alderson, W., 1957) which he called, rather boringly, "functionalism" (perhaps the reason why it did not gain traction or catch imaginations!) but it is no less useful. He argued that mankind is a tribal creature and that markets are examples of group or herd behaviour. Herd behaviour has, for instance, affected investment markets creating boom and bust for many centuries (from the Dutch Tulip bubble and the English South Sea investment craze to the dot com boom and the junk mortgage debacle of the 21st century). Markets develop their own beliefs, language, icons, symbolism, and narratives. Marketing directors, competitors, business leaders, and even customers collude in these group dynamics. An understanding of this is, he argued, vital to marketing strategy and communications.

Voices and further reading

- Alderson, Wroe, *Marketing Behaviour and Executive Action*. Richard D. Irwin Inc., 1957.
- "The Author holds that market behavior is typically group behavior and that individuals generally seek to achieve their purposes through the functioning of organized behavior systems. He draws upon such varied fields as sociology, psychology, anthropology and political science for the elements of group behavior." Alderson, W., 1957.
- Lunn, P., *Basic Instincts: Human Nature and the New Economics*. Marshall Cavendish, 2010.
- "The science of shopping: the way the brain works". *The Economist*, 20 December 2008.
- Lovallo, D. and Sibony, O., "The case for behavioural strategy". *McKinsey Quarterly*, March 2010.
- Zaltman, G., *How Customers Think*. Harvard Business School Press, 2003.
- Welch, N., "A marketer's guide to behavioural economics". *McKinsey Quarterly*, February 2010.
- "Marketers have long been aware that irrationality helps shape consumer behavior. Behavioural economics can make that irrationality more predictable." Welch, ibid.
- Thaler, R. and Sunstein, C., *Nudge*. Penguin, 2009.
- "By treating individuals like so many Robinson Crusoes taking independent, autonomous decisions, traditional economic theory fails to account for the social dimension of human activity." Ormerod, P., 2010.
- Page, G. and Raymond, J., "Cognitive Neuroscience, Marketing and Research: Separating Fact from Fiction". ESOMAR conference 2006.
- Allen, S., "The next discipline: applying behavioural economics to drive growth and profitability". Gallop Consulting, 2009.
- "To make sense of how employees and customers behave, leaders must first begin to understand human nature and accept that human beings do not always react

in rational ways . . . Fortunately, there is an emerging management discipline based on the principles of behavioural economics that can help business leaders and executives make sense of the economic behaviour of real people and serve as a platform for effective management solutions." Allen, ibid.

- "Creative people are, in fact, strong believers in the inverted Maslow pyramid. The definition of spirituality as the 'valuing of the nonmaterial aspects of life and intimations of an enduring reality' really finds its relevance in creative society . . . The rise of the creative scientists and artists, consequently, changes the way human beings see their needs and desires." Kotler, P. et al., 2010.
- Loewenstein, G., *Exotic Preferences*. Oxford University Press, 2008. An edited collection of some of the long standing issues and research projects in behavioural economics by one of the area's leading specialists and other authors.
- Solomon, M., Bamossy, G., Askegaard, S., and Hogg, M. K., *Consumer Behaviour; A European Perspective*. Prentice Hall, 2006. A thorough and well worked review of the field of consumer research which closely relates to and uses many behavioural concepts and their relationship to marketing.

Things you may wish to consider

(i) Various behavioural techniques and models have been chosen and used erratically by both practical marketers and marketing academics over the years. Unfortunately, there does not seem to be the credible, high quality dialogue between marketing and the social sciences that exists in other industries or professions. So, it is rational to step back and take professional, specialist advice on the aspects of behavioural science most relevant to a market or strategic problem, rather than randomly choosing a favourite from the lexicon of concepts.

(ii) At the time of writing, after the credit crunch and the worst recession for seventy years, people are reaching for behavioural economics as a means to explain what went on. (The previous mathematical models of investment markets have, by and large, been discredited.) More serious consideration of behavioural disciplines is being adopted by economists, politicians, financial regulators, and observers. It will be taken more seriously by business leaders and will begin to affect strategy.

(iii) Much of the traditional thinking behind market analysis appears to be based on traditional economics. Behavioural economics yields insights which might create more competitive advantage and distinct opportunities.

(iv) Unlike traditional economics and some marketing theory, behavioural assertions tend to be based on experimentation and research, rather than mathematical models.

 RATING: Practical and powerful

BLUEPRINTING

Application: service design

Blueprinting

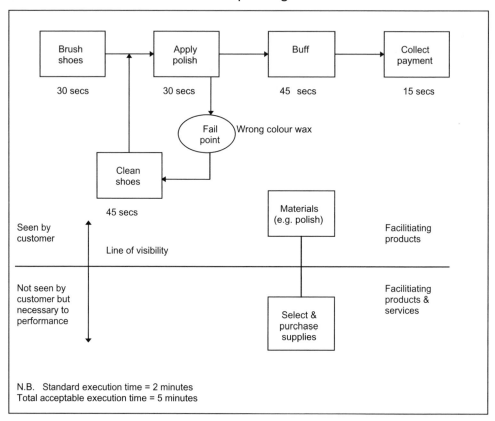

Figure B.2:   Lyn Shostack's representation of a simple service blueprint (from Shostack, G.L., 1982)

The concept

Services, unlike products, contain a process through which a customer must move and that process should be designed or "blueprinted". Process is central to the success of the service and the nature of the experience that the customers receive. When people use a service they must submit themselves to the service provider's process. So, one of the major differences between the purchase of a product and the experience of a service is the process through which the buyer moves (see *services marketing*).

Marketers must plan the service process in detail and educate their customers in the parts of the service they will experience. Potential customers must know how to access the supplier's service system, which has to be designed to encourage use. The firm needs to use clear signage and communicate its meaning to all potential buyers. Educating them to access and use the supplier's process is, therefore, an important aspect of *services marketing*. This ranges from the deployment of branded consumer signage, like McDonald's, to the use of customized web sites as extranets for customers in business-to-business markets.

Once "in the premises", though, the buyer needs direction (even in a virtual environment). If it is not immediately apparent how to use the system (the equivalent of standing helplessly in a foreign shop) the buyer becomes embarrassed and gives up. So, clear signage into the delivery process and a step-by-step guide through it are equally important. On landing, for example, many flights show a video guide through the airport. This ensures that the stress levels of new passengers stay low and any difficulties are seen as aberrations, which can be corrected by excellent service recovery. Finally, marketing communication must concentrate on the "outcomes" of the process rather than the "benefits" emphasized by product marketers.

Service blueprinting needs:

- to identify all the main functions of the service
- to show time dimensions in diagrammatic form
- to precisely define tolerances (i.e. the degree of variation from standards).

A blueprint should be constructed in the following way:

(i) Identify the customer process and map it out.
(ii) Isolate potential fail points and build in sub-processes to tackle possible errors before they occur.
(iii) Establish a time frame or a standard execution time for each task.
(iv) Distinguish between processes which are visible to the user and those which are not. Manage any implications arising from this.
(v) Analyse profitability.

History, context, criticism, and development

The proactive creation of a service through the use of process design techniques has been suggested by several specialists. Lyn Shostack, a practising marketer (a VP of Citibank) rather than an academic, seems to have been the first. She pointed out (Shostack, G.L., 1982) that, whereas it is relatively easy to design a product through engineering specification, there was no "service engineering" technique to which service designers could turn. Services are therefore often launched before they are ready for customers to use. She suggested that, as a service is a process, it can be "blue printed" by using the "Organisation & Methods" (O&M) techniques (a pseudo-scientific process design technique of, largely, the 1960s now superseded) developed to deal with process improvement.

These she suggested, included:

- Time and motion engineering. Shostack suggested that of eight basic charts used by methods engineers, those which were most applicable were the "operations process chart", a "flow process chart", and the "flow diagram".
- "PERT" charting. This is an accepted method of planning detailed projects.
- Systems and software design. It was suggested that many of the software design methodologies could be used to design service processes.

Shostack used a "blueprint for a simple shoeshine service", which is shown in Figure B.2, to illustrate the work she had pioneered at her bank. She originally offered the concept of blueprinting alongside *molecular modelling* and suggested that academics develop and test both for more generic use by business. Later writers on the subject have neglected the latter but developed the use of blueprinting in service design. This may be because the popularity of "O&M" waned somewhat in the 1980s although the concept of process mapping has received attention because of emphasis in senior management circles on the concept of "process re-engineering" (see *thought leadership*).

Yet the process that clients experience is important to both the delivery of good service and to the experience of the customer. It can create opportunities for new services and for new market strategies. Blueprinting is a practical and straightforward method to use in designing these aspects of a service. It is taught in specialist centres (like the Service Management Centre at the University of Arizona) and used throughout the service sector today. It (or a version of it) has also been used to improve generic service and aftercare. In financial services, for instance, marketers have been prompting executives to map the "customer journey" for several years. This charts the progress of customers through their operational processes and distinguishes between "front office" and "back office" in a similar way to Shostack's blueprinting. Moreover, CEM (see *service quality*) techniques also prompt executives to think through the customers' experience of the service process.

Voices and further reading

- "Services are very often defined in terms of poorly articulated oral and written abstractions. From this subjective and superficial start, the conclusion is drawn that 'the service' is now documented and understood, that what is 'known' about the service can be communicated with precision and certainty . . . perhaps this is why so many services go awry . . . What is required is a system which will allow the structure of a service to be mapped in an objective and explicit manner while also capturing all the essential functions to which marketing applies; in other words, a service blueprint." Shostack, 1982.

*   Shostack, G.L., "How to design a service". *European Journal of Marketing*, 1982.
*   "Services are processes consisting of activities or a series of activities rather than things. In order to understand service management and the marketing of services it is critical that one realizes that the consumption of a service is process consumption rather than outcome consumption. The consumer perceives the service process (or production process) as part of the service consumption, not simply the outcome of that process, as in traditional marketing of physical goods . . . the consumption process leads to an outcome for the customer, which is the result of the service process. Thus, the consumption of the service process is a critical part of the service experience." Grönroos, C., 2003.
*   Ziethaml, V. and Bitner, M.J., *Services Marketing*. Irwin McGraw-Hill, 2003.

> ★ **RATING: Practical and powerful**

BOSTON MATRIX

Application: analysis of business portfolios

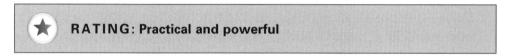

The Boston Matrix

	High	Market Share	Low
High		* Star	? Question Mark
Growth			
		$ Cash Flow	x Pet
Low			

Figure B.3:   The Boston Matrix as it originally appeared (from Stern and Deimler, 2006)

The concept

One of the best known, but poorly understood, *portfolio management* tools is the Boston Consulting Group's "growth-share matrix". It plots relative market share against relative growth, and was an attempt to give corporate strategic planners a way of evaluating different business units in different markets.

First, the annual growth rate of each business unit, in each market, is calculated. This is plotted on the matrix, depending on whether its growth is high or low because that is assumed to be an indication of investment needs. (Note: originally it was suggested that the horizontal axis of the matrix should be a growth rate of 10%.) Secondly, the relative market share of each unit is calculated and plotted on the matrix; that is share relative to the largest competitor. The turnover of each unit is then represented by appropriately sized circles.

The portfolio of business units is then categorized by the matrix into four groups, according to their cash generative ability:

(i)   The "question-marks" (otherwise called "problem children" or "wild cats") have low market share in high growth markets. A business which has just started operations would be a "question mark" because the ability of the management team to improve on its competence would be unproven. These are businesses with long-term potential which may have been recently launched and are being bought primarily by buyers who are willing to experiment. They need large amounts of cash if they are to be developed to their full potential because the company has to keep adding plant, equipment, and personnel to keep up with the fast-growing market.

(ii) The "rising star" is a company that has established itself in the market and is beginning to thrive. It is a leader, with high share in a high growth market. It requires significant investment in order to maintain and grow market share. It does not necessarily produce a positive cash-flow but stars are usually profitable and can become "cash cows".

(iii) The "cash cows" are companies that are well established and profitable. They have high share in low growth markets. They are producing profit but unlikely to achieve much incremental improvement (but see the case study in the *portfolio management* entry). They are generally cash positive and can be used to fund other initiatives.

(iv) The "dogs" (originally "pets", which is slightly less pejorative) have low share in low growth markets. These are companies who were in decline and worthy of withdrawal. They have weak market share in low growth markets and tend to be loss-makers, providing small amounts of cash if any.

This concept can be used to help marketers hone the thinking around their different businesses; to help prioritize resources between the business units that their firm might own. It is argued that a multi-business company needs to balance the needs of its portfolio of businesses or SBUs. It might, for instance, use money gener-ated from the cash cows to invest in newer businesses rather than raising capital or through other means. It is thought that an unbalanced portfolio of businesses can be classified into four areas:

(i)   Too many losers causing poor cash-flow.
(ii) Too many question-marks requiring too much investment.
(iii) Too many profit-producers.
(iv) Too many developing winners.

It was suggested that the matrix be used to develop different business strategies and corporate requirements for each business unit according to its position on the matrix. Objectives, profit targets, investment constraints, and even management style are likely to be different according to their position. Strategies set by the leadership are likely to include:

"Build". This means increasing the market share using cash, resources, marketing programmes and management attention.
"Hold". This means maintaining the market share and is appropriate for strong cash cows if they are to continue to yield cash.
"Harvest". This means using resources to get as much cash from a business unit as is possible regardless of long term effect. It is appropriate for weakening cash cows whose future is uncertain or dim.
"Divest". This means selling or liquidating the business, and is appropriate for dogs and question-marks that are acting as a drag on company resources.

History, context, criticism, and development

The *Boston Matrix* was developed by the Boston Consulting Group and owes its origins largely to the founder of that consultancy, Bruce Henderson, and his fame. Henderson (1915–92), an engineer by training, attended both Vanderbilt and Harvard Universities before joining Westinghouse Corporation; the start of a glittering and influential career. He was asked, for example, by the American President to work on the Marshall Plan, headed Arthur D. Little's management services unit and founded Boston Consulting in 1963 for the Boston Safe Deposit & Trust Company. He was hugely influential and his fame gained attention for the concepts he promulgated. For instance, he was named one of *Time Magazine*'s top 10 news makers under 30 years old and *The Economist* said that he did more to change the way business is done in the United States than any other man in American business history.

In 1965 (two years after the consultancy was founded) he published a piece of thought leadership (Henderson, B.D., 1965) on a concept he called the "experience curve"; something which is similar to, but not the same as, both economies of scale and the learning curve. Through extensive research and analysis, he demonstrated that, over time, companies specializing in an area of expertise became more effective in their market, reducing costs and gaining competitive advantage. A company might be at various points on the experience curve, depending on its maturity and the accumulated investment in its prime area of focus. A management team which was just starting out would be inexperienced (so a "question mark"), whereas one which is fast establishing itself would learn quickly (becoming a "rising star"). This is the source of the terms of the Boston Matrix which was later published (the original format is in Figure B.3 above) in a 1970 perspective (see Stern, C.W. and Deimler, M.S., 2006).

This work was detailed, numeric, and extensive. There was (and is) complexity and maths behind it which could be used to direct the operations of a business. It demonstrated that a relationship exists between the efficiency and the experience of a business unit; that unit costs fall with experience of operating in an industry and with a company's cumulative volume of production. The consultancy invested substantial time into examining many "high growth" industries (including service industries) and used "the scientific method" to validate the concept. It found that, although the percentage may change from industry to industry, it is more or less constant.

Costs decline due to a combination of: economies of scale, accumulated learning in the organization, and the substitution of technology for labour. Executives should plot the firm's prices or costs against unit volume; projecting back in time as far as is sensible. The resultant curve (illustrated in Figure B.4) should reveal the accumulated gains by the firm. The cost decline gives competitive advantage because new competitors can face higher costs if not entering with a major innovative advantage. Some have argued that the advantage is so great that established leaders should drive to gain further advantage through actions such as price cutting.

Although appearing deceptively simple, and intuitively right, the experience curve concept can be used in several ways. It can, for example, be used to set strategic objectives around costs and pricing. It can indicate the sort of cost reduction measures that a management team should be gaining. As a result it can become a benchmark by which the firm can set strategy for business units to improve costs. It can also be used to predict and set prices by giving a directional indication of industry costs and likely competitive responses. Henderson argued, though, that it should be used as a basis of competitive strategy. He linked the ability to reduce costs through the experience curve effect to the need to drive for market share; the bigger the share the lower the costs. This thinking led to the "Growth/share matrix", to give it its proper term.

There is no doubt, that by the time of his 1970 "perspective" on "the product portfolio" (see Stern and Deimler, 2006), Henderson was asserting that products produce cash according to where they rate by market share and growth. It is quite a simple document which asserts that there is a correlation between market share, costs, and success; also that companies need a balanced portfolio of each category. The link to the experience curve and the emphasis on business units is lost in the simplification.

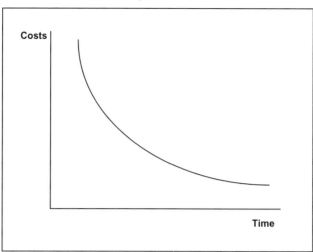

Figure B.4:   A representation of the experience curve

Voices and further reading

* Henderson B.D., *The Growth Share Matrix is Directly Derived from the Experience Curve*. Boston Consulting Group, 1972.
* Morrison, A. and Wensley, R., "Boxing up or boxed in?" *Journal of Marketing Management*, 1991.
* "Many so-called 'dog' and 'question mark' businesses generate cash, while many 'cash cows' are dry." Buzzell, R.D. and Gale, B.T., 1987. This is evidence based on the PIMS database so likely to be reliable.
* ". . . there are circumstances where great caution is required in its use . . . Consider those industries in which market share for any single product in the range has little to do with its profitability. Often a low market-share product enjoys the same production, distribution and marketing economies as other products in the portfolio . . . It is complications such as those outlined above that make the Boston Matrix less relevant to certain situations." Woodburn, D. and McDonald, M.H.B., 2011.

Things you may wish to consider

(i)   The terms of the matrix easily capture the imagination and executives can, perhaps wrongly, label their offers without any analysis at all. Managers can be heard to talk of their products or services as either being a "cash cow" or a "dog". This builds assumptions into the language of a firm which are risky.

(ii) If you are going to use the tool, understand and do the maths behind it.

(iii) Some companies have tried to use this conceptual framework to understand the positioning of their individual products or services rather than business units. This misuse of the tool is dodgy because it muddles two different concepts (the experience curve of a business and the *product life cycle*). The matrix really has nothing much to do with the life cycle of individual products or services, unless those individual offers are a separate business unit. To assume that a long established product is, for example, at the maturity phase of its *life cycle*, and thus a cash cow, risks the misuse of investment. Perhaps if a product or service is the sole focus of a business or SBU, then the experience curve will apply and the thinking behind this concept might be useful. The casual construction of a portfolio of products (using their sales growth rates and their relative market shares) based on the blithe assumption that their individual life cycles are inevitably s-curves, is superficial and poor analysis.

(iv) The tool assumes that market share is important to success. This is based on the experience of consumer product industries in 1970s America, where the likes of Coca-Cola and Pepsi, or Unilever and Procter & Gamble, fought over tiny percentage increases in share. However, market share is not necessarily a critical issue for some businesses. In some cases, such as in serving the public sector, a large share makes it more difficult to win work. In business-to-business marketing, some large customers have a procurement policy to share their work out among suppliers and not rely on one single supplier (such as that adopted by supermarket Sainsbury following the failure of their single supplier outsource to Accenture). Other businesses pursue a strategy of margin maximization rather than growth. In others, market share is not a focus. In law and accountancy, for example, conflict rules will not allow large firms to relentlessly sweep up share with no inhibition. Marketers in these circumstances need to focus on the juiciest opportunity, not every point of market share. This tool is unlikely to be helpful to such organizations.

(v) This assumes that lower costs, linked to lower prices, linked to high market share, is the right strategy. There are, though, other strategic choices. You might want, for instance, to differentiate through brand or take some other position in a market. It is clearly nonsense to argue that every supplier should be cutting prices and driving down costs to kill for an extra percentage point of market share. Life is just too short to be lived fighting for dominance in this boring way.

(vi) The concept is based on analysis of high growth markets with a benchmark of 10% per annum as the horizontal break point. Not all markets grow at that rate so it is probably wise, if using the tool, to agree the growth dimensions of an individual market. Many modern markets are likely to have much more modest growth rates.

(vii) Is it really important to have a "balanced" portfolio? If you have, say, a long lived, branded offer (like Coca-Cola or Stella Artois) which is loved by customers and generates high margin, do you really want to starve it of investment in order to start up questionable new ventures?

RATING: Conceptual

BRANDS

Application: revenue generating, value creation, communication

The relationship of customers to brands

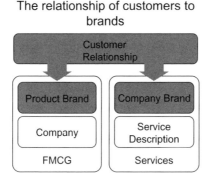

Figure B.5: A representation of Leonard Berry's differences between product and service branding

The concept

A brand is an entity that engenders an emotional response from a group of human beings so that they pay more than they probably should for the purely rational components on offer. It is a changing, multi-faceted entity which creates a variety of impressions in the minds of different human beings through many different stimuli. It causes people to buy again and again, often at an inflated price, creating valuable equity. It forms a bond between a group of human beings and a supplier, creating value from their propensity (supported by findings in experiments by behavioural economists; see *behavioural aspects of marketing*) to stick with what is familiar.

It is beyond dispute that a carefully designed image rests in the memory of buyers and helps them to choose products and services. Numerous firms have proved that, by managing that image carefully, a product or a service will appeal time and time again to a group of interested buyers. It becomes a familiar part of their life, giving them consistent benefits in their day-to-day activities and reducing the risk of purchase. As a result, they will pay a premium for the offer and develop a loyalty towards it. Over time, they become fond of these entities and, if they think about it, regard them as part of the landscape of their life. What starts as simple reassurance about quality or consistency becomes, on a deeper but hard to measure level, an emotional bond in a hectic modern lifestyle. Consequently, there are people who feel warmth towards a tin of paint, a sugar-filled drink, and sports shoes.

Brands are probably the most enduring and valuable entities that marketing skills have created for the business world. They differentiate an offer from competitors, protect against price erosion, and increase margins. Whether they are product brands, service brands, or corporate brands, they are amongst the most valuable, yet least tangible, of assets. Managed carefully, they can be the basis of sustainable competitive advantage by building strong, profitable "relationships" with loyal buyers. Yet, this can only be achieved by creating a branded proposition that stands out from the crowd and consistently delivers what it promises. So, marketers should use brand techniques to claim their space in the most important market of all: the minds and imaginations of their buyers. Experience shows that, with the right visionary leadership and political will, firms can create and manage a branded service proposition in such a way that it gives a clear direction to everyone involved, whether customer or employee.

Effective brands are most common in consumer goods marketing (like Coca-Cola, Nike, and Dove) but are also increasingly found in both mass services (e.g. Virgin, McDonald's, and Thomas Cook), business-to-business services (Goldman Sachs, McKinsey), and even in professional services (Deloitte, Clifford Chance). They affect the price of every product or service these firms offer in every part of the world. They set expectations of quality and communicate subliminal messages of the firm's raison d'être. They are one of their owner's major intangible assets and should there fore be one of the prime strategic issues for marketers to address.

Brand work involves a wide spectrum of specialist skills including:

- Brand strategists
- Creative agencies and consultancies who help to design new images or new names
- Design consultants
- Valuation specialists (from accountants to dedicated agencies who estimate the financial value of brands).

There are several fundamental aspects to brand creation and management:

(i) Financial worth

A successful brand is a very valuable intangible asset comprising the goodwill of buyers and nurturing their future buying intent. In 1996, for example, Professor Alvin Silk (Silk, A.J., 1996) estimated one of the world's most valuable brands, Coca-Cola, to be worth $39 bn; whereas ten years later, Interbrand and *Business Week*'s estimate put it at $67 bn; a remarkable increase in wealth. That Interbrand survey contained a number of brands that were not really consumer goods companies such as IBM (valued at $53 bn in 2004 and $56 bn in 2009), GE ($44 bn and $48 bn), Nokia ($24 bn and $30 bn), and HP (static at around $20 bn). The changing value of this remarkable intangible asset is an addition to normal sales, revenue, and profits.

So, there is a hard financial dynamic to brand work. In the past, marketers and strategists have found it hard to translate brand strategies into clear numeric data which would win the respect of their MD or finance director. Investment in many brand programmes, particularly corporate brand strategies, was based on little more than faith. As a result, worthy brand initiatives did not get the investment they warranted and some non-brand literate companies did not even begin to venture down this path. Yet, with the rise of more service dominated economies, many companies have found that their "intangible assets" have grown in importance and the accountancy profession has become increasingly focused on valuing this type of asset. From this point of view, brands are simply one type of intangible asset in a firm's array of assets and it is possible to use state of the art valuation techniques in order to calculate their value.

There are now a range of credible techniques by which brands can be valued including: historical cost of creation, replacement costs, royalty savings, real option valuation, premium pricing, relief from royalty, and the residual approach. One specialist estimated that there are at least thirty-nine proprietary models to value commercial brands (Salinas, G., 2009). More importantly, it is possible to estimate the likely success of different brand strategies and to estimate the likely future brand value based on the effect of those strategies. In other words, it is possible to put real numbers behind brand strategy and calculate the likely return on investment. However, to do that, it is essential to merge marketing and financial techniques in a profound way. Valuation and economic modelling can be merged with brand positioning tools to give a detailed, manageable route map for one of the company's most important areas of investment.

(ii) Durability

The effect of brands is surprisingly enduring. It is a popular belief amongst business executives that markets are changing very fast and that it is difficult to create a durable and profitable offer. Many assert that companies need to continually innovate because the "product they launch on Monday is a commodity by Wednesday". At the same time, business books routinely suggest that companies must continually innovate risky new products to survive. This is nonsense. There are several brands in existence today that were created over a hundred years ago. Tables B.1 and B.2, for example, show simply the country and date of origin of a number of well known brands (both products and services) that were created before 1950. Some of these entities have been

Table B.1 The durability of some product brands

The product	Category	Country	Date	The product	Category	Country	Date
Product brands: 1900 to 1949				HP: Hewlett Packard	Computers/ tech	USA	1939
Pucci	Fashion/ luxury goods	Italy	1949	Teflon[2]	Kitchenware	USA	1938
Onitsuka Tiger[1]	Sports wear	Japan	1949	Old Spice[3]	Aftershave	USA	1938
Longchamp	Fashion/ luxury goods	France	1948	McDonald's	Fast food	USA	1937
				Valextra	Bags	Italy	1937
Rowntree: Polo Mints	Confectionery	UK	1948	Rowntree: Rolo & Smarties	Sweets	UK	1937
Biro	Ballpoint pens	Hungary/ Argentina	1948	Pickwick[4]	Tea	Netherlands	1937
Lambretta	Scooter	Italy	1947	Orangina	Drink	France/ Algeria	1936
Céline	Fashion/ luxury goods	France	1947	Lux	Soap powder	UK	1936
Dior: Miss Dior	Perfume	France	1947	Mars: Maltesers	Confectionery	USA	1936
Sony	Electronics	Japan	1946	Rowntree: Dairy Box, Quality Street	Confectionery	UK	1936
P&G:Tide	Soap powder	USA	1946				
Estée Lauder	Perfume	USA	1946	Rowntree: Kit Kat & Aero	Confectionery	UK	1935
Vespa	Scooters	Italy	1946				
Dior	Fashion/ luxury goods	France	1946	P&G: Dreft	Soap powder	USA	1933
McVite: the Penguin	Biscuit	UK	1946	Rowntree: Black Magic	Confectionery	UK	1933
White Rabbit	Confectionery	China	1943	Lacoste	Fashion	France	1933
Velcro	Fastening	Switzerland	1941	Mars: 3 Musketeers	Confectionery	USA	1932
Mars: M&Ms	Confectionery	USA	1941	Joy by Patou	Perfume	France	1931
Coach	Fashion	USA	1941	Unilever: PG tips	Tea	UK	1930
Vitasoy	Milk alternative drink	China	1940	Birdseye	Frozen food	USA	1930
				Mars: Snickers	Confectionery	USA	1930
McVitie: Jaffa Cake	Biscuit	UK	1939	Fisher Price	Toys	USA	1930

[1]now ASICS

[2]now part of Du Pont
[3]now P&G
[4]Part of Douwe Egberts

Table B.1   Continued

The product	Category	Country	Date	The product	Category	Country	Date
Ryvita	Biscuits	UK	1930	Union Carbide	Chemicals	USA	1917
Peak Freen: the Twiglet	Biscuits	UK	1929	Nikon	Cameras	Japan	1917
Domestos[5]	Bleach	UK	1929	Harry Winston	Diamonds	USA	1916
Brylcreem	Hair gel	UK	1928	Cadbury: Milk Tray	Confectionery	UK	1915
P&G: Oxydol	Soap powder	USA	1927	Rolex	Watches	UK	1915
Furla	Fashion/ luxury goods	Italy	1927	Lipton	Tea	UK	1915
Spiller's: Winalot	Dog meal	UK	1927	Salvatore Ferragamo	Shoes	USA	1914
Harvard Business Review	Management magazine	USA	1926	Prada	Fashion/ luxury goods	Italy	1913
Godiva	Confectionery	Belgium	1926	Camel	Cigarettes	USA	1913
Camay	Soap	USA	1926	Aga	Cookers	Sweden	1912
Unilever: Lux	Soap	UK	1925	Patou	Fashion	France	1912
Fendi	Luxury goods	Italy	1925	Mars	Confectionery	USA	1911
Chanel No 5	Perfume	France	1924	Gauloises	Cigarettes	France	1910
Belstaff	Leather jackets	UK/Italy	1924	Hallmark	Greeting cards	USA	1910
IBM[6]	Computers	USA	1924	Samsonite	Luggage	USA	1910
Primola	Cheese	Norway	1924	Peek Frean: the Bourbon	Biscuit	UK	1910
Mars: Milky way	Confectionery	USA	1923	Rowntree: Walnut whip	Confectionery	UK	1910
Q-tips	Cotton bud	USA	1923	BP	Oil	UK	1909
Russell Stoner	Chocolates	USA	1923	Mercedes–Benz	Cars	Germany	1909
Time	Magazine/ news	USA	1922	Audi	Cars	Germany	1909
BMW	Cars	Germany	1922	Teacher's	Whisky	UK	1909
Filofax	Stationery	USA	1921	Johnnie Walker red label	Whisky	UK	1909
Gucci	Leather goods	Italy	1921	Lanvin	Fashion	France	1909
Allied Chemical	Food/bio tech	USA	1920	Vogue	Magazine	USA	1909
				Bisto	Gravy	UK	1908

[5] now Unilever
[6] Name applied to entity which had existed for over 20 years

Continued

Table B.1 Continued

The product	Category	Country	Date	The product	Category	Country	Date
Hoover	Vacuum cleaners	USA	1908	Perrier	Drink	UK/France	1902
Amoy	Soy sauce	China	1908	Peak Freen: the Pat-a-cake	Biscuit	UK	1902
Evian[7]	Bottled water	France	1908	Unilever: Marmite[12]	Food stock	UK	1902
Spiller's: Shapes	Dog biscuit	UK	1907	Monsanto	Pesticides	USA	1901
Osram[8]	Lighting	Germany	1906	Hornby	Toys	UK	1901
Kellogg's	Corn flakes	USA	1906	Meccano	Toys	UK	1901
Max Factor	Make up	USA	1906	The Tatler[13]	Society magazine	UK	1901
Warner Bros	Entertainment	USA	1906	Lurpak	Butter	Denmark	1901
Xerox[9]	Copiers & printers	USA	1906	Ever Ready	Batteries	USA	1900
Honeywell	Electronics	USA	1906	Melle	Confectionery	Netherlands	1900
Van Cleef and Arpels	Jewellery	France	1906	Gossard	Intimate apparel	USA	1900
Cadbury: Dairy Milk	Chocolates	UK	1905				

Product brands: 1850 to 1899

The product	Category	Country	Date
Hellman's[10]	Mayonnaise	USA	1905
Batavus	Bicycles	Netherlands	1904
Kiwi	Shoe polish	UK	1904
Ovaltine	Nutritional drink	Switzerland	1904
Noritake	Tableware	Japan	1904
Rolls Royce	Cars	UK	1904
Werther's Originals	Sweets	Germany	1903
Persil[11]	Soap powder	Germany	1903
Typhoo	Tea	UK	1903
Gillette	Male grooming	USA	1903
Ford	Cars	USA	1903

The product	Category	Country	Date
Aspirin	Pharmaceutical	Germany	1899
Renault	Cars	France	1899
Miele	Domestic appliances	Germany	1899
Bassett: All Sorts	Sweets	UK	1899
Bugatti	Cars	France	1899
San Pellegrino[14]	Bottled water	Italy	1899
Castrol[15]	Lubricants	UK	1899
Dentyne	Chewing gum	USA	1899
Dewar's White Label	Whisky	UK	1899
Pepsi	Cola drink	USA	1898

[7]now owned by Danone, A spring since 1789
[8]now part of Siemens
[9]now very much a service brand for over 20 years
[10]now Unilver
[11]now Unilever

[12]originally own brand
[13]Named after Tatler of 1709
[14]local since 1200
[15]originally Wakefield & Co

Table B.1 Continued

The product	Category	Country	Date	The product	Category	Country	Date
Michelin	Tyres	France	1898	San Miguel	Beer	China	1890
Nabisco	Biscuits	USA	1898	Kendal Mint Cake	Biscuit	UK	1890
Lewin	Shirts	UK	1898	Player	Cigarettes	UK	1890
HMV	Entertainment	UK	1897	Canada Dry	Drink	Canada	1890
Chad Valley	Toys	UK	1897	American	Tobacco	USA	1890
Jell-O	Desert	USA	1897	Hovis	Bread	UK	1890
Dow	Chemicals	USA	1897	Nintendo	Entertainment	Japan	1889
Hornby	Toys	UK	1897	Dunlop	Tyres	UK	1889
HP	Sauce	UK	1896	Sharwood	Spices	UK	1889
The Daily Mail	News	UK	1896	Schwartz	Spices	Canada	1889
Lifebuoy	Soap	UK	1894	Woodbine (Wills)	Cigarettes	UK	1888
Barbour	Clothes	UK	1894	Lee Kum Kee	Food sauces	China	1888
Andrew's Liver Salts	Pharmaceutical	UK	1894	Kodak	Cameras	USA	1888
Famous Grouse	Whisky	UK	1894	Bulmers	Cider	UK	1887
Hershey	Confectionery	USA	1894	Glenfiddich	Whisky	UK	1887
Mikimoto	Pearls	Japan	1893	Brighton Rock	Sweets	UK	1886
Pepsi	Drink	USA	1893	Smirnoff	Vodka	Russia	1886
Halls	Cough sweets	UK	1893	Verkade	Chocolate	Netherlands	1886
Tholstrup	Cheese	Denmark	1893	Adler	Jewellery	France	1886
Rowntree: Fruit Gums	Confectionery	UK	1893	Coca-Cola	Drinks	USA	1886
Alfred Dunhill	Men's accessories	UK	1893	Avon	Cosmetics	USA	1886
Shredded Wheat	Food	USA	1893	Del Monte	Food	USA	1886
McVitie: Digestive	Biscuit	UK	1892	Bacardi	Drink	Cuba	1886
Maxwell House	Coffee	USA	1892	Whittard	Tea	UK	1886
Ingersoll	Watches	USA	1892	Anchor	Butter	UK	1886
Philips	Electronics	Netherlands	1891	Raleigh	Bicycles	UK	1886
Wrigley	Confectionery	USA	1891	Lyle's Golden Syrup	Food	UK	1885
Parker	Pens	USA	1891	Johnson Controls	Electronics	USA	1885
				Andrew's	Liver salts	UK	1885

Continued

Table B.1 Continued

The product	Category	Country	Date
The Lady	Magazine	UK	1885
Fabergé	Jewellery	Russia	1885
Dr Pepper	Drink	USA	1885
Bovril[16]	Processed food	UK	1884
NCR	Technology	USA	1884
UHU	Glue	Germany	1884
Black and White	Whisky	UK	1884
Jaeger	Clothes	Germany	1884
Waterman	Pens	USA	1884
Bulgari	Jewellery/ luxury goods	Italy	1884
Breitling	Watches	Switzerland	1884
Tiptree	Jams	UK	1883
VAT 69	Whisky	UK	1882
Cerruti	Watches	Italy	1881
Rowntree: Fruit Pastilles	Confectionery	UK	1881
Scott's	Porridge oats	UK	1880
Maynard	Confectionery	UK	1880
Hovis	Bread	UK	1880
Philadelphia	Cream cheese	USA	1880
Spear's[17]	Games	UK/Germany	1879
Eu Yan Sang	Chinese medicine products	Malaysia	1879
Listerine	Mouth wash	USA	1879
P&G: Ivory	Soap	USA	1879
Quaker Oats	Food	USA	1878
General Electric[18]	Consumer electronics	USA	1876
Ericsson	Technology	Sweden	1876
Budweiser	Beer	USA	1876
Bissell	Cleaners	USA	1876

The product	Category	Country	Date
Tufts	Soda fountain	USA	1876
Toshiba	Technology	Japan	1875
HP	Sauce	UK	1875
Remington	Typewriter	USA	1874
Southern Comfort	Whisky	USA	1874
Church's	Shoes	UK	1873
Beck's	Beer	Germany	1873
Levi Strauss jeans	Clothing	USA	1873
Chivers	Jams	UK	1873
Horlicks	Drink	UK	1873
Eijsbouts	Bells	Netherlands	1872
Stork[19]	Margarine	Netherlands	1872
Folger	Coffee	USA	1872
Adams	Chewing gum	USA	1871
Penhaligon	Men's scent	UK	1870
De Beers	Diamonds	South Africa	1870
Campbell	Soup	USA	1869
Pillsbury	Bakery products	USA	1869
Tabasco	Sauce	USA	1869
Exchange and Mart	Magazine	UK	1868
Jack Daniels	Whisky	USA	1866
Nestlé	Baby milk/ confectionery	Switzerland	1866
Nokia	Electronics	Finland	1865
BASF	Chemicals	Germany	1865
Bertolli[20]	Olive oil	Italy	1865
Bovril	Beef stock	UK	1865
Jacob's: Cream Crackers	Biscuits	Ireland	1865
Fisherman's Friend	Lozenges	UK	1865

[16]now Unilver
[17]now Mattel
[18]Investors backing Edison's experiments

[19]now Unilever
[20]now Unilever

Table B.1   Continued

The product	Category	Country	Date
McDougal's	Flour	UK	1864
Quandude	Food	China	1864
Victory	Lozenges	UK	1864
Robertson's	Marmalade	UK	1864
Heineken	Beer	Netherlands	1864
Benedictine	Brandy	France	1863
Fray Bentos	Processed food	Uruguay	1862
Bacardi	Drink	Cuba	1862
Rowntree	Chocolate	UK	1862
Heinz[21]	Processed food	USA	1861
Peek Frean: Garibaldi	Biscuits	UK	1861
Otis	Elevators	USA	1861
Swan Vesta	Matches	UK	1861
Paneri	Watches	Italy	1860
Amaretti Virginia	Biscuits	Italy	1860
Grenson	Shoes	UK	1860
Peek Frean: Nice	Biscuits	UK	1860
Vaseline[22]	Skin care	UK	1860
Tag Heuer	Watches	Switzerland	1860
Chopard	Watches	Switzerland	1860
Tate & Lyle	Sugar	UK	1859
Canadian Club	Drink	USA	1858
Peak Freen	Biscuits	UK	1857
Smith and Wesson	Guns	USA	1857
Borden's	Condensed milk	USA	1857

The product	Category	Country	Date
Burberry	Clothes	UK	1856
Spiller's: Dog food	Pet foods	UK	1855
Miller	Beer	USA	1855
The Daily Telegraph	Newspaper	UK	1855
Louis Vuitton	Clothing/ fashion	France	1854
Steinway	Pianos	Germany	1853
Aquascutum	Clothes	UK	1851
Kiehl's	Cosmetics	USA	1851
New York Times	Newspaper	USA	1851
Singer	Sewing machines	USA	1851
Bally	Shoes/leather goods	Switzerland	1851
Howden	Engineering products	UK	1851
Lazzaroni Amaretto	Liqueur	Italy	1851
Jacob's	Biscuits	Ireland	1850
Moss Bros	Clothing	UK	1850
Eno's salts[23]	Pharmaceutical	UK	1850

Product brands 1800 to 1850

Oxo	Meat extract	UK/ Uruguay	1850
Bowler	Hats	UK	1850
Schlitz[24]	Beer	USA	1849
Lobb	Shoes	UK	1849
Bally	Fashion	Switzerland	1848

[21]horse radish first
[22]now Unilever

[23]now part of GlaxoSmithKline
[24]acquired by Schlitz in 1858, then by Pabst brewing

Continued

Table B.1   Continued

The product	Category	Country	Date	The product	Category	Country	Date
Morton's	Salt	USA	1848	Bird's	Custard powder	UK	1837
Omega	Watches	Switzerland	1848	Hermés	Fashion/luxury goods	France	1837
Carlsberg	Beer	Denmark	1847				
Siemens	Electronics	Germany	1847	Lea & Perrins	Sauce	UK	1837
Cartier	Jewellery	France	1847				
Maple's	Furniture	UK	1847	Colt	Guns	USA	1835
Pond's[25]	Cosmetics	USA	1846	Earl Grey	Tea	UK	1834
Lindt	Chocolate	Switzerland	1845	Jaeger-leCoultre	Watches	Switzerland	1833
The Economist	Magazine	UK	1843				
				De Koninck	Beer	Belgium	1833
Krug	Champagne	France	1843				
Glenmorangie	Whisky	UK	1843	Bassetts	Confectionery	UK	1832
				Waechtersbach	Tableware	Germany	1832
News of the World	Newspaper	UK	1843				
				Young's[28]	Beer	UK	1831
Bryant May	Matches		1843	Terry's	Confectionery	UK	1830
Pilsner Urquell	Beer	Czech Republic	1842	Flavell's Kitchener	Stoves	UK	1830
Whitman's	Chocolates	USA	1842				
Royal Doulton	Pottery	UK	1842	Price's	Candles	UK	1830
				Baume Mercier	Watches	Switzerland	1830
Beechams Pills	Pharmaceutical	UK	1842	McVitie's	Biscuits	UK	1830
Punch	Magazine	UK	1841	Spiller's[29]	Bakery	UK	1829
Van Melle	Sweets	Netherlands	1841	Guerlain	Perfume	France	1828
Spiller's[26]	Pet food	UK	1840	The Spectator[30]	News/magazine	UK	1828
Maker's Mark	Whisky	USA	1840	The Standard	Newspaper	UK	1827
Britains	Toys	UK	1840	Baedeker	Travel guides	Germany	1827
Pimms	Drink	UK	1840	Herend	Porcelain	Hungary	1826
Kikkoman	Soy sauce	Japan	1838	Suchard	Confectionery	Switzerland	1825
Knorr[27]	Soups & food stuffs		1838	Clarks	Shoes	UK	1825
Hathaway	Shirts	USA	1837	Cadbury	Confectionery	UK	1824
Tiffany	Jewellery	USA	1837	Glenlivet	Whisky	UK	1824
Procter & Gamble	Soap products	USA	1837	Macintosh	Clothes	UK	1823
				Robinson's	Fruit juices	UK	1822

[25] now Unilever
[26] Dog food 1855
[27] now Unilever

[28] Acquired brewer from 1550
[29] later pet food
[30] There was a "Spectator" in 1712

Table B.1   Continued

The product	Category	Country	Date
Tetley	Tea	UK	1822
Huntley & Palmer	Biscuits	UK	1822
The Sunday Times	Newspaper	UK	1821
De La Rue	Stationery & printing	UK	1821
Johnny Walker	Whisky	UK	1820
Puiforcat	Silversmith/ luxury goods	France	1820
Beefeater	Gin	UK	1820
Chubb	Locks	USA	1818
The Scotsman	Newspaper	UK	1817
Armitage Shanks	Toilet ware	UK	1817
Remington	Guns	USA	1816
Royal Doulton	Pottery	UK	1815
Coleman's[31]	Mustard.	UK	1814
The Times	News	UK	1814
Purdey	Guns	UK	1814
Crawford's	Biscuits	UK	1813
Courvoisier	Cognac	France	1811
Heal's	Furniture	UK	1810
Denby	Pottery	UK	1809
Wiley	Publishing	USA	1807
Colgate Palmolive	Toothpaste	USA	1806
Pernod	Drink	France	1805
Veuve Clicquot	Champagne	France	1805
Crombie	Clothing	UK	1805
Du Pont	Chemicals	USA	1802
Chivas	Whisky	UK	1801

The product	Category	Country	Date
Product brands 1750 to 1799			
Greene King	Ale & beer	UK	1799
Jim Beam	Whisky	USA	1795
Sarson's	Vinegar	UK	1794
Oban	Whisky	UK	1794
Hopjes	Sweets	Netherlands	1793
Plymouth	Gin	UK	1793
The Observer	Newspaper	UK	1791
Girard-Perregaux	Watches	Switzerland	1791
Booth's	Gin	UK	1790
Pear's[32]	Soap	UK	1789
Asprey	Jewellery	UK	1789
Waterford	Glass/crystal	Ireland	1783
Schweppes	Carbonated water	Switzerland	1783
Veuve Clicquot	Champagne	France	1782
Bass	Beer	UK	1777
Breguet	Watches	France	1775
Mappin & Webb	Silversmiths	UK	1774
Breguet	Watches	Switzerland	1773
Wilkinson Sword[33]	Armaments	UK	1772
Yardley	Cosmetics	UK	1770
Hennessey	Drink	France	1765
Faber-Castell	Pencils	Germany	1761
Pontefract Cakes	Confectionery	UK	1760
Wedgwood	Pottery	UK	1759

[31]now Unilever

[32]now Unilever
[33]Razors 1898

Continued

Table B.1   Continued

The product	Category	Country	Date
Fry's[34]	Confectionery	UK	1759
Guiness	Beer	Ireland	1759
MAN Group	Engineering/ transport	Germany	1758
Cinzano	Drink	Italy	1757
Dal Negro	Playing cards	Italy	1756
Vacheron Constantin	Watches	Switzerland	1755
Wolsey	Knitwear	UK	1755
Axminster	Carpets	UK	1755
Douwe Egberts	Coffee	Netherlands	1753
Coalport	China/pottery	UK	1750

Product brands 1700 to 1749

The product	Category	Country	Date
J&B	Drink	UK	1749
Villeroy & Boch	Tableware	Luxemburg	1748
Moët et Chandon	Champagne and wine	France	1743
Chippendale	Furniture	UK	1740
Sèvres	Porcelain	France	1738
Blancpain[35]	Watches	Switzerland	1735
Remy Martin	Drink	France	1724
Martel	Drink	France	1715
Cow & Gate[36]	Dairy products	UK	1711
Crosse & Blackwell	Soup	UK	1706
Twining's	Tea	UK	1706
Meissen	Porcelain	Germany	1705

Product brands pre-1700

The product	Category	Country	Date
Cutty Sark	Whisky	UK	1698
Dom Perignon	Champagne	France	1693
Tongren-tang[37]	Pharmaceuticals	China	1669
Kronenbourg	Beer	France	1664
Zhang Xiaoquan	Scissors	China	1664
Pi Lo Chun[38]	Green tea	China	1660
Saint-Nectaire[39]	Regional cheese	France	1650★
Haig	Whisky	UK	1627
Grolsch	Beer	Netherlands	1615
Santa Maria Novella	Perfume	Italy	1612
Bushmills	Whisky	UK	1608
Bols	Gin & Liqueur	Netherlands	1575
Beretta	Guns	Italy	1526
Disaronno originale	Liqueur	Italy	1525
Majolica[40]	Ceramics	Italy	1425
Hacker-pschorr	Beer	Germany	1417
Lowenbrau	Beer	Germany	1383
Stella Artois	Beer	Belgium	1366
Fontina[41]	Regional cheese	Italy	1200★
Murano	Glassware	Italy	1083
Weihens-tephan	Beer	Germany	1040
Brie de Meaux[42]	Regional cheese	France	774★

[34]took over former firm founded in 1728
[35]died and revived in 20th century
[36]started as shop but expanded later

[37]one of China's *laozihos heritage brands*
[38]Brewed for 1,000 years before named by emperor
[39]★introduced to court of Louis XIV around this date
[40]imported through Majorca before
[41]★name first recorded in 1717
[42]★record of tasting by Charle-magne

Table B.2   The durability of some service brands

The service	Category	Country	Date
Service brands 1900 to 1999			
Google	Search engine	USA	1998
Amazon	Book retailer	USA	1995
Virgin	Consumer Services	UK	1970
Russell Reynolds	Executive search	USA	1969
Weight-Watchers	Health	USA	1961
Paul Weiss	Law	USA	1945
Ikea	Furniture retail	Sweden	1943
Tesco	Retail	UK	1931
Allen & Overy	Law	UK	1930
Harry Ramsden's	Fish & chips	UK	1928
Patisserie Valerie	Food & drink	UK	1926
McKinsey	Consulting	USA	1920
J C Penny	Retail	USA	1913
Selfridge	Retail	UK	1909
UPS	Courier services	USA	1907
Ernst & Young	Accountancy	UK	1903
Waitrose	Retail	UK	1904
Burton's	Men's tailoring	UK	1904
Austin Reed	Clothing retail	UK	1900

The service	Category	Country	Date
Service brands 1850 to 1899			
Morrison's	Grocery	UK	1899
Bergdorf Goodman	Retail	USA	1898
Maxim's	Restaurant/ luxury goods	France	1893
Lyons Tea Shops	Hospitality	UK	1894
Sear's Roebuck	Mail order	USA	1893
Fenwick's	Retail	UK	1891
Allianz	Insurance	Germany	1890
Savoy	Hotel	UK	1889
Slaughter & May	Law	UK	1889
Paul	Patisserie chain	France	1889
National Geographic	Information/ membership	USA	1888
Westing-house	Electronics	USA	1886
Sketchley	Cleaning	UK	1885
Marks & Spencer	Retail	UK	1884
Sainsbury's	Retail	UK	1882
Wharton Business School	Education	USA	1881
Sears	Mail order	USA	1880
F.W. Wool-worth[43]	Retail	USA	1879

[43]now Foot Locker Inc

Continued

Table B.2   Continued

The service	Category	Country	Date
DH Evans	Retail	UK	1879
Boots	Pharmacy retail	UK	1877
J Walter Thompson	Advertising	USA	1878
Liberty's	Retail	UK	1875
AT&T	Communications	USA	1875
Bloomingdale's	Retail	USA	1872
Cable and Wireless	Communications	UK	1869
Saks	Retail	USA	1867
KPMG	Accountancy	UK	1867
Marshall Field	Retail	USA	1867
HSBC	Banking	UK/China	1865
John Lewis	Retail	UK	1864
London Underground	Transport	UK	1863
Lillywhite's	Retail	UK	1863
H. Samuel	Jewellery retail	UK	1862
J P Morgan	Banking	USA	1861
Macy's	Retail	USA	1858
Banco Santander	Banking	Spain	1857
Credit Suisse	Banking	Switzerland	1856
The Halifax	Banking	UK	1855
Standard Chartered	Bank	UK/Asia	1853
Le Bon Marché	Retail	France	1852
Wells Fargo	Financial	USA	1852

The service	Category	Country	Date
Reuters	News	UK	1851
Moss Bros	Retail	UK	1851
Pullman	Rail services	USA	1851
Macy's	Retail	USA	1850

Service brands 1800 to 1849

The service	Category	Country	Date
Harrod's	Retail	UK	1849
Pricewaterhouse Coopers	Accountancy	UK	1849
W. H. Smith	Retail	UK	1848
Deloitte	Accountancy	UK	1845
Thomas Cook	Travel	UK	1841
Heal's	Retail	UK	1840
The Co-op	Retail	UK	1840
Linklaters	Law	UK	1838
P&O	Shipping	UK	1837
Tiffany	Retail	USA	1837
John Menzies	Retail	UK	1833
London Zoo	Entertainment	UK	1827
Harvey Nichols	Retail	UK	1820
Debenhams[44]	Retail	UK	1813
Claridges	Hospitality	UK	1812
Citigroup	Banking	USA	1812
Heal's	Retail	UK	1810
Clifford Chance	Law	UK	1802

[44]Previous store 1776

Table B.2 Continued

The service	Category	Country	Date
Service brands from the 1700s			
Hatchards	Bookseller	UK	1797
Norwich Union[45]	Insurance	UK	1797
Lombard Odier	Banking	Switzerland	1796
Dickens and Jones[46]	Retail	UK	1790
CMS Cameron McKenna	Law	UK	1779
Gieves and Hawkes	Tailors	UK	1771
Christies	Art auctioneers	UK	1766
Lloyd's (TSB)	Banking	UK	1763
Rothschild	Banking	UK	1769
Sotheran's	Book sales	UK	1761
Hamley's	Toy shop	UK	1760
Cox & King	Vacations/ tours	UK	1758

[45]now Aviva
[46]closed 2006

The service	Category	Country	Year
Coutts	Banking	UK	1753
The British Museum	Entertainment/ education	UK	1753
Dollond & Aitcheson	Opticians	UK	1750
Sothebys	Auctioneers	UK	1744
Freshfields	Law	UK	1726
RSA	Insurance	UK	1710
Fortnum & Mason	Retail	UK	1707
Service brands pre-1700			
Bank of England	Banking	UK	1694
Barclays	Banking	UK	1690
Pickford	Removals	UK	1690
Mitsuko-shi[47]	Retail	Japan	1673
Lloyd's[48]	Insurance	UK	1668
Harvard	University	USA	1636
Thurn und Taxis[49]	Postal services	Germany	1489

[47]Formerly Echigoya
[48]formalized in 1771
[49]post nationalized 1867. Now cultural icon supporting luxury products/board games

creating wealth by appealing, in a unique way, to a succession of human beings for several centuries. The brands in these tables have commanded the attention of segments of customers and earned relatively high margins for many generations. Admittedly, some of these offers may not have had brand characteristics throughout their long life. It is true too, that, particularly in luxury goods, many were run by artisans with a craft heritage and a commitment to quality but perilous financial track records. Nevertheless, this evidence suggests that brand creation is a powerful way to create substantial, profitable, long-term business. It is striking, for instance, to find brands in modern China, created several hundred years ago, which have survived both communism and the traumas of the Cultural Revolution. Marketers have a responsibility to their shareholders to convince their colleagues to invest in this remarkable approach.

(iii) Brand integrity

The concept of brand integrity is behind the success of all brands. It means that the promise created for buyers by the brand name and its reputation is always delivered when they use that product or service. The perception of consistent delivery of an offer is the fundamental principle from which brands originated; often so obvious that it is taken for granted, unarticulated, and not explicitly managed. In pre-consumer times, at the start of the industrial revolution, most buyers could not rely on purchases of any kind to be consistent, reliable or safe. Food and water, for example, could kill the people who consumed them. Yet, as in the undeveloped world today, a brand gave a much-needed promise of quality and delivery. So, journalists like Naomi Klein (Klein, N., 2001) and similar sceptics, who have challenged the ethics and integrity behind brand building, ought to be more even handed. They have suggested that brands exploit workers and trick buyers, generating outrageous profits for unscrupulous owners. Yet today's enduring brands became market leaders through consistent delivery to the expectations of buyers. It is no exaggeration to say that the concept of branding has saved lives.

Consumer brands have to deliver the promised function of the product, time after time, to be successful. Admittedly, expectations change over time and there is a need to keep pace. For instance, some food products reduced their sugar content dramatically in the last half of the 20th century. However, this happened step by step as consumers' tastes changed, moving in line with expectations so as not to lose the precious brand franchise.

Consistency in delivery is also vital for service brands. It is essential that the promises of the advertising and the expectations raised by promotion are properly reflected in the service experience. This means that the cocktail of service components (the way employees behave, the process through which the customers move, the environment in which the service is experienced, and the technology deployed) must embody the brand promise. Moreover, this must happen every single time that people experience the service process. This is probably the most challenging and difficult aspect of marketing management experienced by any specialist in the field because the delivery of all services is unpredictable and variable. It is hard enough to translate research insights into product propositions. It can also be difficult to communicate the essence of a brief to design agencies and production people in order to create or change a physical product. Once done, however, the factory can normally continue to produce it without difficulty. It is much harder, though, to ensure that a service delivers its promise time and time again. (This has led, incidentally, to the concept of "Customer experience management "; see *service quality*.)

Many mass services (in the airline, fast food, and car hire industries, for example) set out to achieve this by sophisticated process design and the use of technology. They seek to "industrialize" their service. However, this is more complex for business services, especially consultancy services, because they comprise sophisticated employees who do not wear uniforms or adopt any of the behaviours of mass services. The firm has to understand the common values that its professionals employ in their work and embed them in the design of their brand.

Brand integrity, then, rests in the experience of the product or service. It is much more than designing a corporate logo, adjusting a strap-line, or choosing a snappy name. Brand specialists have to focus on attitudes, principles, and values that run through the organization and which buyers actually experience. The emphasis of the firm should be on how the brand is experienced on a day-to-day basis and all its components must be integrated in one programme in order to reinforce the brand claim. Marketers must begin their brand strategy with the integrity of the brand claim; the consistency between the firm's external marketing and its customers' experience of the offer.

(iv) Fame

The familiarity of brands to different groups of buyers is part of their success. In the same way that a consumer might buy Burberry and be a fan of Tom Cruise, a business buyer might buy Pink's shirts, read *The Economist*, and choose McKinsey. The wide knowledge in the general population of what these brands stand for enhances their appeal to those that buy them. It is rather odd, then, that marketing professionals tend to dilute the importance and impact of fame by calling its use in brand work (rather meekly): "brand awareness". In non-marketing companies this allows leaders to under-invest in the creation and promotion of one of their greatest potential assets. In others, fame is a major ingredient in the success of their brands. Firms that have been successful in exploiting this phenomenon have invested, over years, in marketing programmes aimed at making it familiar to as wide a range of people as possible. These might comprise a range of activities from brand awareness advertising, through product placement in feature films to high profile sponsorship. All are aimed at the very simple objective of helping both the potential buyers, and the larger population, to remember the brand and to aspire to have its benefits. In other words, they set out to make their brand famous. In fact, research suggests that sales and revenue decline over time, as memory fades, when these programmes are stopped or paused in difficult times.

The creation, maintenance, and exploitation of brand awareness is, then, a key component of brand strategy. To succeed a brand has to become famous. Yet companies that are inexperienced with brands are often reluctant to spend sufficient funds on marketing and associated work in order to make their brand famous. This attitude has to be changed if successful positioning is to be achieved. They must be prepared to invest.

(v) Brand essence

Each brand has a simple truth or "essence" which it leaves in the mind of its intended buyers and its wider, admiring, audience. This is a promise that creates expectation and demand. For example, the essence of the Disney brand might be "childhood magic", whereas the essence of an accountancy brand might be "financial rigour". In clarifying this brand essence, the firm seeks to understand the fundamental truth about its promise to its buyers and to build its presence in the market around this truth. This is sometimes called the brand message, the main idea communicated to the market about the offer, creating a reason to buy. Over time, this brand essence develops depth and different aspects as buyers use it. It creates a brand "personality", to which buyers relate. Brand personality is distinctive. Offers like Nike and Apple stand for something that is clear to analysts, buyers, and employees. These brands are so rich and meaningful that different aspects of their personality appeal to different segments of customers, extending their effect. The customers themselves often interact with these entities as if they were people, developing, over time, a relationship which becomes part of the backdrop of their lives.

(vi) Brand attributes or values

It is possible to identify a number of attributes or values that will resonate with potential buyers. By making these values explicit and communicating them effectively to the intended customer groups, marketers can make their brand strategy more effective. Some of these characteristics, called hygiene factors, are essential if the firm is to compete in the market. They are likely to be strong in all competitors and discounted by customers. "Motivators", on the other hand, are brand values that are meaningful to customers. They might include soft factors such as "generosity"; describing the tendency of a supplier to give insight and help which is not always charged but is part of a professional approach. On the other hand, they might be matters of style, such as the way relationships are conducted. Emphasis on these will, over time, differentiate the brand from competitors.

Academic researchers have suggested three categories of brand attributes based on their work which seem both practical and useful (Darby, M.R., and Karni, E., 1973). They include "search attributes" (like name, price, and product characteristics) which consumers can understand before purchase. The second group is "experience attributes" (like fun, emotion, and entertainment) which can only be evaluated after purchase and during consumption. A third group is "credence attributes". Although these cannot be directly experienced or evaluated (and are more intangible than others) they are, nonetheless, very important. A number of corporate consumer brands have, for instance, been damaged by the discovery that their product is produced in child labour sweat shops. This damage to their credibility has affected profit and cash flow until repaired.

Corporate branding: the brand strategy for service companies.

One of the world's leading specialists in service marketing, Professor Leonard Berry, concluded, after years of research into different service industries that there is a major difference between the way product and service brands should be created and managed (Berry, L., 1988). A product company can create a brand, which has its own presence in the market and is independent of its owners. When it is properly managed, buyers respond to the proposition itself, incorporating it into their purchase habits and returning again and again. The corporate entity behind the product proposition can be irrelevant to them. At the time of writing, brand house, Unilever, owns, for example, brands as different as: Magnum ice cream, Vienetta, Dove soap, Lipton tea, and Slim fast. It is the image and performance of these product brands themselves, which carves out a position in its market. For other brands, though, the owner's name does become associated with the product brand (e.g. the Mars bar, Heinz ketchup, and Kellogg's cornflakes) but the owner is often unseen and relatively irrelevant to the consumer's interaction with the brand.

Berry suggests, though, that the dynamic with service brands is completely different because the emotions engendered by the buying process are different. Services involve a process through which the buyers and users must move. People must surrender themselves to the service provider and this yielding of control creates anxiety (which increases with the importance of, or unfamiliarity with, the service). As a result of this anxiety, service buyers reach around the service proposition itself to seek emotional reassurance from the entity in charge (without being aware that they are doing so). So, the great service brands tend to be corporate brands (e.g. Virgin and IBM), as represented in Figure B.5.

This has implications for many aspects of brand development and naming strategy. For instance, a product company can organize itself so that brand management is handled by a division of specialists, sometimes under a director of brands. While being integral to the health of the company, the brand group can be managed as one function within it. However, brand management for a service company is about dealing with the corporate brand, the name and reputation of the company itself. It involves a different set of stakeholders, including the firm's leadership, and a mix of responsibility. The corporate reputation might, for example, be the responsibility of a corporate relations director as opposed to the marketing director. As a result, competitive positioning and brand essence for a service company involve the whole firm and are more complicated to handle; especially if the firm is inexperienced in, or unsupportive of, brand approaches.

Naming strategy is also different because the names of individual services have to be simple functional descriptors. Examples might include: business class from Virgin versus business class from American Airlines; or managed services from IBM versus managed services from Fujitsu. It is the corporate brand that gives a promise of style and difference to the service category. Branded service propositions or made up names are unlikely to be successful.

Practicalities: How to create a brand where none exists.

There are a number of steps, which although they sound straightforward, are profound and difficult to achieve if a company has no brand experience. They are:

(i)   Decide which buyer groups to focus on and concentrate on them to the exclusion of others

Clear customer *segmentation* and deep understanding of human motivation are not academic or irrelevant, theoretical ideas. They are the practical foundations of effective brand strategies. Brands appeal to the beliefs, needs, and aspirations of people. They need to be built around a clear, unique human insight. Marketers in non-marketing companies have frequently failed to convince their colleagues and their leaders to invest in choosing a distinct customer segment. Yet, the experience of those who are developing differentiated and exhilarating offers demonstrates that marketers cannot begin to position their brand effectively if they are not prepared to invest time and effort in understanding the human beings that make up a distinct group. Even in business-to-business markets, the start of effective brand development is human insight.

(ii) Invest in understanding the rational and emotional needs of the group of buyers

This should be the source of real *differentiation*. Marketers need to understand the customers whose attention they want to attract. They must commission good quality *research*. This will be needed to identify and validate customer segments as much as to concept-test the emerging brand strategy.

(iii) Develop a brand strategy

The company needs to articulate a specific strategy by which it will create and handle its brand. This strategy needs to articulate: the intended segment of customers, the *positioning*, the rational and emotional promise, brand values, any strap-line, and the managerial plans to ensure that this strategic intent is actually experienced by customers.

They might adopt, for example, a "monolithic" brand strategy. This means that the company will have only one brand, which will be reflected throughout the company's public face (from building livery to the behaviour of its people).

This allows the firm to invest in one intangible asset and to communicate that one entity through all points of contact with buyers. To succeed, all identity and communication pieces must reinforce the values and image of this "master brand". "Sub-branding", by contrast, is the creation of many different brands. These might be offers in their own right or linked to either the company brand or a generic brand. While completely stand-alone brands are unlikely to be successful for service companies, a form of sub-branding that is open to them is to apply the brand to organizational groupings. By applying the corporate name to different business units, the firm signals that the sub-group is operating its business with a similar style and approach as the corporate entity. For example, a group of businesses competing in strategy consultancy could be branded as: "KPMG Advice" or "McKinsey Strategy" or "IBM Business Insights" (all fictitious). Each signals a different approach to consultancy subliminally communicating a different "flavour" of service, based on the main brand's essence. This form of brand architecture can support different organizational groups and their position in different markets.

(iv) Design the brand

The success of a brand rests on the shorthand it creates in the minds of the buyers. So, a clear, unique proposition needs to be designed to represent it. A professionally managed design process needs to be used for this which is not as straightforward as it sounds. First, a designer needs to be employed to create a colour scheme which reflects the mood and style that the marketer wants to achieve. For instance, a company with a long heritage may want a "classic" style, whereas a high tech firm may want a modern image, or a management consultancy may want an open-minded, fresh approach.

Colour gives this subliminal message. A designer should first produce a palette of colours representative of a "mood and style", which reflects the firm's objective, (such as the Helios created to bring BP's repositioning to life, using white, yellow, and green to represent heat, light, and nature). There is added complexity if the firm is international, because colour gives different subliminal messages to different cultures. For example, to British or American eyes pure white means freshness and cleanliness. To a Japanese eye, on the other hand, it is the colour of mourning. The marketer must take on board the subliminal message of the intended colour scheme and not just the aesthetic appeal to its leaders.

The design scheme must cover all of the "public face" of the brand in every physical manifestation its presence. This encompasses such things as: signs on buildings, design of reception halls, letterheads, fax headers, business cards, invoice formats, email, presentation slide format, the web site, proposal documents, report covers, conference appearances, and so on. Some organizations even apply it to briefcases, PCs, vehicles, toolboxes, and other items regularly seen by customers. Large firms often have to undertake an extensive audit of all of the points of contact with their public and are frequently surprised by the extent of the project. A useful technique here is a "*contact audit*", which ensures that all points of interface with the public are identified.

Very often a firm uses a "strap-line", a short statement intended to communicate the essence of the brand, to reinforce the thrust of its approach. For example, at the time of writing, Orange uses "Together we can do more", Nokia uses "Connecting people", bmi uses "Better for business", and Eurostar uses "Little break, big difference". A strap-line should reflect the brand essence. If its claim isn't truly reflective of the firm's approach, then neither staff nor customers will see it as having any relevance and it will have no effect on the brand's asset value.

It is absolutely essential that any words associated with the brand, or any new names, are checked before implementation. This might seem to be common sense but many fail to do it well. There are numerous chances to make mistakes in this area and they can be very costly. Choosing a name, for instance, where the web address is already owned by someone else, or means something obscene in a foreign language, is more common than is usually admitted publicly. Choosing a strap-line that will not translate into other cultures is also very common. Before the project is finalized all names should be trademarked, URLs tested, and translation into important cultures of the world checked.

It can be a huge task to ensure that all contact points with customers in all parts of the firm are subject to the redesign. Once implemented, however, it is essential that someone is responsible for controlling the integrity of the design. There will always be a reason why employees feel they need to adapt a colour, a piece of design, or a strap-line. This should be resisted at all costs as it undermines the subliminal message of the brand and damages the financial value of the asset. Even a slight change in colour will create an impression of confusion and diversity in a buyer's mind once a number of pieces of material are produced differently in different parts of the world.

One common practice is to develop an internal web site where all standards and materials, together with an explanation of the importance of compliance, are set out in full. Executives across the firm can access and download materials from the site. This helps ensure that all aspects of brand design are produced in accordance with the overall design scheme. It is absolutely essential, however, that leaders at all levels of the firm reinforce this necessity. If they do not, they are damaging a valuable intangible asset of the firm and are being negligent.

(v) Concept test

A designer needs to apply the colour scheme to representations (mock ups) of all these items. These must be tested in discussion with customers and employees to gauge their reactions to the design before being finalized. Some companies are hesitant to put unformed propositions about their own business to customers. However, experience suggests that customers are often willing to help a worthy supplier to find their way and the risk of launching an unpopular or negative design is worth the much lesser risk of imposing on a customer's time a little.

(vi) Test, launch, and communicate it

Brand communications must be integrated into the mix of communications that the marketer crafts to influence the generic market and specific customer groups.

Sometimes it will be an objective in its own right, with a dedicated campaign, and at other times it will be a component of a campaign. Yet it must always be a specific ingredient of communications policy and planning if it is going to earn substantial margins over a long period of time.

Political will and leadership vision.

So why hasn't brand strategy been more fully adopted by different companies? Unfortunately, all the famous branding exercises look good in retrospect. Before Nike emerged as a leading sports brand, people bought gym shoes or sneakers. Teenagers (and their parents) would have been astounded to be told that they had to pay over $100 for a pair of "running shoes" and would wear them to go out with friends. Similarly, before Intel, microprocessors were just "chips". It took visionary leaders to invest in the development of those brands, to invest in brand strategies that turned a near commodity into a value proposition. The leaders of firms like Intel and Virgin media had to put their personal political capital behind the risk of a commitment to brand. Large firms with no brand heritage do not typically have the political commitment to alter the balance of power radically in their internal operations in order to achieve this longer term benefit. They often have to be driven there by relentless market forces, going through traumatic management change en route. Smaller companies, on the other hand, can be daunted by the power of better known consumer brands like Pepsi or Nike. They forget that many successful brands (like Body Shop, Chanel, or Estée Lauder) were built from scratch by business leaders with very modest initial resources. However, whether brand success has resulted initially from vision, or luck, or the ravages of the market, the steps needed to succeed are well known. If the firm's leadership is committed to creating effective brands, robust plans can easily be put in place.

History, context, criticism, and development

As Tables B1 and B2 show, brands have a long and impressive history. They have created wealth for many, many decades. It is remarkable that there are brands, like Stella Artois, which have been around for nearly 700 years. Perhaps even more remarkable is a legislative code issued in Japan in 701. In the "Ganshiryō", or "Ganshi" code (which is, apparently, a section of the Daiho code) Article 12 regulated display signs in markets and Articles 17 and 19 introduced consumer protection, something akin to branding, about manufacturer's trade marks: "sellers should not sell defective products or counterfeits. If sellers deal with swords, spears, saddles or lacquered ware, the names of the producers should be written."

It is probably no coincidence that some of the world's greatest brands (like Singer, Wedgwood, Heinz, Coca-Cola, Dell, and Microsoft) were originally created and built by owner operators who took immense pride in the quality of what they offered. (Josiah Wedgwood would walk around his pottery smashing work that was sub-standard and saying it was not good enough for JW). Truly adopting brand management involves visionary leadership, the willingness to invest, and clear organizational emphasis.

Certainly by the early 20th century, branding in the way it is meant today was well understood. One marketing text book of the time (Butler, R.S., 1917) dedicates a chapter to branding and its effect on distribution chains. Yet, branding as a concept was curiously neglected by marketing researchers and theorists in the mid twentieth century. It makes, for instance, no appearance in the four Ps and is virtually neglected as a countervailing force to commoditization. Despite the observable (and obvious) extension of branding techniques on the duration of product sales, it has been largely ignored in debate about the product life cycle. In fact, it is only relatively recently that it has been re-examined as a powerful tool in marketing. Before that, marketing texts largely dealt with branding as an aspect of mere packaging. In the last few decades, though, there has been interesting and powerful work on: brand equity, brand loyalty, corporate brands, service brands, and brand value.

Voices and further reading

* "The problem of national advertising to be examined here is that of packaged goods, branded, identified and advertised by the manufacturer versus packaged goods not so advertised. . . . The transient in a city or a newcomer who has worn a certain brand of clothing, for example, does not hesitate to deal with a strange store that handles the same brand." Butler, R.S., 1917.
* "Much is said in adverting circles, and also in the advertising press, about the value of brand consciousness and the ascendancy of advertised brands . . . Manufacturers spend excessive amounts to create brand acceptance." White, P., 1927.
* "Increasingly customers pay more for a brand because it seems to represent a way of life or a set of ideas. Companies exploit people's emotional needs as well as their desires to consume. Hence Nike's 'Just do it' attempts to persuade runners that it is selling personal achievement or Coca-Cola's relentless effort to associate its fizzy drink with carefree fun. Companies deliberately concoct a story around their service or product, trying to turn a run-of-the-mill purchase into something more thrilling." *The Economist*, 2001.
* "Brands are fiendishly complicated, elusive, slippery, half-real/half-virtual things. When chief executives try to think about them, their brains hurt." Jeremy Bullmore, a director of marketing services group WPP, Annual lecture to the British Brands group 2001.
* Brand personality is . . . "the set of human characteristics associated with a given brand. This includes such characteristics as: gender, age, and socioeconomic class, as well as such classic human personality traits as warmth, concern and sentimentality." Aaker, D., 1996.
* Keller, K.L., "The brand report card". *Harvard Business Review*, January–February 2000.

- Brands are "the future cash flow of the business". Tim Ambler of London Business School, (Ambler, T., 2003).
- "Marketers who have inherited brands built by their predecessors are dealing them to oblivion. Sooner or later they discover that they cannot deal brands which nobody has heard of. Brands are the seed corn they have inherited. They are eating their seed corn." Ogilvy, D., 2004.
- "Service brands should be the firm's name and should not be individualised." Berry, L.L., 1988.
- Salinas, G., The *International Brand Valuation Manual*. John Wiley & Sons Ltd, 2009.
- Hollis, N., *The Global Brand*. MacMillan, 2008.
- "Successful brand building helps profitability by adding values that entice customers to buy. They also provide a firm a base for expansion into product improvements, variants, added services, new countries and so on . . . A successful brand has a name, symbol, or design (or some combination) that identifies the product of an organisation as having a sustainable competitive advantage . . . results in superior profit and market performance." Woodburn, D. and McDonald, M.H.B., 2011.
- Pringle, H. and Field, P., *Brand Immortality*. Kogan Page, 2008. This book draws on the IPA Effectiveness Awards Databank. A key finding is that certain brand strategies are more successful than others depending on the life stage of the market within which the brand is operating.
- Olins, W., *The Brand Handbook*. Thames & Hudson, 2008.
- "Every organization of a substantial size carries out hundreds of thousands of transactions every day . . . In all these transactions, the organization will in some way be presenting itself – or part of itself – to some or all groups of people with whom it has relationships. If it is to be successful in holding all these disparate groups together, it has to be consistent and clear in all these relationships. In other words, if it is to be seen as an entity, it must behave as an entity, and the corporate brand it projects to all of its audiences must be consistent." Olins, ibid.
- Tybout, A.M. and Calkins, T. (eds), *Kellogg on Branding*. John Wiley & Sons Inc., 2005.
- Taylor, D. and Nichols, D., "Brands as market leaders". *Market Leader*, Quarter 2, 2010.
- "People form preferences for a favourite brand and they literally may never change their minds in the course of their lifetime. In a study of the market leader in 30 product categories by the Boston Consulting Group, it was found that 27 of the brands that were number one in 1930 in the United States remain at the top today . . . Brands that dominate their markets are as much as 50 per cent more profitable than their nearest competitors." Solomon, M. et al., 2006.
- "There are in fact two paradigms that now guide (at least imply) the practice of branding . . . Branding by market planning and Branding by advertising. Our purpose is to discuss these two existing paradigms as background to proposing a third approach . . ." Calder, B.J. and Reagan, S.J., "Brand design" in Iacobucci, D. (ed.) *Kellogg on Marketing*. 2001.

Things you may wish to consider

(i)   The evidence suggests that it is possible to create brand entities that command the attention of a group of customers, that are distinctive, that are higher priced, that have higher margins, which see off competitors and last for several hundred years. What else should marketing be doing for its shareholders?

(ii) Increasingly the financial community is appreciating the significant proportion of shareholder value that resides in "intangibles" of which brands are one of the most important components. For example, when Kraft took over Cadbury the Cadbury brand portfolio was worth approximately £3.2bn of the £11.6 bn agreed purchase price for all Cadbury shares in issue (more than a quarter of the total amount paid). Due to highly efficient tangible asset/liability and working capital management by Cadbury plc its balance sheet displayed negative net tangible assets employed. As a result the value of the Intangible Assets acquired by Kraft is £12.0 bn. So, the entire acquisition was based, in effect, on Intangible Assets, the most significant of which was the internally generated brand portfolio. This supported the view of some commentators that the final price paid should have been closer to £10.00 a share rather than £8.50.

(iii) The experience that businesses have with brands self-evidently flies in the face of both some accepted marketing theory (like the product life cycle) and some modern business lore (like "it is difficult to create enduring value" or "you have to keep innovating new products").

IBM: One of the world's most valuable brands

Until very recently, most of the debate about branding has been dominated by consumer product marketing. Marketing media and academic studies have been so full of branding campaigns by the likes of Nike, Dove, and droves of luxury goods that it is felt that they set the ground rules on branding techniques. So, it will surprise many that, according to the respected Interband and *Business Week* survey,* one of the world's most valuable brands is a business-to-business, technology-services brand: IBM (they valued it at $56,201 million in 2010).

The story behind this remarkable success is even more intriguing. IBM is a multi-national company headquartered in New York but operating in over 200 countries. It sells a wide range of computer hardware and software and offers "infrastructure services", "hosting", and consulting services. With almost 400,000 employees worldwide, it is the world's fourth largest technology firm, the second largest by market capitalization and the second most profitable. What is less well known is that it is (at the time of writing) around a hundred years old and many of the brand values that it exhibits today have been in evidence throughout that history. For instance:

1. THE APPLICATION OF EXPERTISE TO LEADING-EDGE TECHNOLOGY CHALLENGES

One of the company's fundamental approaches to business is the idea of progress with technology: making things better through the application of intellect to unique and challenging issues. This is so much an experience of IBM employees and customers that it has become a brand value which has endured throughout the long history of the company. IBM people seem to relish the opportunity to customize their expertise and their technology to a unique and challenging issue that their customers are facing. Two iconic projects (one in its early history and one very recent) demonstrate this approach.

In 1935 the American government passed a Social Security Act which required its representatives to gather and maintain the employment records of twenty-six million people, for the very first time, in order to calculate their benefits. According to the archives of the American social security department, it was described by one newspaper of the time as "the largest bookkeeping operation in the history of the world". For instance, when engineers calculated how much all the paper, filing cabinets, and equipment might weigh, they discovered that there was no building in the United States capable of holding it. President Roosevelt became personally involved in resolving some of the problems with the then executive director of the Social Security Board, Frank Bane; but so did IBM. The work involved handling millions of applications for Social Security and the records of every participating person, taken from quarterly employer reports. (The agency says that, in the next twenty-five years 132 million numbers were issued, 3.7 billion wage records taken, and $51 billion of benefits paid out.) To process this work, the department worked closely with IBM and used what were then state-of-the-art electro-mechanical tabulating machines. Engineers were constantly on site and much of its early office equipment started as a solution to a problem in this massive project.

As the 21st century dawned, the government of the City of the Swedish capital, Stockholm, had a growing problem with traffic congestion (commute times were up 18% on the previous year, for example). It had been studying the effect of congestion charging schemes in London and Singapore; and so announced a trial in 2006. The aim was to reduce congestion, improve public transport, and curb environmental impact. IBM worked with a number of specialized partners to develop an automated charging system. As vehicles passed control points into and out of the city, state-of-the-art technology was used to identify and charge vehicles during specific times. The technology included "transponder tags" which drivers could put in their cars and photographic technology to record licence plates. Typical of the company, this pulled in functions from across the firm. For instance, IBM research had to be involved in developing image enhancement algorithms to cope with Swedish weather.

The subsequent system is easy and not disruptive to traffic patterns. When a vehicle breaks a laser beam at a control point the "transceiver" signals the vehicle's "transponder" recording time date and tax amount, as well as photographing the front. It then hits a second laser which photographs the rear of the vehicle. Payment is debited from the driver's account or paid via web or retailers. All this is done without the car slowing down or being distracted in any way. The trial was a measurable success. It resulted in a 25% drop in traffic, a drop in emissions from road traffic (in excess of 8%), and a 40% fall in greenhouse gases like carbon dioxide.

IBM's current head of brand, Kevin Bishop, says that this customized approach is so endemic in the company and its history that he can publicize one similar story a day throughout its centennial year (2011). So, the award winning "smarter planet" programme is designed to make this brand value explicit and to apply it to the vast challenges of the 21st century. More than just a marketing campaign, the company is supporting public and private sector organizations as they seek to reduce costs, drive innovation, and transform their technology infrastructure. The company's 2008 annual report explains "The economic downturn has intensified this trend, as leaders seek not simply to repair what is broken, but to prepare for a 21st Century economy." Bit by bit, they claim, our planet is getting smarter, driven by the proliferation of technologies used in everyday life, the interconnections between these devices, the information they generate, and the increasing intelligence that can be gleaned from this information. In essence, the company is offering to solve some of the world's most significant problems such as environmental protection, energy consumption, and education.

2. SCALABILITY: THE CONVERSION OF LEADING TECHNOLOGY TRENDS INTO REPLICABLE APPROACHES TO BENEFIT MANY

Another long-standing approach of the firm is the conversion of these unique customized projects into replicable technologies. The Social Security project led to work with other government departments and to the development of products which could be sold around the world. The Swedish congestion project is being developed for other locations. For many decades, IBM has used these pioneering projects with leading-edge customers to identify trends, release new products, and enter new markets. As a result, its innovation and new product development is grounded in reality and the application of technology to emerging needs.

3. LEADERSHIP

This focus on the industrialization of leading-edge technology has meant that the company has been a pioneer and market leader for more than half a century. No book on the behaviour of market leaders or academic study into the success factors in dominating markets can be complete without IBM. It is, and has been, an unquestioned leader in management thinking and practice. One study (Mercer, D., 1988), for instance, tracked its influence on the research and thinking of famous management guru, Peter Drucker; and, in turn, on the economies of the West and the emergent polices of Japan.

The company has led and responded to dramatic changes in the nature and the relevance of technology to business and life. It has set technical standards and invested in research. In the 1930s, for instance, it set up one of the finest research laboratories in the world at Endicott, New York (it now has eight worldwide). As a result the firm holds more patents than any other US-based Technology Company and has earned a number of prestigious awards including five Nobel prizes.

Like market leaders in other industries the IBM brand validates new trends and sets a market standard. The most remarkable example of that was probably the personal computer. There were PCs launched before IBM's and there are very few in the world today that were actually made by the company. Nevertheless, as the PC market began to take off, it was the layout and design of the IBM PC which became the market standard and allowed the market to boom across the world. In the same way that Americans "Fedex" a package and British people "Hoover" up dust, the "IBM PC" became a watchword for an effective personal computer.

IBM has been used for case studies and examples in the field of management and marketing as much as in technology. For decades its sales training was the best in its field and its account management practices were aped around the world in many different industries. For much of its life it has been considered to be simply one of the world's best run companies, leading its sector of the industrial landscape.

4. THE "IBM-ERS"

Another consistent value that seems to have been strong throughout the company's history is the stress put on its people: the "IBM-ers". From its first beginnings, it put emphasis on the way it treated its people. It recruited, trained, and developed people well. It was at the forefront of many human relations policies and underwrote those policies with very practical applications. During the depression of the 1930s for example, it famously kept people on, despite capacity, and had never made anyone involuntarily redundant until the dramatic market traumas right at the end of the 20th century. For much of its history IBM has been a guide to good management practice and "the IBM-er" is still the foundation of the company's brand today.

As one of its global CEOs said: "IBM was the leader in diversity for decades, well before governments even spoke of the need to seek equality in employment, advancement, and compensation. A sense of integrity, of responsibility, flows through the veins of IBM in a way I've never seen in any other company. IBM people are committed – committed to their company, and to what their company does." (Gerstner, 2002).

In fact, although to the outside world, the IBM-er is seen as a loyal corporate employee (and, in earlier decades, even dressed to signal that conformity) within the company there has been a respect for the individual and considerable freedom to act. Some have even called it a "cult of individualism".

The company's respect for and engagement with its people can be seen in its recent, extensive consultation exercises. In 2003, for instance, it embarked on an ambitious project to rewrite company values. Using its "Jam" technology, it hosted internet-based online discussions on key business issues with 50,000 employees over three days. The discussions were analysed by sophisticated text analysis software (eClassifier) to mine online comments for themes. As a result of this, the company's values were updated to: "Dedication to every client's success", "Innovation that matters – for our company and for the world", "Trust and personal responsibility in all relationships". Other "Jams" have been held since to explore other issues in depth.

So, between 1993 and 2009, IBM climbed from the 282nd position in Interbrand's league table of the world's best global brands to number two. It achieved this rise by making huge strides in its marketing strategy and developing impressive global organizational competence in branding and marketing.

Yet, managing this brand through disruptive change has meant guarding the historical brand promise while establishing new brand values. The new campaigns emerged out of things the company was already doing, and the marketing campaigns did the work of distilling these skills down to their essence and presenting them in a powerful way. In other words, the campaigns were authentic and reinforced brand integrity. Kevin Bishop said that "long term success is about understanding a company's enduring purpose and who you serve. In IBM's case that has always been about helping forward thinking people. We can demonstrate that IBM-ers in all the functions of the organization lived those values for many decades. In many ways we have always been a service company; serving the developing needs of our customers. The success in our brand work is making that explicit and recognized."

*The 100 most valuable brands. Business Week/Interband, 2010.

 RATING: Practical and powerful

BUSINESS-TO-BUSINESS MARKETING

Application: the marketing and sale of all offers not aimed at consumers

The concept

Much of the conceptualization, codification, and teaching of marketing has focused on the experience of consumer product companies: soap powder manufacturers, fizzy drink producers, cosmetics and the like. This is because many of its more prominent aspects (like advertising) caught the public imagination during the consumer boom in 1950s America. A vast number of businesses, though, exist to market and sell products and service to other businesses; the so called "B-to-B" markets. In fact, professional associations in many Western countries suggest that there are actually more marketers in business marketing than consumer.

In many respects there are similarities and common practices between consumer and business marketing. Marketing planning, segmentation, NPD/NSD, and communications techniques like advertising or digital marketing are all, for instance, routinely used. Yet, marketing and sales specialists in business-to-business organizations also deal with a range of issues which make them different from consumer markets. They include:

(i) Size

These markets are often smaller than the vast consumer markets. In some, for instance, marketers can virtually name all their buyers. So much so that, this can lead to "conflict issues"; suppliers working for the major organizations operating in a market are unable to work for others. It forces them to prioritize "targets" and makes meaningless the mindless drive for market share prevalent in other markets.

(ii) Intimacy of customers in professional networks

It has been demonstrated by several well framed studies and decades of experience that business–to–business markets comprise numerous inter-related networks of professional relationships. Profit can be increased by deepening these relationships; by increasing trust and developing links between two organizations (see *AAR*). These relationships are the prime focus of many sales people and business-to-business marketing specialists. In fact, many say that "it's all about relationships" (see *relationship marketing*).

(iii) The tendency to attract a number of repeat buyers

The tendency to attract those repeat buyers who dominate the operations of the business and demand special attention (see *account management*). In fact, some business customers have bigger global revenues than some nation states. This fact alone is changing the perspective and priorities of a growing number of business-to-business marketers.

(iv) A more formal *DMU*

Formal sign off processes and the need to get agreement from a group with approval authority is, more or less, routine. Not only do they exist but they are often required by law or regulation. There is some evidence that, particularly in the West, this is lengthening sales cycles as more demanding regulation affects public companies (see *organizational buying behaviour*). The buying process itself is as different as the different organizational structures and cultures of each business. Some might use large, process-based bid techniques while others in exactly the same sector might turn on the whim of a forceful leader. Sales people need the help of marketing communications activities that allow for this variety and warm up different buyers to the point of sale. Good communications are absolutely essential to enable sales teams to function effectively.

(v) The involvement and influence of professional buyers

From IT to professional services, purchasing managers, and directors are becoming increasingly involved in business buying. They introduce their own values, processes and criteria, demanding rigorous approaches from sales and marketing people trying to sell to their company.

(vi) Sector expertise

Without doubt, there is an assumption amongst many buyers that knowledge of their sector is a sign that potential suppliers understand their need. Business customers will expect their suppliers to understand the language, history, key trends, and main competitors in their industry. As a result, most business-to-business marketers have, or are forced to set up, a *sector marketing* programme.

It has been suggested that business-to-business marketing is more "rational" than consumer marketing because formal buying processes exist. Yet, a combination of the recent experience of leading business suppliers, more recent research, and a deeper understanding of human behaviour has challenged this view. Business buyers are human beings who experience emotions at work. The degree of risk, personal enhancement, or political effort in a purchase can be decisive. So, there is a considerable amount of emotion within the decision-making unit of businesses. For many important purchases (such as outsourcing services) the various people in the decision-making unit are influenced as much by emotion as consumers. In fact, some modern behaviourists argue that almost all decisions have an emotional element. Business buyers might, for instance, be worried about the perception of the effectiveness of their work, or their political position, or looking to use the purchase decision as a means of gaining influence.

If decisions are emotional as well as rational, then decision makers can be influenced by appropriate communication. Historically, academics and marketing writers have tended to play down the role of the full marketing communications mix in business markets. They have argued that, because of "industrial buying processes" and the use of specialists (like purchasing managers) the ability of communications to influence decision makers is limited. They have also argued that the sales process has been managed by sophisticated sales people and therefore the supplementary effect of other communications material is negligible. Yet, business marketers in fact use the full range of marketing capabilities to persuade erratic, whimsical human beings to buy. In addition, though, this form of marketing has tended to put greater emphasis on other aspects of marketing like: *relationship marketing*, networking, *sector marketing*, *thought leadership*, *viral marketing*, *hospitality*, and account relationship modelling like the *AAR* technique.

History, context, criticism, and development

Business–to–business (or "industrial marketing") has had a long, healthy record of success. One of the prime examples of its early sophistication is English manufacturer, Mathew Boulton. He made his fame and fortune in the mid-eighteenth century with his direct marketing of "toys" (little silver trinkets). He then became a leading industrialist and set up a pioneering manufacturing plant in his home town (Birmingham, England). He networked extensively and kept his mind open to developing trends. So he was delighted when he came across the Bill Gates of his time; a scientist called James Watt. Watt had solved a number of problems with a new energy source of their time: the steam engine. Boulton recognized that there was a vast business opportunity if they could industrialize it and create markets for it: but they would not be the luxury consumer markets that he was used to, this was business to business marketing and it needed new methods.

It was hard trying to create a market for a true innovation at a time of great international instability and relative poverty. At the heart of their strategy was clear business-to-business marketing which involved: (what would now be called) solutions sales, innovative pricing, word-of-mouth, investment in free trials and business relationships, thought leadership, sales reps, celebrity endorsement, and clear segmentation. For instance, King George III opened their engine for the brewer Whitbread and an early customer (Joseph Jary, an owner of a coal mine) paid nothing, on the condition that he used the engine to "trumpet their name".

The first market segment they truly focused on was the mine owners in Cornwall. Their proposition was a customized solution to their pumping needs based on a unique business model (see Friedel, R., 2007). They would set up the machinery and maintain it. In return, the miners would be able to get to greater depths and have greater yield from their mines. The company would receive an annual royalty, up to the expiry of the patent on the pump, which was calculated as a portion of the savings in fuel costs made possible by the new machine; in other words, from incremental value realized. Historian Jenny Uglow says of them: "Boulton's round marketing phrases ring through the Gazette's 'impartial' report. . . . Slowly the orders came in, from small pumping engines for a London distillery in Bow, to the largest one yet at Hawkesbury colliery . . . The potential market was dizzying." (Uglow, J., 2003).

They even targeted the public sector. They were approached by the French government and, as a result, the *Académiciens* Macquer and Maigny recommended that they be offered a monopoly privilege to erect engines in France for fifteen years. They won a contract to pump the sewage of the City of Paris. This enabled the new French leaders it was the time of the French revolution to demonstrate their enlightened and forward thinking approach to the sciences.

As a result of this precise targeting and pioneering business-to-business marketing, Boulton & Watt engines had 30% of the total UK market by the time their patent expired in 1800. Of the roughly 1,500 machines that were erected, 30% were used in mines, 30% in textiles, and the rest in a range of industries (water supply, brewing, iron works, etc). In twenty years, they had made a fortune by the careful and precise sale of an expensive innovative machine.

Similarly, the beginnings of the German automobile had their roots in successful business-to-business marketing. In 1872, a company called "Gasmotoren-Fabrik Deutz" hired a young engineer called Gottlied Daimler. The rest, as they say, is history. Yet the Deutz company was founded by two people to market engines to businesses. The first was Nicolaus Otto, who started as a travelling salesman representing tea, sugar, and kitchenware. He built a model engine based on earlier innovation by Étienne Lenoir. This attracted the attention of Eugen Langen, a Cologne Sugar refiner. Their machine won a gold medal at the Paris International Exposition in 1867 because it consumed less fuel than competing products and they set about marketing it in Europe to other businesses.

Bankers are another example of an industry that has had long success in business-to-business marketing. Their sector has been financing industrialists for several centuries and they have adopted a range of business-to-business marketing techniques. They have used: elite *relationship marketing*, *PR*, *sales*, and *thought leadership* to achieve this success.

One of the most interesting fields of business marketing is the professions. These outstandingly successful businesses include lawyers, accountants, consultants, and architects. Their industry is dominated by an almost unique form of business ownership: mutual partnership. It means that the business owners, the partners, are intimately tied to its success and engage in work with their clients (as they call them), shifting "management" into a low priority afterthought. These partners have access to the heights of leading organizations, be they family businesses, new start ups, large corporations, or even nation states. They respond to requests, deliver excellent work, and stimulate new enquires. Many are responsible for breathtaking salesmanship, routinely walking away with large, high value deals that dwarf the contracts given to even the world's leading sales people in other industries. Many are, to use the jargon, "unconsciously competent" at revenue generation and routinely use marketing techniques like *relationship marketing*, *PR*, *thought leadership*, *hospitality*, and reputation management (whilst at the same time loathing the idea of their expertise being marketed or sold). Whereas many successful public companies rise and fall in a few decades; and whereas many (in banking or retail for instance) regard net margins of around 10% as success, there are professional practices that are entering their second century of business which routinely return to their owners net margins in excess of 30%. By any measure they are remarkably successful at business-to-business marketing. They just do not call it that.

There is a widely held, but wrong, belief that there is not much unique theory or research in business-to-business marketing. As marketing began to be codified theorists, researchers, and academics began to explore and articulate the differences between consumer marketing and business-to-business marketing. Much of it was originally called "industrial marketing" and confined to a few interested researchers. For several decades now, though, there has been unique and specific work on the dynamics of business markets. Interesting and useful insights on: relationship marketing, segmentation, communications, and sales effectiveness are now available and developing fast. In America, for instance, there was Alexander's "Industrial marketing" (see Alexander, R.S., Cross, J.S., and Cunningham, R.M., 1961) and in Britain an edited book which explored different aspects of the marketing mix with chapters from both practising specialists and academics like Professor Theodore Levitt (see Wilson, A., 1965). In the latter half of the 20th century there has been patient, detailed, and insightful research by the likes of Professors Hakan Håkansson, Evert Gummerson, and Malcolm McDonald which codified the actualities of many aspects of business-to-businesses marketing. Much of it is reliable, practical, and useable.

Voices and further reading

- Wilson, A. (ed.), *The Marketing of Industrial Products*. Hutchinson, 1965.
- "Industrial marketing: all those activities concerned with purchases and sales of goods and services in industrial markets and between organizational buyers and sellers." Wilson, ibid.
- Axelsson, L. and Easton, G., *Industrial Networks: A New View of Reality*. Routledge, 1992.
- Håkansson, H. and Snehota, I., *Developing Relationships in Business Networks*. Routledge, 1995.
- "There is a team effect. Jointly, the two companies can perform activities and utilize resources which none of them could accomplish in isolation. What they can accomplish depends on how the relationship develops. A relationship between two companies does not become automatically a perfect 'team' but the potential is always there. The team effects have to be tried out. They develop as the parties involved experiment with the various connections and learn about their effects.

The quality of the relationship is the extent to which this function will be exploited." Håkansson and Snehota, ibid.

- Purchase, S. and Ward, A., "AAR model: cross cultural developments". *International Marketing Review*, 20:2, January 2002.
- Ford, D., *The Business Marketing Course*. John Wiley & Sons Ltd, 2002.
- "Resource ties can develop gradually and unconsciously as problems are solved within a relationship. These ties can be substantial and important in old relationships, without the companies being aware of them. In contrast, innovation often occurs when the resources are tied together in new ways between companies and this can lead to the development of offerings with wide application. Both of these issues emphasize the importance for the marketer of auditing each important relationship". Ford, ibid.
- Woodburn, D. and McDonald. M.H.B. *Key Account Management: The Definitive Guide*. John Wiley & Sons Ltd, 2011 (3rd edn).
- Minnett, S., *B2B Marketing*. Prentice Hall, 2002.
- Ford, D., *Understanding Business Marketing*. Thomson, 2002.
- Mahin, P.W., *Business-to-business Marketing*. Allyn & Bacon, 1991.
- Boaz, N., Murnane, J., and Nuffer, K. "The basics of Business–to-business sales success" *McKinsey Quarterly*, May 2010.

Things you may wish to consider

(i)   This is as much about people and understanding the desires of human beings as consumer markets, even though organizations are involved.

(ii) The dynamics and effects of *brands* are as much in evidence as in consumer markets.

(iii) Mass advertising has been used and shown results as impressive as in consumer markets.

(iv) There are remarkable effects from mystique and elite media (like Davos, the *McKinsey Quarterly*, and the *Harvard Business Review*) which earn high premiums in business markets.

(v)   Business-to-business marketing has been using *viral marketing* for a number of years, without recognizing it or calling it that. Many, for instance, develop and market ideas or concepts (see *thought leadership*) in order to sell their products or services. They create programmes that spread ideas through conferences, magazines, and other business publications. They are, though, carried virally, through inter-connected networks of business professionals. By developing organizational competence in viral marketing, marketers should be able to make business-to-business campaigns more effective.

(vi) There are a variety of sales models used in business–to business marketing (solutions, consultative, field, and account management). It is vital to understand which is the most appropriate and set it up effectively.

(vii) Large organizations consistently forget that a business buyer's personal experiences create prejudices in their professional life. A telecommunications or computer company that provides awful service to leading individuals can find itself inexplicably shut out of large business opportunities. As a result, a number of experienced business marketers create specific programmes for VIP domestic users, even if they are subtly and discreetly executed. Sometimes, even the customer does not know they are the subject of such a programme.

 RATING: Practical and powerful

C

 CATEGORY MANAGEMENT

Application: sales strategy, marketing strategy, NPD, promotional planning

The category management process

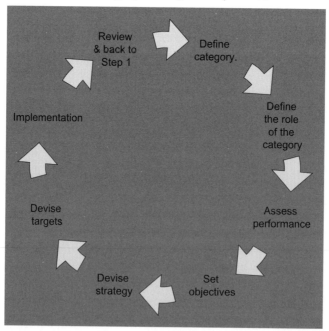

Figure C.1: A representation of the generally accepted category management process

The concept

Category management, which is (at the time of writing) strongest in the retail sector, suggests that a product range is sold with different groups of similar, competitor products. These product categories (like frozen foods or toothpastes) are easily recognized and understood by customers. Each category is run within the organization as a business unit with its own targets and strategies. The introduction of the approach seems to change the relationship between retailers and suppliers; making it more collaborative. It prompts exchange of information, sharing of data, and joint business building. For instance, the emphasis moves to the turnover of the category as whole, not just the sale of individual products. Suppliers are expected to suggest new products or promotions that benefit the turnover of the total category and be beneficial to the shoppers interested in that category.

The idea developed for several reasons. First, retailers wanted suppliers to add value to their business rather than just fight for shelf space with other brands in the shop. Up until then, competition between manufacturers would change share within a product group but yield no incremental gain for the retailer. Secondly, suppliers saw it as a way of countering the rise in power of "own brand" items. It was also realized that there was more profit to be made in increasing the total level of sales in a product group than through harsh, relentless negotiation over price alone. In addition, collaboration meant that suppliers' knowledge of their market could be accessed by retailers, smart marketers also realized that a considerable amount of work in developing a category could be delegated to their suppliers.

In 1992, the research company Nielsen defined category management as: "a process that involves managing product categories as business units and customizing them (on a store by store basis) to satisfy customer needs". This is probably a little off because customizing product groups on a store-by-store basis is logistically difficult and does not seem to be considered a necessary part of category management; it is a concept now referred to as "micromarketing". (The ability to analyse sales data by barcode and by individual store means that the traditional concept of "one range fits all" can be changed to this more flexible approach.) Nevertheless, many retailers manage stores by, say, size, and select product assortments accordingly. The definition does not adequately explain some practicalities for example, where demographic or marketing considerations take precedence, (such as stores tailored to the demographics of a local population).

Nielson also developed a process by which category management could be handled. This "five-step process" included: reviewing the category, targeting consumers, planning merchandising, implementing the strategy, and evaluating the results. It has, though, generally been superseded by an eight-step cycle developed by the Partnering Group and represented in Figure C.1 above. Whilst being very comprehensive and thorough this has been criticized for being rather too unwieldy and time-consuming. Few suppliers say that they use the full process. They seem to use it as a basis to develop their own more streamlined approach, tailored to their own particular products.

It appears to be commonplace for one supplier in a category (normally the one with the highest turnover in the product group) to be nominated by a retailer as a "category captain". They will be expected to have the closest and most regular contact with the retailer and to invest time, effort and, often, money in to the development of the category. In return, they will gain a more influential voice with the retailer. For instance, in order to do the job effectively, they may be granted access to a greater wealth of data-sharing (e.g. more access to an internal sales database).

Interestingly, a similar approach seems to be evolving in service industries. Academics have suggested a number of different ways of categorizing services which will give useful insight into the dynamics of the business. There is evidence that the explicit management of business units within these categories and increased coopera- tion with customers (through a concept called the "co-creation of service") has had beneficial effects similar to category management in product industries. Whilst there is not much evidence of "category captains" in this field, there is no doubt that many large technology providers have, for several years, grown used to an environment where a partner in one deal is a competitor in another. They have had to cooperate for the sake of their customers in different industry sectors. The service groupings are:

- **Customized services versus "industrialized" (i.e. more process-based and packaged) services**. The margins, approach to market, degree of engage- ment with buyers, and personnel used vary enormously between these two types of offers.

- **Infrastructure-based services versus added value services.** Some services are based on an infrastructure, a technology, or a network. They include water supply, computer "platforms" in major companies, telecommunications networks, networks of airline slots, or sets of maintenance contacts. The issues, development, and degree of reliance on that infrastructure affect the nature and the content of those services. Very often there is a core service ("communications" in telecom- munication companies, "support" in computer maintenance companies, and "power supply" in utilities) and opportunities for added value services.

- **Product-based services versus free services.** Some services are adjuncts to product propositions and are therefore intimately tied to the value, development, and pricing of that product. Other services are unique propositions in their own right which will stand alone in the market place.

- **Discrete (project) services versus continuously rendered (annuity) serv- ices.** Some services (such as consultancy) are one-off discrete projects whereas others (like financial audit) are recurring contractual relationships. This difference affects pricing, customer relationship techniques, margins, and business structures.

- **Technology-based services versus people-based services (high tech versus high touch).** Some services (extranets for business buyers, for example) comprise technology through which customers are served. Other services are predominantly reliant on the skills of people.

- **Self-service versus performed service.** Some services are performed on behalf of a buyer, whereas others provide the means by which they can perform the service themselves.
- **A membership relationship versus anonymity.** This classification suggests differences according to the relationship of the buyer to the supplier. Membership may range from formal paid-for inclusion in a club to an emotional attachment to the group or community at whom the service is targeted. However, in many circumstances, buyers prefer anonymity or simple functionality and resist suppliers' attempts to form an intrusive relationship.
- **Transactional versus interaction services.** Some services are short-term "transactions". They are often low value and commoditized purchases. "Interactions", though (a relatively new definition), are higher value, mutually profitable exchanges between a customer and a supplier over a long term.

History, context, criticism, and development

The relatively recent concept seems to have originated in grocery retailing, and has since expanded to other sectors such as DIY, cash and carry, pharmacy and book retailing. It seems to have started in North America in the 1980s and prompted a change in relationships between suppliers and retailers (from adversarial to more collaborative). Nielsen appears to have begun publishing information around 1992, prompting the category management process to gain momentum across the Europe and Canada. At first, it was limited to supermarkets but, as the advantages became clearer, it spread into other sectors.

Two key things were needed in order to enable category management to evolve:

(i) The growing dominance of large retailers like Tesco in the UK and Wal-Mart in the USA. Before then, retailers were focused more on growth through harsh price negotiation and the building of stores. Likewise, suppliers would not have seen a return on investment in relationships with lots of small retailers; but with the emergence of fewer larger clients, the concept became attractive.

(ii) The explosion in information technology which meant that sales data (collected from barcodes) could be more efficiently collected and analysed for trends and information.

It is reported that, during the mid 1990s, category management seemed to be confused with rationalizing and clearing out duplicated products, seen as a one-off "spring-clean". Following this initial hiccup, there was a brief period during which some retailers reverted to old-fashioned trading but category management then regained momentum, embracing many aspects which should have had more prominence the first time around (price architecture, promotional strategy, and shopper understanding). At the time of writing, category management is increasingly becoming a way of doing business. There is even a Category Management Association, formed in 2004, with members that come from a broad range of functions. It connects members with category management peers around the world, is a central resource for information and best practice, and is the only group certifying companies and individual category management professionals according to recognized industry standards.

Voices and further reading

- "Viewed purely as a strategy to reduce waste and therefore costs, CM loses its focus on the end customer as the absolute priority. Concreting on the maximization of shelf-space profitability may not improve customer satisfaction levels and that, in the long run, may reduce profits." McDonald, M.H.B. and Wilson, H., 2011.
- Lovelock, C.H., "Classifying Services to gain strategic marketing insights". *Journal of Marketing*, Summer 1983.

Things you might like to consider

(i) As the amount of data increases category management is becoming highly "technology" and mathematics-orientated.
(ii) There is a large *behavioural marketing* element to the concept (for example in understanding the psychology of shoppers) and there is potential for real development in this technique.
(iii) Some politicians have viewed the increased collaboration between suppliers and retailers with suspicion and, perhaps, as a potential source of anti-competitive behaviour. The UK Competition Commission has, for instance, raised issues on market distortion in principle. They have also acted on milk price-fixing.

★ **RATING: Practical**

 # CELEBRITY ENDORSEMENT

Application: brand positioning, marketing communication, value creation

The concept

Fame is a very powerful tool open to modern marketers. Actors, musicians, singers, politicians, and even criminals are admired and followed for their public recognition as much as for a particular skill or achievement. Some are even famous for little more than continual appearance in the media; famous for being famous. Alongside favourite TV shows and magazines, these celebrities become a familiar part of day-to-day life. They are intriguing, beguiling, and incredibly valuable as a result. (In 2002, for example, Jennifer Anniston is reported to have earned £21 million, see Pringle, H., 2004.) People feel a sense of warmth toward them and follow their own package of celebrity, magazine, style, and soap opera.

In fact, for many, fame is a route to success and achievement which they think is not open to them through any other means (hence the success of Simon Cowell and shows like "X Factor" or "America's Got Talent"). Others follow celebrities and celebrity trends very closely as a guide to their own tastes and lifestyles. Aspiration is an important aspect of the fame and celebrity phenomenon. People mimic their favourite film stars or sports heroes because they want to be associated with the success represented by their lifestyles. This is often subliminal, but nevertheless very powerful. A young woman styling her hair like Jennifer Aniston or teenage boys dressing like British soccer star David Beckham are all associating with perceived success, and buy associated merchandise as a result. It may not be that everyone is consciously aping the lifestyle of celebrities but they become familiar with issues, values, and products or services through media they find fascinating. As a result, this phenomenon is a powerful marketing tool.

Despite the virtual silence in marketing text books or many academic tomes, there is no doubt that marketers in many different industries use celebrity endorsement extensively. They try to use a celebrity close to the personality of their brand or brand aspiration. In luxury goods, fashion, and cosmetics, for example, names like Jennifer Lopez, Thierry Henry, Victoria Beckham, and Tiger Woods have been used to create aspiration. Even in groceries and more routine purchases the likes of chef Jamie Oliver and footballer Gary Lineker have been used.

The Lineker campaign for Walkers crisps is one of the longest running modern UK celebrity campaigns (and has also been used in other countries). The main thought behind it is that "these crisps are so good they can make a nice guy nasty". In choosing the celebrity to play the part the agency sought out the nicest man in football. Gary Lineker; a player who had never even received a yellow card. Using Lineker as the nice person so tempted by the Walkers crisps that he turns nasty and steals them from a young child was a brilliant piece of casting against type and that basic idea has underpinned of the campaign ever since.

There is also a celebrity dynamic in business-to-business markets. Famous business leaders (like Jack Welch, Larry Ellison, Bill Gates, and Richard Branson), famous media (like the *Harvard Business Review*), famous events (like Davos), and famous companies (like McKinsey or Goldman Sachs) attract audiences amongst business leaders willing to learn. They are prime marketing tools. The leader of a modestly sized business who wants a big four firm as their accountant, the director who stands on an awards platform with a well known academic guru, and the chief executive who basks in the glory of the latest acquisition led by one of the big merchant banks, are all reflecting this phenomenon to a certain extent.

A pre-eminent example of the use of celebrity in business-to-business marketing is Accenture's recent use of Tiger Woods. His focus and achievement became the emblem of their alignment with business aspiration through their "high performance" positioning campaign. The campaign matched his drive, expertise, and success with the message that Accenture employed people with similar attitudes who could help business people achieve similar success (and, of course, many of their target market played golf). Accenture's experience also shows, though, some of the dangers of celebrity endorsement. When Mr Woods had marriage difficulties and his public image was tarnished by behaviour that was not received well in the media, Accenture had an agonizing decision as to whether to continue to use him and eventually ended his contract.

The line in the sand seems to be whether or not the celebrity has done something illegal, in which case it is very hard for companies nowadays to retain the relationship. In most cases the furore caused by a celebrity inadvertently using or wearing the wrong brand merely adds more oxygen to the publicity and actually adds value. Kate Moss was not convicted of the illegal use of class A drugs, so while she was dropped by fashion retailer H&M (because it seems Stefan Persson, their Executive Chairman, was closely involved with Mentor, an anti-drugs charity), all her other contractual relationships were renewed. Indeed Moss gained an important new client: Philip Green and Topshop. So, her increased notoriety may have made her more bankable as it reinforced her "edginess" (one of the reasons why she has been a successful model for so long).

There is a hard financial dynamic to this technique. For instance, after Princess Diana was photographed in 1995 carrying the "Lady Dior" handbag, they sold 100,000 at $1,000 each, raising the company's 1996 revenues by 20% (Thomas, D., 2007). Hamish Pringle reports (Pringle, H., 2004) that the celebrity campaign with Gary Lineker made the market share of Walker's crisps rise by 6% and produced a return of £1.70 for every £1 spent; while Sainsbury's tie-up with Jamie Oliver added incremental revenue of a staggering £1.12 billion and a return of £27.25 for every pound spent. (As this data comes from Britain's Institute of Practitioners in Advertising, it is likely to be reliable.) The financial success of celebrity endorsement and the use of fame is so remarkable that it is a disgrace that marketing academics have not substantiated and codified many of the techniques behind it more extensively.

History, context, criticism, and development

As Tom Payne points out (Payne T., 2009), both fame and celebrity have been phenomena of human society for a very long time. He makes associations with, for example, the attitude of the ancient Greeks to the antics of their gods and draws common principles from similarities with modern celebrity culture. Celebrity has, for example, been used pitilessly by ambitious business leaders and marketers for some time. In the 1700s Josiah Wedgwood exploited links with royalty and nobility. After the Queen commissioned a tea service, for instance, he styled himself "potter to the Queen". He also decided that there was a market for cameo portraits of famous people or "illustrious moderns" as he called them. His pottery produced a series of medallions of famous people of the time (Charles Wesley, The King, William Pitt, and members of the aristocracy) and these pieces are still admired today. They were a sort of collectable set of celebrity portraits before *Hello* or *Heat* magazine. As Professor Nancy Koehn said: "Josiah understood the value of celebrity sanction. He worked hard to obtain it, absorbing significant costs in time and money in order to produce highly specialized individual commissions. While other potters avoided such orders, Wedgwood actively sought them. Once he had completed an aristocratic sale, Josiah lost no time in advertising it to a much larger, more profitable market" (Koehn, N. F., 2001).

In the 1800s Lillie Langtry (an A-list celebrity actress, novelist, and mistress to the King of England) amassed a small fortune from her association with Pear's soap. In 1881 she was paid £132 (a princely sum at the time) for her first Pears advertisement in which she said: "Since using Pears' soap for the hands and complexion I have discarded all others" (despite not using the product). Considered to be the most beautiful woman in the world, crowds greeted her all over the USA during her first tour of that country and she took a furnished apartment in exchange for endorsing American Recamier preparations. It is said that she helped to make advertising socially acceptable. In the 1890s Adelina Patti earned the nickname "Testimonial Patti" for the extent of her endorsements (corsets, pianos, toothpaste, olive oil and, of course, Pears soap!). Even the adventurer Scott of the Antarctic took Heinz on his expedition in 1911.

At the end of the 20th century, though, marketers and others seemed to become more aware of this phenomenon and began to develop organizational expertise (such as dedicated agencies and selection processes inside large organizations). In 1988, for instance, Armani hired society editor Wanda McDaniel to get Hollywood players to wear their range. The first impact of this was with producers and executives through informal contacts. Armani took on the dressing of Jodie Foster for awards after she was criticized in the 1989 Oscars (where she won for *The Accused*). Then followed Michelle Pfeiffer, Jessica Tandy, Steve Martin, Dennis Hopper, etc. Their success could not be disguised: between 1990 and 1993 Armani turnover doubled to $442 million. So, from the mid 1990s onward, fashion houses began to routinely dress stars in return for them attending fashion shows and post show parties. With the rise of brand Beckham and the success of god-maker Simon Cowell, the modern celebrity machinery was born. This growing marketing phenomenon, and the organizational competence it requires, particularly in the digital age, needs to be more extensively studied and codified.

Voices and further reading

- Pringle, H., *Celebrity Sells*, John Wiley & Sons Ltd, 2004. (The first "how to" book on the use of celebrity with brands).

- "Marketers and their agencies should be aware that the general public is cynical about the motivations of stars in doing testimonials for brands – they think these celebrities do it for the money, and of course they're right. So the skill is to do everything possible to counteract this cynicism and create a context in which the relationship between the brand and the star has genuine credibility. One of the ways in which this credibility is undermined is if the brand enters into a relationship with a star who already has too many other contractual links with other brands." Pringle, ibid.
- Payne, T., *Fame: From the Bronze Age to Britney*. Vintage Books, 2009.
- "It's possible to see our fascination with even the most fleeting stars as something that bonds us, and which expresses something about how our civilisation works." Payne, ibid.
- "The goal is to show that celebrity is accessible. Readers feel that they 'know' celebrities in a way that they will never know models. There's glamour but not distant glamour. Celebrities are in TV, movies and pop music. They are in people's lives and in people's living rooms. They are not mysterious." Martha Nelson, founding editor of *In Style* (quoted in Thomas, D., 2007).
- "No other malice goes faster than fame; growing with movement, strengthening as it goes, first little, fearful, soon striding the winds, it treads the earth . . . the horrid huge monster has many wings, beneath which . . . are vigilant eyes." Virgil's *Aeneid*.
- "Harry Winston's advertising budget in the US is slightly over \$1 M . . . but if you ask nine out of ten people in this country . . . they'll say: 'oh yea, they are the jeweller that dresses the stars'. Dressing celebrities is an overwhelming way to gain awareness. Uma Thurman put Prada on the map. . . . Americans spend billions of dollars on luxury brands because celebrities do." Carol Brodie, Publicist for Harry Winston diamonds (quoted in Thomas, D., 2007).
- "The bottom line is that celebrities sell much better." Anna Wintour, Editor-in-chief of *Vogue* (quoted in Thomas, D., 2007).
- Sweitzer, M., "Uplifting Makeup: Actresses' testimonials and the cosmetics Industry, 1910–1918". Paper to the business history conference, 2004.

Things you might like to consider

(i) Celebrities need to be selected to reflect the brand values of the product, service, or company to be marketed. It's crucial to cast the right person for the part that needs to be played. There needs to be the right "fit" between the brand, the target audience, and the celebrity (who of course is a brand in their own right). The most effective use of celebrity occurs when the central idea unites the brand and the star; and together they create something of mutual benefit that is also rewarding to the current and potential customers of the company, product, or service involved. When this happens the "back story" that the celebrity brings with them to the campaign accelerates the communication of the core idea and amplifies it enormously.

(ii) This needs as much professional handling and organizational competence as any other aspect of modern marketing.

(iii) The use of a celebrity in advertising is merely one of many different executional types, and therefore the fundamental starting point is that there has to be an underlying idea which is relevant to the brand and motivating to the consumer.

> ★ **RATING: Practical and powerful**

CHANNELS OF DISTRIBUTION

Application: revenue achievement, sales, market access

Different potential channels

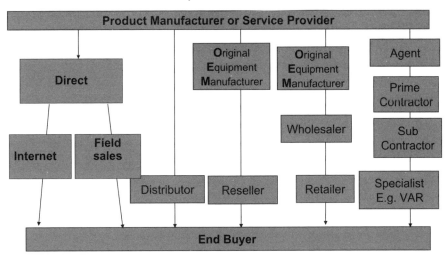

Figure C.2: A depiction of different potential channels of distribution (adapted from McDonald, M.H.B. and Wilson, H., 2011)

The concept

Complex and difficult though channel strategy and management is, it is the "P" for "Place" in the four Ps of the marketing mix; and it needs careful thought. Marketers, more than sales people, have to step back and think through how their product or service is going to reach buyers; how it is going to be "placed" in the market. Figure C.2

depicts the range of direct and indirect channels accessible to marketers. Direct channels involve, for example, field sales, catalogue and, of course, the internet. Indirect ranges from retail to "added value" suppliers. Activities involved in the channel are wide and varied though the basic activities revolve around these general tasks:

- selling
- marketing
- ordering
- handling and shipping
- storage
- display
- promotion
- merchandising
- information feedback
- installation and service.

For many marketers, the distribution decision is primarily about the supply chain's "front-end". Distribution channels are designed to move products or services from the company into the hands of the customer. All activities and organizational helping with this exchange are part of the marketer's channel strategy task components.

The different channels to consider are:

○ **Direct field *sales*** (see entry under "sales"). Companies often take a "field sales" approach to their *sales* organization. This involves sales people being assigned to a geographic territory and handling the approach to all potential customers within that territory. They are often managed by an "area manager" reporting to a "regional manager" who, in turn, reports to the sales director. The ethos behind this approach is efficiency in terms of sales time. This is the most recognizable and, in some ways, straightforward type of selling. A new business sales person is normally briefed and trained on the details of a product or service in order to sell to an intended group of customers. They will usually have a defined "territory" to cover, the size of which depends on the size of the total market, and sales targets to achieve each month or quarter. These sales people have to be managed and motivated through pay, training, administrative back-up, and targets; some form of payment by results being the chief of these. It is then up to them to find and gain access to potential customers who will buy, with the help of "leads" generated by the company's marketing programmes. This approach has been widely used across a range of both product and service businesses (from cars and confectionery to banking and insurance) in a wide range of countries for at least 300 years. Often this type of sale is led by a direct marketing campaign and executed by telesales people, combined with an online sales mechanism.

The sales person can plan what length of time to take to visit customers within a geographic patch and management can assess this efficiency by the number of "sales calls per day" (or its equivalent).

◦ *Account management* (see separate entry) is based on the fact that certain buyers will give a stream of repeat business to a supplier whereas others will not. Three researchers who studied "2,500 businesses in sixty eight countries" (Zoltners, A. A., Sinha, P., and Lorimer, S. A., 2006) claim that companies which move from regional sales to the appointment of account managers find that "the change increases revenues and customer satisfaction whilst reducing the cost of selling".

◦ **Direct retail sales.** Of course, many companies who sell to consumers through retail premises employ people to sell their products. This is a balance between sales skills and service attitude. Whilst sales skills and instincts are self-evidently important, there is evidence that an emphasis on service and achieving the best result for customers has earned long-term positive performance for retailers like Marshall Field, John Lewis, and Marks & Spencer.

◦ **Online selling.** One of the most recent revolutions in channel strategy has obviously been the internet. Many, many companies now sell online, direct to their customers (see *digital marketing*).

◦ **Dealers.** These are small businesses that sell products or services on behalf of manufacturers. They might be tied to one manufacturer in an exclusive deal or they may offer a range of products. They often have, though, limited marketing and sales skills. So, they need effective marketing support from the marketers in the manufacturing company which they are representing. This can range from lead generation campaigns to training and more extensive business support.

◦ **Value added resellers (VARS).** Value added resellers normally buy products and adjust them in some way. For instance, software companies might tailor a basic software product to a particular sector.

◦ **Franchisees.** These are businesses where people pay for the right to sell a tightly designed package in a tightly controlled geographic area. They expect a clearly defined and effective marketing package to assist their sales.

◦ **Consultative selling.** Contrary to popular opinion, the best sales people are the best listeners. Many develop intuitive approaches to get an idea of their potential buyers' needs, and then begin to offer product that best suits those needs, to match the product "benefits" to the "prospect's requirements". With more complex products, this approach has to become more structured and, at its most sophisticated (with, say, complex engineering networks) the listening aspect of the sale is more like consultancy. The sales people who lead these deals, often first class scientists or mathematicians, are taught the sort of diagnostic and discovery approaches which are second nature to leading strategy consultants. Consultative selling is remarkably successful. The majority of product sales people are unable to whisper in the ear of senior people and walk away with the high revenue, high margin deals that many partners in professional practices do every day. "Business generation" (sales) in consultancies is led by their top practitioners who manage client relations. This is called "partnership selling", a term from the professional services industry where it is often the role of partners in the firm to lead the dialogue with clients. The consultancy industry tends to base its sales organization on "industry knowledge"; familiarity with the industrial *sector* in which the buyer works (see the separate entry on *sector marketing*).

Channel design is often detailed, complex, and hard work. Marketers need to understand and model the cost and efficacy of delivering a product or service through each particular channel. They then need to recruit their representatives or partners (whether direct or indirect) and establish the channel infrastructure (perhaps through negotiated contracts). Once underway, they need to create marketing campaigns to support the channel while delivering appropriate levels of stock and measuring performance. Moreover, they need to look out for "channel conflict", damage caused by one means of distribution to another.

There are different types of marketing communications strategies which can be applied to different channels. A "pull" strategy, for instance, communicates directly to the end consumer and tries to attract them to the channel. In America, for instance, pharmaceutical companies can advertise drugs to the general population and encourage them to ask their doctor for them (a practice banned in parts of Europe). A "push" strategy, on the other hand, conducts marketing communication campaigns through the channels.

One of the fundamental aspects of good channel management is clear operational performance monitoring and measurement. Marketers need to be in close contact with the development and activities happening in their channel in order to spot difficulties or aberrations in performance which will affect sales and revenue. Sometimes these are so disastrous that they need to "cull" the channel.

History, context, criticism, and development

Businesses have used different sales mechanisms to reach markets for many years and marketers have thought carefully about the nature and mix of different channels for at least a hundred years. For example, one American marketing text book published at the start of the 20th century (Butler, R.S., 1917) dedicates several chapters to "distribution" including: direct sales, mail order, retail sales, and retail chains. He emphasizes the need to plan them carefully and examines in detail what was then the channel conflict (although he does not use that phrase) between the huge impact of mail order and retail sales. In fact, market access and channels of distribution seemed to be a primary concern of businesses, economists, and marketers in America up until the outbreak of the Second World War as the country grew.

Similar studies continued after the War as new markets were opened up (international distribution) and new methods of market access took off (such as the internet).

Voices and further reading

- "While product innovation continues apace, with the Internet offering many opportunities for providing digitizable products and surrounding services remotely, we believe that the dominant business theme of the next ten years will be innovation in the route to market – the channels by which the customer is communicated with the product delivered." McDonald, M.H.B. and Wilson, H., 2011.
- Pelton, L.E,, Strutton, D., and Lumpkin, J.R., *Marketing Channels: A Relationship Management Approach*. McGraw-Hill, 2002.
- McCally, R.W., *Marketing Channel Management*, Praegar, 1996.
- "To accomplish the task of moving products from one or more points of origin to hundreds of destinations that reach thousands or even millions of consumers requires a formal structure for both marketing and physical distribution. The unified structure, which must accomplish the objectives of these functions, is the marketing channel. The marketing channel includes every aspect of business, from product concept to the guarantee of its value or usefulness to the buyer. It is the obligation of the marketer or manufacturer to create or employ a marketing channel capable of ensuring that all these functions are accomplished." McCally, ibid.
- Coughlin, A.T., Anderson, E., Stern, L.W., and El Ansary, A.I., *Marketing Channels*. Pearson, 2006.
- "The starting point in addressing channel strategy options is to consider objectively who should dictate channel – the customer or the supplier . . . Companies usually select from one of the following broad channel strategies: A mono-channel provider strategy . . . A customer segment channel strategy . . . A graduated account management strategy . . . A channel migratory strategy . . . An activity-based channel strategy . . . An integrated multi-channel strategy." Payne, A., 2006.
- Zoltners, A.A., Sinha, P., and Lorimer, S.A., "Match your sales force structure to your business life cycle". *Harvard Business Review*, July–August 2006. Based on the study of sales structures in 2,500 businesses in 68 countries.
- "The choice of channel/medium is generally a complex one, involving different media for different communications with the same customer. The organization will also frequently want to leave some options in the hands of the customer." McDonald, M.H.B. and Wilson, H., 2011.
- "We view channel partners as complex entities. They are hybrids of companies, consumers and employees. They are also companies with their own missions, visions, values and business models. They are consumers with needs and wants

that need to be served. Moreover, they also sell to end-users and form the consumers' interface just like employees do. Their role is essential in marketing 3.0 as they become collaborators, cultural change agents and creative partners for companies at the same time." Kotler, P, et al., 2010.

Things you might like to consider

(i) There are fluidities and changes between channels that need to be tracked and assessed. These cannot always be tightly defined or understood.

(ii) One of the objectives of channel strategy is to achieve "synergy" between channels; that they mutually reinforce each other and cause greater sales.

(iii) These are often separate businesses run by small entrepreneurs. An issue which marketers need to consider is the way that sales or service people are chosen and motivated by their dealers. Poor motivation can cause poor sales performance. Also, really awful management can affect the reputation and brand of the company that the dealer represents.

(iv) One of the prime issues in channel strategy is the degree of exclusivity that the manufacturer will insist upon.

(v) Modern marketers, particularly in business-to-business markets, have found that their relationship with other suppliers is fluid, that they talk about a distribution and cooperation "eco system".

 RATING: Practical and powerful

CLOSING TECHNIQUES

Application: sales effectiveness

The concept

In all exchanges between sellers and buyers, there comes a moment when buyers need to make up their minds. Very often, success can be improved if that moment occurs with the seller present. So, sales people have evolved tools to help focus on this moment and to understand relative sales effectiveness, marketers ought to be familiar with them. Called "closing techniques", they include:

• Asking for the business. It is obvious, and therefore often forgotten, simply to ask buyers if they want to go ahead. A surprising number of sophisticated and experienced professionals do not do this.

- Overcoming objections. This is based on asking buyers whether there are any reasons why they can't proceed and then handling each and every objection as it arises.
- Open-ended questions. This is an extension of "overcoming objections". A series of questions are asked to get further and further into the buyer's needs and to match the offer closely to those needs.
- Exaggeration to the absurd. Here, the seller may take one of the objections buyers present and exaggerate it to the point of the ridiculous in order to overcome it as a barrier to purchase.
- The "trial close". A method to test the buyer's reaction, often responding to positive signals during a sales conversation. It can take the form of assumed actions and lead to planning of practical issues like delivery.
- The "assumed close". Here a customer's body language signifies that they are happy with the suggestions and want to buy. The supplier moves to talking about next steps and assumes the sale is agreed. (In fact, they may be concerned that, if the customer is asked for the business or asked whether they want to go ahead, barriers will be raised in their mind.)
- The "go-away". In this instance a seller is convinced that the offer matches the needs a buyer has. If the buyer tries to negotiate on price, or cut corners, the seller can suggest that they don't go ahead. This causes the buyer to re-commit to the sale.

Closing techniques developed in product selling have made their way into both business and professional services and are taught in sales courses throughout the world. Books, courses and conferences are alive with them.

History, context, criticism, and development

Different closing techniques have been used as different attitudes to sales have evolved. It seems, for instance, that in the USA at the end of the 19th century sales people were expected to "control the sales presentation". In the early 20th century they were the heroes of commerce, slick, motivated, and convincing. From the 1960s on, though, the questioning and diagnostic approaches, epitomized by Rackham's "SPIN" selling, began to develop.

Voices and further reading

- "The experienced salesman knows how to avoid a direct confrontation with human inertia and reluctance to make a decision. Without asking for a direct yes or no, he may begin to write up the order or ask which of various delivery dates would be preferable. He may inquire about the quantity the customer would like to try in a new display. This may lead the customer into taking action without consciously having to make a direct decision – a difficult step for some people." McCarthy, E.J., 1960.

- McDonald. M.H.B. and Leppard, J.W., *Effective Industrial Selling*. Heinemann, 1988.
- "The sale is closed only when the buyer makes a firm commitment to place an order. The salesman should be constantly looking for opportunities to close the sale at any moment of the sales interview . . . [he/she] needs to have a number of techniques at his disposal." McDonald and Leppard, ibid.
- Shapiro, B. and Posner, R.S., "Making the major sale". *Harvard Business Review*, July–August 2006.
- "Because of the complexity of the selling process and the length of the selling cycle, the close is the first concrete evidence that the sales person is successful. Since the signature may occur anywhere from six months to three years after the start of the sales process the sales person should close on each call . . ." Shapiro and Posner, ibid
- Pickens, J.W., *The Art of Closing a Deal*. PRION, 1989.

Things you might like to consider

(i)   Closing techniques vary according to the complexity and importance of the sale.

(ii) One of the hardest environments in which to close is the formal presentation or beauty parade. Clearly this needs to be professional and well prepared. It also needs to focus on the needs and questions of the people in the room. Obvious though it is, far too many people pontificate about their own expertise and heritage, rather than listening to the customers' priorities.

(iii) Services are intangible offers which, as a result, can prompt unique difficulties for buyers. If the seller is too overwhelming and uses closing techniques too forcefully, once the buyer has a moment to think, he or she is likely to feel cheated and the deal might unravel. These approaches need to be handled with real care in a service context.

★ RATING: Practical

COMPETITIVE STRATEGY

Application: strategy and planning, revenue success

The concept

The ability, style, and will to compete are issues that marketers need to consider as they design their work. There are times when the actions of individual competitors are of immediate concern, such as during a proposal to a customer. More important, however, are the times when changes in the business or the market allow actions by other firms to threaten the health of the business. Competitive response then becomes a major strategic issue which needs to be addressed.

Companies in a range of markets can be complacent and engrossed in internal work. They can develop a tendency to focus more on the improvement and presentation of their own offers rather than any specific attack on vulnerable competitors. Experience suggests that, as mature markets tighten, marketers need to think more explicitly about their competitive strategy. They have to concentrate on how to attract business to them rather than letting it go to other firms. Even more importantly, they need to find processes whereby that competitive strategy, once developed, can be implemented throughout their organization.

For example, it may be that a firm which has been number two in its market decides that the time has come to challenge for leadership. This means taking the position of the established market leader in a deliberate and planned way, backed by proper investment. The rewards of such a move are great. It implies that this "challenger" will seek to gain the leading buyers in the market and aim to have the dominant share of the budgets of those consumers. It must also offer the value proposition which appeals to most of the customers in the market and keep it in line with changing needs. The firm will become the leading authority on technical matters and policy issues within its own market place, advising regulators and industry advisers. In short, it must behave like the market leader. However, such a strategy will not be viable if the leadership espouses it but the firm itself carries on as it has always behaved.

Alternatively, a firm may settle on a "niche position" (see *positioning*) based on some source of *differentiation*. A truly differentiated offer will enable it to earn greater margins and attract more customers than the industry average. However, this will simply not be feasible if the experience the customers have is much the same as it always has been and is no different from other providers.

The challenge of competitive strategy, then, is not just to set direction or to deal with ad hoc competitive threats as they occur but to implement a competitive stance throughout the organization so that it becomes an effective guide to day-to-day management decisions. There are a number of approaches that seem to have proved effective over time.

(i) Porter's three generic strategies

Michael Porter (Porter, M., 1995) has made a major contribution to the thinking on competitive strategy over several decades. These ideas can be used by marketers to shape the firm's strategic focus. Among other things he has argued that firms should focus on one of three generic competitive strategies. They are:

- **Overall cost leadership**. The organization concentrates on gaining the lowest costs of production and distribution, and thus has the ability to set lower prices.

Whether it does that or not depends on its objectives in its market. Some set lower prices to gain volume share; others maintain higher prices to increase margins. Cost leaders achieve their aims by very tight cost control across all areas of the business. This is helped by having a large scale of operations and opportunities for economies of scale, perhaps internationally. The basis of cost control is the "experience curve" (see *Boston Matrix*), globalization of operations (by focusing production in cheaper parts of the world), labour efficiency, the rewards of global brand development, and innovation of design.

◦ **Differentiation**. In this, the supplier focuses on a component of the market offer which is important to buyers and emphasizes it in its business dealings. Normally it is: brand, quality, *innovation*, or technology.

◦ **Focus.** Here the firm concentrates on one or more market *segments*. By doing this, the marketers are able to gain in-depth knowledge of the *segments* and tailor the approach in detail. This best suits small firms, able to focus on a portion of the market.

(ii) Positioning as a competitive tool

Market positioning is based upon customers' views of value, which is a derivative of quality and price. Each company involved in a market takes its own position in that market, whether by design or default (see separate entry). They may become: market leader; market challenger; premium supplier; niche; or least-cost. This is the competitive position of the firm and ought to be the orientation of everyone in it. Also, the prices and features of the offers ought to be different. For example, the offer of a least-cost supplier ought to be very different to that of a features-rich premium supplier. Each makes money in a different way from different groups of customers.

The power of positioning strategies is that they are built upon customers' value perceptions. If constructed using *research*, they can clearly indicate what the firm needs to do to its offer in order to move to one of the long-term viable market positions. If, for example, customers perceive there to be no "premium" supplier or no "least-cost" service, then the marketer has discovered a vacant position into which to move the firm. This can also be used to anticipate the moves of competitors or to understand shifts in the whole market.

(iii) Military analogies as a guide to developing competitive stance

Several academics have suggested that military language and approaches are useful analogies in the development of this competitive stance (see, for instance, Wilson, R.M.S., Gilligan, C., and Pearson, D.J., 1992).

They suggest:

◦ **Market leaders** are in the most powerful position and tend to adopt certain behaviours (see Treacy, M. and Wiersema, F., 1995). They need to maintain their lead by consolidating *brand*, customer relationships, and employee loyalties while honing their offer over time. Although they will be assailed by most competitors, they can, if necessary, affect all of them by changing the rules of the game. If the marketer changes the price and offer of a market leader, all others will have to move because they have changed the value equation of the whole market. The market leader can, for example, initiate a price war in order to damage competitors. Before doing so, it should estimate carefully how far it can afford to reduce margins and how low competitors can afford to go in response. An alternative is to invest in new uses for its skills or to seek to grow the whole market.

Market leaders are, though, constantly under threat from the various competitors. Their competitive strategy is therefore largely defensive. The firm can adopt a "position defence" (holding on to a supposedly impregnable fixed position), although this is thought to be the weakest defensive strategy, causing the firm to progressively retreat. A "mobile defence", on the other hand, is to move into other areas which might prove to be leading offers in the future. Whereas "flanking defence" means attacking vulnerable areas such as an unaddressed part of the market. "Contraction defence" is a withdrawal from a certain area in order to use resources more effectively, "pre-emptive defence" is to make a move before that of a competitor, and "counter-offensive defence" is a response to an attack from a challenger.

◦ **Challengers**, being strong competitors with abundant resources, have a number of competitive strategies open to them. They can attack the market leader, attack peers, attack smaller firms, or seek to maintain the status quo. Their attacking strategies are: a "full frontal assault", a direct challenge for leadership needing superior resources, a "flank attack", using technology or market opportunity to focus on a vulnerable area, an "encirclement attack", striking in several areas of business at once, and a "bypass attack", competing against indirect or less important parts of the market.

Whether or not the strong competitor thinks in these terms, it will need to consider its market position and how it affects the health of its business. It may be that it can hold its position and maintain its earnings by seeking to preserve the status quo in a steady market. However, it may be forced to take business from others to maintain earnings or to satisfy the ambitions of the business owners. If it settles for a "full frontal" attack on the market leader, for instance, it needs to ensure that it has the resources for the battle. If not, it is sensible to consider the benefits of focusing its resources on another competitor's offer.

◦ **Niche** suppliers are normally smaller and more focused firms who, again, have several options. They might adopt an "alliance strategy", working with another firm to challenge the business of others or they might adopt a "guerrilla strategy", gaining the loyalty of one market group. The latter is about using the strength of being small and fleet of foot against the larger competitor. Whether or not these smaller firms use this approach to plan their business development, they need to be obsessive about their point of specialization and use their smaller resources judiciously to secure their business growth.

(iii) Service quality as competitive strategy

It is surprising how many companies, who consider the quality of their after care service to be an important part of their offer, do not think through the place of service in their competitive strategy. Service programmes are often imprecise and vague, thereby losing any potential competitive advantage. It is sensible to develop a clear, competitive strategy for the service of the company which matches the general business strategy; for service style to reflect market position. If the firm is a least-cost, premium, or niche supplier, its competitive position is reinforced if its after care is undertaken in a style similar to that *positioning*.

As important is to recognize the moments in the evolution of a market when there is a strategic opportunity to gain ground by offering a new style of service. Industries appear to develop through an evolution of thought and strategy with regard to service standards. Some have reaped enormous rewards when taking advantage of those moments. The first phase is to reach a national par. This is a common expectation of service quality which is shared by the population as a whole. It is assumed, ill-defined, and emotionally based, but is a common value nonetheless. For various reasons (such as a historic monopoly or legislative distortion) the service provided by an industry may be below this expectation. A service which is far below par will eventually become the subject of national ridicule: the target of comedians and journalists because they recognize that there is a common experience which can be exploited. In an industry where all suppliers are criticized, the first supplier to move to meet national par will gain market share. This has happened in numerous industries in both a national and international context.

These unique strategic opportunities for a few suppliers in passing moments of developing industries have become the examples used by many of the service quality and customer care gurus. Few have gone on to look at the opportunities to use service quality as a strategic asset in other phases of market development. For example, once competitors notice that a company is taking a lead through quality they begin to develop programmes of their own. As a result, the service of competitors begins to catch up. They then look for ways to communicate the efforts that they have made in order to attract them back. The industry goes through a phase where it "markets" the quality of service that it provides.

Once the industry is filled with suppliers communicating common quality of service propositions, it must evolve further. It moves towards "service differentiation". This is a process which results from changes in attitude among both buyers and suppliers. If all suppliers are making similar quality claims, then buyers choose on the basis of service style and price. They are attracted to an ambience, design, or behaviour which suits their taste. Suppliers therefore respond by developing different service offerings for different groups. Clearly, if the industry is not yet at this stage, a marketer can gain competitive advantage by anticipating it. They can choose the most attractive segments and design a service which appeals primarily to them. For instance, in an industry where all services are designed for naïve customers, the service standard comprises: good client care, clear process, smiling people, and a reassuring brand. However, because of the need for emotional control (see *services marketing*), frequent purchasers can become frustrated with this approach. For them, good service is self-service and streamlined process. By constructing a service which has, at its heart, the sense of privilege, of joining a club, the supplier can provide better quality service at less cost. If a marketer introduces a new standard of service for experienced clients, it will attract them from other providers.

There is then a stage of service evolution when "added value" services are offered to the market. Buyers are able to recognize the value of the base service and are thus willing to pay extra for added value service features. Competitive advantage can be gained by launching packages of added value services for the segment that the firm is targeting. The difficulty is that the incremental value of the added value features is eroded over time as standards improve. Buyers then expect them to fall into the base service. Suppliers must continue to create new added value features to distinguish them from the core service in order to maintain their competitive lead in their chosen segments. So, the creation of the new service standard can be a competitive weapon.

(iv) Value chain analysis

This concept suggests that marketers view their businesses as a series of activities, linked in a process or "chain", each of which adds value to raw materials (see Porter, M., 1995). The concept is familiar in manufacturing businesses and is used to find items of extraneous costs. However, it can also be used to identify areas of potentially greater added value and areas of competitive advantage. Theorists have also developed a generic value chain model for service businesses (see Heskett, J.L., Sasser, W.E., and Schlesinger, L. A., 1997).

Competitive tracking and analysis: As with other areas of strategy, decisions about competitive response are more likely to benefit the firm if based on market insight and good analysis. Information which is typically sought about competitors relates to their:

- objectives and plans
- performance
- structure and organization
- senior management changes and the decision-making track record of those assuming leadership roles
- strengths and weaknesses
- products, services, and pricing
- marketing materials and campaigns
- wins and losses
- response profiles, (i.e., are they opportunistic or thoughtful in their selection of business targets?)

Without such a system to inform leadership about competitor response, information can be anecdotal and, quite simply, wrong. More than one business has thought itself to be the market leader in a field of work but, once objective analysis was undertaken, discovered that it had been overtaken. It is sensible to establish a system to gather objective knowledge about competitor moves. To achieve this, specialist agencies, people, and processes exist which can be easily accessed by marketers.

Sources of competitive advantage: One of the most important aspects of competitive strategy is to find sources of competitive advantage. They are likely to include:

(i)   The "core competence" of the business (see Hamel, G. and Prahalad, C.K., 1994) This idea suggests that each company has a skill or function in which it invests over time because it is seen as the most important task of the organization. Often this is made a priority unconsciously because it is so obviously the most important task. It is the area of responsibility which always receives time, attention, and investment, almost without question, in comparison to other functions. Because of investment in both people and resources, this area is likely to improve in both performance and cost. It is represented as an "experience curve" (see *Boston Matrix*). Unfortunately, despite the fact that many strategy experts emphasize the importance of the core competence, there are few recognized techniques to define it. It can usually be determined in discussion, or brainstorming, with senior management. Such discussions can seem vague and difficult but, once the "blinding flash of the obvious" occurs, the simple heart of the company's performance can be exploited as a competitive expression of skill.

(ii) Brand
      A company's *brand* or brands are a source of competitive advantage. They will appeal to the target market causing them to relate to it in such a way as to purchase over time. Customer loyalty is fostered by brands because they give reassurance in any emotional aspect of buying or using a product or service.

(iii) Customer relationships
      The relationship between a company and its customers is also a source of competitive advantage, called by some accountants "customer equity" because it is seen as an intangible asset. The heritage of contact between the people, processes, and systems of the two organizations cannot be duplicated (see *business-to-business marketing, relationship marketing,* and *AAR*). A company's relationships will include some who are very loyal and others who could be made more loyal. They are a source of competitive advantage because they are more inclined to purchase and repurchase. They are also likely to be advocates of the firm. This might be turned into highly profitable growth through a structured relationship programme.

(iv) Distribution
      The way a firm reaches its clients is a source of competitive advantage. This might be the location of a shop to attract the best flow of buyers but a similar dynamic applies in *business-to-business* marketers. A firm might decide that it needs to open

an office in a city or region where it identifies potential demand. It will need to secure a facility, assemble resources, and launch the new presence.

(v) Critical success factors

Any market has established rules of engagement by which the participants in the market survive or prosper. These rules may be imposed by regulatory or market pressures, and usually by a combination of the two. For example, in a professional services industry all of the participants must meet the necessary legal or industry standards of qualifications and behaviour in order to be able to participate. Meeting these criteria is a critical success factor as it is not possible to trade without them. Beyond these basic requirements for being "in the game", suppliers also face certain criteria which enable them to succeed in the market place. However, the critical success factors for this are commercial imperatives resulting from the evolution of forces within the market. The way marketers create, implement, and manage these "motivators" can be a source of competitive advantage.

History, context, criticism, and development

Competitive strategy and behaviour has been a fact of marketing and business life for many hundreds of years. It was in the latter half of the 20th century that many of the concepts related to competitive strategy began to emerge. The fight for market share, for instance, existed in many markets amongst many leading companies well before the PIMS survey and thinkers like Bruce Henderson demonstrated the advantages in terms of profits and success for those with a dominant share. The work by Michael Porter around different sustainable competitive positions similarly articulated viable strategies for business leaders. There are now a range of credible concepts by which marketers can include viable competitive strategies in their plans.

Voices and further reading

"Although the vast majority of marketing strategies acknowledge the importance of competitive analysis, it has long been recognized that less effort is typically put into detailed and formal analysis of competitors than, for example, of customers and their buying patterns. In many cases this is seemingly because marketing managers feel that they know enough about their competitors simply as the result of competing against them on a day-to-day basis. In other cases, there is almost a sense of resignation, with managers believing that it is rarely possible to understand competitors in detail" Wilson et al., 1992.

- Hamel, G. and Prahalad, C.K., *Competing for the Future*. Harvard Business School Press, 1994.
- Porter, M., On Competition, *Harvard Business Review* book, 1995.
- Porter, M., The five competitive forces that shape strategy. *Harvard Business Review*, January 2008.

"Competitive behaviour refers to the attitude adopted by firms in its decision making process, with regard to its competitors actions and reactions. The attitudes deserved in practice can be classified . . . independent behaviour . . . co-operative behaviour . . . follower behaviour . . . leader behaviour . . . aggressive or warfare behaviour" Lambin, J., 2000.

"Competing on capabilities: the new rules of corporate strategy" Stalk, Evans and Shulman, in Stern 2006.

Things you might like to consider

(i) It is possible for the leadership of a firm to give it a competitive emphasis, or a "stance", which permeates the organization.

(ii) Many of these concepts are based on assumptions about market share and growth which may not apply to some markets (see separate entry on market share). There does not yet seem to be the depth and quality of research into their applicability to the unique dynamics of, say, professional service industries as have been applied to other areas of marketing.

(iii) It is clear that strategy is valued by the military and is thought to pay off in success in battle. The direct applicability of these tactics to management and leadership teams while they are constructing day-to-day strategy or policy seems to be less evident. Many of the anecdotes and case studies used in the work to promulgate this militaristic view of competitive strategy appear to be more post event application to illustrate an interesting thesis rather than practical business thinking used proactively.

British Gas competes for the first time

In the late 1990s the senior managers of one of Britain's leading utilities, British Gas, were worried and a little frightened. They had been privatized and their business gas market had been opened to competition. Unfortunately, their experience of that competitive force had not been good. After many decades of having 100% of the market, they had braced themselves for losses. It had been, though, a huge and dramatic loss which had forced the leaders of the organization to tackle a raft of different implications rising from sudden loss of revenue.

Now the government of the day was going further and introducing competition into the domestic market. The trial for this initiative was the West of England and Welsh regions. A large number of suppliers and new entrants had announced their intention to compete and enter the market. Everyone of these had said that they would offer better quality at a cheaper price.

The local regional management team met in a competitive strategy session to discuss their course of action. The corporate board had given them the ability to adjust or discount price should they need to. They needed to work out how they would respond to this frightening and unusual onslaught.

During a competitive strategy workshop they first worked through a "positioning map" (see separate entry) for their region and the strengths (and vulnerabilities) of a market leader. Like many companies they were more critical of their own firm's capabilities than others. One iconic moment was when they realized that the few people in the room had, between them, several hundred years of experience in the gas market. They then broke into teams to examine and position all the competitors that had announced that they would participate in the trial. Every single one had claimed they would offer better quality at cheaper prices.

As one after another was placed at the same position on the map it became obvious that this was not sustainable. These new entrants would have to move their stance to gain a sufficient number of customers and they would trip over each other in fighting for the customers who said they might move supplier. (In the event that turned out to be true. There were appalling and, in some cases, corrupt practices as suppliers fought for the first customers. Several soon withdrew.) Back in the workshop the managers decided to behave like market leaders. They announced a series of packages which reinforced their own heritage and quality. They even made it easy for people to leave, arranging to say goodbye in a manner which made it clear that it would be easy to come back; and they did not take advantage of the price reduction mechanism offered by their board.

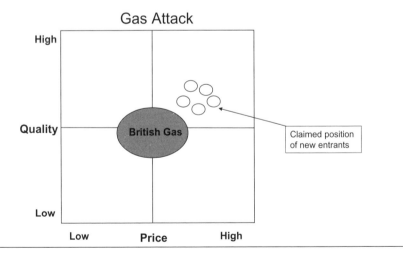

Gas Attack

RATING: Practical and powerful

CONSUMER BEHAVIOUR

Application: strategy, communications, NPD/NSD, sales effectiveness

How consumers buy

Awareness of need → Planning → Evaluation of alternatives → Serious discussion with seller → Purchase

Figure C.3: A depiction of (and over-simplification of) consumer buying

The concept

It is almost impossible to market effectively without understanding how, why, and when people buy. This is not, however, as straightforward as it sounds. It is dangerously easy for a firm to institutionalize a half-baked view of buyer needs or to ignore them because it has succeeded by creating and pushing certain products or services in the past. Human beings are erratic, unpredictable creatures, driven by both their rational and emotional natures when making decisions and, particularly, when buying anything (see *behavioural aspects of marketing*). Sometimes they approach decisions carefully, collecting as much data as possible before they commit to a purchase; at others they return to trusted suppliers or brands; often they join in with the herd, buying to be a part of something; and sometimes they buy, whimsically, on impulse. Although they sometimes have fixed ideas of what they want, it is just as likely that they are unclear on a particular occasion or cannot articulate their needs.

"Consumer behaviour" is a discipline, sometimes seen as an adjunct field of study or semi-detached from mainstream marketing. Nevertheless, considerable research and experimentation has been conducted to understand buying motivations and behaviours. It covers such human issues as: culture, motivation, values, and attitudes. It looks at decision making, shopping, and demographics. Much of it is observed research, and closely related to *behavioural aspects of marketing*. It is extremely useful in giving pointers to practical sales approaches, market opportunities, or the design of marketing programmes. It seeks to understand, for instance, why customers segment, why they respond to brands, how communications affect their purchase behaviour, and a range of other dynamics such as loyalty.

Researchers in this field suggest, for example, that people might have different types of relationship with a product (self-concept attachment, nostalgic attachment, interdependence, and love). They also suggest distinct types of consumption (as an experience, for instance, or as play). The discipline has explored the influence of the five senses on desire and purchase, insights which can be very useful to different aspects of marketing. An understanding, for instance, of the influence of colour, sound, and symbols on the thinking of different segments can affect branding, packaging, and marketing communication.

When consumers shop (whether physically, by telephone, by catalogue, or through the internet) they may have a cluster of needs in their minds, which are not necessarily refined into a fixed product purchase. They might only have an intuitive, confused mix of ideas or preferences and look for the proposition that best fits them. First they become aware of a need. This may happen quickly (perhaps prompted by the breakdown of an old domestic appliance like a vacuum cleaner) or though growing awareness (like an ever-closer house move and the need to arrange a new broadband connection) or, perhaps, over time (say, by the gradual ageing of a water boiler). They will then think through what to buy, when, and how to buy it. They might, for instance, research an involved purchase through the internet or by visiting showrooms. Once they have refined their search they will discuss the potential purchase with the seller before buying.

Marketers and sales people can increase their chance of success if they are able to influence their customer's thinking at the planning or evaluation stage. For instance, suppose a mother wants to buy a home broadband service to meet the needs of her whole family as they move house. She might be very familiar with the latest offers from seeing newspaper advertisements or receiving other forms of publicity. She might, though, savour the experience of spending a morning online, browsing through the offers of the leading suppliers. Or she might be too busy to either read adverts and direct marketing or to do her own online research. However, she is likely to have in mind a number of different attributes that her new service must include. She might consider: the style of equipment provided, the speed of connection, scope of the package (TV, telephone, and broadband), brand, contract flexibility, and price. These attributes vary in nature and importance according to individual preference, occasion, and culture. Different people will describe them differently and rank them in different orders of importance (see *features analysis*).

This thinking process can be represented in Figure C.3. This diagram is, though, only a very broad representation because the intensity and duration of these different stages differs according to their experience, understanding, and view of the purchase. Different and more complex models have been developed over the years to represent the thinking and behaviour of consumers. They are a powerful aid in practical marketing.

History, context, criticism, and development

Specialists in this field say that it grew as a body of work in parallel with psychology and other behavioural sciences. They argue that, before the mid 20th century much thought about consumer buying behaviour was related to classical economics and impersonal market forces.

The beginnings of the current view of this field of work have been credited (see Gabbot, M. in Baker, M.J. and Hart, S. (eds), 2008) to a 1961 study by the Ford Foundation which summarized available research into economics and psychology which applied to consumer buying behaviour. This, together with studies by General Foods and Nestlé, apparently prompted academic studies into consumer buyer behaviour. The first outputs of this work were models of how people approach buying by the likes of Howard and Seth; Engel and Kollatt; and others. They began to frame the relationship of the individual to external stimulants like the social environment and the physical environment. There have since been several fascinating pieces of academic work which have explored each of these aspects and other aspects of decision making, like the influence of family, culture, and emotions.

In recent years the speciality has explored the linkage between modern, personal identity, and consumption; the idea that people get their sense of self-worth from what they buy and own (like branded luxury goods). This "philosophy of consumption" has explored the role of buying in personal identity, as part of identification with a group, and how the subtleties of culture affect identity. At the time of writing, the idea of consumption dictating identity is being challenged in the light of new values emerging around social expectations and concerns like ethical and environmental issues. Refreshingly, there is evidence that this body of work (like relationship marketing) is being integrated with classic marketing training to round out marketing communications, research, and strategy processes.

Voices and further reading

- "But we have to acknowledge that the behavioural sciences have not answered all of the questions. It would be most desirable to have an integrating framework to relate the various influences on buying behavior and theories about these influences. Unfortunately, we do not have such a framework. As of now, after the marketing manager has reviewed all of the behavioural data, he still has to rely on his own intuition and marketing research to help him estimate expected behavior in various market grid boxes." McCarthy, E.J., 1975.
- Solomon, M., Bamossy, G., Askegaard, S., and Hogg, M.K., *Consumer Behaviour; A European Perspective*. Prentice Hall, 2006.
- "The field of consumer behaviour is young, dynamic and in flux. It is constantly being cross-fertilized by perspective from many different disciplines . . . it is the study of the processes involved when individuals or groups select, purchase or dispose of products, services, ideas or experiences to satisfy needs and desires." Solomon et al., ibid.
- "Understanding consumers" by B.J. Calder in Iacobucci, D., *Kellogg on Marketing*. 2001.
- "Consumer behaviour" by M. Gabbot in Baker, M.J. and Hart, S. (eds), 2008.
- ". . . consumer behaviour is a particularly challenging field of study. Not only does it require consideration of a wide range of theoretical material and perspectives, but, like any aspect of human behaviour, it is very difficult to deal in absolutes. That having been said, it is also one of the most interesting, dynamic,

challenging and frustrating areas of study . . . the application of marketing principles in non-traditional spheres of health, public policy, not for profit, international aid, environmental protection, and security, provides demand for more applied understanding of consumers and their consumption behaviour." Gabbot, ibid.

Things you might like to consider

(i)   This is a behavioural field of work which is likely to help with insights into consumer buying behaviour. Its concepts and models are a credible place to start when starting practical marketing programmes or research projects.

(ii) This speciality encompasses a wide body of knowledge about how consumers live, respond, and behave. It ought to be background knowledge for any marketer moving into consumer marketing.

★ **RATING: Practical and powerful**

CONTACT AUDIT

Application: customer service, customer experience, communication

Contact audit

Type	Frequency	Typical reasons	Average quality	Outcomes
Letters				
Invoices				
Brochures etc				
Mailings				
Telephone reception				
Web site and email				
Account meetings				
Project management				
Receptions				
Client service staff				
Buildings, security guards, etc.				
Advertising (TV, press)				
Hospitality events				
Reports				

Figure C.4:   A representation of a contact audit

The concept

Several marketing-related concepts (*CEM*, *brand* integrity, the customer journey, touch-points, and moments of truth – see entry under *service quality*) put great emphasis on a customer's experience of a supplier's offer and distribution methods; the effect of interactions with the firm on the opinion of buyers and repurchase intent. This little idea is a practical method to understand the quality of these interfaces (see Figure C.4).

Marketers should list all the firm's interfaces with its customers. These range from sales and customer service employees, through operational materials (like contracts, statements, or invoices) to attendance at events. This, alone, prompts them to think about the effect of some surprising items. For instance, customers, who visit a scruffy office, are kept waiting by reception staff, or who have to negotiate difficult security staff, can have their confidence in the firm's offer undermined, even if some of these people are clearly employed by contractors.

The tool then causes the firm to think about the frequency with which customers use a particular interface and the reason why. If it is very important or emotionally distressing to them, then the impression it forms is likely to be very influential. If the supplier neglects it, then issues are likely to arise which will affect representation and repurchase rates. Finally, the quality that customers experience and the outcomes they receive are considered. These are best completed in discussion with a sample of them.

This simple tool is a planning mechanism which identifies improvement areas in the firm's interface with its customers. It emphasizes all aspects of the customers' contact with the firm and prompts marketers to think beyond their own functional area.

History, context, criticism, and development

Methods to test and examine the experience that customers have of a business and its products have appeared under many guises. It is as though the contact audit has disguised itself in various different names and functional specialties in order to achieve the same effect: collecting data which will improve the interfaces of the whole organization with its customers. For instance:

(i) **"moments of truth"** (see *service quality*). This was a method made famous by Jan Carsson of SAS in the 1980s to audit and examine the critical interfaces between customers and an organization. It is well known today as a practical quality technique and can be used by marketers as a method to engage other functions of their organization in analysis which will lead to improvements in customers' experiences of the whole company.

(ii) **"brand audit"**. Brand consultancies and strategists now frequently use this method to understand how a company's brand, particularly its corporate brand, affects people's purchase decisions. Although this will involve research into communication issues and brand values, it frequently uncovers the experience of the brand in service encounters or operational processes.

(iii) **the "customer journey"** (see *service quality* entry). This term is commonly found in the financial services industry. It prompts executives to understand the process through which their customers move. It emphasizes the moments when potential buyers first hear of a company or its offers to the point where they disengage, even if that final disengagement is after years of repeat business.

(iv) **CEM "touch points"** (see *service quality* entry). Customer experience management is a very recent concept which links marketing, brand experience, and service quality together. Before the Western credit crunch and global recession it was gaining real traction as a powerful idea to improve customer responsiveness in line with marketing strategy. One important component of it was the need to identify and improve the "touch points" between a company and its customers. Slightly different to generic service quality concepts, like "moments of truth" (because it seeks to ensure that customer experiences are in line with brand positioning), it nevertheless seeks to audit the contact that an organization has with its buyers.

(v) **communities of interest or stakeholder groups.** Often used in PR or senior investor relations, this concept seeks to identify all groups who have an interest in a business and its objectives. Although it is often limited to developing communication strategies which address the concerns of these different groups, the data this exercise elicits can be used to construct more broad-based marketing strategies. Consumer groups might, for instance be one community of interest. Whereas, in the past, PR initiatives might have been used to communicate with them, modern marketers might be just as concerned with how they experience service issues, pricing, or even taxation compliance because of the power of the internet to create strong, negative viral campaigns.

Each of these approaches are similar, in that they set out to understand the full extent of the customers' experiences of the firm; the way the brand is experienced by a company's dealings with its customers.

Voices and further reading

- "Managing Brand Experience: The Market Contact Audit", Chattopadhyay and Laborie 2005.

Things you might like to consider

(i) Operational messages set up by others in the organization can undermine reputation and marketing messages. For example, many companies put messages on their call reception systems which are provided with the technology. Yet a customer that rings late at night and gets a message saying "we are experiencing unprecedented high call volumes at the moment" knows that this is not true. In fact, informed, valuable buyers are likely to know that any company which has been receiving telephone calls for any period of time has sufficient history to estimate volume and resource accordingly. What has actually happened is that the company has decided to keep the costs of call reception staff down by making customers wait longer for an answer; and they have chosen to lie to their customers about their decision. If marketers do not get a grip of this operational nonsense through a technique like a contact audit, the claims of their marketing campaigns will be undermined.

(ii) The performance and attitude of the people in a company, particularly a service company, can affect propensity to buy. This tool and mechanisms like the GAP model identify the relative importance of operational interfaces on purchase intent and revenue growth.

(iii) If a marketer knows the number of contacts between customers and their organization every day, they should be able to commission research which finds out how many are good and bad. From this they can calculate both the impact on reputation in numeric terms and the number of poor, or good, stories circulating about their firm. This rudimentary form of "net promoter" can indicate which interfaces ought to be improved when and how.

 RATING: Practical

CORPORATE SOCIAL RESPONSIBILITY (CSR)

Application: reputation management, positioning

The concept

Corporate social responsibility (CSR) is self-imposed responsible behaviour by businesses and other organizations. It is a marketing issue because, first, it is a response to consumers, employees, communities, stakeholders, and other members of society. Secondly, it has a profound effect on reputation, buyers' willingness to do business with companies and, eventually, profit.

CSR policy ensures that businesses monitor and support law, ethical standards, and international norms. It also prompts them to embrace responsibility for the impact of their activities on the environment. In fact, there is an increasing expectation that businesses will proactively promote the public interest by encouraging community development (particularly in third world nations) and voluntarily cut out dubious practices, regardless of legality (such as the use of child labour by subcontractors). CSR is the deliberate inclusion of public interest in corporate decision making, and the honouring of a "triple bottom line": people, planet, profit. It is also known as: "corporate conscience", "corporate citizenship", "responsible business", "sustainable responsible business" (SRB); or "corporate social performance".

Some argue that CSR distracts from the fundamental aim of a business; others that it is nothing more than superficial window-dressing; others, that it is an attempt to pre-empt the role of governments over powerful multi-national corporations. Yet, this is more than fluff, fashion, or a cynical response to activism. Firstly, there is a strong business case for CSR policies and activities because firms benefit from operating with a broader perspective than their own immediate, short-term profits. It can be a positive help to an organization's reputation as well as a guide to what the company stands for. Secondly, cynics should acknowledge that businesses in a range of sectors have contributed to society for many years. The leaders now coming into power have grown up in a generation concerned with social issues; so business engagement will increase.

There is little doubt that people, particularly in the West, are becoming more aware of the environmental and social implications of their day-to-day consumption and are beginning to adjust their buying decisions to their environmental and ethical concerns. The internet, social networking, and twenty-four hour media are, it seems, creating a consensus on some issues like the treatment of waste. As a result, marketers are having to respond to this even if they are personally cynical toward it.

One common approach to CSR is philanthropy. This includes donations and aid given to local organizations and impoverished communities in developing countries. However, some organizations do not like this approach as it does not help build on the skills of local people. Community-based projects tend to lead to more "sustainable development".

Another approach is to build CSR priorities directly into the business strategy of an organization. For instance, the use of "fair trade" tea and coffee has been adopted by a number of businesses. Another approach is called "Creating Shared Value", or CSV. The shared value model is based on the idea that corporate success and social welfare are interdependent. A business needs a healthy, educated workforce, sustainable resources, and adept government to compete effectively. For society to thrive, profitable and competitive businesses must be developed and supported to create income, wealth, tax revenues, and opportunities for philanthropy. CSV acknowledges the trade-offs between short-term profitability and social goals, but focuses on the competitive advantage that can be gained from building CSR into corporate strategy.

Although many companies are increasingly more socially responsible (because their most important stakeholders expect them to understand and address the social and community issues that are relevant to them) it often takes a crisis to prompt serious, real attention to CSR. These crises can be very costly in terms of money, reputation, and retrospective action. There is a history of major, costly incidents like the Exxon Valdez disaster in Alaska in 1989, the lead poisoning paint used by toy giant Mattel (which required a recall of millions of toys), Shell's manipulation of oil reserve information in 2004, and BP's pollution of the Gulf of Mexico in 2010. Each prompted the companies involved to act in both the short term and the long term.

So, there is an argument for marketers to initiate programmes which will, to some extent, obviate costly catastrophes of this kind.

There are several sensible reasons for a CSR programme:

(i) Risk

Reputations that take decades to build can be ruined in hours through incidents such as corruption scandals or environmental accidents. These can also draw unwanted attention from regulators, courts, governments, and media. Building a genuine culture of "doing the right thing" within a corporation can offset these risks to some extent. Although there are examples of wilful wrongdoing (e.g. the difficulties at Satyam and Enron), despite the views of conspiracy theorists, most problems with large organizations (like the 2010 BP oil spill in the Gulf of Mexico) are accidents created by a series of organizational cock-ups. Yet these can have a dramatic effect on corporate reputation if mishandled. The public impression created by BP during 2010 was awful but it was exacerbated by a series of public gaffes. The argument for a CSR programme is to create a favourable impression as a foundation for any such eventuality. Those companies with a long, self-evident, commitment to social issues have a better track record of surviving catastrophe or commercial embarrassment of this kind than others.

(ii) Employee motivation

As a series of common ethics and values (for example toward global warming or the environment in general) are evolving across the globe, a CSR programme can be an aid to recruitment and retention, particularly within the graduate market. Many recruiters have learnt, for instance, that the current graduate crop, particularly in the West, tends to value self actualization and green issues. They are stressing their charitable work in order to attract them. Potential recruits often ask about a firm's CSR policy during interview, so having a comprehensive policy is an advantage. CSR can also help improve the perception of a company among its employees, particularly when they can become involved through pro bono work, payroll giving, fundraising activities, or community volunteering.

(iii) Brand distinction

CSR can play a role in building customer loyalty based on distinctive ethical values. Several major brands, such as The Co-operative Group and The Body Shop are closely aligned to ethical values. Business service organizations can benefit too from building a reputation for integrity and best practice.

(iv) Interference

By taking substantive voluntary steps, marketers can persuade governments and the wider public that they are taking issues such as health and safety, diversity, or the environment seriously. As good "corporate citizens" with respect for employment standards and impacts on the environment, they might avoid harsh interference in their business through taxation or regulation.

In response to CSR there are a number of emerging practices; measurement for instance. Taking responsibility for its impact on society means that a company must account for its actions. So "social accounting", a concept describing the communication of social and environmental effects of a company's economic actions to particular interest groups, and to society at large, is an element of CSR. There is also an increase in CSR-related regulation and law at both national and international level. Yet regulation in itself is unable to cover every aspect of a corporation's operations. So, another trend is the rise of "ethics training" inside corporations, some of it required by government regulation. The aim of this type of initiative is to guide employees in ethical decisions when the answers are unclear. There is evidence that, like racial or sexual equality initiatives of the past, this is a force which is changing the behaviour and culture of corporations because it helps to diffuse the idea amongst modern workers.

History, context, criticism, and development

There has, it seems, been a philanthropic and social engagement aspect to business for a very long time. One of the early social action programmes in the West was the anti-slavery campaign in Britain at the end of the 1700s. At that time, sugar was a much appreciated, recent luxury which gave flavour to bland food. The voluntary boycott of it by informed people (becuase slaves were used to produce it) was a powerful statement which influenced the debate. Yet it was a CSR programme by the ever market-orientated Josiah Wedgwood which added significant momentum to the campaign. He created a fashionable medallion of a slave raising his hands and saying "Am I not also a man and a brother" (see Figure C.5). As Wedgwood was such a fashion item and a desirable brand it had a powerful impact which added momentum to the anti slavery-campaign.

Lord Lever (founder of Lever Brothers) was a market-orientated business leader of the late 19th century. He pondered who his profit belonged to, despite the fact that he owned the company. As his company boomed he is quoted as saying: "Whose was that money? We had the same works, the same manager, the same soap boiler and the same staff. . . . I want to give it to the man who ought to have it" (Maqueen, A., 2004). This led him to build his "Sunlight" town for his workers. He was typical of the philanthropic approach of many business leaders of the time in both America (like Hershey) and the UK (like Cadbury).

Corporate Social Responsibility has been redefined throughout the years. The term itself came into common use in the early 1970s, after many multi-national corporations formed. Interest in business ethics accelerated dramatically during the 1980s

Figure C.5: Wedgwood's anti-slavery badge

and 1990s, both within major corporations and within academia. Today most major corporate web sites lay emphasis on commitment to promoting non–economic social values under a variety of headings (e.g. ethics codes, social responsibility charters). In some cases, corporations have re-branded their core values in the light of ethical considerations (e.g. BP's "beyond petroleum").

There is even the beginning of thought about international standards which will give grit to these issues; for instance, a draft international IOS standard for CSR (ISO, 26000). A number of reporting guidelines or standards have been developed to serve as frameworks for social accounting, auditing, and reporting. For instance, some countries (like France and Denmark) have developed legal requirements for CSR-related reporting, although international or national consensus on meaningful measurements of social and environmental performance is at the time of writing, still a long way off. Many companies now produce externally audited annual reports that include and CSR issues but the reports vary widely in format, style, and methodology (even within the same industry).

Voices and further reading

- Porter, M.E., *The Link between Competitive Advantage and Corporate Social Responsibility.*
- "Philanthropy and cause marketing have been gaining popularity in recent years. A global survey by Edelman suggests that 85% of consumers prefer socially

responsible brands, 70% will pay more for the brands, and 55% will even recommend the brands to their family and friends. Companies are aware of this fact. They are increasingly recognizing that their employees, consumers, and the public at large develop a view of a company not only based on the quality of its products and services but also on its degree of social responsibility." Kotler, P, et al., 2010.

• "Whether intentionally or not, some marketers do violate their bond of trust with consumers . . . Faced with the rising phenomenon of the political consumers – a consumer who expresses his or her political and ethical viewpoint by selecting and avoiding products from companies which are anti-ethical to those viewpoints – the industry is increasingly coming to realize that ethical behaviour is also good business in the long run, since the trust and satisfaction of consumers translates into years of loyalty from customers." Solomon, M. et al., 2006.

Things you might like to consider

(i) Some companies may implement CSR-type values without a clearly defined team or programme.

(ii) Critics dismiss CSR reports as lip service, citing examples such as Enron's yearly "Corporate Responsibility Annual Report" and tobacco corporations' social reports. Marketing in this field, like any other, has to have integrity of concept or the value of any initiative will be undermined.

(iii) The current enthusiasm for CSR has prompted spend on green or charitable issues. Millions are currently spent in the hope that association with a good cause will induce goodwill toward a firm. Is the money well spent? Is it truly aligned with corporate objectives? Is the CSR programme actually a reflection of the company's customers or simply unrepresentative lobbyists? It takes excellent marketing skills to get the heart of these questions.

Michelin Man rolls into CSR

Michelin is the world's leading tyre company. It has a 20% share of the global tyre market, employs 130,000 people, and operates in more than a 170 countries. With its headquarters in France, it operates seventy-five plants in nineteen different countries which produce 194 million tyres a year. It also publishes nineteen million maps and guides and operates a number of digital services. On top of this it operates the "Michelin star" rating system of restaurants.

The company was founded in 1889 by two brothers, André and Edouard Michelin, and the family is still closely involved today. Their initial focus on excellence in innovation has remained with the firm and has led to numerous technological breakthroughs in mobility over the years, and many new products or services. Yet the replacement tyre market, in the passenger, car, light truck, and truck markets, still represents some 70% of sales in volume.

The company is organized into a number of product lines:

- Passenger, car, and light truck
- Truck
- Speciality product lines, including aircraft, earthmover, agricultural, two-wheel, and components
- Travel publications.

The organization also encompasses:

- Distribution networks: Euromaster in Europe, and TCI in North America;
- Michelin Technology Centre, with three main sites in France, the US and Japan, plus a number of other testing or research facilities around the world;
- Eleven group services such as audit, communications, finance, etc.

As a long-standing French company, driven by private ownership and with a strong reputation, Michelin has long been aware of its role, engagement, and contribution to society. It has always been involved in supporting local communities, both socially (through participation in local initiatives) and in the form of economic development support. So, it has embraced modern expressions of engagement through CSR principles and thinking. One of its initiatives in the UK, Michelin Development (MDL), is a good example.

Michelin Development is a scheme that has been set up to assist with the economic development and long-term prosperity of the regions where their sites are, or have been, located. It provides an opportunity to have a far greater impact on Michelin's ability to support the regeneration of the local business community and in particular the creation of quality sustainable jobs.

Working in conjunction with regional development agencies, local government, and business support agencies, Michelin Development in the UK aims to:

- stimulate employment creation through attracting inward investment;
- generate or safeguard sustainable quality employment within existing and new businesses;

- assist in the shaping and development of projects in conjunction with local business support agencies;
- encourage skills and entrepreneurship able to support the long-term future of the local region.

Support is available for viable projects that can demonstrate the potential to create quality, sustainable jobs. Applications must be supported by a credible business plan together with relevant financial accounting information.

Michelin Development offers access to finance for small and medium-sized enterprises (with up to 250 employees) in areas where it has operations. These businesses can obtain unsecured loans from £5,000 at a highly subsidized interest rate, with a repayment period of three to five years, through the company's associate bank. A Michelin Development loan can be used for a whole range of projects which are linked to the creation of jobs. This could include purchase of capital equipment, process improvement, working capital, and marketing, to name just a few. The funding is private so it can normally be used to "gear up" public and other forms of loan funding. Although, in most cases, the applicants are required to invest some of their her own equity into the project, the initiative gives access to funds that clients would not normally be able to have, because of the backing of the Michelin brand.

Participants in the scheme can also have access to advice and expertise. They might, for instance, get free, independent advice from Michelin's considerable in-house expertise. This ranges from issues like health and safety to recruitment, sales training, or productivity improvement. This type of support could cover the following areas:

- Industrial engineering (Organization)
- Marketing
- Purchasing
- Information technology
- Personnel-related issues
- Environment
- Quality systems
- Training
- Health and safety
- Other areas by discussion.

Moreover, where the product or service is appropriate, the client may be invited to tender for Michelin business. Finally a press release may be created for successful applications, providing valuable publicity. Applicants are free to choose either financial help, expertise support, or both.

Launched in 2002, MDL in the UK was the first country outside of France to embrace this new approach. The first scheme was in Burnley,

North of England, following the closure of the plant in mid 2002. However, the model was successfully developed over the next eighteen months and launched in Dundee, Stoke, and Ballymena in 2004. It has helped over 150 companies to create nearly 2,000 jobs in the UK alone. The fund has, at the time of writing, exceeded a total of £4 million in business loans to small businesses.

Whilst applications can be submitted from any new start-up or existing small/medium-sized business located within or relocating to the areas indicated below, priority is given to those businesses in the manufacturing and service sectors. Its successful clients have, though, been in sectors varying from high precision engineering to construction and from state-of-the-art technology to fine bone china.

The offer of subsidized unsecured loans and free independent advice from experts within Michelin has been a real success. It acts as a catalyst to tempt other funders to back good local entrepreneurial projects. Yet, the real strength of the scheme is in the way that MDL works with local and regional development agencies. An application to the local "MDL steering committee" can lead to support from several of the committee members and, of course, by involving these agencies the MDL message is spread far and wide throughout the local business community.

MDL works closely with all the relevant regional agencies such as AWM at Stoke, NWDA at Burnley, INI at Ballymena, and SE at Dundee. Since the setting up of each scheme, managers from these agencies have been regular contributors and supporters at monthly steering committee meetings at each site. At Burnley this relationship has gone further with Mike Cole sitting on the NWDA Enterprise Forum and invited to attend various events including a small delegation to Clarence House in 2007 for an audience with Prince Charles to discuss strategy for the development of Burnley. It is fair to say that all the regional agencies have been very supportive of the work of MDL and good relationships exist.

The programme has resulted in considerable press coverage. The UK national, regional, and local press, together with TV and radio have been more than happy to feature stories about MDL and its clients because they are positive and successful in hard economic times. Perhaps the highlight, which illustrates the positive impact of CSR on a company's reputation, was a three-quarter page story in Britain's *Sunday Times* (in 2006) with the title "Michelin gives big business a good name".

One recipient of the scheme's help was a Staffordshire-based company called Compact Science Systems Ltd. Their Technical Director, Dennis Leigh, developed part of the technology for the Beagle 2 Mars Lander. The £10,000 cash injection from Michelin Development has been channelled into developing portable spectrometer equipment, the only instrument of its type in the world. The mass spectrometer is used to explore for oil and gas fields by measuring the isotopes of carbon in the gases produced from exploratory bore holes.

The system can measure a sample on the rig in six minutes instead of six days (a typical laboratory turnaround time) and can be operated remotely from a shore-based control room so that the results can be seen by the geoscientists in real time. The analysis of the bore hole gases can signal when the bore hole is about to break through, the quality of the oil field, and even if the oil rights to the field are owned by another company. The fast analysis time can save hundreds of thousands of dollars in drilling costs and massively improve efficiency of energy prospecting.

This breakthrough technology is proving a success for the small North Staffordshire-based firm as they expand into the lucrative oil exploration market and take on the established multi-million pound competition with their unique and innovative equipment. James Leigh, Managing Director of Compact Science, said:

> The Michelin Development loans fund is really important to a company like ours. Although we are considered to be an important company for the future in terms of the innovative, groundbreaking technology we are involved in developing, the support from the traditional lenders does not reflect this.
>
> There is no consistent investment from the banks or the government in a high tech business such as ours and that is why Michelin Development's readiness to approve funding is so crucial in being able to take our ideas forward and compete in the sectors we are involved with.

Mike Cole, Director of Michelin Development, said:

> Supporting progressive, forward thinking companies such as Compact Science who are looking to take their ideas and business to the next level create growth, wealth, and quality sustainable jobs in the region, is what forms the Michelin Development ethos.
>
> We want to create a climate in which other start-ups and enterprises can flourish and in doing so contribute towards successful, local business communities and economies which thrive and grow for many years into the future.

 RATING: Practical

CULTURAL VARIATIONS

Application: International marketing

Individualism x masculinity/femininity

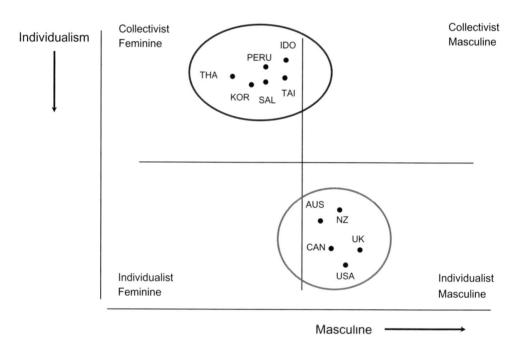

Figure C.6: A representation of Hofstede's cultural variation models

The concept

People in different parts of the world have different languages, mindsets, preferences, attitudes, and prejudices. This "collective programming of the mind", the inculcation of indigenous culture, occurs during childhood and adolescence; and different cultures create different expectations and attitudes in customers. It is often so subtle that people themselves can be unaware of their own cultural perspectives and biases. Yet it has a profound effect on their attitude to life and business. While another country may look misleadingly similar to home territory, there are underlying attitudes to life and business that mean different criteria are used to make judgements. These differences in lifestyle, values, behaviours, and business practices between different geographies and cultures are difficult to identify, digest, and manage. While stereotypes and clichés are often exaggerated, there are genuine differences in taste and approach, which can cause real problems. This is a marketing issue because some products and services are intensely personal and affected by imagination, aspiration, allegiance, atmosphere, intonation, or body language. Cultural differences can affect their success in different countries or regions.

Language is an obvious example. When Coca-Cola first started serious international expansion, for example, it had difficulties with its name alone. The Chinese characters which most closely reproduced the sound of the drink's name actually translated as "bite the wax tadpole"; whereas their slogan ("Refresh yourself with Coca-Cola") translated into Dutch as "Wash your hands with Coca-Cola" (see Pendergrast, M., 1993). Although English is now generally accepted to be the international language of business, different words have different meanings and the subtlety of intent can be lost in translation. However, they are even more likely when a supplier is working, through translation, in a customer's local language.

Even worse, culture and upbringing give different meaning to words which can dramatically affect understanding. Problems can be caused through the ignorance of cultural differences. For example, while the English word "lunch" refers to a meal eaten in the middle of the day, what this signifies varies enormously in European cultures. In Sweden, it is generally a meal at 11:30 am which comprises fish, potatoes, and salad accompanied by a "lättöl" (a light beer). To the English, though, it means a snack, like sandwiches, eaten soon after midday, generally at the desk, or possibly, in the pub. To the French, particularly in Paris, it is still often a three-course meal at 1:00 pm with red wine and, to the Spanish, a big meal at 3:00 pm. The cultural context gives different meanings to the word, complicating life. If an inexperienced Swedish business person says to a Spanish customer: "we'll discuss this over lunch", obvious complications arise. Cultural heritage has an enormous effect on marketing because words are given very different meaning by their cultural context.

Even the ubiquitous American fast food service, McDonald's, has to be customized in different cultures of the world to deliver satisfaction. Although it is thought to be the same the world over, the franchise dynamic of the firm's international operations has not only ensured that the service is varied around the world but also that the fast food menu itself is customized to some degree. As John Travolta's character pointed out in the film *Pulp Fiction*, their products in Paris (and other countries) are different to those in the USA. But there are other aspects of the service that have been adjusted over the years. For instance, in the early years of its expansion into the UK, their employees were trained to say "Have a nice day". In America this is a polite, unremarkable phrase, which is part of day-to-day life. However, this was not natural to employees in the UK and their uncomfortable tone of voice implied insincerity. Unfortunately, as one of the key service assumptions in the UK is sincerity this caused offence and affected trade. (British people will tolerate many other aspects of poor service if the service supplier is sincere or polite.) Eventually, McDonald's publicly apologized to the country through PR and mass advertising media; and dropped the phrase.

What is not often understood is the vast difference that cultural heritage makes to quality expectations. "Quality" to a New Yorker, for example, can mean choice and speed of delivery while to the English it means sincerity and to Germans, thoroughness or accuracy. People approach every service with a set of expectations, which are both emotional and practical. They will only think that a service is good quality if both the technical content and the service performance meet those expectations. Yet they will not make any effort to explain these expectations and, in fact, are often unaware of them themselves. However, they are ruthless in the way they criticize and judge a firm if it does not meet these articulated and unarticulated expectations.

So, cultural differences force a company to consider the customization of service to meet local, cultural expectations. This has serious implications. It may be that, in one culture, the delivery of service is a performance designed to serve the customer with people and take care of all of their needs. In another, however, excellent service may be self-service. In yet another, it may be delivered through advanced technology. So, if a marketer is designing a service that will be received in Scandinavia, Germany, Spain, and France, they need to research the expectations of that service in each of those cultures. The outlook, attitude, and assumptions will be different in each culture and the service must be adjusted to suit those different tastes.

Firms both large and small have been damaged by ill conceived international strategies. Marketers should think through the strategic and managerial aspects of international market approaches with real care. For instance, culture affects demand for different offers. Some cultures, for instance, value strategy and consultancy more than others. The Nordic countries of Europe tend to place emphasis on discussion and debate that leads to consensus. This, in turn, tends to make them value ideas and pay for advice more readily than, say, the British. As a result, the demand for a consultancy service, and the price people are prepared to pay for it, is different in different cultures of the world.

It is often wrongly assumed that, in business-to-business markets, attitudes and expectations are very similar across the world and, as a result, cultural differences are less important. However, there is much evidence that differences occur and affect all aspects of business. One of the most useful and extensive studies to demonstrate this was undertaken by Geert Hofstede (Hofstede, G., 2001). He identified five significant cultural variations and devised matrices by which international business affairs can be planned and managed. Interestingly, his original research was conducted in one business-to-business company (IBM) that perceived itself as a successful market leader with one consistent global culture. So, even in the perceived monoculture of one large international business, cultural variations have a large influence. This has implications for many aspects of business-to-business practice.

In fact there is very little business practice that is not influenced by cultural diversity and, as a result, impacts the markets of suppliers. For instance, different cultures respond differently to colour and this affects any work on international design, advertising, and brand. Similarly, there are indications that business innovation occurs differently in different cultures so that the styling of propositions needs to be adapted. Finally, there appears to be a difference in the adoption of new ideas, affecting the pace at which new offers are launched and accepted by the market in different parts of the world.

History, context, criticism, and development

Market-led companies have been working on the international stage and dealing with cultural variations for many centuries. As late as the mid 20th century, though, the attitude to international marketing amongst marketing theorists and teachers was from their home country out to the rest of the world. A groundbreaking piece of work was undertaken in the 1980s by Geert Hofstede. He researched, developed, and published a number of dimensions of cultural difference. He grouped, tested, and demonstrated the effect of these dimensions on management practice. They can be used to guide international strategy and planning.

The dimensions were:

(i) **Individualism versus collectivism.** Some societies are loosely knit, where individuals are supposed to take care of themselves and their immediate families. Work, career, economic provision, and progress are centred around the individual. Others are more collective. Individuals can expect their relatives, clan, or gang to look after them in exchange for loyalty.

(ii) **Power distance.** This is the extent to which members of a society accept that power in its institutions is distributed unequally. This attitude affects the behaviour of those with and without power. Large power distance cultures accept hierarchical order in which everyone has a place; small power distance cultures strive for equalization. This issue affects how societies handle inequalities when they occur.

(iii) **Uncertainty avoidance.** This is the degree to which members of a society feel uncomfortable with risk, ambiguity, and uncertainty. Uncertainty avoidance cultures maintain rigid codes of belief and behaviour. They are intolerant towards deviants. Weak uncertainty cultures are the opposite.

(iv) **Masculinity versus femininity.** In Hofstede's view, masculine cultures prefer achievement, heroism, and material success. Whereas feminine cultures stand for relationships, modesty, caring for the weak, and quality of life.

This work shows how different cultures cluster and are similar under different dimensions. Figure C.6 represents just one set of pairings (individualism/collectivism with masculinity/femininity). This clearly shows the clustering of the "Anglo Saxon"-influenced cultures of the USA, UK, New Zealand, and Canada. A proposition built on the assumptions of individualistic masculinity (like high-end executive search) is likely to succeed in this group. The model can be used as an aid to almost any international marketing function. It can be used to develop growth and acquisition strategy. It readily reveals compatible cultures that will be low-risk targets. It also shows how communications and product or services need to be adapted to penetrate different cultures.

Voices and further reading

- "Since marketing is part of the social warp and woof of a nation, it is essential to understand all aspects of a people's culture in order to appreciate the structure of their marketing systems and operations. Customs, language, religion, taboos, ethnic relationships and dispositional characteristics can significantly add to the professional insights of the marketer." Carson, D., 1967.
- Fifield, P., "Managing the mix in Europe", in *Perspectives on Marketing Management*, vol. 1 Chapter 5, edited by M.J. Baker. John Wiley & Sons Ltd.
- Hofstede, G., "Cultural dimensions in management and planning". *Asia Pacific Journal of Management*, January 1984.
- Hofstede, G, *Cultural Consequences*. Sage, 2001.
- "Outcome control systems are much better received in some cultures (such as the United States, Canada, Argentina, Italy, Southern Nigeria or parts of India) than in others (such as Sweden, Japan or Korea). A firm with global reach, therefore, should have multiple control systems for its various sales forces". Anderson, E. and Onyemah, V., 2006.
- "In Europe, most of the evidence points to the fact that cultural differences persist in playing a decisive role in forming our consumption patterns and our unique expressions of consumption. At the same time, global competition tends to have a homogenizing effect in some markets such as music, sports, clothing, and entertainment . . . Cultural borders do not always follow national borders. Although national borders are still very important for distinguishing between cultures, there may be important regional differences within a country, as well as overlap between two countries. Add to this immigration and the import of foreign (often American) cultural phenomena and you begin to understand why it is very difficult to talk about European countries being culturally homogenous." Solomon, M. et al., 2006.

Things you might like to consider

(i) Cultural variations exist between regions within geographic boundaries. The differences between the regions with countries like, say, Spain, Italy, and the United States of America can be large and profound. So, it can be dangerous to assume that a nation responds with unanimity to an offer.

(ii) The majority of the fans of British soccer team, Manchester United, are not in Britain or even Europe. Remarkably, a wide range of people in Asia are devoted followers, keeping up with their team's stars and tournament performance through satellite TV. Despite living in the heat of Singapore or Malaysia, in perhaps poor circumstances with Muslim beliefs, many people are part of an excitable group, which charts the course of rich, pampered Western soccer stars. They suspend their cultural heritage and issues for a greater benefit: to be part of an excited tribe. A similar phenomenon occurred just after the Second World War. At the time, America was seen as energetic, modern, and rich. People across the devastated globe wanted to feel part of its exciting modernity. They wanted to belong and, as a result, willingly bought into American exports like Coca–Cola with its promise to a young generation. It is possible, then, to create an offer that has appeal and fame across the world. It is so associated with success that it prompts people to desire it and suppress or suspend their cultural predilections. They want to get in on the experience.

(iii) Is the world truly global in the sense of creating ubiquitous, similar offers? It is certainly very integrated, with formal trading treaties, regional trading blocks, and a growing consensus amongst political representatives. Yet, for the past 3,000 years the thrust of history has been driven by the rise and fall of great powers. At the time of writing, China and India are in the ascendancy. How much is international marketing strategy to be developed within the constraints and opportunities of the evolving nature great powers? Is the world really stable, integrated and "global"?

(iv) The safety created by the evolution of regional entities, like the EU, seems to allow local culture and identity to reassert themselves. And, cultural identity is very powerful and durable. There is, for instance, an annual meeting and celebration of Celtic culture. People travel from Wales, Cornwall in the UK, and parts of France to share music, art, and poetry in common languages. What is remarkable about this enduring cultural identity is that the Celts were largely wiped out some 2,000 years ago. Their sense of community and identity has, it seems, endured and is growing in strength. The same can be said of many cultural groups. So, is bland international sameness really appropriate with a rise in cultural identity?

(v) When business leaders talk of globalization they often use this as shorthand for the world's centres of capital (like New York, London, and Hong Kong). Is the company's ambition really global or focused on some tighter international grouping?

(vi) It is remarkably difficult to identify your own cultural values, beliefs, and prejudices.

Fujitsu evolves into a "transnational" enterprise to grow its global business

Japanese IT giant Fujitsu is a leading provider of IT-based business solutions for the global market place. With approximately 175,000 employees supporting customers in seventy countries, Fujitsu combines a world-wide team of systems and services experts with highly reliable computing and communications products, and advanced microelectronics, to deliver value to their customers. Headquartered in Japan, with revenues of US$47 billion, Fujitsu is the world's fourth largest IT services provider and Japan's market leader.

TIME FOR A NEW GLOBAL BUSINESS STRUCTURE

Global expansion is on of the agenda of most large enterprises, together with how best to organize themselves for international operations. Developing a new strategy-structure relationship in the increasingly complex environment of international business is an enormous challenge. Yet it is one that Fujitsu has taken head-on in order to achieve its aim of becoming a truly global IT company, based in Japan, within a three-year (FY2009–2011) timeframe.

Fujitsu recognized that it needed to adopt a broader, global perspective, rather than focusing so heavily on Japan, and has undertaken a radical shift in the focus of its operations. The process of structural reform has meant an end to a "silo approach" to business inside and outside Japan, with integration enabling the Group's companies to work together better to accelerate global growth. The strategy to clarify responsibilities and strengthen overall group management is reflected in its adoption of a "transnational organisational model". This reinforces Fujitsu's ability to view operations from a global standpoint, while still pursuing business that is responsive to the prevailing conditions in each region, taking customer-centric management to a new level.

President Kuniaki Nozoe explains, "We will expand business globally by leveraging the base Fujitsu has built in developing its worldwide operations over many years, and by instilling the maxim 'Think Globally, Act Locally' in our operations."

Two business imperatives drove this strategic change in organizational structure. First and foremost was the need to organize the group's business to better meet the needs of its global markets and clients. This involved improving its ability to: present a "One Fujitsu" to all customers; to take products and services to market together; to simplify its regional organizations; and to derive lasting benefits from best practice and standardized processes across regions. Second, naturally, was future growth, and the opportunity to significantly increase the percentage of Fujitsu's business outside the Japanese home market.

The expanding global IT market place, where markets are developing at different speeds and in different ways, is driving this increasing demand for both global and local excellence. In IT services, analysis of consumer wealth and IT spend shows the considerable variations and opportunities, (particularly between markets in the West and newly emerging economies). As these markets evolve quite differently, so local requirements vary from market to market, despite the fact that clients also demand the benefits of global scale and coherence. It was the need to address this paradox of "trying to do it all" that was behind Fujitsu's move to become a transnational enterprise; "thinking globally and acting locally". With few truly global IT companies, and none that are wholly successful, Fujitsu saw the potential for differentiation through this approach.

Fujitsu has long worked to develop operations globally, and was one of the first IT vendors in Japan to advance operations abroad. Fujitsu Services, for example, had an impressive track record in securing large-scale outsourcing business deals in Europe. But despite this record, and initiatives such as their "Global Service Innovation Programme", Fujitsu's operations outside Japan were limited to an "Act Locally" mindset.

Pressures for local responsiveness or for global integration lie at the heart of the international strategy-structure choices considered by Fujitsu. They reviewed four models – *Multi-national* (ultimately localized), *Global* (highly centralized), *International* (focused on sharing), and *Transnational* (highly networked) – which differ according to their management structures, external approach to the market, and internal lines of communication and reporting. The *Transnational* organization combines the essential features of the other three models. It is flexible and sensitive to local conditions (like a *Multi-national* company), competitive and efficient (like a *Global* company), and, at the same time, attentive to sharing knowledge across local business units (as in an *International* company).

So, seen as the answer to increasing complexity, the transnational model is a balance between the pressures for global integration and for local responsiveness; centralized control and decentralized autonomy. Described by Fujitsu as an "integrated network", it can deliver simultaneous efficiency and scale benefits for global competitiveness, national responsiveness for flexibility, and the benefits of corporate-wide learning for innovation. As a pure form it is still evolving, but it seemed the obvious route for Fujitsu given the group's multi-national heritage, global aspirations, and unique culture in the world of IT services and solutions.

Fujitsu is now fully embracing the management principles behind the transnational business model. A structural reform is underway, that underpins the global delivery of a "One Fujitsu" to all customers; going to market under one consistent brand, with one single business responsibility. Whereas the "local" component that is the company's heritage helps to simplify and transform their regional operations, providing empowerment but not independence. Global coherence has evolved from a small but powerful set of functions, all supported by a shared incentives programme called the "collective bonds of performance".

Clients undoubtedly benefit from the "Think Global, Act Local" approach. The scale and coherence of the transnational business elevates Fujitsu's global delivery and global client management capabilities. The shared values of the "Fujitsu Way" reinforce the "One Fujitsu" experience. Whilst, the global knowledge and experience-sharing add considerably to the security and confidence that is a function of scale and reach.

At the same time, the local proximity of focused regional operations helps ensure Fujitsu is fully in tune with local market conditions and client requirements. For example, it enabled the successful roll-out of a client relationship initiative, "Field Innovation", which converts IT innovation into real business value. Long-term partnerships are also more manageable.

Fujitsu believes the transnational model works well to balance global scale and local touch. From their experience, it's now feasible to reach the higher number of services, sectors, and geographies on a "global" level, yet with the "local" benefit of greater segment focus and more localized management and delivery systems. Another advantage includes a superior ability to meet key IT purchasing criteria. These include building a deep understanding of the customer's requirements; getting senior executives involved in the sales and delivery process to build relationships and demonstrate commitment locally; pricing competitively at both a global and local level; bringing all the benefits of a tried and tested solution to bear for the customer; and having the scale and flexibility to offer innovative, outcome-based commercials.

Fujitsu continues to push ahead on structural reforms and growth strategies geared to each market while strengthening group management, clarifying responsibilities, and increasing sales. Where previously each region implemented their own strategy, with significant overlapping of functions, now there is unified planning. R&D, sourcing, and supply chain have become "global" integrated functions, with sales and service positioned squarely at the "local" level – Japan, the Americas, APAC, China, EMEA. Taking "Think Global" a step further, the Global Business Group that drives strategy has been organized into four global support functions – namely, Marketing, Delivery, Global Client Management, and Business Management.

The specialization of Group companies has been a major component in the restructuring. Concentration of resources has put Fujitsu in a stronger position to better meet the needs of business markets of all sizes. Converting Fujitsu Business Services into a wholly owned subsidiary, for example, effectively created a one-stop shop for medium-sized businesses in Japan. The acquisition of Fujitsu Siemens Computers, was a catalyst to accelerate the Group's globalization strategy. Through reorganization of this subsidiary, and further realignment of operations outside Japan, Fujitsu aims to double annual IA server sales within two years, and to improve profitability in the longer term by adding services to these deals.

Fujitsu's global value proposition has evolved noticeably alongside the structural changes. An ambitious transformation that is paying dividends, with the cost efficiencies, strengthened management structure and integrated "Think Global, Act Local" capabilities of a transnational enterprise fast being realized.

President Kuniaki Nozoe confirms: "Fujitsu's goal is to get more than 40 per cent of its sales outside of Japan in fiscal 2011, and it will do this through a 'think globally, act locally' strategy."

DECISION-MAKING UNIT (DMU)

Application: sales planning, communications planning, account planning, relationship marketing

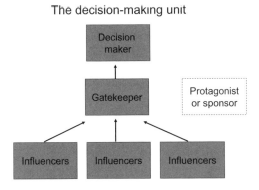

Figure D.1: A representation of the DMU

The concept

The concept of the "decision-making unit" (DMU), sometimes called the "buying centre", attempts to identify the different roles in a "buying group" (see Figure D.1). They exist in both consumer and organizational buying. Marketers can use this tool to identify the influence that different people wield in the buying process. Different approaches to each one can then be designed according to the role each one plays. The idea is to understand who participates and who has influence on buying decisions. There are various roles that have been suggested.

In consumer group buying they are:

(i)   "Initiator": the person who first thinks of an idea.
(ii) "Influencer": someone whose views influence the purchase (like children on the choice of breakfast cereal).
(iii) "Decider": the person who actually decides what to buy.
(iv) "Buyer": this can be different to the decider.
(v)   "User": the person who uses or consumes the purchase.

In business markets:

(i)   "Influencers" are people who have a valid opinion on the purchase or a valid contribution (perhaps a junior employee). They might research or contribute to the evaluation of the proposed purchase.
(ii) The "gatekeeper" is someone who might deal with potential suppliers prior to the decision maker getting involved. It is normally a reasonably senior person who presents a proposition to the decision maker.
(iii) A "sponsor" is someone who is particularly well disposed to the supplier, perhaps an employee who may have no involvement in this particular purchase at all but genuinely believes that the deal or the supplier is good for their company.
(iv) The "decision maker" is the real power in the buying group with authority to give the go ahead. Sometimes this is a group responsibility because of the level of spend and, sometimes, it still needs a particular authority to comply with formal processes.

Some researchers have identified other roles such as "end users" and "specifiers". Professor Jean-Jaques Lambin, for example, distinguishes between "purchasers", "users", and formal "deciders" or "approvers" (Lambin, J., 2000). He points out that the size and nature of the DMU varies according to the nature of a purchase. It differs if it is a new task, a modified rebuy, or a straight rebuy, getting simpler as these states progress.

There are some interesting and consistent themes about DMUs that crop up time and again in studies of it. For instance, in business marketing, the roles, nature, and size of the DMU seem to vary according to the organizational culture and size. As interesting, individuals within it consistently exaggerate their influence. They might imply that they are the decision maker to increase their kudos or add a frisson to their role in the process. In cost constrained environments, purchasing or finance tend to be the main arbiter, whatever others say about their role. In important or politically risky decisions, more senior people are involved.

History, context, criticism, and development

Since the mid 20th century, there have been many studies, starting originally in research around *organizational buying behaviour* that have sought to understand DMUs. There have been both quantitative and qualitative research projects, and detailed observational research. One marketing historian (Sweitzer, R.W., 1997) details the extensive work on the subject, highlighting its strengths and weaknesses. So, this is a reasonably robust concept.

In Western markets there is evidence that decision making has changed since the turn of the 21st century and the Enron debacle; which has prompted changes in corporate governance. New regulations affecting Western companies seem to be increasing this method of buying. For example, as a basis for their article in the *Harvard Business Review* two researchers (Trailer, B. and Dickie, J., 2006) surveyed over 1,200 companies. They found that the individual "economic decision maker" was being replaced by committees and multiple layers of approval, all equally important to the decision to move ahead. This was partly why the length of the average sales cycles was increasing. It affected the sales cycle because the sales team needed to talk to and nurture more people. They found that companies reporting a sales cycle of seven months or more had climbed from 18% in their previous surveys to over 25% and those under three months had dropped from 50% to under 42%.

Voices and further reading

* Webster, F.E. and Wind, Y., *Organizational Buying Behavior*. Prentice Hall 1972.
* "The buying centre is defined as consisting of those individuals who interact for the specific purpose of accomplishing the buying task . . . persons interact on the basis of their particular roles in the buying process". Webster and Wind, ibid.
* "Family members can strongly influence buyer behaviour. We can distinguish between two families in the buyer's life . . . parents make up the family of orientation. The family of procreation have a more direct influence on everyday buying behaviour." Kotler, P. et al., 1999.
* Bonoma, T.V., "Major sales: who really does the buying?" *Harvard Business Review*, July–August 2006.
* "This set of roles can be thought of as a fixed set of behavioral pigeon-holes into which different managers can be placed to aid understanding." Bonoma, ibid.

Things you might like to consider

(i) Research and analysis into DMU's is likely to reveal, when done properly, a group of individuals with personal histories, political power, emotional influences, and idiosyncrasies. This is as much about understanding and communicating with people as any other aspect of marketing; even in complex business-to-business settings.

(ii) There is no doubt that, even in business-to-business environments, marketing communications programmes can be targeted at members of a DMU to influence their thinking. This can help sales people to achieve sales.

 RATING: Practical and powerful

 **DIFFERENTIATION**

Application: strategy, NDP/NSD, pricing, communications

The concept

The concept of differentiation suggests that an offer from a company should be made to be distinct and unique by marketers. It is the exact opposite of a commodity. This uniqueness has several effects:

(i) It sets the offer apart from competing ideas or products.
(ii) It earns superior profits for the business owners.
(iii) It gives the offer its own perceived value, a unique price point. In fact, it is probably true to say that it is not possible to create a real *value proposition* without some form of differentiation.
(iv) It attracts a segment of customers and commands their attention for years.
(v) It commands a unique position in the market.
(vi) It circumvents or obviates price pressure.
(vii) It allows companies to expand into other opportunity areas (see *repositioning*).

There are several ways in which differentiation can be developed:

(i) By *branding* (see separate entry): One of the characteristics of a brand is its uniqueness and its appeal to a group of human beings. The design of a product brand, service brand, or corporate brand involves the creation of a truly differentiated offer which will distinguish it from rivals for many decades.
(ii) Through customer insight (see entry under *behavioural aspects of marketing*): The response to a unique human insight can create a means of differentiation which gives a company a lead over others that can last for quite a considerable time.
(iii) By engineering an attractive features mix: A product or service should be a unique combination of features at a price. This unique combination should create a distinct offer (see *features analysis*).

(iv) Through quality (see separate entry under *service quality*): It is possible to create uniqueness through both product quality and through service quality. The latter might be the style of service or one aspect of its functional performance (like speed of delivery).

(v) Through the people who serve customers: The style and character of the people who serve customers can be a source of differentiation. Companies as different as Disney, Virgin Atlantic, and Deloitte all have a strategy built on the competence of their human capital. The people they recruit, and the way they manage and train them, creates a unique experience.

(vi) By explicitly offering perceived cheapness: Several writers are unduly polite in saying that some "differentiate on cost". They are, in fact, aiming for cheapness. A "value hotel" often means that it is the cheapest possible for a certain standard of accommodation; and customers know that.

(vii) Through attractive design: The use of packaging or advertising which appeals to people's senses, sometimes subliminally, can create a unique and differentiated offer.

History, context, criticism, and development

Although business people have been creating unique offers for at least two centuries, it is hard to find a reference to the term "differentiation" before the 1960s. Leaders who created brands wanted their offer to stand out from the crowd and mean something unique to their customers. It was, it seemed, only in the latter half of the 20th century that the methods, value, and concepts of differentiated offers began to be codified. The PIMS survey highlighted the economic value of differentiated offers and the work by Michael Porter on competitive strategy called real attention to it as a competitive strategy amongst business leaders of significant stature. It is now an accepted part of the canon of marketing thinking. Although there is research and debate about exactly how marketers achieve differentiation, there is, at the time of writing, little serious doubt about its value as a viable strategy and marketing approach.

Voices and further reading

- Levitt, T., "Marketing success through differentiation-of anything". *Harvard Business Review*, January–February 1980.
- "There is no such thing as a commodity. All goods and services are differentiable. Though the usual assumption is that this is more true of consumer goods than of industrial goods and services, the opposite is the actual case." Levitt, T., 1980.
- "To be a practical strategy the difference between the organization's product or services and the competitor's offers must be sustainable and believable over the longer term. Costs for the differentiating organization will probably be slightly higher because of the costs of developing and maintaining a unique position in

the market place but costs will still have to be close to the industry average. It is a mistake to believe that differentiation can be used to disguise inefficiency." Fifield, P., 1992.

- "Competitive advantage in either cost or differentiation is a function of a company's value chain . . . a company's ability to differentiate itself reflects the contribution of each value activity toward the fulfilment of buyer needs. Many of the company's activities – not just its physical product or service – contribute to differentiation." Porter, M.E., 1995.

- Trott, P., *Innovation Management and New Product Development*. Prentice Hall, 2008.

- "Broadly the differentiation sought by competitors could be based upon cost, with a value-for-money proposition, or it could be based upon superior quality, which might encompass better materials, better performance, new features, uncommon availability or better service." Trott, ibid.

- "The conventional view of differentiation is that successful differentiation requires distinguishing a product or brand from competitors on an attribute that is meaningful, relevant and valuable to buyers. Observation, however, reveals that many brands successfully differentiate by introducing an attribute that appears valuable but, on closer examination, is irrelevant." Carpenter, G.S. et al., "Market-driving strategies" in Iacobucci, D. (ed.), *Kellogg on Marketing*, 2001.

- "This [PIMS] study shows that the firms with the lowest return on investment operate in commodity markets where there is no differentiation on quality or anything else, such as the coal industry. Where there is room for differentiation, losers have inferior quality . . . The most highly performing group of companies are 'power companies', which have superior quality in differentiable markets. These are ahead of Nichers . . . Differentiation may be harder in some industries than others but creative firms have shown that any market can be differentiated." Kotler, P., 2003.

Things you might like to consider

(i) Marketers working for a range of different companies (utilities, professional practices, or IT companies for instance) settle too easily with the assumption that their offer is a commodity. This, though, is a result of their companies' and their marketers' policies and behaviours. If they are marketing a commodity it is their fault. Marketers should set out to turn all offers into unique, differentiated, and appealing offers in order to maximize return to shareholders.

(ii) In many conferences in the West over the past few years there has been a mantra based on the underlying assumption that commoditization is inevitable and that it is difficult to create sustainable value. ("Markets are changing very fast, the world is getting more global, customers are demanding more for less, the internet allows people to compare prices more easily . . ." etc. etc.). This does not, though, fit the evidence. As Tables B1 and B2 demonstrate, there are many companies that have created differentiated offers that have endured for many years, centuries even. Marketers should surely not accept that commoditization is inevitable and owe it to the businesses' owners to maximize return by trying to create differentiated offers in the face of this ridiculous but ubiquitous belief.

(iii) The method by which companies achieve real differentiation is sometimes through the systematic application of marketing planning or NSD techniques. Sometimes, though, it is through the driven ambition of a fixated, intuitive business leader. Or it might be through the maddeningly ill-defined insight of a gifted creative specialist. This is an area of marketing where logic, science, and rationality do not necessarily produce the results.

 RATING: Practical and powerful

DIFFUSION OF INNOVATIONS

Application: product strategy, communications strategy

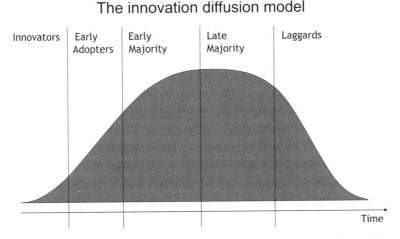

Figure D.2: A representation of the attitudes of people at different phases of the diffusion of innovation

The concept

Diffusion of innovation is the process by which societies learn of new concepts and adjust to them. It is a theory of how, why, and at what rate new ideas and technology spread through cultures. It tracks the course of new ideas and concepts, like water purification or environmental concern, as they grow in influence through a society. It is used by public bodies to help with significant social initiatives like changes in health practice or agricultural techniques.

The phenomenon is, essentially, a communication process which involves word-of-mouth, publicity, and subtle forms of marketing. The social scientists who study this phenomenon recommend the use of opinion leaders, experts, and catalysts to help an idea spread. It is from this, not the product life cycle literature, that the attitudes of various groups of people at different phases of diffusion (which is used so extensively by marketers) are drawn (see Figure D.2). Some are:

- **Innovators**: the first to adopt an innovation. They are willing to take risks and interested in scientific or technological ideas (gadgets).
- **Early Adopters**: the fastest category to adopt an innovation and, generally, a larger group.
- **Early Majority**: taking up the idea after a degree of time, they tend to be slower in the adoption process.
- **Late Majority**: adopting the innovation after the average member of the society, these tend to be more sceptical.
- **Laggards**: the last to adopt an innovation and can take pride in their resistance to new ideas.

Marketers should be aware of this because it is the social communication mechanism which opens the market for any specific product or service. Marketing communication should go with the grain of the attitudes of the dominant group of buyers at that stage in the innovation diffusion process. Marketers can use the knowledge of the phases in the adoption of ideas to help the spread of interest in their product or service amongst a market. If it is, say, at the phase where the "late majority" are taking the concept on board (at the time of writing, for example, internet banking) then the communications strategy and methods would be different to those used if it was a totally new idea which was attracting the attention of innovators (at the time of writing, for example, 3D TV).

History, context, criticism, and development

Study of the phenomenon was explicitly initiated by social scientists like Beal, Bohlen, and Rogers after the Second World War. They trace its foundations and antecedents back to a range of people notable in their field (like August Comte, Herbert Spencer, Gabriel Tarde, James Baldwin, and even Charles Darwin). It has been tested, researched examined and used in many contexts (from first-world drug use to third-world water sanitation). A famous study, reported by Rogers, was, for instance, on the diffusion of the use of hybrid seed corn amongst Iowa farmers in 1943. The primary source on this concept, though, is Everett Rogers (Rogers, E.M., 2003) who gathered massive amounts of data on it. He estimates that, by 2007, there were 6,000 diffusion studies and 600 diffusion publications by academics who study communication. In 1960, for example, Deutschmann and Danielson published ground-breaking research which demonstrated the S-curve in the diffusion of news events through journalism and across society.

There have been attempts to reconcile the stream of research around this concept with that of the product life cycle in marketing (see Spears, N.E. and Germain, R., 1995). Their conclusion is that the two are inter-related where a product is an object, idea, or construct that is entirely new (Rogers, 2003) but they talk of a "higher order construct", the extent to which the market embraces an innovative idea or concept (of which the product or service is a manifestation).

In recent years, a growing body of marketing thinkers, primarily connected with the launch of IT-related products in Silicon Valley (see Moore, G.A., 1991; Rosen, E., 2001; and Godin, S., 2004) have brought attention to the marketing communication techniques relevant in the early adoption phase of a new offer. They argue for the use of viral marketing, PR, and network marketing, particularly through digital methods. Some suggest that this should become the dominant method of marketing because of the rapid increase of new technology, the powerful viral networkers on the internet, and the disruption to established broadcast TV networks. The diffusion of innovation is now becoming an established part of marketing communication theory (see Rogers, E.M., Singhal, A., and Quinlan, M.M., 2009).

Voices and further reading

- Rogers, E.M., *Diffusion of Innovations*. Free Press, 2003.
- "Information about an innovation is often sought from peers, especially information about their subjective evaluations of the innovation. This information exchange about new ideas occurs through a conversation process involving interpersonal networks. The diffusion of innovation is essentially, then, a social process in which subjectively perceived information about a new idea is communicated from person to person. The meaning of an innovation is thus gradually worked out through a process of social construction ...This information exchange about new ideas occurs through a conversation process involving interpersonal networks. The diffusion of innovation is essentially a social process in which subjectively perceived information about a new idea is communicated from person to person." Rogers, ibid.
- ". . . our marketing ventures, despite normally promising starts, drift off course in puzzling ways, eventually causing unexpected and unnerving gaps in sales revenues, and sooner or later leading management to undertake some desperate remedy. . . . the point of greatest peril in the development of a high-tech market lies in making the transition from an early market dominated by a few visionary customers to a mainstream market dominated by a large block of customers who are predominantly pragmatists in orientation." Moore, G.A., 1991.

- Rogers, E.M., Singhal, A., and Quinlan, M.M., *Diffusion of Innovation*. 2009, which explores this process as part of communication theory.
- Trott, P., *Innovation Management and New Product Development*. Prentice Hall, 2008.
- "Innovation diffusion theories try to explain how an innovation is diffused in a social system over time; the adoption of an innovation is therefore a part of the wider diffusion process. . . . There is a considerable amount of confusion with regard to adoption and diffusion. This is largely due to differences in definition. Most researchers in the field, however, view adoption of innovations as a process through which individuals pass from awareness to the final decision to adopt or not adopt; whereas diffusion concerns the communication over time within a wider social system." Trott, ibid.

Things you might like to consider

(i)   This concept is clearly important to the successful creation of marketing strategy. Communications with markets ought to be adjusted as to where each group of people is in its adoption of the innovation that the product or service represents.

(ii) The groupings of different people at different phases in the diffusion of ideas are often presented as established fact because it is supported by numerous research projects. Yet this is just one more concept, developed in the behavioural sciences. Is it actually the case in your market? Human beings are individual as much as they are tribal. Does this always apply?

(iii) Some modern writers suggest that it is best to concentrate exclusively on the early innovators and get them to spread an idea through word-of-mouth because traditional media are breaking down. It seems daft, though, to neglect later phases in the innovation–diffusion–communication–learning process. There is absolutely no doubt that broadcast advertising and brand consolidation (from "to Fedex" in the US and "to Hoover" a carpet in the UK) have helped with the diffusion of new concepts and, consequently, sold millions of products and serv- ices. Communication techniques might need to be adjusted in the light of the forces affecting broadcast media but, even in the light of the communications theory related specifically to diffusion research, it is clearly idiotic to abandon attempts to communicate with the early or late majority (or even laggards) as some suggest.

 RATING: Practical and powerful

DIGITAL MARKETING

Application: marketing communications, branding, NPD/NSD

The concept

At the time of writing, "digital marketing" is the increasingly accepted term for the marketing and selling of products and services through a range of new, rapidly integrating, technologies like mobile telephony and, of course, the internet. It is yet another vast subject which is difficult to capture in this format. It is also fast changing, so it is difficult to come to effective, professional judgement on developments in it. At the time of writing, for instance, Twitter has become a major phenomenon in many Western countries. Celebrities, media personalities, and business people are using it. Many have people following their tweets and connecting with blogs to develop conversations. It is difficult to know, though, the long-term viability of this habit and, as important, how exactly it might be used to market products and services.

Digital marketing uses a range of new technologies and platforms including: the web itself, mobile phones, Skype, email, social networking sites like Facebook, search engines like Google, and YouTube. Each is new. Yet these are not just mechanisms to reach people, they are fast being adopted into the lifestyle of many people on the planet creating new communities, new concepts, and new attitudes to life. Marketers in all disciplines have to understand how their customers are using this range of technologies if they are to succeed. They have no option but to get their mind around this phenomenon.

There are very few buyers, certainly in the West, who do not search for information about potential services and products on the internet (whether for home or work use) before starting the buying process. Younger people, of course, reach for information on the web as easily as breathing but even older, retired people (with a little more time on their hands) have assimilated much of this technology. They will pay bills online, Skype relatives in remote locations, and buy entertainment tickets. Some are more proficient at adopting new web-based practices than their middle-aged sons and daughters who are busy juggling careers and young families.

Even the most staid and stodgy business-to-business markets are alive with people exploring needs on the web. In the older and more hierarchical businesses, for example, it is normal practice for top management to ask more junior employees to research a subject; and they do so, on the web. The professions, for instance, have often been slow to adopt new practices and many still run their firms based on dusty partnership principles. Yet they are absorbed with debate about how this electronic onslaught will change their way of working. They have, for some time, tried to change their recruitment policies to attract high calibre young people that have grown up with the web. These in turn are bringing social networking sites into these businesses. One expert observer, Professor Richard Susskind, thinks that the effect on lawyers, to cite but one speciality, will dramatically change the profession within a few years (Susskind, R., 2008).

There is both a radically new aspect to this and a repetition of old principles and behaviours. The radically new, of course, refers to the behaviour of the human mind in this fabulous new space. People of all ages, all nationalities, and all cultures are not only exploring the ideas, concepts, and services available in the world-wide web, they are also adopting them into their lifestyles. In the past, a young child's continual questions would weary a parent to the point where they might brush them off with superficial answers or push them off to another relative. Now, though, they can get those answers on the web. In the past, a school student would research a project in the library or might catch a relevant programme on TV. They might cut out pictures from old magazines (if they could get hold of a relevant article) or draw by hand. Now all that they need is available at the touch of a button. In the past, special interest groups might meet up from time to time or correspond by mail. Now they can discuss in real time and attract suppliers into their debate. There are new phenomena such as, for instance, people cooperating across vast distances to co-create books (like Wikipedia), campaigns, and events; and, of course, the use of this technology to pompt social reform in countries like Tunisia and Egypt. Businesses are being forced to listen, observe, and respond to the way their customers are using this technology.

There is a logical argument that, to those born in the past two or three decades, this is not new technology. It is simply a way of life. They integrate mobile and internet-based technology into their lives in just the same way that their parents did television or telephony. Don Tapscott (Tapscott, D., 2009) has called this generation the "netgen" (as opposed to "Generation X" or baby boomers) because the internet is redefining how they live, work, and socialize. As his work is based on interviews with 10,000 people and over forty reports, it has credibility. He suggests that this generation has eight new "norms" (they want freedom, to customize, to scrutinize; they insist on corporate integrity, they want to play, to collaborate; they want speed and to innovate). He even asserts that they are measurably (in IQ terms) brighter and better adjusted as a group (with measurably less crime, for instance). It remains to be seen whether these are long-term patterns which marketers can use (several specialists have challenged the findings) but marketers cannot ignore this phenomenon and its implications to their work.

At the same time, though, many of the behaviours in the digital space are the repetition of people behaving in the way they always have and responding to new technology as they always have. One credible writer, an *Economist* correspondent, wrote a well worked analogy around the way technologies like telegraphy were adopted (called *The Victorian Internet*, Standage, T., 2007) in order to argue for sense and perspective amongst businesses considering investment in digital strategy. For instance, although there is incredible creativity and diversity, there are, when objectively analysed, very conservative usage patterns. Suppliers like Google, Facebook, and YouTube are, by far, the most used sites. So, even in this new environment, people are conservative in behaviour, grouping around brands. Another example, reported by Dan Cobley, a director of Google, in his "Ted" lecture, is the use of the internet. One of the most searched categories on the web, he said, is pornography. (A desire and curiosity that powered the development of other new technologies in their time, like the camera and video recorders.) Yet, this is rarely reported in books and conferences on the web, and hardly ever shows up in research reports. People are happily lying to themselves again about their real needs and aspirations. Similarly, in the past, new technology has promulgated ugly and dangerous ideas. There is evidence, for instance, that during construction the trans-Siberian railway encouraged the spread of anti-Jewish sentiment in 19th century Russia. Similarly, it is certain that modern terrorism would not be such an international threat without the web. Marketers must not, it seems, be too captivated with the gloss of the new or exorbitant claims. As ever, markets and marketing are about people and their aspirations.

How far, then, should marketers go with this phenomenon and how far should they wait to see how humanity settles down to use this new technology? Being in early (the so-called "first mover advantage") clearly helps some. Waiting to enter the fray with an effective, well thought out strategy helps others.

The components of digital marketing are inter-related and draw companies further into a digital format. Marketers, for instance, must ensure that they have a superb web presence and produce materials with key words that reflect the culture and aspirations of their firm. This is, in many ways, the very heart of their business and they must ensure that it will be found by search engines. So, they must then invest in search engine optimization. In addition to the generic website, many firms now have web sites created for specific customers, segments, or campaigns. Blogs, RMS feeds, social networking sites (such as LinkedIn) need to be considered as part of a wider online strategy. Professional institutes and universities are stuffed full of courses to understand and deal with this phenomenon. No company can afford to be without an online strategy. This will include not only communication methods, but new offers and new experiences for customers. Its elements are likely to encompass:

- Web sites in all their forms
- Email campaigns
- Search engine maximization
- Presence and influence on social networking sites
- Online advertising
- Viral marketing campaigns
- Real time monitoring of on-line chatter about service quality.

History, context, criticism, and development

Although new communication technology has consistently been used by marketers, there is no doubt that the emergence of the internet created, at the end of the last century, an entirely new space in which human minds can meet. There has been a constant flow of innovation (from web sites to Google, Skype, and Twitter). Unfortunately, in many cases there has been massive over claim when these new technologies arrive, some of it related to the fast adoption of these technologies.

There are, of course, millions of people online at the time of writing. Yet, the internet began amongst a closed group of scientists and innovators in the early 1960s. So, its gestation period was approximately forty years (hardly the overnight sensation that some claim).It began to emerge when Tim Berners-Lee and, later, America's NCSA started to add open standards. It then took off fast, in a similar way to mobile phones, as the diffusion spread across the world. Maddeningly, the wild early claims which emerged as new aspects of this fascinating technology developed, seem to be both idiotically over blown and, eventually, true. Take, for instance, the suggestions when the web first took off that all shopping had to move online. That experience (which led to the "dot com crash") shows how careful marketers need to be with this phenomenon. Some people just love to shop. They set out to explore, browse, hunt bargains, touch, smell, experience, and have fun; in fact, to be entertained. This has been a human desire for many years and even the mighty internet technologies could not afford to ignore it. So, for some geeks to claim, as they did, that the internet is the "death of shopping" was absurd. In fact, very soon most were talking about "click to brick", serious understanding of the relationship between online and high street buying. Nonetheless, companies like Amazon did eventually make a fortune through new forms of shopping (while many went bust) and services like Google have transformed humanity's access to information.

Voices and further reading

- Tapscott, D., *Grown up Digital*. McGraw-Hill, 2009.
- "Net Geners' brains have indeed developed differently than those of their parents." Tapscott, D., ibid.
- ". . . the internet is forcing managers to experiment, invent, plan and change their ideas constantly while they are trying to build complex new products . . . to face the reality that competitive advantage can appear and disappear over-night. . . . however, some of the strategic precepts of the pre-internet world continue to ring true. Several core elements of competitive strategy remain criti-cal. The bewildering pace of the internet may even put a premium on these old fashioned virtues." Cusumano, M.A. and Yoffie, D.B., 1998.
- *The Future of Advertising and Agencies – A 10 year perspective*. IPA, 2007.This report sets out the findings of the extensive research and consultation process conducted by the Future Foundation for the IPA. The report outlines what advertising will mean in the future, what the agency of the future will look like and how agencies may get paid. It also sets out three possible scenarios

for the nature of the advertising and marketing communications. It proposes a new categorization which addresses the convergence that is rendering the traditional definitions increasingly meaningless. For example, how many modern TV commercials do not have some kind of response mechanism and doesn't that mean they should be part of direct marketing? And how many newspapers don't have online versions which increasingly carry video content? So the new specialties are: display v classified; unnamed v named; one-way v two-way; non-screen v screen. Their relative market shares vary depending on the future scenario whether it be the "central", "media-led", or "consumer-led" one. The report suggests that advertisers, agencies, and media owners need to consider which future scenario they think most likely and adjust their strategy accordingly. There's evidence that this report's forecasts are coming true – for instance in the massive increase in "search" advertising at the expense of "display". There's also been a proliferation of devices with screens which has led to a significant increase in screen-based communications.

- Solis, B. and Breakenridge, D., *"Putting the public back in public relations"*. Pearson Education, 2009. An interesting review of the implications to PR of new digital media like social networking sites.

Things you might like to consider

(i) Messages can be more targeted to the audience and the objectives of campaigns with this technology. For instance, marketers, often use "landing sites", which are easy to integrate into a campaign that takes buyers through a relationship to purchase.

(ii) At the time of writing, this new technology can be an excuse for sloppy and ineffective marketing. Some bang out email blasts with little thought or targeting because the "ROI" is good. In other words, they are behaving stupidly because there is very little cost in electronic communication. This method of reaching human beings needs as much thought, professionalism and sophisticated organizational capability as any other aspect of marketing communication.

(iii) Just because it is new, this form of communications need not be given immediate, overdue importance. It needs to be part of the experienced, hard-nosed discipline of marketing communications and aligned with other methods of reaching markets. Marketers need to be open-minded and explorative to the new while keeping a hard-headed perspective of how their human buyers actually behave. Marketers need to take into account the behaviour of the audience in addition to the aspirations of the online marketing team to do something innovative.

(iv) Offline customer acquisition needs to be integrated with online digital communications and any relationship marketing programmes developed for digital execution.

(v) The rise of social networking tools has promoted a rise in "network marketing" and "viral marketing". These allow for techniques which have existed in marketing practice for many years to be used across broader markets. Marketers need to integrate them into other elements of the marketing communications mix and sort out both their suitability and applicability. Although they have been presented as new, universal panaceas, they are unlikely to be so.

The digital river

Contract publishing is a highly specialized part of the marketing supply industry. The companies involved contract with marketers inside large corporations to publish magazines exclusively for their customers. The approach is routinely used by marketing directors in retail, luxury goods, car manufacturing, and business-to-business markets. One of its leading European suppliers, the River Group, was set up in 1994 by two different yet equally passionate, creative and intelligent business women: Dr Nicola Murphy and Jane Wynn. When the pair launched their customer-publishing agency they were very careful with their business plan and cash flow predictions because they were entering a very crowded market, full of established publishers owned by the big agencies. Yet they were convinced that they had a unique and distinctive approach (based on a marketing orientation) which would help them to gain share. It did.

Being marketers, their aim was to concentrate on unique, stylish "content" for their clients by really understanding their clients' customers. As a result, soon after its launch River became the UK's largest independent customer publisher (ranked independently by the UK's *Marketing Magazine*). Within a few years, they had a remarkable client list. It included: News International, Harrods, Barclays, Holland & Barratt, Superdrug, Moss Bros, Lotus, Honda, Virgin, Weight Watchers, the Ramblers, and many more. The feedback from these leading companies is an indication of the success of their focus and emphasis. For instance, Guy Cheston (Harrods' Director of Advertising and Sales) said of their work on Harrods' magazine for its high-end shoppers: "We've seen a marked improvement in the magazine. Not only have River managed to improve the quality, they've actually listened to us as a client, which makes such a difference from our previous experience. Apart from all of that, they're of course lovely people to work with and we've developed a great partnership."

At the time of writing the company still works with many of these original clients and is still the UK's largest independent customer publisher. Yet, the nature of their work with clients has fundamentally changed due to the proliferation of digital media and the increasing use of digital communications by modern consumers. They have had to re-think their business model using their original marketing philosophy to guide them through the demands of this fast developing new environment.

The business of customer publishing had been simple (albeit highly professional and competitive). The publishers created editorial content on behalf of clients which reflected their brands and their marketing objectives; and as a result the industry was dominated by marketing specialists who understood branding. They produced magazines that reflected the brand values of clients and were mailed to high value customers, sold on newsstands, or distributed in stores. The output formed part of both CRM programmes and new acquisition strategies.

Of course, River still produces customer publications, award-winning magazines, and branded content but, as the company celebrated its 16th birthday, it re-launched to become a "full service content agency". That re-launch was prompted largely by the changes in marketing communication amongst its clients due to the advent of digital media and digital marketing. So, in addition to the existing range of offers (magazines, catalogues and books) they have added: website production (in all its forms), mobile and eReader applications, animated digital magazines, viral, video, eRM, social web strategies, and fulfilment. In other words: they are a supplier of "full service digital and print content solutions".

So how did they achieve this? With a major company restructure? A complete overhaul of the business? Completely new staff? New business models? Hardly any of these, actually.

Way back at the beginning of their journey, River's founding partners built their business ethos on traditional marketing strategies. They developed a simple "5-step plan" which was emphasized to clients and employees alike. It was:

1. Listen to the needs of the (potential) client.
2. Help to produce a brief, and set key performance indicators (KPIs).
3. Listen to the needs of the client's customers.
4. Produce content that supports 1 and 3.
5. Review the effectiveness of the content (and start all over again).

One great example of this is the work that has been produced for the Holland & Barrett group. Nicola and Jane approached Holland & Barrett when they first launched River. They researched the needs of H&B's customer base, and presented a concept for a magazine to be sold in-store. "Healthy" magazine has been produced by River and sold in H&B ever since. Peter Aldis, CEO of Holland & Barrett, said of them: "They're very, very, creative, but also very focussed on ensuring that we get a return on our investment".

River made a point of continually listening to the changing needs of H&B's customer base and have evolved and developed the magazine over the years. So much so that it's now the number one selling product in store. Traditional, effective, and commercial marketing at its finest. Yet, they have recently launched for the client: a content-based website and a monthly eRM. They are now looking at wider social web strategies to engage with the customer base on a deeper level.

So the River re-brand and re-launch as a "full service content agency" was, in the eyes of the agency's leaders, just an example of the evolution that's taking place in marketing. The core business principles are the same. They do not believe the evolution of digital products has changed the fundamentals of marketing and communication. Customers, consumers, real people still want to be communicated with. They still have high expectations from brands. Consumers want to be entertained, rewarded, recognized, and spoken to. They just expect to hear through new mechanisms and to be able to respond or even talk back to brands. So, suppliers can no longer afford to just push content at consumers.

The evolving digital world has made marketing and communication more exciting, and no agency or brand can afford to ignore it. But River believe that marketers must not over complicate the process. They still follow their "5-step plan". The only difference is that they now have a wider selection of channels and tools through which they can deliver content. They still aim to deliver the right content, to the right audience, in the right way. The traditional magazine model is still included within the list of tools available to their clients, but they surround these with more interactive, often digital, elements. Nicky Murphy says:

> The real beauty of digital marketing is now we not only have more tools to deliver our content, but we also have many more tools to prove, evaluate and measure the effectiveness of everything we create. The overall processes for digital communications are very similar – we just have to think harder about our content. The content we produce for our clients can be used across multiple devices, read in many countries, interacted with in a multitude of ways. The social web landscape is our new crowded market. Cutting through the extensive array of content available to consumers is a challenge, but we believe we are best placed to do this due to the deep understanding we have of our clients and their customers. We know where our clients' customers are, and we take the time to listen.

River have also found that this perspective has helped them to retrain and reorganize their existing teams (to increase their skill sets to manage the full multi-channel offering) without radical changes in personnel or structure. Long gone are the days when agencies could pitch to clients that they needed to have both on and offline departments. That simply does not work now that digital media are a part of people's everyday life. Production departments may vary in terms of headcounts across digital and print, but an editor can now see his or her beautiful and engaging copy across a magazine, a web site, a blog, or even a little tweet. Admittedly, they have had to employ a few specialists to help produce the technical aspects for some of their clients. But rather than segregate them from the rest of the business, River have integrated them into existing client-facing teams and departments.

River have also launched a new social web agency called "Jack Content". The philosophy behind Jack is to not only create content for brands but also to hunt down the best content that's already out there. They are working with influential bloggers and the rising social web superstars to deliver further branded and engaging content.

So, the content of River is just as creative and relevant today as it was sixteen years ago. With the advent of digital marketing, it's now equally as applicable to new media and multi-channel platforms. The agency is able to offer its clients new services that will help them reach even more customers in even more efficient and effective ways. However, these experienced battle-hardened marketers are not carried away with the hyperbole and the technologies of the digital age. Their view is that people are people; and that marketing is about communicating with people in engaging ways, whether thorough digital or other means. They are still set on providing brilliant, beautiful, and creative content.

RATING: Practical and powerful

DIRECT MARKETING

Application: market communication, sales

The concept

Direct marketing is the practice of communicating to intended buyers through person-alized written or digital messages, as opposed to "above-the-line" broadcast advertising. The most common form of modern direct marketing is, of course, via the web. This is so routine that it is easy to forget that direct marketing is a broad category of work with some common principles. It can range from a letter with a printed insert to elabo-rate creative campaigns, such as sending multi-media messages complete with the MP3 or DVD equipment on which to play them. It includes: database marketing, direct mail, catalogue marketing, telemarketing, direct and response marketing. It can be used with consumers and businesses; it is also used in international marketing campaigns.

Direct communication requires an accurate and up-to-date database of contacts (something harder to achieve than might be imagined), a relevant offer, clear written technique, and a concise message. It is most effective when part of a relationship with customers (see *relationship marketing*) or when the customer has given permission to be contacted in this way. This, though, is an act of trust. Most people detest direct mail, whether physical or email. It irritates and frustrates them to receive unwanted mailers, however attractive. By giving a supplier permission to mail to them, the customer is acting on trust that the marketer will take the trouble to filter out unwanted communications and make their offers relevant. Yet, this is not always achieved, even by leading firms, due to inadequate attention given to systems and planning.

Direct communication is well known in consumer markets but is also used extensively in *business-to business marketing*. For instance, firms routinely invite customers to *hospitality* events and to seminars on technical subjects. They also send research reports or other material. Some use very effective internet-based communication. More than one merchant bank, for example, sends an internet-based newsletter on mergers and acquisition activity in their clients' industries. These are widely appreciated by people at all levels in their customers' organizations, even chief executives, because they are timely, relevant, and give valuable insight.

Email is so much the norm at the time of writing that a printed or mailed piece can stand out from the crowd. One professional membership organization, Europe's "Managing Partner Forum" was planning a conference for busy leaders. This event needed to be high profile and stimulate debate. Rather than the usual email invitation, the organizers printed and posted a high quality card, similar to those used on important social occasions like weddings. Attendance at the event was, perhaps surprisingly, up by nearly 100%. One of the attendees, the managing partner of a large professional partnership, said that the invitation stood out from others and stayed on his desk until he dealt with it; effective retro marketing in a modern age.

Marketers should ensure that direct marketing activities are as effective and well planned as any other aspect of marketing communication. If not, they will be very costly in terms of data manipulation, design, and management time. Worse, it can undermine the prestige of the firm in the minds of customers and cause dissatisfaction. Even leading firms have sent out poorly written communication, or written to dead people still caught on their poorly managed database, or inundated their customers with so much communication that they became annoyed. Most leading firms now invest in a client database with a campaign management facility. The data in this system should be seen as an asset of the firm. It needs to be kept up-to-date by internal disciplines (ensuring that sales staff keep records current) and by a, perhaps six-monthly, check with customers. It also needs to comply with local data protection laws.

History, context, criticism, and development

As with other aspects of marketing, direct marketing has a long history. For instance, Fred Gye had a big win on the British lottery and then fulfilled his dream, setting up in business as a tea merchant. He advertised himself as part of the product, emphasized quality ("Not Bohea", a product used to adulterate better teas), and branded every order over 0.25 lb, which was sent in a sealed pack with the wrapper of his shop. Quality, price, and seal were stamped on it. He soon had 500 agents in principal towns. Interestingly, this successful direct marketing business was established in the mid 1700s.

There were similar business leaders using direct marketing techniques around that time. History does not seem to record, for instance, whether, one morning in 1771, the 1,000 German aristocrats who received an unsolicited sample with a circular letter from British potter Josiah Wedgwood were astonished. It would be fascinating to know whether the language seemed strange to them, how it was packaged, and whether Josiah's designs appealed to the Germanic taste of their families. We do know, however, that the huge risk (a princely £20 per package, at a total cost of £20,000; nearly £2 million at current prices) elicited a fast response which quickly paid back and that, within two years, all but three of those that had purchased had paid in full. A factor in this success was Josiah's long-running after care package. It included a "satisfaction or money back" guarantee, free shipping, and the willingness to replace any broken item without question. Amongst the first recorded examples of service support to product purchase, it was one of the distinctive components of his approach and contributed to the success of this 300-year-old premium brand.

In 1872, American entrepreneur Montgomery Ward started to sell things through mail. His first attempt was a one-sheet mail listing items like cloth and glass. After twenty years his catalogue had grown to 1,000 pages and reached over three quarters of a million isolated American farming families. He was followed by Sears Roebuck. Its first catalogue was published in 1888 and was soon stuffed full of products like sewing machines, bicycles, fridges, dolls, and groceries. As its sales reached nearly a million dollars by the turn of the century, it put a very specific and successful form of marketing on the map. Like any form of direct marketing, it relied on: accurate address lists, a reliable reputation, and a degree of relationship with the customer. It has been estimated that, by that time (1900) there were almost 1,200 mail order businesses in America reaching around six million customers (Koehn, N.F., 2001). It is ridiculous not to regard this as direct marketing.

Later, of course, Reader's Digest took to this method of communication and earned a reputation in the West as an addict of direct marketing. Founded in 1922, its history reflects some of the successes and failures of the direct marketing industry. It grew to a fantastically large business with sales in many different countries and, reputedly reaching in excess of forty million people. Yet its tone was conservative and traditional winning it a large following amongst an elderly segment of populations. This led to recent trouble with regulators and law-makers when its (direct marketing) claims were thought to mislead elderly audiences. Also, like many direct marketers, it was severely challenged by the internet which induced changes in both postal and reading habits. It had to file for Chapter 11 insolvency and, like many direct marketers, had to rethink the way it traded.

Towards the end of the "Madmen" period of notable broadcast advertising in America, Lestor Wunderman gained fame (he is credited with creating the term "direct marketing" and created a successful direct marketing agency as a result of his reputation) through a conflict with McCann Erickson over the account of Columbia Records. It was a vast mail order club and he had handled their account using direct mail techniques for a long time. They were considering using McCann's advertising for late night awareness work. Wunderman proposed a test, which in fact was more like a duel. Two different campaigns were run in different areas. His used direct response techniques (a little gold box in magazines which viewers could find and send in for a prize). The results demonstrated that responses to Wonderman's work were up 80% but only 19.5% for McCann's (source: Gladwell, M., 2006). This prompted a rise in direct marketing and direct marketing agencies which created the impression that it came into its own around that time. It has, though, been successfully used for much longer than that.

Even the conceptual frameworks used today have been around a long time. One early marketing text book, for example, demonstrates the sophistication of direct marketing techniques nearly a hundred years ago. *Direct Mail and Mail Order* was published in the 1930s (Rittenberg, M., 1931). It was published as part of a series called *A Library of Advertising*, by the Incorporated Practitioners in Advertising in order to raise the skills of the profession. It differentiates the practice from broadcast advertising and defines "mail-order" as "selling direct to the consumer without the intervention of a personal salesman". The book covers in detail different approaches (letters, booklets, and catalogues) and different techniques (like copy style, layout, and response mechanisms). It contains detailed and sophisticated graphs on the time-response decay effect of advertising, direct techniques, and combination of the two (it argues for the latter). It even addresses in detail a bugbear of modern marketers: the need for accurate, clean customer records. It takes up considerable space with nearly fifty "discovered principles of advertising". In other words, it was attempting to codify extensive and long established practice. Although it is possible to be sniffy and pedantic about definition, it is clear that the principles of direct marketing are older and more established than many acknowledge today. Marketers of the mid 20th century adapted accumulated direct marketing experience to new technologies (like the computer) as much as today's cohorts are adjusting to the internet and email.

Voices and further reading

- "The approximate total sales of ten of the leading mail-order houses in 1915 were $350,000,000. To this total Sears, Roebuck and Company alone contributed over $100,000,000 . . . A study of marketing methods requires a dispassionate consideration of selling by mail, with particular reference to the following questions: What is its extent? What is its nature? Is it legitimate? What is its competitive strength? . . . How can the manufacturer use it to his own best advantage?" Butler, R.S., 1917.
- Bird, D., *Commonsense Direct and Digital Marketing*. Kogan Page, 2007.
- "Today, however, with the trend towards more narrowly targeted or one-to-one marketing, many companies are adopting direct marketing, either as a primary marketing approach or as a supplement to other approaches . . . [DM] consists of direct communications with carefully targeted individual customers to obtain an immediate response and cultivate lasting customer relationships." Kotler, P., 2005.

- "Direct mail was my first love – and secret weapon in the avalanche of new business acquisitions which made Ogilvy & Mather an instant success". David Ogilvy quoted in Bird, ibid.
- Direct marketing is ". . . any advertising activity which creates and exploits a direct relationship between you and your prospect or customer as an individual." Bird, ibid.
- McDonald, W.J., *Direct Marketing: An Integrated Approach*. McGraw-Hill, 1998.

Things you might like to consider

(i) The mechanisms and methods of direct marketing are old and proven. Despite the new technology, they still apply in the digital age. A good database and, a direct appeal (which combines customer knowledge with attractive creative) work as well in the internet age as they did in the mail. In fact, the disciplines could add to many who try to use digital methods to reach customers.

(ii) Direct marketing is just one aspect of integrated marketing communication which needs to be used appropriately as part of a sensible, clear communication strategy.

(iii) Data and the maintenance of clean, up-to-date records are at the heart of this technique and remain an issue for marketers today. It is not worth attempting to introduce this method of communication without an explicit and robust mechanism to set up, store, and maintain clean customer records.

Age UK is concerned with direct marketing

Age UK is a national British charity. Its purpose is to campaign, research, and provide services to older people while influencing decisions and issues at government policy level. The charity is the largest in a federation of around 300 local, independent Age Concern charities (the "federation"). Age Concern Enterprises Limited ("ACEnt") and Aid-Call Limited (Aid-Call"), wholly-owned trading subsidiaries of the charity, were recently merged to form one trading organization. Their prime purpose is to, cost effectively, raise income for the charity whilst also promoting its aims.

ACEnt's products and services were: general insurance, funeral plans, energy services, legal services, independent advice, and lotteries. (It was authorized by the British Financial Services Authority to conduct general insurance business.) However, all these products were sold under the Age Concern brand (making it easier to integrate the organizations) and all were designed with the needs of the over 50s in mind. The income raised through selling them flows back into Age UK and the members of the Trading Alliance, to support their charitable activities. The two organizations employ about 250 staff, located in London, Ashburton (Devon), and throughout the UK, in field and home-based roles. At the time of writing, there are over a million Age Concern customers, who generate upwards of £40 million in commission and gift aid income, and in excess of 40,000 Aid-Call customers.

One of the most exciting opportunities available to the new organization was the creation of a single, UK-wide database which holds the names of approximately two million people. This, together with the need to keep costs to an absolute minimum in a charity, has prompted the organization to become expert at direct and digital marketing. Direct Marketing is run by the charity's central marketing team and its affinity partners (such as E.ON, Dignity, and Fortis). Response is directed to the Age UK web site where call centres are run by "product partners" such as E.ON, Dignity, and Fortis using ACEnt's brand. The charity has structured its business model so that:

- The products are provided by third party providers (Fortis for insurance, Dignity for funeral plans, E.ON for energy plans) and can be sole or co-branded. The charity is seen by these partners as a large affinity group.
- It provides marketing investment and activity, although some of the third party providers conduct marketing activities themselves, with ACEnt's agreement.
- The main channels to market are through the TAMs. (These are face-to-face channels that look rather like travel agents talking across a desk in locations up and down the high streets of the UK.) They work locally on a face-to-face basis using direct mail shots, outbound telephone marketing, and web site promotion.
- It provides the TAMs with infrastructure support in the form of marketing, compliance, FSA guidance, market information, risk management, and training (particularly sales, marketing, product knowledge, and FSA regulatory compliance).
- In Scotland, and Northern Ireland, it has joint venture companies with the local Age UK charities. These are 50/50 joint venture companies that run the sales activities in those nations, with ACEnt providing infrastructure and financial support.

THE ENERGY OFFER

"Age Concern Energy Services" was launched in September 1999 with the prime aim of helping older people benefit from the savings that could be achieved by switching their energy supply. To do this, the charity joined forces with E.ON, one of the UK's leading energy suppliers, to develop a package of competitive energy prices and customer service designed specifically for older people.

The charity had concerns about the way energy contracts were sold, so the product was only offered via TAMs or direct through the call centre where service standards could be monitored. The product is marketed through direct marketing campaigns with responses directed to direct sales channels and the web site.

Over the last eight years it has had a positive impact on the way energy is sold and influenced the way E.ON does its business. When the industry was affected by rising wholesale costs and had to pass on price increases to customers, Age Concern and E.ON worked together in an effort to mitigate increases for Age Concern customers. On several occasions they were able to achieve a delay in price increases until after the winter months, or a mitigating cash-back to customers. They currently have around 400,000 contracts and the penetration across gas and electricity is two products per customer.

There are three bespoke products which are positioned to give best price either to lower than average or above average higher users. The features of the online proposition (which is the same as the offline product) are:

- Dedicated customer service line, free to call, and not automated, with a facility for the hard of hearing and accessibility to a video phone for the deaf.
- A guaranteed Cold Weather Payment of £10 for all gas customers (£20 for those aged 80 and over).
- Gas customers aged 60 and over may receive an additional payment above this guaranteed amount for each day the temperature drops below zero between December and February each year.
- Free hypothermia thermometer.
- Free carbon monoxide alarm (worth c £20).
- Choice of additional free and discounted energy efficiency measures when customers join the scheme.
- Face-to-face advice and assistance at around 150 Age Concerns across the country.
- Large print bills, bills in Braille, talking bills.
- Free energy efficiency advice.
- Password scheme for meter readings for extra peace of mind.
- Services for customers with priority needs.
- Exclusive discounts from E.ON for Age Concern customers on loft and cavity wall installation. These may also be installed free of charge for customers aged 70 and over or on qualifying benefits.

With Powergen and E.ON, the charity has built a customer base of approximately 220,000 over the last decade. They have gained an average of 65,000 new contracts per year over the last three years. Through this they have gained the detail on their customers' use of energy and that has allowed them to cross-sell their portfolio of products to energy customers using direct marketing. They use sales routes to the older market to develop a customer proposition to reduce energy consumption and modify behaviour. The charity has developed a successful energy efficiency scheme selling the benefits of cavity wall and loft top-up thermal insulation.

Mike Abrey-Bugg, general manager of Age UK says: "Over the last ten years we have proved that you can satisfy customer and charity require-ments whilst satisfying the commercial equation. What I mean is that we have given people in later life the confidence to switch their energy, safe in the knowledge that we a charity will ensure that their interests are looked after and in the process have secured a revenue stream for a charity to actively campaign for the interest of people in later life, a very pleasing result." Direct marketing has been at the heart of this achievement.

RATING: Practical and powerful

DIRECTIONAL POLICY MATRIX

Application: business portfolio strategy, investment, budgeting

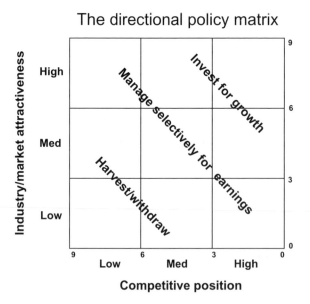

Figure D.3: The directional policy matrix

The concept

Sometimes called the "GE/McKinsey matrix", the directional policy matrix is a way of categorizing and prioritizing opportunities (see Figure D.3). It can be customized to unique content and made relevant to the individual strategic position of the company in its market place. The grid plots "market attractiveness" against "business strength" and allows management to prioritize resources accordingly. It is created in the following way:

(i)   Identify and define the strategic business units in a company.
(ii) Debate and agree the factors contributing to market attractiveness in the markets under discussion.
(iii) Agree the factors contributing to business success.
(iv) Rank and rate the market attractiveness and business strength features.
(v)   Rank each business or product unit against these criteria.
(vi) Plot the SBUs on the matrix.
(vii) Represent the total size of the market and the business's market share by a pie chart at the appropriate plot on the matrix.

Steps (iv) and (v) involve numerically rating the relative importance of each feature. Multiplying these together and totalling them for each business unit gives a composite score which allows marketers to plot the businesses on the matrix.

This visual presentation means that complex information can be presented in an easily understood form and strategy can be deduced from the matrix. Where a business unit scores high or medium on business strength or market attractiveness the firm should maintain or grow investment. Whereas those which score low/low or low/medium should have investment cut. If possible, cash should be harvested from them. Units scoring high/low or medium/medium should be examined to see if selective investment should be made to increase earnings.

History, context, criticism, and development

This tool was developed (by the American coporation GE) soon after the Boston Matrix as a result of inadequacies with it. It was typical of several methods of "multi-factor portfolio models" which were developed at the time. (There is some suggestion, incidentally, that the term "directional policy matrix," originally belonged to a tool developed by oil giant Shell which compared "prospects for sector profitability" against "competitive capability".) The original GE matrix used the market attractiveness and business strength factors which are listed on the next page. GE used these factors because they believed that, taken together, they had the most influence on return on investment in their industry. However, this list should be modified for each company according to its own particular circumstances.

Factors of market attractiveness and business strength used in the original GE matrix

Market attractiveness	Business strength
Size	Size
Growth rates	Growth rate
Competitive intensity	Market share
Profitability	Profitability
Technology impacts	Margins
Social impacts	Technology position
Environmental impacts	Strengths and weaknesses
Legal impacts	Image
Human impacts	Environmental impact
	Management

The fact that this concept uses several dimensions to assess business units instead of two, and that it is based on ROI rather than cash flow, makes it a different, and probably better tool than the Boston Matrix. However it is criticized because:

(i) It offers only broad strategy guidelines with no indication as to precisely what needs to be done to achieve strategy.
(ii) There is no indication of how to weight the scoring of market attractiveness and business strengths. As such it is highly subjective.
(iii) Evaluation of the scoring is also subjective.
(iv) The technique is more complex than the Boston Matrix and requires much more extensive data gathering.
(v) The approach does not take account of inter-relationships between business units.
(vi) It is not supported by empirical research or evidence. For instance there does not seem to be evidence that market attractiveness and business position are related to ROI.
(vii) It pays little attention to business environment.

Voices and further reading

- McDonald, M.H.B. and Wilson, H., "Marketing Plans: How to prepare them, how to use them" John Wiley and Sons Ltd, 2011.
- McDonald, M.H.B., "Some methodological comments on the directional policy matrix" *Journal of Marketing Management*, 6, 1990.
- "The first time managers try using the directional policy matrix, they frequently find that the circles do not come out where expected. One possible reason for this is a misunderstanding concerning the use of market attractiveness factors. Please remember, you will be most concerned about the potential for growth in

volume, growth in profit, and so on for your organization in each of your markets." McDonald, ibid.

- Wilson, M.S. et al, "Strategic marketing management" Butterworth-Heinemann, 1992.
- Johnson, G. and Scholes, K., "Exploring Corporate Strategy, Prentice Hall, 2002.
- "This portfolio logic is about understanding the relative strength of a business in the context of its markets so as to make decisions about investment, acquisition and divestment". Johnson and Scholes, ibid.
- Kotler, P. "Principles of marketing." Pearson, 2005.
- ". . . these approaches focus on classifying current businesses but provide little advice for future planning. Management must still rely on its judgement to set the business objectives . . . ", Kotler, ibid.

Things you might like to consider

(i) This is really powerful as a tool to reach consensus amongst a group of leaders. The definition of business units, the agreement of common criteria and, particularly, the joint scoring exercise stimulate debate which is very valuable. So it is particularly useful in organizations where leadership seeks consensus such as professional partnerships, and some cultures, such as Swedish corporations.

(ii) A major decision in the process of using this tool is the degree to which leaders will be involved in the detail of its construction. Too little involvement means that they will criticize the criteria and scoring; too much and their patience will be tried. This, more than the tool itself, determines the success or failure of any attempt to use it.

Russell Reynolds Associates hunts in sectors

Russell Reynolds Associates is one of the world's leading international executive search firms. Founded in the latter half of the 20th century (1969), it specializes in finding executives for the top jobs of leading companies. It has 31 offices around the world and more than 40 specialist practice areas.

Historically, the firm had grown by the creation of local geographic offices as teams in major cities established and developed client relationships. However, like other professional services firms, the partners found that clients tended to come back to search consultants who had expertise in their industry sector. Also, as searches became increasingly international, clients valued search consultants who knew their industry sector (and key individuals within it) more than a local geography. So they naturally grew specialties in certain industry sectors such as "investment banking", "technology", and "consumer products".

Debate grew within the firm about how to prioritize opportunities and where to invest. How should the firm decide whether "global telecommunications"

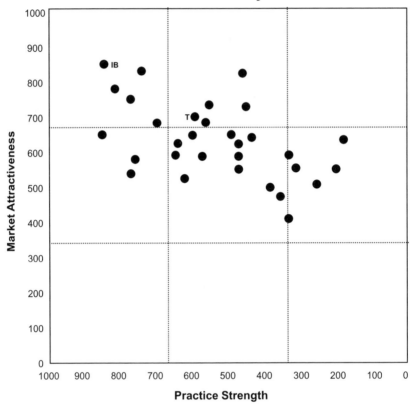

Figure D.4 Directional policy matrix

had more potential than, say "consumer products" or geographies such as the newly liberated Eastern European markets? Where should the leadership team invest partners, staff, and marketing programmes? What was the mechanism by which scarce resources would be allocated?

By the mid 1990s the firm had reached the point where it needed to reach a consensus on how to prioritize the approach to industry sectors. It decided to use the GE/McKinsey matrix as a tool to structure its thinking.

The first step was to define each industry sector, something which the firm hadn't done before. Partners were surprised by two things: the actual number of claimed industry specialisms and the difference in the understanding of what comprised such sectors. The discussion among the industry leaders in the firm revealed differences about which clients would belong to which sector. After debate, the group produced an agreed, defined list of the main sectors.

Lead partners then began to consider the criteria which made any of those markets attractive to them. The technique required the group to produce a clear, ranked, and graded set of criteria. Again, this was a very useful debate because it helped to make explicit different assumptions by partners about what made the markets attractive. The debate produced criteria about what made a market attractive to the firm – these had previously been unarticulated and diverse.

The final list included criteria such as "potential growth", "client size", "ability to earn fees", and "sector turbulence". Once the criteria were agreed, each was then rated out of 10 to produce a prioritized list.

The next step was to decide what characteristics make a practice (whether belonging to Russell Reynolds or its competitors) strong in each of the markets. After debate, the final criteria included: "brand strength", "dominance in sector", and "partner expertise". As with market criteria, the final list was ranked out of 10.

The industry leaders then ranked each practice against those criteria. So, for example, the industry leader for investment banking (the firm's strongest practice) was asked to indicate how the practice stood against each of those criteria by giving marks out of 10. By multiplying each practice's score against the criteria score, a plot on a matrix was produced. Once all the practices were plotted, a final matrix, shown in Figure D.4 above, was agreed.

The final matrix proved to be a useful basis for debate and decisions. Investment strategies were naturally discussed and agreed by the group. For instance, at the time, the technology practice was seen to be in a highly attractive market but it was weaker than investment banking. The group therefore decided to invest partners, staff, and marketing programmes in it. Other, less attractive areas were denied funding or had resources depleted.

The power of the exercise was the use of the tool to generate debate among the leaders of the sectors and to reach consensus about investment strategy. As each practice was ranked, colleagues challenged their peers and reached a workable consensus.

 RATING: Practical and powerful

F

 **FEATURES ANALYSIS**

Application: component design for products and services, value proposition development

Features analysis

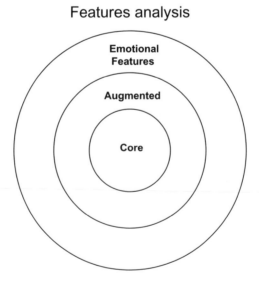

Figure F.1: A representation of the three layers of product or service features

The concept

This is a method used in product and service design to plan the components of an offer. It helps marketers, designers, engineers, and production people to plan the elements of a product or service in great detail. It allows for the fact that buyers often do not know exactly what they are looking for and will explore a range of different options, with a different mix of features at different price points, when researching a purchase (whether for personal or business use). For instance, suppose a business woman wants to buy a new pair of shoes to go with a dark-coloured dress for an important, formal dinner. She is likely to have in mind a number of different attributes that her new shoes must include such as: style, colour, fit, brand, and price (represented in Figure F.2 below).

These attributes vary in nature and importance according to individual preference, occasion, and culture. For example, in this instance, the subtlety of each feature is likely to be different than for a special occasion in a social context. "Fit" might be more sensible and "style" more conservative if senior colleagues or customers will be present. Ideal "colour" though might still be a complete match with the intended outfit. Different people will describe the features differently and rank them in different orders of importance, but "price" will always be ranked after several other features.

Using a research technique called "zones of tolerance" (see Ziethaml, V. and Bitner, M. J., 2003) each of these attributes can be broken down into the customer's "ideal", "acceptable", and "unacceptable" components; as shown in Figure F.3 below.

During the evaluation phase of the purchase, it is likely that the buyer will come across a number of different choices which meet these needs. She may, for example, see three shoes with the features shown in Figure F.4. All three are candidates to fit her varied criteria, despite being very different.

Shoes: A fictional example of graded product features

Features			
Style			
Brand			
Colour			
Fit			
Price			

Figure F.2:   Fictional features in new shoe purchase

Shoes: A fictional example of graded product features

Features	Ideal	Acceptable	Unacceptable
Style	High heel	Lower heel	Flats
Brand	Jimmy Choos	Kurt Geiger	Local discount store
Colour	Perfect match	Black	White
Fit	Perfect	Can only walk in	Too tight
Price	$150	$250	$500

Figure F.3:   Graduated features

Shoes: A fictional example of graded product features

Features	Ideal	Acceptable	Unacceptable
Style	Very high heel	Lower heel	Flats
Brand	Jimmy Choos	Kurt Geiger	Local discount store
Colour	Perfect match	Black	White
Fit	Perfect	Can only walk in	Too tight
Price	$150	$250	$500

Figure F.4:   Different choices of shoes

The generic approach to this technique is normally to use three levels of features, as shown in Figure F.1. They are:

- "The core feature". This is the hub of the offer and is the prime benefit to buyers. In the case of a briefcase it will be to "carry documents", whereas, for a car, it would be "personal transportation".
- "Augmented features". These are the many physical components of the offer which the marketer chooses to use to represent the core feature. A briefcase for example, would compose: choice of leather, latches, nature of stitching, internal construction, etc. A car, of course, would include the engine, the bodywork, the

colour, and the physical layout. This is very much the design and assembly of physical components around identified customer need but may have elements like: process, technology, and remote service access.

- "Emotional features". These are designed to appeal to the buyers' underlying, sometimes unknown and unarticulated, emotional requirements. They are often the most influential aspects of the appeal of the proposition and particularly affect perceptions of value. Without them many offers become commodities. Although these are actually offered through the physical (augmented) features, the emotional ring of the planning tool is there to remind designers to proactively plan their presence. They are particularly tied to the firm's brand values. For example, the emotional promise of a briefcase that is labelled "Gucci" will give a different message than one which is labelled "Wal-Mart".

Figure F.5 represents the design of a product where brand and service are being used as emotional features. The service element (a maintenance or warranty contract) is primarily an emotional reassurance to a product offer. The supplier has accepted (probably because it is based on new technology) that faults will occur in their product. The promise is: "Don't worry, if it goes wrong we'll repair it quickly and efficiently". However, its impact reduces as technology becomes more stable. Few consumers in the West, for example, buy extended warranty with televisions.

There are times, though, when service is engineered into the product; it becomes an augmented feature. This occurred, for example, in the computer industry during the latter half of the 20th century. Suppliers began to provide preventative maintenance through a monitored service involving people, procedures, and technology. In an entirely different market, OTIS elevators launched an "intelligent elevator" which

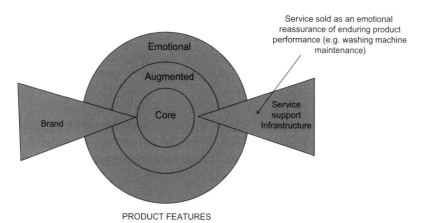

Figure F.5:   A product where brand and service are emotional features

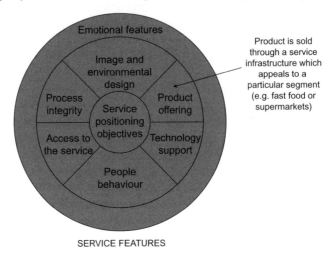

Figure **F.6:**   The hybrid model

had technology as part of its manufacture and allowed a remote service desk to access it to undertake routine, remote diagnostics, as a mechanism to pre-empt any failures. It was sold as part of the product offer so that the product failed less due to self-diagnostic technology and preventative maintenance. Service had become an augmented component of the product offer in an attempt to ensure that the product did not fail at all.

Figure F.6 represents the hybrid, a position where people are buying a mix of service and product, and it is hard to distinguish between the two. It is common in industries which offer a high volume, low margin product. The fast food industry, for example, uses service to sell a cheap product. In places like KFC or MacDonald's, the brand, environmental design, product range, technology support, people behaviour, method of accessing the service, and the process through which the service is provided are all integrated into a holistic experience which people buy. However, hybrids are also seen in complex business-to-business markets. It is quite common, for example, for suppliers to offer their customers systems integration projects or complex, integrated "solutions". Others have sophisticated, world-wide, "chase-the-sun" help desks which allow highly qualified engineers to access customers' facilities in real time. All have the elements of a hybrid model.

On the other hand, some companies offer a proposition (shown in Figure F.7) which has almost no physical or product content. An example would be management consultancy or law, where any physical components (e.g. slides or bound reports) are merely an emotional reassurance to the buyer that good quality and high value exist in the offer. The tangible elements are a reassurance of the intangible benefit, making

A service offer

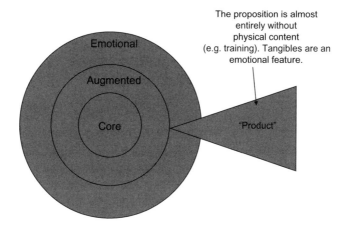

The proposition is almost
entirely without
physical content
(e.g. training). Tangibles are an
emotional feature.

Emotional

Augmented

Core

"Product"

FEATURES OF A SERVICE OFFER

Figure F.7:   A pure service

the intangible offer more tangible, one of the principles of services marketing. Tangible components particularly help with *post purchase distress*.

It is the detailed and proactive management of the mix of features in this way that allows marketers to design increasingly sophisticated versions of their offer in the light of feedback from markets. This allows evolution of real choice and helps marketers to create profit through the creation of differentiated offers

History, context, criticism, and development

Various academics and marketing writers have described this mix of features in various ways. Professor Phillip Kotler (Kotler, P., 2003), for instance, said that products and services are propositions augmented by intangible marketing concepts such as brand and design. His layers of features are: core benefit, basic product, expected product, augmented product, and potential product. Professor Malcolm McDonald, on the other hand, distinguishes between core product and "product surround". In the latter he describes three layers of features as: efficacy, services, and intangibles (McDonald, M.H.B. and Wilson, H., 2011).

Voices and further reading

- "Products are almost always combinations of the tangible and intangible. An automobile is not simply a machine for movement visibly or measurably differentiated by design, size, color, options, horsepower, or mile per gallon. It is also a complex symbol denoting status, taste, rank, achievement, aspiration and (these days) being 'smart' − that is, buying fuel economy rather than display. But the consumer buys even more than these attributes." Levitt, T., 1965.

• "A product is anything that can be offered to a market to satisfy a want or a need. Products . . . include physical goods, services, experiences, places, properties, organizations, information and ideas. The marketer needs to think through five levels of the product. Each adds more customer value . . ." Kotler, P., 2003.

• ". . . product surround can account for as much as 80 per cent of the added value and impact of a product. Often, these only account for about 20 percent of costs, whereas the reverse is often true of the core product." McDonald, M.H.B. and Wilson, H., 2011.

Things you might like to consider

(i) The importance of emotion in the planning of a business-to-business proposition is just as critical as it is in consumer propositions. Human beings are prompted as much by emotional factors at work as at home. The ability of the emotional components of an offer to influence the perceived value business-to-business offers should not be neglected. If it is, the product or service will become a commodity.

(ii) Services are often poorly designed and ill prepared because they are intangible. In some cases, companies simply make up an idea and hope customers will buy it; they would then work out how to deliver it. Features analysis forces marketers to think through the detail of a service proposition and have it engineered as carefully as any manufactured product.

(iii) Experience shows that the identification of the core feature can be one of the most difficult aspects of product and service design. It can be inordinately difficult to settle on the core proposition, even if it seems blindingly obvious once settled.

(iv) This technique needs to be adjusted to take on board the observation by Lynne Shostack (Shostack, G.L., 1977) that propositions from companies are neither all product nor all service. Using her goods/services spectrum of offers (see *services marketing*) different models of different features mixes can be used with real precision.

(v) If a marketer chooses to use features analysis they should use the correct design model. It may be, for example, that market conditions have changed and a service which was once associated with a product offer can be positioned as an entity which has value in its own right; or, vice versa, a service is now being offered through self-service technology. In each, a different features mix must be used.

(vi) Despite what many sales people say when they lose a deal, no-one, in any part of the world, buys products solely "on price". They don't go "looking for a bit of price" but a product or service to meet their needs and there will always be anywhere from two to four product attributes that will be more important than price. If all of these more important attributes are exactly the same as competitor products, then price becomes the only difference. So, if suppliers do compete on price, it's because they haven't understood the cluster of needs that are in their buyers' minds, and created a distinct offer that meets those needs. If they are competing on price or are offering a commodity, it is their own fault.

 RATING: Practical and powerful

 GAP MODEL

Application: diagnosis of client service issues, development of service strategy

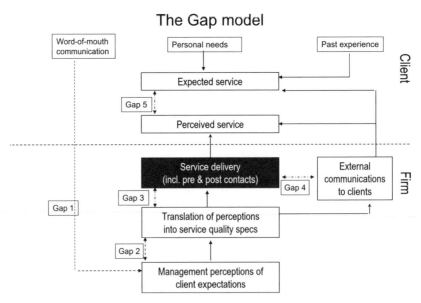

Figure G.1: The Gap model

The concept

This model (see Figure G.1) is a method of diagnosing difficulties with service quality and analysing the source of potential improvements. It was designed and proposed by a group of academics (Parasuraman et al., 1985) who specialize in service marketing studies. It is built on the assumptions that:

- Quality and customer satisfaction is a comparison between the delivery that customers expect to receive and performance they perceive they receive. Satisfaction depends on the degree to which the two match (or not).
- Customers find service quality more difficult to evaluate than product quality because they have few tangible clues so must rely on other evidence of the quality they are likely to receive.
- Quality evaluation by buyers depends on outcomes and processes. Quality can be influenced by technical outcomes and functional or service outcomes. It can also be influenced by physical aspects of the service and by company image as much as by the interaction with service staff.

The original investigation to substantiate the model was conducted in financial and product repair services. It has, however, been widely tested and developed since. It identifies and focuses upon five "gaps":

(i)   The management perception gap
      This is any difference between management's views and those of the customers or the market in general.
(ii) The quality specification gap
      This exists when quality standards, strategy, or plans do not reflect management objectives or views.
(iii) The service delivery gap
      This exists if there is a difference between quality strategy or plans and the firm's delivery to customers.
(iv) The market communications gap
      This tracks any difference between marketing communications (say a lag in customer perception) and service delivery.
(v)   The perceived service gap
      This exists if there is a difference between the service delivery perceived to be experienced by customers and their expectations. Note the emphasis on perception of experience. What they think they experience may not be reality and might be addressed through marketing campaigns.

Research, customer feedback, and accurate data need to be collected at the point of each gap to compare and contrast opinion or experience. This brings into sharp relief the differences between various perceptions and experiences. It allows the leadership

The SERQUAL Model

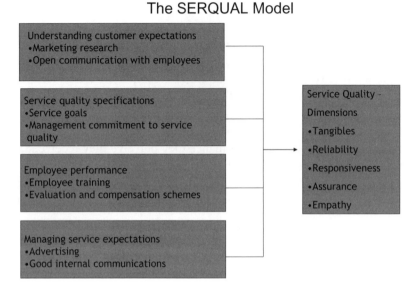

Figure G.2:   The SERVQUAL tracking mechanism

to construct very specific improvement programmes in all relevant areas of business.

History, context, criticism, and development

In the 1980s a group of marketing academics set out to research quality of service in depth. They said that their objectives were to "attack head-on the mystique, mush and myths that surround the service-quality issue" (Ziethaml et al., 1990). They also set out to develop a practical framework by which quality issues could be diagnosed, improved, and managed. After extensive qualitative and large-scale empirical studies they developed the Gap model. Based on that they created an ongoing measurement process called "SERVQUAL" (see Figure G.2).

They suggested ten dimensions of quality which should be measured in a systematic way. They are:

*   Tangibles: appearance of facilities, personnel equipment etc.
*   Reliability: ability to perform the promised service
*   Responsiveness: willingness to help
*   Competence: possession of the required skills
*   Courtesy: politeness, respect etc.
*   Credibility: trustworthiness, believability
*   Security: freedom from danger or risk

- Access: approachability and ease of contact
- Communication: keeping customers informed
- Understanding: making the effort to know customers and their needs.

Voices and further reading

- "The strength of the gap methodology is that it offers generic insights and solutions that can be applied across different industries. What it doesn't attempt, of course, is to identify specific quality failures that may occur in particular service businesses. Each firm must develop its own customized approach to ensure that service quality becomes and remains a key objective." Lovelock et al., 1999.
- "The gaps model of service quality brings customer focus and service excellence together in a structured practical way." Zeithaml and Bitner, 2003.
- Parasuraman, S., Ziethmal, V.A., and Berry, L.L., "A conceptual model of service quality and its implications for future research". *Journal of Marketing*, 49, Fall 1985.
- Zeithaml, V.A., Parasuraman, A., and Berry, L.L., *Delivering Quality Service*. Free Press, 1990.
- "Overnight service-quality miracles are more a figment of lecture-circuit rhetoric than organizational reality. The truth is that it usually takes longer to materially improve service than the sponsors of this change anticipate, and then, it takes longer still for the customers to notice . . . we lay no claims to breakthrough thinking that will quickly raise an organization's SERVQUAL scores. Instead we discuss some practical necessities for giving an organization a decent chance to move forward on quality." Ziethaml et al., ibid.
- "There have been numerous criticisms of SERVQUAL for the inductive nature of the original research in that it failed to draw on the theory base in the disciplines of psychology, social sciences and economics." Palmer, 2005.

Things you might like to consider

(i) This work demonstrated very effectively that customers' perception of quality of service depended on the service they perceived they received compared to their articulated and unarticulated expectations.

(ii) This model was based on extensive exploratory research undertaken by several respected researchers and academics. It has general principles which are likely to be applicable across many situations.

(iii) The original phases of the research were completed in the late 1980s and early 1990s in the United States of America. The geographic limitations and the historical context may mean that it needs to be adapted in certain situations.

(iv) Later concepts around "the customer journey" and "customer experience management" have introduced subtleties into service quality thinking which are very relevant to marketers (the expectations raised by the brand for instance and the importance of emotional empathy). This is, nonetheless, a very practical and grounded planning tool.

(v) This is probably, like other tools of the time, a little too linear and fails to really take into account behavioural issues.

⭐ **RATING: Practical and powerful**

GLOBALIZATION OF MARKETS

Application: Affects pretty much every aspect of cross border marketing work

The concept

In the latter half of the 20th century, it became common to talk about "globalization". The crux of this argument is that a number of powerful forces are driving the world towards convergence and commonality. They include: a growing consensus amongst educated populations (e.g. about sustainability and global warming), the emergence of international trading blocks, greater political integration, and technology (like the internet). These have prompted the free flow of capital and enabled big world-wide markets to evolve. It has allowed suppliers in markets as different as professional services, vacations, information, and commodities (to name but a few) to access much larger groups of customers. A revolution in communications technologies has allowed media like film, music, and the internet to create aspiration amongst massive world-wide audiences; prompting, in turn, the evolution of gigantic markets. In parallel, political initiatives like the GAAT rounds and the emergence of the European Union have added to the creation of common standards in international markets. This has had implications to the capital flows which enable businesses to grow and to the political or legislative frameworks in which they operate. More than one politician and many business leaders have been heard to talk about the inevitability of globalization; that protectionism cannot be resisted, Canute-like, in this fast harmonizing international community.

So, the globalization of markets has become a familiar basis for strategy in the boardroom of businesses throughout the world. It is particularly familiar to technology companies as firms like Microsoft, IBM, Oracle, Nokia, and Ericsson have become famous brands across the world with offices and factories on almost every continent. Marketers must consider how global their offer will be. Is it to be a ubiquitous, world-wide entity which is the same wherever it is used and communicated in the same way with the same methods and message? Many voices would argue that it should.

In the early 1980s, for example, Theodore Levitt published an influential article in the *Harvard Business Review* on the globalization of markets (Levitt, T., 1983). He pointed out that people around the world have similar aspirations for their life and family. He argued that this was an opportunity for international firms to save costs. They should be able to create common processes in brand management, advertising, and distribution, improving profit through a new international strategy: global marketing. The global approach would be owned by no culture but would serve all equally well with a common offer. While demonstrating his sophisticated understanding of *cultural differences*, Levitt argued that these were declining in influence in the face of standardized products, which derive from commonality of preference.

In this view, multi-nationals which accommodate national preferences in their approach are thoughtlessly accommodating poor marketing which "means giving the customer what he says he wants". A global strategy would be to create a cheap, reliable, ubiquitous product, which would appeal to a universal need and would create markets for that proposition by investment in marketing communication or brand advertising. Levitt suggested that marketers should set out to convince different audiences to subsume their cultural tastes; to convince them that a ubiquitous global offer is what they want. Some well established global offers (such as Coca-Cola) were cited as leaders in this approach.

History, context, criticism, and development

Unfortunately we have been here before. Proponents of globalization seem unaware that the world was once very global (enabling the direct marketing of numerous offers and free flow of capital) but drew back from it. In 1920, for instance, the great economist, Maynard Keynes (Keynes, M., 1920) illustrated this by describing the ease of access to international goods in London before the First World War. In the three decades prior to 1910, the world saw an expansion of new, enabling technology (telegraphy, steam ships, and the railway), which created world-wide networks.

This led many to think that there would be an ever closer integration of political structures and greater freedom of trade. H.G. Wells (the scientist and novelist who predicted the internet nearly a century before its advent) even mooted the idea that a "world government" was inevitable. Yet the world community fractured. Around 1880 countries began to introduce tariff barriers to restrict the free flow of goods and (in 1914, with the advent of passports) restrictions on the free flow of people. War and the economic depression then prompted restrictions on the free flow of capital and higher, protectionist, trade barriers.

It is yet to be seen whether the global recession, the credit crunch, and the vast appetite for commodities amongst developing nations, at the start of the 21st century will damage global integration. Nevertheless, there has been a resurgence of national identity and a dislike of some Western offers in much of the world which flies in the face of a ubiquitous, global marketing approach. For the marketer this prompts an horrendous strategic dilemma which could, quite literally, destroy the company. Is the offer going to be presented as a local proposition available in some other countries or a truly global offer? The answer to that question needs to be carefully considered and thoroughly analysed. Investment in the chosen direction needs to be assessed, planned, and carefully controlled. This, combined with high profile failures to achieve global positioning, has caused all but a few established firms to attempt risky investment in truly global strategies. Instead, many are adopting a "think global/act local" strategy, which acknowledges the impact of local *cultural differences* on marketing. The international Japanese technology company, Fujitsu, is, for example, currently adopting a "trans-national" approach to IT services (see case study in the *cultural differences* section) and the Chinese white goods manufacturer Haier (see the case study in the *international marketing* entry) is decentralizing its research, innovation, marketing, and sales capabilities into regional clusters of expertise.

Voices and further reading

- "... and then in London, a man could order by his telephone, sipping his morning tea in bed, the various products of the earth, in various quantities that he might see fit, and reasonably expect their early delivery upon his doorstep." Keynes, M., 1920.
- Levitt, T., "The globalization of markets", *Harvard Business Review*, May 1983.
- "... different cultural preferences, national tastes and standards ... are vestiges of the past. Some die and some become global propositions (Italian food, American rock music, French wine etc)." Levitt, ibid.
- "An all embracing world system of virtually unrestricted flows of capital, labour and goods never actually existed, but between 1860 and 1875 something not too far removed from it came into being." Hobsbawm, E., 1999.
- Aaker, D.A. and Joachimsthaler, E., "The lure of global branding". *Harvard Business Review*, November–December 1999.
- "Managers who stampede blindly toward creating a global brand without considering whether such a move fits well with their company or their markets risk falling off a cliff. There are several reasons for that. First, economies of scale may prove elusive ... Second, forming a successful global brand team can prove difficult. Third, global brands can't just be imposed on all markets ... taking a more nuanced approach is the better course of action." Aaker and Joachimsthaler, ibid.
- Hollis, N., *The Global Brand*. MacMillan, 2008.
- "The formula that makes a brand strong in one country may not travel well. Consumer needs and values still differ dramatically from place to place. Few brand positionings readily stretch across different cultures. The process of going global not only magnifies the complexity of building a strong brand but adds new barriers to success." Hollis, ibid.

- "... globalization creates not a uniform but a diverse culture ... Globalization creates universal global culture while at the same time strengthening traditional culture as a counter balance. This is the socio-cultural paradox of globalization, which has the most direct impact on individuals or consumers." Kotler, P. et al., 2010.

Things you might like to consider

(i) The emphasis on globalization emerged as a forceful concept just after the collapse of the iron curtain. It was particularly strong in America where a wide range of people assumed that democracy, force, and free markets would be universally accepted prompting the "end of history".

(ii) For at least 4,000 years, human history has been about the relationships between great powers. Businesses have been able to trade within negotiated treaties backed by the power of diplomacy and law. Although many parts of the world look uniform, do you really think that has changed very much? How much do international treaties and trade agreements actually harmonize business?

(iii) When some international business people talk about globalization they mean the main centres of capital (New York, London, Hong Kong etc.) only.

(iv) Cultural differences are strong and reasserting themselves (see separate entry). This has massive implications for marketing.

(v) There are, in fact, very few truly global brands and those that develop often do so on the back of a powerful force rather than their own resources. Coca-Cola, for instance, became a global brand on the back of its support for American forces during the Second World War. (General Eisenhower ordered three million cokes and bottling capabilities when planning the invasion of Italy.) Taking the decision to invest in building a global brand is a vast undertaking.

 RATING: Toxic

H

HOSPITALITY AND CUSTOMER ENTERTAINMENT

Application; communication, sales, relationship marketing

The concept

This is the use of social entertainment for commercial advantage. It ranges from large customized events, through packages bought at public events (such as the Ryder Cup or Wimbledon) to smaller, more intimate occasions with like-minded groups of customers, and right down to individual customer entertainment (like taking an individual to dinner or lunch). There is evidence of different hospitality habits in different industries. The legal sector, for instance, tends to wine and dine its clients, while pharmaceutical companies tend to go for team building events.

There are several reasons why this technique helps marketing and sales:

(i) The informal situation can help create a relationship with customers, which will encourage further business. A well managed and customized event can certainly help two people to understand each other better – a major feature of relationship marketing. It is especially effective if part of a wider communications programme and should be planned as an aspect of either *relationship marketing* or *marketing communications*.

(ii) It helps to build trust and undermine wrong impressions. Whether in a consumer or business-to-business situation, a setting which helps people to get to know a company and its executives destroys wrong perceptions and encourages positive impressions which help sales.

(iii) An important principle of human relationships and, particularly, *business-to-business* marketing is reciprocity. It is the mutual giving of one professional to another and it occurs in relationships with buyers and fellow suppliers. In all professions, for instance, reciprocity generates work. Some psychologists have identified it as an important ingredient in human relations and their work has, in turn, seeped into behavioural economics; a field of work which is beginning to affect marketing thinking. Professor Leonard Berry (one of the world's leading specialists in *services marketing*; see Berry, L.L., 1995) said, after years of study into successful service companies, that a prime ingredient in their success was "generosity"; his word for reciprocity. Relationships cannot progress unless there is mutual investment in the professional relationship.

There can, though, be a number of significant problems with hospitality marketing activities. They include:

(i) The wrong attendees at any related event

It is a fact of life that real decision makers are normally very busy and focused on their work. Most achievers in line jobs, including specialties like purchasing directors, don't have time to spare for optional, pleasant events. Sensible senior people allow themselves just one or two a year, particularly if it is to further relationships with one of their trusted suppliers. Other than that, they normally prefer to spend their scarce free time with their family and friends. Attendees from customers can therefore be "stand ins", perhaps using a reward from their boss, or persistent hospitality takers with no real authority. Worse, the recipients of hospitality can be the suppliers own employees, filling numbers at the last moment. As a result it can have no real effect on actual buying decisions.

(ii) Regulatory restrictions

Some people, particularly public sector organizations, cannot accept hospitality.

(iii) Legislation

Modern legislation, such as recent moves in the UK to control bribery, can interfere with this method of marketing.

(iv) Alignment with marketing objectives

It may not be appropriate to the marketing objectives of the organization. According to one specialist (see Robert, J., 2009) tracking of satisfaction scores with a thousand hospitality packages in Britain showed that only 60% were relevant to the needs of the brands which they were intended to promote.

(v) Vulnerability to cost control and volatility

It is easily cut and very sensitive to recession. In 2009, for example, *The Times* reported that hospitality plummeted by 25%; even for blue ribbon events like Wimbledon and Formula One.

(vi) Culpability for poor behaviour

It is an unpleasant fact of life that some customers can behave badly at hospitality events as alcohol flows freely. In these situations, though, it is normally the host that is culpable if, say, there is an accusation of sexual harassment from employees or subcontracted waiting staff at the venue.

(vii) Reputation risk

Some events and some hospitality practices risk damaging the reputation of the firm, and so future revenues. The international marketing leader of one blue chip firm was horrified to find, for instance, that its representatives in one Asian country were routinely spending hospitality budgets on trips to prostitutes with customers.

(viii) Over lavish provision

There can be a lot of waste and indulgence simply because it is designed for customers. This can be a particular problem in a recession. Although elite buyers in some cultures will still expect five-star treatment, others can be perturbed by excess and waste during times of austerity.

History, context, criticism, and development

This method of marketing has been used by marketers and sales people for many, many years. In 1799, for instance, Matthew Boulton, a market-orientated British businessman, was trying to persuade the Russian ambassador to use his machines for the Russian mint. Historian Jenny Uglow describes this as "corporate hospitality on a lavish scale" (Uglow, J., 2003). During one visit they saw Hamlet and a farce, had elegant dinners, musical evenings, daytime tours, and a customized hospitality event.

The latter was a "secret expedition". A specially upholstered barge took the ambassador to see the manufacturing capability, led by another barge crammed with musicians. On the return journey they went through the Dudley tunnel into the huge limestone caverns under Dudley Castle which were suddenly lit by a hundred torches, accompanied by a fanfare from the musicians' boat.

Since then, customer hospitality has routinely been used by marketers, sales people, and business leaders to help cement relationships and sales success. It has been used in a range of industries from banking and the professions to luxury goods and media. In more recent times, marketers have developed organizational competence in this field. Many large firms have dedicated teams that are expert in choosing the appropriate hospitality mechanism to suit strategic objectives and handling the range of administrative details needed to make it successful. They work with an array of specialized agencies that operate in this field, using their expertise in the same way that marketers might use an advertising (or any other) agency.

Over recent years, with increasing experience and sophistication in hospitality and the plethora of options open to customers from competing suppliers, hospitality programmes have changed shape. "One size fits all" packages have been replaced by bespoke experiences for customers. Modern events can, for example, be either "issue-led", bringing customers with similar questions together to share knowledge and approaches, or they are events that customers themselves cannot buy. Several companies have taken advantage of the popularity of the Harry Potter films, for example, offering advanced screenings to customers and their families before the latest film goes on general release. When BT used this approach, it even hired actors in costume to make the event more memorable for important customers and their families.

Voices and further reading

- "Hospitality involves taking care of the customer. It finds its full expression in face-to-face encounters with the customer. The enterprise should show pleasure at meeting new customers and recognizing existing ones when they return. It may include elements such as offer of transport to and from the service site, availability of drinks, and other amenities, customer recognition systems etc. Here there is a need to adopt the Disney philosophy and treat all customers as guests." Payne, A., *Handbook of CRM*. Butterworth-Heinemann, 2006.
- "Companies may take care of customers by offering them gifts, free entertainment or corporate hospitality. Freebies such as a calendar or a fountain pen carrying the supplier's logo are usually accepted by clients without a second thought. A nice dinner merely to build client relations or to keep in touch with a valued customer rarely raises an eyebrow. Corporate entertaining or hospitality is an expected part of business life . . . In the absence of clear corporate or standard guidelines, how would managers decide whether a gift, meal or trip is acceptable or sleazy?" Kotler, P., 2005.

Things you might like to consider

(i) It is probably too obvious to say (and therefore worth saying) that hospitality needs to be well planned, with the objectives, suitability, and intended audience carefully thought through. There is nothing worse than letting customers down by holding a shoddy, poorly planned event. Even a simple lunch with one customer ought to be thought about. What is the most suitable venue in which to hold it and does the intended style of occasion suit the objectives of the discussion? Can the diary allow the main participants time to get there promptly and lavish enough attention on their guests? (More than one customer has been treated to events, by surprisingly large and sophisticated companies, where their hosts were distracted by matters outside the room. Can leaders, for instance, switch their mobiles off while with their guests?)

(ii) This is a marketing technique which is so common and so obvious that it is rarely mentioned in standard marketing theory books and, in practice, is rarely examined to mesh with fundamental objectives or to develop new approaches based on the principles behind it. Most simply use hospitality, within fixed budgets, because it has been done for years and there is a sense that it helps sales. Few step back and consider why. Companies in many sectors frequently pay for their customers to be wined, dined, and entertained in some way, in the hope that they will buy.

(iii) Some companies are small or decentralized. As a result, individuals (partners in professional service firms, for instance) try to arrange this themselves. It may look like just administration but in an event of any size there are complexities and professional processes. As with other aspects of marketing there is sophistication and professional technique behind this approach.

(iv) It is fascinating that, even with the modern emphasis on the value of relationship development, there is so little academic work on the affect of hospitality or entertainment on customers' propensity to buy or repurchase. Marketers and sales people have spent millions on all aspects of hospitality, for many decades, because it feels intuitively right that it eases the marketing process and encourages sales. It would be useful to have sound, systematic, academic concepts and research around this subject in order to help direct this investment more effectively. If there is, for example, a profound, deep, and respected relationship between two professional organizations, which is mutually beneficial, is customer hospitality really needed?

  RATING: Practical and powerful

⊙ INNOVATION MANAGEMENT

Application: new revenues, new products and services, new strategies

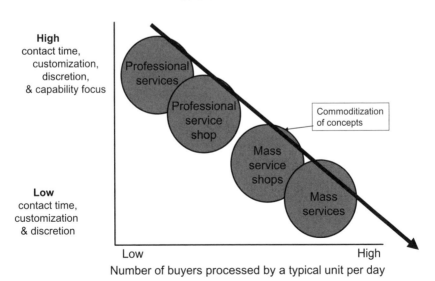

Figure I.1   A representation of the commoditization and diffusion of concepts in the services industry (adapted from Johnston, R. and Clark, G., 2001)

The concept

Innovation is a management process, the mechanism by which an organization captures, cultivates, and exploits initiatives. It is different from creativity itself which is the source of initial insight or ideas on which innovative new offers are founded. Traditionally, people have thought that there is a need to innovate in offerings, process, and market. There are, though, well researched projects and many anecdotal stories about the need to bring innovation to many aspects of businesses. They suggest that innovation in functions like strategy, governance, management, NPD/NSD, operations, marketing, and sales is vital in fast changing markets; that sclerosis can destroy value.

Creativity and innovation are particularly vital to a firm that needs to bring a range of new products and services to market. In fact, some researchers suggest that the ability to innovate new products and services is the key to survival for some companies operating in a number of mature or fast changing markets. In the 2010 results of McKinsey's annual innovation survey of senior executives, for instance, 84% said that innovation was either very or extremely important to the growth of their companies (*McKinsey Quarterly*, July 2010).

In recent years a number of businesses have adopted successful methods of harvesting creative insight, in addition to ensuring that creativity is stimulated in the first place. They vary enormously but can be grouped into several generic approaches.

(i) Innovation founded on a formal process

The proactive creation of new products (NPD) has been established practice for many years in a number of different businesses selling physical products. Leading organizations in markets where new product innovation is a critical success factor, like consumer products, have highly sophisticated processes, which are managed at a senior level in the firm. See *NPD/NSD*.

(ii) Innovation through smallness

Others, by contrast, emphasize smallness as a means to innovation. For instance, in a recent speech, Sir Richard Branson attributed part of the success of his Virgin organization to smallness. His policy, he said, was to break units in two once they had reached "around thirty" people. He had found that it maintained entrepreneurial spirit and kept overheads low. This approach is founded on a story which has become the stuff of business legend. In the 1960s, the American multi-national 3M nearly missed a major opportunity. Its Dr Spencer Silver had produced, a "low-tack reusable adhesive" (glue which didn't stick well). He saw the potential to create what became "Post It" notes. Unfortunately, the concept was rejected by all (including the marketing department). However, he did not give up on the idea but began to manufacture samples, which he gave to the board's secretaries. As they asked for more, word spread and demand grew until the amateurish manufacturing capability for the notes took over his supportive boss's office. The company eventually accepted the innovation, which became one of its most successful products. Then, as a response to the fear that its large, bureaucratic structure might miss a significant product opportunity because of its short-sightedness, it broke down into small cells. It claimed that this was responsible for a number of subsequent innovations.

The approach can be seen in several different industries. In the technology industry, for instance, not only have some large companies sought to create entrepreneurial growth through small business units, but the character of places like Silicon Valley have facilitated interaction between capital investors and numerous start-ups. Leading creative technologists have grown used to the fact that tiny start-ups can grow into massive, valuable businesses like Google. Innovation through smallness has also been the reason for the success of many of the professions. Even in the largest firms, success lies in their individual practices, which, like cells in a living organism, evolve and respond to changes because they are run directly by a partner. As an owner of the business they feel freer than corporate executives to take their own course and refine their own offer. In fact, some leading practices ask partners to write and then implement a "business plan" which sets the direction for their practice; especially if in a completely new field of operation. There is even evidence of partners developing a practice in defiance of the wishes and policies of leaders, sometimes to great effect. So, fostering an innovation by dedicating a practice to it is common in the professions. Typically, though, this is intuitive and not part of structured "innovation management" policies or any managed process. Experience suggests that marketers can improve the success of this approach if they make explicit a mechanism to identify, nurture, and prioritize developing ideas.

(iii) Outsourcing innovation management

There is a view that creativity occurs less in large, bureaucratic, and process-dominated organizations and that innovation management rarely manages to exploit it. So, 47% of the executives who responded to McKinsey's (see McKinsey, 2010) innovation survey said that they sourced innovation externally. This is probably in response to a concept called "open innovation", described by US professor Henry Chesbrough. It was famously prompted at Proctor & Gamble in 1999 when, in response to analysts' pressure, an incoming CEO (Alan Lafly) challenged the organization to source innovation from outside (as opposed to just from its own, extensive R&D facility).

Some product companies have, for example, managed creativity by using an external agency; innovation through outsourcing. These agencies, which came to prominence in the 1970s, are known as "new product development companies".

They take a brief in the same way that advertising agencies or research companies take briefs from marketing departments. These briefs contain requirements to produce new products, offering benefits to new markets for whatever reason. The famous cream and whisky drink, Bailey's Irish Cream was, for instance, created in this way. The then owners of the drink commissioned it from a creative agency because they had spare manufacturing capability in their Irish plant. The original brief, it seems, contained a requirement to produce an alcoholic drink product which contained "typically Irish components". These suppliers have specialist processes to explore the target market, to design the offer, and to specify manufacturing and packaging. They return to the company a researched concept which can be taken, through a detailed business plan, into manufacture.

(iv) Exploiting the *"diffusion of innovation"*

As described in the separate entry, the acceptance and growth of an innovation in society occurs through dialogue amongst a network of inter-related people. Its diffusion depends on relationships and conversation. Marketers can use this phenomenon to develop new services and marketing concepts. There is, for example, a specific type of innovation diffusion which occurs in the professional services industry, represented in Figure I.1. Consultancies which specialize in high-end customized services, like McKinsey, usually undertake complex projects to solve unique client problems. However, if their practice meets a problem several times, the type of engagement will be given a name and a new concept is born in the industry. Other suppliers will then take up the offer, creating processes and tools to handle it. It moves down the "industrialization" line, picking up volume but losing margin. Eventually the approach becomes commonplace, is captured in software tools, is taught in professional academies, and undertaken by customers themselves. It becomes more of a commodity. Offers like double entry book keeping, portfolio planning, and process reengineering have followed this course; and it is seen throughout the industry today. Yet, different offers suit different firms at different stages in the commoditization journey. High-end strategy firms pioneer new concepts, whereas one of the IT-based management consultancies, such as Accenture, might be better suited to volume, process-based offers. Marketers can identify potential innovations for their practice if they have a clear view of the concepts that are appropriate to its competences and by adapting ideas from others as they diffuse across the professions.

In his definitive study on the use of this concept in technology companies, Geoffrey Moore (Moore, G.A., 1991) pointed out the difficulties that companies have in bringing true innovations to market. He emphasizes the need to take different approaches in marketing strategy and technique as diffusion progresses. The differences in the pace of development of high-tech services like Broadband over optical fibre (originally proposed in the 1980s) and either the internet or iPhone apps shows that this level of sophistication in innovation marketing is just as relevant in services marketing.

(v) Innovation through *thought leadership*

As discussed in the separate entry, *thought leadership* is one of the most influential marketing strategies that the world has seen. It is a vast, influential, and diverse range of activities, which, at its best, produces systematic, iconic work like the *McKinsey Quarterly* and the *Harvard Business Review*. It is both a source of innovative new services and a marketing tool that helps sales. Leading consultants like Accenture, IBM Global Services, and Deloitte have skilled staff dedicated to this function. What starts with an idea and a marketing campaign can soon have consultants and leading practitioners dedicated to it. It becomes a "practice" in its own right, sometimes earning millions of dollars in revenues. Leading businesses have, for example, had practices focused on "CRM", "Lean service", and "shareholder value"; each innovative ideas in their own time.

(vi) Innovation through imitation and adaptation

Another valid form of innovation is the adaptation of emerging ideas; when, for instance, a supplier adopts and adapts a new idea, product, or service, which has been created and pioneered by a peer in their industry. As new concepts occur, they are often pioneered by small, flexible businesses or by notable individuals. However, it tends to be when organizations with a huge footprint take them on board, that they have substantial impact and a new market is formed. So it is a natural evolution and a source of real profit to identify emerging ideas and adapt them. Some would argue that this is not true innovation because the results not completely new. Yet, famous strategy professor, Ted Levitt, argued as far back as 1966 (Levitt, T., 1966) that this was a valid form of innovation, which was less risky than blindly pursuing the entirely new idea or offer. Innovation is not only about completely new ideas but also about the sensible adaptation and improvement of concepts pioneered by others. IBM originally moved into computers (and later the PC) through imitation; as did Virgin in air travel (after Freddie Laker) and Ericsson in mobile phones. This is not to argue that the services or products that result are not unique or appealing. These companies adapt a concept without infringing copyright or patents; making it their own and producing a unique new *value proposition*.

(vii) Innovation through co-creation

Creativity tends to occur in all businesses as they interact with customers. As local people (particularly in large, diffuse businesses) respond to needs, solve developing problems, and tackle the unintended consequences of central policy, they frequently find creative new answers to needs. This is particularly common in service companies because of the involvement of human beings in the interaction between the two sides. Unfortunately, these creative answers to local problems are, like fast blooming wild flowers, frequently lost. So some companies put great stress on capturing local innovation across the operations of their company and communicating it across the whole firm. Some marketing VPs, for instance, see part of their role as identifying and legitimizing innovation that occurs in the field. They stress the need to set up mechanisms capable of industrializing it and replicating it across their company. In many cases, this leads them to concentrate on mechanisms by which they can create innovative ideas with customers.

The "co-creation of services", for example, is the practice of developing new services through collaboration between companies and customers. Innovation and value is created by the firm and the customer, rather than being created entirely inside the business. Co-creation not only describes a trend of jointly creating offers but also a movement away from customers buying products and services as transactions. It leads to purchases being made as part of an experience.

It is common for firms to take ideas from their customers and develop the way in which they deliver their products to them. They try to get customer input into the way they enjoy the offer; in fact some create online communities, exploring and understanding how customers use the offer and then seek their ideas on how to improve delivery. This is a way of improving the customer's experience without affecting the product itself. It is also a way to bring the customer inside the business, helping them work with the brand on a part of the experience that matters to them most. Co-creating products and services, however, goes beyond this, it might, like Amazon, allow customers to select and change their delivery times. Many airlines, for instance, allow real-time self-service for their customers, letting them choose and change their seat, meal, and even their flight time. In some business-to-business cases, customers work with suppliers on a deeper level of engagement to create entirely new offers. The suppliers then bring these into their portfolio and offer them across their business.

(viii) Innovation through rivalry

There is an assumption made in much modern business literature that organizations should be efficient, smooth, and harmonious. But life isn't like that. Business organizations are structured in different ways and contain ambitious, driven people who thrive on competitive thrust. In fact, some organizations (law firms for example) are configured to grow by exploiting and nurturing this ambition. There is evidence that this rivalry produces innovation (see Ferrari, B.T. and Goethals, J., 2010).

One credible study amongst British market leaders (Davies, R., 2010) focused on barriers to innovation. They found them to be:

- Lack of knowledge.
- Skill-related barriers
- Lack of trust
- Lack of space (i.e. energy from leadership amongst other priorities)

- Cultural alignment
- Structural barriers.

Marketing leaders need to understand these inhibitions on change in their organization if they are to develop new offers or new approaches to market. The research indicates that in many corporate companies, change management might be an important component in the innovation programme of marketing functions.

History, context, criticism, and development

Innovation of products, services, and strategies has undoubtedly been a part of marketing and business life for many centuries. It is, of course, closely related to innovation in science and technology. As breakthroughs occur in technical fields it allows entrepreneurs to take advantage of business opportunities and create new markets. So, it is clearly related to *diffusion of innovation* of new scientific developments. In fact, since the mid 20th century in particular, governments have created policy and initiatives to encourage cooperation between universities and business entrepreneurs or financial investors. In fact, there is evidence that, in some places, marketing skills can be left out of the thinking of science specialists working to bring innovation to market.

Since the 1960s there has been a recurring belief in many circles that companies have to keep innovating new products and services to survive. Many assert that this is essential to thrive in fast changing and commoditizing markets. This is slightly dubious though. If the studies (from the 1960s and 1970s) showing that a vast percentage of revenues resulted from new products were, in fact, credible, then the companies and sectors involved would have churned their complete portfolios many times by now. Yet, as Tables B1 and B2 show, there are many branded items in all sectors that have survived and thrived for several centuries. It seems, then, that this drive for innovation needs a degree of realistic perspective and balance.

At the start of the 21st century, there was a resurgence of focus on innovation. This was influenced largely by IBM's massive thought leadership campaign on the subject. In 2006, they launched a massive international campaign (which included TV, print, outdoor, and web) "Innovation That Matters". It was their primary campaign for the year, and would have involved spend of several million dollars. The aim was to reposition IBM as supplying the means for corporations to innovate – structurally, financially, or operationally. There is little doubt that it kick-started a renewed interest in innovation. Consultancies developed "white papers" and several creative agencies re-badged themselves as innovation companies.

Voices and further reading

- "We live in a business world that increasingly worships the great tribal god: innovation; lyrically hailing it not just as a desired but necessary condition of a company's survival and growth. This highly agitated confidence in the liberating efficacy of innovation has in some places become an article of faith almost as strong as Natchez Indians' consuming faith in the deity of the sun. Man creates gods according to his needs. Significantly, the businessman's new demigod and the Natchez's more venerable and historic god make identical promises. They both promise renewal and life. Yet before all our R&D energies and imaginations are too one-sidedly directed at the creation of innovations, it is useful to look at the facts of commercial life. Is innovation all that promising? More important, how does a policy of innovation compare in promise to more modest aspirations? What is needed is a sensibly balanced view of the world. Innovation is here to stay, it is necessary, and it can make a lot of sense; but it does not exhaust the whole of reality. Every company needs to recognize the impossibility of sustaining innovative leadership in its industry and the danger of an unbalanced dedication to being the industry's innovator. No single company, regardless of its determination, energy, imagination, or resources, is big enough or solvent enough to do all the productive first things that will ever occur in its industry and to always beat its competitors to all the innovations emanating from the industry." Levitt, T., 1966.

- "Innovation and commercialization, 2010: McKinsey global survey results". *McKinsey Quarterly*, July 2010.
- ". . . innovation processes in large companies stifle exactly those radical developments which the firms seek". Ambler, T., 2003.
- Hamel, G. and Prahalad, C.K., "Corporate imagination and expeditionary marketing". *Harvard Business Review*, July–August 1991.
- Brown, R., "Managing the 'S' curves of innovation". *Journal of Marketing Management*, July 1991.
- Trott, P., *Innovation Management and New Product Development*. Prentice Hall, 2008.
- "Traditional arguments about innovation have centred on two schools of thought. On one hand, the social deterministic school argued that innovations were the result of a combination of external social factors and influences, such as demographic changes, economic influences and cultural changes. . . . On the other hand, the individualistic school argued that innovations were the result of unique, individual talents and such innovators are born . . . The resource-based view of innovation focuses on the firm and its resources, capabilities and skills. It argues that when firms have resources that are valuable, rare and not easily copied they can achieve a sustainable competitive advantage – frequently in the form of innovative new products . . ." Trott, ibid.

Things you might like to consider

(i) The innovation of new products, services, and strategies is undoubtedly a marketing responsibility. Experience suggests that it is not confined to the NPD/NSD processes that are so loved by academics. Marketers needs to find the appropriate style of innovation for their organization.

(ii) It seems important to keep a sensible, judicious perspective on this. Apple, the iconic case study for all advocates of innovation, had a very difficult and vulnerable history until its massive breakthroughs with the iPhone. Not all firms can innovate in this way.

(iii) There are alternative strategies. The nurturing or refreshing of a long-standing brand franchise might also be viable.

(iv) Communication strategies need to match innovation initiatives. If it is a truly novel concept, then all those strategies to promote at that point in the *diffusion of innovation* should be adopted. If it is, say, an innovation in a well established and understood category, then different marketing communications strategies apply.

Allen & Overy grows further

Allen & Overy is one of the world's leading law firms with around 450 partners and nearly 3,000 lawyers working in over thirty-three cities around the globe. It is one of a small group of truly integrated international law firms and one of the UK's "magic circle".

The partnership has grown by offering high end, customized professional services. It is seen as one of the elite practices in its field, built on its partners' reputations for individual excellence. The firm obviously offers a wide range of legal services, from M&A instructions with leading financial Institutions through corporate law to specialities like estates and insolvency. It has sector skills in fields like communications, media, and technology; energy and utilities; financial institutions; hotels and leisure; infrastructure; licensing and gaming; and life sciences. It has partners with expertise in all these fields and has created thought leadership on subjects in many of them.

The core of its client base comprises several thousand significant organizations in a variety of sectors and locations. In fact, it is on the "legal panel" of many of the world's most well-known and influential organizations. Globalization is leading the partnership to concentrate on a core group of clients, common to many of the offices in their network. In this arena they compete with a small number of global and US-origin law firms in addition to leading local law firms. So the firm has well established strategies to concentrate on important clients, to appoint client relationship partners, and to give a more sector-specific orientation to its advice.

The partnership thinks that the international legal services market is changing due to a number of forces; including:

The 2009/10 financial crisis which gave impetus to the drive among clients to reduce legal spend and focus on the efficiency and value delivery of their external law firms

The commoditization of a number of services, leading to new forms of delivery like international outsourcing or technology-based services.
The introduction of professional buying skills into the purchase of legal services.

As a result of these forces, the firm has begun to experience two opposing but related forces.

The first is a tendency toward cost cutting, automation, outsourcing, and process efficiency. Within its field of operations, it has been asked to provide more streamlined, efficient, and competitively priced services. In areas such as syndicated loans to investment grade credits or leveraged loans in private equity, there is a tendency toward standard forms or similar processes. Although A&O is perceived to be one of the few firms with the market knowledge and resources to do this specialized work, and, although clients think they receive personalized, high quality advice, both sides think there is an increasing standardization of delivery. This process is called by academics the "industrialization of services"; a completely different business to individual advisory work, needing completely different processes and competencies.

In response to this, the firm has initiated a "More for less strategy", aimed at delivering service to clients in new ways. It asks: how can A&O deliver more to its clients for less cost and effort using different working practices, processes, technology, document automation, sources of resource and so on?

The leaders think, therefore, that some of the existing services need to be carefully re-engineered, perhaps re-configuring back office processes and the use of technology to improve costs, margin, and client satisfaction.

This industrialization process needs the deployment of new skills and techniques. The practice needs to identify those areas where industrialization is a real phenomenon and ask the following: What technologies and systems are employable here? How can things be designed so that clients and associates can use technology instead of people, systems instead of individual preference or serendipity? Should those services which are already high volume be reconfigured or, perhaps, automated further?

For instance, Allen & Overy announced in 2009 the launch of "CDS deliverability", a tool, sponsored by its innovation committee,[*] that offers the CDS market an indicator of deliverability for the growing universe of frequently traded reference obligations. The online service brings greater transparency and efficiency to the credit derivatives markets by providing rigorous legal analysis of deliverability made available in a one-page report for each obligation. (Historically market participants have conducted this analysis on a unilateral basis, duplicating effort and cost without the benefit of a recognized market standard.) CDS deliverability has been developed in association with Markit, a provider of independent data, portfolio valuations, and OTC derivatives trade processing to the global financial markets.

Simon Haddock, head of Allen & Overy's Derivatives and Structured Finance practice, said: "Quick and efficient mechanisms for delivery of both legal and market data are an integral part of the commoditization of the credit markets. The market has long sought a cost-effective and timely indicator of deliverability for frequently traded obligations. CDS deliverability has been produced to satisfy that demand based on feedback from a number of leading dealers in the credit markets."

Despite the industrialization forces, though, the partners are firmly of the view that there will always be demand for customized, high quality advice from world class experts. So, in parallel with the cost/efficiency strategy it has created a deliberate programme to maintain "high end work".

There are several aspects to the programme which involves equipping partners with new skills and adopting different routes into leading clients. To do this, a partner needs to create a new dialogue with its clients, "moving up the value chain", to discuss emerging legal, regulatory, and risk issues with business leaders, rather than merely taking instructions from in-house legal counsel and deal transactions. In doing so, partners need to adopt "the language of the board room", learn how to identify latent needs, and maintain positive relations with the general counsel's team. This will require new approaches, language, and skills.

*Allen & Overy's innovation committee is a small group of senior partners, with two retained external advisors, which has a mandate and a budget to identify and sponsor innovation across the firm.

 RATING: Practical and powerful

INTERNAL MARKETING

Application: services marketing, marketing communication, employee motivation, achievement of strategic goals

The concept

One of the main communication channels to customers is via the employees of the firm, service firms in particular. If a company has 10,000 employees talking to three customers a day on average, there are 30,000 opportunities through which marketing can communicate with customers every day. Communications planning should therefore take into account the views of employees when preparing any external communications. At the very least, employees should be told about any campaign before it is released, so that they can explain it to their contacts. However, effectiveness is dramatically improved if employees are drawn into the campaign and enthused to talk to customers about it.

Internal engagement and motivation are particularly important in a service industry. As service offers frequently involve the direct engagement of human beings, it is not surprising that, with the rise of the service economies in the West, marketers have created internal marketing functions. Used in some of the leading service businesses with increasing sophistication, these aim to communicate with the internal audience as professionally as the firm communicates with its external audiences. They set up internal communication media, which can range from simple management briefings to sophisticated TV channels or intranet broadcasts. Many create internal communication campaigns linked to external campaigns. This involves all the usual best practices of *marketing communication* including: a specific communications strategy, the creation of clear messages, the segmentation of audiences; and the management of responses from them, all directed at the company's own employees.

Marketing campaigns can be used to keep the atmosphere, motivation, and experience of a service fresh and exhilarating. It helps to keep employees informed of important issues, contributes to a common sense of purpose, and helps develop positive motivation. Internal marketing campaigns are frequently designed in businesses with large, diversified workforces to create internal enthusiasm and achieve really good service. In consultancy firms, by contrast, leaders frequently initiate new concepts, strategies, or ideas to stimulate the interest of restless brains, and these often involve marketing skills.

Internal communication that is ill-conceived, poorly planned, or erratic can have a detrimental effect. If marketers do not ensure that there is good internal communications management, the leaders and the people responsible for various activities will copy emails, send out erratic messages, and pass on ad hoc technical changes, causing confusion. If there is no communication discipline, there will be a multitude of conflicting, disparate messages, which will become a deluge that employees are unable to comprehend. The firm will suffer from over-communication and employees will be overwhelmed by a discordant cascade, which conflicts and confuses.

Marketers need to construct an effective internal marketing programme with similar characteristics to an external programme. Just as with external communications, the firm needs an internal communications strategy. What is it communicating, to whom, and why? What are the objectives of the leadership in communicating with its own people? What are the core messages? What are the outputs and behavioural changes that they want to achieve through the investment in communication? These different elements of communication need to be thought through and included in the overall *marketing communications* strategy. That strategy, as with the general marketing strategy, ought to be produced to suit the style and culture of the firm. For some, it will be a detailed document produced after months of close analysis. For others it will be a lengthy PowerPoint presentation prepared over several collaborative meetings; while, for others still, it will be a short, pithy, statement of intent. Whatever its format, this strategy is likely to encompass: the message, the communication objectives, the aspirations of the human beings it is aimed at, the budget, and the intended outcome. It must, though, give a clear direction to all campaigns and programmes.

Internal communications also needs clear message management. This involves crafting the message to employees and prioritizing against the many other business communications. Since putting out multiple messages can give rise to confusion, it is not only important to make sure these messages are simple and straightforward, but also that they do not conflict with other internal messages. As with external communication, they need to be sustained, simple, and relevant. Yet, with internal communications, one of the most important considerations is credibility. Employees must be able to give some credence to the thrust of senior management claims. The ideas and actions of leaders of the firm need to be properly aligned so that, either overtly or subtly, they don't undermine the professed direction of the firm. If they do that, there is a danger of lowering morale and that, in turn, can have a detrimental effect on customer service. As with external messaging, it takes time for internal audiences to accept and internalize messages. Messages about the firm's values and priorities should be unchanging or, at least, slow to evolve.

Marketers need to be just as careful in planning the use of internal media and methods as in external communications. For instance, modern *marketing communication* techniques (like digital marketing) can be applied to internal communications. The prime and best media, through which to communicate with employees, are their own line management. The second word-of-mouth: the internal "grapevine". Both need to be valued and influenced by communications planners. The marketer sets out to communicate through internal networks, particularly in a large firm which will be dominated by inter-connected relationships of people. These might be people who have been in the same company for a decade or more and have learnt to trust each other by working on projects or in managerial teams. They are circles within circles; networks of trust. There might be, for example, a network of specialists around the world concentrating on one business sector. The people involved have a common interest and rely on their internal network to receive information. Their leaders and the immediate group of contacts with whom they work daily are much more relevant to them than other messages.

So, gossip becomes more effective than the deluge of emails, magazines, and other publications. Marketing specialists can map these networks and target communications through them. This is a form of *viral marketing*, where word-of-mouth is used to influence the behaviour and motivation of a company's people. It is a powerful internal marketing mechanism if used effectively. Moreover, all of these networks will interconnect with customer networks, and so good, credible communications from the leadership through these internal networks will also influence customer thinking.

It is sensible to make a member of the internal communications team responsible for viral and relationship marketing techniques. They need to analyse the internal networks, how those networks communicate, what the word-of-mouth is, and how to influence it. As with external approaches to relationship marketing, the internal approach enables the identification of network nodes, or points at which the networks interconnect. These might be conferences of different employees who focus on industry marketing or an informal meeting of all technical staff interested in one professional area. All are opportunities for the firm's leaders to target communications more effectively.

Other internal media include: "town hall" meetings, internal email, company intranets, blogs and wikis, and staff magazines. Some even design their external advertising with an eye to motivating their own people. This was a consideration, for example, in Accenture's choice of advertising in airline departure halls. Many of their staff fly regularly and gain encouragement from being part of a large firm, able to communicate on this scale.

As with external marketing, internal marketing is improved by the use of communications campaigns. A campaign is a group of activities coordinated together through the available media over a period of time in order to reinforce one message with the internal audience. As with external communications, an internal campaign needs to be planned carefully. The communications manager needs to have a clear idea of who the target audience is, what the key objectives are, and what the available budget is. They need to refine and agree the message and concentrate on the media to be used over whatever period of time. A firm adopting a campaign approach to internal marketing will ensure that its key campaigns are known to the communications manager and there is no conflict when received by the internal audiences.

There also need to be open and reliable methods through which the response to messages from employees can be gathered. Many firms carry out internal staff surveys to get objective measures of reactions to messages. These frequently have to be anonymous, in order to encourage honest feedback. But this is much more than merely measuring whether they have received and understood the leader's messages. The best service companies set out to understand the views, concerns, and motivations of their employees. Just like external communications, effective internal communication is two-way; a dialogue more than a monologue.

History, context, criticism, and development

The advent of internal marketing is closely related to the emergence of the service economy because of the need to motivate employees to give excellent service to customers. Over the past fifty years, the balance in many economically developed countries has shifted to the point where services account for almost three-quarters of their gross domestic product. This comprises a wide array of services, including financial, utility, professional, and consumer services. For instance, American manufacturing is, at the time of writing, reported to be 13% of GDP, a decline from 26% in 1970, whereas the service sector represents around 75% of economic activity, depending on definition. According to the UK's Office of National Statistics, for instance, the services found in the City of London now account for almost a third of the British economy, twice that of the manufacturing sector.

The effect of the service economy is most clearly seen in employment patterns. In the autumn of 2005 the *Economist* magazine published an analysis of the number of people employed in manufacturing as a percentage of the total workforce. It estimated that 10% of American workers were employed in manufacturing as opposed to 25% in 1970 (employment in services was 80%). The estimates for Britain (14% compared to 35% in 1970), France (15%), and Canada (14%) were similar, with other big economies, like Japan, at 18%. They found that the only big economy where more than a fifth of workers were in manufacturing was Germany (23%), which has a lot of innovative companies and a high content of capital goods that are not as easy to copy. Since a number of workers within manufacturing companies still occupy service roles (like marketing, design, and facilities management) the actual employment in manufacturing roles among the developed economies could be much less.

Over the long term, successful first world economies have replaced manufacturing workers with new technology to boost productivity and moved away from labour-intensive products (like textiles) to higher value sectors (like pharmaceuticals and biotechnology). The relatively high percentage of manufacturing jobs in, say, Italy is probably more a sign of economic weakness or protectionism. America led the world in productivity improvement during the last decade of the 20th century and this, in turn, led to higher average incomes. In short, manufacturing is producing more while employing fewer people.

In all the Western economies there is now a wide range of flourishing service businesses. As people grow richer they want more education, better housing, improved healthcare, more restaurants, bars, car dealerships, and shops which carry goods far beyond the mere basic amenities of life. Increasing prosperity unleashes a creative explosion in new service concepts, some of which become massive international chains.

Some of these arise from the growth and adaptation of established services due to social trends. In the last fifty years, for example, the rise of household ownership has been accompanied by growth in services such as legal conveyance, estate agencies/realtors, building, renovation, and decoration (plus TV house makeover shows). Some, on the other hand, are completely new services which would have been unheard of fifty years ago. An educated person returning from war in 1945 might not be surprised by today's fast food chains or modern opticians but psychoanalysts' practices, tanning salons, video rental stores, and internet cafes would probably be a complete revelation. The range of new service businesses appears to be limited only by the power of human creativity.

Government policy has also created a swathe of newly competitive service businesses. In Europe, for instance, apart from progressive legislation to introduce competition to many service sectors like airlines and banking, privatization has had a dramatic impact. It has created a number of large, profitable, and successful service businesses which were once not fully recorded as part of economic activity. These include airlines, rail companies, and utilities such as water, gas, and telecoms. When they were funded by the public purse, all costs (both current and capital) were paid by the Exchequer. However, investment was then artificially restricted by political policy rather than organizational or customer needs. Also, items which would normally increase in value (such as intangible assets like intellectual property, brand, or customer loyalty) had no realizable value. As a result, many of the liberalized industries have grown in revenue, investment, profit, and service provision since being freed from political constraints. The marketing of service is critical to their success.

Another group of businesses which have caused growth in service sector employment are those which were once an integral part of the support functions of major firms: those which have been "outsourced". In the past, most of the support infrastructure of major companies such as Hewlett-Packard, or IBM or ICI would have been owned and run by them. In the 1950s and 1960s, for example, many firms set up staff canteens or restaurants (often with separate facilities for directors and visitors) believing them to reflect the behaviour and policies of responsible, progressive employers. The chefs, waiters, and equipment were all employed and owned by the firm as part of the cost of doing business. In the early 1980s, for instance, British Telecom ran one of the largest catering chains in Britain, comparable to professional suppliers like the then Trust House Forte, but exclusively for its own staff. However, most of these and other services are now invariably outsourced to specialized providers whose business focuses in these areas. They have become competitive service businesses in their own right and the revenue is now recorded as part of the service economy.

This phenomenon distorts the view of both the service sector and manufacturing. If a computer manufacturer outsources its security, estates, or cleaning staff to a private company, manufacturing appears to decline and service grow. There will be some overall productivity improvement because not only will the outsourcing supplier be further down the "experience curve" of its core service business, it will also be able to reap initial economies of scale by integrating with existing operations. Yet the effect on the total economy will not be as dramatic as appears from the overall statistics.

Modern business leaders and managers have to spend so much time responding to the needs of their customers and attending to the motivation of their employees that it is easy to forget how impersonal, detached, and mechanized big business had become. Until the mid 20th century, the Western attitude to business had been influenced by two powerful forces: mass production and scientific management (or "Taylorism"). In all but a few backwaters, manufacturing had become synonymous with mass production and the human element of it reduced to the impersonal term "labour". Employees were "costs of production", undertaking tasks that technology was not yet able to handle. The philosophy of scientific management, routed as it was in the 19th century quest for reason and experimentation, broke their work into routine, planned tasks. These could be measured, demonstrated, and supervised. The pseudo science that resulted from this thinking, "time and motion", was based on the unquestioned drive for efficiency, speed, and mechanization.

It was in the late 1960s and early 1970s that management thinkers were startled to find that human beings worked better and more productively when part of "self-governing work groups"; or (as tested in pioneering organizational models at firms like Volvo) when they worked on complete tasks (like building one car) rather than soul-destroying repetitive tasks. Not only were people more productive, but industrial relations were less strained and profits improved. This led inexorably to today's concern to "compete for talent", to find a "good job fit", and to "develop" the human beings employed by a firm so that they gain satisfaction through work that delivers company objectives.

Modern attitudes are most clearly seen in the professional services industry. Rather than the serried ranks of number crunchers, clerks, or productivity analysts of the past, these huge businesses now regard their people as "human capital". They are, as the term suggests, a rich resource which will create wealth through their views, talents, and skills. The professions compete seriously for the cream of the graduate crop, training and nurturing them to become "lead advisors" to clients and partners of the future firm. Their instinctive drive to keep talent makes them move with the times, introducing state of the art human resources (HR) practices like diversity policy, flexible working contracts, and work/life balance initiatives. They also keep up-to-date with the changing aspirations of the newest generation to reach work. Many are now, for example, trumpeting their environmental or social conscience credentials to attract the ("Generation Y") graduates of the early 21st century. Yet, the professions are only the bellwether of industry, as it learns to employ modern workers effectively.

The motivation of people employed by vast swathes of the service economy is therefore critical to modern profitable growth. The marketing to this internal audience is an important success factor in providing effective, attractive, and competitive services.

Voices and further reading

* Shamir, B., "Between service and servility: role conflict in subordinate service roles". *Journal of Human Relations*, 1980.
* Parkington, J.J. and Schneider, B., "Some correlates of experienced job stress: a boundary role study". *Academy of Management Journal*, 1979.
* "Services are performances and people are the performers. From the customers' perspective, the people performing the service are the company. An incompetent insurance agent is an incompetent insurance company." Berry, L.L., 1995.
* "The term 'internal marketing has come to be widely used to describe the practice of running many of the established techniques of marketing inwardly by focusing on employees . . . viewed as an activity in isolation, internal marketing is unlikely to succeed. For that to happen, the full support of top management is required." Palmer, A., 1994.
* "In a study by Sotrey and Easingwood, 78 marketing managers in financial services firms were surveyed to identify factors distinguishing successful from unsuccessful products . . . the key factors were . . . synergy and Internal marketing (the support given to staff prior to launch to help them understand the new product

and its underlying systems …).” Lovelock, C.H., Vandermere, S., and Lewis, B., *Service Marketing; A European Perspective.* Prentice Hall, 1996.

- “A complex combination of strategies is needed to ensure that service employees are willing and able to deliver quality services and that they stay motivated to perform in customer-orientated, service-minded ways. These strategies for enabling service promises are often referred to as internal marketing . . .” Ziethaml, V. and Bitner, M.J., 2003.
- Ahmed, P.M. and Rafiq, M., *Internal Marketing.* Butterworth-Heinemann, 2002.
- “The internal marketing concept was first proposed in the mid 1970’s as a way of achieving consistent service quality – a major problem in the services area. Its basic premise was ‘to have satisfied customers, the firm must have satisfied employees’ and that this could be best achieved by treating employees as customers, i.e. by applying the principles of marketing to job design and employee motivation.” Ahmed and Rafiq, ibid.
- Varey, R.J. and Barbara, R. (eds), *Internal Marketing.* Routledge, 2000.

Things you might like to consider

(i) Internal communications and mechanisms to gain feedback from employees can often be the responsibility of HR functions. Yet they do not have the professional communication and research skills to do this effectively. This ought to be a dedicated marketing function which works closely with HR specialists.

(ii) If people are employed in manufacturing and treated badly, then their misery will not affect sales unless they take dramatic action like a strike. If they are part of a service which customers buy and experience, it will affect performance. They may be professional and try to hide discontent but their body language and tone of voice will communicate their agony to their customers. It is simply not possible to have bullies or insensitive leaders successfully in charge of a competitive service offer.

(iii) Internal marketing in a service business communicates with employees, getting feedback from them and tuning the company to respond to them. It is a critical competitive capability for those competing in service industries.

(iv) Some regard employees as “internal customers”, part of the value chain of delivery to customers. This gives focus to internal marketing activities.

(v) Some employees (like sales people or consultants) have professional networks which slip over into external customer networks. These need to be specifically targeted by internal marketing strategies as they communicate directly and credibly with buyers.

 RATING: Practical and powerful

INTERNATIONAL MARKETING

Application: all aspects of marketing beyond local borders

The concept

International marketing is the conduct of marketing across geographic borders. Whatever anyone says, this complicates the whole marketing task. There are several broad issues that marketers should consider, as they venture out of home territory.

(i) The business model

There are different models of international business which adopt different growth and marketing strategies. Each is successful in different circumstances.

The exporter, for example, is primarily a domestic firm. Its offer, approach, and underlying business assumptions are a reflection of its domestic culture and perspective. In moving abroad it is normally responding to unsolicited demand or opportunities. Its strategy is to reap new revenue streams with little customization or cost. It normally chooses local representatives (whether individuals or firms) who can service demand. The marketing of the exporter normally involves the use of domestic campaigns through established links and relationships. Any separate marketing into foreign countries has to be carefully examined and justified.

An international network, on the other hand, is a group of companies or individuals working under a similar brand or proposition. This might be a formal franchise structure with very strong controls on local operations, a holding company owning many different decentralized firms, or a federation of locally owned businesses which contribute part of their earnings to a central organization for some greater benefit (usually a shared brand or the ability to service large international clients). A franchise normally has a clearly defined offer and image. Marketing is funded primarily from franchisees' contributions but is centrally prepared, packaged, and launched. It is highly controlled. Marketing in a federal network, however, is almost completely the opposite. Central guidelines and marketing policies can be very weak. The approach is frequently diverse and diffuse, driven largely by the local businesses. The holding company, on the other hand, will vary its approach according to its policy on the effectiveness of brand impact. Some might play down the corporate centre, while others might promote it heavily, depending on the relevance to customer need.

A multi-national is a large firm operating on several continents. It has one consolidated set of accounts, one profit pool, and a corporate function which directs or leads policy. While it seeks to optimize costs (by streamlining processes, locating facilities in areas of cheap labour, and standardizing offers) it also tends to configure its marketing approach to local nationalities and culture.

In fact, the proponents of a global approach cite the degree of product standardization and similarity of marketing as a fundamental difference between the multinational and global firm. A "transnational", by contrast, tries to get the balance between having a consistent global platform and local customization (see the Fujitsu case study in the *cultural differences* entry).

They are different in policy and approach. In fact, muddled thinking, which has confused federal networks with global policy, has damaged the earnings of some large firms over the past few decades. The appropriate marketing and growth strategy should be adopted for the firm's culture, structure, and mentality.

(ii) The allowance that will be made for *cultural differences*

Different cultures create different expectations and attitudes in customers (see separate entry). It affects their attitude to life and business. This has serious implications. Marketers must, therefore, decide the degree of customization they will allow in their approach to international markets.

Businesses have been conducting international marketing campaigns for at least 300 years; and making fundamental mistakes for at least as long. What might look sensible in headquarters can look ridiculous in remote locations. One European vice president of marketing resigned from a leading global technology company soon after the start of the new century because of growing exasperation with this phenomenon. The American chief marketing officer ran worldwide marketing with a very tight "dashboard" approach. Events, mailings, and campaigns were expected to run at set times in different parts of the world and local marketing teams were expected to concentrate entirely on execution and administration of centrally designed programmes. This VP decided to leave when asked to run a seminar in Paris on July 14th (Bastille Day and a national holiday as important to the French as July 4th is to the Americans).

It is essential that the firm's marketing communication strategy covers this subject explicitly. What degree of latitude is necessary to make the message and the emphasis understood in different cultures? Which communication channels will be most effective? How much must the creative execution be adjusted to the taste and prejudice of local audiences? Where is the balance between pragmatic acceptance of customization and the incremental cost of this work? In which countries is any transliteration of communication into local cultural taste uneconomic?

(iii) International growth strategy

The marketer needs to set a clear international growth strategy. They need to consider how aggressive their company is going to be when it comes to overseas opportunities. For instance:

Is it going to refuse international work and remain a domestic practice?

The unarticulated assumption that demand should be serviced is at the heart of many firms. There is, however, the option that international demand could be refused. The leaders of the firm could take the view that margin, not growth, is their prime strategy and that international work risks damaging their margin. In these circumstances it is advisable to know international firms to whom customers can be referred. This will safeguard reputation and the potential for future work from them.

Is it going to service demand entirely from the home territory?

If the firm is only going to service international demand in an opportunistic way, or as a service to domestic customers with international needs, (i.e. without an explicit drive for significant international growth) it has a number of options. It might recruit an employee from the foreign territory and allow them to travel there to service customers. Alternatively, it might make an arrangement with a local agent or partner firm. With the former, the firm needs to recruit an experienced professional with both technical and business development skills. If the latter, it needs to choose carefully who their local agent is and decide the nature of the relationship. This might range from a simple percentage reward for work referred, to a tightly defined franchise agreement. All will involve risk, however, because any poor service or variation in technical standard will damage the reputation of the firm.

Is it going to actively target chosen countries or international markets?

If the firm decides that it wants to actively pursue international growth, then it needs to think through and prioritize its investment. It needs to conduct an initial strategic review and opportunity analysis to decide which the most interesting opportunities are. These might be based on geographic proximity, cultural fit or overriding opportunity for its products and services. It then needs to conduct detailed analysis of the markets it is considering and decide on the first areas it wants to focus upon. Like any area of investment it needs to decide the amount it is prepared to invest and the time it is prepared to give for payback.

Will it take the "follow the customer" strategy?

In *business-to-business* markets, the international growth of many small firms begins with large international customers. A small firm, or a business unit in a large firm, might service a division of a large international organization. As the work and relationship develop, it might find demand for work in many parts of the world from the same customers. This might become the foundation for international offices and employees.

What degree of local expertise will it employ and when?

There will come a time when the leaders will judge that there is continuing demand from an international market. It then needs to plan how it intends to provide local resource to service that demand. It may set up an office using expatriate employees from the home firm. The intention in these circumstances is to eventually hand over to talent developed locally and reap earnings from the profit

of the new entity. Alternatively, it may combine recruited talent with an acquisition to create a new firm.

The style of overseas investment can be affected by the reason for the approach.
Many work internationally because of demand. Others move because of slowing
home markets, declining business or intense competition. However, as there is
increased risk in international work, those moving abroad due to significant problems
in home markets need to ensure that they have secure investment funds for a long
term approach.

(iv) International market analysis and perspective

Any debate about international expansion is better conducted in the light of analysis
and insight into that market. The processes and techniques used in domestic marketing (market research, market audits, etc.) apply as well in international markets.
However, there is increased risk of error in international analysis. Whereas published
research reports and industry data can be freely available, a lack of real local knowledge
can be very costly if the firm is considering a serious investment. At the very least,
there should be a visit to the target countries, discussion with local professionals, and
even a visit to the commercial representatives of embassies in that country. Each will
round out knowledge and yield insight prior to any strategy debate.

Market research studies (see separate entry) can yield as much valuable insight into
international markets as they can into domestic markets. However, they need to be
managed with as much care, creating a clear research brief and using proper selection
processes to choose properly qualified agencies. Questionnaires and responses should
be properly translated, and normally translated back into the original language to check
meaning. The main vulnerability is normally the level of spend that a firm will tolerate. Restrictions on research budgets mean that samples in different foreign countries
can be ridiculously small. One way of handling this issue is to undertake an initial
quantative study to make initial judgements of potential and then to explore one or
two countries in depth.

(v) *Segmentation* of international markets

It would be dangerous and wasteful for any firm to attempt to "target the world" with
a broad and amorphous approach to expansion. All have to start by choosing a portion
of the international market, a group of clients, to concentrate upon. The most obvious
international segmentation method is by country. This has allowed many firms to
grow businesses inside national borders until they are flourishing mature businesses.

Yet choosing a country or a geographic market can also be a limitation. The firm
is, in fact, restricting itself to agreed borders and legal frameworks (many of which

resulted from long forgotten peace conferences which followed centuries-old wars) that are irrelevant to some modern business needs. Some marketers have therefore created a broader grouping of customers based on cultural groups. For example, a Spanish emphasis is likely to appeal in Spain, South America, and certain Spanish-influenced areas such as Miami in the US state of Florida. This segmentation approach might also lead to an emphasis on "Anglo-Saxon", Germanic, and Chinese groups, which involve similar cross-border opportunities. Some firms have found that successful penetration of cultural groups in this way has led them, through trade relationships, into valuable groupings of diasporas which have developed from previous migrations of trading peoples. Others have followed ancient trade routes into new geographies. For example, some firms relate to customers in Southern America through Spanish offices.

In fact, many of the approaches outlined in the separate entry on *segmentation* can apply in the international context. If, for example, a consultancy firm has decided to grow by penetrating a few international clients, it might concentrate on firms with cultures that make them "early adopters" of new concepts. These might be large firms in many different countries which would be attracted to leading conferences. Marketers should, therefore, define the most relevant segmentation for their firm using a method similar to that described in the separate entry on *segmentation*.

(vi) International brand strategy

Marketers have several strategic decisions to take with regard to the positioning of their brand internationally. Each has serious implications for the health of the firm, for the development of brand equity, and for the ease with which revenues will grow.

Is the brand going to be perceived to be indigenous to each country in which it operates?
   It is possible to create a brand which makes the firm appear native to each country in which it operates. It will be American in America, British in Britain, and Australian in Australia. It will be familiar to locals in every country in which it becomes established. This "multi-national brand strategy" can evolve naturally for firms which have strong offices established in countries that are staffed with good local professionals. The reputation from excellent local work will create a local brand in each country. This strategy can be maintained by following the same approach as new countries are penetrated.
Is the brand going to reflect the culture of the corporate or domestic headquarters?
   The brand can simply reflect the values and image of the country in which the firm originated or is headquartered. IBM is unquestionably American, while Ericsson is undeniably Swedish. This has both advantages and disadvantages. Firstly, it is relatively easy to maintain the integrity of a brand which reflects

national identity. It also resonates with certain cultures, creating opportunity. In recent years, for example, the countries of Eastern Europe have been very open to American firms because they thought that they needed to catch up after years of communism. On the other hand, some Asian countries have been cautious of westerners after the last collapse of their economies. Some firms have had to let locals lead work to overcome this prejudice.

Is the brand going to be presented as what a national culture is perceived to be?

People in different countries have perceptions of foreign cultures and their business practice, some of which are unrealistic images based on media received in their home country or cultural heritage. If the brand reflects a dominant culture, the firm needs to decide whether the positioning should embody the reality of that culture or what the local market perceives that culture to be. For example, in some markets American business is perceived to be efficient, process driven, and modern. This may not actually be the case, but the brand positioning which exploits the indigenous market's perception of American business is a strategy open to the firm.

Is the firm going to attempt to create a *"global"* brand?

A global brand is an entity that commands allegiance from buyers in many parts of the world. It has equity and the same identity in many markets. Proponents of the approach argue that the commonality of design, distribution, and advertising allow its owners to reap efficiencies of spend which competitors are unable to achieve. This is based on a number of global brands that have achieved enormous benefits from scale. There appear to be, however, very few clear definitions of a global brand. If simple criteria are applied (such as being present in at least three continents of the world and having more than 40% of revenue outside its originating country) then there appear to be few truly global brands in existence. The risk here is that the brand will be perceived to be Western rather than truly global. This strategy is also hugely expensive because the firm has to invest in all markets in which it operates to create a consistent impression.

(vii) International marketing communication issues

A firm working on the international stage has to communicate with both individual customers and with markets. Just as with domestic market communication, it needs to use communication techniques to plan and execute its messages so that they pave the way for personal dialogue between customers and sales people. It needs a strategic communications plan, good message management, clear media selection, programme management processes, and response mechanisms.

In the international context, however, differences in language, taste, colour preference, and humour need to be accommodated (see *cultural differences*). The design and message of all communication pieces need to be checked with internal representatives of different cultures at the planning stage. There need to be clear processes which engage communications representatives of all the firm's organizational units in the development of both strategy and programmes.

(viii) International sales, business development, and account management strategy

Many of the approaches to *sales* and *account management*, described in the relevant separate entries, apply in the international context. It is possible to use the *pipeline management* tool to focus thinking on the internal management of business development processes. It is also possible to build a personal network of international customers and handle them effectively while at the same time managing the implementation of a customized marketing plan for major accounts.

However, "relationship management" is one of those phrases that, although they use the same words, are heard differently by different cultures. The way an American or British professional manages business relationships is different from the way a French professional manages them and different again from the way some Asian firms work. For example, westerners feel at ease approaching all levels of an organization and would expect to receive honest, clear feedback. Consultants, for example, will often recommend to senior executives that they visit and collect data from front-line employees in order to get a true picture of how a company is performing in its market. By contrast, however, in some Asian cultures there is a sense of people having their place at certain levels of society. Junior employees will not therefore express any view which appears to be a criticism of senior management, even if those views are strongly held. Very often they will be uncomfortable spending any time or developing any relationship with people serving top executives. Relationship management must therefore be different in different cultures.

(ix) International *NPD/NSD*

New proposition development also has to be adjusted when working on the international stage. There is both an international and local management dynamic. For instance, innovation is most likely to occur in local firms or countries because they are close to the market. Local marketers are likely to spot developing needs and to deploy resources to meet individual opportunities. They are unlikely, however, to be successful at spreading that innovation across the firm because they will be limited by their own time constraints, by a lack of local perspective in foreign cultures, by internal politics and, sometimes, petty jealousy.

It is therefore effective to have a small international *NPD/NSD* team who are responsible for service innovation across the international firm. They must have a budget to create or stimulate new ideas and to undertake feasibility studies. Their prime task, however, is to legitimize local innovation and spread it across the firm. They need a clear mandate and international processes to do so. Similarly, the firm's portfolio management and *NPD/NSD* design process must be managed internationally.

There is, however, a local dimension to the design of components. Different cultures respond differently to process, people, colour, image, and technology. These differences need to be built into the *NPD/NSD* processes. The international team needs to decide the degree of standardization or customization which will occur for each offer and in which parts of the world. This will be based on a balance between research needs and affordability. Once the policy is decided for each proposition, tools such as *features design* or *blueprinting* (see separate entries) can be used to modify the offer for local cultures.

History, context, criticism, and development

Business leaders and marketers have been conducting cross-border marketing campaigns for many centuries. Wedgwood issued a multi-lingual catalogue in the 1780s and conducted business in Europe & America. A hundred years later, America's Singer established a Scottish plant as a bridgehead for its international operations (in a similar model to that adopted by modern Chinese white goods manufacturer, Haier, in the case study) in the 1870s, soon after their start. Coca-Cola started its international operations around the same time. Although it was present in Cuba, Canada, and Mexico by 1897, it announced its international intent in a board statement of 1919. During the 1920s Coca-Cola conducted detailed market analysis, tackled mistakes from cultural differences, registered trademarks in foreign companies, and began international marketing on an aggressive scale. Although it famously went global with the American forces during the Second World War the company was among many with serious competence in international marketing by the mid 20th century.

It is odd, then, that the first marketing text books that discussed international marketing, by and large, centred on how Americans could enter other countries. During the 1970s and 1980s there were an abundance of research projects and publications which focused on international marketing. These were polluted somewhat by the global ubiquity/end of history discussions of that period. Most practitioners are now searching, though, for a sensible balance between global infrastructure, with associated economies of scale, and local cultural sensitivity.

Voices and further reading

- Carson, D., *International Marketing: A Comparative Systems Approach*. John Wiley & Sons Inc., 1967.
- "The de-Americanisation of the term marketing has been hastened since the end of World War II as its original, narrow connotation began to be buffeted

about from opposite directions . . . Americans as well as non-Americans have realized increasingly that American marketing techniques do not apply perfectly in Accra, in Yokohama, in Cagliari, or for that matter, in Halifax . . . The identification and analysis of common factors and differences in marketing concepts, systems, and techniques among various societies, including nations, may therefore be considered the main thrust of comparative marketing." Carson, ibid.

- Wells, L.T., "A product life cycle for international trade?" *Journal of Marketing*, July 1968.
- "Companies can no longer afford failure to analyze opportunities for profit offered by exports and the possible threats to their own market posed by imports . . . the manager must have a continuing program to analyze the future directions of international trade in his products so that he may pan early enough for appropriate polices." Wells, ibid.
- Paliwoda, S.J., *International Marketing*. Heinemann, 1986.
- "International marketing concerns itself with the application of marketing operations across national frontiers. . . . [it] involves dealing with societies where politics, beliefs and values may be very different from those in the home market." Paliwoda, ibid.
- Phillips, C., Doole, I., and Lowe, R., *International Marketing Strategy*. Routledge. 1994.
- "The pressures of the international environment are now so great and the bases of competition within many markets are changing so fundamentally that the opportunities to survive with a purely domestic strategy are becoming limited to small and medium-sized companies in local niche markets. Because of this, many companies in both product and service markets are having to develop an international marketing orientation in order to survive." Phillips et al., ibid.

Things you might like to consider

(i) The balance between global and local considerations is one of the hardest things to get right and yet one of the most important.

(ii) There are many prejudices and idiotic assumptions in international markets which can cause real damage. Many wrongly assume, for instance, that the success of international Chinese businesses is largely due to cost and price. That can be far from the truth as the Haier case study shows.

(iii) Regional variances within national or transnational entities can be just as powerful as those differences between countries themselves.

(iv) All aspects of marketing need to be adjusted when working in international markets.

Haier: Chinese home appliance brand going global

Chinese consumer goods manufacturer, Haier Group, was the only white goods sponsor of the 2008 Beijing Olympic Games. It is the world's number one major home appliance manufacturer with a market share of 5.1%. As a direct result of its remarkably successful and recent international marketing strategy, Haier has established sixty-one trading companies worldwide, including nineteen in overseas markets; eight design R&D centres with five overseas; twenty-nine manufacturing plants, including twenty-four in overseas distribution; and four overseas Industrial Parks out of a total of sixteen worldwide. The Global Distribution network spreads into over 160 countries and 58,800 sales outlets. Haier has more than 60,000 employees worldwide. This remarkable international expansion story began with the opening up of the Chinese economy.

Since China's planned economy (which allowed the marketing of only Chinese products) was replaced by a market economy, the country has progressively opened its doors and become a major player in the global economy. Young Chinese brands competing within this new economic framework have experienced an approach to business which was not possible before. Some were eliminated, but many others have thrived in competitive international markets due to continuous self-improvement and rising to the challenge. Haier is one of those that has thrived through excellent international marketing. Today, for instance, one out of every ten refrigerators sold worldwide is a Haier brand.[1] As a result of its remarkable success (and, incidentally, other Chinese brands, like Lenovo[2] who sell one out of every ten of the world's PCs) business leaders have started to view Chinese companies with special interest and admiration.

HAIER'S ROAD TO GLOBAL BRANDING

In the early stages of Haier's development, the Chinese market was still relatively isolated with vast domestic demand exceeding supply. At that time, the price of a refrigerator was higher than the average worker's annual income. Due to the heritage, Haier did not believe that succeeding in the market depended on winning the hearts of consumers with quality products. CEO Zhang Ruimin set out to change that. For instance, he publicly drew attention to quality among all Haier's staff when took the lead in smashing seventy-six defective products. Haier then established its branding strategy and a zero-defect quality standard. As a result, it grew into the top brand in the Chinese refrigerator industry.

The early 1990s witnessed changes in the relationship of supply and demand in the domestic market. Haier expanded from one product to multiple products, from one brand to multiple brands, and from only producing white goods into black household appliances. The company grew from being the first brand in the Chinese refrigerator market to becoming the top brand in the entire Chinese home appliance industry.

In the early 21st century, though, Haier launched its "international strategy": "Three in One". It gradually set up the design, production, and marketing of this "operational framework model" in six regions (the Americas, Europe, Middle East/Africa, Asia, ASEAN, and South Asia). Haier products subsequently entered 160 countries around the world, achieving its arrival on the world stage. Then, in 2005, the business entered what it called a "phase of internationalization". With the rapid development of information technology and the integration of the global economy, it began to view every single market as a microcosm of the global market. Faced with increasingly fierce competition, Haier developed a unique strategy and a shift from quantity to quality in accordance with its own brand values.

HAIER'S OVERSEAS DEVELOPMENT STRATEGY: "THREE STEPS" AND "DIFFICULT FIRST, EASY LATER"

Multi-national companies (characterized by independent intellectual property rights and ownership of well known brands) have become a dominant force in the global economy. Losing a home market leads to instability, while a loss of the overseas market leads to less influence. Haier decided to be a powerful participant in international markets and separated its approach into "Three steps": "Get in", "Stay in", and "Leadership". "Get in" meant entering into mainstream markets using a "Difficult first and easy later" strategy. "Stay in" meant entering the main channels of mainstream markets to sell mainstream products. "Leadership" meant becoming a localized mainstream brand.

"Get in"

Haier used this approach to establish its brand overseas. Different from the "Easy first" strategy of other enterprises, Haier adopted a "Difficult first, easy later" principle in the development of overseas markets. This meant first entering developed countries with mature markets that demanded technology and products with strict requirements; and improving Haier's own technical ability and its products' adaptability in the process. Meanwhile through market segmentation, Haier focused on the products that consumers needed but rivals had missed so as to meet needs which were overlooked. For instance, Haier's first batch of exported products in the early 1990s was sold to Germany. CEO Zhang Ruimin said: "We choose the developed countries first to compete with international well known companies. Only by playing chess with grand masters can one make progress." The successful use of the gap strategy is also an important factor for the "Get in" strategy going so smoothly. Through market segmentation of developed countries, Haier identified and developed the potential demand, and avoided direct conflicts with both local and other strong brands.

Case 1: The US Wine Cellar

A large number of Americans prefer to drink wine and like keeping it at home. Wine cellars, however, can be very inconvenient for their life. Moreover, many families only keep about 10 or 20 bottles of wine at one time. Wine not only needs high placement requirements and cabinet design, but also has particularly stringent requirements on the temperature during the drinking and storage. Due to this particular local demand from US consumers, Haier designers developed a new stand-alone liquor cabinet suitable for the living room, which came into vogue immediately after entering the US market. In less than two years, Haier's liquor cabinet developed from one product into a series of twelve and from the first generation to the fourth. The fourth generation, the masterpiece of a famous French liquor cabinet designer, integrated practical utility, fashion, and European romance. It appeared on the cover of US magazine *International Wine* in 2001. The product took 60% of the US liquor cabinet market, with a price exactly twice that of similar products on the market.

Case 2: Little Smart Washer

Haier's "Little Smart Washer" meets the needs of consumers who want to wash a small amount of laundry at any time. The product has grown from the first generation to the eighth and achieved sales of several million units, creating a unique place for Haier in the washing machine market. The 5kg rotary drum washing machine designed for the Japanese market entered into the major appliance sales channels in Japan, and become the first in its sales category.

"Stay in"

Successful though they have been in entering many international markets, for Haier "Get in" was just the beginning. While they were getting in, rivals did not pay much attention. However, once it was clear that the company was trying to stay in, competitor suppression and resistance followed. Disorder in the competitive environment and trade disputes driven by the competitors' malicious dumping are examples of the resistance the company has experienced when trying to "Stay in". Improved technology levels also posed a challenge for the business at the "Stay in" stage. To solve these difficulties, Haier underpinned its international strategy with consolidation using R&D, production, and sales as its "Three in One" approach, together with localization of products, channels, marketing, and management. They set up twenty-nine manufacturing facilities and four industrial parks in the United States, Europe, Middle East and other places, achieving the manufacturing localization. The company also set up eight design R&D centres in Japan, the United States, Germany, and elsewhere, achieving design localization. It also established sixty-one trading companies and nearly 59,000 sales outlets worldwide, realizing marketing localization.

Product localization: Haier keeps strengthening its technology, R&D, and product innovation, and has launched mainstream products catering to the characteristics of local consumers.

Case 1: Pakistan gown washing machine

In Pakistan, local residents have a preference for big gowns. That local fashion, combined with large families, means that common washing machines are unable to meet the laundry needs of local consumers. The latest washing machine, designed specifically for this market by Haier washing machine developers, can wash more than thirty big gowns. When launched, the product quickly became a favourite of local consumers, reaching the number one sales spot among washing machines with the same capacity in Pakistan during that year alone.

Case 2: "Unbending" refrigerator

During India's hot summers, people like to drink cold drinks and at the same time, due to religious reasons, prefer vegetables and fruits to meat. So the refrigeration function is used much more frequently than freezing. However, common refrigerators are designed with the freezer section at the top of the refrigerator so people need to constantly bend down to get food. Haier fully understands the needs of the Indian market and switched the position of the two parts, keeping Indian people from bending over so much. This type of refrigerator became popular in India the instant it was launched, creating a "marketing miracle"; according to the company.

Channel localization: Due to the "Three in One" framework and subsequent breakthrough of products, Haier entered the top ten distribution channels such as Wal-Mart and BESTBUY in the United States. With its contributions to sustainable, green, and energy-saving product development, production, service, and other aspects, Haier was named the "top sustainable supplier" in 2009 by Wal-Mart.

It also entered the top fifteen European distribution channels in the same way. Haier products were accepted in KESA, Media Market, Carrefour, Expert, and other mainstream channels. In November 2009, for example, Haier's high-end large-capacity drum washing machines with mute function entered smoothly into the Germany's largest home appliance chain MSH, and led other Haier washing machines to realize a turnover growth through that chain of 45%

In Hong Kong, Haier has full access to the mainstream channels including Broadway, Gome, Best Appliances, Time Appliances, and Jusco with networks throughout Hong Kong, providing quality products and services for the residents.

Marketing localization: Haier launched differentiated local marketing programmes based on the characteristics of each market, and injected vitality into brand building and business development.

Case: Haier sponsored NBA

On 10 April 2006, Haier became an NBA strategic partner. Vice Premier Wu Yi attended the global strategic cooperation signing ceremony, underlining the importance of this move. Haier had become the first home appliance brand to sponsor the NBA. Through joining in with a popular American pastime and collaborating with the NBA, the company quickened its pace in becoming a mainstream brand in America. The four-year sponsorship deal contributed to Haier's success in creating a localized young, vibrant, and innovative brand image, and thus Haier entered into the US users' lives and gradually became a favourite brand. According to the research firm Millward Brown in 2010, Haier's brand recognition in the US has reached 35%, with outstanding performance in energy-saving and environmental protection and innovation.

Management localization: Haier attaches great importance to culture inclusiveness and construction, and seizes the essence of management by starting with culture. Having the staff of each localized institution agree with Haier's management and values is a necessary condition for the success of the "Stay in" strategy. As long as the company continues to expand, it will mix with local culture. Without an understanding of the culture or concept of international standards, "cultural collision" is bound to occur. No two cultures are alike, and it is wrong to force one culture to accept the other's ways. An alternative way, acceptable to both sides, has to be found.

Case 1: Staff prayer room in Pakistan industrial park

In Haier Pakistan, many employees are Muslims and they need to follow the religious requirement to pray every few hours. Haier fully respects this demand of local staff and specially sets up prayer rooms for them. This allows the local staff to feel Haier's care for them and enhances the cohesive power of employees.

Case 2: Teddy bears and toy pigs

Haier's management practices include a policy that the staff's performance will be published whether or not they are doing well or badly. However this caused difficulty in the United States where people think that only good performance should be published; otherwise it is seen as disrespectful. However, Haier requires that positive and negative incentives must co-exist. The American manager finally worked out a solution to this clash between global performance and local culture. He used a teddy bear and toy pig. The teddy bear was for good performance and the toy pig was for bad. Apparently, American workers were willing to accept this approach.

"Leadership"

Haier has developed world-wide overseas manufacturing bases and "Three in One" centres to lessen the exchange rate risk and reduce supply chain costs. The company gradually completed more overseas distribution, con-solidating its position in many international markets and laying the founda-tion for further "stay in" strategies. As a result, Haier's overseas market turnover has achieved remarkable, steady growth.

As a result of the financial crisis and the global market slump in 2008, Haier's international development strategy was adapted by upgrading over-seas markets. It sped up the "Get in, stay in and leadership" strategy and accelerated the pace of the development of high-end products. Meanwhile, the business model was reformed. It adopted an approach called: "Individual-goal Combination" to achieve, it says, both "win-win development and customer satisfaction" through establishing independent operations. A team that is committed to business objectives, has access to corporate resources, manages business resources, and shares benefits with the company. The aim is to fully stimulate the staff's enthusiasm and quickly acquire and meet market demands, so that everyone "becomes their own CEO".

Case: Three-door refrigerator

In the European Haier R&D centre, the Haier team, in response to the local needs of European consumers, integrated the talent of European, Asian, and American designers to develop a high-end Italian-style three-door refrigera-tor. This kind of refrigerator features four major elements, including a large capacity, stainless steel, and multi-door and drawer style. It is considered to be a remarkable breakthrough in creativity, appearance, design, and innova-tion. It won the Plus X award (a famous award in Europe) in 2009 because of its genuine European-style design and "human-orientated functions". In September of the same year, the monitoring of the average selling price of the refrigerator on the German market conducted by German statistics agency IFR showed that the average price of mainstream refrigerators was 746 euros, and Haier's refrigerator came in third, with an average price of 855 euros. This was higher than the industry average selling price and ranked third for German mainstream refrigerators. This was mainly due to the Italian-style three-door refrigerator and other innovative products. According to the world's leading monitoring body, GFK, Haier topped Germany's three or above multi-door refrigerator market with a market share of 75.9%.

These remarkable results are due to Haier's internal implementation of their "Individual-goal Combination" business model. As a direct result of this approach, the three-door Independent operation actively communicates with the retail centres of the market, and customizes, on demand, the marketing model instead of sticking to conventional marketing or slavishly following the annual marketing plan. For instance, to enhance the confidence of retail stores, Haier set up advertising signs outside retail outlets in order to increase footfall. Haier also set up a B2B official web site and training centres to enable the staff to fully understand the products. The company says that, at the "leadership" stage, differentiated marketing becomes very important.

Case: Haier and Italian football

Italians love soccer and the Italian Napoli Calcio football team, which Maradona once played for, has many supporters in Italy. In 2009, Haier signed a cooperation contract with the team and became an official partner of Napoli Calciothe which has 7.4 million fans world-wide. In the second half of 2009, the Haier LCD TV with the "Naples" team logo appeared in the Naples club's official web site. The product was in the team's symbolic blue and, without a base, was very convenient to move and watch. Once the colour TV was launched, it attracted the attention and favour of many fans, injecting a young, stylish, and innovative dynamic into Haier's brand image in Europe.

Case: Fashion show in Kobe, Japan

Haier's brand recognition in the Japanese market reached 39% in 2009, increasing 66%. The recognition amongst men compared to women was 50% and 30% respectively. Yet women are the main users of home appliances and decision makers in Japan. So, the aim of this initiative was to further enhance the Haier brand image, improve popularity (especially amongst women), and provide consumers with a philosophy toward home appliances of constant design. The company wanted to strengthen the brand image making it represent: "household appliances for your life". Haier sponsored the "Kobe collection" fashion show in 2010, and had in-depth interaction with the consumers who attended. It deepened the Haier brand image (of "household appliances for your life") in Japan and injected a fashion element into the Haier brand. During the event, Haier achieved year-on-year sales growth of 15% and had in-depth interaction with a total of 15,000 attendees.

SUMMARY

In December 2009, the world's leading consumer market research firm, Euromonitor International, announced the latest market research data of the global home appliance brands. It suggested that the Haier brand, with a global market share of 5.1%, has grown into the world's number one major home appliance brand. Meanwhile, Haier Refrigerator and Haier Washing Machine have both ranked first in the same industry with market share of 10.4% and 8.4% respectively. Haier's brand value reached 81.2 billion Yuan, topping China's most valuable brands for eight consecutive years. In April 2010, the US publication *Business Week* published "The 50 most innovative companies 2010 in the world" results. Haier Group was ranked at twenty-eight and was the only Chinese home appliance brand in the list. So, Haier has demonstrated in its international marketing that it closely follows market dynamics, respects local culture and the pace of changing consumer tastes. It constantly updates and improves itself, and is committed to being the best solution provider for good living conditions.

[1]According to *Euromonitor* data in Dec 2009, Haier is the world's number one brand of home refrigeration appliances with a market share of 10.4%.
[2]This data is from Lenovo.

L

**LOYALTY**

Application: strategy, communication, sales, NPD/NSD

The loyalty ladder

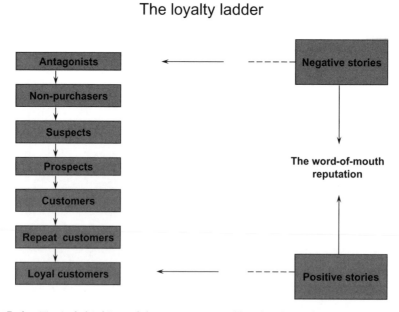

Figure L.1 Typical thinking of the progression of loyalty through repeat purchase and the effect on reputation

The concept

No marketer can put together a strategy or plan for a market of any kind without thinking through the relevance of this interesting concept. It is closely related to *service quality*, *after care*, and *relationship marketing*. It suggests that, if buyers think that they receive good service, they will be loyal to the supplier, returning again and again to buy. Loyalty, a long-term feeling of attachment to a supplier, is thought to occur when buyers are satisfied and have investment in the relationship which is too great to sacrifice for a cheaper or lower quality alternative. This has prompted marketers to think seriously about marketing to existing customers as much as (some would say more than) to new customers.

It has been the thinking behind many discount retail schemes to repeat purchasers and huge investment in customer relationship management (CRM) systems. Some have even asserted that it is the primary determinant of profit and growth because loyal buyers produce greater cash flow, cost less to service, and spread positive word-of-mouth (see Reicheld, F.F., 2003). The positive stories from loyal buyers counteract any negative reputation and, if they outweigh the negative stories, help to grow demand for the product or service (as illustrated in Figure L.1). This net positive reputation has been suggested as a measure called "net promoter" which, at the time of writing, many are examining.

There is evidence that people do become loyal at the point of purchase, feel warmth to a supplier, and return to buy. Yet loyalty is far more than a fabulous IT system, a revamped direct marketing programme, or the launch of a customer magazine. People need something to be loyal to; they need emotional resonance. For instance, by gaining emotional allegiance to some features of a *brand*, product managers have been able to earn incremental revenue over many years. Their brands have remained high in their category's sales leagues due to repeat purchase. The phenomenon also occurs with some corporate brands, such as Virgin. Buyers find that these entities offer them an experience that is reliably the same. It saves them time and effort, meeting a need in their life, time and time again. In fact, some people (like Harley Davidson owners, who tattoo their icon's brand on their own body!) take allegiance to quite astonishing levels, finding their sense of self-worth from identification with a group or perceived lifestyle.

One of the significant developments to emerge from the loyalty emphasis is CRM (customer relationship management) systems. These have been produced by many well regarded technology companies for about two decades. They not only contain and manage changing data on customers but integrate changing buying patterns with marketing management systems. They have been so popular that, at the time of writing, it is rare to find an established company that does not have a "campaign management system" integrated with customer data in this way. As these systems have been adopted, they have been adapted for different types of organizations and have prompted more and more marketers to consider *relationship marketing* and loyalty-based programmes. Yet, there have been serious studies which have questioned their efficacy and a number of marketing thinkers have suggested that CRM smacks of manipulation by suppliers. Nevertheless, the loyalty framework and the foundation of these systems has had a remarkable impact on marketing thought and practice.

History, context, criticism, and development

There is no doubt that the concept of loyalty has been the subject of a massive *thought leadership* programme. Kick-started by the publication of work by Fredrick Reicheld in the *Harvard Business Review*, it grew into a major breakthrough idea. Large consultancies and technology companies committed vast sums to marketing the concept. The prize for the former were significant advisory projects and, for the latter, major system sales. For a while it became very faddish, with many companies adopting it on a wave of publicity. As with all *thought leadership* programmes, though, that does not mean that the idea had no integrity or that it made false claims.

At the time of writing, academics are trying to analyse and digest the data to attempt to develop sound generic principles. Some think that the studies on which loyalty work relies have not, at the time of writing, been thoroughly tested (see Ambler, T., 2003).

Voices and further reading

- Reicheld, F.F., "Loyalty based management". *Harvard Business Review*, March–April 1993.
- Reicheld, F.F., *The Loyalty Effect*. Harvard Business School Press, 1996 and 2006.
- "Customer retention is a subject that simply cannot be confined within narrow limits. . . . business loyalty has three dimensions – customer loyalty, employee loyalty, and investor loyalty – and that are far more powerful, far reaching, and interdependent than we had anticipated or imagined. Loyalty has implications that extend into every corner of every business system that seeks the benefit of steady customers. Retention is not simply one more operating statistic, it is the central gauge that integrates all the dimensions of a business and measures how well the firm is creating value for its customers." Reichheld, 1996.
- "For most companies, customer loyalty is the single most important determinate of long term growth and profit margins." Doyle, P., 2000.
- Reicheld, F.F., "The only number you need to grow". *Harvard Business Review*, December 2003.
- Keiningham, T.L., Vavra, T.G., Aksoy, I., and Wallard, H., *Loyalty Myths*. John Wiley & Sons Inc., 2005.

- "Billions of dollars are spent every year by firms pursuing increased loyalty from their customers. Over 40,000 books have been written espousing the virtues of customer loyalty and offering methods with which to accomplish it . . . The simple truth is that the science studying the subject was incomplete. 'Incomplete' frequently tends to mean 'wrong'." Keiningham et al., ibid.
- "Loyalty segmentation involves identifying customers' loyalty to a brand or product. Customers tend to be very loyal, moderately loyal or disloyal. These groups are then examined to try to identify any common characteristics so the product can be targeted at prospective loyal customers." Payne, A., 2006.
- Shaw, R., "Net promoter" *Journal of Database Marketing and Customer Strategy Management*, August 2008.
- "So where does this leave net promoter? Well, it seems to be a lag indicator, whose cause-and-effect pedigree is poor and which is unlikely to have any serious management value in any except high-involvement purchases where people follow the advice of friends and acquaintances. In those situations, do choose net promoter, but apart from those I'd suggest you ignore it." Shaw, ibid.

Things you might like to consider

(i) If you want unquestioned, enthusiastic loyalty, get a dog. If you want to benefit from loyalty from customers there is a need to be smart, objective, and insightful. Marketers should understand the concept in great detail and master the source of loyalty effectively (whether it be brand, or, say, service).

(ii) There are some difficulties with this concept. Some corporate names and some service firms, for example, have no brand value or emotional allegiance. Trying to engender loyalty in these circumstances is difficult and assumptions can be made which are misleading.

(iii) Some people actually want anonymity. There are some buyers who just want to get on with the purchase and not to be interfered with at all. They want some low-involvement transactions to remain insignificant in their lives and the supplier should recognize that.

(iv) There are some buyers that a supplier does not want. Satisfaction is not an end in itself, but ultimately the basis of shareholder value. It is quite possible to have satisfied buyers who are not at all profitable. Logically, suppliers should choose which buyers they want and discourage those that they don't. This makes *segmentation* a key strategic issue behind loyalty investment.

(v) There is evidence to suggest that a number of customers regard the offers of some competing suppliers as, more or less, similar. Their reluctance to change is more apathy than loyalty. It is risky to try to create loyalty schemes in these circumstances or to rely on the assumption that the business is "all about relationships". If another supplier were to come along with a better scheme or, more effectively, a better value proposition, it would attract these buyers away. Suppliers need to take a hard-headed view of this issue. They need to understand the emotional allegiance of their customers in terms of the relationship and the value of any goodwill in terms of repeat purchase.

 RATING: Toxic

MARKET DEFINITION

Application: strategy, planning, NPD/NSD, communication

The concept

One of the most fundamental issues that marketers need to think about is how they define the market they operate in. This may sound simple, and it is, but there are many examples of businesses being damaged because their owners had not defined their market correctly. It is important because there is an assumption built into the fabric of a business that gives direction to its activities. If this assumption is not aligned to the market, the business will, in a competitive market, ultimately, fail.

Marketing and sales people can be so overwhelmed by the demands of their day-to-day job that they have very little time to investigate other industries or think about the relevance of different ideas to their market. As one of the classic marketing thinkers, Wroe Alderson, pointed out (Alderson, W., 1957), this results in group think and similar behaviours within markets, some of which is decidedly odd. Different beliefs and conventional wisdom grow up within different industry sectors which become the basis of business policy, such as a fascination with technology rather than what it can deliver. Some of these are profoundly idiotic and out of touch with the realities of the world. As a result, marketers, competitors, and buyers collude to conform to established ideas within markets, which can be restrictive.

A consumer might, for example, shop one morning for a branded, luxury good, perhaps as an important gift. In that market, long established brand names like Gucci or Chanel will be sought out. The shopper will expect their purchase to look and feel expensive, reflecting partly its durability and heritage. Some will even spend large sums on second hand branded pens or watches that are decades old. Yet in the same shopping trip they might also buy an over-the-counter drug (where markets are slow to change and investment is on a seven-year life cycle) and a personal computer (where technologists believe the customers are fast changing and only want cheapness). The precepts of each of these markets contradict, but are genuinely believed by the suppliers and, as a result, accepted by shoppers while they engage in that market.

Gerald Zaltman (Zaltman, G., 2003) has called this set of beliefs "the mind of the market" and it inhibits business opportunities. Occasionally, though, new propositions enter markets that shake up these ingrained attitudes. Richard Branson, for example, showed with his Virgin Atlantic service that it was possible to change the competitive landscape of the airline market by thinking differently and contradicting established group think. In their turn, propositions like First Direct (banking) and Direct Line (Insurance) have shown the wealth that marketers can make by challenging the status quo. So, marketers should take a moment to step out of the established beliefs in their market to see if new approaches can shake up their market a little, open up different opportunities, and create substantial wealth for their shareholders. Many do not, and spend their time projecting trends in sales from recent history, jumping to bash out e-marketing campaigns in the current quarter and combing the internet for reports from respected industry analysts which will confirm their preconceptions. Henry Mintzberg (Mintzberg, H., 2005) said that this is like primitive tribes throwing bones or consulting oracles on which way to go hunting. Instinct, history, and luck mean that they are sometimes right, but they frequently inhibit the potential earnings for their business owners by not stepping back and thinking.

So marketers must define for their company the market on which they will focus and this must be done in clear, customer-centric terms. This may be a generic proposition (like Disney's "Childhood Magic"), it may be an aspiration aimed at a wide market (like Black & Decker's famous reorientation to help people make holes rather than merely manufacturing drills), or it may be a carefully defined segment within a wider generic market. Market definition, or re-definition, is a route to profound market insight.

History, context, criticism, and development

The exasperated business professor, Theodore Levitt (Levitt, T., 1960), called the inability to correctly define a market "market myopia" and used the history of American railway companies (the computer companies of their age) to dramatize the damage that such thoughtlessness does. When they first appeared, they were handling a stunning new technology that would revolutionize life in the 19th century as much as (perhaps even more than) computer power did in the 20th. By the end of the 19th century, there were hundreds of thousands of miles of track in the USA alone, some crossing the entire country. The American railway companies then earned huge profits. So anyone approaching the chief executive of one of these companies in, say, 1910, and predicting that there were major new threats to the business that could see them virtually bankrupt by the 1930s/1940s, would be dismissed out of hand. And yet, thanks to the development of the car and the airplane, that is exactly what happened. According to Levitt's analysis, the American railway companies struggled because they defined their businesses as "trains" rather than "transportation". Had they focused their businesses on the "transportation market" they would have invested in these new technologies (perhaps backing a young Henry Ford when he needed funds) and moved their businesses in exciting, different directions.

Voices and further reading

- Alderson, W., *Marketing Behaviour and Executive Action*. Richard D Irwin Inc., 1957.
- Levitt, T., "Market myopia". *Harvard Business Review*, 1960.
- "The general rule for market definition is that it should be described in terms of a customer need which covers the aggregation of all the alternative products or services customers regard as being capable of satisfying the need." McDonald, M. and Dunbar, I., 1998.
- Zaltman G., *How Customers Think*. Harvard Business Press, 2003.
- "The mind of the manager (including both its unconscious and conscious elements) and the mind of the consumer (and its unconscious and conscious elements) interact, forming the mind of the market." Zaltman, ibid.

Things you might like to consider

(i) Experience shows that this can be enormously difficult to clarify but, once agreed, gives direction to innovation, leadership, investment, and service quality.

(ii) A radical market definition can give a new entrant real advantage if it is moving into an established market, which is dominated by complacent suppliers who all have a common view of the market need. The new entrant can quickly gain share by defining its offer more closely to customer needs.

(iii) Market definition can give direction to the whole firm, not just marketing functions.

Agreeing BT's service concept

BT is one of Europe's leading telecommunications companies. Its principal activities include local, national, and international telecommunications services, including high value internet services and complex business IT offers. In the UK, it serves over 20 million business and residential customers with a wide range of communications services including voice, data, internet, multi-media, and a range of managed and packaged communications solutions. It also provides network services, as a wholesaler, to other licensed operators. Its experience over the last twenty years is a good illustration of the need to be clear about the concept a business is putting to a market. Although its early experience of liberalization and privatization has made it one of the global pioneers in competitive telecommunications, it took the company a while to find the most effective direction.

PUBLIC SECTOR RESTRICTIONS

Up until 1984, British Telecom (as it was then known) was a government department, with all that that entailed. For example, prior to privatization, there were no real capital budgets and all investment money was provided by the Treasury. This meant that, like many of the then government institutions, it was often a low priority for funding. Under a right-wing government issues like defence, police, and security were higher priorities. Under a socialist government, on the other hand, issues like health and social benefits came to the fore. As a result, by the mid 1980s the majority of BT's infrastructure was under-funded and out-of-date. For example, throughout its network it was still using the "Strowger" electro-mechanical exchange for telephone switching (invented by a US undertaker in the 1880s) and much of this equipment was in a poor state of repair or in scarce supply. The British public had to apply to this government body for a telephone, which came in either black or cream. It was hard-wired into the network and, called Customer Equipment, was owned by the government (as were the wires and cables in the backbone network). There was also a three-month waiting list for a new phone while repairs could take over a week and were often poorly done.

In addition, the organization reflected its history as an engineering-led government department. For instance, while BT had the biggest fleet of vans in Europe after the then Soviet army, there were few qualified accountants, no appreciable profit, and no marketing department to speak of. Also, customers were served in strict order of request. This meant that a low earning residential customer was given exactly the same priority as a high earning business user.

In the run-up to privatization in 1984, the company embarked on a massive project aimed at separating Customer Equipment from the backbone network by introducing a socket at the entry into the customer's premises. This, coupled with new legislation, enabled the country to create a competitive market in the supply of telecommunications equipment ranging from single telephones to large scale private switches, bought by companies to handle their internal telephone calls.

SURVIVING IN A NEW COMPETITIVE ERA

Upon privatization, BT (together with several new, competitive entrants) started selling communications equipment. The race was on to capture as much of the market as possible before every major buyer had replaced their government rented apparatus with new technology. The company set up an extensive sales and marketing organization which spent all of its time focusing on selling equipment. This market was vibrant from the time of privatization to about 1990 and still exists. As it peaked, however, the company began to wonder what it would earn revenue from. It began to explore the sale of computers and IT equipment because "clearly the telecommunications market is mature".

However, there were even bigger and more dramatic changes to come. The British Telecommunications Act of 1984 had included a provision to introduce network competition. This was the first instance of this anywhere in the world and few believed it was viable. While it might now seem strange, most industry experts thought that competitive network telecommunications was an unrealistic aim and unworkable. Telecommunications businesses were thought to be natural monopolies that would not benefit from competition. This proved to be wrong.

After an initial set-up period, two other network competitors began operating in the UK. As they established their networks, BT began to realize that huge network revenues, which had been taken for granted, were now at risk. Managers at the time were heard to say that if they lost the "dialled revenue" from some of their major customers they may as well have given the equipment away because it affected profits so dramatically. In other words, they had been so focused on revenue from equipment sales that they had neglected the impact of revenue from calls.

MARKETING HUMAN RELATIONSHIPS INSTEAD OF TECHNOLOGICAL PRODUCTS

Ridiculous as it now sounds, it was only about four years after privatization that the company accepted that it was in the market of communications and its service was about communications. The director of advertising at the time, Adrian Hosford, oversaw this dramatic change in emphasis. It included the creation of a series of memorable advertisements, some of which have now become part of British culture. Much of the public, for instance, will still recall those with actress Maureen Lipman starring as "Beattie" and her "ologies". These began to make the process of communication human and had a measurable effect on the amount of telephone calls and therefore increased network revenue.

However, the most dramatic examples were the series of advertisements starring actor Bob Hoskins. These were designed by Hosford's team to exploit a piece of research which showed that men in families (before mobile phones) were often, at the time, the "gatekeepers" of the family's communications by phone, limiting the amount they talked and the amount of time the rest of the family spent on the phone. The campaign included advertisements which showed the positive and negative way a middle-aged man might talk to his elderly mother, and the positive effect of using the phone as part of the full repertoire of human communications in all contexts.

The company continues to use this approach in many of its core programmes. If it had simply limited itself to providing products, the business would have been badly damaged, perhaps irreparably. BT's market is "human communication".

 RATING: Practical and powerful

MARKET MATURITY

Application: strategic insight into market development, NPD/NSP, communications strategy

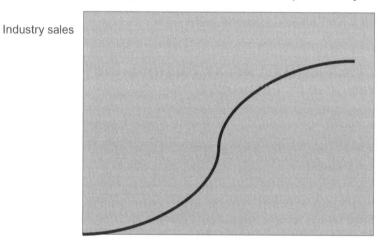

Figure M.1   A representation of market maturity trends

The concept

The phenomenon of market maturity reflects changing patterns in demand and supply, and occurs when there are multiple suppliers and multiple buyers in a market. It is normally represented by an S-curve (as in Figure M.1 above) and, as a result, is frequently confused with the "*product life cycle*" of individual offers. This is also closely related to (and often muddled up with) a sociological phenomenon called "*the diffusion of innovation*". (The latter is directly relevant to marketers because the products and services their companies offer are themselves part of innovative groups of offers which are diffusing across different societies in the world at different speeds.) Market maturity, though, is something distinct and different, the implications of which marketers need to understand.

This concept draws an analogy between biological life cycles and the sales growth of successful product groups, by suggesting that they are born, introduced to a market of human beings, grow in sales, mature (sales growth stops but profit growth continues), and then decline (sales fall). This organic analogy is probably relevant because the trend represents an iterative learning process between the buyers and suppliers in a market which mimics natural, organic growth. For example, a new mobile phone is easily communicated to a mature, sophisticated market which has grown used to the idea of mobile communication as part of life. Yet the extra cost of an iPhone would have been difficult to sell to a developing market where mobile communications did not exist. They would first have to accept the idea of mobile communication just as, at the time of writing, societies are beginning to think about, say, 3D television. So, taking a moment to understand the evolution of the macro market in which marketers operate is vital to the development of marketing strategy and campaigns.

At "birth" (the first introduction of the proposition to the world) a new concept sells poorly. Buyers are unaware of its existence, suspicious of the new idea, or experience problems when ordering (with production capacity, effective distribution, or product quality). Rogers, (who was largely responsible for the concept of diffusion of innovation, see Rogers, E.M., 2003) suggested that "bold" or "innovative" people buy the new product during this stage as a substitute for an existing product or to meet a newly identified need. They need to be shown how to use the innovation and how it is relevant to their lives. Suppliers need to educate the market in the concept and grow their business by inducing customers to try it. In this phase of a market's life, costs are likely to be high and firms can be unprofitable because of the high cost of sale. As a result, it may be wise for any businesses wanting to enter completely new markets to wait for upstarts to burn investment and establish the concept. They can then enter by buying them out. Companies who have successfully marketed true innovations, like Apple with its iPhone, have used a range of concepts to induce trial and spread word-of-mouth like a contagion. They rely heavily, for instance, on *PR* to create demand and mavens (see *viral marketing*), like Apple's "super users" to excite communities. Some argue (see Moore, G.A., 1991; Godin, S., 2004) that, with the disruption to broadcast media like TV and the interactive nature of digital marketing, marketers should concentrate on launching to these pioneers and encourage ideas to spread through viral marketing; to the exclusion of broadcast marketing aimed at later adopters.

As time goes by, customers become familiar with the concept and more buy it. In these early stages they frequently adapt it for different or unforeseen uses. When, for instance, the mobile phone markets began to expand in Western societies, suppliers tried to open new market niches, such as teenagers, with different styles of products. At the time, it was strange for youngsters to be given what was, until then, a luxury item often used only for business. These younger customers, with dextrous fingers from frequent use in computer games, did something unexpected. They started to use a little known facility to communicate (texting) which, at the time, was free in many markets. This opened up a new way to communicate, new patterns of behaviour, and even a new written language. The suppliers observed this behaviour and adjusted their products accordingly. They made keyboards friendlier toward texting, created new tools to help (predictive text), and changed tariffs to make it profitable.

In this phase, sales growth develops as a consequence of "word-of-mouth" communication (see *viral marketing*). Early buyers pass on the good experience of the product to others or re-purchase it. Producers and distributors (whether new to the market or well established) recognize the opportunity and switch over to produce their own version. The market broadens through policies of product differentiation and market segmentation. Profit margins grow as experience reduces unit costs and promotional expenditure is spread over a larger sales volume.

Quite frequently one product becomes the dominant offer and encourages more cautious buyers, "the late majority", to enter the market. This product becomes a market standard elbowing all others into narrow niches or oblivion. The "IBM PC" became, for example, the standard for the personal computer market pushing the Apple Mac into a specific, quirky niche. Similarly "VHS", "Hoover", "Google", and "Fedex" became the shorthand in their own markets for a whole product category.

The adjustments to innovations which come from the interaction between suppliers and early buyers, in turn, cause other people to buy and adapt them to their lifestyle. This increases the volume and the offer enters the growth phase of its market. There is strong natural demand and, in many cases, sales just walk through the door. In this phase of the market's life the firm has to concentrate on servicing demand, so established suppliers will be focused upon obtaining and deploying skilled resource. They must also ensure that there are efficient processes to capture and meet orders. It is possible to concentrate on internal issues, ignoring competitor moves because there is sufficient demand for all. As a result these markets are relatively easy to enter in a low risk way. In fact, natural growth with a small venture is probably the best method of entry, particularly if a supplier has a well known brand or a large number of existing customers who are likely to want their offer.

Maturity occurs because all markets are ultimately finite (in time, volume, and geography), and the market becomes "saturated" (most people have bought their first one). Sales growth becomes more or less flat as sales settle down to a level which reflects the regular volume of new buyers entering the market plus re-purchase rates. Profits can initially decline because companies need to adjust to the number of competitive offers. There can be some market consolidation during this transition which reduces competition. Companies can make cost reductions but those who succeed eventually thrive and become profitable though segmentation and real differentiation, normally achieved by hard trial and error.

Most buyers are familiar with the concept and have made their initial purchases. Sales growth in the market comes from replacement or added value sales, from innovation with new market segments. However, although established businesses in this type of market may be struggling to gain substantial sales, this is often a good time for new entrants to gain a foothold by attracting the attention of a few specific buyers and offering an experience that is truly different. They can, for instance, command the attention of a distinct niche of customers, carving out a profitable and enduring position for their firm by redefining the accepted rules or behaviours in the market (see *market definition*).

Most suggest that "decline" then occurs as buyers switch to new offers which offer advantages or benefits not present in the existing range. Producers initiate a new curve, bringing to an end that of the product group to be displaced. Declining sales are accompanied by falling profit margins as too many competitors fight for the remaining market. Price-cutting is prevalent and marginal competitors move out of the market. However, markets can be redefined or reinvigorated by legislation or new regulation.

Normally, suppliers in a market are buffeted by the forces at play in each phase of its development. However, if marketers understand what stage of development their market is in, they can set strategic direction for their firm in the light of that insight and perform more effectively. An individual product being offered into a market place can then be adjusted in the light and understanding of the relationship to the market conditions. The likely strategies in each phase of market maturity were suggested by Peter Doyle and are summarized in Table M.1 below. Marketers should be cautious, though, of being too prescriptive about the adoption of these strategic stances as the case study below shows. The assumption that markets decline is challenged by both the experience of the British railway industry and some of the detailed analytical studies (see Polli, R. and Cook, C., 1969).

History, context, criticism, and development

The market maturity concept has been tested, examined, criticized, and developed over the past four decades. It was observed by an economist and then brought to prominence by leading marketing writers. In 1962, for instance, Raymond Vernon published a paper in the *Quarterly Journal of Economics* (Vernon, R., 1962) which was "a by-product of the hypothesis stage" of a study into the foreign direct investment of the United States (sponsored by the Ford Foundation at Harvard). Just as significant, though, was the fact that his work was also published as part of a conference held by the American Marketing Association ("Emerging concepts in marketing", December 1962). There is little doubt that this kick-started the interest in *product life cycles, diffusion of innovations*, and market maturity amongst marketing specialists.

Table M.1 Strategic implications of different phases of industry maturity

Characteristics	Introduction	Growth	Maturity	Decline
Sales	Low	Fast growth	Slow growth	Decline
Profits	Negligible	Peak levels	Declining initially but eventually rising	Low or zero
Cash flow	Negative	Moderate	High	Low
Customers	Innovative	Mass market	Mass market	Laggards
Competitors	Few	Growing	Declining	Declining
Responses				
Strategic focus	Expand market	Penetration	Defend share through differentiation	Efficiency
Marketing spend	High	Declining	Rising	Low
Marketing emphasis	Product awareness	Brand preference	Brand loyalty	Selective
Distribution	Patchy	Intensive	Intensity	Selective
Price	High	Lower	Lowest	Rising
Product	Basic	Improved	Differentiated	Rationalized

Source: Doyle P., 1976

He pointed out that, at the time, the relative conditions of the US economy (higher labour costs and high disposable income) had led to the development of products ("the drip-dry shirt") which would not take off in other countries where, say, labour ("laundresses") was cheaper. He reviewed many reasons for starting labour-saving product innovations in the USA and settled on communication as a prime one. He described the "maturing product" and used the standardization of one product group (radios) as an example. His paper also quoted research into the office equipment and electronics industries. It used S-curves to show the phase of development of markets (he described them as: "new product", "maturing product", and "standardized product") and how to understand when to invest abroad. His work was unquestionably about product groups and the development of markets. (Incidentally, there was no assertion in his work that the normal sales pattern of individual products or services was an S-curve.)

There have since been some detailed studies which seemed to substantiate this phenomenon. Two academics at MIT, for example, (Polli, R. and Cook, C., October 1969) reported on tests into the "observed sales in 140 categories of nondurable consumer products". They tried to isolate certain variables like population growth and price changes. They also distinguished between: "product classes" (all those objects which are substitutes for the same need, e.g. cigarettes), "product forms" ("finer partitions of a product class"), and *brands*. Their work was numeric, objective, and thorough. It, by and large, confirmed the tendency toward an S-curve in product classes and product forms. The market maturity phenomenon for product groups appears to be a verifiable trend.

Voices and further reading

- Vernon, R., "International investment and international trade in the product cycle". *Quarterly Journal of Economics*, 1962.
- "All of these considerations tend to argue for a location in which communication between the market and the executives directly concerned with the new product is swift and easy…" Vernon, ibid.
- Wells, L.T., "A product life cycle for international trade?" *Journal of Marketing*, July 1968.
- "Empirical studies of trade in synthetic materials, electronic products, office machinery, consumer durables, and motion pictures have demonstrated that these products follow a cycle of international trade similar to the one which the model describes." Wells, ibid.
- "The product life cycle concept . . . has been formulated as an explicit, verifiable model of sales behavior and tested against actual data in 140 categories of durable goods." Polli, R. and Cook, C., October 1969.
- Swan, J.E. and Rink, D.R., "Fitting market strategy to varying product life cycles". *Business Horizons*, January–February 1982.
- ". . . entire industries have developed ways and means of operating efficiently within a particular PLC. The apparel industry, for example, has developed systems of rapid manufacture and distribution of clothing in order to live with the relatively short fashion cycle." Swan and Rink, ibid.
- "The telephone, the Beatles, the PC, the automobile, and many, many more other great innovations were derided early on. The absolute maximum size of the US car market was once established to be 20,000 since that was the number of those who could afford chauffeurs." Ambler, T., 2003.

Things you might like to consider

(i) The market maturity curve is often mistakenly referred to as the "product life cycle concept". Yet the phenomenon occurs in the sales volume of product groups over time, not individual products. There must be multiple suppliers and multiple buyers in markets that develop over time for it to be observed. (Individual products rarely go through a sales history similar to an S-curve. Most die soon after launch.)

(ii) As the phenomenon occurs when there are independent variables (i.e. groups of suppliers and buyers) it can be used to create marketing strategy. Many have found that the concept can be used to form a judgement about movements in the category's sales growth curve. They can develop marketing strategies appropriate to each stage in the life cycle.

(iii) Changes in the shape of markets, or categories within markets (e.g. filter cigarettes within the overall smoking market or rail journeys in the overall transportation market) may not be straightforward. They may be distorted by other macro economic forces as the case study below shows.

(iv) It is rather a shame that discussion of this subject tends to begin with the "introduction" phase and the "innovators". Marketers should also understand and consider "latent markets"; those that do not exist. For instance, in 1977, Ken Olsen, (the founder of DEC) said that there was "no reason why anyone would want a computer in their home" and, in 1947, the chairman of IBM said that he thought there would only ever be a world market for "about five computers". *The Economist* magazine reported that, in the 1980s, AT&T had asked McKinsey to estimate how many cellular phones would be in use in the world by the year 2000. A consultant (who still works for them at the time of writing and is, apparently, teased mercilessly by colleagues) noted all the problems with the then innovative devices (heavy handsets, poor batteries, awful network coverage, and costs). The advisers estimated the total worldwide mobile phone handset market would be about 900,000 by the year 2000(!), prompting AT&T to pull out of the market. People do not know what they want or desire, logic does not apply to the creation (or timing) of markets. Marketers need to develop clear, professional judgement about their advent and evolution.

Transportation markets in the 20th century

One of the industries that grew enormously during the 19th and 20th centuries was transportation. It enabled the mass movement of millions of people, the creation of new towns, new lifestyles, and new methods of working. Also, as technology evolved (and as Professor Levitt pointed out in his 1960 article) new forms of transportation opened up new markets.

It is possible to see the market maturity curve from long-term perspectives of these evolving markets. The diagram below, for instance, is based largely on figures from a historian (Hobsbawm, E., 1999) and shows passenger rail journeys in Britain since their inception. (The figures since 1999 come from the industry's publicly released results.) The market maturity curve can clearly be seen. Interestingly, though, since the 1990s, changes in socio-demographics, government policy, and the values of society have meant that rail travel in Europe has experienced a renaissance. This alone shows the dangers of using these trends to develop strategy. Rail was in decline in the 1960s as car travel grew and, as a result, rail infrastructure was cut back. At the time of writing, though, there are more rail journeys in Britain than ever before. The graph has kicked back up again. Marketers (contrary to what strategists would have recommended in this "mature/declining" industry) are launching campaigns to compete against both air travel and car journeys. They are growing a supposed falling market.

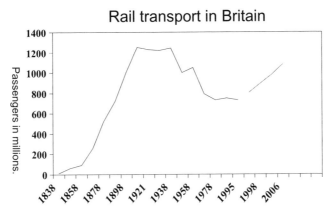

Figure M.2   A graphical representation of passenger rail journeys in Britain since the technology's inception

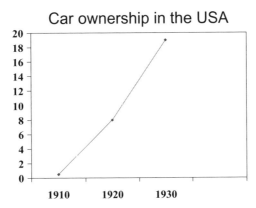

Figure M.3   A graphical representation of the advent of car ownership in the USA

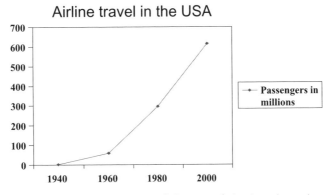

Figure M.4   A graphical representation of the growth in American air travel

The source of the other two graphs is an American business historian (Koehn, N.F., 2001). They chart the rise of American car ownership in the first half of the century and air travel as it changed from a rarity (in the early sixties when Sinatra could convey romance with "Come fly with me") to when it became commonplace (and anything but romantic in the public imagination). The industry maturity curve can clearly be seen. Yet again, though, marketers ought to be cautious about assuming that these booming markets will continue. The problems with oil, the slowly changing values to a greener society, and the Obama administration's policies toward high speed rail, may yet make other transportation options viable careers for marketers of the future.

 RATING: Practical and powerful

 # MARKET SHARE

Application: marketing strategy, NPD direction, sales strategy, communications strategy

The concept

This is one of the most straightforward and simple of concepts. The idea is that marketers measure the percentage of sales in any one market that their product or service takes. By understanding the share that their company has, compared to other competitors, they can adjust their strategy and marketing programmes. For instance, the company with the dominant share, the market leader, has significant advantage. It is thought that large market shares allow economies of scale, cash generation powers, re-investment opportunities, and the chance to dominate a market.

History, context, criticism, and development

Whilst it is possible to find references to "increasing your share of consumption" in early marketing text books (see Butler, R.S., 1917), the emphasis on market share dominance seemed to come to the fore in the mid 20th century. Bruce Henderson, for instance, was a very influential strategy advisor (see the entry under *Boston Matrix*) and reoriented his thinking to argue that share was an important determinate of profit.

He suggested that high share gave large economies of scale which allowed companies to reinvest and grow.

A particularly influential support to the argument in favour of market share dominance was the PIMS (Profit Impact on Market Share) research project. This was a long-term study which was set up as a collaborative research project (by the American Marketing Science Institute and the Harvard Business School) in 1974. In the first few years of operation it comprised about fifty-seven American companies with over 600 participating individuals. (It has since grown to become a broad international programme.) Each was asked to provide data in a strictly defined, comparable format. The first major finding of the survey was a link between explicit strategic planning and profit performance. However, within three years the leaders of the study were reporting a link between market share and profitability. They demonstrated that, in several sectors, dominant players were more profitable than smaller share operations. They suggested that the reasons for this included: economies of scale, market power, and quality of management. They made an explicit link between market share and return on investment. Based on the data, they observed the cost of several marketing strategies related to share and recommended that companies distinguish between: building strategies, holding strategies, and harvesting strategies. They were convinced that there was a level of market share in each market below which participation was not viable and companies withdrew. They also observed remarkable stability. Of the 600 business units that were then in the study only a fifth grew share by two points or more in the previous years. They observed that real share gains were made in all instances by new entrants in new markets, leading to the "first mover advantage" belief amongst many business leaders.

Voices and further reading

- Buzzell, R.D, Bradley, T.G., and Sultan, R.G.M., "Market share – a key to profitability". *Harvard Business Review*, January–February 1975. (This was a report on the fourth year of the PIMS project. By then the project has fifty-seven companies in its ongoing survey. The authors report a strong co-relation between high market share and profitability.)
- Buzzell R.D. and Gale, B.T., *The PIMS Principle*. The Free Press, 1987.
- "The primary reason for the market share-profitability linkage, apart from the connection with relative quality, is that large-share businesses benefit from scale economies. They simply have lower per unit costs than their smaller competitors. These cost advantages are typically much smaller than those once claimed by over-enthusiastic proponents of 'experience curve pricing strategies' but they are nevertheless substantial and are directly reflected in higher profit margins." Buzzell and Gale, ibid.
- "Most business people already understand that there is a direct relationship between relatively high share of any market and high returns on investment.

Clearly, however . . . it is important to be most careful about how 'market' is defined." McDonald, M.H.B. and Wilson, H., 2011 (7th edn).

- "Market share is very valuable. It leads to lower relative cost and therefore higher profits. Unfortunately, most efforts to improve share depress profits, at least short term. There are two principal reasons for a shift in market share between competitors. The most common is lack of capacity. The other reason is a willingness to lose share to maintain price." Bruce Henderson in *The Boston Consulting Group on Strategy*. Wiley, 2006.

- "A company following the market-share leadership strategy tries to reap above-average profitability by becoming one of the few companies remaining in a declining industry. Once a company attains this position, depending on the subsequent pattern of industry sales, it usually switches to holding position or controlled harvest strategy. The underlying premise is that by achieving leadership the company can be more profitable (taking the investment into account) because it can exert more control over the process of decline and avoid destabilising price competition." Porter, M.E., 1995.

Things you might like to consider

(i) In some markets where no external benchmarking exists or where competitive forces are new, it can be very difficult to understand or get detailed numeric measurement of share.

(ii) In some markets, it is not possible to drive for dominant share. Professional service markets, for example, have restrictions such as conflict rules (it is not possible to serve two competing suppliers). Or, where there are no restrictions, large share can be counter-productive. In the executive search market, for instance, if a search consultant wins a mandate to find talent for a company, they will often give an "off limits" guarantee (that their firm will not search for talent in the client company). However, if they won several mandates like this in the same sector, they would reduce their scope to search for candidates. In this market, dominant market share would be counter-productive.

(iii) Where sales and marketing people in business-to-business markets are focusing on one or two major, repeat customers, market share may not be an issue. Large businesses may not like certain suppliers serving their competitors, and so the original account selection is a critically important strategy. If customers restrain a supplier from going to their competitors with their offer then they must be carefully chosen in the first place. This makes "targeting" in any market of this kind a crucial marketing strategy.

(iv) Some marketers concentrate on getting a dominant share of the spend by their customers in a particular category. However, within some large organizations, and particularly public bodies, there are rules restricting the amount that any one supplier may have. This, again, demands smart strategy and planning.

(v) Where there is one supplier with a commanding lead or where there are one or two suppliers which dominate, others need to create viable strategies. Although share might be measured, it may be that they should concentrate on serving a segment of customers, a geographic region, or some other form of *differentiation*.

(vi) This idea has prompted many to fight and invest for incremental increases in share in many market sectors in many markets of the world. Like any marketing concept, though, it ought to be thought through because it is actually very hard to make major gains in "like for like" market share; alternative, less costly and less destructivek strategies might be available.

(vii) This is also not really relevant to the myriad of smaller businesses (or relatively small compared to their own market). They need alternative strategies to the drive for market share.

 RATING: Toxic

 # MARKETING COMMUNICATION

Application: communication with buyers, sales, strategy, revenue generation, brand building

The concept

This is another vast subject in which people, both academics and practitioners, spend their whole careers. It is difficult to capture the subtlety, experience, complexity, and depth of those who do it really well. It is easy to see, though, the crassness of those who do it badly.

It is not an efficient use of resources to rely on sales teams, major account managers, or fee earning partners in professional service firms to generate revenue alone. Nor is short-term, tactical, sales support enough. Numerous businesses in many different markets have demonstrated that the use of carefully designed marketing communication techniques paves the way for sales; that investment in communications saves money. Communication campaigns can be used to attract initial attention, to stimulate interest, and to induce customers to buy, sometimes without the intervention of a sales person at all. Even in markets that are heavily reliant on a sales person, a retailer, or a consultant to close and deliver a sale, the use of marketing communications can, cost-effectively, attract customers to the point of sale and reassure them afterwards that they did the right thing.

Marketers seeking to optimize the contribution of communications to the sales process should take advantage of the complete range of modern communications. But they must think before they do. To communicate effectively with a group of buyers and to influence their purchasing behaviour, marketers must resolve a number of important and sometimes complex strategic issues. These include:

(i) Understanding the intended segment of buyers

One of the most important components of effective communication is a deep under-standing of the human beings for whom it is intended. Marketers must decide which buyer groups to focus on and concentrate on them to the exclusion of others. They must then invest in understanding both the rational and emotional needs of these people. If there is one difference between marketing-literate companies and others, it is their concentration on customer knowledge and their willingness to invest in research to get it. The leadership of their companies knows, through bitter experi-ence, that their sales success hangs upon the intimacy and warmth of their customers' responses to their communication. They invest in regular, deep research to understand this dynamic and to adjust to it. Moreover, they invest in recruiting and training experts whose job it is to understand this relationship.

It is in this field, probably more than any other, that a *behavioural* view of markets is important. Marketers must understand their intended group of customers in as much depth as possible. Who are they? How many are in the group? What do they think, feel, and believe? What are their aspirations, dreams, and ambitions? What do they read? What do they listen to? Which conferences do they attend? Which voices of authority (individuals or organizations) do they respect? What professional associations do they belong to?

Good marketing communication is grounded on data about the human beings at whom it is directed. Most experienced advertisers know exactly how many shoppers they are aiming at and their intended audiences' attitudes to the product through systematic investment in research data or response mechanisms. In modern businesses, there is no reason why marketers should not have data on: their customers' attitudes, the competitive reputation of their offer, the propensity of customers to refer them to others, and the play of their brand in the purchase process. All can be obtained through careful, systematic research and all will increase the effectiveness of com-munications. Marketers should steadily invest in customer knowledge, setting up processes to retain "corporate memory" of customer behaviour. There is no excuse for the arrogance of "gut feel" based on the experience of just a few customers and internal dialogue.

(ii) Creating and managing the message

Effective communication often depends on the use of one simple, relevant message. It has to be relevant to the target group to ensure impact and simple enough to be taken in by people in a brief moment of time. It also needs to be capable of sufficient repetition to become familiar to the intended audience without becoming irritating or boring. The message needs to contain a definite proposition which should be unique and strong enough to persuade people to act. It is likely to contain both rational elements (giving the reasons why the offer should be bought) and emotional appeal. It might be testimonial-based (using examples of others who have bought) and "dramatic" (using a narrative to convey meaning). Some are humorous (using laughter to appeal to humanity and create empathy) whereas others focus on fear (raising concern about consequences). Yet, it takes enormous effort to achieve the elegant simplicity of an effective message. The marketer needs to work with communications specialists in order to frame this message to the market place appropriately.

The timing of the message also needs to be carefully considered. At the lowest level this involves timing in relation to customer needs or in terms of other messages. In Europe, for instance, the culture of many countries is to take long holidays in August and many business people return in September ready to start new initiatives; this is a good time to start communication campaigns. However, suppliers should also think about the timing in terms of the customers' phase of thinking and progress along the buying process. Messages which introduce a new concept, for instance, can be tailored to customers who are at the early phase in their thinking. Whereas, messages aimed at those near purchase will emphasize benefit and include a call to action. Messages aimed at those who have purchased, however, may be about service, process, and post purchase reassurance.

(iii) Allowing for the maturity of the market

Marketing communications strategy needs to be different at different stages in the market maturity process. For instance, when an idea is completely new, a true innovation (as Blue-ray was in the 2000s, mobile phones were in the 1990s, and video recorders in the 1980s), suppliers need to make people comfortable with the idea before they can sell individual products or services. They must use *PR* to educate and *viral marketing* to help the concept diffuse across the country in which their intended market resides. Articles must appear in magazines and newspapers that discuss the innovation and how it has occurred. Exhibition stands and news items should be dedicated to it. The IT industry has been particularly good at stimulating this form of *PR* because of its genuine excitement about new technology and the links between places like Silicon Valley and venture capitalists (which prompt news stories about new technology deals). In parallel with this, sophisticated marketers will focus on individuals who buy new concepts, those "early adopters" (see *diffusion of innovation*) or mavens. They are the geeks who enthuse about new ideas and love to buy new technology, called by some "Freds in sheds".

Marketing communications strategy at another phase of the industry maturity is likely to be completely different however. In a mature market (like perfume, soft drinks, or computer maintenance, at the time of writing) customers are very familiar with the concept. In these market conditions, suppliers are after profit by teasing out defined segments and creating fascinating forms of differentiation.

(iv) *Brand* building

A firm's *brand* is one of its most precious intangible assets, affecting both the price and quality of everything it offers (see separate entry). Part of the strategy to enhance its value is likely to involve programmes that communicate the brand specifically to the general market place in order to make it famous. The main tool for this is, of course, broadcast marketing communications: advertising consistent messages. The marketer should also ensure that regular funds are set aside to enhance their brand through building fame by consistent communication to the chosen market. The brand needs to be a clear and well understood component of all marketing communication; a dominant theme of communication strategy.

(v) Competition, share of voice, and other influences

Suppliers need to consider the impact of their communications and the investment needed in the light of other messages that the intended customers will receive. These might come from direct competition or completely different concepts. Both can influence the customers' attention to the message. Yet the overall demands on people's attention also need to be taken into account. In a busy, modern lifestyle they are assailed by many different messages through many different media. Too little communication will mean that the message will not reach the threshold necessary to command attention, in the light of other demands (as Figure M.5 above tries to represent); on the other hand, too much will lead to saturation, undermining the impact as buyers become bored.

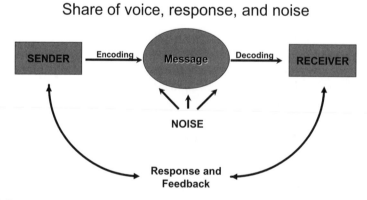

Share of voice, response, and noise

Figure M.5   A representation of marketing communication issues

(vi) Managing the creative execution

One of the aspects of marketing communication which can be the most powerful in convincing customers to respond or buy is the creative components of the campaign. This can range from the text used in emails through to the music and film which are part of a full broadcast advert. It is beyond doubt that the quality and appeal of the creative representation of a message can have a dramatic effect on an audience, affecting buying behaviour and recall. It needs to be taken seriously, even by *business-to-business* marketers.

While some make up their own, most marketers invest heavily in the creative execution of their communications needs. They use graphic designers for proposals or brochures, web designers for internet-based work, video teams for both staff and customer communications, and advertising agencies to design advertisements. The variety and range of work is as wide as the methods used to manage this resource. For instance, some firms have used elaborate design techniques for individual sales proposals. Many have large in-house design teams, often supplemented by ad hoc design consultancies. In an ideal world, creative work ought to be selected using competitive processes and an agency brief. It should follow the brief, not drive it. While many firms work well over many years with small agencies who learn their culture, a new, complex, or significant project should be subject to competitive tender.

(vii) Which media to use and when; how to integrate their cumulative effect on customers' opinions

As important as the creative elements of a communications campaign is the precise and careful planning of which media to use. There is a variety of media that influence the intended market group. They include, for instance, the tools of broadcast *advertising* (TV and newspapers), *digital marketing* (the web), *direct marketing*, PR, the firm's *sales* people, employees, and referrals from people that customers respect (word-of-mouth: see *viral marketing*). All need to be understood and used precisely. The frequency, cumulative impact, and style of the message being communicated through that medium needs to be planned very carefully. In an ideal world an intended customer will receive the same message, whether it is from TV, magazines, or the web. This is well understood in many consumer markets but it also applies in *business-to-business* marketing. A customer might receive the message from the professional association to which they belong, an article they read, an informal discussion with a colleague, or a presentation from the supplier. Well crafted messages will get through to the market place, with a subtlety that hides the calculated planning of appearance in relevant media.

The skill of communications planning is designing the right mix of these different media and different techniques to influence customers' thinking, called recently "Integrated marketing communications" (IMC). By planning an integrated approach and managing various agencies to deliver it, a concerted effort can be made to communicate an idea to a customer. The customer might receive an invitation to an event one day, see a newspaper article the next, read a blog online, notice an advertisement after that and, finally, talk to an employee of the firm. Well planned communications prepare the way for a direct conversation, optimizing both time with the customer and costs. IMC examines all the channels through which people receive messages about the offer and uses models to plan the frequency of communications through different media. This must be done by the firm itself to achieve a good balance of effective communication and spend. Normally marketers will manage a group of different agencies throughout one campaign to achieve this.

At the same time, IMC improves the cost-effectiveness of marketing communications. To date marketing promotion has tended to be a supplier driven industry. External specialist agencies have been hired by companies to carry out one of a wide range of promotional techniques. Developing an integrated approach has been made difficult by the focus these agencies have on their own area of expertise. Most advertising agencies want to do advertising, most direct marketing and public relations consultancies want to do direct marketing or PR, and so on. They all tend to stay in their own silos. (For a time there was a move in the industry toward a "full service agency", or the one-stop shop, but that concept has not really taken hold.) Even the big networks, which own a range of different marketing agencies, have difficulty in combining them effectively to produce the best balance of communications vehicles for their clients. However, a firm that adopts IMC can itself manage the balance of different agencies, saving costs and improving impact. This is at the heart of good "client side" *marketing management*.

(viii) Response management and adjustment in the light of feedback

Modern marketing communications also looks for a response from the buyer. This goes beyond the relatively unsophisticated practice of broadcast marketing promotion in that it plans, from the start, a process of two-way communications between the firm and the buyers. A response, through a database or a dedicated micro site or a response driven promotional campaign, can give the marketers an idea of the effectiveness of the communication. It can also point to improvements the buyer needs from the company in the form of either quality of service or adjustment to the proposition. The company can then improve its profits and brand value by responding to these messages.

So, marketers must develop clear communications strategies which give precision, clarity, narrative, and impact to any practical marketing communications. The essence of good communication is: good strategy, clear objectives, good targeting, a poignant message, and imaginative creative (particularly writing) and effective organizational capabilities. Moreover, these issues need debate and resolution at senior levels in the firm before planning and implementing the detail of any campaign because they have financial implications. Marketers must learn to craft carefully targeted communications that are digestible and easy to understand, while at the same time cutting through the myriad of other messages to reach their intended audience.

History, context, criticism, and development

There is evidence of businesses using different marketing communication techniques for many years. As described in their individual entries, *advertising, direct marketing,* and *PR* have a long history of contribution to brand building and profit. It is arrogant beyond belief to assume that these earlier marketers and business leaders had no understanding of "modern" communication ideas. The success of names like Heinz, Wedgwood, Singer, Pears, Lever, Colt, and Woodruff (Coca-Cola) in creating profit and enduring businesses in dirt poor societies where their markets did not previously exist is, in many ways, much more impressive than the day-to–day functionalized existence of many modern marketers. The behaviour of many of these people (and others) formed the foundation of modern communications theory.

Yet, the way marketing communications was described in the early days of marketing theory ("promotion") is completely inadequate because it implies that any activities are one-way: directed from the supplier to the customer. It is true that suppliers need to put clear, simple propositions to groups of customers. It is also true that they need to be put in attractive, distinctive, and meaningful ways that stimulate their desires and appetites. If suppliers do not communicate effectively, they cannot overcome the noise of other claims on their intended customer's attention. Buying simply cannot begin if potential customers do not know who you are or what you stand for. As the adverts for McGraw-Hill once ran: "I don't know who you are, I don't know where you come from, I don't know how long you have been in business, I don't know who your customers are . . . now, what are you trying to sell me?" (see McCarthy, E.J., 1975).

Toward the end of the 20th century several concepts emerged which affected both theory and practice in marketing communication. Most academic texts, for example, began to adopt the term "integrated marketing communication" to reflect growing consensus that all the aspects of communication need to be carefully deployed and used to convince an audience of a message. The very best practitioners found this to be a statement of the obvious. Despite the biases in the marketing supply industry they had been integrating messages across multiple media for some years. Another emerging concept was the emphasis, on responsive marketing communications. With growing interactive technology, markets began to put greater emphasis on stimulating a response from their customers and responding to that response. Even with large broadcast brands (like TV shows or magazines) it became increasingly recognized that people wanted to engage and respond. This led, for example, to interactive advertising campaigns and a greater emphasis on dialogue through, say, digital media. This, in turn, led to a re-emphasis on word-of-mouth and viral marketing. The advent of social media and an increasing codification of relationship marketing led marketers to explore, in a more structured way, the communication of messages through networks and inter-related communities. If marketers want to capture the imagination of modern buyers, they must also communicate with them by getting a response and adjusting their message in the light of that response. They must listen and respond as much as they plan and pronounce. Effective marketing communication is a two-way process not a one-way broadcast.

Voices and further reading

- "In recent years, the marketing communication environment has experienced the fragmentation of traditional advertising media as well as the emergence of new, non-traditional media, promotion and other communication alternatives . . . As a result of these and other changes, a modern marketing communication program typically employs a host of different communication options." Keller, K.L., 2001.
- Dahlen, M., Lange, F., and Smith, T., *Marketing Communications; A Brand Narrative Approach*. Wiley, 2010. A fascinating and through little text book which emphasizes the power and importance of branding in all aspects of marketing communication.
- ". . . today's marketing communications has to be integrated, must move away from a tactics orientation and must be able to grow with the target audience. Marketing is moving away from managing customer transactions to managing internal and external relationships and from passive to interactive multi-channel marketing communications strategies. Marketing communications is concerned with engagement: the planned, integrated and controlled interactive dialogues with key target audiences to help mutually beneficial objectives." Dahlen et al., ibid.
- "Marketers do not promote simply to inform, educate and entertain; they communicate to facilitate satisfying exchanges-products or services for money or donations." Dibb, S. et al., 2006.
- "A method for the selection of appropriate business-to-business integrated marketing communications mixes." Garber and Dotson, 2002.
- "Advertising strategy", Sternthal, B. in "Kellog on Marketing" (ed) Iacobucci, D., 2001.
- "The shift from mass marketing to segmented marketing has had a dramatic impact on marketing communications. Just as mass marketing gave rise to a new generation of mass-media communications. So the shift towards one-to-one marketing is spawning a new generation of more specialized and highly targeted communications efforts. Given this new communications environment, marketers must rethink the roles of various media and promotion–mix tools." Kotler, P., 2005.

Things you might like to consider

(i) This is a precise and carefully orchestrated, long-term operation, needing a mix of strategy, creativity, and bog-standard managerial capability. The very best combine all three.

(ii) One of the inhibitions that inexperienced firms often have about brand building and brand management is the wrong perception that it is based on expensive advertising alone. Yet several well known, successful brands (like Virgin) have been built without advertising. See, for example, the research by two academics, (Joachimsthaler, E. and Aaker, D.A., 1997) which demonstrates that there are several ways to communicate a brand promise to a market, particularly for service businesses. The first is through the experience of the product or service. Starbucks, for example, launched new coffee shops by handing out free coffee and used no associated advertising. The second is by investing in and managing internal communication so that employees are clear about the firm's position in the market and speak with a common voice to customers. Another tool is PR. There are good examples of brands built through PR and publicity alone because they have gained fame or a strong reputation through a sustained public profile. Several companies which started with a modest budget have, through targeted reputation management, turned their brand into a substantial intangible asset. Their techniques include media relations (proactive work with journalists and editors), sponsorship, and publicity.

(iii) Good communication is carefully planned and sustained. It is simply not effective to put out erratic, short-term tactical programmes hoping that they might elicit responses that lead to sales. Neither is effective communication a collection of ad hoc tactical under-funded programmes such as "email blasts" or "webinars" which change month by month. These techniques work well in the context of a carefully designed, integrated communications programme that has cumulative impact on a well understood group of customers. On their own and out of context, they are almost a complete waste of money.

(iv) If your company has little data on its intended segment of customers, media planning specialists in advertising companies can determine which medium has the most impact upon an individual customer group whereas good quality research will give insight into their attitudes and needs. By understanding this level of detail, marketers will create communications that will be effective and appealing; the investment will be well directed.

MasterCard and "Priceless"

MasterCard is an American multi-national corporation with its headquarters in New York. It processes payments between merchants and their customers who use its debit and credit cards. MasterCard has been a publicly traded company since 2006 but, prior to its IPO, was a membership organization owned by the 25,000 financial institutions that issue its cards. Originally known as MasterCharge, it was created by several California banks as a competitor to the card issued by Bank of America, which later became Visa. MasterCard has created an enduring, distinct, and simple message, which has earned it awards, impact, revenues, and distinction: the "Priceless" campaign.

At the time the campaign was conceived, American Express and VISA were the company's main competitors. Both had strong brand values and personalities built in the 1980s era of materialistic, outer-directed, success-focused values. MasterCard, by contrast, lacked emotional currency or aspiration. It was seen as ordinary, unassuming, unpretentious, and practical. However the consumer climate was changing.

MasterCard's communications strategy, which was started in the US, was based on substantial consumer research and the insight that there had been a significant change since the 1970s attitude of, "You are what you buy". Consumers were focused on lifestyle and quality, and on the concept of "rewarding yourself for what you've earned". Their core values had become: family, security, companionship, and "making time for yourself". At the time, it was unique for a credit card company to say to consumers, "It's not about what you buy; it's about how you take care of yourself." Economic pressure and growing debt began to take its toll, so that the materialistic, outer-directed consumer culture was giving way to a growing search for quality of life, relationships, and greater balance between work, family, and leisure. This, in turn, was leading to a more enlightened, if wary, view of credit cards. MasterCard called the consumers who adopted this mindset, "Good Revolvers" because they used credit cards to acquire the things that mattered to them, things that enriched everyday lives.

Their advertising agency was McCann-Erikson who took stock of the situation. In 1997, MasterCard didn't stand for any one thing. This was partly because their communications effort was diluted. The organization had run through five different advertising campaigns in ten years and was losing a lot of business. At that time, every country in the international organization used a different agency, a different campaign, and a different strategy. The success of "Priceless" as a platform in the US helped persuade other countries in the network to adopt a single approach. So, over time, this became a consistent global positioning. The "Priceless" campaign eventually appeared in nearly a hundred countries and over forty languages. It formed the framework for all the company's brand communications and allowed MasterCard to integrate all its other campaigns and marketing practices. The idea started as an advertising strategy, became a marketing platform, and went on to become a global brand platform.

The purpose of the campaign was to position the card as a friendly credit card company with a sense of humour, as well as a response to the public's worry that everything is being commoditized and that people are becoming too materialistic. They summed up their selling idea as "The best way to pay for everything that matters". Their communication idea, based on a detailed understanding of the people they were aiming at became "Priceless moments"; and this, in turn, translated into a message: "There are some things money can't buy. For everything else there's MasterCard." This became the tagline for the "Priceless" campaign.

The first Priceless adverts were run in 1997, quickly followed by numerous different TV, radio, and print ads. They were so successful that MasterCard actually registered Priceless as a trademark. Interestingly, part of the success of the campaign has been prompted by the parodies it stimulated in various parts of the world. Some were circulated on the internet; others were on broadcast TV – America's Comedy Central, for instance. Despite the fact that these lampoons added to the campaign's momentum, MasterCard threatened legal action against some. Apparently, it took presidential candidate Ralph Nader to court after he produced his own "Priceless" political commercials (he was victorious).

Several things helped their complex (pre-2006) organization to adopt the commercials:

(I) RESEARCH

They found that their US insight held just as true for every other country. The success in this situation came from taking the insight to a level where it cut across every culture and country, based on an extensive understanding of what really matters to people.

(II) THE SUCCESS OF THE US CAMPAIGN

The great success in the US simply grabbed the attention of the organization.

(III) APPEAL

Nobody believed any other alternative campaigns were any better. Most importantly, whenever local marketers saw the campaign, they really liked what they saw.

(IV) RECOGNITION OF LOCAL NEEDS

They empowered each local team by creating a strategy framework within which they could create and focus their own content.

In more recent iterations, the Priceless campaign has been applied to both MasterCard's credit card and debit card products. They also use the "Priceless" description to promote products such as their "Priceless travel" site which features deals and offers for MasterCard holders. The success of the campaign demonstrates the power of a simple, relevant, and memorable idea backed by a clear communications strategy.

Source: constructed from publicly available information.

RATING: Practical and powerful

(🔍)MARKETING CONCEPT

Application: strategy, organizational development

The concept

The marketing concept suggests that the buyers and the market, not exclusively the operations of the firm, should be at the centre of management's attention; and that, by putting attention on the market, long-term profits can be achieved. Over the years it has been called "market-orientated" or "customer-led" but is the antithesis of the internal orientation of many firms. Some are sales–led, some fascinated with technology or product enhancement while others are monopolies, preoccupied with internal rivalry. These approaches can be successful for a time, generating funds for owners, until market conditions change. If new regulation is passed or an aggressive competitor changes market dynamics, or the industry reaches market maturity firms without a market orientation can fail.

This simple concept is in all marketing text books and can sound like wishful thinking by marketing theorists, keen to press for greater influence for their discipline, because, in practice, the experience of many marketers is almost the opposite; that the function is not appreciated or allowed to contribute as it might. They become absorbed with changing daily priorities, tactical rather than strategic work, and the need to engage in internal politics to protect the contribution of their function. But this concept is more than an academic wish, a passing management fad, or theoretical fantasy. Numerous papers (from Professor Benson Shapiro's *Harvard Business Review* article: "What the hell is market orientated?" to Regis McKenna's "Marketing is everything") and long-term tracking surveys (like the PIMS database) have shown that market-orientated companies produce long-term to business owners return.

A market-orientated company understands its market and anticipates future trends, exploiting emerging opportunities. It is forward looking and intimately engaged in understanding the minds and responses of its buyers. Brand management and marketing functions are often lead functions of the business, maintaining a market perspective for all functions.

History, context, criticism, and development

Some attribute this concept to Robert Keith, CEO of America's Pillsbury dough company in 1951 (see Pelton, L.E., Strutton, D., and Lumpkin, J. R., 2002). Whatever its origin, there is no doubt that an announcement by America's massive company, GE, in the 1950s put it on the map (see Vaghefi, M.R. and Huellmantel, A.B., 1998). In 1957, the then CEO, Ralph Cordiner, announced that "marketing would be both the corporate philosophy and the functional discipline to implement the philosophy".

This surprised audiences and needed to be explained. Up until then, he said, all planning had been internally orientated, focused on solving internal problems. This change set the foundation for an externally orientated culture.

Evidence suggests that, since then, each CEO has chosen their successor as a means of continuing this philosophy, amongst others, and the consequent enduring legacy has been the foundation of GE's outstanding success. Under Jack Welch this huge conglomerate routinely exceeded expectations in terms of shareholder return and, for over a decade, came top in survey after survey as the most admired company, particularly amongst CEOs. But this success was built over the long term, with each CEO setting the conditions of the next. Market orientation appears to have been an ingredient in its success. It certainly appeared to start the debate amongst marketing specialists about market orientation.

Many other industries succeed by market orientation. The professions, for example, contain a number of highly successful, remarkably profitable businesses (like McKinsey, Deloitte, and Clifford Chance). Whilst they generally shun recognized marketing techniques, the owners of these businesses, the partners, tend to be very market conscious and responsive. The elite practices put unquestioned emphasis on reputation management and client service. At their heart, though, are the individual practices led by partners with highly specialized skills or experience. These respond very quickly to market need and even ignore internal leadership directions to service their clients. They have their own reputation and the leadership even talks about these partners being "in the market".

Voices and further reading

- "The marketing concept is a philosophy, not a system of marketing or an organizational structure. It is founded on the belief that profitable sales and satisfactory returns on investment can only be achieved by identifying, anticipating and satisfying customer needs and desires – in that order. It is an attitude of mind which places the customer at the very centre of a business activity and automatically orientates a company toward its markets rather than toward its factories. It is a philosophy which rejects the proposition that production is an end in itself, and that products, manufactured to the satisfaction of the manufacturer, merely remain to be sold." Barwell, C. in Wilson, 1965.
- Shapiro, B., "What the hell is market orientated? *Harvard Business Review*, August 1987.
- Pelton, L.E., Strutton, D. and Lumpkin, J.R., Marketing Channels: *A Relationship Management Approach*. McGraw-Hill, 2002.
- McKenna R., "Marketing is everything". *Harvard Business Review*, January–February 1991.
- Vaghefi, M.R. and Huellmantel, A.B., "Strategic leadership at General Electric". *Long Range Planning*, 31, 1998.

- "The business enterprise has two and only two basic functions: marketing and innovation. Marketing and innovation produce results: all the rest are costs." Drucker, P.F., 1954.

Things you might like to consider

(i)   Even at the most senior levels there is little that a marketing specialist can do to turn a company which is not market-led into one that is. This is a process of evolution involving organizational learning and politics.

(ii) Whatever the theorist says there is no doubt that some businesses which are not market-led thrive and produce fabulous, iconic marketing programmes.

(iii) Being market-led does not seem to be the same as having marketing people in charge. There is little evidence that having senior marketing people in charge of major organizations makes them more market-led or improves their actual results. In fact, there have been some memorable disasters, such as Northern Rock, as marketing people have got to the top.

> ★   **RATING: Practical and powerful**

MARKETING MANAGEMENT

Application: practical delivery

The concept

As with any business activity, marketing has to be managed. The function contains a range of activities and components which need to be coordinated in order for it to work effectively. These need to be "managed" by people who know what they are doing. When working inside a business (often called "client side" by the marketing supply industry), it is not good enough just to be a great marketer with creative insight; it is essential, though, to have great management skills. The function, however large, must be stocked with really great marketing managers.

The components of marketing management include:

(i) Managing people

Marketing managers will normally have a number of people working for them to get activities done. These people will have different motivations and capabilities. A good manager needs to work out their own way of getting the best performance from their own people. Modern managers will normally have to set objectives, delegate, review performance, and complete appraisals. There are different theories and concepts on what it takes to manage people well (from "theory X & Y" to "situational leadership") but the very best managers seem to develop their own style of getting the best from their direct reports. One of their prime tasks is to prioritize marketing objectives for their people and, frequently, for others.

(ii) Managing teams

Marketing work frequently involves different functional specialists so a marketing manager can find themselves in, or leading, a number of different teams. There are different roles that people will take in a team which have been studied extensively. For instance, they need to be led well and they normally need to have good administrative support. Theory exists on the detail of these team roles (from "Belbin roles" to "Myers Briggs") and the normative behaviour in teams ("Forming, storming, norming, performing"). Some companies take these very seriously and have found them to be very effective tools for selecting teams. The over-riding view, at the time of writing, seems to be that a team is more effective in marketing work than an outstanding individual or a mere group of individuals.

(iii) Budgets

Every sensible business will have a clear budget setting process. Good marketing managers know how to bid for budgets and how to manage to them. Marketing involves expense and managing the allocated funds well often wins respect which enables marketers to bid for more resources. Yet, this area, probably more than any other, can be open to abuse. Suppliers might offer kick backs and marketers might embezzle funds. It is sensible to have a periodic audit of actual spend against allocated funds.

(iv) Project management

Marketing is, more or less, a project-based function and its version of project management is programme or campaign management. The concept of the marketing programme introduces a discipline into a firm's communications with its market. It ensures that programme managers plan the message, the media, and the duration of the communication, together with its integration with other programmes that customers are likely to receive. Programmes tend to be at least a year, to a year and a half, in duration. The investment of funds into a few well planned programmes of longish duration is more effective than multiple, unplanned, and confusing bursts of activity. It is a case of less is more. Each programme has specific objectives, defined scope, and a delivery programme manager. In planning the programme, all activities and interdependencies should be identified. It may be divided into different fields of activities (thought leadership, PR, etc.) and could be grouped into "campaigns". All programmes and campaigns should then be grouped into a timetable of firm-wide marketing activities to clear any clashes of message to the market or to a customer.

Yet, the use of the terms "campaign management" and "programme management" disguises the fact that a lot of marketing activity is, in fact, conducted as bog standard projects. Project management is a clear, practical, and well researched aspect of management. Serious marketing managers ought to know it well. They ought to clarify objectives, identify milestones, inter-relate activities, and identify the critical path. Again, there is well substantiated and respected theory on what constitutes good, effective project management.

(v) Briefing processes

Like computers, first-class marketing programmes are dependent on the data and programming put into them. Garbage in means garbage out. Marketing agencies, of any kind, are unable to produce good work of any impact if not properly briefed. Some time ago, the leading advertising agency Saatchi & Saatchi was so concerned about this that it created its own client template for firms which were unclear about their needs. They would not develop communications until clients had clearly expressed their needs in terms that communications specialists could understand. Marketers should develop a standard brief for all activities, which is given at the start of a job. This should be discussed and developed by the relevant team members to ensure that it is a clear articulation of the need and the required work. A good supplier will take as much care to ensure that it understands the brief and interprets it correctly.

(vi) Marketing automation

The marketing function needs its own IT and systems strategy to develop its organizational competence in line with the firm's needs. The best known marketing systems are databases to store and hold customer details. Whether this information is held on a Palm Pilot, on an Outlook database, or in a sophisticated CRM system, firms need systems to hold customer data. It is sensible for these systems to have relevant functionality (i.e. the ability to make lists, reminder mechanisms for important events, etc.). There is a need for marketers to set a strategy and framework for the sharing and maintenance of customer data. If not, the control of a very precious intangible asset, customer knowledge, remains with individuals who may leave the firm, rather than the firm itself. It is marketing's responsibility to ensure that this asset is managed on behalf of the business's owners.

Lesser known are marketing systems with other functionality. Systems exist, for example, that can plan and hold data on marketing campaigns, marketing programmes, and materials. This means that, in large firms, best practice can be shared and marketing specialists can see potential clashes of programmes at the planning stage. Also, by storing research reports, advertisements, brochures, and other materials, marketing specialists in smaller parts of the firm (perhaps in international groups) can use and adapt materials developed by others. One major firm, for example, found that large savings in time resulted from having an online "pitchbook". This held key facts and case studies which could be customized for proposals by local people once downloaded. Systems also exist to help with marketing analysis and planning. They can be used to store research and help to focus strategic thinking and decision making.

(vii) Purchasing

Marketing-naïve firms tend to have ad hoc (and hence expensive) relationships with a range of marketing agencies and suppliers. The industry tends to encourage the nonsensical view that these creative agencies should be exempt from the rigours of purchasing and contract negotiations. Yet, all should be subject to proper controls through a managed purchasing process. (A small firm can hire freelance buyers to handle this for them.)

(viii) Organizational adjustment and effectiveness (see separate entry under organizational effectiveness in marketing)

Part of good management is to think about the effectiveness of the organization for which the management is responsible and to adjust it to make it more effective. There are different organizational constructs in marketing depending on whether the firm is, say, a big corporate, a privately owned firm, a professional service partnership, or a smaller company. The leaders of these functional units need the experience and judgement to adjust the structure of their organization to meet the changing needs of the company. One large corporation, for instance, needed to rationalize its many different communication campaigns. It created a "communications unit", structured like an internal agency, to receive briefs from marketing managers across this large corporation and to brief agencies to common standards and strategies.

Yet, the marketing leaders also need to think more broadly about organization. They need to understand the effectiveness and evolving needs of their company as it goes to market. They need to understand how their function works with others (like sales or service) to reach customers and facilitate any changes needed, even those outside their own marketing department.

(ix) *Measurement*

It is a principle of good management that, however vague and esoteric the function, performance mechanisms and measurements be established. There are reasonable mechanisms by which marketing is measured, set out in the separate entry.

(x) Political awareness

Political understanding is an important means of getting anything done in an organization. As marketers progress in their career, they begin to realize that they can only do their job properly by getting others to work with them. That, however, is not always straightforward. Sometimes colleagues do not agree to help with what is the most simple request or senior people will not sanction the most logical course of action. They seem to have a completely different agenda. This can be strange and confusing. It can seem as though they have stepped into a world which has different rules that no-one else is prepared to explain.

Human beings in organizations have power and people behave in different ways when they have it. Organizational politics is simply a fact of life. It is neither good nor bad. It just is. Nor is it new. For instance, one marketing text book of the early 20th century (White, P., 1927) devotes several pages to organizational politics in marketing. He points out that organizations contain people with ambition and drive. No matter how scientific or professional marketers set out to be, they must understand and allow for the political dimension of businesses.

So, marketers can learn to handle this important facet of management. Sadly, many do not understand that and do not make an effort to get to grip with it. Marketers, like any other group in a business, need to negotiate the power bases around them in order to thrive. They need to understand the behaviours and roles people adopt when they have power, and communicate with those individuals appropriately. The most obvious, for example, is "the bully". Bullies are actually very insecure. If they are a peer, they can be confronted and they normally back down. If not, they will almost always have an acolyte or two who gets things done for them. These support people are normally very personable and approachable, because the bullies cannot have strong, threatening people working for them. Marketers can sell their strategy or initiative to them and, quite soon, the bully will be espousing it as though it was their idea. There are a number of other political roles or behaviours that occur again and again: the "good king", the "warrior general", or the "priest visionary". It is a good career investment to become familiar with them.

There are many sources on these power roles but management texts and courses are probably not the best places to look. Creative writers, though, have got it nailed because of their fascination with governmental politics. For instance, Shakespeare's history plays have lessons to teach about the political work place. Some leaders, for example, behave like Richard II: there as a result of a divine right to govern yet, in fact, through their own inadequacy, causing the decay of the organization. Some behave like Hamlet (unable to make up their mind, causing chaos and damage to all around them) whilst others are like Macbeth (driven by another's ambition).

Two academics (Baddeley, S. and James, K., 1987) examined the political competence of executives. They found that under-achievers were people who kept their head down. People who say: "I do not get involved in politics". These people are like innocent sheep, say the academics, in that they get used. If marketers hide from political forces, shareholders are denied their contribution and the firm loses out. They are not doing their job. It is unprofessional not to engage with the powerful debates about resources and priorities. One reason people take that stance is that they see others who are obviously "political" and do not like they way they behave. Yet these people are actually politically "inept", because they are out for themselves rather than keeping the integrity of the job as their prime motivation. They are "donkeys", unpredictable and ugly.

Successful marketers learn to be politically competent and yet act with integrity (likewise "owls"). In fact, most senior business leaders, in all sectors, will privately admit the importance of political skills. They have learnt how to do their job professionally and get colleagues to change direction without being thought to be political. Yet this is rarely discussed publicly or taught on courses. It is a huge yawning gap in marketing training and development programmes. Marketers have a responsibility to quietly practice plus politics: the art of managing the way people react to power in order to achieve job objectives. It is very practical and is a learnt skill. It is a route to achieving positive support for most proposals and will improve marketing's overall contribution to the organization.

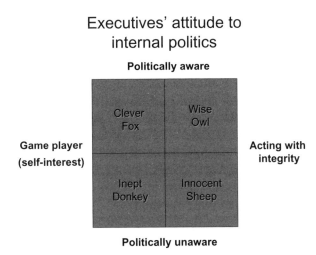

Figure M.6   Attitudes and behaviours toward internal politics (Baddeley, S. and James, K., 1987)

History, context, criticism, and development

Professional management appears to have started, in earnest, in the mid 20th century but the concept has been around for many centuries. (The Borgias in medieval Italian states had, for instance, a partnership structure to their business but handed new operations to managers, trained in a business school, once a partner had established it.) It was, though, in the early 1960s that much of the theory and concept of management began to be codified. The hero of this growing body of work is Peter Drucker. He was a fan and supporter of managers and their value to business. His view was: first learn to manage and then other specialties follow. There is evidence that several large corporations take this approach with their marketing people. They will start them on a graduate training scheme which gives them experience of management at various levels before they move into their chosen speciality. The best continue this view as careers develop. Some marketers are not allowed, for instance, to move into top management if they have not run a business with a full profit line (as opposed to staying in a function throughout their career).

Voices and further reading

- Drucker, P.F., *The Essential Drucker*. Harper Business, 2001.
- "Management is about human beings. Its task is to make people capable of joint performance, to make their strengths effective and their weaknesses irrelevant. This is what organization is all about, and it is the reason that management is the critical determining factor." Drucker, ibid.
- "The marketing manager is responsible for developing and recommending objectives, policies and programmes for sales, sales services and marketing activities; for co-ordinating, developing and maintaining favourable relations with customers and the trade; for recommending all marketing budgets; and for seeing that the marketing aspects of all policies and activities are considered and provided for to achieve the purpose of the company." Lever. E.A. in Wilson, A., 1965.
- "Organization of any kind inevitably has a political aspect. This is true in government, equally true in business and especially applicable to the marketing division. The men who engage in marketing must, of necessity, be versed in the lore of the politician." White, P., 1927.
- Palmer, R., Cockton, J., and Cooper, G., *Managing Marketing: Marketing Success through Good Management Practice*. Butterworth-Heinemann, 2007.

Things you might like to consider

(i) In recent years there has been great emphasis on "leadership" in both HR and general business circles. This has, to some extent, meant that the idea of good management has been neglected. It remains, though, the essence of good, effective marketing. If you can't manage you can't market.

(ii) There has been a tendency, in recent decades, for training to be put online or reduced due to cost constraints. There are, though, some elements of practical management (like team participation and project management) that can only be learnt by doing or classroom-type experiences.

(iii) There are a cluster of management skills (like personal gravitas, communication to groups, presentation skills, writing and flexibility of style) which are crucial to success in client-side marketing management. This is no different to any other aspect of management in large businesses but ambitious marketing specialists need to identify them and develop them.

 RATING: Practical and powerful

MARKETING MEASUREMENT

Application: control, tracking, planning

The concept

This is another controversial, extensive, and important field that it is difficult to do justice to in this format. Marketers undoubtedly need to set up mechanisms whereby they can gain an indication of the effectiveness of their work. There have, though, been some idiotic concepts promulgated as to how they should do that and there remains extensive confusion. The balance of judgement about the most simple of measures, revenue generated, shows how difficult it is to reach a sensible, professional perspective of marketing measurement.

When a new campaign is launched it is, in many environments, relatively easy to track the leads passed to the sales force. So, it should at least be possible to set up a measure of "leads generated" and then to analyse how many turn into sales. There are though a number of considerations which make this crude measure only an indication of success. For instance, the campaign may follow a number of other campaigns and be reaping the momentum of that former investment. Or it may be part of a powerful brand franchise, building its worth on the heritage of brand equity. And what about those sales that the sales force closed? How many were stimulated by this campaign and not by the sales person themselves? How many opportunities were lost because warm leads were passed to hopelessly inadequate sales people who were unable to close? Whereas purists, academics, and large companies might be able to invest in large tracking surveys or to isolate a number of fascinating variables, life and time is normally far too short for the average marketing manager in the average real company. Most normally have to agree with their own line management sensible mechanisms to give an indication of success and, frankly, after nearly a hundred years of obscure "marketing science" or dubious proprietary tools or concepts, there is probably not much wrong with that.

One really good writer on this subject, Tim Ambler (see Ambler, T., 2003), suggests three criteria for assessing marketing effectiveness: internal expectation, external comparison, and adjustments to brand equity. In reality, marketers seem to measure through several broad categories:

(i) Financial measures

The first and most important is some form of financial measure like revenue, price maintenance, margin, or projected sales volume resulting from marketing activities. This is so simple and obvious that it is often neglected. A surprising number of smart people in even the largest companies do not step back and analyse revenue trends or sources of profit. Too many believe their customers to be at different levels than they actually are and far too many are blinded by accepted myths. It *is* possible for new customers to be more profitable than existing customers and it *is* possible that large repeat customers are unprofitable. It is also possible to form a judgement of the cost-effectiveness of certain projects. People also measure: sales volume, sales value, gross revenue, net revenue (i.e. gross revenue less marketing and sales costs), investment, profit, and cost. Yet nearly all specialists in this field have horror stories of marketing managers neglecting the simplest of financial measures. This really ought to be put in place before esoteric tracking programmes are set up.

(ii) Market-based measures

These have to be gained through a reliable research mechanism. They might include: customer value, total number of customers, contribution per customer, share of wallet, satisfaction, propensity to buy again, complaint levels and intensity, and price inelasticity. They might also include mechanisms to measure brand equity, such as: unprompted awareness, prompted awareness, loyalty, lifestyle adoption, and image.

Customer equity is a growing category of market-based measures. It includes: profit per customer, perceived quality, perceived value for money, customer acquisition, visits to new customers, cost per acquisition, contacts before purchases, and life-time value of customers.

Product innovation can be a market-based measure (rather than an internal investment measure). It might include: number of new offers, number of successful launches, average speed of market acceptance, number of competitor imitations, and investment spend in R&D.

Effectiveness of marketing communications might include: share of voice, response, recall, category share. One common way of measuring the effect of marketing campaigns is by having "quiet areas". These are geographic areas where no marketing is undertaken. They are compared against revenues in areas where programmes impact. As the – rather surprising – case study shows, this is not entirely new!

(iii) Internal performance measures

The firm's own operational performance measures can be used to judge the effect of marketing. The marketer can set measures of the progress of marketing tasks and measure marketing output (articles published, conferences spoken at, etc.).

Approaches to the management of marketing measurement inside modern companies seem to include:

(i) Cascade management systems

These align internal management thinking across a firm in common values, objectives, and aims. The simplest is probably KPIs (key performance indicators). These prompt each level of management to identify performance indicators and success measures relevant for their work. They normally work alongside some form of management by objectives. These are so simple and obvious that they are sometimes taken for granted by marketers. They remain, nonetheless, very effective and practical methods of reaching a view on the effectiveness of the marketing operation. A recent, and famous, cascade system is Kaplan and Norton's "balanced score card" (see Figure M.7). This is not normally exclusive to marketing but embraces the whole company; wherein lies it power. It is particularly useful to marketing and sales because "customers" is one of the areas of focus introduced at all levels of the company.

(ii) "Dashboards"

Setting up mechanisms whereby key metrics are available, often in a cascade system, to different levels of marketing management (see Figure M.8). These are blunt instruments which can be questionable and dangerous across large international organizations because they aim to provide one inflexible and consistent view. They are unlikely to allow for local, regional differences.

(iii) Benchmarking

This is the use of external surveys to measure marketing effectiveness. These might be specially commissioned membership surveys, wherein members subscribe and have anonymous comparative data. Or they may be an externally constructed reporting system.

(iv) Research

Some of the most interesting measures are research-based. It is possible to establish research programmes which track changes in the attitudes and intentions of buyers. An ongoing survey which takes, for example, a small monthly sample can build up useful trend data. Key issues to track are: brand strength, competitive reputation, propensity to refer, and propensity to purchase. For instance, one market-based measure is "test" marketing. Groups of customers are either invited to a group discussion or are subject to a small trial run. Response or attitude changes are then assessed.

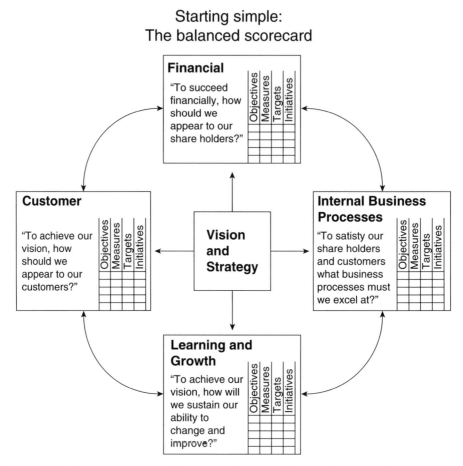

Figure M.7   A representation of Kaplan and Norton's balanced scorecard

Tim Ambler reported that his research showed that company's marketing measurement went through phases of development: first they were unaware, then they started to use financial measure. After a while, they grew to understand that financial measures were not enough and reached for a diversity of measures from different departments. This, however, led to confusion. Most then reached for some form of market-based measure, streamlining financial and non-financial measures into one coherent system. Finally, they adopted some form of "scientific method" of assessment such as comparison of trends against a complex database of past and current metrics.

History, context, criticism, and development

At the start of the 20th century John Wanamaker said: "50% of my advertising budget is wasted but I don't know which 50%" (it has been attributed to several people) and,

The dashboard approach

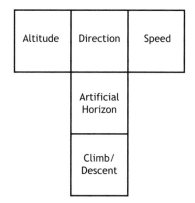

- **Altitude** – are we flying high enough?
- **Direction** – are we flying in the right direction?
- **Speed** – are we flying fast enough?
- **Artificial Horizon** – are we flying in a straight line?
- **Climb/Descent** – are we going up or down?

Figure M.8   Dashboard's in marketing measurement

according to Tim Ambler, at the start of the 21st century the situation has only improved a little. He reported (Ambler, T., 2003) that 63% of the American Marketing Leadership Council were dissatisfied with their marketing performance measurement system and that they were wasting 26% of their spend. So, although nearly a hundred years' research, trial, error, and investment has improved the experience of the best by 100%, there is still a long way to go in understanding the effectiveness and value of marketing activities. There is much further to go in convincing business leaders and financial directors.

During that period marketers and marketing academics have tried various mechanisms to measure the effect and return of marketing. So much so that the Wanamaker comment need no longer apply because there are many ways to get a view on effectiveness. If the marketer is willing to invest time, thought, and effort in progressively developing the necessary processes and systems, satisfactory measures can be set up.

Voices and further reading

- Ambler, T., *Marketing and the Bottom Line*. 2003 (2nd edn).
- When people talk of the ROI from marketing, they usually mean the profit return after deducting the cost of the campaign: it is return minus investment, not return divided by investment. And, of course, we are considering discretionary marketing activities (the budget) not marketing as a whole. In making this point, one

response has been that the ratio is still useful for comparing alternative uses . . . of the same budget. In fact, if the I is constant, then R–I peaks at the same point R/I does, so the ratio is still redundant at best and possibly misleading because the immediate reaction to a high ratio is the supposition that more investment would produce the same ratio." Ambler, ibid.

- Shaw, R. and Merrick, D., *Marketing Payback*. Prentice Hall, 2005.
- "Marketing payback myopia is a common symptom of . . . structural problems. While most marketers get excited talking about creativity, they get immensely bored when costs and budgets are mentioned; their eyes glaze over and their minds shut down. The limited attention span is also widely reflected in the treatment of costs and budgets in books on marketing. Examples of the amount of space devoted to the assessment and evaluation of marketing costs and budgets in some leading text books is shown in Table 2.1.*" Shaw, ibid.
  (*Note: all under 1% except Philip Kotler which was 1.7%.)
- Binet, L. and Field, P., *Marketing in the Era of Accountability*. WARC, 2007. This identifies the marketing practices and metrics that practitioners think truly increase profitability. It draws on key quantitative findings from 880 case studies in the IPA Effectiveness Awards databank in the most comprehensive analysis of the communications process to date. Amongst other things their analysis proves the importance of emotional as opposed to rational communications, the power of "fame" or "buzz" for a brand, and the increased effectiveness of multi-media campaigns.
- Doyle, P., *Value Based Marketing*. John Wiley & Sons Ltd, 2000.
- *How Share of Voice Wins Share of Market*, published by IPA 2009. Central to a successful campaign is setting the right media budget in the first place. This study by the IPA and Nielsen Analytic Consulting shows that share of voice continues to drive brand growth, and without investment here, innovation in media and creativity is wasted. The report indicates that an average fmcg (fast moving consumer goods) campaign for an average brand can be expected to deliver market share growth of 0.5 percentage points for every 10 points of "extra" share of voice (ESOV), where extra share of voice equals the difference between share of voice and share of market. Brands that allow their share of voice to fall below their share of market lose market share in the same proportion. So, any marketer setting goals for their brand must take this into account. Similarly any agency entering into a remuneration agreement involving an element of payment by results needs to ensure that the KPIs are actually achievable on the budget set for the brand. The data also highlights the importance of the quality of advertising alongside the quantity of advertising. Comparison between Nielsen data and data from proven highly effective campaigns in the IPA Databank of IPA Effectiveness Awards cases shows that IPA-grade campaigns are on average about 60% more effective than the "typical" fmcg campaigns in the Nielsen sample. The implication here is that clients can "beat the system" by investing in top quality agency work.
- Farris, P.W., Bendle, N.T., and Reibstein, D.J., *Marketing Metrics*. Wharton School Publishing, 2006.

- Kaplan, R.S. and Norton, D.P., *The Balanced Scorecard*. Harvard Business School Press, 1996.
- Reicheld, F.F., "The only number you need to grow". *Harvard Business Review*. December, 2003.
- "Unfortunately, most accounting systems do not measure what drives customer value." Reicheld, ibid.
- Shaw, R., "Net promoter". *Journal of Database Marketing and Customer Strategy Management*, August 2008. A devastating and forensic analysis of this faddish measure by a marketing professor who started as a PhD mathematician.
- "The need for common metrics becomes more critical as marketing becomes more embedded in the sales process . . . Sales metrics are easier to define and track. Some of the most common measures are percent of sales quota achieved, number of new customers, number of sales closing, average gross profit per customer and sales expense to total sales . . . But how then should the company evaluate the upstream marketers? On the basis of the accuracy of their product forecasting, or the number of new market segments they discover? The metrics will vary according to the type of marketing job." Kotler, P., Rackham, N., and Krishnaswamy, S., 2006.
- "Beware of make-believe marketing metrics . . . On the boards that I sit on I have always argued that we should carefully review marketing metrics such as customer satisfaction, brand equity, and customer loyalty." Kumar, N., 2004.

Things you might like to consider

(i)   It really is possible to set up satisfactory measures of most marketing activities if time is taken to think through what is needed and to invest and test. These measures should be enough to get an operational judgment even though they would not be "scientific" to purists.

(ii) Tracking surveys are the most widely used and, probably, some of the least useful mechanisms used by marketers.

(iii) "ROI" is one of the most widely used and devalued terms in discussions about marketing budgets. Marketing is, in most cases, a current account cost, not an investment. The judgement is whether the expense of these tasks is effective operationally. Physical assets like a CRM system or intangible assets like brand are investments and can be subject to DCF analysis, comparing their internal rate of return against other assets. To continually and casually refer to the ROI on marketing campaigns is sloppy.

(iv) A recent, dubious, idea that has been suggested is ROMI (return on marketing investment). There are several difficulties with this. Firstly, it is, as Robert Shaw points out, often muddled with ROCE (return on marketing expenditure). Secondly, marketing is normally an expense of business not an investment, so it is inappropriate to look for an ROI measure. Thirdly, the technique suggests understanding a "base line of sales" that would exist without marketing, a virtually impossible task in many situations. Finally, it is often difficult to isolate other effects of campaigns in the way purists suggest.

(v)   Another relatively recent concept, and another dubious idea, is linked to the "shareholder value" concept: value-based marketing. The concept of shareholder value rose in the late 20th century and was promulgated as a mechanism to align management action with the levers inside a company that influence the value of its shares (such as "cost of capital"). Value-based marketing is an attempt to align the actions of marketing to these mechanisms. It is argued by some accountants, for instance, that "brand equity" and "customer equity" are important influences on share value. There have, though, been a number of criticisms of shareholder value (most harshly from Jack Welch, ex CEO of GE). One is that it is too narrow a focus; prompting some, in continental Europe, for instance, to concentrate on "stakeholder value". The most obvious fault is, though, that there are many other determinants of share value than the internal actions of management. Linking marketing success to shareholder value may be useful if the company is obsessed with this approach but it is unlikely to be credible in the long term.

(vi)   Clearly marketing needs to be measured in different time scales. Activities aimed at creating customer awareness or building brand equity will have longer term effects than a campaign aimed at immediate quarterly sales stimulation.

(vii)   Digital marketing gives a dangerous appearance of precise measures. It can be easy to track, for instance, the number of visits to a web site or "stickiness" (the amount of time people spend there). Yet how far do these measures reflect buying behaviour and relate to items purchased?

(viii) PR is a discipline which has specific measures which have been developed in their professional silo. There have been various attempts at conceptual work related to PR effectiveness and evaluation, such as: Cutlip's PII model (1985), Watson's continuing model (1997), Watson's unified model (1999), the IPR "pre" model (2001), Lindeman's PR yardstick (1993), the pyramid model (1992, 2000). Specialists tend to discuss and track the advising equivalent effect of their work. Again, it's a matter of seasoned judgement (particularly when deciding how much budget to allocate between different media based on previous successes) as to how credible these different indicators of effectiveness actually are.

(ix)   How much should you go native? Although it is professional to have some form of sensible indicator, there is a case for marketers not to get too anal, precise, financial, and pedantic about their work. There is no doubt that certain aspects of marketing (such as brand, synergistic impact, herd behaviour of markets, and creative appeal) are hard to summarize or capture in precise financial or operational measures. Sensible leaders and CFOs understand that and are willing to discuss pragmatic indicators of effect and return.

(x)   Since the advent of the discussions on loyalty many companies have investigated and adopted Fredrick Reicheld's recommended "net promoter" measure (see Reicheld, F.F., 2003). This is an adaptation of word-of-mouth tracking measures and the propensity of customers to refer their contacts to the product or service. So it should be, in most circumstances, a powerful indicator of satisfaction and growth potential. There are, though, a number of strategic issues which need to be addressed in loyalty management and it is far from a panacea (see separate entry on loyalty). There are also a number of doubters and sceptics about the basis of some of the claims and applicability of this measure (see Ambler, T., 2003 and Shaw, R., 2008). It seems most applicable to areas where word-of-mouth and personal recommendation play an important part in growth.

(xi) There are some very effective measures to indicate and improve customer satisfaction. See the introduction to SERVQUAL under the GAP model entry, for instance, or the description of the public tracking measures under service quality. This is the marketer's province because it affects repurchase intent. Very poor customer service undermines any marketing claims and damages brand equity. At the same time, many of the impromptu satisfaction surveys, such as written sheets left in hotel rooms, ask the wrong questions inadequately. Satisfaction measures are likely to only reveal future buying intent if properly configured. There are several types of these measures that are important to understand and have in place in order to manage ongoing customer satisfaction. They are:

Event driven feedback. These are sometimes called "transaction surveys", because they follow a specific transaction between the supplier and its customer. This is feedback from the buyer in response to a specific event or project (a completed consultancy project, for example, or the installation of a new home service). These feedback mechanisms can either be through some form of questionnaire or response to a telephone survey. Their purpose is to capture the customers' views of their specific experience while it is fresh in their mind. It is therefore important to gather customers' responses as soon after the transaction as possible. The surveys need to be carefully designed using experienced researchers. If not, they are likely to reflect the wrong views and mislead the company. They need to be carefully administered and sent to the correct people. (More suppliers than would admit send these to anonymous departments or invoicing addresses.) The firm should keep careful records and undertake trend analysis as an input to its strategic direction.

Generic perception studies. These are research projects undertaken on a regular basis in order to understand the general view that different groups of buyers have about a supplier. Frequency of surveys varies according to volume (some might be monthly, some might be annual). Quite often suppliers will carry out a number of surveys each month and then have either a quarterly or annual summary of trends. Techniques for conducting this research vary although many suppliers have used conjoint research because it yields powerful insights into changing customer views of different aspects of service. These are very different in style, purpose, and design to event driven research. They are frequently conducted by independent research companies using independent sampling techniques. The aim is to get a generic view of the firm's service performance which can then be compared to the trends in event driven measures.

Internal measures. Firms should establish internal measures of service quality (percentage of projects completed to predicted time scales, for instance). These should be prioritized around customer need and the leadership's objectives. They should be communicated to all, set as individual objectives for each executive and used as a basis for reward. However, they should also be compared with external measures to identify any gaps. If, for instance, a firm's internal measures show excellent performance in an area that customers criticize there are two possible solutions. Either internal results are distorted and need adjustment or customer perception needs to be changed through marketing communication.

Stone and Young (1994) proposed the following method of drawing these elements together as an ongoing management system of satisfaction measurement.

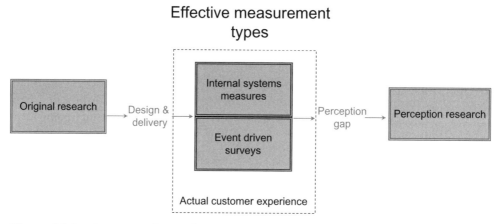

Figure M.9   A structure for satisfaction measurement

Marketing measurement in the Edo period of Japan

Mitsukoshi is a famous Japanese department store in Japan founded as a Kimono shop in the seventeenth century. It claims to be the first retailer in the world to have implemented one-price selling (with its then slogan "Cash sales at fixed prices"). In doing so it repositioned its offer, making a luxury item available to a wider range of Japanese shoppers. Yet that is not the extent of their marketing.

In cities like Edo and Osaka merchants competed with each other using display signs and door-to-door sales. One of their most powerful marketing tools was "hikifuda"; exquisitely painted hand bills. Many of these were created by artists like Santo Kyoden, who have since become prized famous artists (advertising, as ever, supporting artists in their early career).

According to Japan's museum of advertising and marketing, early versions were copied by woodblock cutting and stuck into every gateway in town. Upmarket advertisers, by contrast, handed the beautiful sheets "only to valued customers and neighbourhood leaders". These folk, in turn, were counted on to disseminate the information by word-of-mouth; an early use of viral marketing.

What is startling is the focus on mass advertising and the sophistication of their understanding of its effect. Advertising was routinely used for products like toothpaste, clothing, smoking accessories, and sake (see Pollock, D., 1995). The same copy was used in different media such as hand bills, signs, stories, and theatre, a deliberate attempt at integrated marketing communication.

Mitsukoshi's founders, though, demonstrated why they had the marketing skills to create and nurture a 300-year-old brand. According to Toshio Yamaki (Tokyo University) and Kikuko Fukatsu (University of Iowa) (see Yamaki, T. and Fukatsu, K., 1995) they handed out around 500,000 hikifuda in April of 1673 when they opened a new store and measured a 60% return on revenue by having no advertising at all for another store, to get comparative data. Just over a hundred years later (1794) they were still measuring the effects of advertising on both sales and profits in their Osaka store, and reported the cost of advertising as 4.5% of total sales. There are advertisers today who are not as measured.

MARKETING MIX

Application: market planning

The marketing mix for services

Product	Price
Promotion	Distribution (Place)

People	Presence	Process

Target market

Figure M.10   A representation of the marketing mix for services

The concept

This simple concept focuses on the aspects of marketing which need to be planned, coordinated, and integrated in order to influence the intended buyers. They are:

- The product; or the offer to customers
- The price at which the product is offered
- The promotion of the product to the target buyers
- The placing of the product in the market through sales and distribution channels.

There is, of course, complexity behind the idea which has developed over the years since it was proposed. Each "P" has many detailed aspects.

Classic marketing training emphasizes that all these elements need to be planned in order to achieve success. However, there are two other ingredients. The first is a clear knowledge of the target market. Suppliers need to know, in detail, the attributes and benefits that the buyers will value so that they can customize each "P" to their needs. The second is the "mix" of components that will most appeal to the buyers. This needs to be planned and balanced carefully.

It is generally accepted that there are further aspects of the marketing mix for services, three extra "Ps" in the "extended marketing mix for services". They are:

- The people who deliver the service because the buyer often cannot separate them from the service they buy.
- The physical evidence or tangible aspects of the offer designed to help deliver perceived value to the buyer.
- The process through which the buyer moves while using or buying the service.

Again, all aspects of the mix need to be designed to match the aspirations of the intended buyers.

The marketing mix is most often used in management dialogue or communications. Those involved can use it as an informal checklist to ensure that all aspects of a proposition have been properly considered. However, it can also be used in detailed marketing planning. Simply list the elements of the mix and ensure that they have been considered for the particular target market; try to understand how each set of variables might influence the intended customers' purchase intent. Once strategy has been decided, a full campaign which comprises all elements of the mix should be created for each target market.

History, context, criticism, and development

Although several academics had previously pointed out that marketing was a "mix" of activities aimed at a buyer (see Borden, N.H., 1964), it was Jerome McCarthy (McCarthy, E.J., 1960) that crystallized it into the now famous "four Ps" of marketing. The thrust of his book, *Basic Marketing*, was to demonstrate that it was ineffective to just send sales people to call on customers; that advertising could cost-effectively pave the way. He used a campaign by JWT that was famous at the time and that fame called attention to the four Ps, which seem to have stuck since then, despite their shortcomings. However, it took a while for this to be generally accepted. In his 1965 article, for example, Philip Kotler (Kotler, P., 1965) describes the mix as "the various marketing variables . . . product price, advertising budget, distributing budget . . .". It is, though, regrettably taught as one of the fundamentals of marketing throughout the world.

Service marketing academics later demonstrated that the marketing mix for a service business is different because services have a number of characteristics which make them inherently different from products. First, the offer is not a tangible product but a proposition which is likely to be a mix of intangibles and tangibles; so it is important to create "presence", to try to make the intangible tangible. Secondly, it involves a process through which people might move. It is also likely to involve people in its delivery. This changes marketing dramatically (see *services marketing*) and, it is argued, adds "presence", "process", and "people" to the marketing mix.

What is not often taught is that the simplicity and the content of the marketing mix has been heavily criticized and that it is rarely used in practice.

Voices and further reading

- "How salesmanship and adverting work together: One result of a study of marketing methods is a realization of the single purpose of all selling activities . . . This failure to properly link up salesmanship and advertising is not so general as it used to be, but there is still enough of it to demand warnings against it." Butler, R.S., 1917.
- "An analysis of the problems that face both large and small companies shows that it is possible to reduce the number of variables in the marketing mix to four basic ones: Product, Place, Promotion, Price. It may help to think of the four major ingredients of a marketing mix as the 'four Ps'." McCarthy, E.J., 1975 (original 1960).
- Borden, N.H., "The concept of the marketing mix". *Journal of Advertising Research*, 1964.
- ". . . the phrase 'marketing mix', which I began to use in my teaching and writing some 15 years ago . . . I liked his [a Harvard colleague] idea of calling a marketing executive a mixer of ingredients, one who is constantly engaged in fashioning creatively a mix of marketing procedures and policies in his efforts to produce a profitable enterprise." Borden, ibid.
- "The marketing mix – specifically the four P's – is often considered the cause for embarrassment in marketing academia." Baker, M.J. and Hart, S., 2008.
- "Activities in marketing are usually described as a marketing mix – the 4 or more Ps – including price, sales calls, physical distribution, and other activities

and strategies. . . . Instead of starting with mixing Ps, a company needs to define and review its relationship portfolio. A portfolio is a collection of components and their total benefits should be greater than the sum of the parts; there should be synergy effects . . . The relationship portfolio is a combination of RM activities to be performed during the planning period." Gummerson, E., 2003.

- "Faith in the Four Ps: an alternative." Kent, R.A., 1986.
- "The concept of the Four Ps is just a classification, a handy mnemonic for remembering some of the key elements of the so-called 'marketing mix'. It does not amount to a 'theory' or even a 'model' in the usual sense of these terms . . . The indictment against the four Ps, then, is that they have seriously misled students, researchers, academics and practitioners alike into a false sense of simplicity." Kent, R.A. ibid.

Things you might like to consider

(i) Many marketers, even at the most senior levels, do not have control over all the Ps. In pharmaceutical companies the product might, for instance, be fixed after ten years of research under exacting technical standards and tight laws. In others, pricing may be held by finance people. It is highly likely that marketers will have to try to influence these other elements of the mix, not winning all arguments.

(ii) The concept is superficial and inadequate. Many of the "Ps" are completely inadequate to describe the subtlety and complexity of what marketers need to do.

(iii) The four Ps do not include "brand", a serious omission given that this is one of the most powerful and valuable strategies that marketers can engage in for their employers (see Tables B.1 and B.2 for evidence of this). Branding is much more than merely packaging around the P for product. Professor Borden's original suggestion had twelve elements of the mix and the third was "branding".

(iv) The four Ps say nothing about after care service. This concept dangerously supports the separation of the marketing function from the buyers' experience of the product or service and the effect of after care on repurchase intent.

(v) To represent modern, responsive marketing communication as a "P" called "promotion" is superficial and misleading nonsense.

 RATING: Merely conceptual

MARKETING PLANS AND PLANNING

Application: resource allocation

The concept

Planning is a fundamental process of the marketing function. A plan aligns marketing resources and actions to both the leadership's priorities and budgets available. It makes strategic objectives achievable. However it is developed, there are several issues which will round out and make a marketing plan effective:

Strategic context. The plan must take into account the strategic issues which the firm faces, particularly those with direct market relevance such as: target markets, brand, segmentation, and competitive strategy. The strategic imperatives and corporate objectives of the firm must set the context for the plan. So, marketers must understand the business strategy before creating either marketing strategy or a marketing plan.

Market perspective. No market plan is useful unless its approach is based on insight and perspectives on the market it addresses. A method of gaining market insight (such as *research, a market audit*, or *scenario planning*) ought to be used as a foundation of a market plan. Some academics are probably too rigorous in demanding that a market plan be founded on logical, sequential market analysis but market insight is crucial. It is good discipline to separate market analysis from the synthesis needed to gain profound market insight.

Scope. There are a number of issues the plan needs to address in order to give it maximum impact. They range from communication with different audiences to adjustments to product or service features; from pricing to changes in account selection and revenue targets. The most recognized concept which summarizes the elements that need to be draw into a marketing plan is the *"marketing mix"* but that is seriously inadequate (see separate entry). The marketing team should include all these elements in the marketing plans of the business, even if their part of the organization is not directly responsible for them. The marketing plan is the plan for the whole firm, not just their function.

The content of a marketing plan ought to cover:
- Marketing objectives (including communication take out)
- NPD/NSD programmes and associated pricing changes
- Specific sales initiatives
- External communication programmes
- Internal communication and training programmes
- General brand and public face programmes (including collateral)
- Channel programmes
- Organizational development programmes (e.g. database or HR)
- Measures and targets.

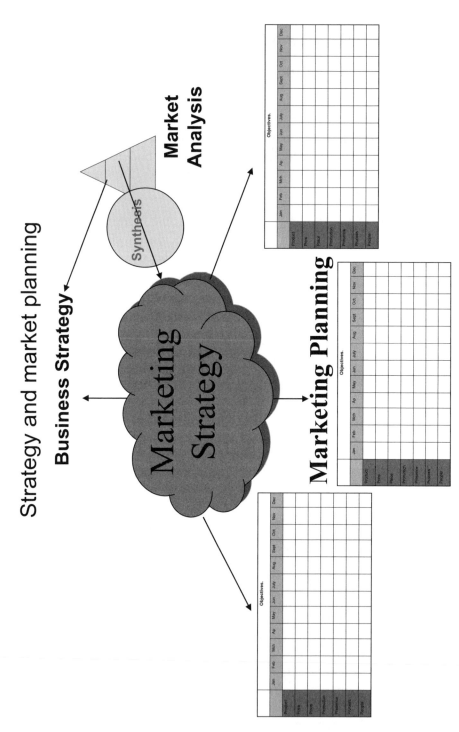

Figure M.11 A representation of modern, systems–based market plans and strategy development

Professor Malcolm McDonald (McDonald, M.H.B. and Wilson, H., 2011) has written extensively on this subject. He proposes a very clear and sequential set of ideas to think through: business vision, corporate objectives, insights from the market audit, market overview, SWOT analysis, assumptions, marketing objectives and strategies, estimated expected results, alternative mixes, budget and detailed implementation programme.

Dialogue. Marketing plans must be constructed in dialogue with key stakeholders. They should be consulted at the start, during the analysis, and as preliminary conclusions are drawn. This communication needs to be two-way, engaging them and including their views. It will ensure that the final plan is approved more easily.

Organizational politics. Most marketing plans involve projects and changes which affect the jobs of many across the organization. This means that market planning is a political process. Significant initiatives could be lost simply through irrational emotional resistance. Any experienced marketer will create a political map *as part of the whole market planning process.*

The things which make market planning effective are:

- Support from senior management
- Simplicity and identification of important strategic priorities
- Political sensitivity
- Shared responsibility across functions
- Long-term goals being recognized and taken on board
- Ambitions are achievable and easily accepted
- There must be built in flexibility to accommodate changing conditions.

The market planning process ought to combine all these features if it is to be successful. It should be based on relevant strategy and analytical insight. It must embrace all relevant activities and create practical, budgeted programmes. A full approach, likely to be adopted by a large, corporate firm, is represented in Figure M.11 above.

History, context, criticism, and development

It is possible to trace reports of effective and detailed market planning back to at least the start of the 20th century. One text book (Butler, R.S., 1917) uses the phrase so easily that it must have been in common use at the time. Although there is no use of the terms "strategy" or "marketing mix", the author stresses the need to make all aspects of marketing (advertising, direct marketing, price, and sales) the subject of a detailed and professional plan. He also argues that it should be based on thorough market analysis.

Much of the detail that is suggested today, evolved though in the latter half of the twentieth century. For those that need it there are extensive, inter-related processes and concepts which lock market planning into corporate strategy, market analysis and marketing strategy.

Voices and further reading

- "Necessity of a marketing plan: . . . there must be definite advance knowledge of the methods to be used in marketing an article or the stock of a store, before the selling starts. Opposed to a planned campaigns that are the hit–or–miss unplanned trials of this scheme or the vacillating, wavering attitude of the man who does not know exactly what he wants to do or how he wants to do it . . ." Butler, R.S., 1917.
- "Just as in modern production management, there is a special division organized for the planning in detail of marketing processes and operations. . . . Planning in marketing, as elsewhere, means setting up policies and objectives, establishing standards, providing suitable means of procedure and arranging for the actual steps involved in carrying out the work in hand." White, P., 1927.
- McDonald, M.H.B. and Wilson, H., *Marketing Plans. How to Prepare Them: How to Use Them*. John Wiley & Sons Ltd, 2011 (7th edn). A very extensive and logical treatise on the subject of market planning.
- "Any manager will readily agree that a sensible way to manage the sales and marketing function is to find a systematic way of identifying a range of options, to choose one or more of them, then to schedule and cost out what has to be done to achieve the objectives. Marketing planning, then, is simply a logical sequence and a series of activities leading to the setting of marketing objectives and the formulation of plans for achieving them. Companies generally go through some kind of management process in developing marketing plans. In small, undiversified companies, this process is usually informal. In larger, more diversified organizations, the process is often systematized. Conceptually this process is very simple, and involves a situation review, the formulation of some basic assumptions, setting objectives for what is being sold and to whom, deciding on how the objectives are to be achieved, and scheduling and costing out the actions necessary for implementation." McDonald, ibid.
- "To carry weight, RM and CRM aspects must be introduced in the marketing planning process. Marketing in the light of relationships, networks and interactions becomes marketing-orientated management, and therefore the marketing plan must be an integral part of the company's overall business plan." Gummerson, E., 2003.

Things you might like to consider

(i) Many modern firms use campaign management systems to plan the details of programmes and campaigns. These electronic tools become default marketing plans. However, it is easy to forget that these are de facto marketing plans and to simply load campaigns and programmes into them. Marketers ought to step back and ensure that they are working through the thinking of both the business strategy and marketing strategy, before they do so.

(ii) Some firms plan rigorously as part of an annual cycle while some are more short-term, not even committing plans to any form of document. Yet, whether it is elaborate, detailed, and long prepared or simply a series of decisions expressed by a leader, all firms should plan their approach to market.

(iii) Some large firms have separate plans for subsets of the marketing function like communications.

(iv) Despite the extensive theoretical body of work on market planning it is without doubt that some organizations thrive and conduct excellent marketing through intuition with hardly any planning at all.

(v) These should probably be separate plans for different segments and geographics.

RATING: Practical and powerful

MARKETING STRATEGY

Application: strategic direction

The concept

Good strategy is a framework of ideas, developed by the leadership, which sets a course that the leadership wants for the firm by creating a common purpose. It involves making decisions about direction, communicating those decisions, and allocating the resources to go in that direction. The firm's marketing strategy should be a component of its overall strategy and, as such, become a touchstone for all decisions throughout the organization about its approach to market. It might address: new market entry, repositioning of a brand, international expansion, or customer retention strategies.

All firms, even when no strategy is explicitly developed or communicated, must take a direction. However, if that direction is a rudderless drift, or if it flies in the face of market realities, or if it is not communicated throughout the firm, the health of the business is likely to be damaged. The leadership of the firm has, therefore, a duty of care to create clear, market-conscious, achievable strategic direction.

Whatever the size and shape of the firm, marketers need to take time to think of the future health of their business and how they go to market. They need to focus on the strategic imperatives relevant at any one time and allocate resources appropriately to chart the next steps of the firm. This should be done in a style and manner geared to the culture of the firm and the judgement of the leadership. It can be elaborate, documented, or intuitive. But it should be done.

Marketing specialists would argue that within business strategy are issues related specifically to the market which require marketing tools, judgement, and experience. For instance, Nirmalya Kumar of the London Business School (Kumar, N., 2004) argues that numerous decisions taken by chief executives are, in fact, marketing decisions which influence the direction of the firm; while Professor Nigel Piercy argues that marketers should influence the strategic direction of the whole company through the interplay of corporate strategy with marketing strategy (Piercy, N., 2001). Leaders should therefore aim to adopt market-orientated strategy and planning.

The development of strategy can be "procedural" (where a number of prescribed steps are followed to arrive at a particular point), "functional" (where it is someone's job to draw up a well presented and detailed strategic document), or "extant" (consisting of a pattern of decisions by a business leader which are largely intuitive and often seen in retrospect). A procedural approach is often present, for example, in large corporate firms, whereas extant strategy is often seen in smaller firms or those that are privately owned. All have their strengths and weaknesses and none is an ideal approach. There is, it seems, no "right way" no panacea, and no proscribed course for the development of strategy.

A rational, procedural approach, recommended by many business schools and followed by many companies, follows a logical, sequential process to determine strategy. It comprises a calendar of inter-related planning activities, often driven by a company's need to report results to financial analysts and shareholders. This approach will often distinguish between different time horizons influenced by the firm's market and investment horizon. There may be a set of "one-year" operational plans focusing upon short-term goals, in addition to medium-term (three- to five-year) plans where investment is needed. The strategic framework needs to embrace them all. It will often distinguish between corporate planning, strategic market planning, and business unit planning.

In the functional approach a function exists which has responsibility for the creation and management of strategy. This may be led by a director of strategy who works closely with the chief executive and may also include an executive responsible for marketing strategy. Such a role will often also include responsibility for research, competitive intelligence, internal reporting, and market analysis. Strategic planning is the focus of the role. The unit is expected to manage the planning timetable, execute ad hoc strategic studies, and share their analytical perspective in appropriate debates. Some large firms have executives dedicated to this role.

Extant strategy, by contrast, can only really be determined by a retrospective view of direction. It is the direction deduced from the decision making of, normally, one dominant business leader. The pattern of past decisions reveals the direction of the firm. Marketers in such firms can feel that they have no strategy to follow because there aren't well crafted written documents or clear planning schedules. Nevertheless, experience shows that firms led in this way can be dramatically successful, achieving their strategic intent, particularly if the leader makes the direction clear to the people in the firm.

Professor Malcolm McDonald (McDonald, M.H.B. and Wilson H., 2011) identifies other approaches such as: an "interpretive model" where, as in the case of private partnerships or mutually owned profit firms, direction emerges from shared values or beliefs; a "political model" where direction emerges from conflict amongst various stakeholders; a "logical incremental model" where strategy emerges from lower level "subsystems"; an "ecological model" where strategies are driven by relentless external forces; and a "visionary leadership" model where a strategic path is set by the senior people.

The SCORPIO model

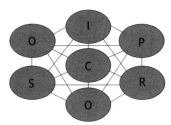

Figure M.12 A representation, from Professor Paul Fifield, of the inter-related components of marketing strategy (see Fifield, P., 2006)

Marketers tend to reach for various concepts to help them think through the contents of a strategic marketing plan. Some, for instance, use the "McKinsey seven S" framework. This is, though, a structure for a corporate strategy and can cause people to muddle the two. The likely content of a marketing strategy is captured well in Professor Paul Fifield's "SCORPIO (segmentation and targeting; customer; offer; retention strategies; positioning and branding; industry or market, and organization) model illustrated in Figure M.12 (Fifield, P. 2006). The power of this particular representation is the fact that each strategic area is seen as inter-related.

Marketing strategy is likely to give direction to: objectives, markets to be addressed, competitive strategy, opportunity analysis, brand strategy, segmentation of markets, resource allocation and channel strategy. These elements of marketing strategy need to be developed and integrated with the business strategy and are rounded out if experienced specialists are engaged in their formulation. This inter-relationship of strategic perspectives is illustrated in Figure M.8 (see *market planning*).

A well crafted corporate strategy might contain:

- Business vision
- Business mission
- Corporate objectives
- Strategic intent
- Target returns
- Business unit targets
- Broad inorganic growth plans
- Organic growth plans
- Potential disinvestments
- Intended market positions
- Corporate brand strategy
- Asset utilization.

A strategic market plan might contain:

- Market objectives
- Key markets and aspirations in them

- Target segments
- Brand development goals
- Positioning intentions
- Organic growth targets
- Inorganic growth intent (M&A)
- Sales and revenue goals
- Target share in key markets
- Portfolio strategy: new products and services, re-launches, withdrawals, and associated activities
- Competitive strategies
- New market entry
- Major strategic programmes and initiatives
- Quality plans and subsequent quality measures
- Exit plans
- Internal and external communication objectives
- General organizational development to meet market demands.

History, context, criticism, and development

It is well known that many strategy techniques came originally from the military, where they evolved over a long period of time to help improve decision making, resource allocation, and success. Military history has shown that success in the heat of battle is more likely if there has been prior thought given to likely scenarios. A little forethought, using methods that have been successful elsewhere, reduces risk and increases the likelihood of success. There is evidence that successful military leaders were versed in the strategies of previous historial victors.

Stunning military successes as diverse as the Roman campaigns against ill-disciplined tribes, Napoleon's conquest of Europe, and General Norman Schwarzkopf's "Operation Desert Storm" in Kuwait, have demonstrated the power of experience and forethought.

Executives returning to civilian life after, particularly, the Second Word War seemed to think that, if good strategy was effective in military endeavours, it was likely to be effective in business. So, business leaders have, over time, adopted and shaped many of the military's strategic techniques in order to improve their chances of success and, subsequently, developed many of their own. If mankind has learnt, after thousands of years of bloody combat, that good strategy is more effective than rushing at the other side with sticks, business leaders should surely acknowledge that good business leadership is a little more than "gut feel" or decisions made on the hoof.

However, strategy as a management discipline appears to have been through several evolutionary phases. Ex servicemen in the 1950s began to apply military terms (like "objectives" and "strategy") to their businesses. They found that this improved effectiveness. Early voices on strategy (such as Ansoff, Henderson, and Minzberg) began to talk about the process of strategy development and the content of good effective business strategy. A consensus emerged that the leaders of a business needed to be involved in the debate for their own firm.

Marketing strategy itself seems to have been an established force by the 1960s. In his 1965 article for example, Philip Kotler (Kotler, P., 1965) referred to nine *"classes"* of marketing strategy. They were: Non-adaptive strategy (where the initial marketing mix is held constant throughout the product's life), Time-dependant strategy (automatic marketing mix adjustments through time), Competitive adaptive strategy (changes to the mix in the light of competitor moves), Sales-responsive strategy (adjustments in the light of sales history), Profit-responsive strategy (adjustments in the light of significant inter-period changes in company profits), Completely-adaptive strategy (monthly changes in the mix responsive to all variables), Diagnostic strategy (changes prompted by analysis of causes of current developments), Adaptive profit-maximizing strategy (optimal marketing mix changes in response to competition), and Joint profit-maximizing strategy (cooperative responses with other players).

In the 1970s, business strategy began to develop its own lexicon of techniques and new management tools (such as the Boston Matrix or scenario planning), focusing largely on the corporate strategy of large corporations. By the 1980s strategy was often overseen by large, central strategic planning functions in multi-nationals running complex strategic models. This was reinforced by the apparent success of Japanese firms and their famed focus upon long-term planning. Professor Henry Mintzberg challenged this routine, analytical approach to strategy in his work. In fact, he engaged in public debate with Igor Ansoff about the validity of a less rigorous, numeric approach.

By contrast, in the 1990s, the combination of recession, the collapse of the Asian model, and a tougher competitive environment, with the perception that business must be more short-term, created much more of a feverish, immediate focus. This culminated in some of the excesses of the dot.com boom, when the lack of a proper business model was no barrier to raising large amounts of capital. After the burst of that bubble and the associated recession, strategy became more short-term and need driven. In fact, many of the strategy houses reported that strategy projects became, a distress purchase, responding, for instance, to hostile bids or the need for turnaround. The appetite for large, long-term strategic planning and analysis diminished in many sectors. Strategy, in the sense of longer term detailed strategic plans, was less valued.

In recent years, though, strategists have begun to think about complexity theory and change through networks of people, as behavioural economics gains recognition and new technologies (like social networking sites on the web) made impacts on human behaviour (see separate entry under digital marketing). So, business strategy seems to be, at the time of writing, undergoing a further evolution and this will profoundly affect attitudes to marketing strategy.

Voices and further reading

- "In warfare first lay plans which will ensure victory and then lead your army to battle; if you will not begin with stratagem but rely on brute strength alone, victory will no longer be assured". Sun Tzu, 500 BC.

- Johnson, G. and Scholes, K., *Exploring Corporate Strategy*. Prentice Hall, 2002 (6th edn). This is one of the most thorough and respected texts on business strategy.
- Mintzberg, H., "The fall and rise of strategic planning". *Harvard Business Review*, January–February 1994.
- "Some sort of consciously intended course of action, a guideline (or set of guidelines) to deal with a situation." Mintzberg, ibid.
- "Study after study has shown that the most effective managers rely on some of the softest forms of information, including gossip, hearsay, and various other intangible scraps of information. My research and that of many others demonstrates that strategy making is an immensely complex process, which involves the most sophisticated, subtle, and at times, subconscious elements of human thinking." Mintzberg, ibid.
- "Marketing strategy is the process by which the organisation translates its business objective and business strategy into market activity." Fifield, P., 1992.
- "Few practising marketers understand the real significance of a strategic marketing plan as opposed to a tactical, or operational marketing plan . . . Preoccupation with preparing a detailed one-year plan first is typical of those many companies who confuse sales forecasting and budgeting with strategic marketing planning – in our experience, the most common mistake of all." McDonald, M.H.B. and Wilson, H., 2011.
- Kumar, N., *Marketing as Strategy: Understanding the CEO's Agenda for Driving Growth and Innovation*. Harvard Business School Press, 2004.
- *The Boston Consulting Group on Strategy*. John Wiley & Sons Inc., 2006.
- Piercy, N., *Market Led Strategic Change: Transforming the Process of Going to Market*. Butterworth-Heinemann, 2001.
- ". . . since most organizations do not do marketing planning, in any serious way, it is worth dwelling on whether our (typically creative, grandiose and exciting) ideas about our marketing strategies ever get translated into recognizably appropriate programmes of action in the market place. The theoretical distinction is between 'intended' and 'realized' strategies. The practical bottom line is that, before we get carried away with ideas about 'market led strategic change', or indeed anything else, perhaps we should get to grips with what are our real, delivered, actual marketing strategies." Piercy, ibid.
- Mintzberg, H., *Strategy Bites Back*. Prentice Hall, 2005. A fascinating (and fun) little book with a wide range of views, quotes, and illustrations of the good and bad aspects of strategy development.

Things you might like to consider

(i) Strategy should give a clear, flexible, and practical direction. It should not be inflexible and rigid.

(ii) A company's strategy should be known to all employees so that it becomes a touchstone for decisions throughout the organization. In fact, all strategic devices and tools are aimed at achieving this common understanding of the firm's strategy. Properly communicated, members of the firm will use it as a reference point when making decisions. Without it, decisions throughout the organization will be based on the judgement of local people with a local perspective and information which, while valid, may conflict with priorities developed from knowledge of the needs of the total firm. Chaos and poor results can then follow.

⬤ **RATING: Practical and powerful**

 # MOLECULAR MODELLING

Application: Product service design

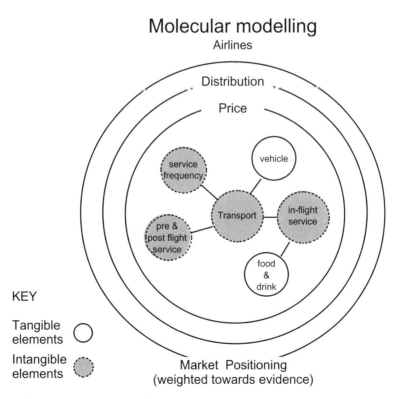

Figure M.13   A representation of molecular modelling

The concept

This is a method used to plan the detailed components of product or service offers. The technique allows marketers to create a picture of the total proposition, whether service or product dominant. It reflects the fact that propositions might have different degrees of physical or service components without diminishing the importance of either. Marketers can adjust their plans according to the degree of service content in the total offer.

The method breaks down the offer into "tangible" and "intangible" elements. Tangible elements are represented by a firm circle whereas intangible elements are represented by dotted lines. The outer rings represent various aspects of marketing such as price, distribution, and market positioning. Lines interconnecting the various elements show the inter-relationship of process in delivering the offer. The classic representation of the technique (for airlines) is reproduced in Figure M.13. above.

Constructing a molecular model involves:

(i) identifying the "nucleus" of the proposition (in the case of cars it is personal transportation);
(ii) identifying physical and intangible elements;
(iii) linking the elements;
(iv) ringing the total entity and defining it by a set value;
(v) clarifying its distribution method, so that its relationship to the market is clarified;
(vi) describing its brand positioning or "face".

History, context, criticism, and development

Molecular modelling was suggested as a technique, based on actual experience, by Lyn Shostack (Shostack. G.L., 1982). It has suffered from a lack of communication rather than being an impractical or irrelevant method. Managers responsible for the creation of new offers might start to use the technique with something which is well known in their company. By breaking it down into its components they may identify new elements of the offer which need to be designed and also ways of adjusting the offer to make it more relevant to new markets or to new segments. Having experimented with the technique, and tested it in anger, they are likely to find it a practical method for the detailed design and planning.

Voices and further reading

- Shostack, G.L., "How to design a service". *European Journal of Marketing*, 1982.

Things you might like to consider

(i) The strength of this little tool is its ability to prompt marketers to think through the linkages between intangible and tangible components of an offer.

(ii) This was created by a practising marketer who had clearly used it in practice. There is little evidence, though, of good academic substantiation of it.

 RATING: Merely conceptual

N

NEW PRODUCT DESIGN/NEW SERVICE DESIGN (NPD/NSD)

Application: new offers, innovation, revenue sources, risk management

An NPD/NSD process

Step 1	Analysis: business backdrop and buyer analysis.
Step 2	Idea generation.
Step 3	Prioritization of ideas against the firm's criteria.
Step 4	Feasability study on each candidate idea.
Step 5	Detailed component design.
Step 6	Create the value proposition.
Step 7	Create the concept representation.
Step 8	Research: Focus groups with buyers to test the concept.
Step 9	Write the "product" plan.
Step 10	Trials.
Step 11	Launch.

Figure N.1: A typical NPD/NSD process

The concept

Marketers need to create new products and new services to offer to their customers and must create the competence to commercialize or "monetize" (to use a dreadful jargon word) them. Unfortunately a large number of new products simply fail. One source estimates a failure rate of 40% across industrial and consumer markets, a stag-gering 95% failure of new consumer products in the United States; and that around

90% of all new European product introductions fail within the first two years (see "Managing new product development for strategic competitive advantage" by D. Jain in Iacobucci, D. (ed.), *Kellogg on Marketing*, 2001).

NPD (new product design) or NSD (new service design) is the managerial process intended to obviate this failure record and minimize lost investment. It is a method of turning ideas and insights into viable offers. One of the business world's most extensively studied fields of work, it is essentially the mechanism by which companies harness creativity and *innovation* for commercial advantage. The thinking and activities involved in this have most often been represented by a process (represented in Figure N.1). Although, as with so many management concepts, the steps in this process ought not to be proscriptive; they are just a way to structure thinking and marshal resources.

The activity of NPD or NSD is often controlled by a sub-committee of the organization's leadership because, done properly, serious investment is involved. The controlling group is given a budget to sponsor potential new offers. Marketers and other executives are given responsibility for each new idea and asked to undertake certain logical steps and return at defined points in the process (normally called "gates").

It is generally accepted that the factors which contribute to the success of new product design include:

- senior management involvement and control;
- a clear and managed new product design process;
- superiority over existing products;
- investment in understanding the market;
- the proficiency of marketing operations;
- the degree of business/project fit;
- effective interaction between R&D and marketing;
- a supportive management environment;
- effective project management.

These factors are now widely recognized. As a result, many companies in many sectors have in place clear and formalized new product creation processes, portfolio management techniques, and dedicated product managers.

Marketers ought to be closely involved in this process. In fact, in some companies, it is the responsibility of the marketing function. They should establish criteria by which the new offers that are created are considered to be effective. The measurements put in place by top management give signals to the organization as to what is important and what gets priority. If the creation of new offers is important to a company appropriate success measures really ought to be created. They might include:

- sales performance;
- ease of market access;
- speed of market acceptance;

- competitive performance;
- revenue growth;
- cost performance;
- "other booster" (i.e. how it affects other sales and costs).

History, context, criticism, and development

The proactive creation of new products has been established practice for many years in a number of different businesses selling physical products. Leading organizations in markets where new product innovation is a critical success factor, like consumer products, have highly sophisticated processes, which are managed at a senior level in the firm. As a result, NPD processes and concepts are well established and known to provide demonstrable value. Research has shown, for example, that a new product design process in manufacturing reduces risk of failure; also that successful innovation is both costly and risky but an NPD process reduces these costs.

In 1991 Canada's Ulrike de Brentani (de Brentani, U., 1991) conducted research designed to apply the "conceptual and research paradigms that have evolved from studies of new manufactured goods to services". He concluded that the strategic issues facing service organizations were similar to those for product companies. While NPD technologies and the detailed steps in the process may vary, the underlying notions behind their use do not. In fact, many leading service organizations now use a formal innovation process; as the Interoute case study demonstrates. They also create as many good ideas as possible and then reduce the number of ideas by careful screening to ensure that only those with the best chances of success get launched. This occurs most commonly in companies that create and industrialize consumer services because the nature of their business demands careful process design and technology deployment.

As a general rule, those services that are high-volume, low-margin, and easily reproducible can more easily be developed using a rigorous development plan than those that are highly customized (like consultancy or other professional services). American Express and Barclay's Bank, for instance, have sophisticated processes with strict controls over development "gates"; while at the other end of the scale, even the venerable British law firm, Allen & Overy (which specializes in highly customized advice) has an "innovation committee", (see the case study under the *innovation* entry) which reports to its leadership team on programmes to capture and exploit creativity. It has successfully sponsored the launch of a series of IT-based services that, at the most sophisticated level, automate a number of their clients' processes.

Voices and further reading

- Kotler, P., "Competitive strategies for new product marketing over the life cycle". *Management Science*, December 1965.
- "An Increasing number of companies are turning to new product development . . . In doing this they are substituting one danger ridden course for another.

Studies seem to indicate that more new products fail than succeed. Each phase in the management of innovation process (search, screening, profit analysis, product development, test marketing and commercialisation) requires a 'go, no go' decision . . ." Kotler, ibid.

- Aaby, N. and Discenza, R., "Strategic marketing and new product development". *Journal of Business and Industrial Marketing*, 1993.
- Levitt, T., "Production-line approach to service". *Harvard Business Review*, September–October 1972.
- Raymond, M.A. and Ellis, B., "Customers, management and resources: keys to new consumer product and service success". *Journal of Product and Brand Management*, 1993.
- Trott, P., *Innovation Management and New Product Development*. Prentice Hall, 2008.
- "The organizational activities undertaken by the company as it embarks on the actual process of new product development have been represented by numerous different models. These have attempted to capture the key activities involved in the process, from idea to commercialization of the product. The representation of these tasks has changed significantly over the past 30 years . . . Virtually all those actually involved with the development of new products dismiss such simple linear models as not being a true representation of reality. More recent research suggests that the process needs to be viewed as a simultaneous and concurrent process with cross-functional interaction." Trott, ibid.
- Middleton, V.T.C., "Product marketing – goods and services compared". *Quarterly Review of Marketing*, Summer 1983.
- Cooper, R.G. and Edgett, S.J., *Product Development for the Service Sector*. Perseus Books, 1999.
- Berentani, U. de, *Success Factors in Developing New Business Services*, 1991.
- G. Lynn Shostack, "How to design a service", *European Journal of Marketing*, 1982.
- G. Lynn Shostack, "Designing services that deliver", *Harvard Business Review*, January–February 1984.
- Easingwood, C.J., "New product development for service companies", *Journal of Product Innovation Management*, 1986.
- Hollins, W., "Design in the service sector", *Managing Service Quality*, March 1993.
- Anderson, J.C. and Narus, J.A., "Capturing the value of supplementary services". *Harvard Business Review*, January–February 1995.
- Brentani, U. de, "The new product process in financial services: strategy for success". *International Journal of Bank Marketing*, 1993.
- Brentani, U. de, "Success factors in developing new business services". *European Journal of Marketing*, 1991,
- Ozment, J. and Morash, E., "The augmented service offering for perceived and actual service quality". *Journal of the Academy of Marketing Science*, 1994.
- Cooke, P.N., "Value added strategies in marketing". *International Journal of Physical Distribution and Logistics Management*, May 1995.
- Quinn, J.B., Doorley, T.L., and Paquette, P.C., "Beyond products: services-based strategy". *Harvard Business Review*, March–April 1990.

- Jain, D., "Managing new product development for strategic competitive advantage" in Iacobucci, D. (ed.), *Kellogg on Marketing*, 2001.
- Holman, R., Kaas, H., and Keeling, D., "The future of product development". *McKinsey Quarterly*, 3, 2003.

Things you might like to consider

(i) This is very much about developing organizational competence. Marketers need to set up systems and processes which are adopted by the company and become part of the innovation processes of the whole firm.

(ii) It is sensible, even in small or informal companies, to have a structured method of commercializing offers, even in very fast changing markets. This is a way of judging the use of shareholder funds and ought to be sensibly managed.

(iii) Even the best NPD/NSD processes and the longest, most sophisticated experience with commercializing new offers does not guarantee success. This is about risk and venture. Executives must expect some failures even if properly researched and professionally prepared.

(iv) Sometimes blind belief and personal passion makes a new product, service, or brand succeed. Offers as different as Coca-Cola, Post-it Notes, Starbucks, and the Body Shop are among many that had to be driven by passionate, obstinate individuals in their early days. It is possible to be too rational about this. Passion and emotional investment have their place in NPD and NSD.

(v) Research can be wrong. People frequently cannot imagine new or latent needs; so even the best designed field research can misjudge the potential of new offers.

(vi) The history of research into new offers ought to prompt anyone considering a new product or service to step back and think. Credible academic research projects in the 1960s, 70s and the last decade suggest that a huge percentage of new offers fail. The waste and disappointment far outweighs the successful case studies. It appears to be exacerbated by the continual, strident insistence on the need to innovate. No one seems to have planned to think and examine this dreadful fifty years of failure and compare it to the remarkable brand success in evidence in Tables B.1 and B.2.

Interoute grows through customizing its core service

Interoute is a fast growing international, communications network which offers "business-class voice and data services at an economy price". Its products and services include: bandwidth, virtual private networks, high speed internet access and transit, managed hosting, communications services, and media streaming. Founded only in the 1990s and privately owned it has 57,000 kilometres of fibre and fifty-nine data centres. It operates in twenty-four countries and ninety cities. The firm's service was, initially, as a niche player in the international telecommunications market. The fact that it has customers that are serious players in that market (Sprint, BT, AT&T, Deutsche Telecom, and China Telecom) demonstrates the quality of its service, technology, and reputation.

It started as a basic "bearer" network offering network capacity to other suppliers. This it regarded as a "wholesale" business because other telecommunication suppliers bought extra network capacity. Yet, although it was successful and respected, the leadership of the firm were dissatisfied with remaining a commodity infrastructure service. They set a ten-year strategy to reposition the services of the firm. They started offering "DIY" technology to telecommunications experts but have climbed through "collocation" and "hosting" to "application management". The long-term vision of the firm is to be a player in the emerging "cloud computing" marketplace, where computing applications will be provided as services which are remotely sourced in internationally hosted data centres. In order to do this, the company had to learn the skill of crafting its core service to different customers; to improve perceived value.

The company has deliberately set out to move from a generic infrastructure service to a higher value, tailored communications service. It identified buyers in individual companies who were either chief finance officers or chief technology officers. It then worked through the products, features, and benefits that would appeal to each person in each organization and tailored its offer to each company. The results were dramatic. Between the period 2004 to 2008, there was a compound average growth rate of 67% and "EBITDA" quadrupled. Over the same period, the percentage of its customers who were "corporate" grew from 8% to 51%. The company has penetrated the corporate sector very effectively by re-configuring its basic, core service to different corporate buyers. It has customers in the public sector (e.g. the European Union), financial services (ING and Morgan Stanley), services (Hilton, Yahoo), retail (WE and Chopard), and manufacturing (Ford and Siemens).

The respected industry observer, Gartner, recognized the effectiveness of the firm's strategy when it said:

> Interoute is pursuing a focused strategy based on extensive infrastructure ownership. It has been expanding its footprint principally through acquisition of long distance and metropolitan fibre assets, such as CECom covering central European countries. Principally a provider of wholesale services to other operators, Interoute also offers a growing range of services to enterprises including MPLS VPNs, internet access, Ethernet, and bandwidth services.

Tony Rogers, Corporate product marketing manager, says:

> The customisation of our core service to different customer groups has been one of the main components in our success. We are now formalising this into a more structured NSD process upon which we can create viable and robust services. We also see this as a tool to create added value services for different customer segments.

The process, illustrated below, starts with idea generation similar to many others. It then, though, undertakes a "quick impact analysis" of the ideas, to prioritize those which might move quickly into the market. The process then moves through similar "gates" to other NSD processes, under-taking research, and constructing business cases at the appropriate time.

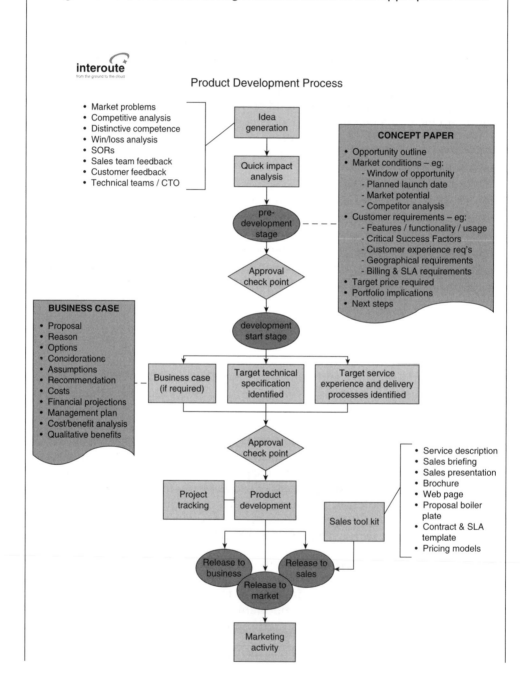

As the firm has grown from a fairly small start-up with a small firm ethos, this more structured approach has become necessary. Rogers says:

> People have seen the effectiveness of this more thoughtful approach and now understand that, as we grow and take on more significant corporate customers, we have to be more thorough and structured. If not, quality might not be so good and money might be wasted on mistakes. We have, though, tried to preserve the small company entrepreneurial spirit which made our services distinctive in the first place.

Interoute's combined network assets now represent one of the largest and most advanced voice and data networks in Europe, and are still growing fast thanks to the tailored strategy. It is now regarded as the operator of Europe's "largest next-generation network". In June 2009 the company won a business innovation award at the Global Telecoms Business Awards, for innovation in the International Service Delivery category. The award was for its "Ground to Cloud" service delivery platform. This gives its customers the ability to take basic fibre services and add their own management layer or buy fully managed services including Interoute's monitoring and reporting tools. In giving the award, the organizers said:

> For those enterprises looking to a partner to take on the management of their critical IT infrastructure Interoute's cloud approach to services removes the complexity of building, managing and changing their infrastructure.

 RATING: Practical and powerful

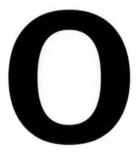

⊙ ORGANIZATIONAL BUYING BEHAVIOUR

Application: sales, marketing communications, strategy

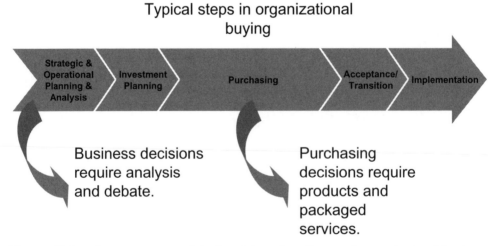

Figure O.1: A representation of the broad (very broad) stages in organizational buying

The concept

One of the main differences between organizational buying and consumer buying is the more formal recognition of the role of different individuals in the business *DMU*. This affects the sales cycle because the sales team needs to talk to and nurture more people (see separate entry under *sales*); and governance rules in Western companies seem to be increasing this method of buying. For their article in the *Harvard Business Review* two researchers (Trailer, B. and Dickie, J., 2006) surveyed over 1,200 companies. They found that the individual "economic decision maker" was being replaced by: "committees and multiple layers of approval, all equally important to the decision to move ahead. This is partly why the length of the average sales cycle keeps increasing." They found that companies reporting a sales cycle of seven months or more had climbed from 18% in their previous surveys to over 25% and those under three months had dropped from 50% to under 42%. Suppliers have to become knowledgeable about the roles of these different people, the weight given to different purchase criteria, and the sources of information used to come to a decision.

Marketers can be particularly troubled by purchasing managers (a significant participant in the organizational buying process) when they first encounter them. These specialists, often professionally trained, are employed to get the best value for their organization. Contrary to popular belief, though, they do not just want the cheapest price. In fact, some deliberately cut out the lowest (and the highest) priced suppliers in any buying process because of concerns over quality of delivery. They will have a clear set of criteria by which they will evaluate and decide. Inordinate effort must be made by sales people to understand those criteria and how their offer is perceived to measure up against them.

There are clear differences in the way different organizational buying groups behave in different sizes of company. For instance, the influence of the chief executive is likely to be more dominant in smaller companies and, because they have limited expertise, they are likely to filter information through trusted advisors or business networks. However, even in the very largest firms, the buying of some offers, such as consultancy, can sometimes be impulsive and individual with little involvement from purchasing specialists, although this is decreasing as corporate governance and risk management become more important to shareholders and policy makers. The situation is complicated by changing business strategies, by the network of relationships between firms, by the interactive nature of dialogue, by governance requirements, and by the influence of the formal purchasing function (particularly in government or other public sector purchases).

History, context, criticism, and development

Although people have been marketing and selling to organizations for several centuries, it is only relatively recently that thoughtful, careful research and conceptual work

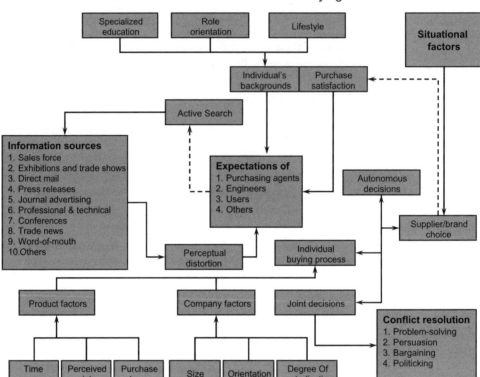

The Howard-Sheth model of industrial buying behaviour

Figure O.2: the Howard-Seth model of organizational buying processes

has begun to emerge around how organizations buy. Some of this is really helpful to practising marketers wanting to think through new strategies and approaches.

One of the earliest and best known models, for instance, is the Howard-Seth model of organizational buying, shown in Figure O.2. Published in 1973 it looks, for instance, at the role of expectations on buying and tries to separate "autonomous decisions" from "joint decisions". Both of these are useful to know in the practical sales and marketing activities aimed at any organization.

Later developments in this field have created different models and explored different, useful issues. One piece of work, for instance, (published by N.C.G. Campbell in 1985) distinguishes between: "competitive buying", "cooperative buying", and "command buying". It challenges the assumption (made by many sales people) that all systematic organizational buying is combative and involves formal proposals aimed at getting the lowest prices.

This field also examines the diffusion of ideas and new products into organizations and how that affects the buying process. This is, though, a young and developing field of work with relatively little reliable and proven work. There also seems to be little to distinguish between the organizational buying of, say, large corporations, national government, local public sector, charities, private firms, and partnerships. Nor does there seem to be extensive work on the effect of variations in international culture on organizational buying.

Voices and further reading

- Wilson, A., *The Marketing of Industrial Products*. Hutchinson, 1965.
- "Organizational buyers are those buyers of goods and services for the specific purpose of industrial or agricultural production or for use in the operation or conduct of a plant, business institution, profession or service. Such buyers act on behalf of organizations for the furtherance of organizational, rather than personal goals." Marrian, J. in Wilson, 1965.
- "Organizational buyers are those buyers of goods and services for the specific purpose of industrial or agricultural production or for use in the operation or conduct of a plant, business, institution, profession or service." Marrian, J. in Wilson, 1965.
- Shapiro, B. and Posner, R.S., "Making the major sale". *Harvard Business Review*, July–August 2006.
- Bonoma, T.V., *"Major sales: who really does the buying?"* *Harvard Business Review*, July–August 2006.
- "Business-to-business marketing, organizational buying behaviour." Woodside, A.G. and Ferris-Costa, K.R. in Baker, M.J. and Hart, S. (eds), 2008.

Things you might like to consider

(i) Some have suggested that organizational buying is more rational and objective than consumer sales because of the existence of objective evaluation processes and the buying function. Yet emotion still plays a part in business sales. People at work make emotional decisions as much as (some would argue more than) logical, objective, and analysis-based decisions. A chief executive may want to buy an IT outsourcing service from a particular firm because he fears acquisition and wants to use the brand of his supplier to reassure shareholders. A business buyer may be worried about the impact of a purchase on their budget, or their political standing after choosing a poor performing supplier. Above all, though, as executives develop in their career they rely more and more heavily on the beliefs, opinion, and intuition that they have developed through long experience in their industry. As they become more senior they deal with more strategic and less clear cut issues, so rely on their judgement (or "gut instinct") even more. This means that, despite governance and rational processes, senior business leaders take intuitive and emotional decisions and must be influenced at that level. Experience suggests that suppliers who understand these emotional dynamics achieve higher value sales.

(ii) The different cultures of different sizes and styles of organization affect their approach to buying. A large centralized organization, will have different buying approaches to, say a decentralized organization like a large private partnership; these will be different again to a privately owned firm or a government or quasi-governmental body.

(iii) A large number of companies in different industrial sectors have avoided some of the cost pressures of formal organizational buying by "going up the value chain" (as they describe it). Companies offering computing, telecommunication, and accounting services to large businesses have developed consultative skills and used them to create a strategic dialogue with senior people. They have found that this has earned them advisory revenues of some size. It has enabled them to advise on any tenders that are issued, giving them the opportunity to influence the tenders more toward their own capabilities. They have also found that, after earning trust at senior levels, through relationship development (see separate entries under *relationship marketing* and *AAR*) they have been given some work without it going to tender at all.

RATING: Practical and powerful

ORGANIZATIONAL COMPETENCE IN MARKETING

Application: marketing effectiveness, strategy

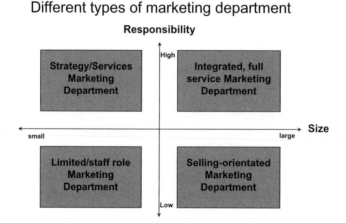

Figure O.3: A representation of the evolution of different marketing departments

The concept

Much of the published work on marketing focuses on theory, concepts, or practice and makes assumptions about the way the function works in a firm. Most assume that there is a well developed organization led by a marketing director or CMO, able to call on financial and human resources to undertake research, manage advertising, or adjust product features in the light of rational, justified arguments. There is little talk of the need to convince organizations of marketing's importance, of competing for resources, or of organizational politics.

The situation is rarely so clear-cut. The marketing function is often under-developed. It has to argue for its role in the organization and has to invest in processes, as well as running projects to generate revenue. Some companies do not understand their own need for certain marketing skills and restrict the contribution that the function makes, limiting it to, say, a minor promotional role. In many firms, marketers spend their time running around making PowerPoint presentations to each other or organizing the mind numbing detail of different events. This is not effective marketing and does not necessarily create wealth.

Responsibility for the organizational competence of the function normally rests with the "chief marketing officer" (CMO). As leader of the function this person has several roles. The first is to provide marketing experience, judgement, and advice to the firm's leaders about policies; to round out and inform decision making and strategy development. The second is to be the voice of the market within the firm, challenging it to embrace opportunities and understand customer needs. The third is to lead the function, ensuring that it is properly resourced and contributes appropriately. There is almost complete unanimity amongst marketing specialists that one of the main roles of the CMO or marketing leader is to maintain a perspective on the market and articulate that to the company; acting as the voice of the market into the organization.

It is less frequently argued (but more frequently experienced by those who do the job) that the CMO has a responsibility to ensure that the firm has the organizational competence to meet the demands of the market. This has two elements. The first is highlighting to the leadership of the firm those areas where it needs new skills or processes, in any part of the firm, to tackle competitive threat or market opportunity. The second is developing the competence of the marketing function itself to tackle strategic imperatives.

The first is likely to arise from the firm's strategic planning process. The leaders need a clear perspective on three things: market trends, competitive moves, and the firm's competences. These are likely to reveal changes which need to be made in order for the firm to thrive. It is the role of the marketing leader to identify these issues and illustrate how their absence threatens the firm. While the development of the organizational capability to meet the problem might not rest with the marketing function, the facilitation of a strategic debate does. Similarly, the function has a responsibility to review the result of the project and to ensure that it has met its intended objective so that it can compete effectively. A tool which helps with this is a *market audit*, a systematic review of the marketing and sales capability of the firm against its competitive backdrop (see separate entry under *market audit*).

Unfortunately, by no means every business has a CMO or even an experienced marketer. Small firms or new start-ups can have very modest marketing resources. Yet, there is evidence that marketing capability increases as companies grow and work through different inflection points in their development. As small firms grow, marketing specialists are recruited into different places in the organization, such as public relations and sales support. Later, this develops into the fully integrated marketing function seen in many corporate firms. A large corporate entity might have several hundred marketing specialists running campaigns, integrated by both a hierarchical senior management team (culminating in a CMO) and by the use of common processes and technology. The development of marketing in many leading companies has been through this evolution as their market situation has changed. So, it is the role of senior people in the function (particularly marketing directors or CMOs) to think about how the marketing function should evolve and, in fact, how the marketing competence of the whole firm should be facilitated.

In publicly owned companies, marketing is likely to be the responsibility of a relatively small specialist unit comprising people who are qualified and experienced. They will be responsible to the management team for creating strategy, plans, budgets, and programmes to grow the business. They will also be expected to balance the skills, resources, and processes of the marketing department to optimum effect and for the benefit of the business in its market. They will have delegated responsibility to manage the function effectively, and will need to ensure that it has good knowledge of relevant concepts, develops appropriate competencies, uses reliable techniques, and installs robust processes or systems. On top of this, they will need to engage with the whole firm to ensure that the customers' experiences are appropriate to meet the firm's objectives. In short, the marketing function needs to keep up-to-date and act as a catalyst for the business in its approach to market.

Figure O.4 tries to show the typical functions within a unit of this kind but these can vary enormously. For instance, brand management might exist within market management (because it focuses on market categories or in marketing communications. Sales and sales support might be combined with marketing under one "sales and marketing" director or vice president. Also, there may be elements of the marketing mix in other parts of the organization. For example, some firms place new product development and pricing under a separate director. Others have directors dedicated to *corporate relations*, responsible for reputation, brand, *corporate social responsibility (CSR)*, and public relations.

Not all marketing is undertaken in the carefully organized departments of large publicly owned companies. In small firms and professional partnerships, the situation tends to be more fluid and less clearly defined. Different people will initiate marketing activities, which are frequently handled by executives who have no specialist marketing knowledge and may not be aware of other marketing initia-

The classic functional shape

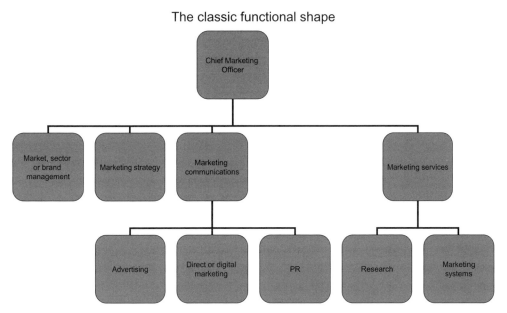

Figure O.4: A representation of the classic shape of a marketing department

tives in different parts of even their own company. If a marketing manager or marketing department exists, which is by no means certain, they may not have exclusive responsibility for all revenue generation tasks. The business world is not uniform. Companies succeed with a huge diversity of products and services, with very different cultures and operating approaches in a wide range of markets. Marketing has to be adjusted to suit these very different environments if it is to be successful.

One of the main business types is, for example, the conglomerate or decentralized business. Figure O.5 represents this type of decentralized organization with devolved business units, (like IBM, Ericsson, or Phillips). These "strategic business units" might be businesses specializing in different disciplines or in different geographies. The effectiveness and behaviour of the marketers depend on the degree of autonomy of the different units. Marketers in these, SBUs, will be expected to work within tight corporate guidelines. They are likely to have a clear job description with defined competences and objectives. They are also likely to report regularly to the corporate function and participate in clear, firm-wide processes. At the other extreme, though, are large conglomerates that own separate firms with different profit pools (like Ingersoll Rand, Virgin, or ABB). The marketers in these firms are likely to have greater autonomy within very broad corporate guidelines.

On the other hand, the majority of businesses range from tiny start-ups to medium-sized companies. In these, any specialist marketing units are limited by resource constraints; often to a single, or isolated, marketer, depicted in Figure O.6.

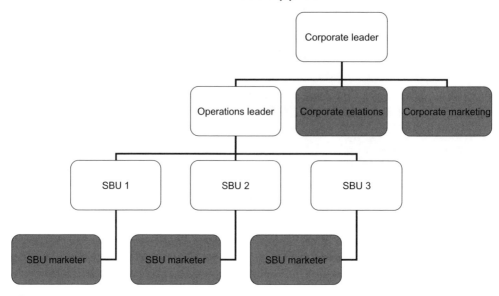

Figure O.5: Marketing in a decentralized organization

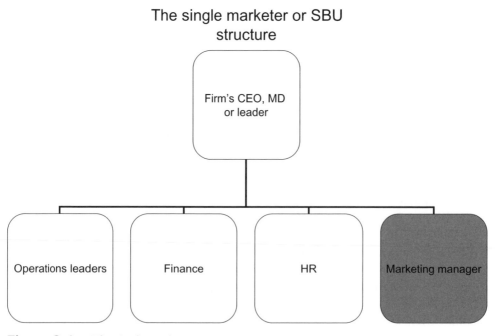

Figure O.6: The single marketer

One person is all that the business can afford, and that person is likely to report to the firm's leader, gaining authority to create programmes, strategy, and change from the closeness of that relationship. Constrained by lack of resources, the single marketer needs influence to get the wider organization to take on work and the budget to rely on external contractors. They need the capability to handle a wide variety of tasks and the humility to do much of the work themselves. In some firms, they report to a functional leader who manages all specialists (HR, finance, IT etc). This, however, tends to be less effective because it weakens the assumed authority behind the speciality, reducing the influence of marketing.

One difficulty in this environment is the marketing skills that small firms can afford. They frequently hire young professionals or marketers from middle management in other firms who have never really progressed in their career. They might lack gravitas and be unable to convince their leaders to invest in needed initiatives or to adopt new policies. Consequently, they tend to focus on promotional work, and are frequently unaware of sophisticated marketing techniques that might be more profitable and effective for their firm. They are often weak at giving credible strategic insight to influence the direction of the firm.

A wide range of companies, both large and small, have yet another form of governance: the intuitive business leader. These creative entrepreneurs tend to use the principles of marketing, based on their business experience and intuition. Individuals (from Richard Branson, Simon Cowell, Alan Sugar, and Phillip Green in Britain to Donald Trump, Bill Gates, Larry Ellison, Michael Dell, and Steve Jobs in the USA) become millionaires, or even billionaires, through an intuitive approach to markets. They are pre-eminent practitioners of marketing, creating enormous wealth for themselves, their investors, their employees, and society as a whole.

They frequently succeed by breaking rules (Harvard would not have advised young pop entrepreneur Branson to go into the airline business, for instance) and shake up or create markets. Their emphasis is on customers and markets, so they push all the elements of their business to focus on external opportunities rather than internal activities. They also tolerate both risk and failure. As their businesses grow, the most successful learn to use specialists (like accountants, lawyers, and merchant bankers) to round out or refine their vision and instinct; and most use marketing specialists (either as employees or through agencies) in a similar way.

The cultures of their highly successful, market-orientated, businesses are focused on understanding and executing the leader's will. Much time is taken to tease out, develop, and communicate their vision and implement it throughout the organization. Their marketing is therefore most often about connecting the leader's vision with a market opportunity. In some cases, the marketing structure is a small, fluid team, in another a trusted agency and, in yet another, the more recognizable structures of big, publicly owned firms. They use novel marketing techniques, frequently exploiting publicity opportunities and, in some cases, breaking away from the rules of consumer product marketing to pioneer other techniques.

Finally, much marketing occurs in the marketing supply industry, working on behalf of their clients. This is a very diverse range of businesses. It includes advertising, direct marketing, and new product development agencies, as well as a variety of consultancies. They range from the huge conglomerates like WPP to single person businesses. Despite the fact that most of the writing and theory of marketing is developed from and for marketing specialists in large companies, much of the real added value comes from agencies. It is the role of leading marketers inside client companies to establish processes and strategies whereby their firm gets the best from these agencies at the optimal cost, making them part of their company's organizational competence in marketing.

History, context, criticism, and development

The ability of the marketing function to contribute effectively to income generation and the health of the business depends on the role it has in the organization and its maturity. In many long-standing consumer goods businesses (Proctor & Gamble, Unilever) or confectioners (Mars), it is a lead function of the business. The firm recruits the cream of the graduate crop into a professional apprenticeship scheme that provides some of the best marketing training in the world. Alumni of the programme progress through the firm from junior brand managers to marketing directors. Their role is to generate income from branded *value propositions*, using wide-ranging and proven marketing techniques. Over many decades, these companies have institutionalized marketing into a leading philosophy of the entire corporation.

In other industries, however, the contribution of specialist marketing people is limited to minor functional roles like sales support, *PR*, or brochure creation. The formal marketing function is not as valued because the income of the business is generated by other means, such as a strong and healthy natural demand for an innovative product or systematic account management. But, there is evidence that this changes as markets mature. For instance, most of the consumer goods companies evolved first rate and leading marketing units because they experienced market maturity in the developed economies during the 1950s and 1960s. Similarly, marketing has become more important to the car industry, the computer industry, and the telecommunications industry, as they, in turn, have faced market maturity. As IBM has adapted to its changing market conditions, for instance, the marketing function within the company has developed its own competence to keep pace. As the case study in the *brand* section shows, starting from a strong heritage in sales, it has progressively become one of the most sophisticated in the IT sector, combining knowledge of marketing concepts with impressive marketing people and real customer insights through growing organizational competence.

Professor Nigel Piercy's research (Piercy, N., 2001) showed that there was rarely consistency about what activities marketing leaders have responsibility for. Nor was there consistency in the shape of organizations. Yet, he found four development phases in the evolution of the competence and significance of marketing departments. They were:

- *Integrated/full service:* closest to the theoretical models and with a wide range of responsibilities and power in the organization;
- *Strategic/services:* smaller units with less power and integration. Their influence is in the area of marketing support services or specific policies/strategies;
- *Selling overhead:* often large numbers and dispersed but primarily engaged in sales support activities;
- *Limited staff role:* small numbers with few responsibilities and engaged in specific staff support such as market research or media relations.

He suggested that marketing departments evolve (from a limited staff role to fully integrated) as firms grow and marketing grows in importance within them. When a company is initially formed, much of the marketing role is undertaken by the founders or specialist subcontractors (like PR agencies). Some time after that a marketing specialist will be hired to manage specific activities such as brochure production, new product launch, and perhaps some advertising. Marketing's leading thinker and educator, Phillip Kotler, has also noticed, through his many years of engaging with different businesses, this evolution of marketing competence (Kotler, P., 2006).

Voices and further reading

- ". . . the nature of the marketing function varies significantly from company to company. Most small businesses (and most businesses are small) don't establish a formal marketing group at all. Their marketing ideas come from managers, the sales force, or an advertising agency. Eventually, successful small businesses add marketing person (or persons) to help relieve the sales force of some chores . . . Both sales and marketing see the marketing group as an adjunct to the sales force at this stage.

  As companies become larger and more successful, executives recognize that there is more to marketing than setting the four P's . . . They determine that effective marketing calls for people skilled in segmentation, targeting and positioning. Once companies hire marketers with those skills, marketing becomes an independent player . . .

  Once the marketing group tackles higher-level tasks like segmentation, it starts to work more closely with other departments, particularly strategic planning, product development, finance and manufacturing. The company starts to think in terms of developing brands rather than products, brand managers become powerful players in the organization. The marketing group is no longer a humble ancillary to the sales department." Kotler, P., 2006.

Things you might like to consider

(i) Marketing managers need to be interested not only in the organizational capability of the marketing function, but also the productivity and effectiveness of sales channels and the general go-to-market capability of the whole organization. These are as much part of strategy development as issues like positioning or segmentation.

(ii) It is part of *marketing management* to review and develop the performance and capability of the marketing organization in the light of the changing needs of the company.

(iii) Really well developed marketing capability and a track record of success do not, it seems, avoid massive marketing mistakes. Coca-Cola is, without question, one of the marketing successes of the 20th century. Successive generations of marketers and marketing-orientated leaders have created enormous wealth from their little black drink. They have used the full extent of all marketing techniques for many decades. This heritage did not stop them, though, from messing up on a grand scale when they tried to drop the original drink for "New Coke" at the end of the 20th century and, later, when they tried to launch bottled water in Britain.

 RATING: Practical and powerful

 PACKAGING

Application: NPD/NSD, branding strategy, sales, marketing communication, post sales service

The concept

For many consumers, packaging is the public face of marketing, capturing the essence of a product or service. It has the ability to tempt, entice, and stimulate desire whilst communicating the functional realities of the offer. It is a blend of hard commercial reality with art and design. This is a vital part of marketing and ought, if there were much credence to be given to them, be another "P" in the four Ps.

Packaging can have several levels: the container for the product itself (Coca-Cola's bottle), any surrounding consumer packaging (such as the cardboard box a scent bottle is given in), and any shipping packaging. Even the latter can be branded and attractive. This packaging needs to serve a number of purposes: it needs to be functionally durable enough to contain the items purchased, it needs to communicate brand messages and values, it needs to be functionally fit for purpose during use, and it needs to convey modernity. The latter can range from innovative ways to supply the product (like the recent launch of the Heinz baked beans fridge storage container) or matching new values (like the lessening use of plastics in the light of environmental concerns).

The development of good packaging involves a series of crucial and practical decisions. There needs to be a "packaging concept", thinking through what the packaging will do and what it will, essentially be. There then needs to be a carefully thought through creative management process which produces: materials, colour, style, size, shape, etc.

Packaging is primarily thought of in terms of consumer goods. Yet, contrary to popular belief, it has been used to market services very effectively for some time. Consumer services like banking, vacations, train travel, and insurance have all used packaging and design to good effect. In many service organizations, though, it is less central to the marketing management process than consumer goods companies. This is a difficulty because, if anything, tangible, attractive packaging is needed in service marketing to help buyers overcome issues raised by the intangibility of the offer (see separate entry under *service marketing*). Marketers in service companies need to create devices to make the intangible more tangible.

One area where packing does not seem to be as strong or sophisticated is in business-to-business markets. In these environments (apart from operational protection during shipping) marketers tend to use "collateral", particularly in professional services and complex business-to-business markets. It is the expression of marketing messages in brochures, case studies, and other physical forms for, primarily, professional buyers. It also includes digital collateral such as web sites and videos. It may be that a customer is in emotionally distressing circumstances, such as a significant business problem, or it may be that the purchase seems expensive. Collateral plays an important reassurance role in these circumstances. For example, if the marketer is presenting credentials during a "beauty parade", they should leave behind a bound copy of the presentation in a format acceptable to the customer, so that they can leaf through it and consider it after the meeting. Also, at the point where the customer is about to make a decision but hasn't yet signed a contract, it makes sense to send a case study of a company which has purchased a similar item from the firm, so that there is something physical to refer to. Finally, after signing the contract, it is sensible to leave behind a directory of the people involved in the project, their experience, and contact numbers in a format that the customer can use internally to show others. At the very least a "thank-you" note should be sent to the customer for their business. Collateral needs to be carefully designed and crafted to communicate benefits clearly. Some business marketers create a "collateral strategy" for the whole firm (as part of a generic brand identity strategy) covering: intended use, design structure, renewal and reprinting methods, plus the types favoured for particular customers.

History, context, criticism, and development

There is a long history of the use of presentation and packaging in sales and marketing. The design of products and services dates back over many decades, so much so, in fact, that there is legislation controlling labelling and packaging which is at least a hundred years old. Packaging is so much part of the marketing process and such an influence on buyer behaviour that it is surprising that it is not a more established part of marketing theory and training.

Voices and further reading

- Kotler, P., *Marketing Management*. Prentice Hall, 2003.
- "Everybody requires the risk-reducing reassurances of tangibilized intangibles." Levitt, T., 1981.

Things you might like to consider

(i) Packaging is particularly important in a digital environment and in services marketing. As both are intangible, customers need physical items to reassure themselves that they have done the right thing.

(ii) Packaging needs to be designed to have international appeal. This can be an issue because colour gives different messages to different cultures.

(iii) Brochures in particular can be an exorbitant waste of money. Many firms produce expensive annual reports with photos of their own people. There are several problems with this approach. Firstly, there are frequently few differences between competitive brochures. They are often filled with the same pictures of people and descriptions of dubious, irrelevant "values". Secondly, these brochures are often written to extol the virtues of the firm and its leaders, rather than focusing on customer needs and the benefits the firm gives them. Thirdly, they are fixed in time, printed, and bound using expensive, high quality print and design techniques. (A more effective strategy, if an electronic format is not an option, is to create a "gate folder", a designed jacket which positions the firm, its values, and benefits. Sales people can then insert pre-prepared descriptions of expertise, case studies, and CVs.)

(iv) Although it might seem simple and obvious, it is important that the firm's representatives understand how to use packaging and collateral and the moments in the customer relationship when it is most effective. For instance, it can be used to overcome post purchase distress. A piece of material, delivered at the right time, can allay concerns and safeguard the value of a sale. Even senior sales people or highly intelligent consultants can get this wrong.

Capturing and communicating customer evidence at Microsoft

The customer evidence programme in the business and marketing organization of Microsoft UK bridged the need for customer stories across both sales and marketing campaigns. The programme linked into Microsoft's "global evidence programme", particularly where large deals were in the pipeline and evidence was needed from the world's biggest organizations in diverse industries around the globe.

DRIVERS FOR THE CUSTOMER EVIDENCE PROGRAMME

The drivers for setting up the customer evidence programme initially came from both the external environment and internal demands. Externally, in business-to-business marketing, references have always been important, but two things happened to make them more important than ever. First, IT procurement became more sophisticated. Driven by the public sector, where there was increasing demand to demonstrate value for money from public funds. The burden for demonstrating that value fell to the supplier of IT, by using past examples and cases as well as ROI modelling tools. Microsoft had a good enough track record in the technology, but was now charged with demonstrating business value. Second, the rise of social media and consumer recommendations, driven by suppliers such as Amazon, also influenced IT decision makers. This meant that the procurement process needed references much earlier on in the buying process and sales cycle.

Internally, the ad hoc process previously used to capture and share evidence of successful projects needed to become more effective and efficient. Sales people had often relied only on the references that they themselves were involved in or knew of from their personal networks. But as sales grew in size and scope, and references increased in importance, this became an inefficient way of working. A new approach was needed. At the same time, there was a drive within Microsoft to improve customer-centricity and satisfaction. The previous approach meant that often the same customers were asked to act as a reference, and hence were overused. It became obvious that at least in the English speaking markets, the top tier of customers were experiencing this, and so needed to be ring-fenced and managed more sensitively.

A SYSTEMATIC, DATA DRIVEN APPROACH

The customer evidence programme was built from the ground up, starting with a process of analysis to determine what the business needed. The first step was to produce a matrix of market sectors against Microsoft products, in order to prioritize where the best opportunities lay and evidence needed. Two further filters were overlaid onto the matrix: the first showed where gaps in sales support materials existed in each cell; and the second showed how tough the competitive situation was in each cell. The completed matrix provided a gap analysis that revealed priorities for investment for the customer evidence programme.

The second step was more granular, looking at the specific nature and needs of each priority cell. For example, local and central government cells needed a different approach to the hi-tech communications cells. From this analysis, the plan for the customer evidence programme was crafted, built on an annual basis with specified quarterly deliverables. The pipeline of evidence stories was represented, showing the timelines and critical milestones in their development. For instance, milestones were created by working back through the sales cycle of large, future deals, to highlight when specific evidence was needed. The pipeline of customer evidence was filled by the sales teams, who were quickly brought in to the new approach once they realized the value of the evidence pro-gramme in their own sales, and their own role in helping to populate the pipeline.

To start the production process, an outline form is now completed that populates a sharepoint system and triggers a series of emails to allow a potential story to be evaluated for its relevancy and potential impact. Then funding is approved and the production process triggered. An external case study writer then contacts the customer and the sharepoint system is updated in real time as the story is drafted, edited, and approved by both Microsoft and the customer. Delays trigger automatic alerts and warnings, so that issues can be ironed out as soon as possible.

Stories are produced in a number of formats, depending on the prefer-ences of the customer. They might be a simple quote, a written case study, an audio or video piece, a live presentation or even site visits to the customer premises. The final milestone is complete once the story is posted to Microsoft's global database, where it triggers emails to thank everyone involved and alert Microsoft people to its availability. But while this is the final milestone in the evidence production, it is only the start of the process of getting value out of the story.

Each story is tracked in terms of how it is used, both internally and externally, and (at the time of writing) a feedback loop is currently being established to identify the return on investment for the story. This is no mean feat, as the stories are used as part of integrated marketing campaigns as well as in specific sales situations.

BENEFITS AND LESSONS FROM THE APPROACH

The UK programme has demonstrated best practice in a number of areas, winning awards for its use of evidence as part of new product launches and for the quality filters that are applied to evidence creation. The latter is a scoring system that drives investment to those stories that can demonstrate value for money delivered, or other key metrics, for the customer. These filters have meant that Microsoft almost never produces a poor case study – poor quality references are weeded out early on in the process.

Microsoft learnt that the task of changing sales behaviour, to use a system rather than their own network and ad hoc approach, is a huge one.

Time and attention is needed to get over this particular hurdle, with a clear demonstration of the link between the value sales people get from using references and their role in developing them. Another lesson is that top management sponsorship of the customer evidence programme is a key to its success. They simply must understand its value as a business asset, and look regularly at high level reports of the evidence pipeline, as well as act as an escalation point for issues, and also as recruiters of customers to feature in the programme.

The final lesson is the importance of the quality filters in the programme. Without these, and despite the systematic approach to evidence production and use, it would still be possible to waste money cranking out a few mediocre stories.

★ RATING: Practical and powerful

PIPELINE MANAGEMENT

Application: sales planning and management

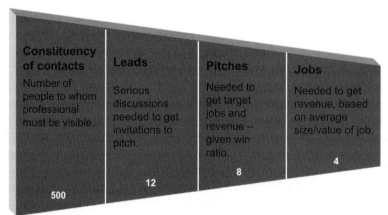

Figure P.1: A representation of pipeline management

The concept

This is a management concept and sales discipline that builds the generation of business into the day-to-day life of a sales team. Based on the concept of the "sales cycle" (the idea that there are progressive stages to the sale of an item) it ensures that there are enough opportunities at each stage to deliver enough sales. It is the foundation of good sales practice and the focus of sales management in many industries. Sometimes called the "sales funnel" and sometimes "the book of business", it is a discipline that translates easily into most business environments, from simple product sales to complex business-to-business services.

The diagram illustrates the concept, which should be approached from a hard-headed, numerically driven perspective. For example, starting from the right hand side, if a sales person has a target of, say, $2 million, and the average value of their sales is $500,000, they need to win four a year. The next section of the pipeline shows that, in order to win four sales a year, they need to propose a bigger number of potential deals to customers. If, in their market place, the conversion ratio is two to one, they need to make eight proposals to win four. In some markets, though, there are no formal proposals and presentations. Sometimes a buyer will simply ask a supplier to start the work. Other times the project can be loosely defined. Nevertheless, there must be some form of discussion, presentation, or scoping of projects that forms the basis of the agreement to go ahead. These all count as part of the "pitches" section of the pipeline, often called "prospects".

The next category refers to "leads" or "serious expression of interest". A sales person will be known to a number of potential customers but, at some stage, those buyers must express an interest in a product or service if there is to be a sale. This might be through email, by telephone, in a meeting, or in a social context. They discuss their needs and ask for more information. That may simply be an invitation to examine the need, or it might be an invitation to take part in a "beauty parade" where the firm has to respond formally to a request for a proposal or presentation of their credentials, or both. If the conversion rate in a market is two to one, there will need to be sixteen expressions of interest to get eight proposals to get four jobs. Already, then, the sales person in this example needs to receive at least one serious expression of interest a month if workflow is to remain healthy.

The final part of the sales pipeline, the wider end of the funnel, is the "constituency of contacts" on which the sales person should focus. This will vary in size and have several components. It might, for instance, be primarily within one major organization, when, for example, a large customer has a dedicated account manager. First, there will be those who are well known business contacts, where there is a close relationship. They will be seen in a social context, and there will be a close relationship of trust, built on mutual value that has been given over the years. Then there will be a wider community who will know the company or sales person to some degree. Finally, there will be a wider group who are in the target market but have very little knowledge of the firm or contact with it. It is in this section that it is cost-effective for marketing campaigns to focus. They should generate leads from the constituency of contacts which feed into each sales person's pipeline.

To use the funnel effectively, sales people need to build these processes into their day-to-day lives. For example, whilst closing deals and developing proposals, they can make sure they maintain regular contact with their intimate professional relationships. They can schedule personal meetings, send information or articles they think will be of interest, and invite them to ad hoc hospitality or professional briefing events.

Pipeline management is also a powerful tool for sales managers. Many build the concept into IT systems so that the pipeline of the business can be seen easily by leaders. They set up performance reviews, between, say, marketing and sales, to keep colleagues focused on the need to manage future business while concluding current projects. Others use it to tie lead generating marketing campaigns into sales plans. In fact, if this sort of joint cooperation between people in the sales and marketing function does not exist in their company, marketers should consider building this concept into their business as part of the development of *organizational competence* and competitive ability.

History, context, criticism, and development

The idea that a flow of sales opportunities can be identified and managed has existed for many years. The argument that marketing activity can, cost-effectively, prepare the way for a sales visit seemed to emerge in the 1960s. The thrust, for example, of Professor E. Jerome McCarthy's famous book, *Basic Marketing* (see McCarthy, 1960 and 1975) was that both advertising and direct marketing campaigns should be used to stimulate interest and leads. His thesis, which was a powerful point at the time, was that the investment in marketing (even broadcast advertising) was cheaper than the abortive cost of sending out sales people cold calling; that by running marketing campaigns a company would save costs and be more effective.

Later, Phillip Kotler (Kotler, P., Rackham, N., and Krishnaswamy, S., 2006) pointed out that marketing and sales functions should be integrated in their ownership of and cooperation in, the sales funnel. His proposed funnel had components in a sequence called: customer awareness, brand awareness, brand consideration, brand preference, purchase intent, purchase, loyalty, and advocacy. He emphasized that it is in the interest of the firm for the sales people to work with the marketing people to create a joint plan of activities. Whatever the detailed components of each company's plan, the use of funnels will avoid the "feast and famine" effect of erratic marketing and sales activities; and use shareholders' funds to best effect.

Voices and further reading

- "Although a marketing manager might prefer to use personal selling exclusively, it can be expensive on a per-contact and a per-sale basis. Mass selling is a way around this roadblock. It is not as pinpointed as personal selling, but it does permit communication to large numbers of potential customers at the same time. Today, most promotion blends contain both personal selling and mass selling." McCarthy, E.J., 1960.
- "Sales and marketing are responsible for a sequence of activities and events (sometimes called a funnel) that leads customers toward purchases and, hopefully, ongoing relationships. . . . Marketing is usually responsible for the first few steps – building customers' brand awareness and brand preference, creating a marketing plan, and generating leads for sales. Then sales executes the marketing plan and follows up on leads." Kotler, Rackham, and Krishnaswamy, 2006.
- Üstüner, T. and Godes, D., "Better sales networks". *Harvard Business Review*, July–August 2006.
- "If salespeople and managers understand how networks function, they can pinpoint the most effective network configuration for each stage of a sale and take the actions necessary to create it." Üstüner, T. and Godes, D., ibid.
- Shapiro, B. and Posner, R.S., "Making the major sale". *Harvard Business Review*, July–August 2006.
- "Strategic selling is an eight-part process that develops the sale from the initial decision to pursue a prospect, through the appropriate strategy for courting an account, to the eventual close of the sale." Shapiro and Posner, ibid.

Things you might like to consider

(i)   This is useful concept to wrap together marketing and sales activities.
(ii) Many CRM and marketing management systems now have this sort of funnel concept built into them. It should seamlessly integrate marketing campaigns with lead generation, sales forecasting, and targeting.
(iii) Without good pipeline management, activity can be erratic. The business experiences peaks and troughs in workflow because there is no consistent focus on the generation of future sales. Pipeline management helps overcome these difficulties.

 RATING: Practical and powerful

PORTER'S COMPETITIVE FORCES

Application: competitive analysis, market analysis, strategy development

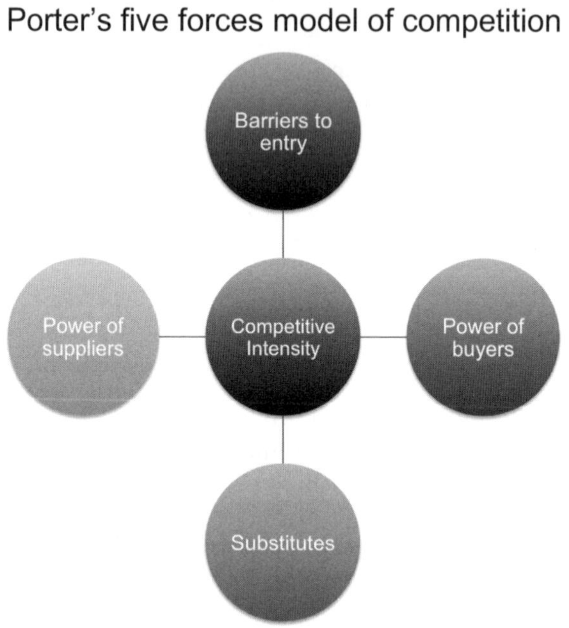

Porter's five forces model of competition

Figure P.2:   A representation of Porter's five forces of competitive intensity (see Porter, M.E., 1990)

The concept

Harvard's Michael Porter is one of the most influential strategy professors living today. Amongst his impressive and prodigious work on competitive strategy he offered a powerful conceptual framework (Porter, M., 1995) which works well as part of the market analysis and strategy development process. His "five forces" of competition are a useful checklist for marketers to work through when analysing a market. They are:

- The power of buyers. Buyers can influence a market by forcing down prices, by demanding higher service and quality, or by playing competitors off against each other. Porter suggested that there are a number of circumstances when a buyer group is powerful including: if they are concentrated, if buying commodities or components, if driven to get price cuts, or if the purchase is unimportant to them.

- The power of suppliers. Suppliers can exert power in a market by raising prices or reducing the quality of the offer. They can squeeze profitability out of the industry. They are powerful if: there are only a few, they have unique offers, are not obliged to compete, threaten forward integration, or are not part of an important industry to the buyers.
- The threat of new entrants: These bring new capacity, the desire for market share and resources. The seriousness of the threat depends on barriers to entry which have six sources: economies of scale, product differentiation, capital requirements, cost advantages, access to distribution, and government policy.
- The threat of substitute offers. These affect the profit of an industry by placing a ceiling on what it can charge through offering an alternative price/feature option. They can reduce demand for a whole product class as new ways of provision suck out demand.

The concept can simply be used as a checklist to prompt marketers to cover relevant issues during market analysis and strategy development. However, it is most powerful when good analysis is put behind the thinking so that judgements can be made with the benefit of real data. Industry reports and original research can be summarized into the model and used as criteria by which to develop competitive responses or critical success factors. The tool can be used to guide debate and is also effective as a communications device. Its clarity summarizes graphically and quickly the competitive landscape and can be used as part of the rationale for competitive programmes. It is best used, though, as a background planning tool in the market planning process.

History, context, criticism, and development

The power of this tool is that it stops marketers or other executives from looking too parochially at competition. They are prompted to think through, for example, fundamental threats from newer competitive forces (such as laser surgery instead of glasses) and the threats to barriers of entry (as, for example, lawyers are experiencing as technology commoditizes their offer and undermines years of training as a barrier to entry).

Where an organization has a range of different businesses, this technique ought to be used to understand the effects on different business units rather than the total organization. Marketers ought to think broadly about the potential forces affecting their businesses and how they might develop into the future. Basing this sort of strategic development around one snapshot in time produced in an informal brainstorming meeting is dangerous. People need to step back and consider how these inter-related factors will, like the earth's tectonic plates, change the fundamental landscape in which the business operates. If not, this form of analysis can be superficial and ineffective.

Some people find this sort of analysis difficult to get a grip on and too complex or technical. It ought to be communicated simply and used as a guide for the intuitive discussion amongst practising executives.

Voices and further reading

*   Porter, M.E., "How competitive forces shape strategy". *Harvard Business Review*, March–April 1979.
*   Porter, M.E., *Competitive Strategy: Techniques for Analyzing Industries and Competitors*. Free Press, 1980.
*   Porter, M.E., *Competitive Advantage of Nations*. Free Press, 1990.
*   Porter, M.E., *On Competition, Harvard Business Review* book, 1995.
*   "The state of competition in an industry depends on five basic forces . . . The collective strength of these forces determines the ultimate profit of an industry . . . Different forces take on prominence, of course, in shaping competition in each industry. . . . Every industry has a underlying structure, or set of fundamental economic and technical characteristics, that gives rice to these competitive forces. The strategist wanting to position his or her company to cope best with its industry environment or to influence that environment in the company's favor, must learn what makes the environment tick." Porter, 1995.
*   "The five forces framework can be used to gain insights into the forces at working the industry environment of an SBU which needs particular attention in the development of strategy. It is important to use the frame for more than simply listing the forces." Johnson, G. and Scholes, K., 2002.

Things you might like to consider

(i)   Prior to the development of this framework, strategists had limited perspectives from classical economics about perfect competition in impersonal markets. They were not always helpful in thinking through strategic options. This is a practical and thought provoking perspective.
(ii) This is well worked and well researched conceptual work which provides useful frameworks in which to discuss and develop strategy.
(iii) There are aspects of modern competitive strategy which are not considered in this work. The ability to create superior value, for instance.
(iv) The framework takes no real notice of the diffusion of innovation or the maturity of markets.

 RATING: Practical and powerful

PORTFOLIO ANALYSIS AND MANAGEMENT

Application: new revenue streams, new offers

The concept

Product portfolio management is a much discussed aspect of marketing theory. It is argued that, in order to stay competitive, a business must continue to offer an up-to-date and broad range of products in a relevant way to a particular market. If a company is offering a range of products that are, for example, all reaching the end of their life, then its survival is threatened; a high risk position. Theorists argue that new offers should be created before this dangerous situation is reached. Logic would imply that such a strategy is relevant to most businesses and that a regular competitive review of the range of offers would benefit the firm.

There are various techniques to help with portfolio planning:

(i)   The *Boston Matrix* is meant for the leadership of firms who own a range of different businesses which each focus on different markets. The varying competencies and phases of development of these different businesses in their different markets allow them to be managed and resourced in different ways. The Boston Matrix conveys complex information, like their position relative to competitors, very easily. (It is technically incorrect to use it on a portfolio of individual products or services that are not SBUs.)

(ii) The "*McKinsey/GE Matrix*" (or Directional policy matrix) can be used to prioritize resources and to approach new markets with new offers. It is particularly powerful at creating a consensus among executives during the ranking of criteria and the rating of individual practices.

(iii) "Line extension" categorizes a firm's products and services according to a "range" or a "line". It is completely independent of the *product life cycle* concept and leads businesses to apply progressive innovation to their business processes. Marketers look for applications based around the competence that produces them, and then try to apply them to new markets or different segments within a market. Theorists argue that the range should have "width and depth". "Width" refers to the number of different lines offered, while "depth" refers to the assortment of offers.

(iv) The product/service spectrum created by Lyn Shostack (see *services marketing*) can be a particularly useful and practical method of planning the strategic direction of a portfolio. Changes in the strategic direction and positioning of the company, or changes in demand, can be incorporated into this concept and used to plan the structure of the company's "proposition portfolio" (i.e. the mix of products and services).

History, development, context, and criticism

Business leaders have brought out new and changing products and services, in response to changing customers' tastes and developing opportunities, for many centuries. It does seem, though, that it was in the 1960s that the idea of proactively managing a "portfolio" of products and services emerged. (Unlike a number of concepts, such as Branding, it does not appear in marketing text books at the start of the 20th century.) The main protagonist of the idea appears to have been Bruce Henderson of Boston Consulting fame (see separate entry under the Boston Matrix). As he had such senior level access this idea was taken up by business leaders and CEOs, so marketing specialists had no choice but to examine it. The idea soon moved into the canon of marketing theory and is routinely taught as one of the fundamentals of marketing.

There does not seem, though, to have been open-minded examination of its limitations or drawbacks. Senior people routinely develop their firms' capabilities and opportunities by other means (M&A), for example. Also, as the case study shows, the term "cash cow" is pejorative and can damage a product or business. A number of entrepreneurs have made substantial fortunes by buying brands or businesses that marketers in other companies have marked down as a result of portfolio reviews. It has to be asked why the owners of these entities couldn't generate the wealth that the new owners could. If there is a substantial reason (like a new strategic capability or greater market access) then the disposal makes sense. If not, it's just sloppy thinking which destroys shareholder returns.

There appears to be very little developed work around the management of a portfolio of services. Within the last ten years, for example, one of the world's leading IT providers had to consult strategy houses, like McKinsey and Boston Consulting, to help develop a mechanism by which the investment in a vast range of services could be decided. There also sees to be little developed work to help marketers think through changes in their portfolio between products or services. Demand and response can move both ways. In the professions, for instance, a number of services (like will preparation or house conveyance) are commoditizing and can be provided through IT products. At the same time, a wide range of different companies have created wealth by providing their customers with managed services as opposed to commodity products. There seems to be little developed work to help with these important strategic changes in the company's offer.

Voices and further reading

- "To be successful, a company should have a portfolio of products with different growth rates and different market shares. The portfolio composition is a function of the balance between cash cows. High growth products require cash inputs to grow. Low growth products should generate excess cash. Both kinds are needed simultaneously." Henderson, B. in *The Boston Consulting Group on Strategy*. John Wiley & Sons Inc., 2006.

- "The idea of a portfolio is for a company to meet its objectives by balancing sales growth, cash flow and risk. As individual products progress or decline and markets grow or shrink, then the overall nature of the company's product portfolio will change. It is therefore essential that the whole portfolio is reviewed regularly and that an active policy towards new product development and divestment of old products is pursued." McDonald, M.H.B., 2007.
- "The trend in management thinking has been to move away from focusing mainly on the balance and attractiveness criteria . . . toward focusing on the fit criteria . . . Many companies diversified in the 1970's and 1980's in order to get into more attractive businesses and balance their portfolios. Most of these initiatives failed and the late 1980's and 1990's were periods of unbundling, break-ups and de-mergers of portfolios that had, at best, spurious relatedness." Johnson, G. and Scholes, K., 2002.

Things you might like to consider

(i)   Academics arguing that money should be taken from "cash cows" and invested into the development of "rising stars" are suggesting that successful products be denuded of funding so that executives can have adventures with risky new ideas. Is that really sensible?

(ii)   Much of this thinking is predicated on a dubious concept, the product life cycle of individual products or services (see separate entry). Marketers should be cautious about coming to conclusions that their offer is "mature" or "dying".

(iii) There are offers which have developed into brands and lasted several hundred years (see the evidence in Tables B.1 and B.2). Is it not sensible to first investigate the potential of turning any offer into a brand? It is certainly very important to understand and protect any existing brand franchise.

(iv)   Theorists have asserted that it is risky to have only one type of product or business (all "cash cows" for instance) but there is very little evidence presented to back this up. In fact, some companies have survived very effectively for many years with one prime, branded offer.

(v)   It does not seem that the very senior leaders of companies use product portfolio strategy alone to grow their business. Acquisition of brands or companies is probably more frequently successful. Investors, banks and, particularly private equity, judge the viability of an investment plan as much on the capability of the management team as on any existing products. Cost of capital is therefore as important an issue to understand as the perceived "life cycles" of any individual products or services.

(vi)   It seems logical and sensible to conduct portfolio reviews and to prioritize investment. But, as the case study shows, numerous individuals and companies have demonstrated that, in buying and reinvigorating so-called "cash cows" or "mature products" or "dying brands", substantial profit can be made. People like Sir Paul Judge, Lord Hanson, Mike Jatania of Lornamead, and Bernard Arnault of LMVH have shown that it is possible to create enormous wealth by injecting sensible investment and good management into entities dismissed by others following idiotically conducted portfolio reviews. Their experience suggests that there is something profoundly muddled and sloppy in the application of portfolio theory. Why could the marketers in the companies that owned these brands not generate the wealth themselves? Why were such valuable entities subject to neglect and decline because they were believed to be "cash cows" or ageing brands?

(vii) This approach is also dangerous in recessions or slow growth markets where mistakes can be very costly or catastrophic.

Sir Paul correctly judges Cadbury's portfolio

Sir Paul Judge is, today, a senior business and political figure in the UK and Europe. Amongst other responsibilities, he is Chairman of Schroder Income Growth Fund plc and a director of ENRC plc, of the United Kingdom Accreditation Service, of Standard Bank Group Ltd of Johannesburg, of Tempur-Pedic International of Kentucky, and of Abraaj Capital of Dubai. His honorary appointments include being an Alderman of the City of London, President of the Chartered Institute of Marketing and of the Association of MBAs, and Deputy Chairman of the American Management Association. He was Chairman of the venerable Royal Society of Arts (founded in 1754) between 2003 and 2006 and is a special adviser to the Royal Institute of International Affairs (Chatham House). He was also the principal benefactor of the Judge Business School at the University of Cambridge.

He is most famous, though, as "the businessman who turned a £90,000 investment into £45 m in just three years". What is not so well known is that this pivotal point in his career emerged as a result of a portfolio review at Cadbury.

Sir Paul's early career was with Cadbury Schweppes, working initially in the overseas group finance department and eventually becoming group deputy finance director at the age of 28. He later went on to become Managing Director of Cadbury Schweppes Kenya which had three factories and 600 employees. In 1982 he was appointed Managing Director of Cadbury Typhoo, a business which had 3000 employees and a turnover of £150 million. In 1984 he became group planning director and a member of the group executive committee. This was to become a dramatic and significant turning point in his career.

Back in 1976 Cadbury Schweppes had undertaken a strategic review of its business which Sir Paul describes as "similar to the Boston matrix analysis". The company had grown through merger and acquisitions. It needed to rationalize its businesses and prioritize investment. As a result, the company decided to concentrate on confectionery and soft drinks. The foods business became a low priority because it was so culturally and operationally different. Chocolate and drinks were international whereas the foods business was largely centred on the UK. So, despite the fact that the food business included a roll-call of some of the most famous brand names in the grocery trade (Typhoo tea, Chivers marmalade, and the Cadbury food products like biscuits, drinking chocolate, and Bournvita) between 1977–85 the company reduced its investment as the business became known as a "cash cow".

As a result of the relative neglect, the financial performance declined over time. Turnover was static and trading profit progressively decreased. By 1985 the £6.4 million of trading profit meant that the trading margin had dropped to only 2.1 % and that the return on £67.5 million of assets was less than 10%. Sir Paul says: "One important consequence of low commitment is that it is difficult to obtain development funding for major capital projects or acquisitions in a low priority business. As a result of low investment, the company then tends to achieve a lower return. Although for the total corporation its role as a cash generator may indeed be the best for the business, there will almost inevitably be a deterioration in its competitive ability, something not always taken into account when considering cash cows."

In 1985, (nearly a decade after the portfolio review) Cadbury Schweppes was prompted, for a number of reasons, to sell some non-core businesses. They included the Jeyes hygiene businesses plus the British, Irish, and French food businesses. So, Sir Paul proposed the £97 million buyout of the food businesses to form "Premier Brands", the largest buy-out of any kind in the UK during 1986. The new entity manufactured and marketed products for fifty million cups of tea per day, fourteen million portions of whitener, and two million cups of cocoa. To go with these drinks were nearly three million finger biscuits, 400,000 helpings of potato, thirteen million dollops of jam and marmalade, assorted helpings of baked beans and jellies, and many other product lines. It initially had 4,000 employees and a turnover of £300 million.

The actual £97 million buyout was of course nerve racking, risky, hard work. There were rival bids, vast amounts of detail to resolve, complex negotiations, and personal risk for the directors of the new entity.

Sir Paul says: "People who work in big companies are used to knocking the last three or even six noughts off the numbers on financial reports. But when you begin to understand that it's your own money, you start putting all of those noughts right back. The personal involvement is high. Obviously the bankers have to be convinced about the business plan, but also they want to make sure they have got the management on their side. That means money, which led to all of the directors having to arrange second mortgages on their houses so that the bankers knew that we were committed, and that our partners and families were right behind us."

The new team won through, though, and began to give the business the attention and investment it deserved. They were taking a substantial risk, but their strategy was based on the belief that competition is, in the end, between workforces. They believed that they could achieve a substantial turnaround and that they could do this through better management of the people in the business. So, in addition to judicious investment and experienced management who focused on the business, they placed a great emphasis on people, generating huge enthusiasm amongst their employees, not least with a generous share option scheme.

By 1989 the company had been transformed and was being described as the most successful buy-out in the UK. This success was recognized in February 1989 by Premier Brands receiving the biannual Award, sponsored by the *Grocer* magazine in conjunction with the International Food Exhibition, as the company with "the best overall performance in the whole UK food and drink industry in the last two years". In 1988 turnover reached £393 million as a result of both organic growth and acquisitions. Trading profit had grown to £31.8 million, more than quadrupling the 1985 figure. In both 1987 and 1988 the return on assets was above 50%. So, in June 1989 Premier Brands was sold for £310 million to Hillsdown Holdings. The initial equity of £330,000 put in by the nine directors was multiplied into £165 million as part of that sale, a 500 to 1 increase. In addition Cadbury Schweppes received £22 million for the 10% it had retained and the employees shared £33 million as a result of their one-penny share options turning into actual shares worth £5.

 RATING: Toxic

 **POSITIONING**

Application: Strategy development, competitive strategy

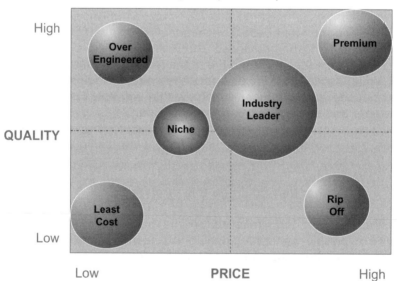

Figure P.3: A generic perceptual map of a market to indicate positioning
Adapted from Lambin's Figure 6.12, 2000

The concept

The "position" of a businesses in a market is based on buyers' perceptions of the value of its offer. By gaining and holding a clear position in a market, a firm can maximize its margins and create a long-term sustainable competitive stance. "Perceptual maps" are used by marketers in many different businesses to determine market position, set strategy, and gain insight. By understanding and ranking the buyers' views of all the significant offers, marketers can deduce and set direction for their own offer. The diagram above (adapted from Lambin, J., 2000) is a generic "perceptual" map of buyer views ("perceptual" because it concentrates on their perceptions of value). The tool is best constructed using detailed conjoint research amongst representatives of all buyers in the market and by understanding their values (see value propositions). It uses two axes (quality and price) which together form buyers' views of value (i.e. value f price x quality).

The "market leader" (like IBM, BA, Microsoft, and Centrica) normally takes centre stage with the offer by which all are judged. It has dominant share and the ability to influence the rules of engagement in the total market. It sets the price/ quality expectations and has the power to change the whole market. The market leader serves the majority of buyers and, as a result, sets both price expectations and service standards for the whole market. A "follower" (like Fujitsu, or Scottish Power) is smaller than the market leader and able to earn a profitable existence by providing a healthy alternative either in terms of price or the mix of features.

The "premium" position (normally a heritage brand like Rolls Royce or Harrods) is taken by a features–rich offer at a high price, whilst the "least cost" supplier (Easyjet, Ryan Air, Costcutter, etc.) strips out all that is possible to achieve low price. Various niche providers (like Virgin Atlantic) set themselves against the market leader and survive by providing a different offer. Each company, either by design or default, eventually commands its own position in a market by serving one group of customers with a particular value proposition.

There are two unsustainable positions. The "rip off" has low quality at high price. It normally exists because of some distortion or recent trauma in the market. However, it cannot keep this position in the long term because buyers will compare offers and desert it for other suppliers with an offer nearer to their values. The "over engineered" supplier might be a naïve new entrant or a recently privatized or de-monopolized supplier. Again it must move in the long term.

The perceptual map can be used in several ways.

(i) Strategy development

The tool can be used to create both corporate and competitive strategy. The leadership can use it to reach consensus on the position that they want the firm to take in the market. It is therefore a very powerful input to strategy debate amongst leadership teams. For instance, the leadership may find that, through acquisition, their company can become the volume market leader of an industry. However, to maintain that position, it must adopt the behaviour of a market leader, taking a stance on price, quality, and leading industry issues. Alternatively, a firm might find that it can maximize margins by taking a position as a niche provider. In this case it needs to determine exactly how its offer will be different from the market leader, communicating that to buyers. Marketers can work out where the target buyers' values lie and move the firm's offer towards them. "Positioning" the firm in this way, is a guide for NPD and NSD policy.

(ii) Communication planning

This tool can also leads communication and marketing programmes. It gives real direction to message planning and creative content.

(iii) Forecasting

Perceptual maps can also be used to determine the number of buyers the firm should expect and what the value proposition should be. The customer insights around value perceptions can take forecasting beyond mere statistical modelling based on historic data.

(iv) Competitive strategy

These perceptual maps can also be used to understand competitive forces (the likely manoeuvres of other businesses in the market) and to work out competitive strategy. Markets are not static. It is dangerous, for example, for the market leader to assume its position is inviolable, since niche providers can progressively capture segments of the market and mount a challenge for leadership. Or a follower, which finds itself number two in a market with a vulnerable market leader, might decide to mount a challenge. So this tool can be used to anticipate the likely reaction of competitors when the firm makes any move. It is a powerful strategic insight, which can clarify strategic intent and give real focus to marketing programmes.

(v) Internal communication and training

The tool can also be used as an internal communication aid. Firstly, it is a very simple and clear summary of the market and the firm's ambitions which can be used effectively in internal meetings. Secondly, it can be used as a diagnostic tool to develop internal communications programmes. By using it as a basis for internal research of employee opinion, it can be contrasted against customers' views. Training and communications programmes can then be designed to address any gap in view. Finally, and particularly important to service firms, is the fact that a clear position communicates to the recruitment market, attracting the right calibre of service employees; this, in turn, enhances quality and margins.

History, context, criticism, and development

Positioning has been a recognized technique since the 1960s. In practice it is closely related to both brand and segmentation strategies. Consumer marketers have used it to command a space for their offers in retail environments and in the mind of their consumers. Towards the end of the 20th century it was increasingly applied to corporate brands and to service offers. At the start of the 21st century, though, it has taken on a more subtle tone as global audiences have become more demanding on social issues and responsiveness. Marketers have increasingly had to think about positioning their company or their offers in line with the values of both their buyers and their employees.

Voices and further reading

- "Market leaders develop unique competitive strategies and have higher prices for their higher-quality products than do small-share businesses." Buzzell, R.D., Bradley, T.G., and Sultan, R.G.M., 1975 (reporting the results of the first years of the PIMS database).
- Taylor, D. and Nichols, D., "Brands as market leaders". *Market Leader*, Quarter 2, 2010.
- "The positioning in the target segment can be crafted in numerous ways. The company can be positioned as a 'hero for the poor' or as a company 'that teaches people how to fish instead of giving them free fish'. The main message is the same . . . if it is a multinational company; the positioning should be localized to the community level." Kotler, P. et al., 2010.
- "Positioning is about developing a unique selling proposition (USP) for the target segment. . . . the inability to do so results in either a price negotiation with the customer or a loss of a sale." Kumar, N., 2004.
- "Product positioning refers to the perceptions customers have about the product. It is a relative term that describes customer perceptions of the product's position in the market relative to rival products. It is founded upon understanding how customers discriminate between alternative products and it considers the factors customers use in making judgments or choices between products in the market being investigated." Trott, P., 2008.
- "In many cases, consumers use a few basic dimensions to categorize competing products or services, and then evaluate each alternative in terms of its relative standing on these dimensions. This tendency has led to the use of a very useful positioning tool – a perceptual map. By identifying the important dimensions and then asking consumers to place competitors within this space, marketers can answer some crucial strategic questions . . ." Solomon, M. et al., 2006.
- Tybout, A.M. and Sternthal, B., "Brand Positioning" in Iacobucci, D. (ed.), *Kellogg on Marketing*. 2001.

Things you might like to consider

(i) This is critically dependant on effective segmentation. It is quite normal for marketers to have different positioning maps for different segments in different markets. This is very powerful when idiotic competitors are taking bland generic approaches to a market. It is relatively easy to gain a prominent position by dominating a segment at a time.

(ii) In reality, the two axes used in most companies' work are often a derivative of critical issues or success factors in the market. They are normally issues which are uppermost in the minds of most buyers rather than generic indicators of quality and value.

(iii) There is a clear inter-relationship between good segmentation, targeting that segment and positioning the offer to them; which is the foundation of many marketing programmes. Some use the mnemonic "STP" (segmentation, targeting, positioning) to prompt thinking around the clarity of it in planning cycles.

(iv) This technique is dependent on getting an understanding of buyers' perceptions, sometimes a very difficult task which is progressive. It can be misleading and dangerous until a reliable view of perception can be formed. Refusal to invest in research methods to get at perception undermines this important strategic perspective.

The accountants position themselves

The UK market for insolvency services illustrates how useful value maps can be in alerting firms to potential dangers. This is a sophisticated processional services market which focuses on helping businesses or individuals to avoid bankruptcy or getting the best return for creditors if problems are irresolvable.

In the 1990s the market was divided between the big firms and boutiques dedicated to insolvency practices at the higher end; and individual practitioners who dealt with the lower end of the market (about 40%).

The big accountancy firms had become accustomed to being given insolvency business from the leading banks, which dealt with problems in companies to which they had lent money. These banks tended to use a virtual rotation system, choosing partners from an approved list of firms to lead assignments. Larger insolvencies went to the bigger firms (either because of perceived complexity or international reach), whereas boutiques tended to be awarded smaller, more price-sensitive jobs.

But the market was changing. First, many of the banks had changed their strategy and had a "cleaner" lending portfolio than previously. Secondly, there was a growing emphasis on turnaround, requiring different management skills. Thirdly, there were new lenders entering the market, both foreign banks and "asset-based lenders" who were not so tied to traditional suppliers. In addition, a new insolvency law was mooted which would change the responsibility for choosing an insolvency firm, swinging the influence on the buying decision away from the large, highly centralized banks towards their smaller, often regionally-based clients.

All these factors would disrupt this tidy market and change behaviour. The barrier between the big firms and the individual practitioners would begin to disappear. This, in turn, would mean that they could no longer be complacent about business and would have to find ways to market to this new audience. The perceptual map, if constructed using client data, would give insight into market conditions and help to chart a course through the changes.

For instance, at least two of the then "Big Five" firms claimed to be market leader, but analysis showed they were not. Based on the perceptual map in Figure P.4 below, once the semi-monopolistic distortion was removed from the market, a new market leader would emerge, threatening the position of the bigger firms. It could move into this position by increasing its volume through finding a new value proposition. Alternatively, one of the niche providers could take a more dominant position because they were nearer to market pricing expectations and more in tune with the new buyers emerging in the market.

Figure P.4:   The UK insolvency market in the 1990s

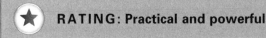

POST PURCHASE DISTRESS

Application: marketing communication, sales methods

The concept

If the purchase of any item is emotionally challenging or if it is expensive, buyers experience post purchase distress. This is worry or anxiety caused by the purchase. However, it can be allayed by the buyer admiring the product or showing it to others. Some buyers of new cars, for example, return to the showroom to collect the brochure of the car they bought. It is also helped by good quality *collateral*. So, marketers should think through the moments of anxiety that their customer might experience and create physical devices to allay this discomfort. A marketing manager anticipates and obviates such concern.

It also occurs in *business-to-business* markets. Business buyers may be concerned about the effect of a purchase on their budgets, the effort to justify the item to others, damage to their credibility, or risk to their political capital. If this anxiety is not managed, then problems occur. It can cause them to re-examine the deal and query value. The "tombstones" routinely created after mergers or acquisitions epitomize the achievement of a well completed, possibly worrisome project. They are a tangible embodiment of "post purchase distress".

History, context, criticism, and development

It is hard to find any substantial theory or marketing programmes around this concept prior to the mid 20th century. It was, perhaps, first taken seriously after Leon Festinger published on "cognitive dissonance". Dissonance takes place when customers have difficulty with a purchase decision they have made. It might be because they are dissatisfied with aspects of the purchase, like price. They might, for instance, come across an alternative which gives them a better outcome at a cheaper price. Or they may have made the purchase on impulse and the regret it because of the effect on their budget. Smart marketers now recognize that, if this is not handled by methods to reassure buyers, negative word-of-mouth can build up affecting reputation, brand, and repurchase rates.

Voices and further reading

- "Post purchase dissonance – the belief by the purchaser that he or she may have made the wrong decision – is a well known phenomenon for such consumer products as automobiles and appliances. However, a study in which this writer participated revealed that 44% of the industrial purchasers also experienced this feeling to some extent, especially those with little previous knowledge of the product purchased or with little experience as a purchasing agent for their company." Hise, R., 1977.

- "Dissonance theory can help to explain why evaluations of a product tend to increase after it has been purchased, i.e. post purchase dissonance. The cognitive element 'I made a stupid decision' is dissonant with the element 'I am not a stupid person', so people tend to find even more reasons to like something after buying it." Solomon, M. et al., 2006.

Things you might like to consider

(i)   This simple human emotion can cause deals to unravel, prices to be renegotiated, and repeat purchases destroyed. It needs to be taken seriously at both the tactical level, in each individual sale, and as part of strategic marketing communications planning.

(ii) This is a very specific use for packaging collateral. It turns an idea or concept into something tangible which provides post purchase reassurance.

(iii) This phenomenon is a particular issue in service markets because services are intangible. There is nothing to offset anxiety and nothing to show off. As a result, methods of summarizing the emotional relief of a well executed project have evolved in some business markets. It is from this that the "P" for "Presence" cameos in the "extended marketing mix" for services.

(iv) Intangibility can cause difficulty in the time between a contract being signed and a business service being delivered. Their anxiety is increased if the supplier is operating in unfamiliar territory. The executive who buys consulting from an accountancy firm may be anxious due more to the risk of using a familiar supplier in unfamiliar circumstances than to normal post purchase distress. If this anxiety is not managed, then problems occur.

 RATING: Practical

PRICING

Application: NPD/NSD, revenue planning, sales, communication

Factors affecting pricing decisions

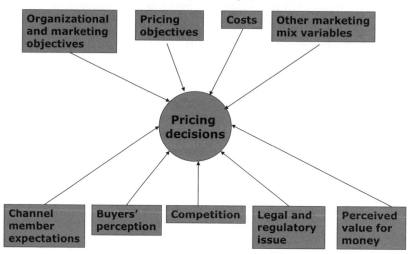

Figure P.5:   Factors affecting pricing decisions
Source: Dibb, S. et al., 2006

The concept

Obviously, a very important part of the perceived value of an offer is the price that customers are charged and the way that it is charged. This is a complex mix of the costs of creating the offer, demand and supply economics in the industry, industry custom and practice, segmentation variables, and brand dynamics. Marketers ought to step back and consider all of these factors in setting prices. For instance, as discussed in the *market definition* entry, different industries create their own beliefs and practices with which customers collude. The pricing of flights in the airline industry, for example, is a complex process of different deals, add-ons, and fixed prices which confuses and annoys. It is a complete contrast to, say, some retail practices. It is sensible, and not academic or theoretical, to step back and consider whether the right mix of *features* (see separate entry) and right pricing mechanism have been used to create a sense of perceived value for the segment for which the offer is designed.

Too many marketers, it seems, take a tactical approach to pricing or leave it to other functions (like finance). Pricing, though, is an important part of product and service design. Different mixes of features create different potential *value propositions* at different prices. In fact, as many companies have demonstrated (e.g. The John Lewis partnership and "Never knowingly undersold") it can be a very important marketing strategy.

There are, in fact, many different approaches to pricing:

(i)   Cost-plus pricing
      This involves estimating the cost of each component of a product or service (often using techniques like "activity-based costing") and then adding a margin. It is, by far, the most commonly used approach.

(ii) Value realized
      Sometimes called "shared reward", the supplier receives part of their payment if certain criteria, agreed with the customer, are met. This has been used, for example, by marketers that are focused on achieving efficiency and cost savings for their customers. They can get paid for the costs they save. It was famously pioneered in the outsourcing market by EDS (now part of HP) taking over the parking ticket processing for a city in America. EDS was able to increase the proportion of parking tickets and fines collected, and as a result shared in the additional revenues that flowed to the city. Interestingly, this is also applied the other way (in terms of "shared risk contracts") whereby if an outsourcer does not deliver the benefits promised, they incur a penalty on their fees.

(iii) Competitive or "market-based" approaches
      Some price on the basis of what they think is appropriate in the market based on what their competitors will charge ("what the market will bear"). The drawbacks to this are serious. First, in some markets, they are unlikely to know exactly what others will charge and risk cutting prices too far. Secondly, they are unlikely to know the competitor's cost base, and may cut prices to a point that profits are eroded because they have a higher cost base than their competitors. Thirdly, the offer is unlikely to meet the customer's view of value and could become a commodity over time.

(iv) Differential pricing
      This includes individual negotiated prices, secondary market pricing, periodic pricing, and random discounting. Prices ought to vary according to market position, segment, or even location.

(v)   Experience-curve pricing
      As the entry under the *Boston Matrix* shows, this concept demonstrated that costs decline as business units gather momentum, gain managerial experience, and invest in technology or processes This can be used as a basis of pricing strategy.

(vi) New product pricing
      Price penetration might be used to launch, for instance, a new offer or gain share. Price skimming might be used to reap profit from some form of short-term competitive advantage created by a new product.

(vii) Bundling
      A company with a wide range of product and services can create packages of offers (with a mix of features and costs) which attract customers. This can put

competitors at a real disadvantage. For instance, some of the annuity services which many companies have created are a form of bundling. The French tyre company, Michelin, for example, has created a service for its large fleet customers across Europe. One of their fastest growing and most profitable offers, it means that they check and replace the tyres for their heavy users (rather than just selling them a product). The customers get increased value because properly inflated tyres last longer but they have to contract for an ongoing service of different monitoring capabilities.

(viii) Psychological pricing

This takes advantage of behavioural insights which appeal to buyers like "everyday low prices". Reference pricing, for example, uses testimonials and word-of-mouth because of their influence on purchase decisions. Prestige pricing, on the other hand, takes advantage of the human desire for status or heritage.

(ix) Loyalty pricing

The information collected about repeat buyers and people who feel loyal to a brand or company can be used to calculate cost of service to these groups of buyers. It is frequently cheaper to serve repeat buyers because there is low cost of sale, they become familiar with the supplier's processes and, in many case will take on board some of the methods of provision (learning, for example, self-service technology). This can be used as a basis for pricing strategies which, in turn, encourage further repeat purchase. A pricing strategy as part of a sensible loyalty programme can create a powerful virtuous circle of mutual reward for the supplier and its customers.

(x) Promotional pricing

This is a very familiar pricing strategy for marketers where price is related to a specific campaign. Organizations that use this routinely tend to become sophisticated and expert at it, prompting their customers to look for their offers. (Although there are still some remarkably stupid mistakes where, for instance, the reward is out of proportion to the product price.) Dynamic pricing is a specific form of promotional pricing. Prices are changed as the moment of use gets nearer. It needs, though, a deep understanding of margin costs. "Price leaders", "special event pricing", and "comparison discounting" are all parts of promotional pricing.

History, context, criticism, and development

After many centuries of barter and negation, fixed prices seemed to begin to grow primarily in retail, in different parts of the world, over a hundred years ago. They were seen in Japan in the early history of Mitsukoshi, for example, that is in the early 1700s. The store, in fact, claims to have invented the practice. They were also evident in Paris, where, during the mid 1800s the Bon Marché department store set a trend in clear pricing.

Voices and further reading

- "Low prices must beget a low quality in the manufacture, which will beget contempt, which will beget neglect and disuse; and there is an end of trade." Josiah Wedgwood, 1772 (quoted in Koehn, N.F., 2001).
- Winkler, J., *Pricing for Results*. Heinemann, 1988.
- "Prices are a function of power. If your demand is strong, you are free to move upwards on price. If your profits are good, you are free to move downwards on price because you can afford it. You have power because options are available to you." Winkler, ibid.
- Rao, A.R., Bergen, M.E., and Davis, S., "How to fight a price war". *Harvard Business Review*, March–April, 2000.
- "There are several ways to stop a price war before it starts. One is to make sure your competitors understand the rationale behind your pricing policies. In other words, reveal your strategic intentions." Rao et al., ibid.
- Morel, G., Stalk, G., Stanger, P., and Wetenhall, P., "Pricing myopia" in *The Boston Consulting Group on Strategy*. John Wiley & Sons Inc., 2006.
- "Executives often suffer from pricing myopia. They underestimate their power to manage pricing, mistakenly believe that their customers are paying the amounts stipulated by their pricing guidelines, passively accept prevailing approaches to pricing in their industries, or neglect to consider how they could use pricing to change the competitive game." Morel et al., ibid.
- ". . . both volume and cost are easier to change than industry prices. Effort to change industry prices can cause them to ebb and flow like the tide, with equal net effect on mean sea level. Above average prices inevitable attract additional capacity until prices become depressed. Depressed prices inhibit capacity replacement or additions until prices fall." Henderson, B. in *The Boston Consulting Group on Strategy*. John Wiley & Sons Inc., 2006.
- Mann, M.V, Roegner, E.V., and Zawada, C.C., "The power of pricing". *McKinsey Quarterly*, 1, 2003.

Things you might like to consider

(i) Important though this is, it is still only one aspect of the design of a product or service; and only one of the features that customers will consider. No buyer in any part of the world, in consumer or business markets, ever bought anything on price alone. Buyers look for a cluster or mix of features (see *features analysis*) which serve their needs and aspirations best. They search, often intuitively, for received value. Price only becomes a determining factor if all the elements of the various offers are exactly the same.

(ii) In many companies pricing is managed by the financial function and individual deal discounts controlled by sales people. The voice of marketing in these decisions (particularly in a firm where the marketing function is restricted to just promotional activity or is not valued or respected) can be very weak. In these situations the use of detailed research techniques (like conjoint research or "zones of tolerance") can be seriously helpful in creating a sense of value. Customers are often more willing to pay for the right mix of features than operations executives, finance specialists or even sales people expect. Other functions will often welcome and adopt these techniques if sold to them properly.

(iii) In leading business-to-business companies many senior people now insist that their sales teams construct a "value proposition" that can be used by marketers to influence their thinking in this direction.

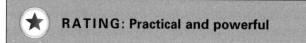

RATING: Practical and powerful

PRODUCT LIFE CYCLE (PLC)

Application: investment analysis, strategy, planning

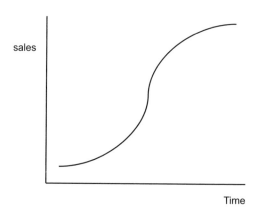

Figure P.6: The typical S-curve depiction of a PLC

The concept

This irritatingly well known concept suggests that the sales of individual products or services follow a pattern over a period of time, represented by the simple S-curve above. The horizontal axis is time and the vertical is total sales volume.

During the first phase of a product's life, it is taught, profits are likely to be low because the firm is investing in creating a market, establishing new sales channels, and developing new manufacturing capability. It is suggested that the customers in this early stage are likely to be "early adopters", who are interested in the new technology and open to new ideas. As their friends, relations, and business contacts see them using the new product, word-of-mouth spreads and demand increases. A moment then comes in the development of the product's history when it becomes a reliable, familiar proposition and sales boom.

During this phase of the product's history the suppliers are focused on sales. They are selling almost all they can manufacture as their offer takes off. Profits, which are initially low, improve as the supplier becomes more efficient and processes improve. Customers are an "early majority" and then a "late majority" as the offer penetrates the market.

Yet all markets are, ultimately, finite and there comes a point where every customer has bought their initial version of the product; the market has become "saturated" or "mature". The growth in sales falls, sometimes quite rapidly. Initially the suppliers can be damaged because they may not accept that the good times are over. They may invest in massive advertising or sales programmes to stimulate demand. Eventually, though, a shake out in the market leaves a few successful suppliers. Once their position is established they can become very profitable, maintaining their position and gearing up to a market held at replacement levels. Some try to create "added value" from their offers, as mobile phone providers did by offering internet access and other services once Western consumers had bought their initial handset. Eventually even the most successful products are replaced by newer items. Examples are used to illustrate this supposed phenomenon, like the way VHS cassettes gave way to DVD and CDs gave way to music downloads. Yet, even in this dying stage, products can make money.

This concept suggests that the sales volume of individual products or services normally follows a similar pattern. Yet, although that idea has a strong hold on management thinking and executives can often be heard to talk about their product as, for instance, "mature" or a "cash cow", it remains unproven and controversial (and completely muddle-headed) for individual products or services. In 1983, for instance, Professor Baker reported that around 80% of all new product launches in each year failed (Baker, M. J., 1983). For those many thousand products and their marketers, then, life was anything but a smooth S-curve. Several research projects have offered many different shaped patterns, including a cycle-recycle effect (in which sales did not decline at maturity but simply restarted a new cycle).

History, context, criticism, and development

Unfortunately this concept is constantly muddled with other ideas like a sociological phenomenon called the *diffusion of innovations* (customers are "early adopters" etc.) or with the *Boston Matrix* (people talk about their offer being "mature" or a "cash cow") and with the sales curve of a "product class" (see *market maturity*). It is routinely taught as fact, frequently misunderstood, and sometimes causes real damage. It is important to unpick the confusion and nonsense that has built up around this idea before trying to use it.

The origin of this concept has been attributed to Joel Dean, an academic who published an article around the theme in 1950 (Dean, J., 1950) and Conrad Jones (a consultant from Booze Allen) who presented at the 39th conference of the American Marketing Association in 1957. Jones said that his work was based on extensive study of client projects (300 "client reports" and 600 written sources). At the conference, he presented the now familiar S-curve with profit margins tracking the phases of product growth (see Muha, W.F., 1985). In December 1962 an economist, Raymond Vernon, presented at an American Marketing Association conference, called "Emerging concepts in marketing" (Vernon, R., 1962). There is little doubt that this kick-started the interest in product life cycles and industry maturity amongst marketing specialists.

Even one of the defining articles of the time, by Professor Theodore Levitt, called "Exploit the product life cycle" (Levitt, T. 1965) did not distinguish between the life of individual products or services and the trends in product classes. He described the phases of the life cycle as they have been subsequently taught and recommended strategies for each phase. His examples, though, are a product group (nylon) and brands (Jell-O and Scotch tape) which, as he describes in the article, were developed into product classes by their owners. Although he uses the phrase "product life cycle" throughout, there is no evidence in his article that the sales volumes of individual products are always S-curves.

It is seldom taught that, after nearly ten years of assertion that the PLC was an observable phenomenon, several credible pieces of work in the early 1970s debunked it. The HBR article by two planners from JWT (Dhalla, N.K. and Yuspeh, S., 1976) rehearsed the arguments well. They pointed out that most advocates of the proposition had little empirical data and that there were credible research projects that had failed to find a correlation. Their article contains several data driven models which show no S-curve at all in individual products or services. Mankind looks for patterns to confirm its prejudices and there seem to be several writers who were looking for S-curves in product data because they were keen to promote marketing as a science.

By contrast, one academic writer who specialized in product strategy pointed out that individual products or services have different shapes to their sales pattern. Some establish a niche early and continue in that pattern (a straight line), others are cyclical or seasonal, and others decline fast after an initial high profile launch. He identified at least five common patterns which were radically different to the PLC and suggested that, in practice, marketers use this concept "as an abstraction". In other words it is theoretical nonsense of dubious practical use (Hise, R.T., 1977).

Voices and further reading

- Vernon, R., "International investment and international trade in the product cycle". *Quarterly Journal of Economics*, 1962.

- Levitt, T., "Exploit the product life cycle". *Harvard Business Review*, November–December 1965.
- ". . . a recent survey I took of some such executives found none who used the concept in any strategic way whatever, and pitifully few who used it in any kind of tactical way. It has remained – as have so many fascinating theories in economics, physics and sex – a remarkably durable but almost totally unemployable piece of professional baggage whose presence in the rhetoric of professional discussions adds a much coveted but apparently unattainable legitimacy to the idea that marketing management is somehow a profession. There is, further-more, a persistent feeling that the life cycle concept adds luster and believability to the insentient claim in certain circles that marketing is close to being some sort of science." Levitt, T., ibid.
- Kotler, P., "Competitive strategies for new product marketing over the life cycle." *Management Science*, December 1965.
- Wells, L.T., "A product life cycle for international trade?" *Journal of Marketing*, July 1968.
- Dhalla, N.K. and Yuspeh, S., "Forget the product life cycle concept!" *Harvard Business Review*, January–February 1976.
- "Most writers present the PLC concept in qualitative terms . . . without any empirical backing . . . it is not possible to validate the model at any of these levels of aggregation." Dhalla and Yuspeh, ibid.
- Doyle, P., "The realities of the product life cycle". *Quarterly Review of Marketing*, Summer 1976.
- ". . . definitional problems need to be clarified in collecting such evidence. First, one must distinguish between product classes (e.g. cigarettes), product form (e.g. filter cigarettes) and brand (e.g. Embassy) . . . there is often little similarity between cycles at different levels of aggregation." Doyle, ibid.
- Swan, J.E. and Rink, D.R., "Fitting market strategy to varying product life cycles". *Business Horizons*. January–February 1982.
- ". . . reliance on the classical product life cycle for marketing decisions can be misleading. Our research shows that there are eleven different product life cycles, each one having different implications for marketing decisions." Swan and Rink, ibid.
- Muha, W.F., "The product life cycle concept: origin and early antecedents". CHARM conference paper, 1985.
- Wood, L., "The end of the product life cycle? Education says goodbye to an old friend". *Journal of Marketing Management*, 2, 1990.
- "With the broadening of the marketing concept over time, weaknesses have become increasingly evident in attempting to universally fit the application of PLC theory to the specific areas of high-tech products, and consumer durables, and the additional areas of industrial products, services and Not For Profits. . . . Marketing is an adaptive concept, yet it would appear that in attempting to adapt PLC theory to its broadening base, we as marketers, may have been guilty of PLC myopia." Wood, ibid.

- Spears, N.E. and Germain, R., "A review of the product life cycle and diffusion of innovation: current and historical perspectives." Paper presented at the 7th Marketing History conference proceedings, Vol. VII, 1995.

Things you might like to consider

(i) There is no logical reason why the sales pattern of an individual product or service should be shaped like an "S-curve". If so, it's probably an unusual aberration. (The sales profile for a product group does tend toward that; see *market maturity*.)

(ii) There is no logical reason why the sales history of an individual product or service should behave like a biological life cycle. (Again that tends to happen with markets of product groups because the iterative conversations between human beings, the customers and the suppliers, mimic organic growth).

(iii) There is no logical reason why the customers for an individual product or service should be "innovators", early adopters or any of the other groups. (That refers to the diffusion of innovation.) It's important to properly understand the diffusion of innovation concept. A brand new product launched as part of a diffused and well understood concept (like a mobile phone or a PC) might well be targeted at the "late majority" and not "early adopters".

(iv) Is your product or service a true innovation? In which case, understand the diffusion of the idea that it encapsulates and set marketing programmes accordingly.

(v) Are you working with a branded offer? In which case, the brand franchise could be many hundreds of years old. Or, you could pass it on to the next generation of brand managers so that it does turn into a long-term durable offer. In any case, it is most likely to live out your tenure of the job by many years.

(vi) Is your product or service "mature"? Really? Even so, do you really want to denude it of investment to support risky new ideas? Can you turn it into a brand instead? Can you focus it on defined segments of customers?

(vii) This simplistic concept is so well known that your competitors are likely to believe it. Can you use their ignorance to exploit your competitive position?

(viii) When first launched, an offer might take a long time to gain traction in the market. Sales of facsimile machines took off, for instance, in the 1970s. Yet the first patents for them were registered in 1842 – an early development stage of over a hundred years. The iPhone, the mobile phone, and the internet all had, by contrast, a much shorter gestation period. In fact some commentators argue that the speed of acceptance of new products is speeding up as accomplished consumers become more adept at assessing and adopting new technologies.

(ix) Although many are familiar with this idea, it is still controversial and unproven. In reality, it is usually an aberration if an individual product or service follows the S-curve pattern and this muddle-headed thinking causes damage and mistaken investment.

The PLC and the black nectars

If the life cycle of individual products or services is an S-curve, and decline is inevitable, then it should be seen in the sales history of long-term, popular products. The history of two famous, and remarkably successful, products demonstrates that this is not straightforward. Figures P.7 and P.8 show the early history of the 20th century's most successful marketing phenomenon: Coca-Cola (source: Pendergrast, 1993). Sales are measured in gallons of syrup sold because, in the early days, the drink was sold to consumers in soda fountains more than bottles.

The rationale for the drink had been to find something simply pleasurable during an alcohol prohibition phase in Atlanta; but by the 1920s (nearly forty years after its invention) that had changed. There were many reasons to think that the decline in sales (see graph below) was because the product was "mature". The government was beginning to respond to constant negative publicity about the effects of the drink and investigate its contents (because there were constant allegations that it contained cocaine). Costly legal actions were being considered, which would add to problems over ownership of the patent. There were cheap competitors and imitators. In addition, global events (the First World War, for example) were affecting the optimism of the nation. "Classic marketing training" (had it existed then) would clearly prompt marketers of the time to consider whether this decades-old product was starting its decline phase and should be replaced. (When the leaders of the firm attempted that at the end of the 20th century with "New Coke", of course, one of the most remarkable examples of consumer antagonism followed.)

Yet, the second graph clearly demonstrates how idiotic it would be to follow classic marketing training with this wonderful product. Just thirty years later the company was selling billions of gallons of syrup and the so-called PLC blip vanished in the rounding. The company's leaders had a passion for their drink and invested in some of the most aggressive and

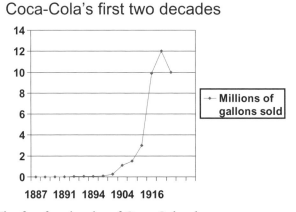

Figure P.7: The first few decades of Coca–Cola sales

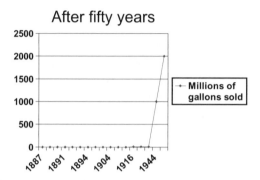

Figure P.8: The first half century of Coca–Cola sales

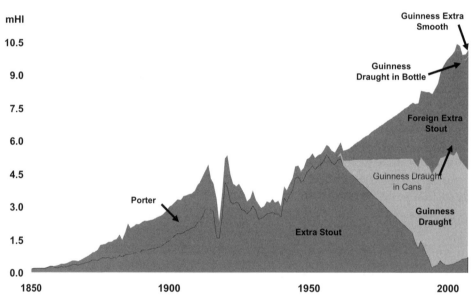

Figure P.9: The first two centuries of Guinness sales

focused marketing possible. They used: segmentation, research, extensive advertising, PR, and thought leadership in the half century before the so-called "marketing concept" phase of thinking.

Figure P.9 shows 150 years of sales history for one of the world's other favourite black drinks: Guinness. It demonstrates the complexity behind marketing strategies and the actions that marketers have to take in order to grow their revenues. Firstly, it can clearly be seen that sales have been climbing for 150 years, defying the simple PLC concept. The brand has clearly played a part in the endurance of this long-term success. Like the other brands in Tables B1 and B2, it has developed equity which has attracted generations of customers into its franchise. Yet, those responsible for the drink have also modernized its nature and packaging. The volume changes between "Porter", "Stout", and "draught in cans" show the investment in innovation and marketing behind this successful product and hint at both the complexity and subtlety needed to succeed in product or service marketing. For instance, Arthur Guinness started selling the dark beer porter in 1778 and the first Guinness beers to use the term were Single Stout and Double Stout in the 1840s. Guinness brewed their last porter in 1974.

The sound bites and "key leanings" that are so prevalent in many marketing books are not enough; and the simple assertion of an S-curve PLC for individual products or services is dangerous.

Source: Diageo; used with permission.

RATING: Toxic

PUBLIC RELATIONS (PR)

Application: reputation management, marketing communications, perceived value, thought leadership

The concept

PR is a generic term for a range of specialist and sophisticated skills involved in communication with publics through, primarily, broadcast, published media. "Media relations", for example, is the process of managing a firm's relationship with public media like newspapers and news channels. This will involve regular contact with journalists and editors, fielding a range of enquiries on new business ventures, the chief executive's press programme and handling embarrassing aberrations or professional errors. It is rare to find a company that does not have at least a "press officer", dealing with these enquires. As specialists, they develop their own skills and their own professional networks to handle the media. In fact, their expertise is often better judged by what they keep out of the press than what appears in it.

It is in the field of proactive media relations that many firms fall down. Some press officers, particularly in smaller firms, find it difficult to get time away from the demands of ad hoc events and enquiries to take any initiative. When they do, it is often to issue press releases that go out to general circulation lists. Unfortunately, journalists receive so many press releases that they rarely give these much attention. It is better to create a proactive media relations plan. This will identify which messages will be emphasized by the firm and which media it will focus on. The aim of the plan is to develop good relationships between principals in the firm and the editors of key media. In fact some take an approach similar to client account management with important publications.

A typical PR plan aims to influence opinion formers through carefully targeted communications with a clear message. It might include:

- News releases on new business or contract wins;
- News releases on new offers;
- Publicity opportunities and photo opportunities to attract media attention;
- Publicity profile on people of note within the organization;
- Trying to get employees speaking on industry conference platforms that the intended customers attend. This puts the audience in the position of pupil to teacher and will increase respect for the suppliers' personnel;
- Relationships with influential professional associations. Company representatives can use them to speak to their members;
- Communications with management institutes or groups representing opinion formers;
- Feature coverage inside the internal magazines of major customers. (If features on the company's strategy appear in the internal magazines of major organizations then there will strong implicit endorsement.)

Clearly, though, the messages developed and promulgated through these mechanisms must be a part of the overall communication strategy of the firm. The style and nature of the message might be adapted to fit the needs of the journalists or specific titles, but it needs to be an articulation of exactly the same message that the marketing department is emphasizing through other media.

An important aspect of communications is when a business has to deal with a serious problem that attracts significant press attention. This might be when a client takes legal action, or a regulator is publicly critical, or a significant individual in the firm receives adverse attention. The first step is to plan to avoid this happening. Standby communications plans, a little like the disaster recovery plans put in place for IT facilities, should be prepared alongside regulatory or policy guidelines. These should include:

- Editorial relationships
  When a negative story appears it is the editors who decide how to treat it. The firm should set up mechanisms to develop relationships between key individuals in the firm and editors of print and broadcast media in the major world centres. Such relationships (apart from helping to raise the profile of the firm) will not

stop a negative story running altogether but will minimize damage and enable the firm to put its point of view more easily.

- Rehearse the leadership
  Evidence suggests that it is the one word ("shredding" in the case of the now defunct but massive accountancy firm Andersen) spoken by a leading figure which can cause catastrophic damage. Leaders should be well rehearsed in media management and publicists should have control over how to respond to media interest.
- Preventative management of sensitive issues
  Meetings should be established between the firm's media team and the firm's leadership to discuss how to handle potential issues.

The creation, maintenance, and exploitation of fame are often key aims of sustained PR and publicity. Yet it is unlikely that people handling reactive PR in the press office will be able to find the space to create and handle complex three-year, proactive programmes. So the marketing leader should define these separately and initiate them for relevant subjects within the firm. Proactive reputation management then becomes part of the marketing mix alongside other well used techniques.

One really useful piece of work by two academics (Grunig and Hunt, 1984) distinguishes between four "models" of PR that are used in practice: the press/agency model, the public information model, the "one-way asymmetrical" model (using persuasion and manipulation to influence audiences), and the two-way symmetrical model. The latter is seen as interactive, negotiating with audiences to influence opinion by dialogue and engagement. There have also been various theoretical models developed to understand and evaluate PR: Cutlip's PII model (1985), Watson's continuing model (1997), Watson's unified model (1999), the IPR "pre" model (2001), Lindeman's PR yardstick (1993), the pyramid model (1992).

History, context, criticism, and development

PR is a marketing practice and concept with long established techniques and a credible heritage. Napoleon, for instance, had a "bureau of public opinion" to create political trends. The UK's Grand Central Rail set up a "publicity department" in 1902 and Selfridge hired a full-time PR officer when he opened his London store in 1909. America's GM established a professional PR department in 1931, sparking a trend in professional press management amongst large US companies. One American marketing textbook of the 1920s talks of companies' "publicity departments" as if they were an established part of large, leading businesses at that time (White, P., 1927).

Two of the early proponents of PR were Ivy lee and Edward Bernays. Lee developed the first press releases but thought of PR as two-way, a conversation with publics. Bernays, a nephew of Sigmund Freud, thought of it as connected to psychology and dealing with the group mentality of publics. Later in life he seemed to regret and retract some of his views but he clearly saw PR as a management discipline which was closely related to the social sciences. They stimulated a century of theory, practice, and research into the way companies (and other organizations) can effectively communicate with publics to their best advantage.

More recently, a complementary activity has developed alongside PR to reach other influencers such as industry analysts or third party procurement advisors. Called "Analyst or Influencer relations", these activities often fall into the remit of the PR group, with specialists focused on these different audiences. The same group of activities is often directed at these audiences, including direct marketing to announce company news or provide in-depth information on specific issues or topics, individual briefings by senior personnel, and annual events to update the audience on recent performance and future plans.

As with other forms of communication, PR has been affected by the advent of the internet and other forms of digital media. Journalists are blogging, consumers are chatting in social networks, and opinion formers are cooperating in virtual groups. PR specialists and the companies they represent have to engage with this new manifestation of reputation and opinion development.

Voices and further reading

- Bernays, E., *Propaganda*. IG Publishing, 2005 (first published in 1928).
- "The public relations counsel, then, is the agent who, working with modern media of communications and the group formations of society, brings an idea to the consciousness of the public. But he is a great deal more than that. He is concerned with courses of action, doctrines, systems and opinions, and securing the public support for them . . . He functions primarily as an advisor to his client, very much as a lawyer does . . . Every phase of his client's ideas, products or activities which may affect the public or in which the public may have an interest is part of his function." Bernays, ibid.
- Solis, B. and Breakenridge, D., *Putting the Public Back in Public Relations*. Pearson Education, 2009. An interesting review of the implications to PR of new digital media like social networking sites.
- "In all honesty, most PR and marketing models are not designed to engage with people directly, nor are they equipped to do so in a way that doesn't insult those they try to reach. But this doesn't mean that the future represents doom and gloom for us. Social media requires one-on-one conversations and unfortunately many marketers and PR 'pros', until recently, have cowered in the shadows, hurling messaging in bulk at people, hoping that some would stick. This is our

chance to not only work with the traditional journalists but to also engage directly with a new set of organic influencers using media channels (traditional and social) that reach them." Solis, et al., ibid.

- "Public relations has a broader remit than certain older elements of marketing communication being both strategic – in relating to the long term building of brand image and creating lasting positive associations – as well as tactical – in responding ad hoc to unplanned environmental threats. The establishment of status and positive linkages for a company is a continuing, coherent process involving many elements of the brand and the organisation's narrative." Dahlen, M. Lange, F., and Smith, T., 2010.

Things you might like to consider

(i) Corporate relations and press management now have their own processes and professional institutes. Many people who work in them have press backgrounds. So, they can be detached from the marketing function in large companies. Effort needs to be made at senior levels to ensure that messages and timing are integrated; and that conflict between people in both functions is minimized.

(ii) PR can be used as part of integrated marketing communications, supplementing any digital campaigns or broadcast advertising to make impact more effective.

 RATING: Practical and powerful

R

Application: marketing communication, NPD/NSD, sales

Relationship networks

Client firm

Competitor

Trade
association

Supplier

Buyer's network

Figure R.1: A representation of the inter-relationships between the principles in two business-to-business relationships

The concept

Relationship marketing (RM) is a relatively recent addition to the more established marketing theory. It suggests that companies can have a relationship with their customers, whether businesses or consumers. By understanding their customers in a systematic way, and by managing deepening levels of interaction with them, revenue and profit will increase. For many firms (particularly in *business-to-business* marketing) this has codified intuitive approaches that have been at the heart of their business for many years.

RM is an approach to marketing based around ongoing relationships with customers. It is, or should be, radically different from the "four Ps"-based, throw it out there, broadcast marketing techniques of the mid 20th century. This focuses on the buyer as a human being and gives attention to the interaction between human beings in transactions. It suggests that organizations seek to understand their buyers' motivations and purchase habits through, among other things, *research* and analysis of buying data. They then create communications programmes directed at these buyers which are more targeted, personalized, and relevant. As buyers respond to these, the supplier can adjust their plans further, creating a virtuous circle of improved profitable engagement.

The approach is based on the assumption that long-term mutual value is created for both sides if the buyer, and an interactive relationship with the buyer, become a focus of the supplier's policies, processes, and people. The marketing of the firm then stresses enduring profitable relationships, rather than individual random transactions.

Profssor Evert Gummerson (Gummerson, E., 2003) suggests that relationship marketing *"is based on interaction within networks of relationships"*. In other words, effective marketing needs to emphasize communication between people who know each other, and others, to varying degrees. From this perspective, markets are a set of networks comprising relationships between people. The complex inter-related sets of different relationships, and their influence on decision making, need to be understood, mapped, and enhanced. This has led, in some circles, to the phrase, "network marketing". In fact, there is evidence (in the professions, for instance) that this view of a market (which is nearer to behavioural economics, see *behavioural aspects of marketing*) has allowed certain suppliers to buck economic trends by stimulating and exciting networks of premium customers during recession.

The basis of relationship marketing is the interaction between two people, at least one of whom represents an organization. (In consumer marketing, for instance, a marketing manager is trying to establish relationships between the firm and many individuals.) However, as these people have interaction with others, there are really two interconnecting networks of relationships through which information flows. These networks flow in and out of the supplier firm, embracing competitors, industry commentators, and professional associations. Figure R.1 tries to show, for instance, a representative in a firm who has a business relationship with a representative in a customer firm; they, in turn, have links to both a competitor and the trade association.

The supplier can strengthen the messages and input to the contact by developing a link through the trade association. However, they need to be aware that any innovative ideas and proposals are likely to be communicated to a competitor.

These relationship networks have "nodes" where suppliers can bring great influence to bear. The web sites of industry commentators, influential conferences, and industry-specific research groups are examples of these. They should be identified and influenced by marketers. In fact, mapping relationships and networks is fundamental to the success of the approach. For instance, academics have proposed three levels of categorization which describe the development of relationships in business marketing: "activity links", essentially normal business transactions; "resource ties", exchanging and sharing resources, and "actor bonds" which are created between people who influence each other (see *AAR* model). These concepts can be used to map and categorize communities and networks which are valuable to the firm. For example, non-executive directors are very influential in the purchase of many items. Some suppliers therefore buy databases of board representatives and then map those who influence their customers. Proactive marketing programmes are then created to reach these people.

Marketing communication should be planned and developed as part of RM strategies. For example, an important fundamental tool of RM is database marketing, often based on "Customer Relationship Management (CRM)" systems. These systems hold details of customers and have a facility (called "campaign management") which controls communication with them. They register customers' interests and preferences. They also allow marketing managers or account managers the chance to edit communications from their firm before they are sent. They can edit out communication pieces which are unwanted or irrelevant to individual customers. This facility alone can solve a very common service problem: erratic and uncoordinated mailings to customers. Once these systems are in place, marketers planning any communications to customers (from *hospitality* invitations, through to generic campaigns) must iron out any conflicts with other communications at the planning stage. Relationship marketing therefore introduces a discipline into the communications processes of the firm that removes potential dissatisfaction.

The marketer should use specific techniques to communicate through the mapped networks. For instance, "word-of-mouth" is one of the most powerful determinants of reputation. The marketer sets out to influence this through *PR*, *viral marketing*, and publicity. They seek to use the networks and moments of contact with customers to enhance reputation. Business buyers, for instance, use their professional networks to gain information on service providers. In fact, these networks are often the most influential source used prior to purchase. A strong reputation and positive word-of-mouth will therefore yield work for suppliers. It will increase the propensity to buy.

The marketer can also communicate to customers through internal networks (see *internal marketing*), particularly in a large firm which will be dominated by interconnected relationships of people. These might be people who have been in the same firm for a decade or more, who have learnt to trust each other by working on projects or in managerial teams. They are circles within circles and networks of trust. There might be, for example, a network of specialists around the world concentrating on one business sector. The people involved have a common interest and rely on their internal network to receive information. Their leaders and the immediate group of contacts with whom they work daily are much more relevant to them than other messages. So gossip becomes more effective than the deluge of emails, magazines, and other publications. Marketing specialists can map these internal networks and target communications through them. This is a form of *viral marketing*, where word-of-mouth is used to influence the behaviour and motivation of a company's people. It is a powerful *internal marketing* mechanism if used effectively. Moreover, all of these networks will interconnect with customer networks, and so good, credible communications from the leadership through these internal networks will also influence customer thinking.

History, context, criticism, and development

Many successful business leaders have adopted approaches similar to RM before it was identified and codified. For instance, Lord Sieff, who ran the famous British retailer, Marks & Spencer, during some of its most prosperous years, was asked why, in the mid 20th century he put such emphasis on service and offered no argument refunds on defective goods. He is reported to have said that, if a young couple marry and move into an area, there is the likelihood of many years of profitable purchases from their growing family. Why damage that over an argument about one defective sweater? (see Sieff, M., 1986). This early example of what later become known as the "lifetime value of buyers" epitomizes relationship marketing. The life cycle of the buyer's engagement with the firm is the priority, rather than one transaction.

RM began to emerge during the 1970s and 1980s from several sources. First, consumerism in various Western economies forced companies to respond to their needs more. This, tied to a greater emphasis on customer service and responsiveness across many businesses, forced marketers to consider ways in which they might communicate with their customers more effectively. Secondly, a growing emphasis on database marketing and *direct marketing*, together with increasingly sophisticated technology, allowed them to move away from solely using broadcast marketing communication. Finally, *research* and thinking from the developing body of knowledge around *services marketing* and *business-to-business* marketing, contributed to this trend. In academia, researchers studying these fields began to uncover the effect of networks of relationships and the importance of repeat customers. The growth in research around services marketing and network marketing gradually became integrated into the modern view of relationship marketing.

In the real world, though, the concept itself started largely in the consumer products industry, and led to the creation of tools such as Customer Relationship

Management (CRM) systems and data warehousing. It has since been applied to many different markets, including business-to-business and professional services. For many it fills a large gap in marketing theory by recognizing the role of human relationships and communications in the buying and selling process. Since the early 1980s marketing practitioners and academics have been exploring, researching, and testing RM. Marketing thinking steadily moved away from an emphasis on broadcast mass communications using the 4Ps and principles founded on the consumer markets of mid-century America. It had a profound effect on many marketing practices. It changes marketing communication, for instance, from erratic broadcast messages to personal and intimate, two-way communication. This has led in some places to it being called "interactive" or "responsive marketing".

Voices and further reading

- Gummerson, E., *Total Relationship Marketing*. Butterworth-Heinemann, 2003.
- "Relationship marketing is marketing based on interaction within networks of relationships." Gummerson, ibid.
- "In practice, relationships and networks and interaction have been at the core of business since time immemorial. . . . The sad story is that relationships have too long gone noticed in research and education. Are we beginning to discern the marketing content of Japanese keiretsus, Chinese guanxies, global ethnic networks, the British school tie, trade between friends, loyalty to the local pub, and so on?" Gummerson, ibid.
- Payne, A., *Handbook of CRM*. Butterworth-Heinemann, 2006.
- "Although the term CRM . . . only came into use in the latter part of the 1990's, the principles on which it has been based have existed for much longer. CRM builds especially on the principles of relationship marketing, the formal study of which goes back 20 years but the origins of it, involving building relationships of mutual value between suppliers and customers, have existed since the start of commerce. However, what has changed over the past decade is a series of significant trends that collectively shaped the opportunity better to serve customers through information-enabled relationship marketing, or CRM." Payne, ibid.
- Üstüner, T. and Godes, D., "Better sales networks". *Harvard Business Review*, July–August 2006.
- "The term 'social network' refers to a person's set of direct and indirect contacts . . . Managers often view sales networks only in terms of numbers of direct contacts. But someone who knows a lot of people doesn't necessarily have an effective network, because networks often pay off most handsomely through indirect contacts". Üstüner and Godes, ibid.
- "Relationship management can be institutionalized, but in the process it must also be humanized." Levitt, T., 1983.

Things you might like to consider

(i) This approach, as much as any other, demands that marketers understand and communicate with the human beings to whom they intend to present their products or services. Human insight and interaction with people must be at the centre of this approach.

(ii) The phrase "customer relationship management", as presented by some systems providers and as discussed by some companies can seem manipulative. This is not about controlling interactions with customers. It is about finding mutual profitability from understanding warm, trusting, and mutually profitable interactions with them.

(iii) The design and implementation of CRM systems, without an overarching strategy or intent to move toward proper relationship management, can be a waste of time and effort. A number of studies have found such projects to be ineffectual.

(iv) In *business-to-business* marketing there is evidence of a progression in relationships which is mutually profitable. Buyers, at some point, must place their trust in a supplier and buy. If they then turn into a repeat buyer, trust develops between the two people who represent the companies involved. This can lead to greater sales and more work; called by many "cross-selling". It can also lead to special deals on prices and discounts; and eventually to the meshing of the two organizations in mutually profitable cooperation. One academic, David Maister (Maister, D. et al., 2001), demonstrated the value of this developing relationship in the professional service and consultancy sales. He argued that professional suppliers should aim to become a "trusted advisor" to their clients.

(v) Several business suppliers have found that, as they have adopted relationship marketing, they have been able to "climb the value chain" and work around formal buying processes.

Satyam uses a diamond relationship programme to recover from disaster

Satyam Computer Services (Mahindra Satyam) is a leading Indian business that has grown into a global business and information technology services company. In the early part of the 21st century it was the subject of an embarrassing and significant scandal involving one of its leading figures. The scandal nearly destroyed the company but, as it had grown into such a significant organization, it needed to be persevered with. Many actions were taken but one which clearly helped was its customer relationship programme.

Mahindra Satyam is part of the $6.3 billion Mahindra Group, a global industrial conglomerate and one of the top 10 industrial firms based in India. The company leverages deep industry and functional expertise, leading technology practices, and an advanced, global delivery model to help clients transform their highest-value business processes and improve their business performance.

Widely viewed as code crunchers who saved the IT world from collective embarrassment of the Y2K crisis, Satyam needed to evolve its image and communicate its assets to a market that had pigeonholed it as a basic, commoditized service provider. Satyam also had its eye on the bigger prize: "mission critical" IT initiatives that would help elevate the company's reputation, develop new clients in different industries, and muscle in on the business that had been the traditional domain of IBM, EDS, and Accenture.

So how do you move an IT-orientated company from a developing nation onto the global stage, surmount cultural resistance, and change the conversation from commoditized services to value-added consulting and ultimately trusted partners? You leverage every current customer relationship basing your enterprise growth strategy on what is working with your top current customers and your account management. You turn your back on traditional media approaches and completely surround the customer, leverage hard-won customer loyalty, and showcase the reasons behind it to prospective new customers.

In essence, "The Diamond Customer-Engagement Strategy", was a growth and marketing model that Satyam created to drive this remarkable transformation. The programme was designed to systematically deal with four key areas (Business, Technology, Industry, and Culture) through a "high-touch" approach and execution. Its goal was to move current clients from strictly transactional relationships to consulting relationships and ultimately, to completely seamless integrated cooperative relationships, as well as showcasing the process to prospective customers.

The objective was to push forward all four points of the "diamond" with equal energy surrounding the client, changing the client's view of Satyam and achieving a fully integrated leading global brand. As Satyam's marketing group began the journey, it understood that it was strong on the "technology" component but weak on the "business", "industry", and "cultural" components of the plan.

It was a daunting objective, which no other Indian peer had approached as systematically or holistically. Others had chosen to focus on hiring in-country talent to short cut cultural challenges and appear more "American". Some were pushing forward simply on their technological merit and price advantage. Some were building in higher-level business messaging, but their ability to deliver was being received sceptically by the US market.

From 2001–2003 Satyam worked hard at getting account planning and management right and that meant understanding customer objectives in detail and putting the right managers in place to execute flawlessly. Marketing reviewed all client plans and categorized them into four growth-potential levels, allocating more dollars to those with the most potential. To be considered for execution, every marketing initiative had to address at least one of the four points of the diamond.

When considering a message strategy, early planning and research concentrated on historical cases of foreign companies in other industries entering the US market. As a result of this analysis it was decided that to be
successful, it was important not to downplay Satyam's Indian culture. Rather
the intention was to align its most compelling aspects with those most
admired by American business, doing for Satyam what "German Engineering"
did for Mercedes and BMW. These were attributes, the marketing department understood from client interviews, were admired; and that also aligned
well with Indian culture.

A new, streamlined tagline was launched: *What Business Demands*. All
messaging expanded on the tagline or landed on it, providing a focus for
both clients and Satyam. Most importantly it addressed two points of the
diamond, head on: business and culture.

With budgets tight, the main focus turned to exploiting every internal
asset available and that meant building and leveraging relationships at every
level inside of Satyam. Marketing systematically met with technical and
industry-specific practice directors to enlist their support for the Diamond
Strategy that, by then, incorporated the best practices of Satyam's long-term
client relationships and comprehensive account management.

A number of initiatives were undertaken within each area of the strategy,
most working to address more than one point of the diamond.

1. **Technology**: Satyam had proven its technology excellence and was on
    the road to increasing its high tech credentials. It was also aggressively
    cultivating relationships with key industry partners; SAP being the first,
    with others following in quick succession. At the risk of appearing overly
    tactical, Satyam relentlessly communicated every new certification and
    partnership to its market, presenting an overall tracking message that
    Satyam was a company on the move with unquestioned technology
    credentials.
2. **Business**: Satyam set out to change the conversation from "technology
    as competitive advantage" to "technology as an industry enabler" –
    driving industry-wide costs down, enhancing revenues and value crea-
    tion across specific industries. With a need to focus business on
    competing on core competencies, this component was tackled through
    exclusive high-touch customer events, thought leadership publications,
    and a modest intra-IT industry advertising programme on the subject of
    business transformation.
3. **Industry**: With strong domain expertise established in several key areas,
    (manufacturing and finance for instance), Satyam moved aggressively
    into new industries, and systematically acquiring expertise to break into
    new accounts. To build its credentials, marketing worked to achieve
    industry-specific leadership positions through forums, "customer boot
    camps", tradeshow participation, and aggressively courting industry
    analysts.

4. **Culture**: Here marketing had to weave the Satyam culture and the client into one seamless fabric. They needed to elevate Satyam beyond simply being viewed as an outsourcing vendor or even as a strategic partner, but as a fully integrated division of the client company. Satyam did this through creating identical copies of customer locations, making it easy for clients to move between their home offices and locations in India, and creating comprehensive India visiting programmes for customers as well as hosted "customer appreciation" social events.

Some of its most compelling components were:

- Premier annual customer event: Satyam World
  Diamond Points: business and culture
      Satyam created their own highly successful premier annual customer event, "Satyam World", modelling it on what they learned worked from other major industry events to attract top decision makers. Although it is more expensive to run a custom event, Stayam had undivided attention and controlled the messaging – for three days the world revolved around Satyam's clients, carefully selected prospective clients, and the Satyam brand.
- Geo Sourcing Forums: cross industry gatherings
  Diamond Points: technology and industry
      Through its "Geo Sourcing Forums" Satyam demonstrated its expertise through action, with each forum a reflection of its industry, technology, or region. These small workshop gatherings provided a crucial venue for those actively engaged in executing IT initiatives; a place where Satyam could listen to client needs, analysts could present views and intra-industry problems solved. Satyam clients chose the topics and as each forum matured, it became an entity in itself, independent of, but underwritten by, Satyam. Several forums have grown to multiple chapters, while some are global in scope and video-conferenced. The most mature forums invite executives from companies that are not yet Satyam clients.
- Customer boot camps: client-specific gatherings
  Diamond Points: technology and industry
      Customer "boot camps" were serious problem-solving gatherings held specifically to solve customers' across their enterprise. Satyam often invited an analyst or an independent expert along to the workshop. Brainstorming, problem solving, planning, and solution roadmap development were the main focus, while customer service and intimacy were the benefits. A Satyam customer-specific intranet provided deep Satyam- and customer- specific resources as well as a forum to continue the work.

- Location replication
  Diamond Points: culture and industry
    Replication of its customers' headquarters at Satyam's offices in India made customers feel at home and surrounded relevant Satyam employees with the customer's brand. Every detail of the client's head-quarters location were replicated and client branded; from product display cases, corporate colours, and office furniture to coasters. It created a seamless experience between Satyam and its clients; no longer a client/customer experience, but a corporate headquarters/corporate division experience.
- Comprehensive customer visiting programmes
  Diamond Points: culture and industry
    Customer visiting programmes provided a comprehensive door-to-door Satyam experience demonstrating service through action. Programmes were planned down to the last detail from the pre-travel communications packages to the events scheduled while in India, with all materials co-branded to communicate partnership and intimacy.
- Customer appreciation events
  Diamond Points: culture
    Satyam hosted clients at major sporting events in the client's home country; in-country marketing ensured Indian managers were fully briefed in both the sport and cultural nuances, resulting in successful customer experiences and a closer bond between Indian and in-country management.

In less than five years, Satyam had moved from code crunchers to business leaders, more than tripled its annual revenues and expanded its workforce by 30,000 employees.

The four points of the Diamond Customer-Engagement Strategy were not only marketing's mantra but, importantly, shared by people across the Satyam organization. Over the five years to 2008, for example, Satyam's Financial Practice experienced 92% growth from their existing 150 customers, a direct result of trust built on the Diamond Client-Engagement initiatives. A large proportion of clients were "moved up the value chain", from transactional to deeply cooperative, with sophisticated joint venture relationships as a direct result of the efforts in the Diamond programme.

Using The Diamond Customer-Engagement Strategy as their guide Satyam's marketing group effectively:

- Embraced its Indian culture when competitors were running from it, aligned and leveraged it to its advantage resulting in changing the market mindset.
- Changed the conversation from technology to business issues through leadership events.

- Changed industry competitors to cross industry cooperators, developing industry transforming solutions and becoming an industry leader in the process.
- Built a global brand that is looked to by global enterprises for advice, counsel, leadership, and solutions.

 RATING: Practical and powerful

REPOSITIONING

Application: new market entry, brand extension, competitive strategy

The concept

Marketers that work with companies that already have strong brands or a company reputation can "reposition" their offer to command the attention of other customer segments, other market niches, or completely different markets. They can convince existing customers, and new buyers, that they have viable new offers.

Repositioning can also, of course, mean moving to a new area of focus in an existing market. Some fall from a premium or heritage position to niche as forces in the market buffet their brand. Others move in a clear and deliberate strategic manoeuvre. British supermarket, Tesco, was started, for instance, as a least cost ("pile 'em high, sell 'em cheap") provider. In the past few decades, though, its innovation, marketing, and impressive management skills have turned it into the unquestioned market leader which, at the time of writing, is also intent on a strong global position.

Repositioning is no small task (as the case study of Virgin Media shows) and the start of this risky process is a clear understanding that the brand exists in the most important place of all: the imagination of its customers and potential buyers. Years of successful business and rewarding transactions for both the business and its buyers have created a valuable heritage; a brand equity. The goodwill towards the company might have a slightly different meaning to each buyer but each nuance is encapsulated in its reputation. It is this that the firm needs to move progressively into the new market or the new market position.

This manoeuvre needs to be undertaken carefully, taking customers with the strategy. Moreover, under no circumstances must it endanger the existing business or brand franchise. A poorly executed programme is likely to cast doubts on the competence of the firm. It will cause customers to wonder if the company can still run its existing business effectively. The marketer needs to demonstrate that their firm is applying its normal business approach, resources, and skills to the new market. It might have been "innovative" or "respectful" or "fun" or "thoughtful" in its previous ventures. It needs to be the same in the new space. For example, at the time of writing, the Finnish mobile manufacturer, Nokia, is moving into services. As its established reputation is for excellent design and fashionable products, it needs to approach services in the same way.

There are several steps to successful brand repositioning. They are:

Step 1: Undertake a brand audit and identify transferable brand values

The marketer needs to understand the strengths of the company's brand and the franchise it holds with four distinct audiences: its existing customers, its employees, city investors, and the general public. A "brand audit" is a research process that determines this. It identifies the image that each audience has and reduces these to identifiable values. It also highlights any areas where there may be inconsistencies. These range from items where the design conflicts with perception to operational issues such as flaws in customer service.

The marketer must use this data to identify brand values that might be a basis for a new position in a market. For instance, the firm might be seen as "responsive", after years of listening to customers and responding to them. Or it may be perceived to be "high integrity" or "high quality". These might be used in the new position. Any negatives that are identified by the brand audit should be confronted honestly. If they are major perceptions or impediments, they must be confronted by the future strategy and by clear, effective communication plans.

Step 2: Identify the intended brand position

Perceptual maps (see the entry under *positioning*) can be used to clarify an intended market position. The maps can be used to determine the likely number of customers, the most relevant *value proposition*, and to anticipate the likely reaction of other competitors. They can also be used to work out the brand style which is appropriate for the firm's strategic position. This highlights any gaps between what the firm believes and what the buyers actually experience. So it enables the firm to create *internal marketing* and education programmes.

Step 3: Create a transition strategy

There are a number of ways in which a brand can be moved into new markets or a new market space. The first is a phased transition. If the firm has a strong brand, it can create its new business by association with that brand. It can, for instance, create a separate division, which specializes in the new field. IBM used this strategy as it moved substantially into services. As a result of nearly a decade's investment, "IBM Global Services" is now one of the world's largest services businesses and has a healthy brand reputation. The juxtaposition of the company name with "services" signalled to buyers that the approach and values of the firm were to be applied to the service market. The heritage, quality, and expertise of the world market leader could be experienced in the service market.

A second transition strategy is the dramatic move. This might be achieved through a memorable and visible launch, an acquisition, or a joint venture. A firm may not have the competences to successfully set up and run a new business very quickly. So a less risky investment is through purchase or mutual partnership. Each has its strengths and weaknesses. Acquisition is an immediate commitment. It gives the firm the ability to create its own direction with the new business from day one and, as importantly, signals its intention firmly to its customers. It can change the brand name immediately or it can phase the change.

A third transition strategy is to build on gradual organic growth. A firm might have some elements of the new business. This can be used as a basis to build. However, it is usually difficult to convince the market.

Step 4: Launch and communicate the brand

Whichever transition strategy is chosen, the firm must invest in communicating the new brand. This involves serious investment in convincing the market that it now has a viable new position. When, for instance, in 2000, Accenture was first set up from the then accountancy firm Andersen, it was launched with an adverting and sponsorship budget of $100 million. Since then, it has consistently invested in its brand, communicating its "High Performance Delivered" promise. This campaign was intended to demonstrate how the company draws on its work with clients in numerous industries around the world to help transform their businesses. The communication strategy must match the transition strategy though. The communications plan to match a dramatic move, like an acquisition, must be shaped very differently to that supporting a phased transition.

Step 5: Measure the brand change

The firm needs to know the view of customers in the intended market of its brand relative to competitor brands. As the brand is such an important asset, it is sensible to set up measures of its health in the market place. It is normal to establish some form of brand tracking survey. These surveys allow the firm to adjust the strategy in light of changing customer views and competitor actions.

History, context, criticism, and development

Consumer product companies have been very successful at repositioning product brands for many decades. They have used, for example, brand extension strategies as a tool to change their market position. Buyers seek a familiar taste or style in the new category of product. For example, the extension of the Dove range of personal hygiene products from one soap turned it into a market leader. Others have gained new customers and a new lease of life for products by repositioning. The health drink, Lucozade, was, for example, languishing as an old-fashioned tonic for ill people until it was repositioned, in modern packaging, in the health drink market. While Mars conquered a seasonal summer hole in its revenues by positioning its Mars Bar brand in the ice cream market. In fact, it was so successful that it created a whole category of products.

Some service companies have also succeeded at penetrating markets through similar brand repositioning. Richard Branson's Virgin Group has moved from entertainment into airlines into trains and into many other retail areas, such as communications services. This took it from a niche supplier to a major player in the international consumer services market. Each move had a sound business reason (normally based on shaking up a stodgy, cosy market) but each time the brand took existing buyers into that market and picked up others *en route*. For instance, the early Virgin flyers were young business people who had learnt the group's style by experiencing its entertainment before they started their career. They also moved with it when they were ready to invest in financial services. Yet, with each move, the brand picked up new customers too.

Voices and further reading

- "Finding new positions: the entrepreneurial edge. Strategic competition can be thought of as the process of perceived new positions that woo customers from established positions or draw new customers into the market. . . . In principle, incumbents and entrepreneurs face the same challenges in finding new strategic positions. In practice, new entrants often have the edge. Strategic positionings are often not obvious and finding them requires creativity and insight. New entrants often discover unique positions that have been available but simply overlooked by established competitors." Porter, M.E., "On competition". *Harvard Business Review* book, 1995.
- "Repositioning: addressing other segments with different threshold requirements . . . As with resources, some organisations may have inadequate (redundant) competences as customer requirements move on. This could lead to business failure. However, these competences may be adequate to service customers in different segments (repositioning) for example in developing markets." Johnson, G. and Scholes, K., 2002.

Things you might like to consider

(i)   As the case study shows, repositioning can involve much more than just the creation of a new product or a new branded item. It can involve substantial investment in all aspects of the direction of a company or business unit.

(ii) Handled badly, repositioning can seriously mess up existing business and the existing reputation of the firm.

(iii) Surprisingly large companies let themselves be subject to the whims of a market or see market forces as inevitable and irresistible. Their firm or their offer is repositioned by external forces such as the moves of competitors or commoditization effects. In these circumstances, it ought to be the role of marketers to point out that portion that can be influenced by explicit strategy and managerial actions.

Positioning Virgin in the media market

Almost 10 million customers choose Virgin Media in the UK today, which makes it one of the largest residential broadband providers in the country; the UK's largest mobile virtual network operator, and the second largest home phone and pay TV provider. In cabled areas, its advanced fibre optic cable network reaches 12.6 million homes, delivering high quality TV with pioneering, on-demand, content as well as broadband services up to 50 Mb. In addition, Virgin Media offers ADSL broadband and telephony throughout the country, delivered over telephone lines.

But it's not all about size. Virgin Media is a company that understands people as much as technology. In other words, it's a typical Virgin company (in fact the largest Virgin branded company in the world with revenues just over £4 bn in 2008) even though it was created from six very different companies as recently as 2006.

CREATING A NEW VIRGIN COMPANY

In November 1999, Virgin Mobile launched as the world's first mobile virtual network operator, listing on the London stock exchange in July 2004. In March 2006, ntl and Telewest, the UK's two leading cable companies, announced the completion of their merger (which also included Flextech Television, responsible for channels such as Living, Challenge, and Bravo, Virgin.net an ADSL based national internet service provider, and ntl: Telewest business – providing business to business IT, data, voice, and telephony products and services). On 4 July 2006, ntl: Telewest completed its acquisition of Virgin Mobile.

At this point, planning began to re-launch the group of companies as a Virgin branded company. The newly merged exective board wanted a re-launch within three months, and a new Managing Director of Brand, Ashley

Stockwell was hired to lead change workstreams across the company. He quickly reset expectations on the executive team that a brand launch like this one was about more than a logo, and as such would take much longer than they had planned. The re-launch would have to cover more than 15,000 staff, 100 buildings, and a fleet of over 5,500 vehicles.

Coming from the Virgin Group, the new MD understood his first job was to make sure that everyone inside the new organization knew what it meant to be a Virgin company. A cultural change programme was designed to brief all staff on Virgin's core values:

- value for money;
- competitively challenging;
- innovative;
- brilliant customer service;
- good quality;
- fun.

All of the companies involved had very different cultures, so the merger and creation of a new single culture under the Virgin brand was a critical success factor. Luckily, most people were thrilled to represent the Virgin brand, and welcomed Virgin as a distinctive and attractive company for which to work.

Perhaps more challenging was the need to consolidate legacy systems and processes across the new company. Members of the newly formed brand team collaborated with workstream leaders on a number of change projects to make sure the customer experience would deliver on the Virgin brand promise. For example, in the billing workstream, a number of legacy systems were consolidated with the aim of simplifying bills so that customers would quickly be able to understand their bill and have charges for all the services they used in one place.

Brand team members reviewed all services and propositions to customers, again making sure that they represented the Virgin brand and values, and would meet customers' expectations around great service and value for money.

As the re-launch date loomed, an internal teaser campaign began with the words "Start the revolution". All the usual internal communications channels were used in addition to more guerilla tactics such as stickers appearing behind toilet doors. For managers, the campaign was titled "Lead the revolution" and involved a special programme of workshops to brief them on how to lead in a Virgin company. This was followed up with the do-it-yourself "Revolution takeaway" in a Chinese takeout-style bag, containing tools and props to help managers work through with their teams what being Virgin meant in their area of the business.

One key message that all managers received was that expectations internally and externally would be high with the creation of a new Virgin company. Known for coming into markets and shaking things up on behalf of the consumer, everyone expects change overnight when a Virgin company launches. Stockwell made it clear to all that the launch was more of a journey, which would take the company 3–5 years to complete.

THE BIRTH OF VIRGIN MEDIA

The combined company re-launched as Virgin Media in February 2007. Virgin Media was a new entertainment and communications company offering consumers a great choice of the latest products and technology, outstanding customer service, and great value.

Internally, the launch campaign built on the teaser campaign, with the rallying cry "Start the revolution". On launch day, everyone received a "Party in a box" containing bunting, streamers, balloons, coasters, and a shot glass along with a little red book that explained what it meant to be a Virgin company.

Externally, a teaser campaign led up to the launch on 8th February 2007, using advertising, direct marketing, and press coverage to announce the arrival of Virgin Media and demonstrate with both the look and feel, and the tonality of the communications, that this really was a new company built from the best of the companies that merged to create it.

Just as he had done many times before for other Virgin companies, Richard Branson took part in a publicity stunt on launch day. He spent 8 February in a glass box in Covent Garden, London, alternatively using his mobile, broadband, and TV to spread the word about Virgin Media, and receiving celebrity visitors through the day.

A special package was sent to existing customers letting them know that Virgin Media was now their supplier, summarizing what had changed, and how the changes would benefit them. For most existing customers, the visible change occurred when they turned on their television or went online. Where once they saw an ntl or Telewest home screen, they now saw the new Virgin Media electronic programme guide, and the old ntl and Telewest portals were replaced with virginmedia.com.

The old Virgin Mobile stores were re-branded and began to sell the other three services now available to customers. Signage on all other premises in the estate was changed over a two-month period. Perhaps the most challenging external re-brand was on the fleet of vehicles, which took longer to change simply because it was a working fleet and so needed to be tackled gradually to avoid any drop in customer service.

REPOSITIONING THE BRAND AS IT GROWS

When Virgin Media launched, its focus was on announcing its arrival and its points of difference to challenge competitors in the market. The competitors were tough – and had deep pockets with which to fight back once Virgin

Media was established in their industry. With customer churn a vital industry performance indicator, it wasn't long before things became very competitive and frenetic, with everyone competing for more customers at the expense of creating real value throughout 2008. For example, everyone was leading their advertising with price messages, and then with the technological features of the offer – benefits were hard to spot and so customers increasingly treated the services on offer as commodities.

Virgin is used to this type of competitive response from larger, more established players, having only roughly 20% of its major competitor's resources in most of the markets in which it competes. And so, while its early offers to customers were around better value and led with price, over time the company began to reposition itself around its other differentiators. In April 2009, Virgin Media began to emphasize its great service, the entertainment aspects of its offers, and its benefits. The message to customers was clear – Virgin was different and worth paying more for.

Today, the brand team remains at the heart of the business, looking after corporate identity, core brand look and feel, tone of voice, championing the customer's experience, and delivering the brand via internal communications. The team regularly gets involved in new product development, for example taking the lead on the design of a new modem to support the new ultrafast 50 Mb internet access, the UK's fastest broadband service, in December 2008.

CREATING VALUE THE VIRGIN WAY

At the heart of Virgin's ethos is the idea that if you look after your staff, they will look after your customers, and your shareholders will be happy. This has certainly worked at Virgin Media.

Brand tracking measures show a steep climb for the brand since it launched in February 2007: *Marketing* magazine's "Best Loved Brand" survey showed a leap from 53rd in the UK to the 6th in just 12 months, and a recent *Readers Digest* survey showed Virgin Media on a par with the BT brand; quite something in just two years.

Customer Churn is significantly down from the ntl: Telewest days. Virgin Media also uses the "net promoter score" (NPS) to keep track of how it is doing. The company tracks NPS through every part of the "customer journey", and can score individual agents, giving them specific feedback on what they're doing well and what they need to improve.

As more people join the company, it remains just as important to share what it means to be a Virgin employee, and this is reinforced in the recruitment process, induction programmes, training, and performance reviews. When he can, Richard Branson will call in to see staff around the country, listening in on their conversations with customers to keep in touch with what they expect from Virgin.

He also gets involved in helping customers use the services on offer, creating "webisodes" that can be viewed online, which explain how to get the best out of the services available.

So, by being the first people in the UK to offer customers TV, broadband, phone, and mobile, Virgin Media sees the future as bursting with fresh entertainment and communication possibilities. Their ongoing mission is to bring customers all the excitement possible and make their entertainment the brilliant experience it should be.

 RATING: Practical and powerful

 **RESEARCH**

Application: client, competitor, or market insight

Importance ratings of IT professional services firms' attributes

When you and your company are selecting a professional services consultant or solution provider, how important is it that this vendor ___?

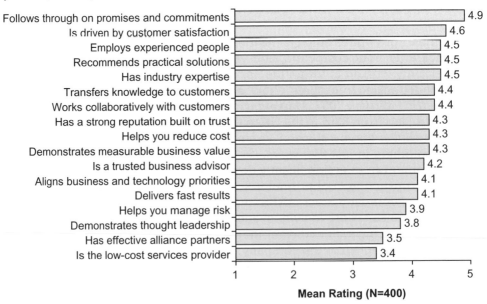

Figure R.2: A representation of an actual result of one question in a conjoint survey (published with the permission of ITSMA)

The concept

It is difficult to capture the complexity, organizational competence, and variety of technique used in well run and properly commissioned research. This highly specialized field combines managerial competence, agency specialization, acquired professional insight, sophisticated statistical analysis, and hard won insight into markets and/or human behaviour. Where it is done well, it is highly valued. Surprisingly large and well run companies, though, do not invest in research and do not set out to understand or adopt appropriate techniques. Too many either neglect it or try to get insight for bottom dollar prices. Others use it to justify established views; like the proverbial drunk using a lamp post for support rather than illumination.

Field research is familiar not only to marketers but also to many business leaders. They may have seen results of research presented at internal meetings or read many research reports. Unfortunately, familiarity can breed contempt, making the processes, the techniques, and the outcomes seem deceptively simple. As a result, there are many unconvincing or poor research reports resulting from poor specification or poor use of the research industry.

Yet, undertaken properly, field research yields insights into human needs, customer views (which can be different to needs), competitor performance, and market trends. It can reveal the different elements of an offer which customers value and how they combine with different price points to form packages that they will buy. Moreover it can reveal how these vary between different customer groups, creating opportunities through variation of offer in different market segments. It can also save money by stopping new ideas and marketing initiatives which the market will reject. Yet to do all this it has to be properly specified and managed. It needs a brief and a managerial process if it is going to produce results. This needs to ensure that the sample frame, the approach, the technique, and the questionnaires are appropriate.

A typical, well run research process includes the following steps:

(i)   Agree objectives and research needs.
(ii)   Write brief for agencies. Brief includes:
  • Research objectives
  • Summary description of the market
  • Description of the research problem and desired output
  • Description of existing knowledge and previous research
  • Budget constraints
  • Time scales
  • Report requirements
  • Constraints (e.g. interviews must be arranged via client relationship managers).
(iii) Shortlist potential agencies.
(iv)   Contact and invite to pitch.
(v)   Create selection criteria. These might include:

- Technical skills
- Previous experience
- Interpretation of the brief
- Proposed approach
- Team fit (will the firm's people be able to work with them?)

(vi) Hold presentations by agencies with selection team.
(vii) Choose and confirm agency.
(viii) Negotiate contract.

There are two main types of research. The first is the qualitative or "in depth" approach. This involves spending time with a relatively small number of people and seeking deep answers to questions. It gives colour to views and can reveal underlying feelings and motivations that can be enormously valuable. Quantitative research, on the other hand, involves a wider number of contacts, normally to investigate trends. Both have their strengths and their weaknesses. Companies also tend to reach for two main types of research approaches: ongoing trend surveys and ad hoc research projects. The first involves clear managerial processes to set up and run the research mechanism, especially if it is a specifically commissioned piece of work rather than the purchase of external questions in an established external programme.

However, methods used to collect and analyse research data vary enormously. They range from face-to-face interviews and observed discussion groups to telephone, postal, or internet surveys. For example:

(i)   Multivariate techniques
       These seem to be the most common approaches in use at the time of writing. They include approaches such as: cluster analysis, factor analysis, and latent analysis. They enable marketers to obtain and analyse complex data sets. Factor analysis, for example, is a tool to reduce a large number of data points to a few understandable trends.

(ii)   Conjoint research
       A form of multivariate analysis, this uses questions (either in face-to-face meetings or via email or telephone) designed to trade off different pairs of values or ideas. Figure R.2 shows (with permission) one part of a conjoint study undertaken by America's "ITSMA". It demonstrates the richness of data that this technique yields. As interviewees are forced to choose, the approach can mimic the thought processes of customers when considering purchase and can provide powerful insight into new needs and adjustments needed to specific offers. It can also identify potential bundles of features/price mixes for different groups of customers.

(iii) "Zones of Tolerance"
       Created by Valerie Ziethaml and Mary Jo Bitner (see Ziethaml, V. and Bitner, M. J., 2003) this is a very specific form of conjoint. It differentiates between customers' "ideal", "acceptable", and "unacceptable" tolerances.

(iv)   Observational research
       As the name suggests this involves a researcher observing the behaviour of people. It can give real insight into human needs and behaviours which are not

picked up by other methods because customer views and beliefs are often different to what they actually do. There is, in this particular method, debate about
the effect of the observer on the results. It is suggested that it is more objective
than, say, interviews, but there is credible evidence that the process of observation, and the observers themselves, influence results.

(v)   Explorative research
Sometimes known as deterministic "operational research methods", this is normally used in developing a new proposition or identifying a new customer
segment. It follows issues until a trend suggests that they are likely to be substantive. The work can be iterative, checking back and adjusting the idea as inter-
viewees respond. It is intended to develop initial ideas and insights.

(vi)   Concept testing
This involves testing ideas for new propositions or approaches with customers
before launch. They are shown an idea or marketing programme and asked to
comment on it in a structured way.

(vii) Depth interviews
These are individual conversations with people who represent the sample of
customers. They are intended to understand issues in depth and, like other
qualitative techniques, cannot be set down too prescriptively. Although interview guides might be agreed it is unlikely that the interviewer will be able to
stick to them as issues and ideas surface.

(viii) Focus groups
These are facilitated discussions of groups of people who represent the sample
of customers. They ought to be led by an expert and can be observed in a
research lab. They give a deeper and more rounded view of a segment's view
than individual conversations because of the interactive conversation.

(ix)   Cluster analysis
This is a generic name given to a range of approaches which identify similar
groupings and relationships between them. It is particularly good, for example,
at finding similar attitudes as part of a good piece of segmentation research; or
grouping various price tolerances amongst different customers; or identifying
potential market positions. Academics and researchers will understand that there
are different types of clustering procedures. The strength of the technique is that
it identifies patterns in data which can be easily presented in graphical form;
communicating complex data easily. That, though, is perhaps also the weakness
of it. Executives might be too quick to jump to conclusions and actions where
subtlety and interpretation are needed.

(x)   Correspondence analysis
This is a technique which is able to represent "multi-dimensional tables"
in digestible form. It is a process by which tables of raw data are related on
relevant dimension. The inter-relationships of various results are then plotted
in graphical form. It is, again, a powerful way of reducing complex data
(like segment needs or competitive brand positions) in easily communicated
constructs.

(xi) Various regression analysis techniques

These include things like multiple regression, automatic interaction detection, etc.

(xii) Artificial intelligence

One of the big disappointments in the development of technology is AI. (In the 1960s, it was credible to believe that there would be an operating, conscious computer, like HAL, by "2001".) Nevertheless, there is experience of trying to use the current AI technology to solve marketing problems. They tend to be the answer to problems needing complex simulations.

(xiii) "Fuzzy sets"

This is a modern mathematical technique used to tackle abstract concepts. As this is deliberately designed to tackle vagueness, it can help with a number of marketing issues around human behaviour and response – if you can get near to understanding it!

(xiv) Simulation

This involves the creation of a model, usually a computer model, which mimics real marketing problems. The approach might help test various marketing strategies which might involve heavy initial investment or help decide between various strategic options. Some of the models used by bankers to assess viable alternatives in markets open to candidates of aggressive acquisition are near to these sorts of simulations.

(xv) Hybrid techniques

These might include: dynamic programming and Heuristic programming.

Clearly the appropriate approach and technique ought to be chosen with an experienced and specialist researcher. One practical way to pull together this complex array of possibilities might be around the pragmatic purposes for which the marketer wants to use research, as indicated in Table R.1 below:

Table R.1 Illustration of the linkage of research purpose to technique

Purpose	Potential general methods	Potential technique
Explore	Focus groups Depth interviews Observational Ethnographic	Omnibus (say, online) Phone questionnaires
Develop	Sequential recycling Online labs Deprivation/switching/trial/user experience	Online labs Conjoint Quali–quant
Evaluate		Online concept test Full potential test Simulated test market (STM) Equity tracking NPS surveys

Research needs to be used properly and fill a gap in knowledge. It is sensible to first conduct an exhaustive "desk review" to see if an internet search can point to libraries, professional societies, or academic institutions that have already conducted research or provided commentary on the subject in question. In fact, many people in large companies which lack a structured research library find, after a brief search, that their own company has conducted research near to the subject in question on previous occasions.

Once this preliminary work has been completed, the gap in knowledge ought to be clearly defined in a brief to a specialist research agency. This should specify the purpose of the research. It might be to test a new idea, to test segmentation dimensions, to understand a new concept, or to identify client needs. The exercise will be confused if there are too many objectives. In particular, the information yield that is expected must be made clear to the supplier.

Once results come through, careful interpretation is needed. It is important to understand, not only the statistically valid representation of results but also their meaning. Human beings often do not know what they want and, sometimes, why they behave in a particular way. They will say they want cheapness yet spend outrageous sums on branded luxury goods or, in business, on a consultancy project from an elite, branded supplier. So research needs careful commissioning, good execution, and enlightened interpretation. Yet the expense and effort is more than worthwhile. It can lead to profitable new insights that build strong future revenue streams and can obviate mistakes.

History, context, criticism, and development

Companies in America and Europe have been conducting structured research since the start of the 20th century. In 1923, for instance, Robert Woodruff of Coca-Cola expanded the former "Information department" to conduct pioneering market research (see Pendergrast, M., 1993). In 1927, this department studied 15,500 retail outlets over a three-year period to establish that there was a relationship between traffic flow and sales volume. They demonstrated both this and the Pareto effect (a third of outlets accounted for 60% of sales volume). The highest performing outlets were in the best locations but also had few Coca-Cola signs. Sales strategy was revised after the survey (sales people visited four times a year offering special support) and an extensive consumer research project initiated (into 42,000 drug store customers).

There were established market research departments, market research agencies, and marketing consultants who appear to have been a routine part of American business in the 1920s.

It is, perhaps, not surprising, then, that a 1927 American marketing text book (White, P., 1927) talks freely about the "regular market research department" and some of the challenges presented to it by "modern, scientific marketing methods". As a result of nearly a century of research practice and academic study there is now a vast range of acquired knowledge and practice which is available to modern marketers.

Research is also, of course, used extensively by academics investigating aspects of marketing and sales. Their techniques are usually rigorous and peer-reviewed, mimicking the approach of scientific disciplines. It is sensible for practising marketers to access their work and understand academic studies relevant to their own information needs. It is rare that there is not some study in some part of the world which is close to a developing need and even rarer that an experienced academic is not willing to cooperate with a company in solving a knotty research problem at reasonable prices. Too many neglect this route.

Voices and further reading

- ". . . there will be special research problems to be met and solved. Some of these will come up in the course of routine work, but in general these problems should be organized in some fashion or other, so that the most important ones be undertaken first. Thus the marketing manager may well suggest to the director of research certain pressing problems, or the director of research may submit to the marketing manager the problems which he considers of the greatest importance." White, P., 1927.

- "Market research has proved a valuable role in assessing incremental improvements but has proved unreliable for radical marketing ideas. Baileys Irish Cream now dominates the global liqueurs market, but when it was introduced in the mid-70's it had already been rejected in all market research tests. Luckily the Baileys marketers had learned to interpret that as an encouraging sign." Ambler, T., 2003.

- "One general way to classify consumer research is in terms of the fundamental assumption the researchers make about what they are studying and how to study it . . . The basic set of assumptions underlying the dominant paradigm at this point in time is positivism . . . that human reason is supreme and that there is a single, objective truth that can be discovered by science . . . The newer paradigm is interpretivism . . . that our society places too much emphasis on science and technology, and that this ordered rational view of consumers denies the complexity of the social and cultural world in which we live." Solomon, M. et al., 2006.

- "We need to broaden our thinking about understanding consumers beyond the perspective of market research's conventional wisdom . . . Understanding consumers is not about data and the superiority of one method over another. The amount of data we collect, or the number of interviews we conduct, is not the critical success factor. Understanding consumers is about creating explanations that can be inspired by data but equally well come from experience and intuition." "Understanding consumers" by Calder, B.J. in Iacobucci, D., *Kellogg on Marketing*, 2001.

- Sherry, J. and Kozinets, R.V., "Qualitative inquiry in marketing and consumer research in Iacobucci, D. (ed.), *Kellogg on Marketing*. 2001.
- Moutinho, Luiz, "Quantitative methods in marketing" in Baker, M.J. and Hart, S. (eds), *The Marketing Book*. Butterworth-Heinemann, 2008.

Things you might like to consider

(i) Field research ought to carry an arrogance warning. Managers and leaders in all sectors of industry can be very dismissive of it. Many have been heard to remark that there is little that field research can tell them about their buyers. Yet they are almost always wrong. In fact, some very senior business leaders have been chastened by the direct comments they have heard their buyers make when sitting behind two-way mirrors watching focus groups.

(ii) There are numerous examples of mistakes due to poor interpretation, as shown by the inability to see latent markets (see the market maturity section).

(iii) Customers often do not know what they want. Poorly designed research will not uncover latent needs that they are unaware of.

(iv) Research has its limitations. Some companies have found innovation and new offers through explorative interaction with their customers rather than field research. Sometimes, a visionary creates a market by intuitively understanding latent need. Hence Henry Ford's famous comment that, if he had asked people what they wanted, they would have asked for faster horses.

(v) This is as much about developing organizational competence as any other part of marketing. Marketers ought to set up processes which contribute to progressive organizational learning in research methods.

(vi) There is evidence that, even in the most market-orientated companies sclerosis can damage the potential yield from field research. At the time of writing, for instance, some specialists in large research departments are unduly sceptical of behavioural economics and its implications whilst agencies report that a number of large product companies have become so bound up in process that creative insight and interpretation of opportunity have been lost or outsourced.

(vii) Filed research can give marketers political power. Properly conducted and communicated, it can give direction to other functions and their work. Few are able to challenge that the work represents customer views and should be taken seriously. It can be used to influence the priorities of other functions toward market need.

 RATING: Practical and powerful

S

SALES AND SELLING

Application: revenue generation

The concept

Selling is not an erratic, ad hoc activity, nor is it best undertaken by a loud mouth in a suit that shouts just as loud. It is not exaggeration, lies, false claims, or pressurizing people to buy things they do not want. All of these constitute poor salesmanship, which causes bad word of mouth, terrible reputation, law suits and, eventually, business failure. Selling is a credible business function with particular skills, processes, and concepts that need to be as rigorously applied as those in other specialities.

During the evaluation phase of a purchase, it is likely that any buyer will come across a number of different choices that meet their needs. Several will be candidates to fit their varied criteria, despite being very different mixes of features at different price points. Some will have few features at a low price, and some will be features-rich at a high price. Some will have components that the buyer has not thought of before, stimulating curiosity or desire. In fact, it is quite possible that a well packaged mix of features could entice someone to pay more than their original "unacceptable" price.

Successful sales people understand this and are able to delicately elicit these needs, suggesting an offer from their own company that best meets them. They must (through technique, experience, or intuition) learn ways to understand their customers' preferences. They have to listen, observe, and diagnose before they "sell". Neil Rackham's (Rackham, N., 1995) famous and exhaustive research (he spent twelve years studying 35,000 sales transactions) emphasizes the importance of listening and questioning in sales success. His "SPIN" model, which has been at the heart of much sales strategy in Western companies for several decades, codified four categories of questions: "situation", "problem", "implication", and "need–payoff" questions. Once the customer's situation is clear, the sales person scopes the need and then identifies the implications for the customer if it isn't resolved. Finally, the sales person will establish the benefits of resolving the problem and create an urgent need to do so in the mind of the customer.

There are a number of different sales concepts that marketers need to understand and get a grip on in their careers. They need expertise in understanding:

(i) The *decision-making unit* (see separate entry)

Whether *business-to-business* or consumer marketing, marketers must help sales people to understand the roles and importance of the different people in the DMU if they are to succeed. For instance, even used car sales people are taught to watch any new family coming onto the sales forecourt before approaching them. Their behaviour, and their answers to a few simple questions about what they are looking for, will reveal who is the actual decision maker, who holds the purse strings, and the degrees of influence of other members of the family in this particular purchase. As a result, marketers working for car manufacturers have, at times, set in place programmes for their dealers to help their sales employees to understand, and keep pace with this dynamic.

(ii) *Closing techniques* (see separate entry) and other aspects of individual sales performance

It is a simple fact that marketing and sales campaigns can fail because individual sales people are not very good. Marketers must develop methods by which they come to judgments about the performance of their direct and indirect sales *channels*. This might range from the capability of an individual to close a deal to their productivity whilst on the road (the number of visits in a day, for instance). There will be many reasons given from within the sales community as to why revenue targets are not achieved; some of which will be utter nonsense. Marketers need to develop objective, comparative performance data.

(iii) *Major account sales* (see separate entry)

It is a simple fact that many businesses are dominated by a few, significant, repeat customers. The sales approaches employed in this situation are unique and different from other sales environments. They demand that marketing operates in unique ways and marketers need to understand this in-depth.

(iv) Different types of sales organization and *channels* (see separate entry)

There are a number of different types of sales organization and sales capability which need different support and interventions from marketers. Marketers tend to get the job of assessing sales effectiveness, predicting revenues, setting sales targets supporting lead generation, and establishing new market access. They need to understand the pros and cons of each channel in these activities.

(v) Solutions selling (see separate entry)

This is a recent phenomenon seen largely in *business-to-business* markets. It is an attempt to customize offers to individual customers which has had mixed results.

(vi) Sales support

Many firms employ specialists who assist with various aspects of the sales process. Some simply provide administrative support, helping sales people or consultants to spend as much time with customers as possible. Others arrange seminars or *hospitality* events aimed at providing opportunities to sell. They have one over-riding objective: to maintain focus on developing sales opportunities. They may assist with account planning (preparing, attending, and participating in planning sessions) and they may manage the production of proposals. Specialist teams are often set up in large *business-to-business* firms specifically to handle bid management, forming part of a sales or account team. Sales support people also participate in account development, visiting contacts to create relationships and open doors. In some companies, these functions make up for faults, inadequacies, and gaps in the marketing department.

(vii) Sales or revenue forecasting

It is often marketing people who have to forecast the revenues of the firm. Some use sophisticated statistical techniques, others use common sense based on field knowledge and seasonal trends.

History, context, criticism, and development

Many successful business people had travelling sales representatives in the 18th and 19th century. Josiah Wedgwood, for example, alongside his retail sales staff in his shop in central London (whom he paid on commission), employed Tom Byerley as his provincial travelling sales rep in the 1770s. One hundred years later, a pioneer of the German car industry, Nicolaus Otto, was originally a travelling salesman (representing tea, sugar, and kitchenware) in the 1860s.

Henry Heinz, who hired his first two sales people in 1877, had 357 by 1901 and nearly 1,000 by 1919. Each one was expected to build trusted relationships with retailers. They helped them manage inventory, choose advertising, and improve merchandising displays. They also reported back to their headquarters on changing demand, competitors' actions, and product performance. The whole Heinz sales force received ongoing training and regular sales meetings. There were company instructions on dress code, job responsibilities, and sales techniques (the "seven steps" that will help ensure a well rounded sales call). There were annual sales conventions and regional meetings, involving senior management, with presentations on subjects like "Broader salesmanship" (see Koehn, 2001).

An early cosmetics pioneer, Celeste Walker (the daughter of slaves), built her successful business (by the time of her death in 1919 she was worth several million dollars) on the door-to-door sales of 25,000 African-American women. Marshall Field issued his first guide to his retail sales staff in 1873 and established travelling sales people soon after. By 1905, Singer (even then a global firm, making sewing machines in eight factories around the world) sold 2.5 million machines a year through 61,444 sales people and 800 retail stores in America alone (See Edgerton, E., 2007 and Butler, R.S., 1917).

One researcher (Powers, T., 1997) documented the professionalization and development of sales practice in early and mid 20th century America. His analysis shows why the idea of a "sales period" grew in the thinking about the development of marketing. Field sales people became more prevalent in the 1920s and 1930s, and were expected to "control the sales conversation". After some doubts during the depression and Second World War they became a major force in American commerce although attitudes to the sale itself seemed to change. There is evidence, for instance, that particularly in "industrial selling" sales practice moved toward the sort of questioning and diagnostic approach best illustrated by Rackham's "SPIN" approach. In the 1960s field sales began to be more integrated with mass advertising and, later, with other aspects of the mix, like direct marketing, as a lead generation tool.

Voices and further reading

- "The kind of service that results from the size of the chain is indicated by the sort of salesmanship that is found in some of the chains . . . Somewhere in these great chains is a man who specializes in retail salesmanship who has studied the problem until he has reduced it to an art. This art he teaches to his salespeople. The salesmanship is standardized for the benefit of the customers." Butler, R.S., 1917.

- ". . . the conception of training in selling has grown and broadened. It has not developed until it tends to include not only the process of salesmanship itself but also the most scientific methods of selecting salesmen, of job analysis by test, and of a concerted attempt to maintain morale in the most effective manner." White, P., 1927.

- "Increasingly good salesmen don't try to sell the customer, rather they try to help him buy by presenting both the advantages and disadvantages of their products and showing how they will satisfy his needs. They find this helpfulness results in satisfied customer and long-term relationships. This new approach recognizes the growing sophistication of buyers, especially industrial buyers." McCarthy, E.J., 1960.

- Üstüner, T. and Godes, D., "Better sales networks". *Harvard Business Review*, July–August 2006.

- Boaz, N., Murnane, J., and Nuffer, K., "The basics of Business-to-business sales success". *McKinsey Quarterly*, May 2010.

- Bonoma, T.V., "Major sales: who really does the buying?" *Harvard Business Review*, July–August 2006.

- Kotler, P., Rackham, N. and Krishnaswamy, S., "Ending the war between sales and marketing". *Harvard Business Review*, July–August 2006.

- "There are two sources of friction between Sales and Marketing. One is economic, and the other is cultural. The economic friction is generated by the need to divide the total budget granted by senior management to support sales and marketing . . . The cultural conflict . . . is, if anything, even more entrenched than the economic conflict . . . Marketers . . . are highly analytical, data orientated, and project focused . . . Salespeople, in contrast, spend their time talking to existing and potential customers. They're skilled relationship builders; they're not only savvy about customers' willingness to buy but also attuned to which product features will fly and which will die." Kotler, Rackham, and Krishnaswamy, ibid.

- Anderson, E., and Onyemah, V., "How right should the customer be?" *Harvard Business Review*, July–August 2006. Work based on 2,500 sales people in 38 countries and working in 500 different companies.

- "When customers are solving a new problem or contemplating new solutions to existing problems, they need a great deal of information. They don't know what they don't know, but they realize their decisions have high stakes. Such customers will take their time, gather information, and process it. In this situation, a good salesperson slowly and invisibly frames the customer's thinking . . ." Anderson and Onyemah, ibid.

- Rackham, N., *SPIN selling*. Gower, 1995. Analysis of 35,000 sales transactions.

Things you might like to consider

(i) There is some unquantified and unresearched evidence, that the best client-side marketers are those that have "carried a bag" (i.e. spent some time in sales) during their early career. An understanding of the sales process and direct experience of customers tends to make marketers less detached and theoretical.

(ii) A marketer must understand how to apply the relevant, credible sales principles to different sales environments in order to achieve revenue growth. They cannot design elements of the mix, new propositions, or effective strategy without an understanding of sales dynamics. This is a crucial part of a marketer's professional expertise.

 RATING: Practical and powerful

SCENARIO PLANNING

Application: market analysis, strategic planning

The concept

Scenario planning is an analytical tool which helps firms to think about potential futures in the light of change, complexity, and uncertainty. Less linear than the *market audit*, it allows marketers to explore likely scenarios which might develop from current market forces. Scenarios can be thought of as stories which help marketers to develop different potential futures based on both knowledge and people's assumptions about the present. They are not forecasts, but possible outcomes which provide a common perspective and language (Ringland, 2006).

Usually, a team comprising people from across the firm is formed to construct scenarios. In a session led by someone experienced in the process, the participants brainstorm potential futures. Input to their debate includes evidence from futurologists, research studies, customer views, and pertinent data. The team is normally encouraged to think widely before scenarios are grouped and ranked. A firm moving into a new market can create different scenarios of how that market might develop and how competitors might react to their entry. These different scenarios can then be worked into a market entry plan which anticipates risk.

History, context, criticism, and development

With its roots in the military, this approach was first developed successfully as a management tool in the strategy process of oil giant Shell during the 1970s. Scenario planning creates a framework in which potential strategies can be developed and tested in the light of future uncertainties. It has, to date, largely been a corporate planning tool used to develop perspectives for the corporate plans of, mainly large, corporations. The approach has been used in the oil, telecommunications, professional services, and public sectors. It is only in recent years that marketers have begun to assess its applicability to their function (Ringland, G. and Young, L., 2006). One writer (Seybold, P.B., 2001), for instance, argued that marketers should create "customer scenarios" to develop human insight for interactive campaigns and for new product development.

Voices and further reading

* Ringland, G., *Scenario Planning* (2nd edition). John Wiley & Sons Ltd, 2006.
* Ringland, G. and Young, L., *Scenarios in Marketing*. John Wiley & Sons Ltd, 2006.

Things you might like to consider

(i) Scenarios become stories which convey complex information very easily. They are an excellent way of communicating strategic opportunities and challenges.

(ii) Scenarios, unlike more generally recognized market analysis techniques, allow for uncertainty, choice, and risk. They are much better than, say, a market audit, at capturing the essence of the complexities and vagaries of a market.

(iii) Scenarios create a language and perspective for executives at all levels in an organization. They can become de facto frameworks for planning and decision making. If marketers use them, their work can influence other functions very effectively.

Ericsson develops service scenarios

Ericsson is a leading provider of telecommunications equipment and related services to mobile and fixed network operators across the world, operating in over 140 countries with over 130,000 employees. In the 1990s, the company recognized that, to maintain its leadership over time, it would need to shift from a product-orientated to a more service driven culture. Further, this culture must be prepared to compete in an increasingly complex, and therefore uncertain, convergent technology industry.

BACKGROUND

Growing beyond its relatively small, local market in Sweden, Ericsson had developed into a truly global firm before many Western companies. As a result, it developed a culture that accommodated a reasonable degree of local-market, organizational input. Still, like other telecom equipment manufacturers, it had succeeded in part because it had established an efficiently streamlined, centralized command structure. The organization and culture were geared to the logistics of undifferentiated product manufacturing and distribution.

However, as the communications industry converged with the information technology industry, Ericsson was increasingly required to deal with more complex and faster changing products and markets. Ericsson's traditional "fixed-lines", or "wire-line", business had been augmented and changed by its mobile business. And the company had been required to establish a position in the Internet Protocol (IP) networking market.

These products required the company to provide increasingly sophisticated and varied support at its many different customer locations. To maintain its competitiveness, Ericsson believed that it needed to change its culture, particularly to make it more distributed and responsive in its decision making. As scenario planning engaged employees throughout an organization in open-minded thought about possible, uncertain futures, the scenario-planning process was deemed an especially appropriate vehicle for Ericsson's work.

THE PROCESS GETS UNDERWAY

Employee involvement was considered to be the most important element in Ericsson's planning process and for that process to be of greater importance than any specific predictions or ideas that might come from it. Not only was broad employee participation actively sought, but the team also solicited outside ideas and perspectives to enrich the scenario planning. However, external input was kept in check so that the initiative and results of the project belonged to the company and its employees. The process also involved discussions of:

- elements of the wider environment, including global, social, and economic factors;
- certain and uncertain factors.

In addition, Ericsson identified eight driving forces that it judged to be certain and critical factors within its future market:

- Increasingly capable microelectronics
- Computer paradigm expansion
- The internet
- Consumer orientation
- Globalization and internationalization

- Mobility
- Continuing deregulation of telecommunications
- Increasingly blurred boundaries between the fields of telecommunications, media, and data.

However, Ericsson considered the timing and specific direction of these forces to be uncertain and variable, particularly in different geographic regions.

One baseline assumption that Ericsson had made was strongly reinforced by all this evaluation: the telecom, IT, and media industries were universally expected to continue converging into one combined industry, which Ericsson called the "Infocom" industry.

The next step was to classify those trends that were possible, but not certain, within three clusters of direction in which it believed its industry could develop. Each of these three "scenarios" formed an internally consistent world as it might evolve. Interestingly, Ericsson did not believe that any one of these scenarios would prevail completely. Rather, it believed that some mixture of these three trends would manifest itself, and that that mix would vary by product segment, geographic region, and time. However, services played an important and growing role in each of the three scenarios that Ericsson developed.

THE THREE SCENARIOS

These scenarios would form the platform for further work within the planning process. They were:

- **"Service Mania"**. In this scenario, end users (individuals as well as companies) would turn to a broker for help in gaining access to an appropriate package containing information and interactive services.
- **"Gran Tradizione"**. If this trait controlled developments, the end customer would rely on his or her traditional operator to provide the basic services he or she considered essential, and purchase the necessary terminal equipment.
- **"Up and Away-Full Speed Ahead"**. In this scenario, end users would gain access to advanced communications systems virtually free of charge; as a rule, they would pay only for the terminal equipment. The manufacturers of the equipment would pay for the communications and for end users' access to the communications network. Advertising would cover the cost of the content as well as gateways. This "Futurenet", a broadband network, would handle everything: multi-media, video, television broadcasts, ordinary telephone calls, etc. A significant percentage of end users would prefer wireless access to the Futurenet, since this would not involve any limitation either of the services offered or of the system's "functionality."

STRATEGIC AND ORGANIZATIONAL DIRECTION

As a result of this, Ericsson identified itself as a "total solutions" firm, and accordingly repositioned itself on the industry's value chain:

- By the turn of the century Ericsson had positioned itself as a full service telecom outsourcer in selected markets, with its greatest success to date posted in its Enterprise Systems business unit.
- The company had taken steps to divest itself of a number of manu-facturing functions (e.g., outsourcing cable assembly tasks to Volex and a number of circuit-board manufacturing responsibilities to Flextronics).
- Ericsson had identified mobile internet access as a core capability by which to leverage the firm's mobile strengths within an IP world.
- The company had formed a consortium with other key players to develop the Wireless Application Protocol (WAP) for furthering the development of mobile internet capabilities.

This case study is published with the permission of ITSMA.

RATING: Practical and powerful

SECTOR MARKETING

Application: strategy, communications, sales, NPD

The concept

Sector marketing is an approach which involves the construction of programmes around the knowledge of a particular industrial sector. It is routinely found in *business-to-business marketing*, where firms, of all shapes and sizes, have "line of business" or "industry" specialists who focus on different industrial sectors. They try to understand issues within it and to customize their firm's offer to businesses within them. This can range from, on one hand, an informal grouping of professionals across the firm who take an interest in an industrial sector to, on the other hand, a highly qualified specialist designing well researched and well funded marketing programmes. Many companies put significant investment into initiatives which demonstrate their under-standing of a sector. It may involve research into trends commissioned by marketers with deep knowledge of a sector or dissemination of the deep knowledge of an expert. Merchant banks, for instance, tend to send out to senior people frequent updates on structural changes in a particular market. Many board level people appreciate these insights and read them avidly.

There are several reasons why sector marketing is valuable:

(i) Perspective

Part of the value to buyers of outside advisors or suppliers is the perspective they develop from handling the problems of several companies in the same industry sector. Business customers are often curious about how they stand when compared to peers and have an open ear to issues or trends that outsiders can spot from such deep engagement. They will even attend confidential discussion sessions and briefing programmes with competitors present if facilitated by a supplier they trust and if there are clear rules for the meeting.

(ii) Opportunity

Such a powerful position as industry expert is a very rich source of sales projects and fees. There is, however, a greater reason for deep knowledge of the sector in which customers operate. Buyers rarely know the full scope of the products or services offered by a supplier and often have latent needs, which, they think, cannot be resolved easily. They may not have even formulated them into potential projects or a request for proposal. An account manager or consultant, who understands the priorities of firms working in a sector, is likely to spot these latent needs and identify those that their firm can meet. They can then create projects, as yet unimagined by the buyer, to solve problems they identity through sector knowledge.

(iii) Empathy

Consultancies and other professional service firms tend to base their sales approach on "industry knowledge"; familiarity with the industrial sector in which the buyer works. As problem diagnosis is at the heart of the consultative approach, clients need to be reassured that the consultants with whom they work have a deep personal knowledge of their industry. So, most consultancies have a sector approach to organizing their practices. Very often there will be a "practice head" who leads a group of specialists dedicated to a business sector such as telecommunications, computing, or banking. Unlike field sales organizations, this organization is not really interested in efficiency within a defined territory. "Virtual" teams can be dedicated to an industry's specific problem from across the world. For them, the incremental revenue that can be gained from greater industry knowledge outweighs any consideration of the number of "sales calls" that can be achieved in any one day.

As sector focus affects all methods of marketing communication (from proposals and beauty parades to PR and digital marketing) it is sensible to develop a clear communications strategy to tackle it. What are the buzz-words in the intended industrial sector? Who do they respect, what do they believe (however daft), and what progressive learning has there been in their little corner of the industrial landscape? People in financial services, technology, luxury goods, public service, and pharmaceuticals have very different views and assumptions. What are they?

There is then a very important decision to be made. Is the marketer going to adopt the technical language of the herd? Marketing agencies frequently complain that they are asked to use jargon in their work and boast about how they brought common sense and simple English to a communication piece. Yet that may not be the right thing to do. If buyers in an industrial sector are wedded to certain words and use them to represent their strategies and assumptions, then they have to be used. In fact, demonstrating that you understand, that you are part of the herd, is an important way of displaying that most important essential element of good marketing and income growth: empathy. You simply cannot develop relationships, pitch, or advise if you cannot communicate.

There is an alternative strategy though. Sometimes it is possible to shock or gain attention with one piece of communication which deliberately misuses industry language. Some organizations set out to challenge and shake up markets. In consumer markets companies as different as Virgin, First Direct, and Apple have deliberately cut a lone and different path. It is striking, too, that in nearly all the professions, respected and outstanding performers exist who are contrarians, standing out from the crowd.

History, context, criticism, and development

Business leaders and marketers have distinguished between the needs of different business types for some time. As described in the *business-to-business* entry, for example, British technology pioneers, Boulton and Watt, focused their new steam pumps on the needs of mining, brewing, public sector sanitation, and clothing manufacture (to name but a few). It was a deliberate attempt to craft features and benefits to different business communities and would have been called sector marketing if the term had existed then.

Voices and further reading

- "... the starting point is the question of which industry to serve, followed by a series of decisions on customer size and purchase criteria. This methodology has been employed to great effect by, among others, IBM . . . they segment the market by commercial type: banking, transportation, insurance, processing industry and so on . . ." Wilson, R.M.S., Gilligan, C., and Pearson, D.J., *Strategic Marketing Management*. Butterworth-Heinemann, 1992.

- "SIC codes are used by direct marketers to segment lists and to target promotions . . . What the code cannot tell the direct marketer is whether a business is engaged only in that activity defined by the SIC code or whether the code represents only a primary business activity. If the latter is the case, there may be other marketing opportunities pertaining to that firm not identified by the SIC code." Imbler, J. and Toffler, B., 2000.
- "An efficient method of estimating area market potential makes use of the standard industrial classification (SIC) system, developed by the U.S. bureau of the census. The SIC classes all manufacturing in 20 major industry groups, each with a two-digit code . . . we must be careful not to confuse a segment and a sector." Kotler, P., *Marketing Management*. Prentice Hall, 2003 (11th edn).

Things you might like to consider

(i) Companies often use SIC (standard industry classifications) to define their approach to sectors. These are, though, set by statisticians and economists in government departments. Are they really the best source for teasing out insight into the common needs of groups of companies? Do they need to be modified? They might not be appropriate or effective representations of the views and wishes of a group of companies.

(ii) Industry sectors can break down as new technologies change categorizations. As a result it can be difficult to tell which company is in which industry sector. For example, some retailers are moving into banking, so are they now in the financial services sector? And, with the convergence of telecommunications and computing, exactly what sectors are internet retailers or publishing companies in?

(iii) Often, the definition of industrial groups is so broad as to make it meaningless in terms of marketing issues. In addition, not all businesses within the same industry sector will have the same requirements. For example, a firm trying to sell new training concepts or management consultancy might be better placed to identify "innovative" companies receptive to new ideas. Yet this promising segment could be in any industry sector.

 RATING: Merely conceptual

⌕ SEGMENTATION

Application: strategy, communication, positioning, NSD/NPD

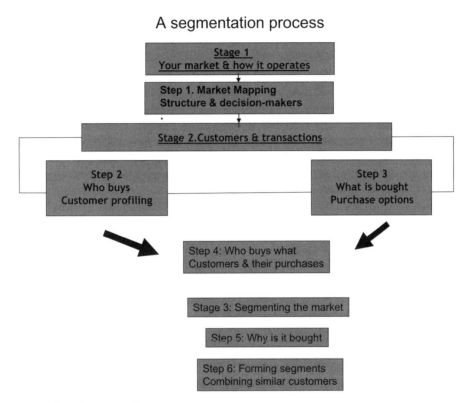

Figure S.1:   A suggested segmentation process

The concept

The segmentation of markets into groups of buyers which can be easily reached by suppliers is a powerful concept which has improved the profit of many businesses. It suggests that buyers can be grouped around common needs. Then, by customizing the firm's offer to meet those common needs, suppliers can both gain competitive advantage and save costs because they are only addressing a portion of the market. Customer segmentation is one of the fundamental building blocks of marketing. It is the basis of: effective marketing communication, innovative offers, and appealing brands. The human insight which follows from deep knowledge of a group of human beings is the source of real competitive advantage. Segmentation, to some extent, *is* marketing.

There appear to be few developed and well accepted approaches to producing effective segmentation. Some advertising agencies arrive at it through creative insight, more logical minds through a review of patterns in data, while others observe and analyse behaviours. The process shown in Figure S.1 was published by Professor Malcolm McDonald (McDonald, M.H.B., 1998). In a very practical book he argued that marketers should first define and map their generic market. They should then take an objective view of the customers and their buying behaviour before doing detailed *research*.

Experience suggests that marketers should approach this with an idea of how they think their market might segment; with an hypothesis. They will need to think about how customers behave and discuss different attitudes or behaviours that they have observed. Eventually they will reach an hypothesis which can be tested. The marketer should then create a set of "segmentation dimensions" by which these differences will manifest themselves. Segmentation dimensions are the ways in which the buyers will behave towards the firm and its offers. As far as possible, they should be values, beliefs, or cultural biases (whether amongst consumers or *organizations*) because they determine behaviour. These can then be scaled using sensible scoring of the extremes. For example, if a supplier was segmenting a *business-to-business* market on the basis of "organization style", they might hypothesize that there are centralized and de-centralized organizations. This would manifest itself in different business practices, one of which would be purchasing style and this would become a segmentation dimension. For a centralized organization, buying would be controlled by a central purchasing department, whereas in a de-centralized organization it would be devolved to business units. If the segmentation is effective, each group will exhibit these in different ways.

The hypothesis can first be tested by examining any existing customers and scoring their behaviour against segmentation dimensions. It should be possible to conduct a fast, inexpensive test on the validity of the dimensions, where different clusters appear. If no clustering is apparent in this first test, then new dimensions, or maybe a new hypothesis, need to be created. Any clustering should be confirmed with direct *research*. This is best conducted in two phases: first, a qualitative phase, testing the dimension in depth with a few potential customers; secondly, a large quantitative project using a trade-off technique such as conjoint research. Through this method different clusters of potential buyer groups will become evident. Again, if clustering does not appear the marketer should revisit the initial hypothesis. However, research itself is not really sufficient to confirm such an important phenomenon as customer segmentation. Potential segments should also be confirmed in a more practical way, imitating as far as possible the rough and tumble of the real market place. A number of test marketing programmes should be designed in order to ensure that the buyers identify with the proposed groups that they are in and respond to propositions specifically designed for them.

Marketers should then create a full investment and marketing implementation plan. Segmentation has implications to: the market proposition for each group, the ideal method of marketing communication, sales strategy, IT systems, operational processes, pricing, and the most appropriate customer service methods for each group. Taken seriously, it affects every aspect of the way the firm approaches its intended market. Each aspect needs to be carefully thought through, costed, and built into all the operational plans of the business. This needs to be treated like any other hard-headed investment strategy. The pros and cons, benefits, and return on investment need to be assessed and drawn together into an investment plan, which should be submitted to the appropriate leadership team for formal approval. As part of imple-mentation of the plan, everyone in the organization will eventually need to be familiar with the new segments and how they should be handled.

Clear tests have been developed to check whether a particular segmentation is appropriate for a particular company in a particular market. They include:

- **Homogeneity:** To what extent will the members of the segment act in the same way?
- **Measurability:** How big and valuable is the segment?
- **Accessibility:** Is it possible to reach the segment with marketing or sales programmes?
- **Profitability:** Is the segment substantial enough for the supplier to profit from?
- **Attractiveness or relevance:** Is the segment something customers will want to identify with?

History, context criticism, and development

There have been several methods of consumer segmentation developed and publicized over the past decades. They include:

Demographics and socioeconomics: The grouping of people according to physical characteristics (age, sex) or circumstances (income, occupation, or education). This is commonly used in developed nations. In the US and Europe, for example, there is currently much emphasis on the design of products and services for ageing populations.

Life stage: This is a more precise form of demographics. It groups buyers according to the phase they have reached in their life such as "married", "home building", or "retired". They might become "freedom seekers", "dropouts", or "tra-ditionalists" according to their phase of life.

Psychographics: The grouping of people according to various personal char-acteristics such as personality or social class. In the 1980s, for instance, the "British National Readership Survey" categorized the population as "A" (higher managerial), "B" (middle class), "C" (lower middle class), and "D" (working class). However, this has now broken down.

Geographic/location: Grouping people according to their country of birth or area of residence. This can focus on the region, population density, and climate. It can involve county, town, or even street.

Behavioural or attitudinal: Grouping according to a particular behaviour which may affect product usage or price sensitivity, or values and attitudes. A good example was created by the marketing agency McCann-Erickson in the latter half of the 20th century. It identified: "avant guardians" (concerned with change and well being), "pontificators" (who have strongly held traditional views), and "self-exploiters" (who have high self-esteem).

"Tribal": A specific example of behavioural segmentation which groups customers according to the social groups or cultures with which they identify. For example, in the 1990s, one of Europe's premier television companies, the BBC, started to commission programmes for tribes in society (such as young, independent women) based on how they communicate and live.

Benefits sought: The grouping of people according to the advantages they are seeking from the product or service. For instance, as early as 1968, Russell Haley (Haley, R.I., 1968) published segmentation for the toothpaste market based on this approach. Customers were in the "sensory" segment (seeking flavour or product appearance) or the "sociable" segment (seeking brightness of teeth), or the "worriers" (seeking decay prevention).

Lifestyle: Grouping customers by a common approach to life. One famous example of this type of segmentation was developed by Young & Rubican in the 1980s. It was this advertising agency which developed, among others, the famous, but now defunct term, "Yuppie" (Young Urban Professional). Incidentally, this also illustrates an important point about customer segmentation: it dates easily. Whereas people revelled in being a Yuppie in the early 1980s, it is now considered out-of-date and unattractive.

Context: Proposed by Professor Paul Fifield in the early 1990s (Fifield, P., 1992), this method groups customers according to the context in which they use a product or service. It focuses attention on things that bring people together, exploiting shared interests. For instance, one cursory glance at people on a fishing bank will show that they have little in common other than the sport itself.

Business-to-business segmentation types have included:

Industry sector: Grouping businesses according to the industry in which they specialize. These sectors are often formally set by government economists as a means of defining and recording activities in different areas of the economy (see *sector marketing*).

Organization style: Grouping businesses according to the culture or prevailing climate of the company. They may be centralized or de-centralized or "innovative" versus "conservative". The Myers Briggs organizational types ("fraternal", "collegial", "bureaucratic", or "entrepreneurial") have, for example, been used as a basis for segmentation;

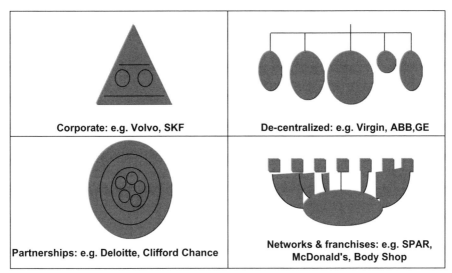

Basis for the segmentation: business culture

Corporate: e.g. Volvo, SKF	De-centralized: e.g. Virgin, ABB,GE
Partnerships: e.g. Deloitte, Clifford Chance	Networks & franchises: e.g. SPAR, McDonald's, Body Shop

Figure S.2: An hypothesis for business-to-business segmentation based on organizational style

Organizational size: Grouping businesses according to the number of employees, assets, or revenue.

Organizational structure: Grouping businesses according to the way they choose to organize and structure their company. There are significant differences (as illustrated in Figure S.2) which can be used to create effective segmentation programmes.

Company life cycle: Companies, like product groups, seem to have "life cycles" through which they evolve. They go from birth to death at different rates, struggling to get through "inflection points" to increase revenue and margin. They have similar characteristics (e.g. management style) in each phase and this has been used as a basis for segmentation.

Industry maturity: Industries and markets also move through different phases (see market maturity). For instance, in developed economies, their agricultural or manufacturing industries are at a different phase of evolution to, say, biotechnology. The phase of growth affects the behaviour of suppliers in it and has also been used as a basis for segmentation.

Context: As with consumers, grouping businesses according to the context in which they use the product or service.

Needs–/benefits–based: Based on underlying needs or benefits sought by the company from its suppliers.

Voices and further reading

- McDonald, M.H.B. and Dunbar, I., *Market Segmentation: How to Do it, How to Profit from it*. MacMillan, 1998.
- "Segmentation is a creative and iterative process, the purpose of which is to satisfy customer needs more closely and, in so doing, create competitive advantage for the company. It is defined by customers' needs and requirements, not the company's, and should be revisited periodically. The importance of segmentation to any business should not be underestimated." McDonald and Dunbar, ibid.
- "Segmentation variables can be broadly classified into two categories: identifier and response. Identifier variables begin by segmenting the market based on who the customers are . . . in contrast, post hoc segmentation starts by using response variables to divide the market on the basis of how customers behave." Kumar, N., 2004.
- "Segmentation is a critical aspect of corporate strategy. It is essential in visualizing the competitive arena and analyzing the preferred strategic emphasis. The goal is to find a way to convert differences from competitors into a cost differential that can be maintained." Stern, L. in *The Boston Consulting Group on Strategy*. John Wiley & Sons Inc., 2006.
- "Whether within or across national boundaries, effective market segmentation delineates segments whose members are similar to one another in one or more characteristics and different from other segments." Solomon, M. et al., 2006.
- Sternthal, B. and Tybout, A.M., "Segmentation and targeting" in Iacobucci, D. (ed.), *Kellogg on Marketing*. 2001.

Things you might like to consider

(i) There are many ways to segment any one market. Like a Rubik's cube, the marketer needs to find their own effective segmentation for their own unique position in their market.

(ii) It is professionally wrong and very limiting to regard products as segments. There is no such thing as a "big systems market" or the "executive car market". There are human beings who buy these things and they have a multiplicity of different needs, wants, and aspirations.

(iii) People have a herd instinct and can identify with a segment. If the target group can be expanded by people who aspire to belong, demand for the proposition will be increased.

(iv) In the past few decades, marketing thinkers have begun to emphasize the "market of one" and mass customization. It is argued that companies need to respond to each individual need. Whilst Amazon has been able to create and deploy technology which is able to take this approach, many have not. There is little evidence that people are ceasing to follow trends and behave without group mentality, so, at the time of writing, the segmentation concept does not yet seem to be debunked.

 RATING: Practical and powerful

 # SERVICE QUALITY

Application: part of marketing mix, strategic defence, proactive relationship building, part of a service offer

The concept

The concepts and policies of service quality have several different generic names: "customer care", "after care", "the after market", "service recovery", and "customer experience management". All capture the fact that the experience of a product or service can contribute to how well or badly a business does in its market. It is a marketing issue because it affects the growth of the firm. A poor experience will undermine any marketing, no matter how good, because negative word-of-mouth will work against any marketing claims.

There are a number of quality issues that need to be understood and acted upon, including the type of after care being offered and how it resonates with customers, the determinants of customer expectations, and all the different aspects that make up the firm's relationships with them. This is not a vague or imprecise after thought, nor is it an unrefined, passionate desire to give buyers everything they want. As in every other area of marketing, the design of strategies and processes which produce an appropriate service experience and excellent after care is essentially very practical. This is as much about setting policy and installing processes as any other aspect of sensible marketing.

Customer care and service quality are important for several reasons. First, service quality affects the attitude of buyers toward repurchase. If they have a good experience they are more likely to buy again and, if a poor experience, they are less likely. This simple fact can be surprisingly neglected and mismanaged by even the largest and most well intentioned firms. Secondly, customers may judge the service they receive on different criteria from that of the provider. Whereas the marketer might focus on product performance, technical expertise or, say, speed of execution, the customer might value "bedside manner", the way they are treated and the perceived attitude of employees, just as highly. In fact, the latter can cause customers to question the former, if unsatisfactory.

Academic researchers have explored the effect of quality of service initiatives on the propensity of people to repurchase from the same supplier. Their particular initial area of interest was in transactional measures, such as satisfaction surveys, which are often sent to buyers asking for an opinion of the way they performed or, say, left in an hotel room for visitors to complete. They found that these are, generally, poorly designed research questionnaires, asking the wrong questions about the wrong issues and giving no manageable data which the supplier could use to improve service still further. Worse, they found that it cannot be assumed that satisfied buyers will return to buy again. They found that there was very little evidence that good quality of service increased the propensity of people to buy again. It was quite possible for a buyer to be entirely satisfied with service and yet next time buy from an alternative supplier because there is a better *value proposition*. Many now argue that quality of service feedback mechanisms must therefore look at underlying motivations and tease out the rational and emotional needs that buyers want satisfied.

Some recent specialists have suggested that the customers' reaction to service quality induces *loyalty* to the supplier, which can be measured and managed. Frederick Reicheld (Reicheld, F., 2003), has even suggested that it is the "only measure necessary". Whatever the reality of these claims, marketers need to determine which issues influence their customers' views sufficiently to enhance or degrade reputation. They have to understand the components of the service which lead to repeat business and referrals (and thus future revenues) and which processes or techniques should be employed to improve them.

As a result of recent history, a number of concepts, policies and, frankly, ill-founded beliefs have built up around the concept of service quality and customer care. There is lexicography around the subject which rests in the back of the mind of many senior executives, affecting policy formulation. Before constructing a strategy or integrating service quality concepts into marketing programmes, marketers should take a clear-headed view of these concepts. They are:

(i) Total quality management (TQM)

This approach to quality came to prominence in the West during the 1980s, led by prominent specialists such as Edward Deming, Joseph Juran, and Philip Crosby. It can dramatically improve customers' experience of products and services. Analytical in emphasis, it suggests that quality issues should be resolved prior to affecting operations, not checked and counted after they occur. It calculates the cost of quality" in the organization and sets out to reduce failure in a systematic way, using multi-disciplined teams of people. In fact, the prime aim of a TQM system is "zero defects, achieved by progressively examining smaller and smaller errors in an objective and numerate way, using a range of specialist techniques. Its "kaizen" principle of continuous improvement based on analysis, "quality circles" (mixed discussion groups), and open suggestion boxes, are fundamental to its success and must be supported by senior management. Where TQM is particularly powerful is in its philosophy of engaging the whole organization in guaranteeing and improving quality. If companies have a serious quality problem, then marketers can use this approach as a rallying cry for the whole organization.

(ii) "Six Sigma"

Six Sigma, an extension of TQM, was pioneered by Motorola and Allied Signal, although it rose to prominence when implemented by GE in the 1990s. It is a measurement-based strategy that focuses on process improvement by applying a model of: "design, measure, analyse, improve and control". It appears to have helped many manufacturing companies improve the quality and effectiveness of their operations.

(iii) Moments of truth

A moment of truth is any moment of interface between a buyer and the firm. These range from interfaces with customer service, reception, and support employees through to administrative processes like invoicing or contracts. All can positively or negatively affect customers' impression of the service, enhancing or damaging reputation. It is sensible to conduct a periodic review of all moments of truth to ensure that all contribute to the health of the firm. Introduced in the 1980s this is very similar to "customer experience management".

(iv) The perceived transaction period

This is the time that the buyer thinks they are engaged with the supplier. Service issues arise if the customer thinks that their engagement with the supplier is longer or shorter than the supplier does.

(v) Employee behaviour and emotional empathy

"Emotional empathy" is the term used by service strategists to ensure that employees who serve customers are competent and responsive. This not only means that they listen to the needs of people but also that they demonstrate empathy; that their tone of voice and demeanour show that they sympathize. Interactions need to be warm and flexible, encouraging positive interchanges between people. If a dull, mechanistic approach is taken, buyers will not respond positively to their experience and will, ultimately, move away. As important, but more difficult, this sense of spontaneity needs to continue after the honeymoon period of the initial launch of any new or improved service.

(vi) Empowerment

Uncertainties about script and boundary can be very damaging to the relationship between customer and supplier. One of the roles of employees is to know when and where they can deviate from the script and break rules to give buyers better service without affecting the overall efficiency of operations. So, operational procedures should "empower" front office workers to meet any unforeseen needs by giving them the right to make concessions, within a controlled framework. "Empowerment" is the discretion given to employees to respond to individual customer needs. This concept arose as service organizations needed to communicate their desire to respond to service needs and in response to strong evidence that any inflexibility in employees' behaviour damages both reputation and future business. John Bateson (Bateson and Hoffman, 1999) suggests that there are three levels to it:

- **Routine discretion**, where employees are given a list of alternative actions to choose from;
- **Creative discretion**, which requires an employee to create a list of alternatives as well as choosing between them;
- **Deviant discretion**, which expects people to do things which are not part of their job description or management's expectations.

The latter are normally most noticed and appreciated by buyers. Yet, if good service depends on experienced employees consistently breaking the rules, the marketer has not done their job properly. They should ensure that concessions are recorded, so that the fundamental processes of the organization can be re-examined in the light of the type and frequency of concession.

(vii) Delight factor

A term which is closely related to Tom Peters (Peters, T.J. and Waterman, R.H., 1982), and which sets out to measure the emotional pleasure or pleasant surprise given to customers by a service experience; some even claim that they have "customer delight measures". The long-term problem with this is twofold. First, it builds cost into the business. Secondly, it introduces an upward spiral of exceeding expectations, with expectations being increased and delivery having to be increased further still. This eventually becomes unsustainable, and the momentum of the company to provide excellent service eventually runs out. Nearly all the examples held up in Peters' original book have, for example, had massive difficulties since publication, damaging the crux of his thesis.

A practical alternative would be to use communication and marketing techniques to lower expectations. The chief executive of cut price airline, Ryanair, is continually making controversial announcements about planned changes to their policy. They considered charging overweight people more, charging to use the toilet on a flight, and for very precise excess baggage. Many of these ruminations do not actually get implemented but it sets the expectations of potential passengers very low. Some are pleasantly surprised when the experience of such cheap travel is not as bad as they feared.

(viii) Customer experience management (CEM)

This is a relatively new term which, at the time of writing, seems to have no clear or generally accepted definition, leaving room for a number of different interpretations. Some think that it is quite simple: every time a company and a customer interact, the customer learns something about the company that will either strengthen or weaken the future relationship. This accumulated experience will affect that customer's desire to return, spend more, and recommend it to others.

Others distinguish it from generic customer service. They point out that even if customers are served well, they might still buy from competitors next time. They see customer service as limited to the quality of the last transaction but CEM as a framework for building an organizational capability to deliver a distinctive service experience. Much of their writing emphasizes the need for the service experience to deliver the promises raised by customers' perception of the company's brand; a practical application of the brand integrity concept (see *brand*).

(ix) Personalization

This concept argues that, in the modern world, consumers expect communication and service to be personalized to themselves through the smart use of technology. Pre-eminent in this is Amazon, a company that has driven personalization of service on a technical infrastructure to new heights through its Amazon.com experience. With the combination of technological sophistication and proliferation of messages and products competing for consumers' attention, the idea that "you no longer find products and services, they find you" is becoming reality through Amazon's approach. Even consumer product companies are adopting this approach. Nike, for instance, has its NikeID facility, through which customers can design their own trainers, adapting the colours and features to suit their personal preferences.

History, context, criticism, and development

Some proponents of service quality concepts normally suggest that an emphasis on customer care was not necessary before the 20th century and only developed as consumerism grew. That is not the case though. For instance, British Potter Josiah Wedgwood routinely used international direct marketing in the 18th century. His offers included a "money back guarantee" and free replacement of breakages, despite there being such poor infrastructure for transporting dinner services. American processed food producer, Henry Heinz, saw lobbying for quality as a foundation for the creation of his brand in the 19th century.

A remarkable example is Chicago's "up-market store" entrepreneur, Marshall Field, who built a service business on outstanding courtesy and quality at the start of the 20th century. The store offered a money back guarantee and was publicly committed to a "guarantee of satisfaction". Sales were backed by courteous, unquestioning service. Greeters were employed to meet shoppers at the State Street entrance and expected to learn the names of returning customers. Sales people were instructed to be attentive and courteous to every person they encountered, no matter how lowly they appeared to be dressed and were prohibited from using aggressive sales techniques (see Koehn, N.F., 2001).

Early theoretical work also stressed service. One of the first marketing text books (White, P., 1927) dedicates a whole chapter to the marketer's responsibility for service and after care; and says that the marketing trend was "towards giving greater service and the establishment of competition upon a service and price basis".

It seems that difficulty occurred as distribution chains grew and marketing was functionalized in the mid 20th century. As a result, leaders of businesses became more remote from their customers' experience of their products and marketers grew distant from the responsibility for service quality. In the latter half of the 20th century, this began to change as the result of a number of developments. They included:

(i) An evolution in customers' standards and expectations, prompting a rise in consumerism after the austerity of the mid–century world-wide conflict.

(ii) The then-steady decline in the performance of much of Western manufacturing in the light of the success of certain Asian, particularly Japanese, companies.

(iii) Emphasis on after care and service in some sectors, particularly retail and computing. One of the early examples was British retailer Marks & Spencer. They gained market leadership and the affections of the entire nation for many decades because of a commitment to service. In the mid 20th century, a time when consumer spending power in Britain was beginning to increase again, they met one of the emotional needs of their buyers with a money back guarantee. This meant that consumers were happy to buy and felt a warmth and loyalty to the company, which underpinned their profits for many years to come.

In business-to-business, IBM made similar strides through quality commitments in the early computer industry. It met an emotional need amongst business buyers when the technology was new and unstable by using leasing to finance many of its early sales. This made it easy and low risk for buyers to invest in the new technology. It also put enormous emphasis on the quality of its maintenance and installation work. This approach has given the company world-wide market leadership for nearly thirty years.

(iv) The publicity gained in the 1980s by several populist writers and speakers on service quality, particularly Tom Peters (Peters, T., 1982), who modelled the dynamics of successful businesses, creating general principles out of case studies. His primary emphasis was on quality of service and customer care. He thought that much Western business had moved away from an emphasis on serving their buyers and had lost world leadership as a result.

(v) Certain well publicized, dramatic improvements in service which affected the share price of the firms involved. Two dramatic examples were in the European airline industry. One was BA and the other SAS.

BA famously improved its market position with a service quality programme called "putting people first". The importance of excellent service to passengers was stressed and barriers to such service were removed from the employees. This was one aspect of a broader marketing programme which encompassed a new brand initiative and new quality measures, based on extensive market research. Before the programme, BA had a terrible reputation for punctuality, was beset by industrial disputes, and was losing substantial money (£140 million in 1981). A decade later, it was not only popular with customers, it was the world's most profitable airline. Although there were clearly other factors which contributed to this performance (see, for example Gruglis and Wilkinson, 2001) the impact of the programme caught management attention throughout the world.

At SAS, the new chief executive of this Scandinavian airline, Jan Carlzon, introduced a similar programme under the banner "moments of truth". Carlzon introduced a company-wide programme to enhance all moments of truth, which had a major impact on the company's market position. In one year, the airline became the most punctual in Europe and the first choice of its intended segment (business travellers). Just as important, though, corporate overheads were reduced 25% and before tax profit went from a loss of $10 million to a profit of $70 million (Vandermerwe, S., 1988).

(vi) The publication of a number of influential research reports. One was, for example, conducted by TARP (Technical Assistance and Research Programmes) in the United States and Canada, for the White House Office of Consumer Affairs. Interestingly, this research has become part of management rhetoric and is still, often unknowingly, quoted at conferences because, at the time, it was given so much attention. The work, which interviewed 200 companies, showed that:

- The average business did not hear from 96% of its unhappy customers;
- For every complaint received, there were twenty-six other people with problems and six with serious problems;

- People with problems who failed to complain were far less likely to repeat their orders and were likely to stop completely their business with that supplier;
- People who complained and whose problems were handled well were much more likely to continue doing business;
- People with bad experiences were twice as likely to tell others about it as those with good experiences.

(vii) Substantive academic analysis and research. This combination of factors attracted the attention of management throughout Western businesses and put a spotlight on quality of service principles; so, for a period of time, service quality and customer care became a popular management fad. Some of the stories told of employees delighting customers were so anarchic that a number of concerned academics set out to research the field and develop credible principles that could be applied within it. For instance, Sri Parasuraman and a group of academics that specialize in services marketing produced their "*GAP model*" (Parasuraman, S. et al., 1985) as an analytical tool; Heskett and Sasser applied value chain analysis to service businesses with the "service profit chain" (Heskett et al., 1997) and Fredrick Reicheld published on his "loyalty effect" (Reicheld, F., 2006). Although each has been evaluated, tested, and critiqued since, they provide a range of practical management concepts which ensure that service quality issues can be tackled in as pragmatic and realistic a way as any other aspect of business.

(viii) Public metrics of service quality were then developed. The American Customer Satisfaction Index (ACSI) is an economic indicator that measures the satisfaction of consumers across the US economy. Set up in 1994, it is produced by the National Quality research centre, University of Michigan. The ACSI interviews about 80,000 Americans annually and asks about their satisfaction with the goods and services they have consumed. Respondents are screened to cover a wide range of consumer products and services, including goods, services, local government services, and federal government agencies. The results are published each quarter. The programme measures customer satisfaction for more than 200 companies in forty-three industries and ten sectors. The ACSI aims to represent the satisfaction of the "average American consumer". It was based on a model originally set up in Sweden, in 1989, called the Swedish Customer Satisfaction Barometer (SCSB) and versions now exist in other countries. The UK version, for example, is based on a representative sample of 25,000 adults surveyed over the internet. The British Institute of Customer Service calls its version the UK Customer Satisfaction Index (UKCSI).

Voices and further reading

- "Services are performances and people are the performers. From the customers' perspective, the people performing the service are the company. An incompetent insurance agent is an incompetent insurance company." Berry, L.L., 1995.

- Luchs, R., "Successful businesses compete on quality – not costs". *Long Range Planning*, February 1986.
- Zeithaml, V.A., Parasuraman, A., and Berry, L.L., "Problems and strategies in services marketing". *Journal of Marketing*, 1985.
- Szmigin, I., "Managing quality in business-to-business services". *European Journal of Marketing*, 1993.
- Schlesinger, L.D. and Heskett, J.L., "Breaking the cycle of failure in service". *Harvard Business Review*, March–April 1991.
- Rust, R.T. and Oliver, R.L., "Service quality". Sage, 1994.
- "Service quality is by nature a subjective concept, which means that understanding how the customer thinks about service quality is essential to effective management. Three related concepts are crucial to this understanding: customer satisfaction, service quality and customer value. . . . they are quite distinct, which has important implications for management and measurement. Rust and Oliver, ibid.
- DeSouza, G., "Now service businesses must manage quality". *Journal of Business Strategy*, May 1989.
- Zemke, R. and Woods, J.A.*, Best Practice in Customer Service*, Amacom, 1999.

Things you might like to consider

(i)   Prior to the functionalization of marketing in early 20th century America, many business leaders seem to have regarded after care and service quality as part of their marketing mix. CEM gets near to the application of marketing principles to service experience but it is not nearly enough. Service really ought to be the province of marketing and routinely understood by marketers.

(ii) There are moments (like with BA and the opening of Terminal 5 or BP and the oil spill disaster in the Gulf of Mexico) when a major service aberration affects the perception and profit of the whole firm. The rapid and immediate marketing strategy and activities in these circumstances is unique and critical. Marketing and PR have a crucial role to play in these circumstances. PR skills have to manage the relationship with the media and marketing people have to communicate with customers. A properly run, concerted effort can avoid catastrophic disaster.

British Airways ensures that its T5 disaster is not terminal

British Airways (BA) is one of the world's largest international airlines, carrying more than 33 million passengers worldwide in the twelve months to 31 March 2009. Together with its partners, BA flies to more than 300 destinations worldwide.

The airline's two main operating bases are London's two principal airports, Heathrow (one of the world's biggest international airports) and Gatwick. In 2008/09, it earned nearly £9 billion in revenue, up 2.7% on the previous year. Passenger traffic accounted for 87.1% of this revenue, while 7.5% came from cargo and 5.4% from other activities. At the end of March 2009, it had 245 aircraft in service.

As one of the world's longest established airlines, it has always been regarded as an industry leader. The company's commitment to customer service, and its strong brand, were perhaps two reasons why it was able to ride out the storm that occurred around the chaotic opening of Heathrow's Terminal 5 in 2008, and why it has since been able to recover its position and the goodwill of its customers.

SERVICE QUALITY HISTORY

In the airline market of the 1980s, passengers had a dreary time. Each airline's service was as bad as every other, providing stodgy food from harassed staff, with awful track records in luggage safety. It is even reported that some staff referred to their passengers as "SLC": self-loading cargo. Industry research at the time showed that frequent flyers would tolerate one airline for a while, then switch and switch again until they rotated back to the original carrier. Into this market came Colin Marshall from the ocean cruise market as MD of the recently privatized British Airways, a government-owned engineering-led service. Backed by his chairman, Lord King, he set out to revolutionize air travel through a massive customer care programme. Called "putting people first" it changed the fortunes of BA's service and had a dramatic impact on its profits. BA shot to market leadership and became "the world's favourite airline".

In the following years, BA became a watchword for service quality and an iconic case study for management thinkers. As time went by, though, (like many other firms that have attracted attention through exceptional quality initiatives) that heritage did not make it immune from the forces which buffeted its industry or errors. It has had difficulties from rising fuel prices, environmental pressure, and employee unrest. It has also muddled, for instance, its attempt to be "global" rather than British, earning negative publicity when Premier Margaret Thatcher threw a handkerchief over a model of its new, anodyne, tail plane designs. One dramatic and highly visible mistake was the opening of Terminal 5 at Heathrow.

DISASTER STRIKES AS T5 OPENS FOR BUSINESS

2008 was a difficult year for everyone, not least for airlines. In addition to the credit crisis that spread quickly from the US, the value of sterling plunged, consumer confidence collapsed, and companies like BA faced record fuel prices. Many went bust, including the UK's third largest travel operator, XL Airways, leaving 90,000 holidaymakers stranded abroad. The disastrous opening of Heathrow's Terminal 5 came in sharp contrast to an industry-defying, successful year for BA, as the airline reported great financial results with profits up 45% and operating margins up to an industry-leading 10%.

It started so well. The opening of Terminal 5 was the result of twenty years of planning. It was the largest construction project in Europe, and over £4 billion of investment. BA saw it as a chance to redefine air travel, "replacing the queues, crowds and stress with space, light and calm". It was the largest freestanding building in the UK, designed with both customers and sustainability in mind, and the promise that check-in would take less than five minutes.

A press release, embargoed to coincide with the touchdown of the first flight at the terminal, BA026 from Hong Kong, announced the opening of the terminal with its headline, "Celebrations as Terminal 5 opens for business". And yet, rather than the celebration envisaged, the opening gave way to one service failure after another, until images from Terminal 5 were transmitted around the world showing the chaos ensuing and damaging the reputation of BA.

A number of factors contributed to the service failures on the day, including:

* Baggage handlers and staff not being able to get into BAA car parks, consequently arriving late for work;
* Poor signage making it hard for BA staff to navigate the building;
* Terminal 5's computer system not recognizing staff identification cards, meaning that doors that should have opened remained locked;
* 17 out of the 18 terminal lifts jamming;
* The transit system moving passengers from the main terminal to Terminal 5 breaking down;
* A programming error preventing staff from logging onto the baggage system;
* The baggage handling system crashing;
* Staff with already low morale becoming stressed and unhelpful as the problems unfolded.

Passengers became frustrated by a lack of communication around the service failures. Baggage systems crashed and flights were cancelled and yet only two of the twenty-six information desks were operational. Some passengers arrived at the airport to be told their flights were delayed, while others were told their flight was cancelled when it was actually scheduled to take off.

By mid afternoon on 27 May BA had cancelled thirty-three of the 534 services it planned to operate from the terminal. In the early evening, passengers were told that no one would be allowed to fly with their hold baggage for the rest of the day. At one stage during the day, 28,000 bags were separated from their owners and 19,000 were sent to Milan to be sorted.

As a result, five days after the crisis, 250 flights had been cancelled and there was a backlog of 15,000 bags. Thousands of passengers had their travel plans disrupted, with some stranded for days, and BA were unable to find them hotel rooms.

Alistair Carmichael, a UK Member of Parliament, described the failure as, "a national disgrace, a national humiliation". More seriously for BA, with passenger choice set to increase, particularly on trans-Atlantic routes in the future, the risk of losing customers forever as a result of the fiasco was high.

WORK BEGINS TO RECOVER BOTH SERVICE AND REPUTATION

In sharp contrast to the celebratory press release issued the day before, BA CEO Willie Walsh apologized in a press release the following day, saying, "We disappointed many people and I apologise sincerely. I take responsibility for what happened. The buck stops with me."

Despite many of the service failures having their basis in issues to do with the terminal operator, BAA, throughout the crisis Walsh did not attempt to blame BAA, saying instead. ". . . there were a lot of angry customers out there. They buy their tickets from BA, not BAA, so we had to deal with it."

Later, when facing a Parliamentary Committee, Walsh acknowledged that risks had been sanctioned by him and that, with hindsight, the opening should have been delayed to allow for more training and familiarization for BA staff. He also announced that he would forgo his £700,000 bonus.

Work began to put right the operational issues that had caused the failures on the day. BA announced that they would appoint a new chief operations officer. The airline gave away thousands of free flights in a desperate attempt to retain passengers in the wake of the disaster. Walsh and chairman, Martin Broughton, both set aside time to personally review a significant number of customer letters and emails so that they could drive the necessary improvements to service.

Once the service failures were corrected, there was naturally a lag in public perception, with many people still assuming that Terminal 5 was a failure. To that end, the airline launched an advertising campaign to announce "Terminal 5 is working", backed by a series of metrics, released daily to prove the claim. The campaign initially ran across a seven-week period in July and August 2008, using a wide range of digital formats. Key metrics from the terminal, such as the percentage of flights departing on time, or the time taken to get through check-in, were sent to media owners at the end of the day before the ads were due to run. The emotions of customers were also drawn on, with roving reporters asking customers to say how they felt about Terminal 5, from a choice of "happy, excited, calm, impressed, frustrated, disappointed or angry". Their emotions featured on a web site, promoted through web and press advertising. Then head of BA global marketing communications, Katherine Whitton, explained. "As a premium service-driven organization, we understand that we need to deliver not only the rational benefits of flying, but also engage our customers emotionally."

THE HARD WORK PAYS OFF

The "Terminal 5 is working" advertising campaign resulted in 62% of respondents in a Millward Brown survey agreeing with key statements such as "most flights arrive on time" and 58% agreed that the ads made the brand seem more appealing. Readers of the UK's *Daily Telegraph* went so far as to vote the opening of Heathrow's Terminal 5 one of the travel highlights of the year, having "found its feet". At the end of 2008, 80% of readers polled felt positive about T5.

   Some 21 million passengers passed through Terminal 5 in its first year. Satisfaction levels among them have risen steadily through the year to 76% as over 82% of flights departed the terminal within 15 minutes of their scheduled time, and BA achieved more than 99% regularity.

Source: constructed with publicly available data.

RATING: Practical and powerful

SERVICES MARKETING

Application: all marketing activities in the service sector

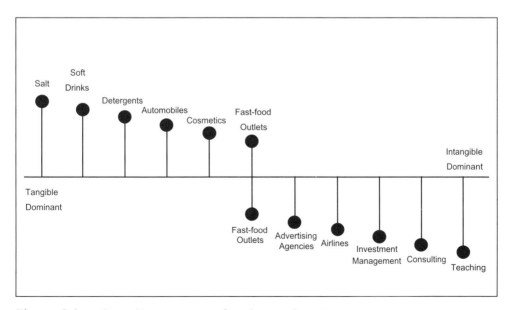

Figure S.3:   Shostack's continuum of products and services

The concept

This concept suggests that the methods to create, run, communicate, sell, and grow a service business are different from those used to handle a product business. The major differences reported by marketers working in the field and by researchers who have studied it are as follows.

(i) Intangibility

Pure services are intangible. They have no physical presence and cannot be experienced or detected by the five senses. So it is not possible to taste, feel, see, hear, or smell them. As a result, they are communicated, sold, and bought in the customer's imagination.

This lack of physical components affects marketing in several ways, the first being pre-purchase assessment. Human beings seem to need physical clues to help them assess benefits and compare *value propositions*. People find it hard to accept or engage with a concept until it is reality, presented to them in physical form. They need to see it and touch it to understand it. In fact, the comparison of physical elements (in a new car for example) often clinches the sale. So, potential customers of a service business need help if they are to understand and grasp the offer. When buying an intangible service, they will often seek the opinion of people they respect before purchase and will buy again only if their initial experience of the service is good. So the reputation of the service, the quality of the experience, and the appeal of the packaging are all very important. The supplier needs to make its intangible service seem both tangible and testable.

Some service marketers create sales promotion materials that represent the service. For example, a recent trend in the retail market is the sale of "experiences" as gifts. People can buy days at spas and race tracks for others. These services are sold in attractive packages which can be displayed on promotion racks and easily taken, by the buyer, to tills. In *business-to-business* markets there have been similar packaging attempts. Over the past two decades, for instance, a number of the leading IT firms have offered their maintenance and project management services in attractive, packaged form. Even leading professional service providers, who generally detest the idea of their service being "marketed", use *collateral* in the form of expensive brochures and case studies to convey the spirit and skill of their offer. Packaging and promotion are therefore one of the prime communication tactics used to market intangible services; to make the intangible, tangible.

More important, though, is the need to understand and emphasize the buyers' experiences of an intangible service. Just as people want to understand how a product might work in practice, they need to understand what their experience of a service might be; and this should be an important focus of service marketing. When launching a new service, for instance, many suppliers create ways to encourage potential buyers to take part in free trials or test runs. They are an essential part of the launch. Some famous hairdressers, like Vidal Sassoon and Nicky Clark, started their remarkably successful franchises by giving free service to celebrities and other opinion formers.

Once the buyer has experienced the service, they are in a good position to assess it for their own future needs and, just as importantly, for the needs of friends or relatives. So, free trials overcome many of the difficulties caused by intangibility because they reduce the perceived risk of purchase. They are also a way of starting one of the most important service marketing tools: word-of-mouth (see *viral marketing*). If customers have a good experience they will talk about it to others and the reputation of the new service will begin to spread. (A bad experience, by contrast, will create negative stories that undermine any effort to grow the business.) After launch, the most important marketing strategy is to amplify this natural reputation. It can be captured in testimonials or printed case studies but it is most effective when word-of-mouth is amplified through *viral marketing*.

Also, as there is no physical product, sales people cannot emphasize benefits but must communicate the experience and outcome of the service process. The selling of an intangible service must therefore be very different from the selling of a product. In fact, if the routine *closing techniques* of product sales are used to clinch service deals, due to intangibility, the buyers tend to feel coerced or cheated and, as a result, might challenge the price or have second thoughts. In some cases, the deal can unravel altogether.

The intangibility of services exaggerates "*post purchase distress*". So, marketers dealing with services have to ensure that they develop techniques by which they mitigate it. Many put emphasis on good after care and others produce printed examples of previous contented buyers; these are given to new buyers soon after purchase. Both provide valuable reassurance.

Finally, as it is often not possible to patent intangible services, suppliers have to find other mechanisms to protect their investment. Failure to do so will mean that services commoditize quickly and markets will be dominated by price wars. Successful service companies therefore create powerful brands which cannot be copied. Some companies that are not skilful at brand creation and management, like some in the IT industry, have damaged their business by moving into service with very little means of maintaining differentiation.

Yet, as with a number of the differences between products and services that are proposed by academics, there are "shades of grey" which complicate life for marketers. (Lynn Shostack captured this in her product/services spectrum shown in Figure S.3). In a number of services, for instance, there are physical components which mitigate the effects of intangibility. It might be that the service itself exists to support a physical product (as in the case of a maintenance service) or has important physical components (like the seat, cabin, and meal in an airline service). These can be used in the marketing of the service to help underline its benefits and overcome buyers' fears or hesitations. They are tangible manifestations of the intangible service and can be used as marketing aides. As a result, airlines will advertise the seat or the meal, and consultancies their people.

In fact, despite academic assertions that intangibility fundamentally changes marketing, there can be little difference in practice between the marketing of product-based services and the marketing of some products. Many products are a mix of physical, conceptual, and service components. A washing machine, for example, is bought because of its functionality, the physical components, the design, the brand, and the service support package. It is also bought through the service system of a retailer. So, the white goods industry has learnt to offer extended warranty as part of product purchase, maintaining total return from the product line through service margins whilst actual product prices have fallen. Although the warranty service is intangible, it is presented as any other retail concept tied to a major product purchase.

Moreover, the marketing industry already has great experience in communicating conceptual, intangible offers. Most brand managers in successful consumer goods companies, like Unilever or Procter & Gamble, would argue that they are in the business of making intangible offers; that a branded product is a concept offering valuable intangible benefits to buyers. A product such as Heinz Baked Beans is, for example, a combination of: haricot beans, sauce, packaging, easy distribution, image, and consistency of familiar taste. It is tangible in the sense that it contains physical components that customers can eat but enormous value is created for Heinz by careful management of the intangible brand concept. Over years the company has invested time, money, and skill in building the brand in the minds of a group of customers. As a result, there is a heritage and equity that causes customers to buy repeatedly at higher prices. So, in order to tackle intangibility, marketers should imitate many of the successful techniques of branded goods such as: excellent brand management, *positioning*, packaging, and progressive investment in fame.

(ii) Variability (or heterogeneity)

Once a product has been designed and the manufacturing process set up, it will be produced time and again by a factory with little variation. Customers know what they are buying and it is consistently delivered. Any aberrations in product quality tend to be few and easily (or relatively easily) driven out by quality control and improvement processes.

Services, though, are rarely as consistently produced as manufactured products. Even those service businesses that try to "industrialize" (see Levitt, T., 1972) their offer through efficient and robust processes find it hard to deliver reliable, consistent service every time. For instance, one of the essential components of many services is the people who serve customers. But people tend to think for themselves, adjusting behaviours and outcomes to suit unique circumstances. Moreover, in certain cases, customers are involved in the process of service production. As people take initiative and change or customize the service, it is unusual for one service experience to be identical to another.

This has implications to the way services are taken to market. For instance, people need to be given clear guidelines on how much they can vary the service. Some businesses want little variation and give their employees little discretion. Others, "mass service shops" like Burger King, for example, see competitive advantage in allowing a degree of customization but are aware that too much will damage the economics of their business. So, marketers need to specify processes which streamline as much as possible but allow people to vary delivery and anticipate failures. They also need to set expectations and communicate the degree of consistency that customers might expect. Their main tool in this is their brand because it sets expectations of a standard of quality. Consumer brands like easyJet and business brands like Accenture, set different expectations. The *brand positioning*, for example, attracts different buyers. A cut-price airline will not be expected to provide high quality food or good landing access to the heart of key cities, whereas the service experience from Accenture's consultants must be as excellent as the business outcomes they offer.

One particularly powerful brand strategy, which sets expectations to suit service variability, is to introduce an element of humanity or responsiveness, which acknowledges that errors might occur. Many high volume consumer services emphasize in their advertising that buyers should complain, if errors occur, so that they can be quickly put right. The Virgin organization, for example, grew through a commitment to contemporary service, which was prepared to be *avant garde* while promising that any human errors would be remedied well. Their humour and humanity, embodied by their brand icon Sir Richard Branson, ensured that buyers were unconcerned by minor quality errors.

Branded volume services use advertising and signage in their premises to signal their intent to provide as consistent and as reliable a service as possible; but also to redress any errors. Some show examples of the processes or systems they use to produce the service. Others use practical documents, like a railway timetable, to set expectations of delivery. As important, though, is the appearance of the service and any physical elements in it. The design and cleanliness of trains and the uniform of employees, for instance, must be carefully managed. A run-down, scruffy service creates entirely different expectations to one which looks organized and professional. A volume service which is clean, reliable, and well packaged will be more readily forgiven for unusual and minor inconsistencies.

At the other end of the scale, the prime mechanism by which professional services, like law, try to achieve consistency is through the recruitment and training of people who will deliver a certain quality and style of service. The delivery of the service might be highly individual and customized to a client's unique situation, but the style of service and manner of delivery must be consistent. Young professionals are schooled in both the technical skills of the firm and its approach to business. Many practices have rigorous control procedures and detailed ethical guidelines that attempt to deliver consistent standards. Yet the heart of their business is the recruitment, development, and motivation of high quality "human capital" which, without close supervision, will deliver the style of service that reflects the firm's position in the market. As a result, the main device used by leading professional service firms to obviate heterogeneity of service is their investment in sophisticated and consistent recruitment marketing aimed at graduates from leading universities.

Other attempts to handle variability include the nature of the contract and guarantees about quality standards, offering financial compensation if errors occur. Excellent, responsive post purchase customer care is also seen as essential to the effective marketing of variable services and forces marketers to focus on quality of service, service experience, and service recovery.

(iii) Simultaneous consumption

A product can be manufactured and stored or passed through a distribution system until it is bought. Once bought, it can then be stored by the customer and used at a later date. By far the majority of services, however, have to be used as they are created. They cannot be stored by either the supplier or buyer. In order to deliver, resources must be prepared and deployed ready for erratic demand. A maintenance service, for instance, must have computer systems able to receive fault reports, trained technicians with appropriate tools able to tackle technical difficulties, and carefully calculated caches of spare parts. Moreover, much of this investment is unseen by the customer before, during, or after the service experience. This means that service companies need to develop techniques that communicate the value of this stored investment.

Simultaneous consumption also means that marketers must focus on demand forecasting and demand management so that resources are available when needed by buyers. They frequently use statistical modelling techniques to predict likely demand based on previous purchase patterns. Some, though, work with key buyers to share the risk of demand fluctuations while others try to influence demand by different pricing patterns. The airline industry, for example, uses different ticket types to get commitment to purchase weeks in advance. In many cases they over-book flights, using incentives to get some passengers to change their flight if necessary. Some marketers also seek to communicate the extent of their stored infrastructure as an asset at their customer's disposal and others use that asset to underscore pricing and value messages. Many use downtime to create other value for their customers. Maintenance services, for example, will fill troughs in demand with routine or preventative maintenance.

As the service is produced while the buyer uses it, the customer is effectively "in the factory", able to see the production process and unable to see the finished result. So the production process must be well prepared and tested, able to host customers and engage them professionally without causing anxiety. Simultaneous consumption also contributes to the need for marketers to manage expectations. They must explain the key steps in the service process and any tasks that the customer must undertake.

In fact, one mistake made by many is their failure to sufficiently plan or design the process through which their customers will move (see *blueprinting*).

Simultaneous consumption has implications for quality management because recovery must happen in real time. Quality processes cannot be the same as manufacturers' post production sampling and correction because any error will be immediately experienced by the customer. Any marketing messages will be undermined if the actual experience is poor or the firm is slow to remedy service errors. So simultaneous consumption concentrates marketers' thoughts on ensuring a quality experience; it reinforces the need to understand and exploit quality of service issues in their work.

(iv) Inseparability

Credible academic researchers (see, for instance, Zeithaml and Bitner, 2003 and Berry, L.L., 1995) suggest that, in the customers' mind, most services cannot be separated from the person they encounter when they buy and use them. So people are not only important to the design and management of a service, they are a critical part of the service itself. Their motivation, behaviour, and appearance are part of the benefit package offered to customers. In many ways they are an essential element in the value that customers seek, part of the bought service, and their behaviour affects the customers' perceptions of price and quality. They are so intimately involved in delivering the service experience that their body language and appearance will communicate messages to the customers about the service as much as their words or the firm's marketing claims.

So, at the front line of interaction with customers, a firm's employees must embody its intentions and, as a result, the appropriate treatment of employees is very important to service businesses. If employees of a production company are treated as mechanized "units of production" their boredom or dissatisfaction will not be passed on to the buyers. But in a service business it will. If their leaders treat them badly then it will be communicated, even if they try to be professional and disguise their unease. Conversely, if they are treated like human beings there is a strong chance that the customers will be too.

Managing employee behaviour in line with changing customer expectations is a major focus and challenge for service businesses. Good service managers understand that front line people can cause customers to turn to or away from a service. Many put real effort, investment. and resources into programmes designed to improve the impressions caused by their people. In fact, it is probably no exaggeration to say that service companies invest in this "intangible asset" the way manufacturers invest in tangible assets.

On the other hand, an increasing number of services are based on self-service technology, with no people involved in day-to-day delivery. From web services to airline check-in, the range of self-administered services is steadily growing. Clearly, in this rapidly increasing category of services, the "people" element of the service marketing mix is less prevalent. For these, the personality of the company brand is used to replace the people who normally deliver service. Marketers must invest heavily in branding this type of service at all points of visibility. The emotional reassurance of major, high quality brands like IBM, Ericsson, or Virgin implies a reliable response should self-service technology fail.

However, there is evidence that self-service technology only penetrates a market if the first buyers are shown how to use it by personable people or their proxy. They need help with the initial socialization process, and in overcoming any technology fear, from specifically designed marketing initiatives. At the time of writing, for instance, most airlines are introducing self-service check-in technology that is very simple to use. They generally place the machines near the "hand luggage only" queue. Employees are trained to approach people in the queue, often frequent flyers, and show them how to use the fast, easy machines. Although many refuse the original offer to use the technology, they are happy to comply once a demonstration overcomes their technology fear and potential embarrassment. Once a sufficient number of people have leant the process, they communicate it to others and the self-service technology penetrates the market.

(v) Perishability

Generally services cannot be stored or saved for other occasions. Once an empty airline seat has flown over the Atlantic, the opportunity is passed; the moment cannot be recaptured. So, services are time bound and the management of time is an important task of a service business. In fact, one researcher (see Ruskin Brown, I., 2005) suggests that there are several "flavours of time" that service businesses need to manage: punctuality, duration, availability, speed of response, and speed of innovation. Of these, punctuality or reliability, in the sense of delivering the service when promised, has been shown in many studies to be one of the most important influences on the way customers judge the quality of a service.

Perishable services must be marketed in the same way as perishable products like fresh food or flowers. Quality difficulties must be dealt with through an immediate, responsive recovery process and inventory must be carefully managed through forecasting and capacity management. This characteristic reinforces the need for good demand forecasting in a service business. It probably has to be more accurate than a product company that can store excess items in a factory until they are used. Maximum capacity must be carefully calculated, balancing the highest anticipated demand against the cost of investment. Marketers have to cope with variations in demand and develop techniques to sell spare capacity such as empty hotel rooms for off-season or weekend capacity. Emphasis should also be put on easy and efficient distribution and the benefit of a new, premium service.

However, the real implication of this is that the supplier must become expert in differential pricing. They need clear communication methods to potential buyers, which demonstrate why the immediate "fresh" service needs to cost a different amount to those accessing it at a later time. They need to produce special price offers, reductions to use up spare capacity, and understand marginal pricing. Moreover, they need to communicate the rationale and, particularly, the fairness of these pricing practices to their customers. This is particularly important for companies with repeat customers who become increasingly sophisticated, holding off purchase to get better offers.

(vi) Ownership

When people buy a product, ownership of it passes to them. They can store it, use it, or give it away. This simply doesn't happen with a service though. The people who are part of a training or consultancy service cannot be owned by the buyer. Nor are airline or train seats bought; they are rented for a moment in time as part of the service. Payment is for use, access, or hire of items. People will talk as if there is a sense of ownership (my flight, my broadband service, my pension or our training) yet there is not the same sense of possession as with a product purchase. This lack of ownership will cause buyers to question value and price. They will look for greater added value or ask for price reductions. As a result, the marketer must dramatize the moment of contract and find mechanisms to emphasize value as the service progresses or they will struggle continually with price pressure. This is one area which many firms find hard to manage. In a variety of businesses, numerous valuable services have been turned into commodities because the suppliers have been incompetent at communicating value.

(vii) Process

One of the major differences between the purchase of a product and the experience of a service is the process through which the buyer moves. A product is an entity, which is bought through a process but is independent of it. Customers can use it, break it, give it away, and ignore the instructions on how to use it. Services, however, have a process inherent in their design through which the customer must pass. So when people use a service they must submit themselves to the service provider's process.

So, marketers must plan the service process in detail and educate their customers in the parts of the service they will experience. Potential customers must know how to access the supplier's service system, which has to be designed to encourage use. The firm needs to use clear signage and communicate its meaning to all potential buyers. Educating them to access and use the supplier's process is, therefore, an important aspect of service marketing. This ranges from the deployment of branded consumer signage, like McDonald's, to the use of customized web sites for client extranets in *business-to-business* marketing. Once "in the premises", though, the customer needs direction (even in a virtual environment). If it is not immediately apparent how to use the system (the equivalent of standing helplessly in a foreign shop) they become embarrassed and give up. So, clear signage into the delivery process and a step-by-step guide through it are equally important. On landing, for example, many flights show a video guide through the airport. This ensures that the stress levels of new passengers stay low and any difficulties are seen as aberrations, which can be corrected by excellent service recovery. Finally, marketing communication must concentrate on the "outcomes" of the process rather than the product benefits emphasized by product marketers.

(viii) Control

When a customer buys a product, they normally have complete control as to when and how to use it. They might keep it, use it immediately, or give it to someone else. When they buy services, though, they do not have such freedom. They must surrender themselves to the service delivery process, which the supplier has designed for them. In doing this they cede control of themselves to the service provider and human beings detest being out of control. The purchase and use of a service therefore invades their personal space and raises emotional issues that service suppliers must learn to tackle (see Bateson and Hoffman, 1999 and Bateson, 1985).

This lack of control means that marketers must take steps to allay the anxiety of new users. They can, for example, design a simple, clear process and choose competent employees to perform the service. Both will help to alleviate anxiety. Many of the well known customer service and after care techniques (see *service quality*) may be used to allay fears and criticisms arising from this underlying emotion. Yet, although the character, reputation, and professionalism of service employees can inspire confidence in the quality of the service to be received, the corporate brand also allays stress.

Unfortunately, customers who use a service repeatedly assert an unconscious need to regain control. They try to cut corners, look to serve themselves, and get irritated if the process is inflexible. In fact they can become annoyed with the simple, clear steps that they first found so enticing and necessary. So, service for the experienced user is very different to that for the new customer. It must be inclusive and respectful; a streamlined club, similar to frequent flyer programmes, which allows as much self-service as possible. This has profound implications. In fact, in some markets, the arrival of a supplier offering, for the first time, a service designed for the experienced user has had major strategic impact.

For experienced buyers, marketers must ensure that mechanisms are designed whereby, as the customer becomes familiar with the service process, he or she can do more themselves or cut out steps. The design of progressive self-service into the service system will reduce costs because some of the effort of performing the service will come from the customer. Yet, it will also improve perceived quality because the service performance is within the control of the customer and thus closer to perceptions of timely delivery. So, it is possible for marketers to provide repeat customers with better service at lower cost.

(ix) Environment

For many services the environment in which they are performed is an important part of the experience for customers. The design and ambience of a restaurant and the layout and style of an airline cabin set expectations of quality and value. Retailers, hoteliers, and managers of holiday resorts are just a few of the service businesses who have to think carefully about the physical setting of their service. It affects the behaviour of employees, sets the expectations of buyers and can be a source of differentiation.

There is a wealth of research on the effect of the physical setting on the health of a service business. A complex and sophisticated process is involved in creating a new one because the marketer must take into account and balance a range of factors including: "sight appeal", "size perception", shape, colour, sound, scent, spatial layout, flexibility, brand, and signs or symbols. They must also calculate operational factors such as capacity, crowding, and queuing. In fact, some businesses use complex statistical techniques like queuing theory (that are used to design the capacity of sophisticated communications and computer equipment) on the flow of people through their premises. Yet in international or ethnic markets, they also have to allow for subtle cultural preferences which influence a range of ambient and behavioural factors.

For those services where the physical setting is important, these complex considerations are unavoidable because they affect buying behaviour. Credible experiments have demonstrated the effect of these different factors on sales. People buy more, for instance, if different music is played, if different colours are used, and even if different smells are deployed.

Some services, though, are experienced in more subtle and flexible environments: the virtual vagaries of the internet or the customers' imaginations. Yet, just as in a real, physical environment, impressions need to be created which set expectations of value. This needs careful design and sophisticated marketing if it is going to influence sales and price perceptions.

After initial design and launch, the "service-scape", the environment visible to customers, must be kept fresh and inviting by marketers. It must continue to reflect the ambitions of the service provider. Marketers must design sales promotion campaigns and point-of-sale materials to stimulate sales, to increase the margin of purchases and to maintain excitement in the service. They must routinely audit the facility, ensuring that it maintains its enticing nature to customers.

(x) Performance

Services tend to occur at a moment in time and involve the attention of one person on another. Many are "performed", not produced. From representation in negotiation, to service at the restaurant table, people perform a service for others and the style of performance affects the customers' views of both quality and value. Moreover, the energy, art, and style of the performance influence the price that can be charged and the degree of customer satisfaction. As a result, the service industry puts great emphasis on the "service encounter"; that "moment of truth" when the supplier's employees interact with the buyers. It is a moment when the firm has a chance to impress and deepen a relationship with a buyer, in addition to delivering the promised benefit. It is this area, probably, more than any of the others, that creates exhilarating, enticing services. A service can be researched, blueprinted, and engineered but those which go the extra step of creating a performance tend to entrance their customers and earn higher margins.

History, context, criticism, and development

Early experience of service marketing and understanding of it in marketing text books (one 1920s text examines the "intangible product", see White, P., 1927) seemed to get lost in a fascination for consumer product marketing in the mid 20th century. As a result, until recently, the majority of marketing theory, language, and practice derived from either the experience of firms offering physical goods (particularly consumer products) or from economic theory. Consequently, many marketing techniques are modelled on product experience (particularly in consumer markets) and most marketing teachers at leading institutes had their early career in a product environment. It is in the past three decades, as Western economies have become more service dominated, that marketers have begun to move from traditional product disciplines to service environments in any significant numbers. So, coupled with the emergence of competitive service sectors in the developed economies, there has been a growing interest of marketers in this field. They are adapting marketing practice to a wider range of service businesses (whether in business-to-business or consumer, profit, or non-profit industries) and to an increasing number of activities within different service businesses.

Until the 1970s there were few well researched and objective analyses of either the role of marketing in service industries or service marketing practice. This was changed by two groundbreaking pieces of work. The first was a paper produced by G. Lynn Shostack (see Shostack, G.L., 1977) when she was a vice president of Citibank in New York and marketing director for the Investment Management Group of America. It was a set of detailed recommendations based on the experience of a senior manager working in a service industry. Shostack clearly used the processes and procedures outlined in her article to design new services and had some success with them. She suggested a number of ideas which have formed the basis of much service marketing thinking ever since. Figure S.3, for example, is her illustration of the range of offers beyond mere physical products. Her primary idea was that there are features of a service which make its creation and marketing different from the creation and marketing of products. In particular Shostack talked about the concept of "intangibility". She suggested that the intangibility of a service is a state which makes the offer fundamentally different from a product offer; "it is not corporeal". This has since become part of the fundamental philosophy of service marketing.

The next significant contribution appears to be a 1983 symposium of the American Marketing Association which debated in detail the marketing of services. The full agenda covered the creation of new services, the management of innovation, and the differences between the marketing of services and products. The meeting was clearly held as a result of growing interest in service marketing stimulated by the Shostack article and a concern that the marketing community was not addressing some of the key issues involved in the move to a service economy. The symposium stimulated various academics to contribute to this field. In particular, there appeared publications by Leonard Berry, Sri Parasuraman, Christian Grönroos, Christopher Lovelock, Donald Cowell, Roland Rust, Stephen Brown, and Valerie Zeithaml. These people in turn sponsored many research projects into service phenomena and set up high quality institutes with industry.

It is not too much of an exaggeration to say that there are now three academic "schools" following this field: the American school, the Scandinavian school, and the French school. Each has a different emphasis but all cooperate in a wide body of research, much of which is conducted in tandem with people in actual service businesses in a variety of countries and economic sectors. There is, then, science behind the marketing of services. Marketers wanting to adopt many of the approaches can generally rely on the applicability and relevance of much that is suggested.

In recent decades larger companies in service sectors have begun to establish substantial marketing departments similar to those in consumer goods industries. Banks, utilities, travel firms, and retailers have learnt to use these structures to market services as their industries have experienced greater competition or, as in the case of newly privatized utilities, market forces for the first time. Some of these firms appear to be adopting the processes of marketing seen in consumer goods companies, and embarking on decades-long organizational learning in marketing effectiveness. BT, for example, had no marketing resource at all when, in 1984, it was a government-owned engineering organization. It now has several hundred marketers working on brand, communication, and strategy programmes; and has a number of highly successful, award-winning campaigns to its name. More importantly, though, it has sophisticated campaign management processes which are progressively improved alongside other operational capabilities. In parallel with all this, though, the marketing profession as a whole has been exploring how different the marketing of services is from the marketing of consumer products.

Voices and further reading

- ". . . I have worked in service companies (McKinsey and American Express) and product companies (RJR Nabisco and IBM). I will state unequivocally that service businesses are much more difficult to manage. In services you don't make a product and then sell it. You sell capability. You sell knowledge. You create it at the same time you deliver it. The business is different. The economics are entirely different." (Gerstner, L.V., 2002).

- Thomas, D.R.E., "Strategy is different in service businesses". *Harvard Business Review*, July–August 1978.

- "To the buyer, then, services . . . are necessary to enable him to develop the full economic value of the goods, and he is generally aware of this. Most buyers of industrial goods recognize that part of the price they pay represents the value of accompanying services, even where those services are not paid for as an individual item." Rose, D., in Wilson, A., 1965.

- Lovelock, C.H., *Service Marketing*. Prentice Hall, 1991.

- "The concept of 'service' evokes, from the opaque recesses of the mind, time worn images of personal ministration and attendance. It refers generally to deeds one individual performs personally for another. It carries historical connotations of charity, gallantry, and selflessness, or of obedience, subordination and subjugation." Levitt, T., 1972.

- "It is wrong to imply that services are just like products except for intangibility. By such logic, apples are just like oranges except for their 'appleness'. Intangibility is not a modifier; it is a state. Intangibles may come with tangible wrappings but no amount of money can buy physical ownership of . . . experience . . . time . . . or process. Tangible means palpable and material. Intangible is . . . impalpable and not corporeal. This distinction has profound implications." Shostack, G.L., 1977.

- Levitt, T., "Marketing intangible products and product intangibles". *Harvard Business Review*, May–June 1981.

- Cowell, D.W., *The Marketing of Services*. Butterworth-Heinemann, 1984.

- "Goods are produced, sold and consumed whereas services are sold and then produced and consumed." Cowell, ibid.

- Grönroos, C., "Applied service marketing theory". *European Journal of Marketing*, 1982.

- "Services are processes consisting of activities or a series of activities rather than things. In order to understand service management and the marketing of services it is critical that one realises that the consumption of a service is process consumption rather than outcome consumption. The consumer perceives the service process (or production process) as part of the service consumption, not simply the outcome of that process, as in traditional marketing of physical goods . . . the consumption process leads to an outcome for the customer, which is the result of the service process. Thus, the consumption of the service process is a critical part of the service experience." Grönroos, C., 2003.

- Palmer, A., *Principles of Services Marketing*. McGraw-Hill, 1994
- Payne, A., *The Essence of Services Marketing*. Prentice Hall, 1993.
- Bateson, J.E.G., *Managing Services Marketing* (text and readings). Dryden Press 1989.
- Woodruffe, H., *Services Marketing*. Pitman, 1995.
- Irons, K., *Managing Service Companies*. The Economist Intelligence Unit, 1993.
- Ziethaml, V. and Bitner, M. J., *Services Marketing*. McGraw-Hill, 2003.

Service marketing: Victorian Jim reforms the Midland

It is very hard for modern people to really understand (especially any that have been stuck on an Amtrak train during a snow storm) just how revolutionary, scientific, and advanced the railways were when they first appeared. This was the first time in human history that mankind could travel faster than a galloping horse, and it is no exaggeration to say that the railway transformed society.

The first real railway line went operational in Britain (Darlington to Stockton) in 1825 and proved to be a fabulous investment for its Quaker owners (returns of 15% between 1839–41). It prompted a railway mania and investment boom. By 1840, 200,000 people were involved in railway construction in the UK alone. British Iron output doubled as a result of it and, by 1850, £240 million had been Invested. By 1869, the first transcontinental railway had been completed in the USA and, in 1891 the construction of the massive trans-Siberian railway had begun in Russia.

The railways created new towns, new concepts, and new jobs. In London, for instance, a young insolvency specialist called William Deloitte created a new system of accounting for these industrialized service businesses and, through such advanced thinking, created the major accounting firm that still bears his name today. The railways introduced consistent time, holidays, commuting, and new concepts like the word "class". Historian Eric Hobsbawm says of them (Hobsbawm, E., 1999):

> By 1850 the railways had reached a standard of performance not seriously improved upon until the abandonment of steam in the mid twentieth century, their organization and methods were on a scale unparalleled in any other industry, their use of novel and science-based technology (such as the electric telegraph) unprecedented. They appeared to be several generations ahead of the rest of the economy, and indeed 'railway' became a sort of synonym for ultramodernity in the 1840's, as 'atomic' was to be after the second world

war. Their sheer size and scale staggered the imagination and dwarfed the most gigantic public works of the past.

Despite the work of novelists like Thomas Hardy and Charles Dickens, it is also hard for modern audiences to understand the attitude of educated and wealthy people to the poor during that period. Many resisted, for example, any education initiatives because they feared that it would cause unrest. There were, though, a number enlightened souls pushing for reform. Victoria's husband, Prince Albert, caused outrage and concern, for instance, when he insisted on there being days when the poor and uneducated could visit his "Great Exhibition". Another reformer was James Allport, who ran Britain's Midland railway in the mid century.

His first significant act caused as much outrage and concern as Albert's. At the time, "third class" was for the poor and working people. It normally consisted of simple open carriages with wooden benches, which were given low priority. There are reported instances of third class trains being shunted into sidings to let even cattle or freight pass them by. Allport abolished this. He had covered carriages, all of which had upholstered seats, partitioning, and more leg room. His peers in the industry hated him for it because (as BA did with flat beds in business class a century later) he set a new standard for the basic service offered on this new and exciting network of technology; and they had to keep up. For him, it was not enough just to offer carriage any more. He wanted to serve people.

He contracted with a successful catering company, Spiers & Pond, to ensure that wealthier travellers could enjoy a food service. They had begun their business with sporting events like Wimbledon and opened the Criterion restaurant which still operates in London's Piccadilly. Passengers could buy one of their hampers at one station and drop it at another after eating the contents on the train. Their service became a social occasion, famous in Victorian England. In his extensive history of advertising (Sampson, H., 1875), Victorian author Henry Samson could have been describing the answer to airplane food:

> Ten years ago no man in his senses would have dreamt of applying for food or drink at a railway buffet while he could go elsewhere; now Spiers & Pond daily serve thousands who desert the old familiar taverns and crowd the bars at the various city stations. . . . the old regime of mouldy pork-pies and stale Banbury cakes has made us feel very well disposed to a firm whose name has already passed into a proverb.

The following personal advert from the Daily Telegraph of 1874 shows how much this service had become part of social life:

> The lady, who travelled from Bedford to London by Midland train on the night of the 4th inst, can now meet the gentleman who shared with her the contents of his railway luncheon basket. She enjoys the

recollection of that pleasant meal, and would like to know if he is going on another journey. Will keep any appointment made at the Criterion in Piccadilly.

Allport's other remarkable innovation was to create a premium service on his railway. He constructed an outsourcing contract (yes, an outsourcing contract in the 1870s!) with America's famous Pullman trains. They provided a "hotel standard service" for an extra fee, using their own carriages and attendants. In fact, Allport had been so effective at increasing the return on the basic rail service that he was eventually asked to run another innovation, the railway clearing house, which handled ticketing and pricing across the whole national network. He repositioned the value of the core service based on a novel network infrastructure and created attractive added value services. An outstanding services marketer.

 RATING: Practical and powerful

SOLUTIONS MARKETING

Application: sales strategy, NPD/NSD

The concept

This is an attempt to sell a customized package of products and services rather than a pre-defined product. It aims to capture additional revenue from associated services or, perhaps more importantly, by understanding the real needs of buyers. Suppliers frequently edge competitors out of their customers' installations by offering packages that work across all technologies. As a result, the word "solutions" is common parlance in many industries and conferences. A "solution", a customized offer, should be an attractive, high margin experience for which the buyer is pleased to pay more than the individual components. It should be a firm's equivalent of a Saville Row suit or custom car; something expensive, sexy, and enjoyable. Self-evidently it should be more expensive than any pre-packaged offers available in the market and, glitteringly expensive though it is, it should tempt customers to buy.

History, context, development, and criticism

"Solutions marketing and selling" evolved from the need to approach customers, particularly business customers, at the moment when their requirements are ill defined;

to "move up the value chain" (see *organizational buying behaviour*). It first appeared as a concept in the computer industry during the 1980s. For example, in his 1986 book about his career at IBM, the retiring global head of sales and marketing dedicated a whole chapter to "solution-minded selling" (Rodgers, B., 1986). At that time suppliers' main proposition to customers was to buy a new product because it would be faster and cheaper than the one they already had; but what was often missing was any analysis of changing needs. They were not, generally, listening to their customers or taking care to understand their real needs.

The "solutions" approach was created to encourage sales people (who had become used to focusing on the upgrade of existing products or overhauling their "installed base") to learn to focus on real customer needs. Because customers had a mish-mash of different technologies and products that had to be taken into account, a process evolved whereby the seller conducted a technical audit of customers' needs and proposed a "solution", initially called a systems integration project, which customized new and existing technology to meet changing requirements. "Solutions marketing" has since been successfully used by a wide range of different companies in a host of different industries, to act as a catalyst for a change in the behaviours of their sales force. It has been seen in: computing, telecommunications, document management, healthcare, and heavy engineering, to name but a few.

However, in the enthusiasm to adopt this approach, and use it as a catalyst of change, the difficulties it causes have been disguised, neglected, or ignored. The first, and most important, is that it can cause an erosion of margin and a fall in price. When companies sell products there are established prices and controlled discounts which a sales person can apply. But when putting together a package of products and services, the discount is frequently applied to supplementary items outside the discount controls on products; services for instance. When a company moves wholeheartedly into "solution selling", their own products can be a small percentage of most orders. If it has no cost information on the other elements of the sale or, perhaps more importantly, no discount controls in place for service items or competitor equipment, the move to solutions will lose money.

Secondly, if a supplier is seeking to run or grow a large business on volume sales, then one of its keys to success is scalability. It needs to "industrialize" its products and services, packaging its offer to customers as much as possible. Many large companies are based on this ethos. Their marketing, sales, distribution, and delivery are all based on volume. Yet, this is in conflict with a sales approach that customizes every single sale through a solutions selling philosophy. Unless the company genuinely uses some form of mass customization process and technology, the conflict in this strategic emphasis will cause inefficiency, higher costs, and poor quality. A company which has spent fifty years making money through volume production simply cannot customize each sale to each customer without major change to its internal processes and attitudes, together with serious investment in technology.

The third problem is that the marketing of solutions doesn't tend to create or communicate a clear *value proposition*. Customers need a simple proposition if they are not clear about what they are looking for or if they are going to change their buying habits. An appealing description and attractive packaging are important ingredients in the marketing of even complex business offers and service experiences (see *features analysis* and *value propostions*). Solutions marketing has led, by contrast, to extravagant claims, odd sounding marketing messages, and some ridiculous product names. The satirical British magazine, *Private Eye* regularly listed some of the sillier examples, such as:

- "Accommodation solutions": Flats/apartments.
- "Integrated care solutions": Residential, day-care.
- "Extra-care solutions": Nursing homes.
- "Chilled food solutions": Ready meals.
- "Outsourced vehicle movement solutions": Car deliveries.
- "Carestream radiology solutions": X-rays.
- "Integrated vegetable supply solutions": Greengrocers.
- "Client solutions team": Complaints department.
- "Integrated solutions, Oiling the wheels of industry with the knowledge to care for the environment": Consultants.
- "Intelligent solutions. A complete IT solution, including hardware, networking and e-commerce": Consultants.
- "Inbound solutions guarantee to take the pain away from all telephony and application-related aspects of your organization": Consultants.

Voices and further reading

- "An IBM marketing rep's success depends totally on his ability to understand a prospect's business so well that he can identify and analyze its problems and then come up with a solution that makes sense to the customer . . . the people in the field have to be a combination of analyst, consultant, application specialist, technologist and salesperson . . ." Rodgers, B., 1986.
- Stone, M. and Carasle, M., *Business Solutions on Demand: Creating Value at the Speed of Light*. Kogan Page, 2004.
- "Transforming the organization into a solutions provider is tricky. Few executives truly comprehend the enormity of the challenge, let alone what 'solution provider' really means." Kumar, N., 2004.

Things you might like to consider

(i) The king really does have no clothes. This is poor English, bad marketing, and really idiotic businesses strategy. Architects take an approach to their work that is similar to the "solutions methodologies" suggested by those who have specialized in this field. They understand their client's needs, often helping them to craft a "requirements specification". They then analyse the site and design a "solution" to their needs, before assembling a multi-disciplinary team to build the building. Yet at the end of the project they deliver a house, a garage, or an office block; not an odd sounding, meaningless package. Marketers need to get a grip on this and make up their mind what their market claim really is. Are they offering a bespoke, customized, expensive offer or more of an industrialized, streamlined, and pack-aged experience?

(ii) It is easy for firms to take a share in markets dominated by companies who have taken a customized, solutions approach to every sale. If they package their offers, they are likely to be able to undercut the price of established suppliers and improve their own profit.

(iii) Some present this concept as though "the move from products to services to solutions" is an inevitable evolution in any industry. It clearly is nothing of the kind. Some customers are quite satisfied with a packaged offer and some companies are geared to produce only packaged volume offers. This is as much about getting the best mix of features as in the creation of any other marketing offer.

Nokia Services' Business Solutions Portfolio

Nokia is a world leader in mobile communications best known for its con-sumer handsets. Yet, in 2005, it embarked on a major change programme for its business-to-business networks division (since combined with Siemens into a new venture) to differentiate itself from its competition by shifting focus from selling technology to providing customer-orientated services. Fundamental to this change was the creation of a "Nokia Services organization" in the company's networks division. At that stage, several service organizations and capabilities were combined from across the company into one business unit. This amalgamation made the existing service businesses more visible because it represented over 25% of the Nokia Networks' revenues.

The company had started to put in place "solution selling" some years before, encouraging sales people to work systematically with its customers, defining their needs, and combining different stand-alone offers into more customized and comprehensive projects. By 2005, the company had trained 1,200 people in "solution selling" methods and practices, so (in 2006), Nokia Networks was prepared for an extensive roll-out of its newly formed "Business Solutions Portfolio". By June of that year, Nokia Services repre-sented more than a third of the Nokia Networks' total revenues with very strong potential growth.

BACKGROUND

The international "mobile network infrastructure" industry had been under-going a number of significant changes, driven by technology, consumer demand, and increasing competition. In mature markets, the boom years had passed and network operators (Nokia's customers) were entering a phase of stability and saturation. Faced with declining revenues from tradi-tional voice services and increasing encroachment from other communica-tions and media industries, they were under enormous pressure to cut costs and earn revenue through new data and entertainment-based services. In developing economies, by contrast, the number of consumers continued to expand very fast, so operators needed to deliver profits from a growing number of low revenue customers, while also updating their service portfo-lios to attract and retain higher value users.

As consumer expectations rose, and as technological convergence enabled new competitors to enter the market, these pressures on operators were increasing. To meet the new challenges, they needed more than mere technology vendors. They needed what Nokia called "strategic solution providers" who could help them determine which markets they should be in, which services would maximize profits, and which combination of com-ponents (infrastructure, applications, content, and user devices) would yield the greatest long-term competitive advantage. In short, they needed a sup-plier who could take a true end-to-end view of their business and work closely with them to help deliver their strategic goals.

Historically, though, operators of mobile networks had seen little change in the way their suppliers had behaved and communicated with them. For example, as recently as February 2005, it was clear that most participants at an industry exhibition called 3GSM (the single most important event in the mobile telecom industry calendar) still had little to differentiate their offer-ings and were relying more on "technology push" rather than "customer pull". Even Nokia, whose "customer first" strategy had been launched in 2000, had not fully articulated its service-led approach, and this despite the fact that (as the world's no 2 mobile networks infrastructure provider and no 1 handset manufacturer) its capabilities and skills made the company better qualified than anyone to deliver true end-to-end "solutions".

Although Nokia thought there was still an opportunity in the mobile market place to create the innovation, excitement, and growth of a few years ago; a new approach was needed. This should be from a new, customer driven, "outside-in" perspective (rather than the traditional technology driven "inside-out" perspective). And the only things preventing the company from taking this approach were its own way of working and own way of thinking. The company therefore set itself the goal of transforming its thinking, processes, and tools to support true cross-business synergy in a way that addressed actual customer needs, and delivered the full business value they required in the com-petitive environment they now faced. It was that transformation that led directly to the creation of the "Nokia Services Business Solutions Portfolio".

THE FIRST STEPS: UNDERSTANDING CUSTOMER/MARKET NEED

Understanding customers and their needs is the cornerstone of all opportunity analysis. But the radical nature of the new "Business Solutions Portfolio" programme demanded a re-think of the process by which this information was collected. Traditionally, the company's view of markets had been gained through globally standardized tracking research into customer satisfaction, customer loyalty, market size, and other metrics. However, all these processes were driven by the global organizational structures and, thanks to Nokia's heritage, took a predominantly product-related perspective. The challenge was, therefore, firstly, to re-orient processes around business challenges (rather than simply analysing customers' purchasing behaviour) and secondly, to localize the collection of information in order to anchor it in the realities of market and customer experiences.

For the first step, market information which the company already owned (for example, research on customer efficiency and end-user behaviour) was used to understand the reality and challenges of the company's customers. This was important because this knowledge could now be drawn upon to define "market opportunity hotspots". For the second step, Nokia used the "eyes and ears" of the organization (the customer account teams) to de-centralize market understanding and gather relevant information on an operator-by-operator basis. By mid 2005, five area meetings, with around thirty participants in each, had been run, including Nokia Networks' sales directors, "solution managers", and "solution consultants". On the agenda were the hottest themes and challenges the company's customers were facing in their markets.

By the end of the programme Nokia had distilled a wealth of new knowledge into approximately fifty clearly identified business challenges. This data was consolidated into five important "customer challenge domains" which, Nokia believed, addressed the industry's toughest issues. It was these five domains that formed the platform on which the Business Solutions Portfolio was built and communicated to the market. The results of this long and detailed process were tested in around ten customer workshops and the feedback was extremely positive.

MAKING IT HAPPEN

The first step toward the "Solutions Portfolio" was to create a dedicated team and a few quick wins with a handful of solutions that the company knew it could rapidly bring to market. Initially this "Solution Marketing Team" was created in the services marketing function, working with the individual business lines to create solutions that addressed customer issues of cost-efficiency and market differentiation. These first offers were the starting point of the new portfolio and were used for illustrative purposes in customer workshops and external events and communications. They were also the basis of the first "Solutions Portfolio" brochure and the business challenges-based Portfolio development work mentioned previously.

CHANGING INTERNAL PERCEPTIONS

Since the primary challenges facing Nokia were within its own walls and across its many internal boundaries, it became clear that it was necessary to send out a concrete internal message and raise the innovative spirit needed to create the new approach. This in turn meant additional work with management to ensure full buy-in and support for the project.

The goal was to create a clear identity and associated behaviour to support the programme. Through a series of management workshops and with creative help from one of the agencies, the "Solutioneer" concept was born. More than a marketer, more than an engineer, more than a sales person, the Solutioneer identity pointed at a combination of a strong and proud engineering heritage with a commitment to solve the customers' business challenges in a holistic way and symbolically defined who the company was. The idea was launched internally throughout the Nokia Networks division and set the scene for the solution-based thinking needed in order to deliver the external promise. To support the message, a range of collateral (giveaway puzzles, T-shirts, etc.) and an internal "inspirational video" was developed to help explain the shift the company was taking in interacting with customers.

ORGANIZATIONAL RE-TOOLING

As the programme moved forward, the resourcing for solutions work needed to move beyond the marketing organization and into the individual business lines, in order to make the promise real. This phase was the most difficult, and although the Solutioneer campaign helped oil the machinery, it was nevertheless probably the single true test of whether or not the Solutions Portfolio would fly. Marketing continued to lead the project, but now business lines needed to take responsibility for practical delivery to customers.

Identifying business owners for solutions which crossed several organizational boundaries was a major milestone, and through this work alone Nokia made significant progress in bringing down walls and silos within its organization. As responsibilities were clarified and delivery work continued, a "Solutions Portfolio Council" was created to oversee the development and approve new proposals.

THE IMPORTANCE OF CREDENTIALS

Providing proof that the solutions actually worked was just as important as creating and developing the Portfolio itself. As solutions were piloted, rolled out, and delivered, a special campaign was launched in which sales had to generate and agree customer testimonials on business successes (with the best examples given awards by management in sales meetings). In this way, the company not only generated a critical element of its external marketing tool kit, but also helped to sustain internal momentum and encourage further buy-in.

BRINGING THE STORY TO MARKET

As a major pillar of the external communication programme, a new sales tool was developed, the Services Sales Kit, to make it as easy as possible for account teams to put the new Solutions Portfolio approach into action. Using a new user interface, sales people could access appropriate materials by defining the customer challenge, specifying the document type, or by asking questions and prompting answers from within the Sales Kit solutions, using a dynamic search engine.

CONCLUSION

From the beginning, the project took a twin-track approach: on the one hand re-positioning the Services organization within the mobile networking market place as a true solution provider, while on the other hand working internally at every level of the organization to develop full understanding and buy-in for the changes required to deliver the external promise. By ensuring equal clarity of communication for both external and internal audiences, and by engaging all levels of management in evangelizing the Business Solutions Portfolio story, the project has been instrumental in aligning real customer needs with real Nokia skills and capabilities.

 RATING: Toxic

 SPONSORSHIP

Application: sales support, marketing communications, brand positioning

The concept

Sponsorship is the support of sporting, charity, and artistic events for commercial advantage. It is such a substantial means of marketing that some organizations thrive through it. Sponsorship is, for example, an important revenue source for sports clubs. There are sponsors of players, kit, stadia, leagues, and whole clubs.

Some marketers see it as a useful and different mechanism to extend their footprint and reach. For instance, in July 2010, P&G announced a ten-year sponsorship of the Olympic Games. They say that they reach 4.2 billion consumers and see this as a way of reaching five billion.

Sponsorship has many uses. It can be used, for example, when building the awareness of a *brand*. Brands need fame to succeed. The wide knowledge in the general population of what these brands stand for enhances their appeal to those that buy them. In this context, sponsorship is a cost-effective means of helping an intended group of people to become familiar with a brand name. It makes business sense when it is based on a clear case and has defined objectives. The sponsorship has context. It can be part of a well articulated, long- term brand strategy.

Another valid use of sponsorship is in areas where there are restrictions on other forms of marketing. Cigarette companies, for example, now have very few opportunities to promote their wares, so they use sponsorship extensively. Some professions are similarly restricted due to the nature of their work. Few clients want to let it be known that they have been helped by an insolvency practitioner or that a forensic accountant has uncovered a fraud. Marketing in these cases needs to be subtle, restrained, and appealing. Sponsorship is a useful tool for these practices if targeted properly.

Businesses sponsor a wide range of activities, including:

(i)   Sports
(ii)   The arts
(iii)   Broadcasting
(iv)   Books and publications
(v)   Competitions and prizes
(vi)   Expeditions
(vii)   Record attempts
(viii) Education
(ix)   Environmental initiatives
(x)   Community affairs
(xi)   Charities.

This is a large category of expenditure. In 2008, for example, the total value of the UK sports sponsorship market had grown from £353 million in 1986 to £486 and was estimated to grow to £600 million in 2013. (However, the number of deals was down from 1,172 to 574 putting the average value of deals up from £322 K to 847 K.) Football took 38% of this spend, motor sport 20.4%, rugby union 8.05%, athletics 5.3%, cricket 4.7%, horse racing 4.35%, golf 3.3%, and tennis 2.7%. Sports sponsorship also shows how sector spend varies: Financial services is about 15.7%, IT, communications and utilities 13.8%, alcohol 11.5%, sports goods 10.8%, transport and tourism 10.8% and autos 4.7%.

There are, though, several difficulties with sponsorship:

• It is highly personal and very visible. It can be the subject of whim and preference at very senior levels and tough to apply professional measurement or judgment to.

- Some sponsorship is unnecessary if other marketing is effective. For example, the sponsorship of public conferences, with the attendant presentation spot, is questionable. If executives are expert enough to speak on a topic they should be invited without the need to pay. The sponsorship of annual award ceremonies can also be of minimal effect. There are many awards in many disciplines and they can prompt both cynicism and low attendance. Sponsors of awards, unless they are highly prestigious or attract huge media attention, ought to be judicious in their use of sponsorship. Many attendees have difficulty remembering later who was behind what.
- Many hospitality venues are ineffective. The box at the concert hall actually allows little time to talk with guests.
- Many sporting sponsorships are distinctly "macho" in flavour and unappealing to the growing number of female buyers.
- If poorly organized, sponsored events end up being used mostly by employees because the invitation process is badly handled or the tone of the event is unattractive to the intended audience.

History, context, criticism, and development

Sponsorship has, like other marketing activities, existed for more than a hundred years. Three academic researchers at Queen's University have tracked much of its early development (see Cunningham et al., 1997). For example, the caterers Spiers & Pond sponsored a British cricket tour of Australia in 1861 to the tune of £11,000 (a princely sum at the time). Whereas *The Times* of 1850 thought that the example of Curriers Company in putting £100 of sponsorship to the "Exhibition of the products of Industry of all Nations" might be *"an example which other corporate companies might follow with advantage"* (*London Times*, 19 January 1850). It was also evident in America around this time. For example, the Remington Rifle company donated a prize for marksmanship in New York in 1878 and Tiffany donated twelve prizes to support a charity doll show in 1890. Coca-Cola sponsored baseball from the start of the 20th century and invested heavily in the 1928 Olympics.

The word "sponsorship" itself seemed to emerge through press reporting in 1920s America (it entered the *Oxford Dictionary* around 1930). Once the term emerged, frequency and amount also seemed to accelerate. It was also encouraged by the development of new media. In America, for example, Firestone and Standard Oil sponsored auto racing to take advantage of the spread of radio. Whereas, in 1957 Britain, the only sponsored event on television was the Whitbread Gold Cup. The method was taken up by tobacco firms as they were increasingly constrained in their advertising (a third of all sponsorship in Britain in the 1970s) and it had exploded as a marketing mechanism within two decades.

In the latter half of the 20th century, though, the practice began to get more structured. It seems that, prior to the 1980s, sponsorship was generally the responsibility of PR departments and approached in a rather ad hoc way. Signage, presence, and awareness were seen as its main benefits. After that, it became more common practice, particularly in America, for sponsorship to move into the province of marketing and used as just another part of the communications mix. Some called it "event marketing" and specialist roles emerged in marketing departments. The 1984 Los Angeles Olympics (the first to turn a profit) seem to have been a turning point. Companies like Fuji photo and Budget rent-a-car gained a particular boost through sponsorship there. Afterward, agencies and client side marketers began to build organizational competence to ensure that commercial sponsorship became a respected part of marketing campaigns.

Exhibition organizers have, for many years, sought sponsors for elements of their shows. It has, though, become an increasingly important part of their revenue. Some sponsor whole shows or complete tournaments, others complete venues (like the O2 entertainment arena in London). Some brands have created their own television content.

A recent emphasis has been on the development of "sponsorship partners". Disney pioneered this by forging partnerships with sponsors since the early 1950s. For instance, Walt Disney himself brought Coca-Cola in to help with the construction of his first theme park in 1955. As of 2009, they had about twenty "global sponsoring partners" including Visa, Nestlé, Kodak, and HP. These agreements cover a range of items from themed attractions in the parks and product placement in shows or films. Their prime criterion is association with the brand. This approach seems to be supported by research. One study (Engage research, July 2010) found that those who developed an ongoing relationship with football did better in terms of consumer recognition than short-term ad campaigns.

Voices and further reading

- Gillies, C., *Business Sponsorship*. Butterworth-Heinemann. 1991.
- "Sponsorship is a highly effective and imaginative communications medium which uses all the marketing disciplines under one umbrella." Gillies, ibid.
- Beck-Burridge, M. and Walton, J., *Sports Sponsorship and Brand Development*. Palgrave, 2001.
- "Sponsorship has been a popular means of supporting a product or organization's position in its chosen markets since the 1980's. The impetus to seek a wider variety of communication channels to promote a name or product derived mostly from the growing cost of media advertising. In addition, sponsoring the right kind of person or activity often gave global coverage that would have been difficult to achieve elsewhere, and sponsorship also offered tobacco companies exposure that was increasingly difficult to achieve as they were banned from TV advertising." McDonald, M.H.B., 2007.
- Collett, P. and Fenton, W., *The Sponsorship Handbook*. John Wiley & Sons Ltd. 2011.

- "Sponsorship is a complex marketing tool and the work required to implement effective sponsorship programmes on behalf of an organization should not be underestimated. Nevertheless, it is currently one of the most powerful ways for brands to connect with their customers in the multi-channel, experience-orientated environment in which we live today." Collett and Fenton, ibid.

Things you might like to consider

(i) When it comes to sponsorship pure rationality rarely applies. The decision to sponsor can come from a leader's personal interests (one leading consultancy puts millions into show jumping because a lead partner is an equestrian) or social ambitions (the passage of more than one knighthood was eased by charitable sponsorship). So, sponsorship can be politically ingrained and hard to rationalize. Few projects are based on realistic business cases and, in many instances, the spend is simply not justified. Marketers ought to be a little more hard headed and, within political constraints (or they won't have a head), ensure that any spend is really effective.

(ii) Again, this should be about developing professional processes and organizational capability. Sponsorship can be structured to be part of the campaign management process; i.e. broken down into project components. It can, without doubt, be subject to all the standard rigours of budgeting and authorization. The company can also gear up organizational competence by hiring a specialist team and using sponsorship consultancies or agencies.

(iii) Sponsorship specialists and proponents use convoluted arguments to support their programmes; often based on a distortion of the PR cost-effectiveness argument. Some, for example, argue that the relative cost of getting a name seen at sporting event is much less expensive than, say, advertising on a cost per view basis. This comparison with advertising is probably fallacious though. When advertising is properly planned, it conveys an engaging message which no board at a stadium can get near to matching. Most of the people that attend football or rugby matches have no idea what some companies stand for and don't need to because they are not in the target market. Those that do know what these firms are about might wonder why they pay high fees if their suppliers can be so lavish.

(iv) In a de-centralized organization it can be costly, erratic, and poorly organized. One marketer, conducting a review of sponsorship, found that their firm had sponsorship at every single football ground north of London and many rugby grounds too. They sponsored players, boxes, events, and young teams. Each had been sanctioned by local leaders on little more than a whim. Even when the total cost was totted up and the fiasco made clear it was hard to make individual executives behave rationally about their own pet sporting fixture.

 RATING: Practical

THOUGHT LEADERSHIP

Application: marketing communication, diffusion of an innovation, NSD

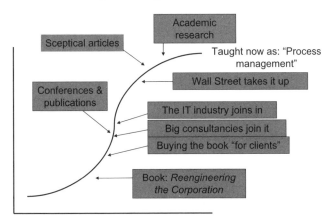

Figure T.1: An illustration of the development of the thought leadership work around "process re-engineering"

The concept

Thought leadership is a term used commonly within the professions, consultancy firms, and the technology industries for the publication and dissemination of ideas for commercial advantage. The communication programmes that surround it can range from an article in a magazine to a major, sponsored PR programme or a complete book. Many management ideas, both credible and not-so-credible, have been developed and promoted in this way. Some then fail; others become established concepts, validated by academic research. The "*Boston Matrix*" as a strategic planning tool, process management, and quality strategy are but a few principles that are now taught routinely at business school but were developed in this way.

This is probably one of the most influential and successful marketing strategies that the world has seen and it is surprising that it appears so rarely in text books on the principles of marketing or publications on marketing communication. It is a vast, influential, and diverse range of activities, which, at its best, produces systematic, iconic work like the *McKinsey Quarterly*. The worst, though, has been mocked by the *Economist* magazine as "Thought Followship" because it is frequently just the erratic, whimsical jottings of professionals from different disciplines tying to "market" themselves between projects; some of it is not leadership and some of it isn't even clear thought. Yet the power of this approach to amplify an excellent reputation and draw in customers is undeniable. It has been used by marketers in all industries at different points in the diffusion of new ideas into their markets. In fact, the energy and resources put into this activity by modern businesses mean that it could be considered to be the market place for ideas.

Despite the vast range of thought leadership activities, some significant ideas "break through". They command the attention of a world-wide audience and seem to match the *diffusion of innovation* process in terms of their own acceptance patterns. A few years ago, for instance, a thought called "business process re-engineering" (BPR) came to prominence. It started in the 1990s and can be credited largely to Professor Michael Hammer and a consultancy called CSC (originally Computer Science Corporation of America). In 1990 Hammer published a Harvard business article (Hammer, M., 1990) after teaching computer science at MIT. He suggested that radical improvements in productivity could be achieved if top management reformed and streamlined the operational processes of their business. An approach was developed which involved designing the operational processes of a future vision of the business. An audit would then be conducted of the existing operational processes and an interception strategy created. He developed this thinking into a book (Hammer M. and Champy, J., 1992) which became a runaway success. It became one of the most famous business books of the time and spent many weeks at the top of the *New York Times* best seller list.

In fact, the prominence of that position illustrates some of the dilemmas that marketers have with thought leadership. There are persistent allegations that those involved in the book (and a subsequent one from the same stable) purchased it for clients in shops where *The Times* measured sales of books. The implication is that such a method would be unethical, distorting the picture of demand for the book. Yet, even if this were true, if the idea was sound and the promulgators believed it would genuinely benefit the business community, is this not just smart marketing? Some of the negative press the consultancy subsequently received shows the difficulty in getting this balance right; the awkward relationship between the integrity of an idea and its promotion is part of the challenge of thought leadership.

The computer industry began to adopt the idea because they realized they could sell computers through re-engineering projects by introducing systems analysis techniques. Marketers in technology companies took the case studies they had used as examples of the effectiveness of the previous influential idea (called "Total Quality Management", TQM) and re-packaged them as "Process re-engineering", because it would sell computers. Again, this was not necessarily dubious practice because TQM undoubtedly had an effect on the quality of operational processes. Technology marketers presented at conferences and wrote articles as if BPR had been happening for years; adding to the cacophony of voices. In fact, as conference companies employ "product managers" (an aspect of marketing) whose job is to spot developing trends which will attract audiences, they were soon dedicating whole conferences to BPR.

Finally, analysts in Wall Street and other financial centres became involved in the idea. They were convinced of its applicability and started to mark down the shares of companies who had not "re-engineered". This prompted yet more companies to take on the approach, improving many. It is difficult to exaggerate the prominence given to this idea in the mid 1990s and the number of American companies that embarked on a BPR project. In fact, there is evidence that this trend helped the United States to achieve the remarkable gains in manufacturing productivity that it did during that decade. It also paved the way for approaches like Six Sigma. However, it became, for a while, a populist dogma as business leaders were expected to have adopted it. As a result it damaged some companies because they were either not ready for it or because change was handled in a ham-fisted way. CSC's own statistics at the time indicated that as much as 25% of BPR projects were ineffective.

At the height of the diffusion of this idea, two things happened. Firstly, academics started to get research budgets to investigate the concept using proper, peer-reviewed methodologies. Now, as a result, most business schools tend to teach "process management", assimilated with proactive quality techniques like TQM and Six Sigma, in their operations faculty. Secondly, sceptics wrote articles like "Has process re-engineering damaged corporate America?" These iconoclasts make money by challenging an idea and saying that it is not a panacea which will change the whole of business. Using PR they suggested, for example, that it dehumanized the work place and acted as an excuse for downsizing.

It is strange that it is so rarely recognized that Thought Leadership is a marketing technique. Marketers can use it to gain revenue and competitive advantage. They can pioneer ideas (the most costly approach), validate new ideas (an approach open to leading brands), join the wave of breakthrough ideas as a sales tool (most powerful when professional services, IT, and City firms all join in), or play the sceptic. They can aim communications programmes about specific ideas at different customer groups. For instance, certain – generally large – corporations are nearly always the same "early adopters" (see *diffusion of innovations*) of a new idea and are ideal targets for innovative ideas. Yet it is not just a PR or communications technique. It has been the source of new services and new businesses (earning many millions of dollars) amongst thousands of professional practices alone.

Thought leadership works because ideas which resonate have powerful influence on both consumers and business leaders. The technology industries have convinced the world, for example (largely through this method) that we all need a PC and a mobile phone, and will be retarded if we are not on the internet. In business-to-business markets, on the other hand, it has generated the business equivalent of "urban myths"; causing, in some cases, immense damage. For instance, most management audiences will recognize:

- "50% of my advertising budget is wasted, I don't know which 50%"; or
- "It costs more to recruit a new customer than retain an existing one"; and:
- "The average dissatisfied customer tells 13 other people if they experience bad service."

Each of these is a manufactured idea which circulates amongst management networks gaining influence. In a busy job where leaders do not get time to think, they make decisions, policy arguments, and presentations, with these propositions clustered in the back of their mind. So, the ideas become *de facto* strategies and, as a result, they have wide impact on businesses creating interest and demand for help from the firms that promulgate them.

Where advice is needed, thought leadership can be an important marketing tool. Leading consultancies like Deloitte, PwC, and Accenture create dedicated groups of specialists to lead this function. Their job is to look across the work in their firm and create new concepts from different projects underway in their practice. They turn emerging themes into services or concepts that will help clients create value in their business. In other words, they fashion ideas to sell to clients; and they do it very well. However, even at this level, actually gaining traction is difficult. It has been estimated, for instance, that the number of "white papers" produced by industry every month is around 10,000. Ideas which have stood out from the crowd (like: TQM, the millennium bug, shareholder value, the dot com revolution, CRM, customer loyalty, and many others) have therefore gained traction through powerful, respected media. One of these is, for example, the *Harvard Business Review* and another is the annual conference of the World Economic Forum in Davos. Ideas presented through media that are respected by senior audiences tend to catch on and flourish. Contrary to popular belief, many CEOs and other senior executives read, listen, and explore developing ideas or policies. Some see a major part of their role as introducing change and reform to their organization in order to meet future demands and are thus prepared to investigate developing trends.

The steps to effective thought leadership appear to start with the choice of an idea. This can come from deep personal knowledge of an industry sector or a leadership team's personal prioritization of candidate concepts. More often it is an adaptation of an important or popular subject to particular circumstances. However, all who succeed with this approach have to put investment behind their work to gain appropriate impact.

Thought leadership can be expensive in terms of both cash and time costs. So, it is sensible to create a discipline to manage the investment. This might include:

- Cost management. Cash costs include: research, printing, promotion, and publication. Time costs include the opportunity cost of employees taken away from chargeable work, subcontractors, and support staff.
- Criteria for approval. These might involve: payback, commercial opportunity, quality, reputation enhancement.
- Anticipated revenue or leads stimulated.
- Timetable of all projects.

History, context, criticism, and development

The idea should have sold itself. At the time (the late 1880s) clothes washing was an arduous, manual, and back breaking process which took a whole day. (It was so awful, in fact, that one of the ad campaigns for the revolutionary new product had a strapline which screamed, in huge letters: "Why does a woman look old sooner than a man?"). It was done in a vast trough, with bucket after bucket of water heated over a range. Soap (which did not lather) had to be flaked into a mixture with soda or lye to burn away stains (urine or pig manure if these were not available). So, the pleasant smelling "Sunlight Self-Washer" soap should have been an immediate runaway success. Yet William Lever (the marketing genius who founded Lever Brothers) knew that such an innovation needed more than just sales and advertising. He had to educate the public in the concept of a self-lathering soap. In 1886, for example, Lever wrote a promotional booklet for customers (see Macqueen, A., 2004) called "Sunlight soap and how to use it" which was distributed to potential customers. It gave instructions, "brought down to the level of the working man's needs" on how the product could be used for a range of household tasks. As the product boomed his growing company went on to produce *The Sunlight Year Book* a "multi-purpose guide to life" which was printed annually.

Created by a pharmacist in 1886, it became the world-wide marketing success of the 20th century. Yet Coca-Cola's early days were marred by controversy. Opinion leaders were critical of its health effects and there were persistent rumours that the early version of the top secret recipe contained actual cocaine. Apart from vast advertising investment (by 1912 it was the most extensively advertised product in the USA) the manufacturers set out to educate the public in its use and possibilities. Apart from PR, celebrity endorsement, and free trials, they used thought leadership (even though they didn't call it that). In 1909, for instance, the company wrote a "book of information" about the product and distributed millions (Pendergrast, M., 1993). In 1932, they gave away millions of copies of a book by a celebrity homemaker, Ida Bailey Allan. (She had a syndicated radio show "The radio homemaker's club".) Her book was a guide to entertaining (neighbours and the husband's boss) for a new generation of post war homemakers for what was then a new, modern outlook. It covered meals and etiquette; and Coca-Cola featured prominently. They were searching for an American cuisine and mode of entertainment at the start of the American century; and Coca-Cola was leading this thinking.

There is no doubt that, in business–to-business markets too, the creation, exploration, and dissemination of ideas have been used very effectively for many years. At the start of the industrial revolution, for example, a group of influential British friends (including Josiah Wedgwood, Matthew Boulton, Erasmus Darwin [grandfather of Charles], James Watt, and Joseph Priestley) formed the "lunar society" (see Uglow, J., 2003). This was, in fact, a regular dinner held at the full moon so that attendees could find their way home more easily. It was part of an elite network which embraced developing ideas across business, science, and the arts. They explored botany, chemistry, geography, manufacturing, sales, and marketing techniques. Each published extensively, promoting ideas through influential bodies (like the Royal Society) and they were influential in the invention or development of number of ideas (like the copying machine, carbonated water and, thank goodness, the coffee percolator). Their thought leadership produced new products and new businesses. It led directly, for example, to the success of one of the most important business-to-business companies of their time: the Boulton & Watt steam power company.

Business books, text books, and magazines disseminated business concepts (like *AIDA*) across the leaders of the world throughout the 19th century and into the 20th, the *Harvard Business Review* being, of course, one of the most influential. After the Second World War, though, in parallel with the creation of a class of professional managers, there seemed to be an explosion of these new business concepts. They included, *inter alia*, brainstorming, decision trees, theory X&Y, MBO, experience curves, zero based budgeting, excellence, TQM, MBWA, Kaban, and intrapreneuring. As a result, many executives, wearied by this deluge of concepts, began to become suspicious of fads and fashions in management thinking. This seemed to lead, in the latter half of the 20th century, to the development of organizational capability amongst elite, high quality organizations. In response to the then pre-eminence of Bane, for example, McKinsey established its high quality thought leadership programme, the *McKinsey Quarterly*.

In many cases, though, breakthrough ideas were still developed by charismatic individuals. These were the source of the ideas mentioned earlier, for example. "50% of my advertising budget . . ." was made famous by David Ogilvy, in his 1963 book,

Confessions of an Advertising Man, which sold a million copies. "The average dissatisfied customer tells . . ." was made famous by ex-McKinsey partner, Tom Peters in presentations about his book *In Search of Excellence*. He was quoting 1980s research into American supermarket shoppers, unlikely to be relevant to modern businesses. "It costs more to gain a new customer…" came from Frederick Reichheld's book *The Loyalty Effect*. Interestingly, although each of these ideas is not relevant in all business situations, they still influence decisions. This tradition continues at the time of writing with celebrity authors like Malcolm Gladwell, whose thought leadership and influence cross between business, politics, and general interest; in the style of the lunar men.

Voices and further reading

- Shapiro, E.C. *Fad Surfing in the Boardroom.* Addison Wesley, 1997.
- Hansen, M.T., Nohria, N., and Tierney, T., "What's your strategy for managing knowledge?" Harvard Business Review, March–April 1999.
- "Some knowledge-intensive products and services – like reengineering consulting, for example – mature over time and become commodities." Hansen, Nohria, and Tierney, ibid.

Things you might like to consider

(i)   Although marketing is important to thought leadership, the integrity of the idea is of over-riding importance. In all cases of breakthrough concepts, the proponents seem to have genuinely and passionately believed in their concept and its importance to their time.

(ii)   This does seem to be a way in which mankind in general, and business in particular, learns. As a new concept is adopted, evaluated, and adjusted, it seems to sink into the lexicon of business education.

(iii)   This is a good source of revenue. Funds can flow from breakthrough books, speaking engagements, and advisory practices dedicated to a concept. With a breakthrough idea, the earnings can be many millions.

(iv)   This is closely aligned to work by PR specialists around "opinion formers" and "opinion pieces".

(v)   Time and again, this approach has been used by marketers (in both consumer and business-to-business markets) in the early days of an innovation to educate markets in a new concept.

(vi)   There is virtually no good quality research or academic work on this technique. Despite its self-evident power it does not normally appear in marketing text books on communication. As a result, most techniques and principles employed by marketers today are based on trial and error.

(vii) Certain cultures (e.g. California and Scandinavian countries), certain businesses, and certain individuals (see mavens in diffusion of innovations) always respond well to a new idea or concept. They can be explicitly targeted.

(viii) There is a risk to a firm's reputation if they are seen as being too closely associated with exploiting an insubstantial fad.

Interbrand thinks about brand value

Interbrand was founded in 1974 in London as a specialist brand consultancy and now has offices in 35 countries around the world. Over the years it has developed expertise in a diverse range of brand skills, including: brand development and management, naming, design, corporate identity, communications, and brand valuation, a discipline which it pioneered (Interbrand was the first company to put a value on a brand publicly).

One of the main techniques the company has used to differentiate itself from competitors and be seen as a thought leader in all aspects of branding has been a continuous and consistent programme of reputation-enhancing materials. For example, its professionals publish up to two books every year, write numerous articles for publication in different countries, speak at conferences, and are quoted regularly in the media.

The firm also runs themed evenings for clients and the media in some of its main offices. In addition, it set up brandchannel.com, which publishes papers on a wide range of branding topics, as well as acting as the conduit for a worldwide exchange of views on brands and branding.

What has really secured Interbrand's place as an authority on brands is the annual survey of the world's 100 most valuable global brands, a survey it has been carrying out since 1997. For the first two years it was done in conjunction with the *Financial Times* but, in 1999, it formed an association with *Business Week* to get more of a global scope and wider exposure.

In the survey, Interbrand uses its now well established brand valuation process to determine, as closely as possible, the true economic value of what it describes as the "complex array of forces that make up a brand". There are also a number of local league tables done with local publications in countries such as France, Brazil, Mexico, Spain, Australia, Singapore, and Taiwan. Additional regional surveys are used to help introduce the firm into new markets.

One of Interbrand's advantages is that when people think about brands, they will often think about the company's league table valuation. This can not only be used as a calling card to attract new clients, but it also gives Interbrand credibility in the boardroom of those target clients. This is in line with the company's objective of creating more in-depth relationships with clients, traditionally the preserve of management consultancies, as branding becomes more integrated into overall business strategy.

Evidence of the headway made by this Thought Leadership programme comes from a US survey of chief executive officers which found that while the first and second most admired tables were the *Fortune* 500 and *Fortune's* America's Most Admired Companies respectively, Interbrand's Top 100 brands came third.

 RATING: Practical and powerful

V

 **VALUE PROPOSITIONS**

**Application: revenue and margin maximization, repositioning
commodities. NPD/NSD, innovation management, pricing, sales**

Developing a value proposition

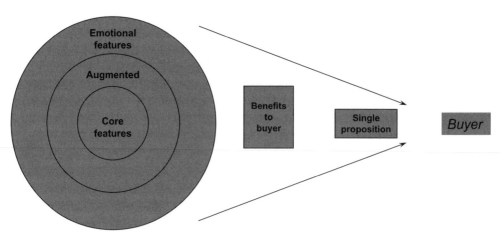

Figure V.1: A representation of a method to reach a clear value proposition

The concept

Surprisingly, the term "value proposition" (which is common parlance among marketers in many different industries) appears in very few marketing texts. A value proposition is an offer to customers which meets their buying criteria at a price that they regard, however illogically or unfairly they form that judgement, as "value for money". Contrary to popular opinion, *price*, or more accurately, cheapness is not a buyer's prime consideration. Sometimes they are willing to pay more for a particular item and sometimes they deliberately choose an "expensive" offer. It depends on the value of the offer to them.

Some new offers fail to make money, not through poor planning or inadequate component design, but because they are misrepresented in the market place: there is not a clear, simple, appealing value proposition. The marketing and sales literature is merely a description of the various components and features. To succeed, it is essential that the raw elements of the offer are turned into a proposition to which buyers can relate. It would be ridiculous, for example, to describe a fast food outlet as follows: "Our service contains people in a carefully designed uniform who prepare a limited range of food very quickly using the latest technology to cook; it is both hot and ready to eat very quickly." Buyers would be bored by the time they reached the end. Yet this is exactly what many marketers, particularly in *business-to-business* markets, do with their offer.

One fundamental reason for this failure is that the creation of a value proposition is frequently fragmented. Engineers or operations specialists will create the components of the offer, an accountant will agree pricing, different sales people will work out the benefits to customers, marketers will create promotional material which pulls all the details together, and an advertising agency will create a one-line summary of the proposition. As a result, a haphazard and unclear proposition is put to the market and fails to gain traction. This crucially important function should be managed within the firm by marketers. An attractive proposition, which summarizes the offer in clear terms, should be created and put to the market.

Most important of all, though, it must be based on what customers value. They will want a mix of features and price which represents value to them. If this was the subject of research, the output in most markets would be a scatter diagram which resembled Figure V.2 below. The horizontal axis is "perceived price", and the vertical "perceived quality"; both of which are components of value. The buyers' ideal purchases will be scattered around a line (the line on which suppliers can achieve long-term position; see separate entry for "positioning"). In a market which is not distorted by monopoly or regulation, most buyers cluster around the middle, a position that the market leader can dominate. Some, though, will want a no-frills, least-cost offer, whereas others want something that is features-rich. A shopper at Harrods food hall in London will think the quality of product justifies the higher prices, whereas someone who shops at a local market, because they are more interested in lower prices, will be just as satisfied. Both think that they get value for money. This

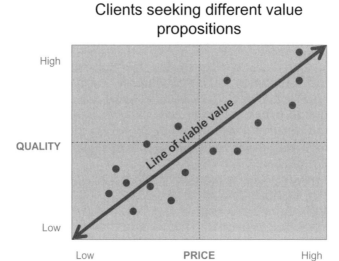

Figure V.2: Customers' perceptions of value

scattering occurs in any given market and allows suppliers to create different offers at different prices.

The map represents buyers' views of the issues that are important to them and the way suppliers should respond to them. It is the job of the marketer to create a value proposition that meets one or more of these different expressions of perceived value.

In his book on marketing strategy Professor Kumar (Kumar, N., 2004) points out that value propositions need to be developed for each customer segment and he uses "value curves" to compare the offers of competitors to those segments. He argues that marketers should work through several issues (attributes the industry takes for granted, attributes which could be reduced, attributes which could be increased above industry standard, and possible new attributes) in developing value propositions.

History, context, criticism, and development

Some of the FMCG companies, like Gillette for example, have long excelled at the creation of clear value poosyions ("three blades, fewer strokes, less irritation"). However, at the time of writing, marketers in different marketing environments, particularly *business-to-business*, are tackling this issue. They will often hold, for example, a "value proposition workshop" to clarify the promise to customers before any offer goes anywhere near the market. Many will even use this approach with individual sales deals to significant customers. They think through the components of a dynamic model shown in Figure V.1. They are:

- A clear understanding of the buyers the value proposition is aimed at, including their rational and emotional needs;
- An integrated view of the tangible and intangible components of the offer, and their value to the buyers (see separate entry for *features analysis*);
- The benefits of the proposition;
- An understanding of the *differentiation* and "unique selling proposition" of the offer;
- A short market-based description of the offer, sometimes called the elevator pitch.

Voices and further reading

- "After the general plan has been made, the product must again be the subject of careful inquiry for that purpose of finding the selling points that will be most effective in making sales. The salesman and the advertising man must pick the product to pieces so that its every aspect, its every use, may be known and utilized in marketing appeal." Butler, R.S., *Marketing Methods; Modern Business*. Alexander Hamilton Institute, 1917.
- Barnes, C., Blake, H., and Pinder, D., *Creating and Delivering your Value Proposition*. Kogan Page, 2009.
- "A value proposition is a clear, compelling and credible expression of the experience that a customer will receive from a supplier's measurably value-creating offering, where Value = Benefits minus cost. It is not a description of what your organization does for a customer." Barnes, Blake, and Pinder, ibid.
- "Ultimately it is perceived value that attracts a customer or lures a customer away from a competitor. In this sense, perceived value and satisfaction vie for attention in managerial strategy. . . . Value may be conceptualized as arising from both quality and price or from what one gets and what one gives. Value increases as quality increases and price decreases yet exactly how quality and price combine to form value is not well understood." Rust, R.T. and Oliver, R.L., 1994.
- "The value to the customer resides not in any single product but in the reassurance that the company will continue to offer them a stream of products tailored to their particular needs . . . By continually offering superior customer value to the customer in an extended relationship, the financial or physiological cost to the customer of switching to another supplier rises dramatically. The result is increased levels of customer retention and profitability and a potential decrease in customer sensitivity to price." Payne, A., 2006.
- "The next two processes define the core of the value proposition to the customer. While they can occur in either order, organizations typically start by defining the value they hope to receive from the segment: . . . the other half of the equation is defining the value to be delivered to the customer in return. This price/value proposition can be thought of using the four Cs: 'cost', 'convenience', 'communication' and 'consumer wants and needs'." McDonald, M.H.B., 2007.

Things you might like to consider

(i) Customers' views may not be technically correct or factually accurate because they represent perception. It may be that there are offers which provide excellent technical performance (one version of quality) but are not perceived to be the leading offer or the best quality offer by the majority of the market.

(ii) For something which is so important to margin and revenue growth it is surprising that there is so little conceptual work around "value propositions".

> ★ **RATING: Practical**

VIRAL MARKETING (BUZZ)

Application: communications

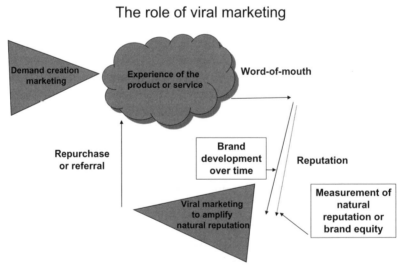

The role of viral marketing

Figure V.3: The role of viral marketing

The concept

This is the deliberate dissemination of ideas and concepts through networks of human beings to promote products and services. "Viral marketing" (viral because the aim is to spread an idea among a target community in much the same way as a virus spreads in a body) exploits social communications and gossip. It is a deliberate attempt to spread positive recommendations, and different messages, through informal customer networks. It can create excitement, respect, and demand for a brand, a product, or a service. It aims to amplify word-of-mouth and is, at the time of writing, one of the newest areas of emphasis among marketers. Although successful business leaders and marketers have been intuitively nurturing word-of-mouth for many years, marketing specialists are only now beginning to properly understand and codify successful techniques to exploit it. For instance, academic research has demonstrated that "word-of-mouth" plays a particularly important role in building services revenue.

History, context, criticism, and development

Marketers and business leaders have known of the value of "word-of-mouth" (WOM), the natural reputation which develops form the use of a product or service, for many centuries. If WOM is positive, then a positive reputation will grow and other customers will buy; so, consequently, sales will grow.

John Pears, for instance, was a hairdresser in London who had a really exciting innovation: a new soap which his upmarket customers loved. They loved it so much, in fact, that it turned into a very successful 200-year-old brand. In his time, there was an economic boom, stimulated by the industrial revolution; there was a fast changing society and new shopping habits prompted by people with newly acquired wealth and international visitors to London's exciting shops. He wanted to find a way to kick-start the sales of his lovely new product and hit on a form a viral marketing: he paid children to run around London with catch phrases ("What's up Pear's soap"; see: Macqueen, A., 2004).

During the Edo period of Japan, advertisers also used viral marketing. One of their most powerful marketing tools were "hikifuda"; exquisitely painted hand bills. According to Japan's museum of advertising and marketing, upmarket advertisers handed the beautiful sheets "only to valued customers and neighbourhood leaders. These folk, in turn, were counted on to disseminate the information by word-of-mouth" – an early use of viral marketing. This method was routinely used at the time to market products like toothpaste, clothing, smoking accessories, and sake (see Pollock, D., 1995).

Viral marketing has also been used in business-to-business markets. Consultants and IT companies have used it to market *thought leadership* output: the marketing of business ideas. A new idea will emerge from a business thinker or a consultancy in the form of a "white paper" or book. It will be presented at a few leading conferences. (It is most powerful if it gets a hearing at chief executive-level conferences such as the World Economic Forum held each year at Davos.) Product managers in conference companies then spot the idea, allowing time on agendas for it to be presented. Soon whole conferences are dedicated to it, articles published, and books authored. Leading consultancies then dedicate partners and staff to practice in the area. They adjust case studies from past projects and present briefs to their clients. At this stage, academics get funding for reputable research into the idea and add to its visibility. The new idea is "viral", carried and reinforced by debate in the business community which can enhance the reputation and position of the firm if properly resourced and managed. So, viral marketing has been the primary tool for communicating thought leadership pieces to business buyers.

Another significant manifestation of viral marketing has occurred time and again between venture capitalists and the technology entrepreneurs in America's Silicon Valley. They have promulgated new concepts in order to sell technology and create funding for new technology companies.

Yet the technique was made famous through the growing interconnections on the internet. As email, YouTube, social networking sites, and Twitter enhanced people's ability to chatter and gossip through wide interconnected networks, the ability to spread ideas, concepts, and events also grew. People could circulate images, ideas, and jokes very easily. There have, for example, been several famous instances of sexual indiscretions being discussed in emails with friends and then being copied to so many people that, within days, they are reported in national newspapers. Some companies have exploited this phenomenon by creating short, humorous video clips that are for the internet alone. As the technique involves the transportation of an idea from person to person, it is a powerful way of judging popularity.

Several writers have picked up on the phenomenon and prompted marketers to think in a structured way about it. The most famous was the author of *The Tipping Point*, Malcolm Gladwell. In his highly successful book (Gladwell, M., 2006) he charts the history of word-of-mouth in spreading new ideas, including new products and services. He suggests several common characteristics of effective word-of-mouth: "contagiousness", "little changes have big effects", and "change happens at a dramatic moment". He also gave names to different types of people who play important parts in spreading an idea: "connectors", "mavens", and "salesmen". There is evidence that some companies have succeeded in marketing innovations by identifying and connecting with these different types; as Apple has done, for instance, with its work with "super users".

Conceptually, this technique is obviously closely connected to the *diffusion of innovations* (see separate entry and Rogers E.M., 2003). With the rise of the internet and social networking tools, it became a very popular, almost faddish technique and became known as "buzz marketing" (Rosen, E., 2001). In fact, some have argued that this ought to be the prime method of marketing in the 21st century. They cite the fact that broadcast TV networks are disrupted and that customers are demanding new offers which are distinctive (see Godin S., 2004). This does, though, seem a little extreme. It seems very risky to neglect other tools of communication and brand building; and to ignore the majority in markets. At the time of writing, evidence suggests, for instance, that big budget marketing companies are returning to highly targeted broadcast marketing, integrated with online and digital strategies. It may turn out then that viral marketing is the codification and explicit use of one communication technique in the marketer's armoury at particular phases in the development of a market, something that smart marketers having been doing, intuitively, for many decades.

Voices and further reading

* "Word of mouth: understanding and managing referral marketing." Buttle, F.A., *Journal of Strategic Marketing*, 6, 1998.
* Reicheld, F.F., "The only number you need to grow". *Harvard Business Review*, December 2003.
* "Research shows that, in most industries, there is a strong correlation between a company's growth rate and the percentage of its customers who are 'promoters'- that is, those who say they are extremely likely to recommend the company to a friend or colleague." Reicheld, F.F., ibid.
* "Neither company practice nor academic research pay sufficient attention to the important area of advocacy and referral marketing. Few organizations have any formal processes that utilise referrals from existing customers. Though many organizations recognize that customers can be the most legitimate source of referrals to their prospective customers, most tend to simply let referrals happen rather than proactively developing marketing activities to leverage the power of advocacy." (Payne, A. 2006.)
* Shaw, R., "Net promoter". *Journal of Database Marketing and Customer Strategy Management*, August 2008.
* "Involvement is a fundamental aspect of consumer behavior, and low-involvement purchasing behavior is entirely different from high-involvement purchasing. The vast majority of purchases are low-involvement and habit is often the guiding force for the consumer. These low-involvement purchases by their nature don't generate WOM buzz and therefore net promoter can be ruled out as a useful measure on cause and effect grounds. High-involvement purchases are items that are important to the purchaser and are closely tied to their ego and self-image . . . and WOM is more likely." Shaw, ibid.
* Gladwell, M., *The Tipping Point*. Abacus, 2006.
* "The tipping point is the biography of an idea, and the idea is very simple. It is the best way to understand the emergence of fashion trends, the ebb and flow of crime waves, or for that matter, the transformation of unknown books into best sellers, or the rise of teenage smoking or the phenomenon of word-of-mouth, or any number of the other mysterious changes that mark everyday life is to think of them as epidemics. Ideas and products and messages and behaviors spread just like viruses do." Gladwell, ibid.
* Rosen, E., *The Anatomy of Buzz: Creating Word-of-mouth Marketing*. HarperCollins, 2001.
* Buzz doesn't affect all businesses in the same way. The role it plays in your business depends on four factors: the nature of your product, the people you're trying

to reach, your customer connectivity, and the strategies used in your industry. Since these factors can change over time, the importance of buzz to your business and industry can fluctuate." Rosen, ibid.

• Godin, S., *Purple Cow*. Penguin, 2004.
• ". . . marketers need to use word-of-mouth marketing to create hypes and a snowball effect to reach the growth stage." Kotler, P. et al., 2010.

Things you might like to consider

(i) This is closely associated with the diffusion of innovation concept.
(ii) A recommendation from a respected source gives a message credibility which can be achieved in few other ways.
(iii) This is now becoming an accepted part of the full marketing communications strategy and mix. It clearly needs to be used to suit some markets that are dominated by some technologies and behaviours or are at, say, a very early phase in their maturity.

 RATING: Practical and powerful

IN CONCLUSION

So, after thirty years of using these concepts and trying to understand both their genesis and applicability, what am I left with? There are a number of issues that marketers ought, I think, to take into account.

THE SOURCE OF MARKETING CONCEPTS

It is noticeable how many of these tools seem to arrive in text books and on marketing courses through fame. The entry under "thought leadership" explores the market for ideas and how, through elite media (like the *Harvard Business Review*) ideas catch on and become adopted. Concepts like the Ansoff Matrix, AIDA, and the Boston Matrix have clearly gained attention in this way. Contrast these with an idea like the AAR model which is a powerful and well researched little tool or Wroe Alderson's remarkable insights into the herd behaviour of markets, neither of which has had similar fame or attention but which are just as useful.

More worrying, though, are those concepts which business leaders and practising marketers have used to create wealth for many decades but have been equally neglected. Nearly two centuries ago, for example, Pears soap clearly used "viral marketing" as a technique to kick-start this highly successful, 200-year-old brand. Why then, after at least a hundred years of text books on marketing and its principles, do modern marketers think they are creating this technique with the internet under the term "Buzz"? Another example is thought leadership. This technique has been used for nearly two centuries and, particularly in business-to-business marketing, has had extensive and remarkable influence. There is no doubt that it has created enormous fortunes for accountants, consultants, and technologists. It has yet, though, to make an appearance in marketing texts or serious academic studies into the impact of marketing techniques. What else is out there which is undiscovered, uncodified, or neglected?

In a busy job, where it's hard to keep up with emails let alone take time out to think, it's easy to get swept up with fashionable thinking or to fall back on well known concepts, without considering their origins or reliability. These can, though, cause marketing programmes to go dangerously awry. It is sensible, if not professional, to understand, as far as possible, the source and credibility of the tools and concepts that are supposed to make shareholders profit. Fame, enthusiasm, and faddish allegiance are simply not good enough foundations to create any concepts reliable enough to make good money for shareholders.

HISTORICAL CONTEXT MATTERS

Many of these tools and the ideas taught around them are creatures of their context. Some, for instance, were developed when the business world was dominated by Western manufacturing companies. They are probably not directly applicable to service companies in, say, China or India with very different assumptions and outlooks.

Just as important is the historical context of the codification of much that is taught as marketing theory. It is routinely suggested, for instance, that there was an evolution of marketing thought. This unsophisticated outlook suggests that in the industrial revolution (the "manufacturing phase") markets were growing very fast and companies could sell all they could make. This was followed by a "sales phase" but markets became saturated and so a "marketing phase" emerged, largely in America, in the mid 20th century (see, for instance, Dibb, S., Simkin, L., Pride, W.M, and Ferrell, O.C., 2006).

Unfortunately this simply does not fit with the historical evidence. Sophisticated branded marketing and advertising were used in various countries from at least the 1700s. Business leaders like Josiah Wedgwood, Matthew Boulton, Robert Woodruff, and Henry Heinz used well rounded marketing programmes to gain insight into customer needs and to build brands. In many cases they created markets or developed nascent opportunities. Marketing text books existed from the early 1900s and there were effective marketing and advertising consultants, certainly in America and the UK, during the late Victorian period. Whilst discussing, for example, the development of complex dyeing techniques during the 1870s (in his remarkable thousand-year history of technology: see Friedel, R., 2007), Professor Robert Friedel says: "In a pattern discernable at least since Wedgwood's day, the expansion of production, the lowering of prices, and the subsequent extension of markets into new segments of society was often accompanied by a growing concern for fashion. This affected a great range of commodities and a wide spectrum of markets, from fine china and furniture to celluloid collars and factory-made clothing." But why does it take a technology professor to see that markets and marketing existed well before the so-called "marketing phase" of mid 20th century America?

What does seem to have happened is that, as American industry boomed in the early and mid 20th century, distribution lines lengthened and enormous mass markets emerged. At the same time, a functional approach to marketing developed. Business owners seemed to get more systematic and separated from their brands, while marketing, as a function, was separated from post purchase service experience. At the same time, leaders like Sloane and Ford promoted a science-based, logical approach to marketing and selling which reflected the views of the time and their mechanistic attitude to both business and people.

Some marketing concepts (like the product life cycle) were born in this context. They emanate from the attempt to turn marketing into a rational, measurable "science". The restrictions of this dogmatic, logical, inhuman approach to markets of emotional, irrational human beings needs to be borne in mind if you are attempting to use the tools created in this environment in any modern context.

In the past fifty years a change in attitude among individuals in Western society, prompted largely by better educational standards, has caused many to challenge authority, to question professionals, and to lobby for individual rights. Gaining momentum largely in the late 1960s and epitomized by the questioning "baby boomer" generation, the "I" society has had a profound effect on many areas of life, business included. Aided by protective consumer legislation and amplified dramatically by the internet, it has enabled customers to challenge the behaviour and attitudes of businesses. Business leaders have had to respond to a range of issues from product performance and after care to governance and environmental issues. Coupled with an expectation among employees that they will be treated as individuals and adults, the mighty industrial machines have been forced to be more responsive to buyers. Marketing principles and practice have had to adjust to this too.

In the last two decades, for instance, debate about the "market of one" has caused practice in consumer businesses to change dramatically. There has been an increasing view that people want to be treated as individuals, to be offered choice based on an understanding of their needs and aspirations. As a result, many firms have revolutionized their marketing, trying to create a two-way dialogue with their customers, which tries to understand their buying patterns, customize offers, and encourage loyalty. Many have invested huge sums in data warehouses and CRM systems to serve restless buyers better.

A similar change has occurred in business-to-business industries, driving suppliers to be more responsive. For example, the leading IT players have run "user groups" for their large buyers for many years. They represent a huge investment by these firms in terms of time, event management, and marketing materials. Often led by a committee of the customers themselves, they create a rich dialogue about investment directions, product development, performance, and future trends. Many are rightly proud of these programmes and market them as an investment in service and responsiveness. What has been forgotten in history is that they began with frustration among key buyers at the lack of responsiveness of systems providers who had a large "installed base". Important customers, held captive by switching costs, began to meet up and lobby for response.

This unwillingness to be the victim of a remote industrial supplier is reflected in the demand for "solutions". Rather than buying the latest machine or piece of software, buyers in markets as different as communications, IT, healthcare, and office machinery expect a customized package which meets a specific need. The suppliers have had to go back to school to learn how to become a "solutions supplier", deploying their people to create unique packages of product, software, and services for their customers. This approach has damaged some, causing prices and margins to plummet. It has also prompted some appalling marketing and brought business language to new depths of awful jargon. Nevertheless, the move to "solutions" is a reflection of the demand from modern business buyers for suppliers to be responsive.

Concepts like "CRM", "solutions marketing", "customer loyalty", "network marketing", "relationship marketing", "inter-active marketing", and "the market of one" all evolved during this time. They may yet turn out to be short–term management fads. Yet all are a reflection of a major and profound change in Western society which has forced industry to treat the individual employee and buyer as human beings. While they might not translate into other cultures, they have caused many firms to completely reassess their approach to market.

In one of his latest books (Kotler, P. et al., 2010), leading marketing guru Philip Kotler has explored this development of marketing ideas and techniques. He relates, for instance, the marketing mix, the product life cycle, segmentation, and the marketing audit to the 1950s. He then relates various other concepts to different decades (e.g. the four Ps to the 1960s; positioning to the 1970s; global marketing and CRM to the 1980s; experiential marketing, internet marketing, and sponsorship to the 1990s; and ROI customer equity, consumer empowerment, and co-creation to the 2000s). In its latest iteration, several writers of the Chartered Institute of Marketing's *Marketing Book* (Baker, M.J. and Hart, S., 2008) also chart this development in marketing thinking to take on issues like services marketing, customization, digital environments, business-to-business marketing, and relationship marketing. This might turn out to be the emergence of an academic, peer-reviewed consensus as seen in other disciplines; or it may not. It does, though, point to the time-dependant applicability of some of the treasures of the marketing canon. These thoughts got us here and were either useful rungs on a ladder or quirky diversions. They are not, though, all valid nor are they universal truths on which practitioners can rely without serious thought.

So, the common concepts and tools of marketing, developed a few decades ago, are not universally applicable nor is it safe to assume that they are equally valid. As a professional, taking decisions about the use of shareholder funds, it is important to ask about their age, context, and applicability. Is a 19th century concept (like AIDA) or an engineering approach to strategy (like Ansoff) really appropriate? It may be, but you ought to know how and why.

THE USEFULNESS OF ACADEMIC WORK ON MARKETING

It is idiotic and unprofessional for marketers, in any discipline, to dismiss or ignore the work of academics. Many of their studies are thorough, relevant, applicable, and practical. Their prime contribution for the practitioner is their ability to spot trends, validate them, and crystallize their observations into general principles, concepts, and tools. Their work has saved many businesses the cost of introducing half baked schemes or mindlessly adopting the latest fad from the latest guru.

If a professional is about to test a new concept (like, say, CEM or viral marketing) and then set about building it into their organization's processes, it is surely important to know that it hasn't just been made up by a loudmouth with something to sell (even if that loudmouth is a member of a respected consultancy firm). If there are well calibrated research projects comprising a hundred, two hundred, or thousands of people, testing a tool that is about to be used, it is sensible to understand some of their implications.

There are problems though:

(i) Sloppiness

It is apparent that some concepts taught today have become distorted through time. One disgraceful example is the simplistic representation of Ansoff's work and the continual reference to his diagram in a 1957 article where it does not actually appear. For the work of a PhD mathematician and respected corporate strategy professor to be so diluted is very poor. It shuts practising marketers out of high level debates about diversification, M&A, and disposal. Another is AIDA. This concept was made up by a marketing consultant around 1889 and is still taught today due to undue fame. The fact that many texts cite the source as a 1925 psychology article, which was debunking it, is very sloppy. It is apparent that some writers simply have not read the sources they quote. Such sloppiness is unacceptable to people who actually try to use these techniques. It damages businesses.

(ii) Bias

There are a number of biases, it seems, in the canon of marketing knowledge. For instance, much of it originates from consumer product marketing in the United States of America during the mid 20th century and much has changed since then. The world's economies are more service dominated and there is greater need for international marketing. Much of modern practice has its heart in very different cultures (like China, India, or Japan). So, the cultural bias in many of the models and concepts needs to be understood and allowed for.

(iii) Lack of an overarching theoretical perspective

In many of the sciences there is a growing body of knowledge against which new hypotheses are tested. Yet despite early attempts to create a "theory of marketing", there is no credible unifying theme in our field. Like the elephant in the poem, each explores an aspect of the entity and presents an incomplete picture.

Whether there will be such a universal perspective on marketing in the foreseeable future is impossible to predict but, until then, practising marketers are left to judge whether one particular concept or tool is applicable in each situation. It's part of the job.

(iv) Isolation of work and concepts

The world-wide marketing landscape seems like a stage lit by a number of limited, precise spotlights. Researchers do cooperate, discuss, and conference. For a practitioner, though, it is very difficult to access excellent valuable, inter-connected concepts.

(v) Lack of rigorous historical context and research

It is exceptionally helpful to learn how enduring techniques have been deployed down the decades and to understand which have been forged by experience. The advent of marketing historians and conferences like the annual CHARM gatherings provide valuable insight to practising marketers. They identify long-term trends and enduring (i.e. non-faddish) practices. They are, though, too few and hard for practitioners to access.

Professor Evert Gummerson is one of the most critical (see Gummerson, E., 2003 and his article in Baker, M J. and Hart, S., 2008). He has suggested that the textbook presentations of marketing are based on limited real world data. He also pointed out that "goods" account for a minor part of all marketing but the textbook presentations are focused on them while services are treated as a special case. He reported that marketing to consumers dominates text books; that business-to-business marketing is treated as a special case, rather than a routine and well developed aspect of the discipline. Most alarmingly he says that the textbook presentations are a patchwork; new knowledge is piled on top of existing knowledge but not integrated with it. They have a clever pedagogical design; the form is better than the content.

Professor Malcolm McDonald speculated about the effect of poor teaching on the actual use of practical concepts. He said: "The DPM can easily be misused and misunderstood, in spite of the technique being described in most marketing texts and taught on courses. The fault appears to lie more with those responsible for writing about and teaching the subject than with those who try to use it. Similar problems caused the somewhat simpler Boston Consulting Matrix to fall into misuse" (McDonald, M.H.B., 1993).

Whereas Professor Paul Fifield thinks the attempt to squeeze marketing into a consistent "scientific" theory is the problem: "The main reason for this apparent confusion is the writers' attempts to try and force every possible situation into a generalized blueprint concept. Marketing is littered with attempts to force theories out of observed good practice and thus make the teacher's and the consultant's job that much easier. We should once and for all accept that this scientific approach just doesn't work in areas like marketing. Marketing success depends on consumer acceptance and this is just not predictable in any scientific sense within scientific limits of accuracy" (Fifield, 1992).

Professor David Carson of the University of Ulster pointed out the disparity between the academic view of marketing and the professionals in the field. He said (in correspondence about this book) that academics assert that it is important to:

(i)   carry out a situation analysis;
(ii) do a SWOT analysis;
(iii) present findings and recommendations which are invariably a radical change such as introducing new products or entering new markets.

Professor Carson contrasts this with the reality in marketing departments. Based on his research they:

(i)   don't advocate radical change;
(ii) don't change the product (immediately);
(iii) look for solutions within the firm's systems;
(iv) promote without heavy spend;
(v)   emphasize: availability, suitability, value perception, and communication;
(vi) focus thinking on what to do and what will work rather than the theoretical marketing process.

It is sensible for professionals to use validated academic work but it is also important to understand the limitations of these concepts.

EMERGING IDEAS AND PROPRIETARY TOOLS

As in any other field of work, marketing is adapting and changing all the time. At the time of writing there are fast emerging ideas, for example, in the fields of research (scanner observations of reactions in the brain of subjects for instance), behavioural economics, loyalty, and digital marketing. Agencies in the marketing supply industry tend to spot credible new trends and create proprietary concepts from which they can profit. These may later be discredited and forgotten; or validated into the broad canon of accepted knowledge. This text has largely tried to steer clear of these but marketers need to make a judgement on their relevance to their work.

THE BEST AND WORST TECHNIQUES

After this long, detailed exploratory journey, my three top tools are:

*   **Brand:** I think the ability to create a distinctive entity which commands customer loyalty and a price premium for several centuries has got to be the best achievement in marketing.

- **Behavioural insights:** Markets are mostly about people and anything which gives insight into their mystifying jumble of wants, needs, demands, and behaviour is potentially profitable.
- **Diffusion of innovation/market maturity:** Understanding the interaction between buyers and suppliers in a social system like a market is fundamental to segmentation, communication, NPD/NSD, and the long-term health of a business.

My bottom three are:

- **PLC:** the idea that each *individual* product or service has a life cycle similar to an s-curve is dangerous and can misdirect investment.
- **AIDA:** It looks easy and logical; and many still use it but does it really reflect human behaviour and should we really rely on a technique made up by an advertising consultant in 1899?
- **Portfolio theory:** Terms like "cash cow" are far too easily and sloppily applied and have, sometimes without analysis, prompted firms to neglect or denude businesses of capital investment. To teach young marketers (who are likely to be in any job for a far shorter time than any of the products, services, or brands they will handle) that it is routine to take money from long-term successful entities to invest in creating risky innovations is daft and naive. The fact that smart entrepreneurs have been able to make millions (even billions) by buying up the resultant orphan brands (see the case study under *portfolio management*) suggests that there is something fundamentally wrong with this approach.

In my view, marketing is not merely management, common sense, art, or an academic field of study. It is a profession. Like accountancy and law it needs deep knowledge of techniques backed by the experience to know when and how to apply those techniques. There is complexity, contradiction, and hard work in grappling with these ideas in order to get the best return for shareholders. I hope that this text makes that task a little easier because, in the end, a professional only has their own judgement to rely on.

REFERENCES

Aaby, N. and Discenza, R., Strategic marketing and new product development. *Journal of Business and Industrial Marketing*, 1993.

Aaker, D., *Building Strong Brands*, The Free Press, 1996.

Aaker, D.A. and Joachimsthaler, E., The lure of global branding, *Harvard Business Review*, November–December 1999.

Ahmed, P.M. and Rafiq, M., *Internal Marketing*, Butterworth-Heinemann, 2002.

Alderson, W., *Marketing Behaviour and Executive Action*, Richard D. Irwin Inc., 1957.

Alexander, R.S., Cross, J.S. and Cunningham, R.M., *Industrial Marketing*, Homewood, 1961.

Allen, S., *The Next Discipline: Applying Behavioural Economics to Drive Growth and Profitability*, Gallop Consulting, 2009.

Ambler, T., *Marketing and the Bottom Line*, FT Prentice Hall, 2003 (2nd edn).

Anderson, E. and Onyemah, V., How right should the customer be?, *Harvard Business Review*, July–August 2006.

Anderson, J.C. and James A.N., Capturing the value of supplementary services, *Harvard Business Review*, January–February 1995.

Ansoff, H.I., Strategies for diversification, *Harvard Business Review*, 35:5, September–October 1957.

Ansoff, H.I., A model for diversification, *Management Science*, 4:1, July 1958.

Ansoff, H.I., *Business Strategy*, Penguin, 1969.

Ansoff, H.I., *Twenty Years of Acquisition Behavior in America*, Cassell, 1972. A long term study (1946–65) into the effectiveness of corporate mergers and acquisitions as a means of business growth.

Ansoff, H.I., *Corporate Strategy*, McGraw-Hill, USA, 1965 and Penguin Books, UK, 1985.

Axelsson, L. and Easton, G., *Industrial Networks: A New View of Reality*, Routledge, 1992.

Baddeley, S. and James, K., Owl, fox, donkey or sheep: political skills for managers, *Management Education and Development*, 18, 1987.

Baker, M.J., *Market development*, Penguin, 1983.

Baker, M.J. and Hart, S. (ed.), *The Marketing Book*, Butterworth-Heinemann, 2008.

Barnes, C., Blake, H. and Pinder, D., *Creating and Delivering your Value Proposition*, Kogan Page, 2009.

Bateson, J.E.G., *Perceived control and the service encounter in The Service Encounter*, Heath, 1985.

Bateson, J.E.G., *Managing Services Marketing (text and readings)*, Dryden Press, 1989.

Bateson, J.E.G. and Hoffman, D.K., *Managing Services Marketing*, Thomson Learning, 1999.

Beck-Burridge, M. and Walton, J., *Sports Sponsorship and Brand Development*, Palgrave, 2001.

Bernays, E., *Propaganda*, IG publishing, 2005 (original 1928).

Berry L.L., In services what's in a name, *Harvard Business Review*, 66, September–October 1988, 28–30.

Berry, L.L., *On Great Service*, The Free Press, 1995.

Binet, L. and Field, P., *Marketing in the Era of Accountability*, WARC, 2007.

Bird, D., *Commonsense Direct and Digital Marketing*, Kogan Page, 2007.

Boaz, N., Murnane, J. and Nuffer, K., The basics of Business-to-business sales success, *McKinsey Quarterly*, May 2010.

Bonoma, T.V., Major sales: who really does the buying?, *Harvard Business Review*, July–August 2006.

Borden, N.H., The concept of the marketing mix, *Journal of Advertising Research*, 1964 (reprinted in *Classics*, Volume II, September 1984).

Brown, R., Managing the 'S' curves of innovation, *Journal of Marketing Management*, July 1991.

Butler, R.S., *Marketing Methods; Modern Business*, Alexander Hamilton Institute, 1917.

Buttle, F.A., Word of mouth: Understanding and managing referred marketing, *Journal of Strategic Marketing*, 1998.

Buzzell R.D. and Gale, B.T., *The PIMS Principle*, The Free Press, 1987.

Buzzell, R.D., Bradley, T.G., and Sultan, R.G.M., Market share – a key to profitability, *Harvard Business Review*, January–February 1975.

Campbell, N.C.G., An interaction approach to organizational buying behaviour, *Journal of Business Research*, 13:1 February, 35–48, 1985.

Carson, D., *International Marketing*, John Wiley & Sons, Inc., 1967.

Cheverton, P., *Key Account Management*, Kogan Page, 1999.

Chattopadhyay, A. and Laboric, J., Managing Brand Experience. the market contact audit, *Journal of Advertising Research*, 45, 2005.

Collett, P. and Fenton, W., *The Sponsorship Handbook*, John Wiley & Sons Ltd, 2011.

Cooke, P.N., Value added strategies in marketing, *International Journal of Physical Distribution and Logistics Management*, May 1995.

Cooper, R.G. and Edgett, S.J., *Product Development for the Service Sector*, Perseus Books, 1999.

Coughlan, A.T., Anderson, E., Stern, L.W. and El Ansary, A.I., *Marketing Channels*, Pearson, 2006.

Cowell, D.W., *The Marketing of Services*, Heinemann, 1984.

Cunningham, P., Taylor, S. and Reeder, C. Event marketing: The evolution of sponsorship from Philanthropy to strategic promotion, presentation paper at the CHARM history of marketing conference, 1997.

Cusumano, M.A. and Yoffie, D.B., Competing on the Internet: lessons from Netscape and its battle with Microsoft, Free Press, 1998.

Dahlen, M., Lange, F. and Smith, T., *Marketing Communications; A Brand Narrative Approach*, John Wiley & Sons, Ltd, 2010.

Darby M.R. and Karni, E., Free competition and the optimal amount of fraud, *Journal of Law and Economics*, 16, April 1973.

Davies, R., *Innovation: Mapping the Role of the Corporate Leader*, Cass Business School, 2010.

Dean, J., Pricing policies for new products, *Harvard Business Review*, November–December 1950.

De Brentani, U., Success factors in developing new business services, *European Journal of Marketing*, 25:2, 1991.

De Brentani, U., The new product process in financial services: strategy for success, *International Journal of Bank Marketing*, 1993.

DeSouza, G., Now service businesses must manage quality, *Journal of Business Strategy*, May 1989.

Deutschmann, P.J. and Danielson W.A., Diffusion of knowledge of the major news story, *Journalism Quarterly*, 37, 1960.

Dhalla N.K. and Yuspeh S., Forget the product life cycle concept!, *Harvard Business Review*, January–February 1976.

Dibb, S., Simkin, L., Pride, W.M. and Ferrell, O.C., *Marketing Concepts and Strategies*, Houghton Mifflin, 2006 (5th edn).

Doyle, P., The realities of the product life cycle, *Quarterly Review of Marketing*, Summer 1976.

Doyle, P., *Value Based Marketing*, John Wiley & Sons, Ltd, 2000.

Drucker, P.F., *The Practice of Management*, Harper Collins, 1954.

Drucker, P.F., *The Essential Drucker*, Harper Business, 2001.

Easingwood, C.J., New product development for service companies, *Journal of Product Innovation Management*, 1986.

Edgerton, D., *The Shock of the Old*, Profile Books, 2007.

Farris, P.W., Bendle, N.T. and Reibstein, D.J., *Marketing Metrics*, Wharton School Publishing, 2006.

Ferrari, B.T. and Goethals, J., Using rivalry to spur innovation, *McKinsey Quarterly*, May 2010.

Field, P., *The Link between Creativity and Effectiveness*, IPA, 2010.

Fifield, P., *Managing the mix in Europe in Perspectives on Marketing Management*, vol. 1, ch. 5, edited by M.J. Baker, John Wiley & Sons, Ltd, 1992.

Fifield, P., *Marketing Strategy: How to Prepare It – How to Implement It*, Butterworth-Heinemann, 1992, 1998 (2nd edn).

Fifield, P., *Collected Essays in Marketing Strategy*, Fifield Organisation, 2006.

Ford, D., *Understanding Business Marketing*, Thomson, 2002

Ford, D., *The Business Marketing Course*, John Wiley & Sons, Ltd, 2002.

Friedel, R., *A Culture of Improvement: Technology and the Western Millennium*, The MIT Press, 2007

Garber, L.L. and Dotson, M.J., A method for the selection of appropriate business-to-business integrated marketing communication mixes, *Journal of Marketing Communications*, 8, 2002.

Gerstner, L.V., *Who Says Elephants Can't Dance? Inside IBM's Historic Turnaround*, Harper Business, 2002.

Gillies, C., *Business Sponsorship*, Butterworth-Heinemann, 1991.

Gladwell, M., *The Tipping Point*, Abacus, 2006.

Godin, S., *Purple Cow*, Penguin, 2004.

Grönroos, C., Applied service marketing theory, *European Journal of Marketing*, 16:7, 1982.

Grönroos, C., *Service Management and Marketing*, John Wiley & Sons, Ltd, 2003.

Gruglis, I. and Wilkinson, A., British Airways: culture and structure, published research paper, Loughborough University, 2001.

Grunig, J.E. and Hunt, T.T., *Managing Public Relations*, Thomson Learning, 1984.

Gummerson, E., *Total Relationship Marketing*, Butterworth-Heineman, 2003.

Håkansson, H. and Snehota, I., *Developing Relationships in Business Networks*, International Thompson Business Press, 1995.

Haley, R. I., Benefit Segmentation: A Decision-Oriented Tool, *Journal of Marketing*, July 1968, 30–35.

Hamel, G. and Prahalad, C.K., Corporate imagination and expeditionary marketing, *Harvard Business Review*, July–August 1991.

Hamel, G. and Prahalad, C.K., *Competing for the Future*, Harvard Business School Press, 1994.

Hammer, M., Reengineering work: Don't automate, obliterate, *Harvard Business Review*, July–August 1990.

Hammer, M. and Champy, J., *Reengineering the Corporation*, Harper Business, 1992.

Hansen, M.T., Nohria, N. and Tierney, T., What's your strategy for managing knowledge?, *Harvard Business Review*, March–April, 1999.

Harris, T.A., *The Book of Choice* (later called *I'm OK, You're OK*), Jonathan Cape, 1973.

Henderson, B.D., *Perspectives on Experience*, The Boston Consulting Group, 1965.

Henderson, B.D., *The Experience Curve Reviewed*, The Boston Consulting Group, 1972.

Heskett, J.L., Sasser, W.E. and Schlesinger, L.A., *The Service Profit Chain*, Free Press, 1997.

Hise, R.T., *Product/Services Strategy*, Petrocello/Charter, 1977.

Hobsbawm, E., *Industry and Empire*, Penguin, 1999.

Hofstede, G., Cultural dimensions in management and planning, *Asia Pacific Journal of Management*, January 1984.

Hofstede, G., *Cultural Consequences*, Sage, 2001.

Hollins, W., Design in the service sector, *Managing Service Quality*, March 1993.

Hollis, N., *The Global Brand*, Macmillan, 2008.

Holman, R., Kaas, H., and Keeling, D., The future of product development, *McKinsey Quarterly*, 3, 2003.

Iacobucci, D., *Kellogg on Marketing*, John Wiley & Sons, Inc., 2001.

Imbler, J. and Toffler, B., *Dictionary of Marketing Terms*, Barron's, 2000.

Irons, K., *Managing Service Companies*, Economist Intelligence Unit, 1993.

Joachimsthaler, E. and Aaker, D.A., Building brands without mass media, *Harvard Business Review*, January–February 1997.

Johnson, G. and Scholes, K., *Exploring Corporate Strategy*, Prentice Hall, 2002 (6th edn).

Johnston, R. and Clark, G., *Service Operations Management*, Prentice Hall, 2001.

Kaplan, R.S. and Norton, D.P., *The Balanced Scorecard*, Harvard Business School Press, 1996.

Keiningham, T.L., Vavra, T.G., Aksoy, L. and Wallard, H., *Loyalty Myths*, John Wiley & Sons, Inc., 2005.

Keller, K.L., The brand report card, *Harvard Business Review*, January–February 2000.

Keller, K.L., Mastering the marketing communications mix: micro and macro perspectives on integrated marketing communications programs, *Journal of Marketing Management*, 17, 2001.

Kent, R.P., Faith in the Four Ps: an alternative, *Journal of Marketing Management*, 2, 1986.

Keynes, M., *The Economic Consequences of the Peace*, 1920.

Klein, N., *No Logo*, Flamingo, 2001.

Koehn, N.F., *Brand New*, Harvard Business School Press, 2001.

Kotler, P., Competitive strategies for new product marketing over the life cycle, *Management Science*, December 1965.

Kotler, P., *Marketing Management*, Prentice Hall, 2003 (11th edn).

Kotler, P., *Principles of Marketing*, Pearson, 2005.

Kotler, P., Armstrong, G., Saunders, J. and Wong, V., *Principles of Marketing, Second European Edition*, Prentice Hall, 1999.

Kotler, P., Kartajaya, H. and Setiawan, I., *Marketing 3.0*, John Wiley & Sons, Inc., 2010.

Kotler, P., Rackham, N. and Krishnaswamy, S., Ending the war between sales and marketing, *Harvard Business Review*, July–August 2006.

Kumar, N., *Marketing Strategy: Understanding the CEO's Agenda for Driving Growth and Innovation*, Harvard Business School Press, 2004.

Lambin, J., *Market Driven Management*, Macmillan, 2000.

Levitt, T., Market myopia, *Harvard Business Review*, July–August 1960.

Levitt, T., Exploit the product life cycle, *Harvard Business Review*, November–December 1965.

Levitt, T., Innovative imitation, *Harvard Business Review*, September–October 1966.

Levitt, T., Production line approach to service, *Harvard Business Review*, September–October 1972.

Levitt, T., Marketing success through differentiation of anything, *Harvard Business Review*, January–February 1980.

Levitt, T., Marketing intangible products and product intangibles, *Harvard Business Review*, May–June 1981.

Levitt, T., The globalization of markets, *Harvard Business Review*, May 1983.

Levitt, T., After the sale is over . . ., *Harvard Business Review*, September–October 1983.

Loewenstein, G., *Exotic Preferences*, Oxford University Press, 2008.

Lovallo, D. and Sibony, O., The case for behavioural strategy, *McKinsey Quarterley*, March, 2010.

Lovelock, C.H., Classifying Services to gain strategic marketing insights, *Journal of Marketing*, Summer 1983.

Lovelock, C.H., *Service Marketing*, Prentice Hall, 1991.

Lovelock, C.H., Vandermerwe, S. and Lewis, B., *Service Marketing; A European Perspective*, Prentice Hall, 1996.

Luchs, R., Successful businesses compete on quality – not costs, *Long Range Planning*, February 1986.

Lunn, P., *Basic Instincts, Human Nature and the New Economics*, Marshall Cavendish, 2010.

Macqueen, A., *The King of Sunlight*, Bantam Books, 2004.

Mahin, P.W., *Business-to-business Marketing*, Allyn & Bacon, 1991.

Maister, D.H., Green, C.H. and Galford, R.M., *The Trusted Advisor*, The Free Press, 2001.

Mann, M.V., Roegner, E.V. and Zawada, C.C., The power of pricing, *McKinsey Quarterly*, 1, 2003.

Maslow, A., *Motivation and Personality*, Harper Row, 1970.

McCally, R.W., *Marketing Channel Management*, Praegar, 1996.

McCarthy, E.J., *Basic Marketing*, Richard D. Irwin, Inc., 1975 (5th edn) (original 1960).

McDonald, M.H.B., Some methodological comments on the directional policy matrix, *Journal of Marketing Management*, 6, 1990.

McDonald, M.H.B., Portfolio analysis and marketing management, *Science of Marketing*, May 1993.

McDonald, M.H.B. and Dunbar, I., *Market Segmentation: How to Do it, How to Profit from it*, Butterworth-Heinemann, 1998.

McDonald, M.H.B. and Leppard, J.W., *Effective Industrial Selling*, Heinemann, 1988.

McDonald, M.H.B. and Wilson, H., *Marketing Plans: How to Prepare Them, How to Use Them*, John Wiley & Sons Ltd, 2011 (7th edn).

McDonald, W.J., *Direct Marketing: An Integrated Approach*, McGraw-Hill, 1998.

McKenna, R., Marketing is everything, *Harvard Business Review*, January–February 1991.

McKinsey, Innovation and commercialization, 2010: McKinsey global survey results, *McKinsey Quarterly*, July 2010.

Mercer, D., *IBM: How the World's Most Successful Corporation is Managed*, Kogan Page, 1988.

Middleton, V.T.C., Product marketing-goods and services compared, *Quarterly Review of Marketing*, Summer 1983.

Minnett, S., *B2B Marketing*, Prentice Hall, 2002.

Mintzberg, H., The fall and rise of strategic planning, *Harvard Business Review*, January–February 1994.

Mintzberg, H., *Strategy Bites Back*, Prentice Hall, 2005.

Moore, G.A., *Crossing the Chasm*, Harper Business, 1991.

Morel, P., Stalk, G., Stanger, P. and Wetenhall, P., Pricing Myopia in *The Boston Consulting Group on Strategy*, Stern, C.W. and Deimler, M.S. (eds), John Wiley & Sons Inc, 2006.

Morrison, A. and Wensley, R., Boxing up or boxed in? *Journal of Marketing Management*, 1991.

Muha, W.F., The product life cycle concept: origin and early antecedents, CHARM conference paper, 1985.

Ogilvy, D., *Confessions of an Advertising Man*, Southbank Publishing, 2004 (original 1963).

Olins, W., *The Brand Handbook*, Thames & Hudson, 2008.

Ormerod, P., Nudge Plus networks, *Journal of the Royal Society of Arts*, Autumn 2010.

Ozment, J. and Morash, E., The Augmented Service Offering for Perceived and Actual Service Quality, *Journal of the Academy of Marketing Science*, 22:4 Fall, 352–363, 1994.

Page, G. and Raymond, J., Cognitive Neuroscience, Marketing and research: separating fact from fiction, ESOMAR conference 2006.

Paliwoda, S.J., International Marketing, Heineman, 1986.

Palmer, A., *Principles of Services Marketing*, McGraw-Hill, 2005.

Palmer, R., Cockton, J. and Cooper, G., *Managing Marketing: Marketing Success through Good Management Practice*, Butterworth-Heinemann, 2007.

Parasuraman, S., Ziethmal, V.A. and Berry, L., A conceptual model of service quality and its implications for future research, *Journal of Marketing*, 49, Fall 1985.

Parkington, J.J. and Schneider, B., Some correlates of experienced job stress: a boundary role study, *Academy of Management Journal*, 1979.

Payne, A., *The Essence of Services Marketing*, Prentice Hall, 1993.

Payne, A., *Handbook of CRM*, Butterworth-Heinemann, 2006.

Payne, T., *Fame: From the Bronze Age to Britney*, Vintage Books, 2009.

Pelton, L.E., Strutton, D. and Lumpkin, J.R., *Marketing Channels: A Relationship Management Approach*, McGraw-Hill, 2002.

Pendergrast, M., *For God, Country and Coca-Cola*, Macmillan, 1993.

Peters, T.J. and Waterman, R.H., *In Search of Excellence: Lessons from America's Best Run Companies*, Harper & Row, 1982.

Phillips, C., Doole, I. and Lowe, R., *International Marketing Strategy*, Routledge, 1994.

Pickens, J.W., *The Art of Closing a Deal*, PRION, 1989.

Piercy, N., *Market Led Strategic Change: Transforming the Process of Going to Market*, Butterworth-Heinemann, 2001.

Polli, R. and Cook, C., Validity of the product life cycle, *The Journal of Business*, October 1969.

Pollock, D., A note on advertising in the Edo period, *Obegaki*, April 1995.

Porter, M.E., How competitive forces shape strategy, *Harvard Business Review*, March–April 1979.

Porter, M.E., *Competitive Strategy: Techniques for Analyzing Industries and Competitors*, Free Press, 1980.

Porter, M.E., *Competitive Advantage of Nations*, Free Press, 1990.

Porter, M.E., *On Competition*, Harvard Business School Press, 1995.

Porter, M.E., The five competitive forces that shape strategy, *Harvard Business Review*, January, 2008.

Powers, T., Personal selling in the early twentieth century; from America's darling t its scapegoat, presentation paper at the CHARM, history of marketing conference, 1997.

Pringle, H., *Celebrity Sells*, John Wiley & Sons, Inc., 2004.

Pringle, H. and Field, P., *Brand Immortality*, Kogan Page, 2008.

Purchase, S. and Ward, A., AAR model: cross cultural developments, *International Marketing Review*, 20:2, January 2002.

Quinn, J.B., Doorley, T.L. and Paquette, P.C., Beyond products: services-based strategy, *Harvard Business Review*, March–April 1990.

Rackham, N., *SPIN Selling*, Gower, 1995.

Rao, A.R., Bergen, M.E. and Davis, S., How to fight a price war, *Harvard Business Review*, March–April, 2000.

Raymond, M.A. and Ellis, B., Customers, management and resources: keys to new consumer product and service success, *Journal of Product and Brand Management*, 1993.

Reicheld, F.F., Loyalty based management, *Harvard Business Review*, March–April, 1993.

Reicheld, F.F., The only number you need to grow, *Harvard Business Review*, December 2003.

Reicheld, F.F., *The Loyalty Effect*, Harvard Business School Press, 1996 and 2006.

Ringland, G., *Scenario Planning*, John Wiley & Sons, Ltd, 2006 (2nd edn).

Ringland, G. and Young, L., *Scenarios in Marketing*, John Wiley & Sons, Ltd, 2006.

Rittenburge, M., *Direct Mail and Mail Order*, Butterworth & Co, 1931.

Robert, J., Put diversification down to experience, *Marketing Week*, 17 August 2009.

Rodgers, B., *The IBM Way*, Harper and Row, 1986.

Rogers, E.M., *Diffusion of Innovations*, Free Press, 2003.

Rogers, E.M., Singhal, A. and Quinlan, M.M., *Diffusion of innovation in An Integrated Approach to Communication Theory and Research*, Routledge, 2009 (2nd edn).

Rosen, E., *The Anatomy of Buzz: Creating Word-of-mouth Marketing*, HarperCollins, 2001.

Ruskin Brown, I., *Marketing your Service Business*, Thorogood, 2005.

Rust, R.T. and Oliver, R.L., *Service Quality*, Sage, 1994.

Salinas, G., *The International Brand Valuation Manual*, John Wiley & Sons, Ltd, 2009.

Sampson, H., *A History of Advertising*, Chatto and Windus, 1875.

Schlesinger, L.D. and Heskett, J.L., Breaking the cycle of failure in service, *Harvard Business Review*, March–April 1991.

Seybold, P.B., Get inside the lives of your customers, *Harvard Business Review*, May 2001.

Shamir, B., Between service and servility: role conflict in subordinate service roles, *Journal of Human Relations*, 1980.

Shapiro, B., What the hell is market orientated?, *Harvard Business Review*, August 1987.

Shapiro, B. and Posner, R.S., Making the major sale, *Harvard Business Review*, July–August 2006.

Shaw, R., *Marketing Payback*, FT, 1995.

Shaw, R., Net promoter, *Journal of Database Marketing and Customer Strategy Management*, August 2008.

Shaw, R. and Merrick, D., *Marketing Payback*, Prentice Hall, 2005.

Shostack, G.L., Breaking free from product marketing, *Journal of Marketing*, April 1977.

Shostack, G.L., How to design a service, *European Journal of Marketing*, 1982.

Shostack, G.L., Designing services that deliver, *Harvard Business Review*, January–February 1984.

Sieff, M., *Don't Ask The Price: The Memoirs of the President of Marks and Spencer*, Weidenfield and Nicolson, London, 1986.

Silk, A.J., Brand valuation a simple example, Harvard Business School note N9-596-092, 1996.

Solis, B. and Breakenridge, D., *Putting the Public Back in Public Relations*, Pearson Education, 2009.

Solomon, M., Bamossy, G., Askegaard, S. and Hogg, M.K., *Consumer Behaviour; A European Perspective*, Prentice Hall, 2006.

Spears, N.E. and Germain, R., A review of the product life cycle and diffusion of innovation: current and historical perspectives, paper presented at the 7th Marketing history conference proceedings, vol. vii, 1995.

Standage, T., *The Victorian Internet*, Walker & Co, 2007.

Stern, C.W. and Deimler, M.S., *The Boston Consulting Group on Strategy*, John Wiley & Sons, Inc., 2006.

Stone, M. and Carasle, M., *Business Solutions on Demand: Creating Value at the Speed of Light*, Kogan Page, 2004.

Stone, M. and Young, L., *Competitive customer care*, Croner, 1994.

Strong, E.K., Theories of selling, *Journal of Applied Psychology*, 9, 1925, 75–76.

Susskind, R., *The End of Lawyers?*. Oxford University Press, 2008.

Swan, J.E. and Rink, D.R., Fitting market strategy to varying product life cycles, *Business Horizons*, January–February 1982.

Sweitzer, M., Uplifting Makeup: Actresses' testimonials and the cosmetics Industry, 1910–1918, paper to the business history conference, 2004.

Sweitzer, R.W., Interactions in the DMU, presentation paper at the CHARM history of marketing conference, 1997.

Szmigin, I., Managing quality in business-to-business services, *European Journal of Marketing*, 1993.

Tapscott, D., *Grown Up digital*, McGraw-Hill, 2009.

Taylor, D. and Nichols, C., Brands as market leaders, *Market Leader*, Quarter 2, 2010.

Thaler, R. and Sunstein, C., *Nudge*, Penguin, 2007.

Thomas, D., *Deluxe; How Luxury Lost its Lustre*, The Penguin Press, 2007.

Thomas, D.R.E., Strategy is different in service businesses, *Harvard Business Review*, July–August 1978.

Tipper, H., Hollingworth, H., Hotchkiss, G.B. and Parsons, F.A., *Principles of Advertising*, The Ronald Press, 1922.

Trailer B. and Dickie, J., Understanding what your sales manager is up against, *Harvard Business Review*, July–August 2006.

Trott, P., *Innovation Management and New Product Development*, Prentice Hall, 2008.

Treacy, M. and Wiersema, F., *The Discipline of Market Leaders*, Addison-Wesley, 1995.

Turner, E.S., *The Shocking History of Advertising*, Penguin, 1968.

Tybout, A.M. and Calkins, T. (eds), *Kellogg on Branding*, John Wiley & Sons, Inc., 2005.

Uglow, J., *The Lunar Men*, Farrar, Straus and Giroux, 2003.

Üstüner, T. and Godes, D., Better sales networks, *Harvard Business Review*, July–August 2006.

Vandermerwe, S., Scandinavian Airlines System, published Harvard case study 8-388-162, 1988.

Vaghefi, M.R. and Huellmantel, A.B., Strategic leadership at General Electric, *Long Range Planning*, 31, 1998.

Varey, R.J. and Barbara, R., *Internal Marketing*, Routledge, 2000.

Vernon, R., International investment and international trade in the product cycle, *Quarterly Journal of Economics*, 1962.

Webster, F.E. and Wind, Y., *Organizational Buying Behaviour*, Prentice Hall, 1972.

Welch, N., A marketer's guide to behavioural economics, *McKinsey Quarterly*, February, 2010.

Wells, L.T., A product life cycle for international trade?, *Journal of Marketing*, July 1968.

White, P., *Scientific Marketing Management*, Harper & Brothers, 1927.

Wilson, A., *The Marketing of Industrial Products*, Hutchinson, 1965.

Wilson, R.M.S., Gilligan, C. and Pearson, D.J., *Strategic Marketing Management*, Butterworth-Heinemann, 1992.

Winkler, J., *Pricing for Results*, Heinemann, 1988.

Wood, L., The end of the product life cycle? Education says goodbye to an old friend, *Journal of Marketing Management*, 2, 1990.

Woodburn, D. and McDonald, M.H.B., *Key Account Management: The Definitive Guide*, John Wiley & Sons, Ltd, 2011 (3rd edn).

Woodruffe, H., *Services Marketing*, Pitman, 1995.

Yamaki, T. and Fukatsu, K., History of advertising in Japan, 701–189 67, an international comparative study, paper presented at 7th conference on historical research in marketing and marketing thought, 1995.

Zaltman G., *How Customers Think*, Harvard Business Press, 2003.

Ziethaml, V. and Bitner, M.J., *Services Marketing*, McGraw-Hill, 2003.

Zeithaml, V.A., Parasuraman, A. and Berry, L.L., Problems and strategies in services marketing, *Journal of Marketing*, 1985.

Zeithaml, V.A., Parasuraman, A. and Berry, L.L., *Delivering Quality Service*, Free Press, 1990.

Zemke, R. and Woods, J.A., *Best Practice in Customer Service*, Amacom, 1999.

Zoltners, A.A., Sinha, P. and Lorimer, S.A., Match your sales force structure to your business life cycle, *Harvard Business Review*, July–August 2006.

INDEX

Index compiled by Indexing Specialists (UK) Ltd